The Definitive AFC BOURNEMOUTH

The Complete Record of 80 Years in the Football League

Leigh Edwards & John Treleven

Volume 18 in a series of club histories
A *SoccerData* Publication from Tony Brown

Published in Great Britain by Tony Brown,
4 Adrian Close, Beeston, Nottingham NG9 6FL.
Telephone 0115 973 6086. E-mail soccer@innotts.co.uk
First published 2003

SoccerData is a specialist publisher of statistical books on football. This volume is the eighteenth in a series of 'definitive' club histories. Other publications include season-by-season annuals of Football League clubs and the complete results of the F.A. Cup, Trophy and Vase competitions. Please visit the SoccerData website or write to the publisher for news of future volumes.

ISBN 1 899468 18 8

CONTENTS

Mention of 'Bournemouth' in this book should be taken as referring to 'Boscombe FC', 'Bournemouth & Boscombe Athletic FC' and 'AFC Bournemouth' (the Cherries) and not the long-established 'Bournemouth FC' (the Poppies), unless otherwise clear from the context.

The player details following pages 15 and 182 are 'as at' the end of June 2003.

THE AUTHORS

Leigh Edwards is a leading football historian based in Bransgore. He is a regular contributor to over fifty club programmes ranging from Arsenal to Yeovil Town, F.A. Cup final and England programmes as well as several newspapers including the 'Daily Echo'. His books include the Official Centenary History of the Southern League and he organises past-player reunions for many clubs.

John Treleven was brought up in Parkstone and first went to see Bournemouth play in 1961. He has always had an interest in sporting statistics first inspired by cricket and now also including football and tennis. He lives with his family in Jersey and works for The International Tennis Federation where he looks after the results and rankings section.

This is the authors' second book on AFC Bournemouth; they also wrote the official club history and championship souvenir in 1987.

ACKNOWLEDGEMENTS

The authors and publisher have many people and organisations to thank, too many to name individually we fear. Without their help, books like this could not be written. In particular, we wish to extend our thanks to the following: the Bournemouth Daily Echo for its general support; the staff at the British Library Newspaper Library and the Bournemouth Library; the players, staff and supporters of AFC Bournemouth, with a special thanks to Neil Vacher and Mick Cunningham; many fellow football statisticians up and down the land, particularly Mike Davage and Jim Creasy; finally, Michael Joyce and Brian Tabner, regular contributors to this series of books.

Mick Cunningham kindly supplied many of the photographs, the copyright of Sporting Media. The line drawings from the 1920s are the copyright of the Daily Echo. It has not been possible to establish who owns the copyright of some of the vintage photographs; apologies are offered in advance if infringements have occurred.

John Treleven would like to express his special thanks to Jean, Morwenna, Jenna and his parents who have had to tolerate his obsession over the years.

AFC BOURNEMOUTH RECORDS PAGE

PLAYERS:

Most Appearances	Sean O'Driscoll, 511 (423 League, 31 FA Cup, 33 FL Cup, 24 other) Ray Bumstead, 465 (415 League, 28 FA Cup, 22 FL Cup)
Most Goals	Ron Eyre, 229 (202 League, 27 FA Cup) Ted MacDougall, 144 (119 League, 19 FA Cup, 6 FL Cup)
Most League Goals in a Season	Ted MacDougall, 42, 1970/71
Most International caps	Gerry Peyton, 7, Republic of Ireland

THE CLUB:

Honours	Division Three champions, 1986/87 Division Three Play-off winners 2002/03 Winners, Associate Members' Cup 1983/84 Division Three (South) Cup winners 1945/46
Best League performance	12th in Division Two, 1988/89
Best F.A. Cup performance	Round 6 (quarter-finals) 1956/57
Best League Cup performance	Round 4 1961/62 and 1963/64
Most League points	62 (2 for a win) Division 3, 1971/72 97 (3 for a win) Division 3, 1986/87
Most League goals	88 Division Three (South), 1956/57
Most League wins in a season	29 Division 3, 1986/87
Best League win	7-0 v Swindon Town, 22 September 1956 *A 10-0 win over Northampton Town in 1939/40 was expunged from the records when the season was cancelled.*
Best League away win	7-2 v Rotherham United, 10 October 1972
Best F.A. Cup win	11-0 v Margate, Round One, 20 November 1971
Best League run undefeated	18, 6 March 1982 to 28 August 1982
Undefeated League games, home	33, from 7 April 1962
Undefeated League games, away	13, from 11 March 1961
Best run of League wins	7, 22 August 1970 to 23 September 1970
Best run of home League wins	12, from 28 August 1968 and 9 April 1971
Longest run of League draws	5, from 10 November 1979 and 25 April 2000

Most appearances;
Sean O'Driscoll

A BRIEF HISTORY

HOW IT ALL BEGAN

Boscombe Football Club was formed from the remnants of the disbanded Boscombe St John's Lads Institute FC during the summer of 1899. The first meeting, held at 60 Gladstone Road, was attended by about a dozen enthusiasts. It was unanimously decided to form the club and a public meeting was held at the Colonnade restaurant for the purpose of enrolling members and electing officers. The first president was Mr C Nutt, while Charlie Hembrey became captain.

Boscombe competed in the Bournemouth & District Junior League in 1899/00, with home matches played on a ground at Castlemain Road, Pokesdown. Teams were selected beneath street lamps to save the cost of hiring a committee room. Prior to the start of the fifth season, Wilf Hayward became honorary secretary. His appointment coincided with the start of an amazing run of success in competitions including the Hampshire Junior Cup, Hampshire League, Hampshire Senior Cup, Dorset Senior Cup and Russell Cotes Cup. A builder by trade, Wilf Hayward remained as secretary then chairman until his death in 1941, at which time his eldest son Reg became a director. Another son, Doug, later became chairman and the Hayward family connection continued for more than ninety years. Grandsons Peter Hayward and Geoffrey Hayward were directors, while Norman Hayward had a spell as chairman.

MOVING TO DEAN COURT

By 1910 the club was making quite a name for itself in local football, attracting the support of many eminent townsfolk. One such man was JE Cooper-Dean JP and that year he kindly granted the club a long lease on a waste piece of land near King's Park, enabling a home ground to be built. This was named Dean Court after the owner who was made the club's president. The hard work put in by supporters enabled Dean Court to be converted into a football ground. The arduous tasks of levelling the ground and laying the turf were done by voluntary labour, then a stand to seat 300 spectators and a surrounding fence was erected under the supervision of Wilf Hayward.

Dean Court was officially opened on 31st December 1910 with a match against Southampton Reserves. An admission charge of 3d was charged, the first gate receipts totalling £65. The players changed in the Portman Hotel before the game, then walked the half a mile across the park to the ground. Baven Penton became the club's first professional player in January 1912 when he was signed from Southampton for a fee of £10. Season tickets were first issued in 1912/13 when grandstand season tickets were 10s 6d per year and ground season tickets cost 5s. Eight more professional were engaged in July 1913 as Boscombe became members of the South-Eastern League but the standard was higher than expected and the club finished bottom of the table.

In 1914 the club was formed into a limited liability company with a capital of £1,000. Wilf Hayward became chairman and Vincent Kitcher, who had shared the secretarial work with Hayward since 1911, was appointed secretary.

Because of the First World War, the South-Eastern League became defunct after 1914/15 and the club ceased playing for the remainder of the hostilities. At the conclusion of the First World War, Boscombe FC returned to the Hampshire League for the 1919/20 campaign before joining the Southern League in 1920 when all its previous members left to form the new Third Division.

THE FOOTBALL LEAGUE

The first two seasons in the Southern League - now composed largely of the new Football League Third Division reserve sides - saw Boscombe struggle with a poor away record. New signings such as Billy James and Hugh Davey gave the side a boost and Boscombe's third season in the competition was more successful. Loyal servant George Parsley received a well-deserved benefit match against Southampton in November 1922 and the Christmas Day win at home to Southampton Reserves attracted more than 5,000 spectators. Overcoming the departure of star defender Vince Matthews to Bolton Wanderers in an exchange deal involving Charles Smith, the team maintained their Southern League title challenge but defeat at rivals Bristol City Reserves left them as runners-up.

With the Football League increasing its membership by two clubs for the 1923/24 season, an application by Torquay United sparked off Boscombe's candidature and Wilf Hayward canvassed representatives of the League clubs prior to their annual meeting. The club was fortunate to enlist the support of local resident William

Pickford, who later became president of the Football Association, and Arsenal's manager Leslie Knighton. Boscombe were elected to the Third Division (South) on 28th May 1923. At a shareholders meeting afterwards a new share capital was authorised and the club was re-named Bournemouth & Boscombe Athletic, with directors later approving the nickname 'The Cherries' after the club was referred to as the Cherry Stripes in the local press. Managed by Harry Kinghorn, new signings included Coventry City pair Foster Robinson and William Leitch, Jim Lister from Hearts, Jim Miller from Chesterfield and Victory internationalist Bill Voisey from Millwall. Builder-chairman Wilf Hayward supervised ground improvements including the new stand to accommodate 1,600 people.

The Cherries' first League game was at Swindon Town on 25th August 1923 and they lost 3-1, with Jim Lister the first player to score for the club. The first League fixture at Dean Court against Watford was postponed when a thunderstorm waterlogged the ground. The following Saturday's return fixture against Swindon, a curtain-raiser on League football at Dean Court, ended in a goalless draw in front of a 6,614 crowd. Bournemouth's first League victory was 2-0 at Exeter City. A week later Exeter gave them their first home win and first League 'double'. Cherries had to seek re-election at the end of their first League season and were struggling in 1924/25 before persuading Sheffield Wednesday's reserve centre-forward Ron Eyre to join them. He scored on his debut in a 2-0 win at Luton Town and results improved significantly. In eight consecutive seasons, Eyre scored a club record 202 goals in 302 League games for Bournemouth. Other notable contributions to the upturn in results were former Merthyr Town pair Leslie Roberts and Pat Clifford.

In July 1925 Kinghorn became trainer and former Arsenal boss Leslie Knighton was appointed manager at Dean Court. He recruited former Arsenal players Arthur Roe and George Collin as well as right-back Jack Hayward of Bradford City. Cherries defeated Merthyr, Brentford and Reading en route to an FA Cup fourth round tie at home to Bolton Wanderers - the first time a First Division club had visited Dean Court in the competition. Bolton scored a late equaliser in a 2-2 draw watched by 10,165 and Cherries lost the replay 6-2 as Wanderers went on to triumph at the Wembley final.

Boosted by right-half Cliff Halliwell from Sheffield United, Cherries had another exciting Cup run in 1926/27 and ex-Scottish international left-back Jimmy Blair was signed before the third round visit of Liverpool. A 13,409 crowd saw Bournemouth lead 1-0 until the dying minutes when Liverpool equalised with a disputed goal and won 4-1 in the replay at Anfield.

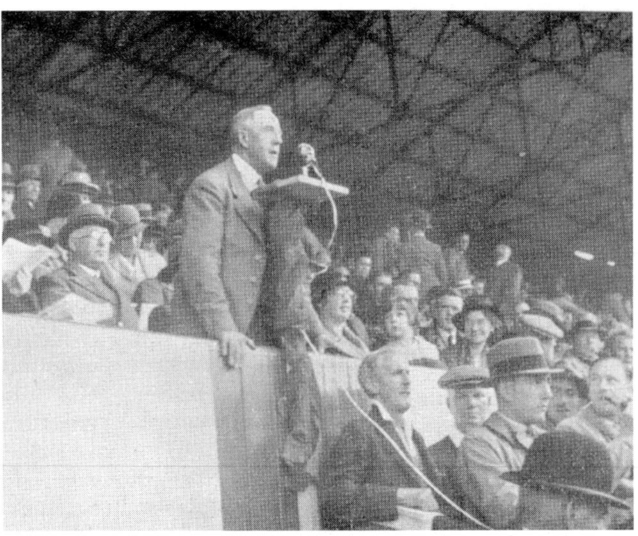

1927: Mr. Sutcliffe opens the grandstand

At the start of the 1927/28 season Mr CE Sutcliffe, vice-president of the Football League, opened the new grandstand. It was put up with the steel framework of the restaurant at the British Empire Exhibition at Wembley. Bought for nearly £12,000 it remained the main stand at Dean Court until the ground was redeveloped.

Manager Leslie Knighton left to take charge of Birmingham in July 1928 and was succeeded by ex-Birmingham boss Frank Richards. Cherries defeated Poole, Guildford City, Accrington Stanley and Watford en route to an FA Cup fifth round tie at home to West Ham in 1928/29. The First Division side were held to a 1-1 draw but won 3-1 in the replay.

THE WOLVES CONNECTION

Former Raith Rovers manager Billy Birrell succeeded Frank Richards in charge at Dean Court in July 1930 but a couple of disappointing seasons led to players being put up for sale and talented young full-back Reg Trim moved to Arsenal. The 1933/34 campaign went down as the worst in the club's history and Cherries were forced to seek re-election for the second time.

In April 1935, Billy Birrell resigned as manager to take up a similar post at QPR. The famous ex-Blackburn Rovers and England full-back Bob Crompton was appointed in his place and new centre-forward Joe Riley spearheaded a significant improvement in results before the club was shocked by Crompton's resignation in February 1936.

The covered stand at the South End of the ground was opened prior to the match at home to Swindon Town on 5th September 1936. Cherries finished in sixth place that season under new manager Charlie Bell, with just one home defeat. Much of the success was due to an influx of players from Wolverhampton Wanderers as Bell was a close friend of their manager Major Frank Buckley. Many of these players were destined for stardom, including centre-forward Jack Rowley, who was capped six times by England while at Manchester United. Right-half Joe Harvey later gave Newcastle United inspirational service as captain and manager, while ex-Wolves junior Billy Elliott arrived from Dudley Town and subsequently starred for West Bromwich Albion. Former Wolves players who gave Cherries long service included Ernie Whittam, Bob Redfern, Jack McDonald, Ernie Tagg and Dai Woodward. But the best remembered were goalkeeper Ken Bird, right-back Fred Marsden and centre-half Fred Wilson. Together with left-back Joe Sanaghan from Bradford PA, they formed arguably the best defence in the club's history.

The club sustained a severe loss when manager Charlie Bell died in June 1939. Former boss Harry Kinghorn took charge again but only three matches of the 1939/40 campaign were played before war was declared. The last of these, at home to Northampton Town, resulted in an amazing 10-0 victory. After the outbreak of the Second World War, Bournemouth continued in the Southern Regional League competition and several guest players appeared for the club including legendary goalkeeper Sam Bartram. A reorganisation of the war-time competition in 1942 ensured that for the second time the club would have to suspend activities. Many players joined the forces and played for other clubs as 'guest players' when possible.

POST-WAR BOOM

When Cherries resumed activities for the 1945/46 season they had to call on guest players. The most famous of these was Liverpool's right-half Matt Busby who became a managerial legend with Manchester United. Tragically one player did not return as Peter Monaghan was killed in the Netherlands during the war. 1945/46 was designated as a 'transition season' by the Football League because of the shortage of players and the difficulty of travel. The Third Division (South) was divided into two and a League cup competition played. The FA Cup for 1945/46 was played on a two-legged basis and Cherries suffered an embarrassing first round defeat by non-League Lovell's Athletic. They had more success in the Third Division (South) Cup, beating QPR in a marathon semi-final replay at Loftus Road before defeating Walsall 1-0 with an early goal by Jack McDonald in the final at Stamford Bridge.

1946: The Bournemouth players with the Division 3 (South) Cup. Back; Dai Woodward, Fred Rowell, Fred Wilson, Ken Bird, Joe Sanaghan, Paddy Gallacher. Front; Tommy Paton, Jack Kirkham, Fred Marsden, Ernie Tagg, Jack McDonald.

The early post-war boom in attendances helped to place the club on its feet and the famed defensive quartet of Bird, Marsden, Sanaghan and Wilson were all ever-present in the 1946/47 campaign. Manager Harry Kinghorn finally severed his connection with the club in July 1947 and was replaced by Harry Lowe. He quickly made three signings - Johnny MacKenzie, Dudley Milligan and Jack Percival - who helped to transform Bournemouth into a promotion-challenging team. The 1947/48 FA Cup third round visit of Wolves was made even more exciting by the fact that the Cherries side included five former Wolves players. A 23,782 crowd saw the First Division side win 2-1. Bournemouth were top of the table by the end of February. By the time the rearranged match against title rivals QPR came round on 14th April 1948, the promotion race had clearly developed into a two-team affair. It was the biggest match in the club's history to that date and the 25,495 attendance remains a record for a League match at Dean Court. A further 6,000 locked outside received a running loud-speaker commentary on the game from secretary Tommy Locks. Rangers triumphed 1-0 and went on to clinch the Third Division (South) title.

Newcomers for the 1948/49 season included right-back Laurie Cunningham from Barnsley. Cherries were exempt from the first two rounds of the FA Cup and they travelled to Manchester to play holders United at Maine Road in the third round - Old Trafford having been badly damaged during the war. A huge crowd of 55,012 saw Cherries beaten 6-0 and they faded in the League to finish third.

CUP GIANTKILLERS

December 1949: Ken Bird and Tommy Lawton of Notts County, on the occasion of Ken's benefit match and 200th first team appearance.

The 1949/50 season marked the club's Golden Jubilee and the home game against Nottingham Forest in November 1949 was designated the Golden Jubilee match. Bournemouth lost 2-1 in front of an 18,452 crowd that included a number of distinguished guests. Jack Bruton succeeded Harry Lowe as manager in March 1950 and brought ex-England international Arthur Cunliffe with him as trainer. Harry Stace became secretary.

Inconsistency marred the next few seasons, with Republic of Ireland international Tommy Godwin replacing Ken Bird in goal and the likes of Peter Harrison, Harry Hughes, Albert Keetley and Stan Newsham also signed. The long awaited first meeting with Southampton came in the FA Cup first round in 1953/54. Cherries drew 1-1 at The Dell, then triumphed 3-1 in the replay at Dean Court.

The highlight of the 1954/55 campaign was the FA Cup third round visit of holders West Brom who triumphed 1-0. Newcomers for the 1955/56 season included Lew Clayton, Nelson Stiffle and Ollie Norris. Goalkeeper Godwin became the club's first full international when he was recalled to the Republic of Ireland team that beat the Netherlands 4-1 in May 1956. Ex-Arsenal winger Freddie Cox arrived from West Bromwich Albion to replace Bruton as manager in April 1956. The new attacking policy was quick to pay dividends with several convincing League wins. The FA Cup trail began with an 8-0 victory at home to non-League Burton Albion and further wins over Swindon and Accrington Stanley earned the Cherries a fourth round tie at First Division high-fliers Wolves. After only six minutes Reg Cutler almost finished the game when he crashed into the goalpost that Wolves were defending and the goal collapsed! It took seven minutes of comic relief to repair the damage and then the game restarted. Cutler scored the first-half goal that clinched the Cherries' remarkable 1-0 win. A 3-1 victory in the fifth round tie at home to Spurs secured Bournemouth a place in the sixth round for the only time to date in the club's history. Freddie Cox's 'Pippins' were drawn at home to reigning League Champions Manchester United and Brian Bedford gave Cherries a 1-0 half-time lead in front of a record 28,799 crowd. The Busby Babes hit back and triumphed 2-1 en route to that year's final.

Bournemouth finished fifth in the Third Division (South) and that summer saw the formation of a new Supporters Club with the aim of ensuring that the £10,000 overdraft was wiped out, a target that was achieved within a year. Cox left to take charge of Portsmouth in July 1958 and former Liverpool boss Don Welsh replaced him as manager. But the Cup run side began to break up and with Cherries fighting relegation, interest in the club was at a low ebb when former Huddersfield Town and England star Bill McGarry was appointed player-manager in March 1961.

1957: The Wolves players survey the damage after Reg Cutler 'hit the post'!

PROMOTION NEAR-MISS

McGarry quickly restored stability and purpose to the side - his driving determination spurred the players to greater effort as he masterminded a sensational about-turn in playing fortunes. Although forward John Archer was his only major summer signing, Bournemouth were unbeaten in their opening 14 games of the 1961/62 season and beat top-flight Cardiff City in the League Cup.

Success stemmed from his 'umbrella defence' with all the players retreating to form a barrier around the penalty-area. The conversion of midfielder Bryn Jones to resolute left-back proved a master-stroke and with the brilliant young David Best replacing Tommy Godwin in goal and experienced Brian Farmer added at right-back, the defence boasted the best record in the division. Promotion would probably have followed but for injuries to key players Ray Bumstead, Chris Weller, Dickie Dowsett, Billy Coxon and John Archer in the vital closing stages of the campaign. Cherries were left to reflect that had a 3-2 defeat at home to rivals Grimsby Town in late March been reversed, they would have gone up instead of the Mariners.

McGarry rebuilt the forward line for the 1962/63 promotion challenge, signing Charlie Crickmore, Jimmy Singer, Ronnie Bolton, Charlie Woods and Derek Reeves. In defence, tough-tackling Roy Gater replaced Tony Nelson but the 'Big Freeze' disrupted the rhythm of the side and they finished fifth. McGarry accepted a lucrative offer to manage Watford in July 1963 and Stockport County boss Reg Flewin succeeded him at Dean Court.

Despite a fine start to the 1963/64 campaign, Cherries again finished just short of promotion in fourth place. Newcastle United were beaten 2-1 in the League Cup as they reached the fourth round for the second time in three years, but the next couple of seasons saw a mid-table placing in the Third Division.

When Flewin resigned through ill-health, Freddie Cox returned to Dean Court as manager in April 1965. The likes of Jimmy White, David Stocks, Rodney Taylor and later Ralph Miller followed him from Gillingham, while Charlie Crickmore moved in the opposite direction and Ken Pound joined from Swansea in exchange for Denis Coughlin. Goalkeeper David Best was sold to Oldham Athletic in September 1966 and replaced by outstanding youngster Roger Jones. He was a key figure as Cherries held Bill Shankly's Liverpool to a goalless draw in the 1967/68 FA Cup third round.

Freddie Cox boosted his attack with the bargain £10,000 signing of Ted MacDougall from York City in July 1969. Bournemouth defeated top-flight Sheffield Wednesday 1-0 in the 1969/70 League Cup second round replay watched by 15,894 but the mid-season sale of England Under-23 keeper Roger Jones to Blackburn Rovers left the club without adequate cover and struggling Cherries were relegated for the first time.

THE JOHN BOND ERA

Relegation came as a bitter blow for everyone, not least newly-installed chairman Harold Walker. He dismissed manager Freddie Cox and long-serving winger Ray Bumstead moved to Weymouth after a then record 415 appearances. John Bond was named as Cox's successor, with former West Ham team-mate Ken Brown as coach. They introduced modern coaching techniques that had a marked effect, notably on Ted MacDougall. Newcomers during the 1970/71 season included goalkeeper Fred Davies, Keith Miller, Mel Machin, Tony Scott and John Benson. Phil Boyer arrived in December 1970 and formed a lethal striking partnership with MacDougall. The latter netted six goals in the 8-1 FA Cup first round replay win against Oxford City and was the country's leading marksman with 49 League and cup goals as Cherries regained Third Division status at the first attempt.

1972: Ted MacDougall scores at Villa Park

Mickey Cave and Bill Kitchener followed the well-worn trail from Torquay United as Bond prepared for the 1971/72 season and the newly re-named AFC Bournemouth were soon top of the table. They made national headlines with an 11-0 annihilation of Margate in the FA Cup first round when MacDougall scored a record nine goals! A then record Third Division attendance of 48,110 watched Cherries visit promotion rivals Aston Villa in February 1972, with the match televised on Match of the Day. Bond's side lost 2-1 but the game will always be remembered for MacDougall's classic diving-header goal. Brighton pipped AFC Bournemouth to promotion after a 1-1 draw at Dean Court watched by 22,540. MacDougall was again the League's leading scorer with 35 goals and moved to Manchester United in a record £200,000 deal in September 1972.

John Bond had signed First Division stars Harry Redknapp and Jimmy Gabriel that summer and invested much of the MacDougall fee in Brian Clark, Ian Gibson and Alan Groves. Cherries narrowly missed out on promotion for the second year running in 1972/73 and Bond left to manage Norwich City in December 1973. Mel Machin, John Benson, Fred Davies, Tony Powell, Phil Boyer and David Jones followed him to Carrow Road, angering fans. Trevor Hartley spent a difficult year as the League's youngest manager before John Benson returned as player-boss in January 1975, assisted by Fred Davies.

AFC Bournemouth were relegated that season and deep in debt. The failure to regain Third Division status in 1975/76 prompted drastic cost-saving measures, with several key players including future England star Kevin Reeves allowed to leave. Ted MacDougall returned from Southampton in November 1978 but Benson resigned two months later with Cherries still struggling in the Fourth Division. Alec Stock was appointed as his successor and his first game was a 7-1 victory at home to Doncaster Rovers, the club's biggest League win for 22 years! Cherries finished mid-table in 1979/80 and ex-Chelsea star David Webb arrived as player-coach in May 1980.

TITLE TRIUMPH

Webb became manager seven months later as Stock was elevated to director and Harry Redknapp returned as coach. The likes of Nigel Spackman, Trevor Morgan, Paul Compton and Chris Sulley were signed and a 14-match unbeaten run augured well for the 1981/82 campaign. Tony Funnell arrived from Brentford in September 1981 and a run of 17 unbeaten matches saw promotion clinched in the 2-2 draw at Bradford City.

Manchester United visited Dean Court in the 1982/83 Milk Cup second round second-leg, which ended 2-2. David Webb was dismissed in December 1982 and Harry Redknapp was caretaker-boss as Cherries crashed to a record 9-0 defeat at Lincoln City in their next game. Brian Tiler was put in charge of the club's administration and Don Megson became manager. Former Manchester United superstar George Best made five appearances for AFC Bournemouth during the closing weeks of the campaign.

1984: The players celebrate one of the great F.A. Cup upsets of all time; Cherries 2, Manchester United 0.

Megson resigned after a poor start to the 1983/84 season and Harry Redknapp began his notable managerial reign in November 1983. Roger Brown returned from Fulham and Cherries shocked the football world with a 2-0 FA Cup third round win over holders Manchester United at Dean Court. United avenged the shock defeat with a 3-0 FA Cup win at Old Trafford in 1984/85 and Redknapp shrewdly signed striker Colin Clarke from Tranmere Rovers that summer. Clarke was leading marksman in 1985/86 and played for Northern Ireland in the 1986 World Cup. On his return from Mexico, Clarke joined Southampton in a record £400,000 deal with David Puckett and Mark Whitlock moving in the opposite direction. Other new signings included Republic of Ireland international keeper Gerry Peyton, Carl Richards, Tony Pulis and Trevor Aylott.

AFC Bournemouth's new-look team lost just one of their opening 12 games of the 1986/87 campaign to emerge as early pace-setters. Redknapp's side remained in pole position and clinched promotion with a win at Fulham in the penultimate match. Cherries were crowned Third Division champions with a record 97 points.

A bright start to the 1987/88 campaign included an aggregate 3-2 win over Southampton in the Littlewoods Cup second round but AFC Bournemouth slipped down the table after injury sidelined ex-England star David Armstrong and only managed to secure Second Division safety in the last fortnight.

Cherries looked set to struggle again in 1988/89 until the arrival of former England striker Luther Blissett from Watford for £60,000 in November 1988. He scored four goals on his home debut. Another notable signing was defender Shaun Teale and the final placing of 12th in the Second Division was the club's highest-ever position.

Ace midfielder Ian Bishop moved to Manchester City in a record £465,000 deal in August 1989 with Paul Moulden moving in the opposite direction, then Redknapp splashed out a record £210,000 on Gavin Peacock. Injuries to key players contributed to AFC Bournemouth's relegation in 1989/90 as they won just one of their final 16 matches.

WEMBLEY FINALISTS

Brian Tiler was tragically killed in a car crash in Rome during the 1990 World Cup shortly after resigning as Cherries' managing director. Manager Harry Redknapp was seriously injured and missed the opening weeks of the 1990/91 season, with Tony Pulis returning from Gillingham as player-coach. The play-offs remained just beyond AFC Bournemouth despite newcomers such as international strikers Andy Jones and Jimmy Quinn, together with Efan Ekoku, Alex Watson, Vince Bartram, Mark Morris and Jimmy Case. Highly-rated pair Jamie Redknapp and Shaun Teale joined Liverpool and Aston Villa respectively.

Cherries were stunned by Harry Redknapp's resignation in June 1992. Tony Pulis replaced him in charge but with the club sinking in debt was forced to offload leading players. Striker Efan Ekoku was sold to Norwich City, Joe Parkinson to Everton and Vince Bartram to Arsenal, while Matty Holmes, Keith Rowland and Paul Mitchell followed Redknapp to West Ham.

Mel Machin returned as manager in August 1994 with Cherries at the foot of the table. They gained only nine points by Christmas but with new signings Ian Andrews, Neil Young, Steve Jones, Steve Robinson, Jason Brissett and Matt Holland making a significant contribution, managed to complete the 'Great Escape' and scramble clear of relegation.

By January 1997 the club, with debts of almost £5 million, was put into receivership by their bank. But fans pledged their support and an independent trust fund headed by Trevor Watkins started negotiations with the administrators to save AFC Bournemouth. Despite problems and no assurances that players would be paid, Mel Machin got the best out of his team. The club was saved, with Machin putting his own money in, and the 1997/98 season was memorable. Despite the £800,000 sale of skipper Matt Holland to Ipswich Town, Cherries defeated Leyton Orient, Bristol City, Luton Town and Walsall en route to the Auto Windscreens Shield final. A year after fans were throwing pennies into buckets to keep the club alive, AFC Bournemouth faced Second Division rivals Grimsby Town at Wembley Stadium. Grimsby triumphed 2-1, scoring the golden goal winner in the 20th minute of extra-time.

PLAY-OFF FINAL GLORY

Cherries narrowly failed to qualify for the Second Division play-offs for the second consecutive season in 1998/99 but defeated Wolves and West Brom in the Worthington Cup and FA Cup respectively. AFC Bournemouth beat Charlton Athletic on penalties in the 1999/2000 Worthington Cup second round but finished a disappointing 16th in the Second Division and Sean O'Driscoll replaced Mel Machin as manager in August 2000, with Machin becoming director of football.

With the departure of leading players such as Ian Cox, Steve Robinson, Mark Ovendale and Mark Stein, Cherries looked likely to struggle in 2000/01 until the arrival of brilliant young striker Jermain Defoe on loan from West Ham in October 2000 sparked a dramatic improvement. He scored in a club record ten consecutive matches and AFC Bournemouth narrowly failed to reach the Second Division play-offs that season after being held to a 3-3 draw at Reading in their final game of the campaign.

AFC Bournemouth shared Dorchester Town's Avenue Stadium during the early weeks of the 2001/02 season as Dean Court was demolished and the site redeveloped with the pitch turned 90 degrees. The sponsored Fitness First Stadium, built at a cost of £6.5 million, was opened in November 2001. Cherries returned home in sensational style with a rousing 3-0 win over fellow strugglers Wrexham, with Brian Stock scoring the first-ever goal in the new all-seater stadium.

The absence of influential striker Steve Fletcher with a long-term knee injury contributed to AFC Bournemouth's relegation as a 2-1 defeat in the end of season return fixture at Wrexham condemned Cherries to the Third Division. They kicked off the 2002/03 campaign with a visit to new-boys Boston United and overcame a disappointing start to emerge as pace setters with Steve Fletcher returning from injury.

Wrexham pipped Cherries to the third automatic promotion slot behind Rushden & Diamonds and Hartlepool United but Sean O'Driscoll's young side defeated Bury 3-1 on aggregate in the play-off semi-finals and faced Lincoln City in the 2002/03 Third Division play-off final at the Millennium Stadium in Cardiff. Two goals by inspirational captain Carl Fletcher plus others from Steve Fletcher, Stephen Purches and Garreth O'Connor gave Cherries a thrilling 5-2 victory in front of 32,148 as they regained Second Division status at the first attempt.

Boscombe 1899/1900. Back: E Skeets (trainer), Jack Spicer, JC Nutt (President), S Davis, E Francis, S Draper (Hon. Secretary). Centre: C Smith, Charlie Stevenson (vice-captain), Charlie Hembury (captain), Charles Kerley, "Jumbo" Hookey, Eddie Richardson. Front: L Coxon, Ted Kerley, H Hannam

Boscombe 1912/13: Back:Barnes, G Alsford, G Dolman, HPT Hockey, C Wallis, Clapham Next to back: J Joy, EA Hockey, J Nightingale, RH Britton, G Parsley, W Clarkson, PS Giles, RG Dolman, F Jenkins, H Cull, J Steele, J Brown Seated: Franklin, W Hayward, R Scott, J Bleathman, B Tarrant, P Taylor, F Whiterow, H Phillips, C Marsh, H Hutchings, V Kitcher. Front: C Franklin, JP New, JC Small, Miss Franklin

Boscombe 1921/22. Back; V Kitcher, EE Brighton, RH Britton, G Kitchen, JT Steele, W Hayward, E Wuytack, R Parsons, EA Hockey, T Franklin. Centre; W Caldwell, E Saxton, JF Lamb, G Parsley, AA Heron, WR Colbourne, KC Marshall, H White, HV Frost, AG Watts, F Perrett. Front: F Wakeley, JP New, ER Dunford, AH Noble, HJ Leavey, WG Lewry, WG Bailey, JR Cartmell, G Smith, HJ Meyer, S Francis. Ground: W Young, EE Ramsay, HG Brighton.

An unnamed team group from 1933. Amongst them are Moralee (back, second from left), Gold (centre, third from right), Chalmers (front, fourth from left) and Russell (front, right).

1934/35. Back; WE Moralee, RW Parker, John Richardson, AT Messer, FC Pincott, J Randle, Jack Richardson, JE Parris. Centre: A White, W Gold, J Fletcher, R Mortimer, WR Chalmers, RD Mellors, WC Richmond, TD Moore. Front; JT Turner, AW Ritchie, GH Farrow, T Tait, WT Cameron, R Twiss, W Smith.

1975/76: Back; Fred Davies (coach), Keith Miller, John Rudge, Stuart Morgan, David Best, Keiron Baker, Neil Hague, Les Parodi, John O'Rourke, John Benson (player/manager). Front: Howard Goddard, Harry Redknapp, Trevor Howard, Clive Payne, Steve Buttle, Mark Nightingale, Derek Rickard.

LEADING BOURNEMOUTH PLAYERS: AN A-Z

PAUL AIMSON

Experienced striker Paul Aimson briefly partnered Phil Boyer in AFC Bournemouth's attack. Signing professional for Manchester City in August 1960, he played in the top-flight prior to joining York City for £2,500 in July 1964. He was leading marksman in York's 1964/65 promotion success and moved to Bury for £10,000 in March 1966, then Bradford City for £4,000 in September 1967. Sold to Huddersfield Town for £20,000 in March 1968, he rejoined York for £11,000 in August 1969 and starred in their 1970/71 promotion campaign. He was reunited with Boyer at Dean Court for £12,000 in March 1973 in a vain bid to boost fading promotion hopes and scored two goals in nine Third Division games for Cherries. A knee injury ended his playing career soon after moving to Colchester United for £8,000 in August 1973. Now living in Christchurch, he was a sales rep for Anglo-Dutch Cigars, then spent 13 years as a physical recreation officer for Dorset probation service until retiring on medical advice in January 1995.

DENIS ALLEN

Inside-forward Denis Allen was an experienced member of AFC Bournemouth's 1970/71 promotion squad. From a notable footballing family with strong QPR links, he signed professional for Charlton Athletic in August 1956 and scored on his League debut at Cardiff City in September 1957. He moved to Reading in June 1961 and was leading marksman four times, starring in successive promotion near-misses before following John Sainty to Dean Court on a free transfer in August 1970. Scoring three goals in 17 Fourth Division games for Cherries, he was displaced by the arrival of Phil Boyer and released by John Bond at the end of the promotion campaign. He had a spell in Belgian soccer with Ostend before managing Cheltenham Town for five years, then scouted for several clubs from his Reading base and was an England scout under Terry Venables until his death from cancer in July 1995. His son Martin played for QPR, West Ham and Portsmouth, then coached at Reading and is now managing Barnet.

IAN ALLEN

Scottish winger Ian Allen contested a first-team slot with the likes of Peter Harrison and Roy Littlejohn while at Dean Court. He impressed with Beith Juniors prior to joining QPR in September 1952 and made his League debut in their 1-0 victory at Bournemouth in April 1954. Jack Bruton snapped him up on a free transfer three months later and he created numerous goalscoring chances for leading marksman Stan Newsham as Bournemouth's team was unchanged for the opening 15 matches of the 1954/55 campaign. He netted 11 times in 52 Third Division (South) games overall for Cherries before moving to Salisbury with Peter Rushworth in July 1957 and starred in their 1957/58 Western League title triumph. Subsequently a local joiner with GW Chilcott builders, Kandic Design & Construction, the Ambassador Hotel and Prowting Homes until retiring in January 1997, he now lives in West Parley.

KENNY ALLEN

Giant goalkeeper Kenny Allen was ever-present for AFC Bournemouth in 1978/79. He represented Durham Schools and had spells with Tow Law, Hartlepool, Hellenic (SA), West Brom and Workington prior to joining Bath City in September 1973. A key figure in their 1973/74 promotion success and 1977/78 Southern League title triumph, he moved to Dean Court for £7,000 as Keiron Baker's replacement in August 1978. He contested the goalkeeping slot with Ian Leigh during the 1981/82 promotion campaign, making 152 League appearances for Cherries. Following spells at Bury and Peterborough United, he reunited with David Webb at Torquay United in March 1984 and moved to Swindon Town in September 1985. He starred in their 1985/86 Fourth Division title triumph, then rejoined Torquay and helped them to reach the Fourth Division play-offs in 1987/88 and played at Wembley in the 1989 Sherpa Van Trophy final. Later with Bath again and Salisbury, he became a postman in Newton Abbot and has since been a driver for a hospital.

IAN ANDREWS

Keeper Ian Andrews made a significant contribution to AFC Bournemouth's 1994/95 relegation escape. An ex-Leicester City apprentice, he signed professional in December 1982 and was ever-present in the top-flight in 1986/87. He was displaced by Paul Cooper and joined Celtic for £300,000 in July 1988 where he understudied Irish international Pat Bonner. Following a loan spell at Leeds United, he moved to Southampton for £200,000 in December 1989 but had limited opportunities as cover for

England star Tim Flowers and was Mel Machin's first signing for AFC Bournemouth at £15,000 in September 1994. He replaced the inexperienced Neil Moss in goal and helped to strengthen a defence weakened by the sale of Vince Bartram to Arsenal. Making 64 Second Division appearances for Cherries, he was given compassionate leave to care for his dying wife towards the end of the following season and Jimmy Glass arrived as his successor. His contract was eventually cancelled by mutual consent and he is now physio at Leicester's Academy.

JOHN ARCHER

Inside-left John Archer was an influential figure in Bournemouth's 1961/62 promotion near-miss under Bill McGarry. A former Port Vale junior, 'Dan' scored twice on his home debut and moved to Dean Court on a free transfer with winger Peter Hall in July 1961. He partnered the likes of Dickie Dowsett and Ken Hodgson in Cherries' attack, helping to beat Newcastle United in the 1963/64 League Cup third round and scoring 37 goals in 139 Third Division games before being sold to Crewe Alexandra for £3,000 in September 1966. He joined Huddersfield Town in an exchange deal involving Kevin McHale in January 1968, then moved to Chesterfield for £1000 in May 1969 and skippered their 1969/70 Fourth Division title triumph. Subsequently player-manager of Sandbach Ramblers and Nantwich Town, he was able to indulge his passion for golf as greenkeeper of the Malkins Bank course near Sandbach until recent retirement and is also president of the Wrekin Federation of Pigeon Fanciers.

JOHN ARNOTT

Versatile right-half John Arnott was a great favourite during six seasons at Dean Court. Initially with Churchfield Old Boys in Beckenham, he made his Second Division debut before signing professional for West Ham in July 1954 and moved to Shrewsbury Town in August 1955. He was an early Freddie Cox signing for Bournemouth in July 1956 and helped Cherries to qualify for the newly-formed Third Division in 1958, scoring 21 times in 173 League outings prior to reuniting with Cox at Gillingham in August 1962. He starred in their 1963/64 Fourth Division title triumph and played alongside several one-time Cherries while at Priestfield Stadium, moving to Dover as player-coach in June 1969. Subsequently following Terry Adlington to Maidstone United as coach, he still lives in Gillingham and spent 23 years as a PE teacher at Kingsdale Secondary School in Dulwich until retiring in July 1998.

JOE ASHWORTH

Tall, versatile left-half Joe Ashworth played alongside the likes of Roy Gater and Jimmy White while at Dean Court. Signing professional for Bradford PA in January 1960, he joined York City in May 1962 and helped to win promotion in 1964/65. Freddie Cox signed him in June 1965, shortly after returning to Bournemouth as manager, and he scored twice in 60 Third Division games for Cherries before reuniting with Ernie Shepherd at Southend United in July 1967. Moving to Rochdale in July 1968, he starred in their 1968/69 promotion triumph and 1970/71 FA Cup run before joining Chester in December 1971. Joining Stockport County six months later, an Achilles tendon injury during the 1972/73 League Cup run ended his playing career. He spent 23 years as a prison officer at Hull, Strangeways and New Hall before retiring in November 1997 and resided in Rochdale until his death in May 2002.

PHIL ASHWORTH

Much-travelled striker Phil Ashworth was a member of AFC Bournemouth's squad that went close to regaining Third Division status at the first attempt in 1975/76. He impressed with Nelson prior to joining Blackburn Rovers in January 1975 but failed to secure a first-team place at Ewood Park and John Benson paid £2,000 for him eight months later. Scoring twice in 31 Fourth Division games for Cherries, he moved to Workington in July 1976 and was leading marksman as they lost Football League status in 1976/77. He suffered a similar fate with Southport in 1977/78, then had a season with Rochdale before featuring in Portsmouth's 1979/80 promotion campaign. Moving to Scunthorpe United in July 1980, he subsequently played for Swedish side GAIS, Cambridge City, Rossendale United, Clitheroe, Bottesford Town, Brigg Town and had a spell as Burnley's commercial manager. Now living in Brigg, he is a driver for a stationery business and his wife owns a travel agency.

WARREN ASPINALL

Former England Youth international midfielder Warren Aspinall was an experienced member of Tony Pulis' squad at Dean Court. An ex-Wigan Athletic apprentice, he helped to win the Freight Rover Trophy at Wembley two months before signing professional in August 1985 and was leading marksman in 1985/86. He joined Everton for £150,000 in May 1986, then Aston Villa for £300,000 in February 1987 and was top scorer in their 1987/88 promotion triumph. Sold to Portsmouth for £315,000 in August 1988, he featured in their 1991/92

FA Cup run and 1992/93 promotion challenge prior to joining Cherries for £20,000 in December 1993 after a loan spell. He scored nine goals in 33 games before moving to Carlisle United in March 1995 and was an influential figure in their 1996/97 promotion and Auto Windscreens Shield double success. Sold to Brentford for £50,000 in November 1997, he reunited with Mick Wadsworth at Colchester United in February 1999 and later played for Brighton until injury ended his career.

TREVOR AYLOTT

Experienced striker Trevor Aylott was an influential figure in AFC Bournemouth's 1986/87 Third Division title triumph. Signing professional for Chelsea in July 1976, he moved to Barnsley for £50,000 in November 1979 and starred in their 1980/81 promotion campaign. He was sold to Millwall for a record £150,000 in August 1982, then joined Luton Town for £55,000 in March 1983 and Crystal Palace in exchange for Vince Hilaire in July 1984. Leading marksman in 1984/85, he was loaned back to Barnsley before Harry Redknapp paid £15,000 for him in August 1986. An excellent targetman alongside the likes of Carl Richards and Luther Blissett, he also featured prominently in Cherries' 1988/89 FA Cup run and scored 27 goals in 147 League games before being sold to Birmingham City for £40,000 in October 1990. Subsequently with Oxford United, Gillingham, Wycombe Wanderers (on loan) and Bromley, he is now a London black cab driver.

JOHN BAILEY

Tigerish midfielder John Bailey scored AFC Bournemouth's goal at Wembley in the 1998 Auto Windscreens Shield final. He played for Croydon and Dagenham prior to joining Enfield in July 1992 and was their 'Player of the Year' in 1992/93. Featuring prominently as Enfield won the Diadora League title and beat Cardiff City and Torquay United en route to the FA Cup third round in 1994/95, Mel Machin paid £40,000 for him in July 1995. He came on as a substitute for his Second Division debut in Cherries' 1-0 defeat at Bradford City a month later. He easily made the transition from non-League football, impressing with his commitment and delivery of telling crosses from the right side of midfield. An influential figure as AFC Bournemouth challenged strongly for the Second Division play-offs in two consecutive seasons, he scored six goals in 148 League outings until a back injury ended his League career in October 2000. He has since played for Brockenhurst, Poole Town and Bashley reserves.

KEIRON BAKER

Popular goalkeeper Keiron Baker gave AFC Bournemouth loyal service over 11 years. A former Fulham amateur, he signed professional at Dean Court in July 1967 and made his League debut in place of Roger Jones at Orient in November 1969. He subsequently provided reliable cover for Fred Davies and was loaned to Brentford prior to becoming Cherries' first-choice keeper in 1973/74, making 217 League appearances before a surprise £20,000 move to FA Cup holders Ipswich Town in August 1978. He briefly understudied Paul Cooper but a back injury dashed his hopes of appearing in the top-flight and he had spells with Harry Redknapp at Phoenix Fire and Oxford City before reuniting with Stuart Morgan at Weymouth in June 1981. Starring in their 1982/83 FA Cup run, he followed Trevor Finnigan to Yeovil Town in July 1983. Now living near Ringwood, he installs fibre optic cabling for communication systems in partnership with Finnigan.

FRANK BARTON

Experienced, versatile midfielder Frank Barton had two spells at AFC Bournemouth. An England Youth international, he made his League debut six months before signing professional for Scunthorpe United in August 1965 and was top scorer in 1966/67. He joined Carlisle United for £8,000 in January 1968 and scored in both legs of the 1969/70 League Cup semi-final, following Bob Stokoe to Blackpool for £23,000 in July 1972. Moving to Grimsby Town in June 1973, he joined AFC Bournemouth for £6,000 in June 1976 and was leading marksman in 1976/77. He was sold to Hereford

United for £8,000 in January 1978, then rejoined Cherries for a similar fee eight months later and netted 15 goals in 88 Fourth Division games overall for the club prior to joining Jimmy Gabriel's Seattle Sounders for £5,000 in March 1979. He has settled in the United States and is now assistant-manager in the services department of a car company in nearby Belle Vue.

VINCE BARTRAM

Highly-rated goalkeeper Vince Bartram was ever-present for AFC Bournemouth in 1991/92. Signing professional for Wolverhampton Wanderers in August 1985, he made his League debut in their first-ever Fourth Division game a year later but had limited opportunities behind Mark Kendall and Mike Stowell. He was loaned to Blackpool, Cheltenham Town and West Brom before Harry Redknapp paid £65,000 for him in July 1991 to replace Eire international Gerry Peyton. Making 132 League appearances for Cherries prior to joining Arsenal for £400,000 in August 1994, he gained Premiership experience as David Seaman's understudy. Following a loan spell at Huddersfield Town, he reunited with Tony Pulis at Gillingham on a free transfer in March 1998 and featured in successive Second Division play-off finals. He starred in their 1999/2000 Wembley triumph as they reached the First Division for the first time and remains a member of their squad.

RUSSELL BEARDSMORE

Versatile former England U-21 midfielder Russell Beardsmore played for Cherries in the 1998 Auto Windscreens Shield final. He starred for Wigan Schoolboys and was a Manchester United apprentice under the guidance of ex-Cherry Joe Brown, signing professional at Old Trafford in September 1986. Given his First Division debut two years later, he featured in their triumphant 1990/91 European Cup Winners' Cup campaign and was loaned to Kenny Dalglish's Blackburn Rovers in December 1991. Unable to maintain a regular first team slot with United behind the likes of Ryan Giggs and Andrei Kanchelskis, he was snapped up by Tony

Pulis on a free transfer in June 1993. He made a significant contribution to AFC Bournemouth's 1994/95 relegation escape and became captain, scoring four goals in 178 Second Division games until a serious back problem ended his career in December 1999. He became an assistant community development officer at Bolton Wanderers, then settled back in Bransgore.

JOHN BECK

Midfielder John Beck was an experienced figure in AFC Bournemouth's 1984 Associate Members Cup final triumph. Signing professional for Queen's Park Rangers in May 1972, he played alongside England internationals like Gerry Francis and Stan Bowles before being sold to First Division rivals Coventry City for £40,000 in June 1976. He joined Fulham for £80,000 in October 1978 and was a member of their 1981/82 promotion squad, joining Cherries on a free transfer in February 1983 after a loan spell. Appointed captain at Dean Court, he scored 13 times in 137 Third Division games and moved to Cambridge United in July 1986. He succeeded Chris Turner as manager in January 1990 and plotted their meteoric rise, then took charge of Preston North End for two years in December 1992 and guided them to the Third Division play-off final in 1993/94. Subsequently Lincoln City's manager between October 1995 and March 1998, he was briefly in charge of Barrow and then had another spell in charge of Cambridge United.

BRIAN BEDFORD

Centre-forward Brian Bedford scored Cherries' goal against Manchester United in the 1956/57 FA Cup sixth round. Initially with Beddau Youth Club, he signed professional for Reading in April 1954 and moved to Southampton in July 1955. Freddie Cox signed him in August 1956 and he partnered the likes of Stan Newsham and Dickie Dowsett in Bournemouth's attack, scoring 32 times in 75 League outings before being sold to QPR for £750 in July 1959. Leading marksman in each of his six seasons at Loftus Road including successive promotion near-misses under Alec Stock, he joined Scunthorpe United in September 1965 and was top scorer alongside Frank Barton in 1965/66. He moved to Brentford in September 1966, then played in the United States with Atlanta Chiefs and was Bexley United's leading scorer in 1968/69. Subsequently coaching tennis for the LEA in Barnes, he returned to QPR as clerk of the works for five years until June 1992, then worked in Arsenal's ticket office and now lives in Cardiff in retirement.

GEORGE BELLIS

Strong-tackling left-back George Bellis was ever-present for Cherries in 1935/36. Born in India where his father was a Company Sergeant-Major in the Royal Engineers, he grew up on Merseyside and developed in local football prior to joining Southport in August 1923. He made his League debut in their 5-1 defeat at Accrington Stanley in November 1924 and moved to Wrexham in May 1927. Joining Wolverhampton Wanderers in June 1929, he helped to clinch the Second Division title in 1931/32 and joined Burnley in December 1932. He starred in the heart of defence as they reached the FA Cup sixth round in 1932/33 and became captain at Turf Moor. Switched to a full-back role, he joined Bournemouth in July 1935 and made 56 League appearances prior to joining Wellington Town in July 1937. He settled in Liverpool and spent 27 years working at Napiers (English Electric) until retiring just six days before his death in January 1969.

JOHN BENSON

Experienced, versatile defender John Benson had two spells with AFC Bournemouth. Signing professional for Manchester City in July 1961, he sampled top-flight soccer prior to joining Torquay United for £5,000 in July 1964. He starred alongside John Bond in their 1965/66 promotion success and reunited with him at Dean Court for £12,000 in October 1970, featuring in Cherries' 1970/71 promotion campaign. After a loan spell at Exeter City, he followed Bond to Norwich City with Fred Davies and Mel Machin in December 1973 and rejoined AFC Bournemouth as player-boss in January 1975. He made 150 League appearances overall until resigning in January 1979 and returned to Norwich as youth coach, then assisted Bond at Manchester City and Burnley

before briefly succeeding him in charge at both. After coaching in the Arab Emirates, he was Barnsley's chief scout under Mel Machin and assisted John Deehan at Norwich and Wigan Athletic where he became manager. He is now assisting Steve Bruce at Birmingham City.

DAVID BEST

Brilliant young goalkeeper David Best was ever-present for Cherries in three consecutive seasons. Initially with Wareham, he signed professional at Dean Court in October 1960 and made his League debut at Watford six months later. He displaced veteran keeper Tommy Godwin and starred in Cherries' 1961/62 promotion near-miss under Bill McGarry, playing 230 Third Division games before being sold to Oldham Athletic for £15,000 in September 1966. Reunited with McGarry at Ipswich Town for £25,000 in October 1968, he had the dubious distinction of conceding the 'goal that never was' at Chelsea in September 1970 and helped Ipswich to qualify for the UEFA Cup in 1972/73. He moved to Portsmouth in February 1974, then rejoined AFC Bournemouth in July 1975 and made two further League appearances.

Appointed Dorchester Town player-manager in February 1976, he subsequently managed Portesham, Poole Town, Cranborne and Parley Sports and is now a driver for Westwind Air Bearings in Holton Heath.

GEORGE BEST

Former Manchester United superstar George Best is arguably the most famous player ever to appear for AFC Bournemouth. Signing professional at Old Trafford in May 1963, he starred as Matt Busby's side won the League Championship in 1963/64 and 1966/67, then crowned a glorious era by lifting the European Cup at Wembley in 1968. Voted 'Footballer of the Year' and 'European Player of the Year', he was capped 37 times by Northern Ireland but a rift developed between club and player after Busby retired. He then had spells with Los Angeles Aztecs, Fulham, Fort Lauderdale Strikers, Hibernian, San Jose Earthquakes and Golden Bay. Moving to Cherries in March 1983, his debut in that month's 1-0 defeat at home to Newport Court attracted double the average attendance and he made five League appearances while at Dean Court. He joined Brisbane Lions in July 1983 and has since worked in the media, also touring with the likes of Rodney Marsh and Jimmy Greaves.

KEN BIRD

Popular goalkeeper Ken Bird was a key figure in Bournemouth's 1947/48 promotion near-miss. Initially with Willenhall Rovers, the ex-England Schoolboy international joined Wolverhampton Wanderers in May 1937 but failed to secure a First Division slot behind Alex Scott and followed the well-worn trail to Dean Court in October 1938. He formed a memorable defensive quartet with Fred Marsden, Joe Sanaghan and Fred Wilson and helped Cherries to win the Third Division (South) Cup in 1945/46. Twice ever-present, he made 249 League appearances prior to becoming Dorchester Town's player-manager in August 1954. He guided them to the Western League title in 1954/55 and was landlord of the Royal Oak pub in Dorchester, then a sales rep for Southern Tiling before moving to the United States to be with his wife's family in Seattle. Subsequently returning to Swanage, he was the local piermaster for 10 years until retiring in September 1980 and died of lung cancer in October 1987.

IAN BISHOP

Skilful mldfielder Ian Bishop starred as AFC Bournemouth took Manchester United to an FA Cup fifth round replay in 1988/89. A former Everton apprentice, he signed professional in May 1983 and was loaned to Crewe Alexandra prior to joining Carlisle United for £15,000 in October 1984. He impressed in a struggling side and Harry Redknapp paid £35,000 for him in July 1988, scoring twice in 44 Second Division games as Cherries finished in their highest-ever League position before moving to Mel Machin's Manchester City in a record £465,000 deal involving Paul Moulden in August 1989. Joining West Ham with Trevor Morley in exchange for Mark Ward four months later, he skippered their 1990/91 and 1992/93 promotion successes and gained England B recognition under Redknapp's guidance prior to rejoining Manchester City in March 1998. He featured in their 1998/99 Second Division play-off final triumph at Wembley and then played for United States' side Miami Fusion and Rochdale. He is now assisting Mike Marsh at Burscough.

JIMMY BLAIR (Snr)

Former Scottish international left back Jimmy Blair was an experienced figure as Cherries took Liverpool to an FA Cup third round replay in 1926/27. Initially with Bonnyrigg Thistle and Glasgow Ashfield, he twice represented the Scottish League while at Clyde and moved to Sheffield Wednesday for £2,000 in July 1914. He followed Jimmy Gill to Cardiff City for a record £3,500 in November 1920 and starred in their 1920/21 promotion success. Capped eight times, Leslie Knighton signed him as a replacement for the injured George Collin in December 1926 and he made 61 Third Division (South) appearances for Bournemouth until retiring in May 1928. He subsequently rejoined Cardiff City as trainer-coach. After his wife's death in October 1948, he returned to Sheffield and lived with his daughter Margaret until his death in February 1964. His son of the same name was a Scottish international who played for Cherries during the early post-war era.

JIMMY BLAIR (Jnr)

Skilful ex-Scottish international inside-forward Jimmy Blair featured prominently in Bournemouth's 1947/48 promotion near-miss. A former amateur with Cardiff City where his father was trainer-coach, he signed professional for Blackpool in June 1935 and was briefly joined by his younger brother Doug. He served on RAF radar in North Africa during the war and was capped by Scotland against Wales in October 1946. Harry Lowe paid £5,000 for him in October 1947 and he quickly became a favourite at Dean Court, scoring eight goals in 80 Third Division (South) games for Cherries prior to joining Alec Stock's Leyton Orient in December 1949. He moved to Ramsgate Athletic as player-manager in July 1953, then joined Canterbury City in August 1959 and was landlord of the Cherry Tree pub in Faversham. Subsequently a prison officer at Dover Borstal and Ham Remand Centre in Richmond until December 1977, he then lived with his son Jimmy near Llanelli until dying from motor neurone disease in July 1983.

LUTHER BLISSETT

Popular ex-England international striker Luther Blissett was Cherries' leading marksman in three consecutive seasons. Signing professional for Watford in July 1975, he was a key figure in their meteoric rise from the Fourth Division to First under Graham Taylor and moved to AC Milan for a record £1,000,000 in June 1983. He rejoined Watford for £550,000 in August 1984 and was capped 14 times by his country before Harry Redknapp paid £60,000 for him in November 1988. Scoring four goals on his home debut against Hull City, he starred in that season's FA Cup run and netted 56 goals in 121 League games for Cherries prior to rejoining Watford for £40,000 in August 1991. He set their appearance and goalscoring records and was loaned to West Brom before moving to Bury in August 1993, then had spells with Derry City, Southport and Fakenham Town. Subsequently Watford's assistant-manager, he briefly coached York City during the 2002/03 campaign.

RONNIE BOLTON

Versatile left-half Ronnie Bolton gave fine service during two spells with Bournemouth. Initially with Crompton Recs, he signed professional at Dean Court as an inside-left in April 1958 and made his League debut at Halifax Town five months later. He was top scorer in 1960/61 and featured in the 1961/62 promotion near-miss, switching to left-half after injury prior to reuniting with Bill McGarry at Ipswich Town for £10,000 in October 1965. Rejoining Cherries for £5,000 in September 1967, he scored 48 times in 264 Third Division games overall for the club before moving to Johnny Byrne's Durban City in May 1969. He played alongside Johnny Haynes as they achieved South African League and Cup success, then joined Poole Town in October 1971 and had two seasons with Andover before becoming Dorchester Town's player-manager in August 1974. Subsequently with Tony Priscott's Ringwood Town, he is now a semi-retired carpenter in Bournemouth.

JOHN BOND

Outspoken manager John Bond plotted Bournemouth's 1970/71 promotion success during an exciting reign at Dean Court. A notable graduate from West Ham's 'Academy', he joined them from Colchester Casuals in March 1950 and starred at full-back as the Hammers won the Second Division title in 1957/58 and FA Cup in 1963/64. He represented the Football League before reuniting with Frank O'Farrell at Torquay in January 1966, helping to clinch promotion that season. After briefly coaching Gillingham, he succeeded Freddie Cox as Bournemouth's manager in May 1970. He so nearly guided Cherries into the Second Division in 1971/72 with Ted MacDougall and Phil Boyer forming a lethal striking partnership. Several key players followed when he left to manage Norwich City in November 1973, guiding them to promotion and the League Cup final in 1974/75. He moved to Manchester City in October 1980 and led them to that season's FA Cup final, then managed Burnley, Swansea City, Birmingham City and Shrewsbury Town.

KEVIN BOND

Former England B defender Kevin Bond was AFC Bournemouth's 'Player of the Year' in 1991/92. Initially an apprentice at Dean Court, he followed his father John to Norwich City in June 1974 and established a regular place in the top flight. He was sold to Seattle Sounders for £200,000 in February 1981, then rejoined his father at Manchester City for £350,000 in September 1981 and moved to Southampton for £60,000 three years later. An influential figure as Saints were semi-finalists in the FA Cup in 1985/86 and Littlewoods Cup in 1986/87, he returned to AFC Bournemouth for £50,000 in August 1988. He helped Cherries to finish in their highest-ever League position and take Manchester United to an FA Cup fifth round replay in 1988/89, scoring 4 goals in 126 League games prior to joining Exeter City in July 1992.

After spells with Sittingbourne and Dover Athletic, he rejoined Manchester City as reserve team boss, then managed Stafford Rangers and is now assisting Harry Redknapp at Portsmouth.

GARY BORTHWICK

Much-travelled midfielder Gary Borthwick was a popular member of John Benson's squad at AFC Bournemouth. Starting with Windsor & Eton, he had spells with Portsmouth and Southend United before a recurring knee injury caused him to temporarily stop playing. He resumed playing with Harrow Borough and moved via Aylesbury United to Barnet, tempting Benson to pay £1,500 for him in March 1978. Given his League debut in that months defeat at Wimbledon, he scored four times in 74 Fourth Division games for Cherries prior to joining Yeovil Town in July 1980. He joined Stuart Morgan's Weymouth in April 1981 and starred in their 1982/83 FA Cup run, then followed Trevor Finnigan back to Yeovil in July 1983 and had a further spell with Weymouth before reuniting with Keith Miller at Dorchester Town in June 1986. Featuring prominently as they won promotion in 1986/87 and were Southern League Cup finalists in 1991/92, he then played for Havant Town (player/coach), Weymouth (player/manager) and Bridport prior to rejoining Dorchester and is employed in the building trade.

DANNY BOXSHALL

Versatile winger Danny Boxshall created numerous goalscoring chances for Doug McGibbon while at Dean Court. Initially a right-back, he developed in the Bradford Amateur League with Alston Works, Wilsden and Salem Athletic and represented the British Army on the Rhine prior to joining QPR in January 1946. He made his League debut 11 months later and helped them to pip Bournemouth to the Third Division (South) title in 1947/48, also featuring in that season's FA Cup run before moving to Bristol City in May 1948. An early Jack Bruton signing in July 1950, he contested a first team slot with the likes of Denis Cheney and Derek Stroud and netted eight goals in 51 Third Division (South) games for Cherries before being displaced by the arrival of Tommy Tippett. He joined Rochdale in July 1952, then played for Chelmsford City in the Southern League. Employed as an insurance agent for Prudential in Chelmsford for 25 years until retiring in April 1981, he now lives in Shipley, West Yorkshire.

PHIL BOYER

Phil Boyer formed a lethal striking partnership with Ted MacDougall while at AFC Bournemouth. A former Derby County apprentice, he joined York City in July 1968 and followed MacDougall to Dean Court for £20,000 in December 1970. He helped Cherries to clinch promotion that season and was ever-present in the 1971/72 promotion near-miss, scoring 46 goals in 141 League games prior to reuniting with MacDougall at John Bond's Norwich City for £140,000 in February 1974. Starring as they won promotion and reached the League Cup final in 1974/75, he became Norwich's first England international before following MacDougall to Southampton for £130,000 in August 1977. He was leading marksman in their 1977/78 promotion success and a League Cup finalist again in 1978/79, then rejoined Bond at Manchester City for £220,000 in November 1980. Subsequently with Bulova (HK), Grantham, Stamford, Shepshed Charterhouse and Spalding United, he scouted for Graham Carr at several clubs and is now a bank courier in Nottingham.

JACK BRADFORD

Experienced left-half Jack Bradford was an influential figure as Cherries took West Ham to an FA Cup fifth round replay in 1928/29. He impressed with Hucknall Byron prior to joining Grimsby Town in May 1920 and made his League debut in their 3-1 win at home to Bristol Rovers four months later. Moving to Wolverhampton Wanderers in March 1924, he helped them clinch the Third Division (North) title that season and take Arsenal to an FA Cup third round replay in 1925/26. Leslie

Knighton brought him to Dean Court in October 1927 and he was ever-present for Bournemouth in 1929/30. His solitary goal in 113 Third Division (South) games came in that season's 4-2 victory at home to Merthyr Town and he moved to Letchworth Town as player-coach in May 1931. A cousin of Bill Bradford, who made over 300 League appearances for Walsall during the inter-war era, he resided in Hitchin until his death in August 1969.

PHIL BRIGNULL

Central defender Phil Brignull featured prominently in AFC Bournemouth's 1981/82 promotion success. An England Schoolboy international, he signed professional for West Ham in September 1978 and made his League debut eight months later. His second cousin David Webb snapped him up on a free transfer in August 1981 and he was ever present in 1982/83, then 'Player of the Year' in 1983/84 as Cherries beat holders Manchester United in the FA Cup third round and won the Associate Members Cup. He scored 11 goals in 129 League games until losing his place with injury and was loaned to Wrexham before moving to Cardiff City in February 1986. Joining Newport County in August 1987, he then had a spell with Merthyr Tydfil before briefly reuniting with Ian Thompson at Newport on a non-contract basis. Subsequently with AFC Cardiff and Weymouth, he became a senior sales manager for Allied Dunbar in Cardiff and Cheltenham and since July 1998 has been group manager in Oxford.

JASON BRISSETT

Enigmatic winger Jason Brissett played for AFC Bournemouth in the 1998 Auto Windscreens Shield final. He represented Essex Schoolboys and joined Arsenal as a trainee in July 1991, featuring in the 1992/93 Southern Junior Floodlight Cup final. Moving to Peterborough United in June 1993, he made his League debut two months later and displaced ex-Cherry Bobby Barnes in their First Division side. He featured in the 1993/94 Coca-Cola Cup run and Mel Machin snapped him up on a free transfer in December 1994, making a significant contribution to Cherries' relegation escape that season. He created numerous goalscoring opportunities for the likes of Steve Jones and Steve Fletcher and regularly featured as a substitute, netting eight times in 124 Second Division games while at Dean Court. Disciplinary problems led to him joining Walsall in August 1998 and he was an influential figure in their 1998/99 promotion triumph, then had spells at Cheltenham Town, Leyton Orient and Stevenage Borough.

KARL BROADHURST

Versatile central defender Karl Broadhurst made a significant contribution as AFC Bournemouth narrowly failed to qualify for the Second Division play-offs in 2000/01. A former trainee at Dean Court, he signed professional under Mel Machin in July 1998 and was given his senior debut in the 1999/2000 Worthington Cup second round first-leg tie at home to Charlton Athletic. He also appeared in the second-leg as Cherries defeated their top-flight opponents in a penalty shoot-out and made his League debut in the 0-0 draw at Blackpool. Replacing the injured Eddie Howe in the heart of AFC Bournemouth's defence, he later featured in a right-back role until sidelined with successive injuries. He forged an impressive central defensive partnership with Carl Fletcher during the 2002/03 promotion campaign but a shoulder injury ruled him out of the Third Division play-off final triumph. He has scored once in 90 League outings for Cherries.

SHAUN BROOKS

Skilful midfielder Shaun Brooks helped Cherries to finish in their highest-ever position in 1988/89. The son of former England star Johnny Brooks, he gained England Schoolboy and Youth honours and signed professional for Terry Venables' Crystal Palace in October 1979. He sampled top-flight soccer prior to joining Orient in October 1983 and his impressive displays tempted Harry Redknapp to pay £20,000 for him in June 1987. An influential figure in the memorable Cup wins against Southampton in 1987/88 and Newcastle United in 1991/92, he scored 13 goals in 128 League games for Cherries before being released by Tony Pulis in May 1993. Following spells with Wimborne Town, Salisbury City, and Dorchester Town, he returned to Dean Court on trial in October 1994 and made one further League appearance prior to rejoining Leyton Orient a month later. He joined Poole Town in November 1996 and then was Ringwood Town's player-coach with Keith Williams. Now running a personal training business.

IRVIN BROWN

Versatile defender Irvin Brown was a popular member of Don Welsh's squad at Dean Court. The eldest of three footballing brothers, he represented East Sussex Schools prior to signing professional for Brighton in October 1952. He had limited opportunities as Ken Whitfield's understudy and reunited with Welsh at Bournemouth for £2,000 in September 1958, scoring twice in 65 Third Division games for Cherries before moving to Poole Town in June 1963. Ever-present in their 1964/65 promotion campaign, he also starred in Poole's 1966/67 FA Cup run and successive relegation escapes prior to joining Harnworthy United in June 1971. He plotted Dorset Combination Cup success during a 14-year managerial reign, then became their physio and subsequently linked up with Alex Pike in a similar capacity at Bournemouth Poppies and Wimborne Town. Still living in Poole, he was a joiner-foreman for Rawlings Builders, then Lytchett Minster Joinery until December 1998.

JOE BROWN

Influential left-half Joe Brown starred as Cherries reached the FA Cup sixth round in 1956/57. Signing professional for Middlesbrough in April 1946, he helped them to finish in their highest post-war position in 1950/51 and remained in the top-flight after moving to Burnley in August 1952. Jack Bruton brought him to Dean Court in June 1954 and he was twice ever-present for Bournemouth, scoring five times in 215 League outings prior to joining Aldershot in July 1960. He returned to Burnley in a coaching capacity a year later, then was chief scout and assisted Jimmy Adamson before succeeding him as manager for a year in January 1976. Appointed Manchester United's youth team coach in September 1977, he became chief scout and during 10 years as youth development officer recruited stars Ryan Giggs, David Beckham and the Neville brothers. He had a serious car accident in December 1990 and continued in a part-time role at Old Trafford until retiring in May 1996.

ROGER BROWN

Central defender Roger Brown skippered Cherries' 1984 Associate Members Cup final triumph. A former Walsall apprentice, he moved via Paget Rangers to AP Leamington in September 1974 and starred in their 1975/76 promotion success and 1977/78 FA Cup run. John Benson paid £10,000 for him in February 1978 and he was a favourite at Dean Court before following the well-worn trail to John Bond's Norwich City for £85,000 in July 1979, gaining top-flight experience. Sold to Fulham for £100,000 in March 1980, he was ever-present with Gerry Peyton and Sean O'Driscoll in their 1981/82 promotion success and rejoined AFC Bournemouth in December 1983. He was a key figure as Cherries beat Manchester United in that season's FA Cup third round, scoring eight goals in 147 League games before briefly joining Weymouth in March 1987. Subsequently manager of Poole Town, Colchester United and Bolehall Swifts while working in the family building business in Tamworth, he is now a probation officer in Norwich.

MARCUS BROWNING

Former Welsh international midfielder Marcus Browning was awarded 'Man of the Match' in AFC Bournemouth's 2002/03 Third Division play-off final success. Signing professional for Bristol Rovers in July 1989, he was a key figure as they reached the Second Division play-off final in 1994/95 and gained the first of five caps against Italy in November 1995. He followed Marcus Stewart to Huddersfield Town for £500,000 in February 1997 and joined Gillingham for £150,000 in March 1999 after a loan spell, helping them qualify for the Second Division play-offs that season. A member of their 1999/2000 promotion squad, he moved to AFC Bournemouth initially on trial in August 2002 and scored his first goal for the club against Brentford in the Worthington Cup, taking over in goal later in the same game. He was an experienced figure as Cherries regained Second Division status at the first attempt, scoring once in 43 League games in 2002/03.

JACK BRUTON

Former England international outside-right Jack Bruton spent six seasons as Bournemouth's manager. An ex-miner, he had spells with Wigan Borough and Horwich RMI prior to joining Burnley in March 1925. He scored on his First Division debut that month and was ever-present in 1926/27, capped three times by his country before being sold to Blackburn Rovers for £6,500 in December 1929. Ever-present and top scorer on three occasions, he became Blackburn's assistant-secretary after the war and was manager at Ewood Park from December 1947 until May 1949. He succeeded Harry Lowe as Cherries manager in March 1950 and brought fellow ex-England winger Arthur Cunliffe with him as trainer to replace Dick Mellors. His shrewd signings included Tommy Godwin, Stan Newsham, Johnny Crosland, Joe Brown and Ollie Norris but he left Dean Court by mutual consent in March 1956 and subsequently worked for Chalwyn Ltd in Parkstone until retirement in 1968, remaining local until his death in March 1986.

CAMERON BUCHANAN

Scottish inside-right Cameron Buchanan played alongside Jack Cross in Bournemouth's attack. A former Wolverhampton Wanderers junior, he was the youngest-ever debutant in English senior soccer at 14 years 57 days against West Brom in September 1942 and signed professional at Molineux in May 1946. He represented the Army during National Service and Harry Lowe snapped him up on a free transfer in August 1949, making his League debut at home to Ipswich Town four months later. Securing a regular first-team slot with Cherries in 1951/52, he scored 19 goals in 83 Third Division (South) games before moving to Canada in April 1955 as Montreal Ukraina player-coach. He joined Norwich City in October 1956, then became player-manager of Barnstaple Town for seven years in July 1957. Subsequently employed in the laundry business, he spent 15 years as linen service manager at Ninewells Hospital in Dundee until retiring in July 1993. He moved back to Barnstaple for a while and has now settled in Tayport.

RAY BUMSTEAD

Long-serving outside-right Ray Bumstead starred in Cherries' 1961/62 promotion near-miss. He impressed with Ringwood Town in the Hampshire League before Freddie Cox brought him to Dean Court in May 1958 and made his League debut at Doncaster Rovers nine months later. Twice ever-present and joint top scorer in 1959/60, he was an influential figure as Bournemouth gained League Cup wins against Newcastle United in 1963/64 and Sheffield Wednesday in 1969/70 and took mighty Liverpool to an FA Cup third round replay in 1967/68. Given a testimonial against Wolverhampton Wanderers in December 1969, he scored 55 goals in a then record 415 League games for the club before moving to Weymouth on a free transfer in June 1970. He played alongside ex-Cherries like Dave Bennett, Rodney Adams, Ralph Miller and John Hill as they were Southern League Cup finalists in 1970/71. Still living in his native Ringwood, he owned two hairdressing salons and is now a semi-retired property developer.

MIKE BURGESS

Versatile centre-forward Mike Burgess was Bournemouth's leading marksman in 1958/59. Born in Montreal, he grew up in Bradford and played for Frickley Colliery during national service in the RAF before signing professional for Bradford Park Avenue in August 1952. He joined Leyton Orient in July 1953 and was swapped for Newport County's Tom Johnston in February 1956, moving to Dean Court for £1,000 in June 1957. Partnering Dickie Dowsett in Cherries' attack, he scored 34 times in 109 League outings prior to joining Halifax Town in July 1961. Switched to central defence, he reunited with Freddie Cox at Gillingham in March 1963 and was ever-present in their 1963/64 Fourth Division title triumph. He had spells with Aldershot and Canterbury City, then made integrated systems for Elliotts in Rochester before working on flight simulators at Crawley and Heathrow. Now living in Broadstone, he spent 18 years as an electronics technician on defence projects for Plessey at Poole and Christchurch until November 1993.

GEOFF BUTLER

Popular right-back Geoff Butler was an experienced member of John Benson's squad at AFC Bournemouth. Signing professional for hometown Middlesbrough in May 1964, he starred in their 1966/67 promotion success and moved to Chelsea for £57,000 in September 1967. He remained in the top-flight when sold to Sunderland for £65,000 four months later, then joined Norwich City for £30,000 in October 1968 and played alongside Clive Payne as they won the Second Division title in 1971/72 and were League Cup finalists in 1972/73. He contested a first-team slot with Mel Machin in their 1974/75 promotion campaign under John Bond and had a spell with Baltimore Comets before reuniting with Benson at Dean Court in March 1976. Scoring once in 119 Fourth Division games for Cherries, he joined Peterborough United as player-coach in August 1981. He had a spell with Trowbridge Town and became Salisbury's player-boss in February 1983, guiding them to promotion in 1985/86 and 1994/95, then managed Weymouth.

MICK BUTLER

Popular striker Mick Butler was AFC Bournemouth's leading marksman in two consecutive seasons. Impressing with Worsbrough Bridge Miners Welfare while employed as an electrician at Dodworth Colliery, he joined Barnsley initially as an amateur and scored on his League debut in February 1973. He was twice top scorer at Oakwell and moved to Huddersfield Town for £30,000 in March 1976, finishing as leading marksman in 1977/78. John Benson paid £15,000 for him in July 1978 and he partnered Ted MacDougall in Cherries' attack, netting 19 goals in 69 Fourth Division games before being sold to Bury for £8,000 in August 1980. He played alongside record goalscorer Craig Madden during two seasons at Gigg Lane, then returned to his native Barnsley and went back to mining while playing local football for Ward Green. Now living in nearby Royston, he was an electrician at Woolley Colliery until it closed in 1987 and has since been a chargehand at Riccall Mine near Selby.

LEN BUTT

Small right-half Len Butt was ever-present in Cherries' 1923/24 Football League debut campaign. He impressed with Shirley St James and signed professional for hometown Southampton in April 1912, serving with the 5th Hampshire Regiment in India during the First World War. On his return, he worked and played for Thornycrofts before rejoining Saints in August 1920, helping to win the Third Division (South) title in 1921/22. Moving to Boscombe on a free transfer in June 1922, he skippered the 1922/23 Southern League title challenge and played in the club's first-ever Football League game at Swindon Town in August 1923. He was an influential figure as Cherries took eventual winners Bolton Wanderers to an FA Cup fourth round replay in 1925/26, scoring twice in 139 Third Division (South) games prior to joining Cowes in June 1928. Subsequently a publican at The Sailors Home and Edinburgh Hotel in Southampton, he resided in Sholing until his death just 17 days short of his 100th birthday in December 1993.

STEVE BUTTLE

Winger Steve Buttle starred as AFC Bournemouth went close to regaining Third Division status in 1975/76. A former Ipswich Town apprentice, he signed professional in January 1971 but failed to secure a First Division slot under Bobby Robson and moved to Dean Court for £8,000 in August 1973 on the recommendation of assistant-manager Reg Tyrrell. He made his League debut in Cherries' 2-0 win at Brighton a month later and featured in that season's promotion challenge. Scoring 12 goals in 139 League games for AFC Bournemouth, he reunited with Jimmy Gabriel at Seattle Sounders for £10,000 in February 1977 and played alongside ex-Cherries Mickey Cave, Bobby Howe, Mel Machin and Harry Redknapp as they reached the Soccer Bowl that season. Subsequently Pittsburgh Spirit's player-coach, he then assisted Alan Hinton at Tacoma Stars and worked for a medical delivery company in Washington State until returning to his native Norwich in May 1994. He is now an active member of the Trade Union movement in East Anglia.

JIMMY CASE

Former England U-23 midfielder Jimmy Case was an experienced figure in AFC Bournemouth's 1991/92 FA Cup run. Impressing with South Liverpool, he joined Liverpool in May 1973 and amassed a vast collection of domestic and European honours before moving to Brighton as part of the £900,000 Mark Lawrenson deal in August 1981. He was an FA Cup finalist in 1983, then joined Southampton for £30,000 in March 1985 and starred in successive Cup runs, voted 'Player of the Year' in 1989/90. Also representing the Football League, Harry Redknapp brought him to Dean Court on a free transfer in June 1991 and his solitary goal in 40 Third Division games clinched Cherries' 2-2 draw at Preston North End three months later. He moved to Halifax Town as player-coach in July 1992, then had spells with Wrexham, Darlington and Sittingbourne before rejoining Brighton in December 1993 and became manager for a year. Appointed Bashley player-boss in May 1997, he was their director of football and is now a part-time analyst for the Press Association.

TOM CASEY

Tough-tackling left-half Tom Casey was capped 12 times by Northern Ireland after leaving Dean Court. He developed with Belfast YMCA, East Belfast and Bangor prior to joining Leeds United in May 1949 and made his League debut three months later. An early Jack Bruton signing in August 1950, his solitary goal in 66 Third Division (South) games clinched Bournemouth's 2-1 win at home to Southend United in January 1952 and he was sold to Newcastle United for £7,000 in August 1952. He played in their 1955 FA Cup final triumph and the World Cup quarter-finals shortly before moving to Portsmouth for £8,500 in June 1958, then joined Bristol City in March 1959. Appointed Gloucester City's player-manager in July 1963, he was subsequently Swansea Town trainer, Ammanford Town and Distillery player-boss, then coached Everton and Coventry City before managing Grimsby Town, KR (Reykjavik) and Harstead. He was a mobile fishmonger based in Portbury for 17 years until retiring in February 1997 and now lives in Nailsea.

MICKEY CAVE

Popular midfielder Mickey Cave had two spells at AFC Bournemouth. Initially with hometown Weymouth while studying engineering, he was leading marksman in 1967/68 and followed Frank O'Farrell to Torquay United in July 1968. He starred in their 1970/71 FA Cup run and reunited with John Bond at Dean Court for £15,000 in July 1971, featuring in Cherries' 1971/72 promotion near-miss. Following a loan spell at Plymouth Argyle, he moved to York City for a record £18,000 in August 1974 and was top scorer in 1975/76. He rejoined Bournemouth for £10,000 in February 1977 and spent that summer on loan to Jimmy Gabriel's Seattle Sounders, playing in the 1977 Soccer Bowl with ex-Cherries Steve Buttle and Mel Machin. Netting 20 goals in 141 League games overall for Cherries, he returned to Seattle for £10,000 in February 1978 and subsequently coached Pittsburgh Spirit until his tragic death from carbon monoxide poisoning in November 1985. AFC Bournemouth's 'Player of the Season' award is named in his memory.

BRIAN CHAMBERS

Midfielder Brian Chambers was an experienced member of Alec Stock's squad at Dean Court. An England Schoolboy international, he signed professional for Sunderland in August 1967 and was sold to Arsenal for £30,000 in May 1973. He remained in the top flight after joining Luton Town for a similar fee in July 1974, then moved to Millwall for £25,000 in July 1977 and featured in their 1977/78 FA Cup run. Alec Stock paid £12,000 for him in July 1979 and he scored seven goals in 42 Fourth Division games for Cherries prior to joining Halifax Town in March 1981. He joined Poole Town four months later and starred in their 1983/84 FA Cup run, then reunited with Geoff Butler at Salisbury in November 1985. Helping to win promotion in 1985/86, he joined Keith Miller's Dorchester Town in November 1986 and repeated the feat in 1986/87. He moved to Swanage in July 1989, then returned to Poole as player-manager in June 1991. Now living in Ferndown, he is a financial planning consultant for Allied Dunbar.

DENIS CHENEY

Versatile forward Denis Cheney partnered Doug McGibbon and Jack Cross in Bournemouth's attack. Signing professional for Leicester City in November 1941, he was leading marksman as they won the Football League (South) title in 1941/42 and served in the Royal Artillery. He gained Second Division experience as Charlie Adams' understudy and was loaned to Watford where he played alongside ex-Cherry Tommy Paton before Harry Lowe paid £2,500 for him in October 1948. A popular figure at Dean Court, he scored 47 goals in 157 Third Division (South) games for Bournemouth prior to joining Aldershot in June 1954. He reunited with Ken Bird at Dorchester Town in July 1956 and topped their goalscoring charts in three consecutive seasons before moving to Portland United in June 1959. Later a chargehand with Cliff Marsh at Vigar & Co timber merchants in Winton, he then worked for Max Factor in Wallisdown and Poole Pottery until early retirement in July 1985 and now lives in Christchurch.

BRIAN CLARK

Experienced striker Brian Clark was AFC Bournemouth's leading marksman in 1972/73. The son of ex-Bristol City star Don Clark, he skippered Bristol Boys and signed professional at Ashton Gate in March 1960. Top scorer in City's 1964/65 promotion triumph, he joined Huddersfield Town in October 1966 and joined Cardiff City for £68,000 in February 1968. He formed a lethal partnership with John Toshack and was leading marksman three times, scoring against Real Madrid in the 1970/71 ECWC quarter-final. John Bond paid £100,000 for him and Ian Gibson in October 1972 and he replaced Ted MacDougall in Cherries' attack alongside Phil Boyer, netting 12 goals in 30 Third Division games before being sold to Millwall for £30,000 in September 1973. He was top scorer in 1974/75, then rejoined Cardiff in May 1975 and featured in their 1975/76 promotion and Welsh Cup 'double' triumph prior to joining Newport County in August 1976. Subsequently manager/coach of Maesteg, AFC Cardiff and Bridgend Town, he still lives in Cardiff and is now a sales rep for safety equipment.

COLIN CLARKE

Northern Ireland international striker Colin Clarke was Cherries' leading goalscorer in 1985/86. A former Ipswich Town apprentice, he signed professional in October 1980 but failed to secure a first-team slot under Bobby Robson and moved to Peterborough United in July 1981. He was loaned to Gillingham prior to joining Tranmere Rovers in July 1984 and Harry Redknapp paid £22,500 for him in June 1985. Scoring 26 goals in 46 Third Division games for AFC Bournemouth, he was capped six times while at Dean Court and starred for his country in the 1986 World Cup. Sold to Southampton for a record £400,000 in July 1986, he was top scorer in two consecutive seasons and briefly rejoined Cherries on loan in December 1988 before moving to QPR for a record £800,000 in March 1989. He joined Portsmouth for £450,000 in June 1990 and featured in their 1991/92 FA Cup run, breaking his country's goalscoring record before injury ended his career. He ran the Queen's Arms pub in

East Garston and has since coached Richmond Kickers, San Diego Flash and Dallas Burn in the United States.

LEW CLAYTON

Right-half Lew Clayton featured prominently as Cherries reached the FA Cup sixth round in 1956/57. Initially with Monkton Athletic, he joined Barnsley in March 1942 and moved to Carlisle United in September 1946. He returned to Barnsley in June 1947 and played alongside Danny Blanchflower for his hometown club, joining Second Division rivals QPR in August 1950. Unable to prevent relegation in 1951/52, Jack Bruton brought him to Dean Court on a free transfer in May 1955 and his solitary goal in 40 Third Division (South) games came in Bournemouth's 3-2 defeat at Southampton nine months later. He moved to Swindon Town in June 1957, then had a spell with Wisbech Town before reuniting with Roy Littlejohn at Poole Town in June 1959 and joined Gainsborough Trinity a year later. Subsequently trainer at Cambridge City, Doncaster Rovers and Cardiff City (with ex-Cherry Peter Harrison), he was then physio at Middlesbrough, Swansea City and Darlington until retiring in May 1989 and now lives in Redcar.

PAT CLIFFORD

Outside-right Pat Clifford starred as Cherries took West Ham to an FA Cup fifth round replay in 1928/29. Initially with his local club Merthyr Town, he joined Bournemouth with right-wing partner Leslie Roberts in December 1924 after they impressed in the League match against Cherries and their arrival contributed to a significant improvement in results. He created numerous goalscoring opportunities for ace marksman Ron Eyre and also helped Bournemouth to take eventual winners Bolton Wanderers to an FA Cup fourth round replay in 1925/26, netting 17 goals in 188 Third Division (South) games while at Dean Court. Moving to Chester in May 1930, he was an influential figure in their 1930/31 Cheshire League title challenge but left as they gained Football League status and joined Stalybridge Celtic in August 1931. Joining Prescot Cables in August 1933, he then played for Bacup Borough and was subsequently a porter at Stalybridge railway station until his sudden death from a heart attack.

DAVID COLEMAN

Young left-back David Colernan provided reliable defensive cover during Harry Redknapp's reign at Dean Court. Signing professional for AFC Bournemouth in September 1984, he made his League debut in the 2-0 defeat at Blackpool in April 1986 and was briefly recalled from a loan period at Poole Town during the injury crisis midway through Cherries' 1986/87 Third Division title campaign. He reunited with Roger Brown on loan at Colchester United in February 1988, then deputised for Paul Morrell during the 1989/90 campaign. Scoring twice in 50 League outings for Cherries, he spent the 1991/92 season sidelined with a knee injury and joined Farnborough Town in August 1992. He moved to Dorchester Town a year later, then featured in Salisbury City's 1994/95 promotion campaign and played for Wimborne Town, Amesbury Town (P/M) and Warminster Town while managing the sports shop at Southampton University until his tragic death from meningitis in May 1997. A team named in his memory competes in the Salisbury & District League.

GEORGE COLLIN

Left-back George Collin starred as Cherries took Bolton Wanderers to a FA Cup fourth round replay in 1925/26. He impressed with West Stanley in his native North-East prior to joining Arsenal in February 1924 but failed to make an impact at Highbury and followed Leslie Knighton to Dean Court with Arthur Roe in August 1925. Forming a notable defensive partnership with Jack Hayward, he made 48 Third Division (South) appearances for Bournemouth before breaking a leg in the FA Cup second round tie at Bristol City in December 1926. He resurrected his career back at West Stanley prior to joining Derby County in November 1927 and starred alongside England international Tommy Cooper as they were First Division runners-up in 1929/30 and 1935/36. Displaced by Steve Fletcher's grandfather Jack Howe, he moved to League Champions Sunderland in June 1936 and featured in their triumphant 1936/37 FA Cup run. He joined Port Vale in June 1938 and became Burton Town's player-boss, residing in Derby until his death in February 1989.

PAUL COMPTON

Central defender Paul Compton featured in AFC Bournemouth's 1981/82 promotion campaign. A former Cardiff City apprentice, he impressed with Trowbridge Town before moving to Dean Court for £10,000 in October 1980 and was given his League debut in that month's 0-0 draw at home to Crewe Alexandra. He partnered John Impey in the heart of Cherries' defence and made 64 League appearances prior to joining Aldershot in December 1983 after a knee injury. Reunited with David Webb and several ex-Cherries at Torquay United in February 1984, he joined Newport

County in December 1986 and was a Welsh Cup finalist that season. He joined Weymouth in July 1987 and became their player-manager, moving via Bashley back to Torquay in August 1991. Appointed manager in May 1992, he was then youth team coach before assisting Eddie May at Plainmoor. He spent a year as Preston's youth team coach until returning to Torquay as youth development officer, since holding similar posts at Swansea City and Cirencester Town.

ALAN CONNELL

Young striker Alan Connell made a significant contribution as AFC Bournemouth regained Second Division status at the first attempt in 2002/03. A graduate from Ipswich Town's Academy, he was a prolific goalscorer in the youth ranks at Portman Road before Sean O'Driscoll snapped him up on a free transfer in July 2002 after he had made several reserve appearances on trial the previous season. He made his League debut as a substitute in the 0-0 draw at home to Kidderminster Harriers in August 2002 and scored the first League goal of his career in that month's 1-0 win at Macclesfield Town. Leading marksman with six goals in 13 Third Division games for AFC Bournemouth when he suffered a cruciate ligament injury during the 0-0 draw at Leyton Orient in October 2002, he missed six months of the season before returning to reserve team football in April 2003. He watched as Cherries defeated Lincoln City 5-2 in the Third Division play-off final.

RICHARD COOKE

England U-21 winger Richard Cooke featured prominently in Cherries' 1986/87 Third Division title triumph. Signing professional for Tottenham Hotspur in May 1983, he scored on his First Division debut at Luton Town six months later but failed to secure a regular first-team slot and was loaned to Birmingham City before Harry Redknapp paid £27,500 for him in January 1987. He scored the decisive goal as Cherries beat Southampton in the 1987/88 Littlewoods Cup second round, then helped to take Manchester United to an FA Cup fifth round replay in 1988/89. Sold to Luton Town for £75,000 in March 1989, he featured regularly as a substitute in the top-flight prior to rejoining AFC Bournemouth in March 1991 and helped to beat Newcastle United in the 1991/92 FA Cup third round. He netted 17 times in 125 League games overall for Cherries until a knee injury ended his League career in March 1993. Briefly with Bashley, he had a testimonial against Spurs in July 1994 and still lives locally, working as a London taxi driver.

STEVE COTTERILL

Striker Steve Cotterill was AFC Bournemouth's leading goalscorer and 'Player of the Year' in 1993/94. Initially with hometown Cheltenham, he featured in their 1984/85 Southern League title campaign and moved via Alvechurch to Burton Albion where his impressive displays led to him joining Wimbledon in a joint £30,000 deal with John Gayle in February 1989. He made his First Division debut two months later and provided reliable cover for John Fashanu, then was loaned to Brighton before Tony Pulis paid £80,000 for him in August 1993. Partnering Steve Fletcher in Cherries' attack, he scored 15 times in 45 Second Division games before a third serious knee injury ended his League career and he became manager of Sligo Rovers for a year in August 1995. Following spells with Dorchester Town, Salisbury City and Cirencester Town, he became Cheltenham's boss in February 1997 and plotted their meteoric rise, then had a spell in charge of Stoke City before assisting Howard Wilkinson at Sunderland.

DENIS COUGHLIN

Popular centre-forward Denis Coughlin was twice leading marksman while at Dean Court. He represented England Boys Clubs and developed with Shiney Row St Oswalds prior to joining Barnsley in October 1957 but failed to make an impact at Oakwell. During national service in the Army, he played for Yeovil Town and his impressive displays tempted Bill McGarry to pay £1,500 for him in March 1963. He made his League debut in Bournemouth's 1-1 draw at home to Bristol Rovers a month later and starred in the 1963/64 promotion challenge, scoring 41 goals in 88 Third Division games before being swapped for Swansea's Ken Pound in August 1966. Following a loan spell at Exeter City, he joined Southern League Champions Chelmsford City in July 1968 and subsequently played for King's Lynn, Bedford Town and South Shields. Now living in Hetton-le-Hole, he worked for Blackett Charlton at Billingham ICI, then spent 15 years as a pipe-fitter with Amec Offshore Oil Rigs in Wallsend until early retirement in June 1994.

FREDDIE COX

Manager Freddie Cox guided Cherries to the FA Cup sixth round in 1956/57. Signing professional as an outside-right for Tottenham Hotspur in August 1938, he guested for Fulham, Manchester City, Reading and Swindon Town during the Second World War and was a Flight Lieutenant in the RAF. He moved to Arsenal for £12,000 in September 1949 and was an FA Cup winner in 1950, then a finalist again in 1952 before reuniting with Vic Buckingham as West Brom's player-coach in July 1953. Helping to plot their 1954 FA Cup final triumph, he succeeded Jack Bruton as Bournemouth's manager in April 1956 and his 'Pippins' defeated Wolves and Spurs en route to an epic FA Cup sixth round clash with the Busby Babes the following season. He took charge of Portsmouth in August 1958, then became Gillingham's manager in June 1962 and guided them to the Fourth Division title in 1963/64. Returning to Dean Court as manager in April 1965, he was sacked after relegation in May 1970 and ran a newsagents in Charminster until suffering a fatal heart-attack in August 1973.

IAN COX

Stylish central defender Ian Cox skippered Cherries at Wembley in the 1998 Auto Windscreens Shield final. He impressed as an attacking midfielder in non-League soccer with Whyteleafe and Carshalton Athletic prior to joining Crystal Palace for £35,000 in March 1994 and made his Premiership debut at Norwich City five months later. Despite featuring as a substitute in the 1994/95 FA Cup semi-final replay against Manchester United, he failed to secure a regular first-team slot at Selhurst Park and Mel Machin snapped him up on a free transfer in March 1996. Successfully switched to a central defensive role at Dean Court, he was leading marksman and 'Player of the Season' in 1996/97 and was ever-present as Cherries challenged for the Second Division play-offs in two consecutive seasons. He scored 16 goals in 172 Second Division games before being sold to Burnley for £500,000 in February 2000 and helped them to clinch promotion that season. He then moved to Gillingham in June 2003.

JACK COXFORD

Commanding centre-half Jack Coxford made a significant contribution as Cherries reached the FA Cup fourth round in 1931/32. Initially with North Seaton Colliery, he impressed with Stakeford United prior to joining Sunderland in May 1924. He made his First Division debut in their 1-1 draw at Blackburn Rovers in April 1925 and moved to Birmingham in April 1927, but again found it difficult to gain a first-team slot and followed Frank Richards to Dean Court in May 1930. A distinctive figure in the heart of defence with his high forehead, he starred as Bournemouth went top of the table after a seven match unbeaten start to the 1931/32 campaign which included a 3-0 win over QPR in the first-ever League game at the White City Stadium. He netted three goals in 134 Third Division (South) games for Cherries prior to briefly joining Poole Town in May 1934, then played for Northfleet United. He died in Bury St Edmunds in 1978.

BILLY COXON

Outside-left Billy Coxon featured prominently in Cherries' 1961/62 promotion near-miss. Signing professional for hometown Derby County in May 1950, he failed to secure a First Division slot and moved via Ilkeston Town to Norwich City in May 1952. He scored on his League debut at Aldershot seven months later and became their regular penalty-taker thanks to his powerful shot, playing alongside Ralph Hunt while at Carrow Road. Sold to Lincoln City for £4,000 in March 1958, he helped them to avoid relegation that season and Don Welsh brought him to Dean Court in November 1958. He created numerous goalscoring chances for the likes of Mike Burgess and Dickie Dowsett, also featuring in Bournemouth's League Cup third round wins at home to Cardiff City in 1961/62 and Newcastle United in 1963/64. Netting 37 goals in 200 Third Division games before joining Poole Town in June 1966, he became Parley Sports' player-coach a year later. He was a local hotelier and taxi driver until returning to his native Derbyshire three years ago and now lives in Spondon.

ANDY CRAWFORD

Striker Andy Crawford was an influential figure in AFC Bournemouth's 1981/82 promotion success. Initially with hometown Filey, he signed professional for Derby County in January 1977 and scored on his First Division debut at home to Liverpool a year later. He moved to Blackburn Rovers for £50,000 in October 1979 and was leading marksman alongside record goalscorer Simon Garner in their 1979/80 promotion campaign, reunited with David Webb at Dean Court for £40,000 in November 1981. Partnering Tony Funnell in Cherries' attack, he scored ten goals in 33 League outings prior to joining Cardiff City in August 1983 and had spells with Middlesbrough, Scarborough and Stockport County before briefly linking up with Webb again at Torquay United in February 1985. He returned to local Scarborough football, then rejoined Funnell at Poole Town in August 1988 and featured in their 1989/90 promotion success. Subsequently with Bournemouth Sports and AFC Lymington, he has since settled back in Filey as a builder and still plays local soccer.

CHARLIE CRICKMORE

Fast, skilful outside-left Charlie Crickmore starred in consecutive promotion challenges while at Dean Court. Signing professional for hometown Hull City in February 1959, he made his League debut seven months later and Bill McGarry paid £3,000 for him in July 1962. He helped Cherries to beat Newcastle United in the 1963/64 League Cup third round and scored 17 times in 128 Third Division games prior to joining Gillingham in June 1966 as Jimmy White, David Stocks and Rodney Taylor followed Freddie Cox in the opposite direction. Playing in the same Gills side as Mel Machin, he joined Rotherham United for £25,000 in November 1967 and Tommy Docherty sold him to Norwich City for £15,000 two months later. He moved to Notts County for £7,500 in March 1970 and was ever-present in their 1970/71

Fourth Division title triumph but lost his place to Steve Carter after an ankle injury. Subsequently a fireman in Hull for 22 years until retiring in July 1994, he now lives in nearby Thorngumbald.

JOHNNY CROSLAND

Former England B international centre-half Johnny Crosland was ever-present for Cherries in two consecutive seasons. Initially with St Annes United, he was awarded the DSC during war-time service as a pilot in the Fleet Air Arm and joined Blackpool in May 1946. He deputised for Ron Suart at left-back in the 1948 FA Cup final but struggled to secure a regular First Division slot behind Eric Hayward, then Harry Johnston and Jack Bruton signed him in June 1954 on the recommendation of Stanley Matthews. Appointed captain at Dean Court, he made 106 Third Division (South) appearances for Bournemouth until losing his place to Harry Hughes for the epic 1956/57 FA Cup run and joined Wisbech Town in July 1957. He starred in their 1957/58 FA Cup run, then reunited with Stan Mortensen at Lancaster City whilst running The Shovels pub in Blackpool. Subsequently a hotelier, he then ran his own taxi business in Blackpool until retiring in December 1982 and now lives near his family in Huntingdon.

JACK CROSS

Popular centre-forward Jack Cross was Cherries' leading goalscorer in two consecutive seasons. A former Blackpool amateur, he played for Hendon and Guildford City during national service in the Army at Pirbright and followed Harry Lowe to Dean Court in June 1947. He made his League debut against Swansea in the opening match of Bournemouth's memorable 1947/48 campaign and partnered the likes of Doug McGibbon and Denis Cheney in Cherries' attack, scoring 64 goals in 137 Third Division (South) games before being sold to Northampton Town for £4,000 in October 1953. He joined Sheffield United for £13,000 four months later and gained top-flight experience alongside England star Jimmy Hagan prior to joining Reading in October 1955, then had spells with Headington United, Weymouth and Poole Town. Now living in Broadstone, he spent 31 years with the UK Atomic Energy Authority based at Harwell, Winfrith, Risley and their London headquarters before returning to Winfrith where he was management services officer until retiring in March 1987.

WARREN CUMMINGS

Scottish U-21 international left-back Warren Cummings featured in AFC Bournemouth's 2002/03 Third Division play-off final triumph. A former Chelsea trainee, he signed professional at Stamford Bridge in July 1999 but failed to secure a Premiership slot and was loaned to Cherries in October 2000. He made his League debut in that month's 5--2 victory at Bury and scored once in ten Second Division games during a three-month spell at Dean Court. After a brief period back at Chelsea, he was loaned to West Brom in March 2001 and helped them to qualify for the First Division play-offs that season. He rejoined the Baggies for another loan spell in July 2001 and featured in their 2001/02 promotion campaign. After a period on loan to Dundee United, he returned to Dean Court on loan in February 2003 and moved permanently the following month. He made 20 League appearances as Cherries regained Second Division status at the first attempt.

IAN CUNNINGHAM

Ex-Scottish Youth right-back Ian Cunningham was a popular member of John Benson's squad at Dean Court. 'Jock' captained AFC Bournemouth's youth team and helped the reserves to win the Football Combination title in 1973/74, signing professional in August 1974. Given his Third Division debut in Cherries' 3-2 defeat at Halifax Town four months later, he featured in the 1975/76 promotion challenge and scored four goals in 188 League games until a knee injury curtailed his League career in May 1981. He then spent seven years with Swanage T&H alongside Terry Shanahan and Neil Prosser, helping to win the Western League First Division title in 1986/87. Later with Poole Town and Bournemouth 'Poppies', he became Sturminster Marshall's player-boss and guided them to the Dorset Combination League title in 1997/98 with ex-Cherries Wayne Fereday, Tom Heffernan and Paul Morrell. He managed the Dorset Soldier pub for 10 years and now has his own taxi business in Corfe Mullen as well as managing Cobham Sports.

LAURIE CUNNINGHAM

Long-serving right-back Laurie Cunningham was ever-present four times while at Dean Court. Initially with Consett, he flew Mosquitos as an RAF pilot in 151 Squadron during the war and joined Barnsley in November 1945. He secured a regular slot in their Second Division side before Harry Lowe signed him in June 1948 as a replacement for Fred Marsden. Forming a notable defensive partnership with Ian Drummond, he played for Cherries in the FA Cup third round ties against holders Manchester United in 1948/49 and West Brom in 1954/55. He made 273 Third Division (South) appearances prior to reuniting with Ken Bird at

Dorchester Town in July 1957 and was an experienced figure in their 1957/58 FA Cup run. Moving to Wareham Rangers as player-manager in June 1959, he briefly rejoined Bournemouth as 'A' team coach during Bill McGarry's reign. Still living locally, he ran a newsagents in Bennett Road until retiring in April 1987 and remains a regular visitor to Dean Court.

REG CUTLER

Outside-left Reg Cutler made a significant contribution as Cherries reached the FA Cup sixth round in 1956/57. Signing professional for West Brom in February 1952, he gained top-flight experience as George Lee's understudy and followed Freddie Cox to Bournemouth for £500 in June 1956. He made headlines when he brought a goal crashing down during that season's FA Cup fourth-round triumph at Wolves. Creating numerous goalscoring chances for the likes of Stan Newsham and Dickie Dowsett while at Dean Court, he netted 21 times in 96 League games before linking up with Cox again at Portsmouth for £27,500 in September 1958. He featured in their 1961/62 Third Division title campaign and reunited with Reg Flewin at Stockport County in July 1962, moving to Worcester City in July 1963. Subsequently with Dudley Town and Bromsgrove Rovers, he became a supervisor for Seamless Tubes in Wednesfield and then ran Oakvale Nurseries near Wolverley until retiring in February 2000.

FRED DAVIES

Experienced goalkeeper Fred Davies was a key figure in Cherries' 1970/71 promotion success. Initially with Llandudno, he joined Wolves in April 1957 and contested their goalkeeping slot with Malcolm Finlayson and Dave MacLaren. He helped them to regain top-flight status in 1966/67 and sampled European soccer after moving to Cardiff City for £10,000 in January 1968. John Bond paid £6,000 for him in July 1970 and he was ever-present in Bournemouth's 1971/72 promotion near-miss, making 134 League appearances before following Bond to Norwich City with John Benson and Mel Machin in December 1973. He returned to Dean Court in January 1975 as Benson's assistant for four years, then coached Blackpool and Cardiff City prior to managing Merthyr Tydfil. Later assisting John Bond at Swansea City, Birmingham City and Shrewsbury Town before succeeding him as manager of the latter in May 1993. He subsequently had two spells in charge of Weymouth.

KEVIN DAWTRY

Midfielder Kevin Dawtry made a significant contribution to Cherries' 1981/82 promotion triumph. Signing professional for Southampton in June 1976, he made his First Division debut at Nottingham Forest almost three years later and followed Tony Sealy to Terry Venables' Crystal Palace in May 1980 but failed to make an impact at Selhurst Park. David Webb snapped him up on a free transfer in March 1981 and he scored 11 goals in 65 League outings for Cherries prior to joining Road Sea Southampton in August 1983 after a loan spell at Reading. He helped them to win promotion in 1983/84, then repeated the feat with Geoff Butler's Salisbury in 1985/86 and joined Fareham Town in October 1986. Playing at Dean Court in that season's FA Cup first round, he had a spell with Gosport Borough prior to rejoining Salisbury in September 1988 and was subsequently Blackfield & Langley player-coach. He is now a production planner for Exxon Chemical at Fawley Oil Refinery.

JERMAIN DEFOE

England Youth international striker Jermain Defoe scored in ten consecutive matches for AFC Bournemouth during the 2000/01 campaign. A former trainee at Charlton Athletic, he moved to West Ham for an initial £400,000 in October 1999 and starred in their U-19 team that won the FA Academy play-offs in 1999/2000. He scored on his first-team debut in the Worthington Cup second round tie at Walsall in September 2000 and joined Cherries on loan the following month. Netting in each of his first ten League games to break a 74 year-old club record, AFC Bournemouth narrowly failed to qualify for the Second Division play-offs as his total of 18 goals in 29 League outings included a brilliant solo strike at Oxford United on Boxing Day. Returning to Upton Park, he scored on his England U-21 debut against Mexico that summer and was West Ham's 'Young Player of the Year' in 2001/02 but unable to prevent relegation in 2002/03.

JOHN DELANEY

Ex-England Amateur international centre-half John Delaney had a spell as AFC Bournemouth's captain. Following an unsuccessful spell at OPR, he played for works teams Horlicks and Coopers prior to joining Slough Town in July 1963 and helped them to win promotion in 1964/65. He moved to Wycombe Wanderers in July 1969 and skippered them to two consecutive Isthmian League titles as well as the Amateur Cup semi-finals in 1971/72. Capped 17 times by his country, he also represented Great Britain in an Olympic qualifier before John Bond signed him in August 1973 and captained Cherries at Wycombe in the 1974/75 FA Cup second round. He made 25 Third Division appearances while at Dean Court prior to rejoining Wycombe in July 1975, then moved to Hayes in July 1976. Subsequently with Sutton United and Oxford City (with Harry Redknapp), he then managed Tring Town and Chesham United and is now a cargo agent for Plane Handling at Heathrow Airport.

DICKIE DOWSETT

Popular centre-forward Dickie Dowsett was leading marksman three times while at Dean Court. Real name Gilbert, he impressed with Sudbury Town prior to joining Tottenham Hotspur in May 1952 and scored on his First Division debut at Aston Villa in August 1954. He moved to Southend United in May 1955, then joined Southampton in July 1956 and Freddie Cox signed him as a replacement for Stan Newsham in June 1957. A key figure in Cherries' 1961/62 promotion near-miss, he scored 79 goals in 169 League games before being sold to Crystal Palace for £3,500 in November 1962. He joined Weymouth in June 1965 and featured prominently as they retained the Southern League title in 1965/66, then returned to Dean Court as commercial manager in June 1968. Instrumental in changing the club's name to AFC Bournemouth, he held the post until January 1984 and his wife Cynthia became club secretary. He still lives locally and was production manager of Icarus (Toys) in West Howe until retiring in December 2000.

IAN DRUMMOND

Long-serving Scottish left-back Ian Drummond was ever-present for Cherries in 1954/55. Initially with Jeanfield Swifts, he joined Portsmouth in May 1945 and represented the Royal Navy during national service as an engineer on HMS Victorious. His only first-team appearance for Pompey was as cover for Harry Ferrier in their FA Cup third round win at home to Brighton in 1947/48 and Harry Lowe brought him to Dean Court in June 1949. He formed a notable defensive pairing with Laurie Cunningham and the first of his two goals in 265 Third Division (South) games came in Bournemouth's 5-1 win at home to Newport County in September 1951. Moving to Poole Town in July 1956, he featured in their 1956/57 Western League title triumph and had a spell as Bluebird Sports player-boss before returning to Poole as assistant-trainer to John Kirk. Still living in Oakdale, he spent nearly 20 years as a supervisor/foreman during two spells with Bluebird Caravans and was then a storeman for a local engineering firm until retiring in August 1988.

MICHAEL DUBERRY

Highly-rated young central defender Michael Duberry had a loan spell at AFC Bournemouth during the 1995/96 season. A former Chelsea trainee, he signed professional at Stamford Bridge in June 1993 and made his Premiership debut as the FA Cup finalists lost 2-1 at home to Coventry City in May 1994. He moved to Dean Court on loan in September 1995 and made his debut in that month's 3-1 defeat at Stockport County, playing seven consecutive Second Division games for Cherries before being recalled by Chelsea in response to an injury crisis. Starring as the Blues were FA Cup semi-finalists that season, the England U-21 international helped them win the Coca-Cola Cup and ECWC in 1997/98. He moved to Leeds United for £4,000,000 in July 1999 and helped to beat AC Milan in the 2000/01 European Champions League shortly before being sidelined by an Achilles tendon injury, then had to endure the club's much publicised off-field problems.

KEITH EAST

Much-travelled striker Keith East was Cherries' leading marksman in 1968/69. A former Portsmouth apprentice, he signed professional in June 1963 but failed to secure a first-team slot at Fratton Park and moved to Swindon Town in May 1964. He was top scorer alongside Don Rogers in 1965/66 and joined Stockport County in December 1966, helping to clinch the Fourth Division title that season. Freddie Cox signed him in November 1967 and he starred as Bournemouth took Liverpool to an FA Cup third round replay two months later, netting 34 goals in 94 Third Division games prior to joining Northampton Town for £5,000 in July 1970. He joined Crewe Alexandra in July 1971, then had a spell with Folkestone before playing in South Africa with Johannesburg Rangers and Berrea Park. Returning to Poole Town in August 1976, he then joined Corinthian Casuals and set up his own car sales business in Holland Park. He has spent the past 16 years selling cars for the Dovercourt (Volkswagen) dealership in Battersea and is now sales controller.

EFAN EKOKU

Striker Efan Ekoku starred in Cherries' 1991/92 FA Cup third round replay win at Newcastle United. Initially spotted as a winger in Merton intermediate football, he joined Sutton United in December 1986 and switched to a central role alongside Paul McKinnon. He was leading marksman in 1989/90 and a member of the England Semi-Professional squad, moving to AFC Bournemouth for £100,000 in May 1990. Overcoming a serious ankle injury, 'The Chief' impressed with his devastating pace and scored 21 times in 62 League games before being sold to Norwich City for a record £765,000 in March 1993. He netted a then Premiership record four goals at Everton six months later and partnered Chris Sutton in their attack, moving to Wimbledon for a record £920,000 in October 1994. Twice top scorer including 1996/97 when the Dons were FA Cup and Coca-Cola Cup semi-finalists, he gained Nigerian international recognition and has since played for Grasshoppers Zurich, Sheffield Wednesday and Brentford.

WADE ELLIOTT

Exciting winger Wade Elliott was an influential figure in AFC Bournemouth's 2002/03 Third Division play-off final success. A former England Schoolboy international, he was midway through a course in sociology and communications at Goldsmith's College in Lewisham when he moved from Bashley to Dean Court for £5,000 in February 2000. He scored on his full League debut in the 2-0 win over Wycombe Wanderers and capped a remarkable first full season by being named 'Player of the Year' as Cherries narrowly failed to reach the Second Division play-offs in 2000/01. He suffered a loss of form during the 2001/02 campaign but showed great character after missing a vital last-minute penalty at Reading to score two more from the spot during the closing weeks of the season. Starring as Sean O'Driscoll's side regained Second Division status at the first attempt in 2002/03, he has netted 24 goals in 139 League outings for AFC Bournemouth.

JOHN EVANSON

Midfielder John Evanson was an experienced member of Alec Stock's squad at Dean Court. Starting with Towcester, he signed professional for Oxford United in February 1965 and was a member of their 1967/68 Third Division title squad. He starred in their 1970/71 FA Cup run and moved to Blackpool for a record £40,000 in February 1974, featuring in that season's promotion near-miss. Sold to Fulham for £50,000 in August 1976, he played alongside the likes of Bobby Moore, George Best and Rodney Marsh before following Alec Stock to AFC Bournemouth for £20,000 in July 1979. He scored twice in 53 Fourth Division games for Cherries prior to joining Poole Town in March 1981 and played in that season's Anglo-Italian Tournament final. Subsequently running the Carpenters Arms in Burghclere for nine years until November 1992, he was then a partner in the Key Eating house in Hamble before managing the Owl & Pussycat pub in Shoreditch. He has since been mine host at the Kentish Horse pub in Markbeech, Kent.

LES EYRE

Versatile inside-left Les Eyre partnered Jack Cross in Cherries' early post-war attack. Initially with Bilsthorpe Colliery, he represented the RAF during wartime service in India and was briefly an amateur with Cardiff City before following Cyril Spiers to Norwich City in July 1946. He made his League debut at home to Crystal Palace two months later and was leading marksman in his first two seasons at Carrow Road, scoring five times in their 1946/47 FA Cup first round win over Brighton. Jack Bruton paid £5,500 for him in November 1951 and he netted 10 goals in 38 Third Division (South) games for Bournemouth before moving to Chelmsford City in July 1953. He soon returned to coal mining at Bilsthorpe Colliery for five years, then settled back in Norwich and became mine host at the Horse Barracks Pub. Subsequently employed at Colmans until retirement in January 1987, he remained in Norwich until his death in November 1991.

RON EYRE

Centre-forward Ron Eyre set Cherries' all-time goalscoring record during nine seasons at Dean Court. Real name Roland, he impressed with Hucknall Colliery prior to joining Sheffield Wednesday in August 1923 and made his solitary Second Division appearance as cover for Sid Binks at home to Oldham Athletic seven months later. Harry Kinghorn signed him for struggling Bournemouth in January 1925 and his arrival sparked a significant improvement in results. Starring as Cherries took eventual winners Bolton Wanderers to an FA Cup fourth round replay in 1925/26 and Liverpool to a third round replay the following year, he also helped them to reach the fifth round in 1928/29. He was leading marksman in eight successive seasons and scored a record 202 goals in 302 Third Division (South) games before being released in May 1933. Subsequently with Christchurch, he spent 30 years as a foreman ganger in the construction department of Southern Electricity Board until retiring in November 1966 and remained local until his death in August 1969.

BRIAN FARMER

Right-back Brian Farmer was an experienced figure in Cherries' 1961/62 promotion near-miss. Initially with Stourbridge, he signed professional for Birmingham City in July 1954 and made his First Division debut at home to Bolton Wanderers in October 1956. He secured a regular first-team slot at St Andrews after Jeff Hall's tragic death in April 1959 and was a Fairs Cup finalist in two consecutive seasons. Bill McGarry paid £3,800 for him in January 1962 and he replaced Arnold Woollard in Bournemouth's defence, helping to beat Newcastle United in the 1963/64 League Cup third round. He made 132 Third Division appearances for Cherries prior to becoming Christchurch player-coach in June 1965. Joining the Save & Prosper investment group, he rose to executive director and then spent five years as Southern Region director with Guardian Royal Exchange until early retirement in February 1993. Still living locally, he coached Parley Sports, then became chairman of Christchurch and Alresford Town as well as scouting for Aston Villa.

GEORGE FARROW

A long throw expert, right-hall George Farrow was Cherries' joint leading marksman in 1934/35. He represented Whitburn Boys prior to signing professional for Stockport County in October 1930 and made his League debut at home to Carlisle United on Christmas Day 1931. Major Buckley signed him for Wolverhampton Wanderers the following month and he gained top-flight experience as Dickie Rhodes' understudy before moving to Dean Court in July 1933. He impressed in a struggling side and became Bournemouth's regular penalty taker, scoring 12 goals in 106 Third Division (South) games prior to joining Blackpool in June 1936. Featuring in their 1936/37 promotion success, he starred alongside internationals like Stanley Matthews and Stan Mortensen before being swapped for Sheffield United's Walter Rickett in January 1948. He became Bacup Borough's player-manager and was later a progress chaser at Whitburn Area Workshops until retiring in October 1975, remaining in Whitburn until his death in December 1980.

WARREN FEENEY

Northern Ireland international striker Warren Feeney was AFC Bournemouth's leading marksman and 'Player of the Year' in 2001/02. Initially with St Andrew's Boys Club, he signed professional for Leeds United in January 1998 and joined Cherries on loan in March 2001. He made his League debut as a substitute in that month's 1-0 victory at home to Bury and came off the bench to score in the next two games, including the decisive goal in the 4-3 win over Oxford United. Signing a permanent deal for AFC Bournemouth in July 2001, he made his debut for Northern Ireland against Liechtenstein in March 2002 and joined his grandfather (Jim Feeney) and father (Warren Feeney) as a full international. He had a series of ankle problems and missed the 2002/03 promotion run-in after injuring his knee playing for Northern Ireland U-21's against Greece in April 2003. He has scored 24 goals in 68 League outings for the club.

RIO FERDINAND

Outstanding young central defender Rio Ferdinand had a loan spell at AFC Bournemouth during the 1996/97 campaign. A cousin of England international Les Ferdinand, he signed professional for West Ham in November 1995 and made his Premiership debut against Sheffield Wednesday in the final game of the 1995/96 season. He was loaned to Cherries in November 1996 and played ten consecutive Second Division games while at Dean Court. Capped at England Youth and U-21 level, he made his full international debut against Cameroon in November 1997 was West Ham's 'Player of the Year' in 1997/98. He moved to Leeds United for a record £18,000,000 in November 2000, helping them to reach the European Champion's League semi-finals that season. Starring for England in the World Cup finals shortly before joining Manchester United for a British record £30,000,000 in July 2002, he was a key figure in their 2002/03 Premiership title triumph.

PHIL FERNS (Snr)

Versatile right-half Phil Ferns was ever-present for Cherries in 1965/66. Initially an amateur with Everton and Manchester City, he signed professional for Liverpool in September 1957 and skippered their reserves before national service in the Royal Artillery. He made his First Division debut at home to Manchester City in August 1962 and won a League Championship medal in 1963/64, unlucky not to play in the 1965 FA Cup final after injury sidelined Gordon Milne. Freddie Cox brought him to Dean Court in August 1965 and he helped Bournemouth take Burnley to an FA Cup third round replay, making 46 Third Division appearances prior to joining Mansfield Town in August 1966. He became Rhyl's player-manager in July 1968, then joined Poole Town as player-coach a year later and was an experienced figure in successive relegation escapes. Still living in Poole, he spent 24 years as a machine operator with Hamworthy Engineering until September 1996 and was then a security man at the B&Q Supercentre in Fleets Lane.

PHIL FERNS (Jnr)

Young left-back Phil Ferns played alongside Ian Cunningham in AFC Bournemouth's defence. The son of ex-Cherry Phil Ferns, he impressed with Poole Town prior to signing professional at Dean Court in February 1979 and featured in that month's 7-1 win at home to Doncaster Rovers. He scored six goals in 95 Fourth Division games for Cherries before being sold to Charlton Athletic for £20,000 in August 1981 and was loaned to Wimbledon prior to joining Blackpool in August 1983. Featuring in their 1984/85 promotion triumph, he joined Aldershot in July 1985 and Yeovil Town a year later. He skippered the 1987/88 Vauxhall-Opel League and Cup 'double' success, then rejoined Poole in November 1989 and helped to win promotion in 1989/90. Returning to Yeovil in July 1991, he starred in their 1992/93 FA Cup run and joined Trowbridge Town in March 1995 but a broken leg ended his playing career in December 1996. He has since been a constable with Hampshire Police and now Dorset Police.

FRANK FIDLER

Centre-forward Frank Fidler was Cherries' leading marksman in 1953/54. A former Manchester United amateur, he joined Witton Albion in exchange for Joe Dale in June 1947 after wartime service in the Irish Guards and set their goalscoring record as they were Cheshire League champions in two consecutive seasons. He moved to Wrexham in May 1950, then joined Leeds United in October 1951 but lost his place when John Charles switched to centre-forward and Jack Bruton brought him to Dean Court in December 1952. Playing alongside the likes of Denis Cheney and Stan Newsham in Bournemouth's attack, he netted 32 goals in 61 Third Division (South) games before moving to Yeovil Town in July 1955. He was top scorer as they were Southern League Cup finalists in 1955/56, then joined Hereford United in July 1957 and starred in their 1958/59 Southern League Cup success prior to joining Bridgwater Town. Employed by Westlands in Yeovil, he then worked for the Post Office until retiring in August 1989 and has settled in Farnborough.

TREVOR FINNIGAN

Striker Trevor Finnigan was a popular member of John Benson's squad at Dean Court. A former Port Vale apprentice under Sir Stanley Matthews, he signed professional for Everton in May 1971 but failed to secure a First Division slot at Goodison Park and revived his career with Runcorn. He moved to Blackpool in March 1977 and John Benson paid £3,000 for him in January 1978, scoring five goals in 25 Fourth Division games for AFC Bournemouth before being sold to Yeovil Town for £2,000 in January 1979. Moving to Stuart Morgan's Weymouth for £5,000 in July 1980, he was one of several ex-Cherries who featured in their 1982/83 FA Cup run and gained England Semi-Professional recognition prior to rejoining Yeovil as player-manager in July 1983. He subsequently played for Bath City, Keith Miller's Dorchester Town, Wimborne Town (P/M), Brian Chambers' Swanage T & H and Lyme Regis. Still living locally, he now installs fibre-optic cabling for communication systems in partnership with Keiron Baker.

JACK FISHER

Hard-tackling left-back Jack Fisher partnered Laurie Cunningham in Cherries' defence. After representing the Royal Navy during wartime service in the Middle East, he signed professional for Millwall in May 1946 and played alongside his twin brother George before Harry Lowe paid £1,000 for him in June 1949. He made 52 Third Division (South) appearances for Bournemouth and also captained the reserves before reuniting with Jimmy Blair at Ramsgate Athletic in June 1954, starring in their 1955/56 Kent League title triumph. Moving to Weymouth in July 1956, he joined Yeovil Town a year later and then became Longfleet St Mary's player-coach. He succeeded John Kirk as Poole Town's trainer in October 1964 and combined this with floor-laying for Sherry & Haycock until returning to Dean Court as a coach under his son-in-law David Webb in July 1981. Still living in Poole, he was subsequently a self-employed carpenter until retiring in June 1992 and his grandson Danny Webb has graduated from Southampton's youth team.

CARL FLETCHER

Inspirational skipper Carl Fletcher scored twice in AFC Bournemouth's 2002/03 Third Division play-off final triumph. He came through the ranks at Dean Court and was still a trainee when he made his League debut as a substitute in Cherries' 2-1 defeat at Grimsby Town in February 1998. Signing professional five months later, he secured a regular first-team slot during the 1999/2000 season and formed an excellent midfield partnership with Richard Hughes as AFC Bournemouth narrowly failed to qualify for the Second Division play-offs in 2000/01. He became Cherries' youngest-ever captain against Blackpool in January 2002 and scored twice in a 4-3 defeat. Appointed skipper for the 2002/03 campaign, he impressed after being switched to a central defensive role due to injury problems at the club. He was 'Player of the Season' as Cherries regained Second Division status at the first attempt and has netted 15 goals in 147 League outings.

STEVE FLETCHER

Big striker Steve Fletcher scored in AFC Bournemouth's 2002/03 Third Division play-off final triumph. The grandson of former England international left-back Jack Howe, he signed professional for hometown Hartlepool United in August 1990 and scored on his League debut to

clinch that month's 3-2 win at Chesterfield. He was a member of Hartlepool's 1990/91 promotion squad and helped take Ipswich Town to an FA Cup third round replay the following season prior to becoming Tony Pulis' first signing at £30,000 in July 1992. Impressing with his aerial strength, he was 'Player of the Season' in the 1994/95 relegation escape and leading marksman as Cherries were Auto Windscreens Shield finalists in 1997/98. Also featuring in successive promotion challenges, a knee injury sidelined the popular skipper for virtually the whole of the 2001/02 season and he is now the club's longest-serving player with 65 goals in 348 League outings. He had a testimonial against Portsmouth in July 2003.

CHRIS FOOTE

Young midfielder Chris Foote helped Cherries to beat Sheffield Wednesday in the 1969/70 League Cup second round. Born locally, he signed professional at Dean Court in August 1968 and made his League debut in the 3-0 defeat at Swindon Town eight months later. He made a significant contribution as Bournemouth were FA Youth Cup semi-finalists in 1968/69 but was unable to prevent relegation under Freddie Cox the following season. Scoring twice in 44 Third Division games for Cherries, John Bond allowed him to join Cambridge United on a free transfer in March 1971. A prominent member of their 1972/73 promotion squad with Brian Greenhalgh, he joined Weymouth in July 1974 and was a member of their side that took Peterborough United to an FA Cup first round second replay in 1974/75. Quitting football at the age of 25 in May 1976, he became a director of Coplead Ltd plumbing & heating contractors in Bournemouth and for the past 18 years has been a self-employed plumbing and heating engineer.

JACK FRIAR

Scottish outside-right Jack Friar was a promising young member of Billy Birrell's squad at Dean Court. Initially with Carluke Juniors, he joined Bradford City in September 1929 but failed to make an impact at Valley Parade and had a spell with Hibernian before moving to Portsmouth in April 1932. He scored on his First Division debut at Middlesbrough six months later and Birrell signed him in July 1933, netting 11 goals in 34 Third Division (South) games that season for struggling Bournemouth prior to joining Port Vale in July 1934. Returning to the top-flight with Preston NE in exchange for Eddie Critchley plus £3,500 five months later, he was sold to Norwich City for £2,000 in December 1935 and secured a regular Second Division slot at Carrow Road before moving to East Anglian rivals Ipswich Town in June 1939. He subsequently returned to Scotland and worked at a pit-head in Lanark until retiring in July 1976, residing in Bathgate until his death in May 1979.

TONY FUNNELL

Popular striker Tony Funnell was leading marksman in AFC Bournemouth's 1981/82 promotion success. Initially with Eastbourne United, he joined Southampton in January 1977 and returned from a loan spell with Vancouver Whitecaps to score on his League debut at Notts County eight months later. He partnered Ted MacDougall and Phil Boyer in Saints' attack and netted their promotion-clinching goal at Orient in April 1978, moving to Gillingham for a record £50,000 in March 1979. Sold to Brentford for a similar fee in March 1980, David Webb paid £5,000 for him in September 1981 and he scored 22 goals in 64 League outings for the Cherries until a back injury curtailed his professional career. He joined Poole Town in November 1984 and was ever-present in their 1989/90 promotion success, setting their goalscoring record before his testimonial in May 1991. Later manager/coach of Hamworthy United, Poole Town and Wimborne Town, he has since run his own community coaching scheme in Poole as well as a private soccer school.

JIMMY GABRIEL

Former Scottish international wing-half Jimmy Gabriel was a key figure in AFC Bournemouth's 1972/73 promotion challenge. A footballing son, he impressed as a teenager with hometown Dundee prior to joining Everton for £30,000 in March 1960. He featured prominently as they won the League Championship in 1962/63 and FA Cup in 1965/66, moving to Southampton for £45,000 in July 1967. Capped twice by his country, he helped Saints to qualify for Europe before John Bond paid £20,000 for him in July 1972. He scored four goals in 53 Third Division games for Cherries and was loaned to Swindon Town prior to joining Brentford in March 1974. Moving to Seattle Sounders two months later, he coached their side including several ex-Cherries to the

NASL Soccer Bowl in 1977. He subsequently coached San Jose Earthquakes before returning to Dean Court as assistant-manager to Harry Redknapp in March 1987. Rejoining Everton in a similar capacity in June 1990, he has been coaching back in the United States since February 1997.

PADDY GALLACHER

Popular inside-forward Paddy Gallacher played for Cherries either side of the Second World War. Born in Glasgow, he impressed with Third Lanark as they won the Scottish Second Division title in 1934/35 and were Scottish Cup finalists in 1935/36. He moved to Blackburn Rovers in October 1936 and played alongside Jack Bruton in their attack before Rovers' manager Bob Crompton recommended him to his former club in June 1938. A member of Bournemouth's squad that narrowly missed promotion under Harry Lowe in 1947/48, he scored three times in 35 Third Division (South) games while at Dean Court and moved to Weymouth as player-manager in June 1948. He guided their side - including ex-Cherries Glan Jones, Ronnie Ranson and Fred Marsden - to an FA Cup third round tie at Manchester United in 1949/50, then joined Dundalk as player coach in June 1950. Subsequently settling in Bexhill-on-Sea, he was an HGV driver until retiring in December 1977 and remained in Sussex until his death in June 1983.

ROY GATER

Tough-tackling centre-half Roy Gater was twice ever-present for Cherries. A former Port Vale junior, he signed professional in April 1958 and made his League debut at Coventry City three years later. He failed to secure a regular first-team slot at Vale Park and followed John Archer and Peter Hall to Bournemouth for £5,000 in July 1962, succeeding Tony Nelson in the heart of defence. An influential figure in successive promotion challenges, he scored three goals in 216 Third Division games while at Dean Court before moving to Crewe Alexandra in January 1969. He reunited with Ralph Miller at Weymouth in November 1972 and helped to win the

Southern League Cup in 1972/73, then joined Dorchester Town in February 1974. Ever-present in 1974/75, he achieved managerial success during seven years at Christchurch and was assistant-boss at Poole Town and Bournemouth 'Poppies' before rejoining Christchurch as manager. Still living locally, he was a painter and decorator for Furneaux Builders until retiring in November 2001.

LEN GAYNOR

Inside-forward Len Gaynor partnered the likes of Jack Cross and Frank Fidler in Cherries' attack. He had spells with Ilkeston Town, Brinsley and Eastwood Colliery prior to joining Hull City in April 1948, gaining Second Division experience alongside the likes of Raich Carter and Don Revie before Jack Bruton brought him to Dean Court in June 1951. Scoring 12 goals in 51 Third Division (South) games for Bournemouth, he joined Southampton in March 1954 and was an influential figure as their reserves won the Combination Cup in 1954/55. Linking up again with Denis Cheney at Aldershot in February 1955, he skippered them until joining Oldham Athletic in July 1957 and moved to Yeovil Town in January 1958 but a broken leg suffered in a Southern League game at Poole Town effectively ended his playing career nine months later. Still living locally, he became a self-employed carpenter and has more recently been in partnership with his eldest son Gary as L&G Builders.

BRIAN GIBBS

Inside-forward Brian Gibbs featured in Cherries' 1961/62 promotion near-miss under Bill McGarry. A former Portsmouth junior, he had a spell with Gosport Borough prior to joining Bournemouth in October 1957 and made his League debut in the 4-1 defeat at Newport County two months later. He provided reliable forward cover for the likes of Mike Burgess and Dickie Dowsett, scoring 15 goals in 58 League games while at Dean Court before reuniting with Freddie Cox at Gillingham for £4,000 in October 1962. Leading marksman in five consecutive seasons including their 1963/64 Fourth Division title triumph, he played alongside several one-time Cherries prior to joining Colchester United for £6,000 in September 1968. He featured in their epic 1970/71 FA Cup fifth round victory over Leeds United as well as their 1971/72 Watney Cup final success, joining Bletchley Town as player-boss in June 1972. Still living near Milton Keynes, he spent 23 years in meat industry management until retiring in December 1995.

IAN GIBSON

Former Scotland U-23 midfielder Ian Gibson was an experienced member of John Bond's squad at Dean Court. Initially with Accrington Stanley, he was their youngest Football League debutant at 15 years 358 days against Norwich City in March 1959 and controversially moved to Bradford Park Avenue four months later. He starred in their 1960/61 promotion success and joined Middlesbrough for £20,000 in March 1962, finishing top scorer in 1963/64. Sold to Coventry City for £57,500 in July 1966, he was a key figure in their 1966/67 Second Division title triumph and 1969/70 Fairs Cup qualification before reuniting with Jimmy Scoular at Cardiff City for £35,000 in July 1970. Helping them to reach the ECWC quarter-finals in 1970/71, he joined AFC Bournemouth in a joint £100,000 deal with Brian Clark in October 1972 and made 20 Third Division appearances prior to joining South African side Berea Park in May 1974. Later with Gateshead and Whitby Town (P/M), he now lives in Redcar and fits new seals in gasometers.

JIMMY GLASS

Goalkeeper Jimmy Glass played for AFC Bournemouth at Wembley in the 1998 Auto Windscreens Shield final. A former Crystal Palace trainee, he signed professional in July 1991 and made his League debut while on loan to Portsmouth in February 1995. Also loaned to Gillingham and Burnley, Mel Machin signed him in March 1996 to replace Ian Andrews and he quickly impressed with his agility. He suffered a loss of form during the 1996/97 campaign and Andy Marshall arrived on loan from Norwich City but soon regained his first-team slot. Ever-present for Cherries in 1997/98, he made 94 Second Division appearances before moving to Swindon Town in June 1998. He ended the 1998/99 season on loan to Carlisle United and scored the dramatic last-gasp winner against Plymouth Argyle that preserved their Football League status. He then had spells with Cambridge United, Brentford, Oxford United, Crawley Town, Kingstonian, Salisbury and Brockenhurst and is now a salesman for Spire Technology in Verwood.

PETER GLEDSTONE

Long-serving left-back Peter Gledstone featured in Cherries' 1961/62 promotion near-miss under Bill McGarry. Born locally, he helped Bournemouth Gasworks to win the Hampshire Senior Cup in 1953/54 and gained Dorset County honours prior to joining Bournemouth in November 1955. He returned from national service in the Royal Berkshire Regiment to make his League debut at home to Port Vale in April 1958 and partnered the likes of Jack Gregory and Arnold Woollard in defence. He scored twice in 131 League games for Cherries before a knee injury curtailed his playing career in June 1964, then had a period with Bournemouth Fire Brigade until emigrating to New Zealand in March 1967. Settling in Auckland, he had two spells as an aircraft technician with Air New Zealand either side of a year back in Bournemouth as a typewriter technician. For the past 23 years he has lived in Australia, employed as a maintenance engineer until retiring in May 1999 and now lives in Cabarita Beach, New South Wales.

HOWARD GODDARD

Striker Howard Goddard formed an exciting young partnership with Kevin Reeves while at Dean Court. A former apprentice, he made his League debut as a 15 year-old in Cherries' 2-0 defeat at Halifax Town in April 1973 and signed professional in July 1974. He was leading marksman in 1974/75 but cost-saving measures led to him joining Swindon Town in June 1976 and he moved to Newport County in August 1977, finishing top scorer in two consecutive seasons. He played alongside John Aldridge in their 1979/80 promotion campaign until suffering a broken leg and had a loan spell at Blackpool before David Webb brought him back to Dean Court in December 1981. Helping to clinch promotion that season, he scored 20 goals in 76 League games overall for Cherries prior to joining Aldershot in August 1982 and subsequently played for Kapa (Finland), Andover, Sliema (Malta) and then coached various Dutch sides whilst working for a computer company in Den Bosch. He is now managing Andover.

TOMMY GODWIN

Republic of Ireland international goalkeeper Tommy Godwin starred as Cherries reached the FA Cup sixth round in 1956/57. Initially with Home Farm in his native Dublin, he represented the League of Ireland while at Shamrock Rovers but broke a leg in the 1947/48 FAI Cup semi-final. He helped Eire to beat England shortly before moving to Leicester City in September 1949 and contested their goalkeeping slot with Johnny Anderson until Jack Bruton signed him in June 1952. Ever-present in three consecutive seasons, he became Bournemouth's first full international when selected to play against the Netherlands in May 1956 and gained the last four of his 13 caps while at Dean Court. He was given a testimonial in May 1962, making 357 League appearances for Cherries before moving to Dorchester Town in June 1963. Subsequently manager of Portfield Athletic, he spent 20 years at British Aerospace (Hurn) and was then a parks patrolman for Bournemouth Corporation until retiring in August 1992. He remained local until his death in August 1996.

MILTON GRAHAM

Young midfielder Milton Graham scored in Cherries' epic 1983/84 FA Cup third round win over holders Manchester United. Initially a striker with Chelsea and Tottenham schoolboys, he signed professional at Dean Court in May 1981 and netted twice on his League debut in Cherries' 3-2 win at home to Bury five months later. He helped to clinch promotion that season and also scored in the 1984 Associate Members Cup final triumph, managing 12 goals in 73 League outings for AFC Bournemouth before moving to Chester City in August 1985. He featured in their 1985/86 promotion success and 1986/87 FA Cup run, then joined Peterborough United in July 1989 but an ankle injury effectively ended his League career the following season and he briefly joined Brian Chambers' Poole Town in April 1992. Subsequently with Spalding United, Bourne Town, Grantham Town, Holbeach United, Corby Town and Stamford, he then managed local side Pearl Assurance and now works for a boat building company in Oundle.

BRIAN GREENHALGH

Much-travelled striker Brian Greenhalgh replaced Phil Boyer in AFC Bournemouth's attack. Signing professional for Preston NE in February 1965, he joined Aston Villa in a joint £35,000 deal with Brian Godfrey in September 1967 and was sold to Leicester City for £15,000 in February 1969. Moving to Huddersfield Town for a similar fee four months later, he featured in their 1969/70 Second Division title campaign and joined Cambridge United in July 1971. He was leading marksman in three consecutive seasons including their 1972/73 promotion success and Trevor Hartley paid £35,000 for him in February 1974. Scoring seven times in 24 Third Division games for Cherries, he moved to Watford for £5,000 in March 1975 and then played for Dartford, Bedford Town, Hillingdon Borough, Staines Town, Wealdstone, Cambridge City, Carshalton Athletic, Maidenhead United and Chesham United. He was Everton's chief scout for nine years until July 1999 and has since scouted for Watford and Aston Villa.

JACK GREGORY

Full-back Jack Gregory was an experienced member of Don Welsh's squad at Dean Court. Initially with Woolston Youth Club, he signed professional for Southampton in December 1944 and became captain at The Dell during the 1953/54 campaign. He was displaced by Tommy Traynor and joined Alec Stock's Leyton Orient in July 1955, featuring in their 1955/56 Third Division (South) title triumph alongside Les Blizzard. Moving to Bournemouth on a free transfer in July 1959, he partnered Peter Gledstone in defence and made 17 Third Division appearances for Cherries before reuniting with Ted Ballard at Ashford Town in August 1960. He made a significant contribution to their 1961/62 FA Cup run, then followed Ballard to Hastings United in July 1962 and helped them to win promotion in 1962/63. Subsequently with Cowes, he then managed Sholing Sports and worked as a boilermaker welder for Vospers ship repairs at Southampton Docks until made redundant in June 1984. He still lives in Southampton.

BILL GRIPTON

Centre-half Bill Gripton succeeded Jim Stirling in the heart of Cherries' defence. Initially with Toll End Wesley, he signed professional for West Brom in November 1937 and was given his League debut at home to Millwall in April 1939. He made the most wartime appearances for Albion but failed to hold a regular first-team slot at The Hawthorns after the war and moved to Luton Town in June 1948. Jack Bruton snapped him up on a free transfer in July 1950. Playing alongside the likes of Laurie Cunningham and Ian Drummond while at Dean Court, he made 79 Third Division (South) appearances for Bournemouth prior to joining Worcester City in June 1952 and became their groundsman. He was subsequently groundsman for Vono bedding company in his native Tipton as well as coaching Vono Sports but motor neurone disease forced his early retirement and he died in February 1980. His younger brother Joe is the long-serving chairman of Tipton Harriers athletics club.

ALAN GROVES

Exciting winger Alan Groves featured in AFC Bournemouth's 1972/73 promotion challenge. Signing professional for hometown Southport in December 1968, he made his League debut at Northampton Town three months later but was allowed to join Chester on a free transfer in July 1970. He featured in their 1970/71 promotion near-miss before moving to Shrewsbury Town in February 1971 and was ever-present in 1971/72. John Bond paid £44,000 for him in October 1972 and he scored twice on his debut as Cherries triumphed 7-2 at Rotherham United, netting four goals in 36 Third Division games while at Dean Court before being controversially sold to promotion rivals Oldham Athletic for £10,000 in February 1974. He helped them to clinch the Third Division title that season and was a favourite at Boundary Park prior to joining Blackpool in November 1977. Shortly after clashing with the Education Authority for refusing to allow his 16-year-old bride to attend school, he tragically suffered a fatal heart attack in June 1978.

JOHN GROVES

Experienced right-half John Groves helped Cherries to beat Newcastle United in the 1963/64 League Cup third round. The son of former Derby County star Arthur Groves, he represented Derbyshire Schools with Billy

Coxon and signed professional as a forward for Luton Town in October 1950. Given his League debut at Leeds United in April 1954, he featured in their 1954/55 promotion success and played alongside skipper Syd Owen in the 1959 FA Cup final. Reg Flewin paid £2,750 for him in September 1963 and he was reunited with Coxon at Dean Court, also featuring prominently in Bournemouth's 1963/64 promotion challenge. He made 54 Third Division appearances until a back injury curtailed his playing career in June 1965 and he settled back in his native Derby. Subsequently assistant manager of Burton Albion, he then scouted for Brighton and Charlton Athletic and spent 30 years working for Courtaulds until retiring in December 1995. He is now a Derby County season-ticket holder.

TERRY GULLIVER

Popular right-back Terry Gulliver featured in Cherries' 1970/71 promotion success. Initially with Shaftesbury Boys, he joined Weymouth in June 1961 and starred as they won the Southern League title in two consecutive seasons. Freddie Cox signed him in August 1966 and he made his League debut in that month's 1--1 draw at Oxford United, partnering the likes of David Stocks and Ralph Miller in Bournemouth's defence. He helped Cherries take Liverpool to an FA Cup third round replay in 1967/68 and beat Sheffield Wednesday in the 1969/70 League Cup second round. Displaced by the arrival of Mel Machin, he scored twice in 163 League outings before moving to Cape Town City in June 1972. An influential figure as they won the South African title, he joined Hellenic for six seasons in June 1978 and then coached junior soccer in Cape Town. He was sales manager for M&B Pump Company in South Africa until returning to the Bournemouth area in March 1986 and still lives locally, now national sales manager for KSB pump manufacturers.

ALISTAIR GUNN

Scottish outside-right Alistair Gunn was an experienced member of Jack Bruton's squad at Dean Court. A former classmate of Ian Drummond at Grove Academy in Broughty Ferry, he played for Dundee Elmwood before wartime service in the Royal Marines on Admiralty Islands and joined Dundee in July 1946. He starred as they won the Scottish 'B' Division title in 1946/47, then were 'A' (First) Division runners-up in 1948/49 and moved to Huddersfield Town for £10,000 in January 1951. Helping them to regain top-flight status in 1952/53, he was displaced by Gerry Burrell and joined Bournemouth for £2,000 in June 1954. He created numerous goalscoring chances for Stan Newsham and netted twice in 27 Third Division (South) games for Cherries before leaving in May 1955 to qualify as an accountant with a jute firm in Dundee. Briefly reviving his playing career with Arbroath under ex-Dundee team-mate Tommy Gray, he still lives in Broughty Ferry and spent 23 years as an accountant with NCR in Dundee until early retirement in May 1984.

NEIL HAGUE

Ex-England Youth international defender Neil Hague was ever-present for AFC Bournemouth in 1975/76. Signing professional for Rotherham United in December 1966, Tommy Docherty gave him his League debut at Millwall eleven months later and he helped to take Leicester City to an FA Cup fifth round replay in 1967/68. He was sold to Plymouth Argyle for £15,000 in November 1971 and featured prominently as they were League Cup semi-finalists in 1973/74. He followed Alan Welsh to Dean Court with Derek Rickard for £9,000 in July 1974. Unable to prevent Cherries' relegation in 1974/75, he scored seven times in 89 League games prior to joining Huddersfield Town in June 1976. He moved to Darlington in May 1977, then reunited with Harry Redknapp and Keiron Baker at Jimmy Gabriel's Phoenix Fire in May 1979 and also played in the United States for Columbus Ohio. Returning to County Durham in August 1981, he became a builder near Barnard Castle and for the past 19 years has been a self-employed property developer in Plymouth.

GORDON HAIGH

Hard-working inside-forward Gordon Haigh was an early Jack Bruton signing for the Cherries. Born in Barnsley, he developed in local soccer with Worsbrough Bridge and Ward Green before wartime service as a wireless operator in the RAF in Canada. He had a spell with Ransom & Marles in Newark prior to joining Burnley in November 1945 and scored on his League debut at home to Newport County ten months later. Helping the Clarets to win promotion in 1946/47, he gained top-flight experience as Harry Potts' understudy before moving to Dean Court in April 1950. Playing alongside Doug McGibbon in Bournemouth's attack, he netted three goals in 17 Third Division (South) games for Jack Bruton's side prior to joining Watford in August 1951 and then played for Rossendale United and Nelson. He ran two fruit and fish shops in Burnley until they were demolished to make way for the M65 link road, then spent 20 years as caretaker at Reedley County Primary School until retiring in August 1986 and now lives in Brierfield.

CLIFF HALLIWELL

Popular right-half Cliff Halliwell starred as Cherries took West Ham to an FA Cup fifth round replay in 1928/29. A former Sheffield Wednesday junior, he served in the Royal Navy during the Great War before impressing with leading Sheffield amateur side Darnall Old Boys. He joined Sheffield United in June 1920 and made his First Division debut at Burnley in October 1921, understudying England international Harold Pantling at Bramall Lane before Leslie Knighton signed him in October 1926. A key figure as Bournemouth took Liverpool to an FA Cup third round replay in 1926/27, he played alongside the likes of Jack Bradford and Charles Smith while at Dean Court and scored twice in 214 Third Division (South) games until a knee injury ended his playing career in May 1932. He was briefly landlord of the Old Crown Inn in Sheffield, then spent 38 years at Firth Vickers steelworks and resided in his native city until his death in June 1984. Cricket legend Ian Botham is his great-nephew.

WALLY HANLON

Popular outside-left Wally Hanlon created numerous goalscoring chances for Doug McGibbon while at Dean Court. A former Dundee junior, he was captured by the Italians during wartime service in the Army and spent four years as a prisoner of war. He joined Clyde in April 1945 and moved to Brighton in August 1946, quickly impressing with his skilful wing play before Harry Lowe signed him in May 1948. Contesting a first-team slot with Denis Cheney, he netted three goals in 19 Third Division (South) games as Cherries finished third in 1948/49 and joined Crystal Palace in July 1949. He became a favourite at Selhurst Park and had a testimonial in April 1954, moving to Sudbury Town as player-manager in July 1955. Plotting their 1957 Suffolk Senior Cup success, he then coached Chelmsford City before settling in Ferndown and spent 20 years as a check weighman for Fatstock Marketing Corporation until early retirement in September 1979. He was a keen golfer but developed Alzheimer's disease and died in April 1999.

BOB HARDY

Centre-half Bob Hardy skippered Cherries 1953/54 FA Cup first round replay win over Southampton. Real name Gordon, he served in the RAF during the Second World War and had spells as a full-back with Hawker Athletic, Charlton Rovers and Brodsworth Colliery prior to joining Millwall in August 1945. He made his Second Division debut at home to Sheffield Wednesday in September 1946 and joined Southport in July 1948. Jack Bruton signed him in June 1950 and he succeeded Bill Gripton in the heart of Bournemouth's defence, making 76 Third Division (South) appearances while at Dean Court prior to joining Yeovil Town in July 1954. Playing alongside Billy Lunn and Cliff Marsh in their 1954/55 Southern League and Cup 'double' campaign, he was then player-manager of Street, Frome Town and Salisbury before scouting for his brother-in-law Fred Ford at Bristol City. He became a sales rep for golf equipment, then ran Premier Sports Agency in Charminster until retiring in May 1988 and still lives locally.

PETER HARRISON

Fast, skilful outside-left Peter Harrison was ever-present for Cherries in 1952/53. A former Notts County amateur under Major Buckley, he represented Western Command and the RAOC during national service in the Army and reunited with Buckley at Leeds United in August 1948. He made his League debut against Alf Ramsey at Spurs in September 1949 and secured a regular Second Division slot alongside his best man John Charles at Elland Road, moving to Bournemouth for £1,500 in August 1952. Creating numerous goalscoring chances for the likes of Jack Cross and Stan Newsham while at Dean Court, he netted 34 times in 172 Third Division (South) games prior to joining Reading in June 1957 after being displaced by Reg Cutler. He moved to Southport in July 1959, then played for Macclesfield Town and Runcorn. Reunited with Lew Clayton as Cardiff City's reserve and youth team trainer for five years in July 1970, he still lives in Cardiff and was a chargehand at Tremorfa steelworks until retiring after a heart attack in June 1984.

TREVOR HARTLEY

Versatile winger Trevor Hartley featured in Cherries' 1970/71 promotion campaign under John Bond. A former West Ham junior, he signed professional in July 1964 and gained top-flight experience before Freddie Cox paid £5,000 for him in July 1969. He scored twice in 42 League outings for Bournemouth prior to joining the coaching staff after injury curtailed his playing career in June 1972. The League's youngest manager at 26 when succeeding John Bond in November 1973, he was assisted by his brother-in-law Bobby Howe and remained in charge at Dean Court until sacked in January 1975. He became Technical Adviser/Director of Coaching for the Singapore FA, then spent six years on Luton Town's coaching staff before following David Pleat to Tottenham Hotspur as assistant manager in May 1986. Subsequently the Malaysian national coach, he was an England scout under Graham Taylor and coached Sunderland until June 1995. He then scouted for Sheffield Wednesday and Bolton Wanderers before coaching back at Luton.

JAMES HAYTER

Versatile striker James Hayter starred in Cherries' 2002/03 Third Division play-off final triumph. Born on the Isle of Wight, he spent 18 months on schoolboy terms with Brighton before being released as a 16-year-old. He also had trials at Luton Town and Wycombe Wanderers prior to joining Cherries as a trainee and was a prolific goalscorer in the youth team, making his League debut as substitute in the 3-1 defeat at Peterborough United in April 1997. He was loaned to Geoff Butler's Salisbury in

December 1998 to gain further experience and quickly recalled after showing impressive form in the Dr Martens League. Scoring his first senior goal in Cherries' 4-0 victory at home to Stoke City in February 1999, he netted four times in the 5-2 win at Bury in October 2000 and featured in midfield after Jermain Defoe joined on loan to spark a rapid climb up the table. He also had a spell deputising for Neil Young at right wing-back and has scored 31 goals in 186 League outings for AFC Bournemouth.

HAYWARD FAMILY

The Hayward family made a significant contribution to AFC Bournemouth throughout the club's first 100 years. Local builder Wilf Hayward was an influential figure in the club's early days and his appointment as secretary coincided with the start of an amazing run of success in local competitions. He became chairman in 1914 when the club was formed into a limited liability company and oversaw the development of Dean Court after the Cherries gained Football League status in 1923, remaining as chairman until his death in November 1941. His eldest son Reg was elected to the board a year later and served as chairman from September 1947 until his death in November 1960, then another son Doug was chairman until Harold Walker succeeded with a takeover bid in May 1970. Doug's son Peter Hayward became a director and was briefly chairman until leaving the board in June 1991. Reg's youngest son Geoffrey was a director until the recent financial crisis and played an important role in the club's recovery, subsequently life president until his death in September 1999. A distant relation, Norman Hayward, also had a spell as chairman in recent times.

JACK HAYWARD

Tough tackling right-back Jack Hayward starred as Cherries took West Ham to an FA Cup fifth round replay in 1928/29. Born in Mansfield, he developed in local soccer with Welbeck Colliery, and Shirebrook prior to joining Bradford City as an amateur in March 1924. He failed to make an impact at Valley Parade and signed professional for Bournemouth in May 1925, quickly securing a first-team slot in place of Edgar Saxton. Helping to take eventual winners Bolton Wanderers to an FA Cup fourth round replay in 1925/26, he also featured prominently as Liverpool were held to a 1-1 third round draw at Dean Court in 1926/27. Partnering the likes of George Collin, Jimmy Blair and Sam Brown in Cherries' defence, he became the regular penalty-taker and scored 28 goals in 247 Third Division (South) games prior to joining Crystal Palace in May 1933 after being displaced by Jack Proctor. He settled in the Bournemouth area and was a security police guard at MEXE in Christchurch until retiring in May 1969, remaining local until his death in March 1974.

BILL HEATH

Young goalkeeper Bill Heath understudied Eire international Tommy Godwin while at Dean Court. Born locally, he signed professional for Bournemouth in December 1951 and impressed in the reserves before Freddie Cox gave him his League debut in the 2-2 draw at home to Crystal Palace five years later. He played 34 Third Division (South) games for Cherries prior to joining Lincoln City in an exchange deal involving Billy Coxon in November 1958, helping them to take League Champions Burnley to an FA Cup third round replay in 1959/60. Unable to prevent relegation the following season, he joined Cambridge City in July 1962 and was a key figure as they pipped local rivals Cambridge United to the Southern League title in 1962/63. He followed Frank Cruickshank to Newmarket Town in July 1966 and succeeded him as player-manager two years later. Still living in Cambridge, he was a self-employed school and sportswear agent until retiring in February 2000 and is a keen member of Links Golf Club in Newmarket.

TOM HEFFERNAN

Popular Irish right-back Tom Heffernan was an influential figure in AFC Bournemouth's 1981/82 promotion success. He initially impressed as a midfielder with Dunleary Celtic and joined Tottenham Hotspur in October 1977 but failed to secure a first-team slot at White Hart Lane. Alec Stock snapped him up on a free transfer in May 1979 and he made his League debut in Cherries' 2-0 win at Rochdale three months later. He was ever-present in 1980/81 and became captain before being sold to Sheffield United for £20,000 in August 1983. He starred in their 1983/84 promotion campaign and returned to Dean Court in June 1985, featuring in the 1986/87 Third Division title triumph. Scoring 27 goals in 217 League games overall for Cherries, he reunited with Ian Cunningham at Swanage T&H in July 1988 and then played for Bournemouth 'Poppies', Downton, Sturminster Marshall, Hamworthy Engineering and Parley Sports while employed as a driver for Allied Bakeries in Bournemouth. He is now a painter and decorator back in Ireland.

KEN HODGSON

Centre-forward Ken Hodgson was Cherries' leading marksman in 1964/65. A former Newcastle United junior, he signed professional in May 1959 and gained top-flight experience before being sold to Scunthorpe United for £3,000 in December 1961. He helped them to finish in their highest-ever League position that season and was top scorer in 1963/64, moving to Bournemouth for £5,000 in June 1964. Replacing Jimmy Singer in attack, he netted 24 goals in 78 Third Division games while at Dean Court prior to joining Colchester United for £4,000 in July 1966. He joined Poole Town in July 1969 and was leading marksman in 1969/70, then played for Christchurch and Parley Sports before moving to New Zealand in April 1974. Appointed player-coach of Eastern Suburbs in Auckland, he returned to Ringwood Town in February 1979 and was a branch manager for Amplivox Ultratone hearing aids in Bournemouth, Leeds and Newcastle until the onset of Alzheimer's disease in June 1997. He now lives in Wilmslow.

JOHN HOLD

Striker John Hold scored Cherries' winner against Sheffield Wednesday in the 1969/70 League Cup second round replay. Initially with Fareham Town, he signed professional for Bournemouth in November 1964 and made his League debut in the 1-0 defeat at Watford in April 1966. He was leading marksman in 1967/68 and had a loan spell at Ernie Tagg's Crewe Alexandra before briefly featuring alongside Ted MacDougall in Cherries 1970/71 promotion campaign. Scoring 25 goals in 85 League games while at Dean Court, he moved to Northampton Town in August 1971. He joined Margate in July 1973 and was an influential figure as they reached the Southern League Cup semi-finals in 1973/74, then joined Ashford Town and was top scorer in 1974/75. After playing in Canada for London City and Toronto Portuguese, he spent 16 years with Asda in Waterlooville, Chapeltown (Yorks) and Lincoln where he was senior food hall manager until being made redundant in March 1996. He is now a salesman at Golfers World in Lincoln.

PHIL HOLDER

Diminutive midfielder Phil Holder skippered AFC Bournemouth during Alec Stock's reign at Dean Court. An England Youth international, he signed professional for Tottenham Hotspur in February 1969 and made his First Division debut at Liverpool in December 1971. He featured in the 1974 UEFA Cup final and reunited with Terry Venables at Crystal Palace in February 1975, helping them to reach the FA Cup semi-finals in 1975/76 and win promotion in 1976/77. He had a spell in the United States with Memphis Rogues before Alec Stock signed him in March 1979. He scored four goals in 58 Fourth Division games for Cherries until injury ended his League career in November 1980, then rejoined Palace as a coach. Subsequently assisting Steve Perryman at Brentford, he succeeded him as manager for three years in August 1990 and plotted their 1991/92 Third Division title triumph. He has since coached at Watford, Southend United and Reading, then scouted for West Ham before assisting Steve Perryman at Japanese club Hiroshima.

MATT HOLLAND

Influential midfielder Matt Holland was AFC Bournemouth's 'Player of the Season' in 1995/96. A former West Ham trainee, he signed professional in July 1992 but failed to make an impact at Upton Park under Harry Redknapp and joined struggling Cherries initially on loan in January 1995. He made his League debut in that month's 2-0 defeat at Huddersfield Town and Mel Machin signed him on a permanent basis in April 1995 as he impressed with his versatility in that season's dramatic relegation escape. Appointed captain, he became a favourite with his wholehearted endeavour and scored 18 goals in 104 Second Division games while at Dean Court before financial problems forced his record £800,000 sale to Ipswich Town in July 1997. The Republic of Ireland international was 'Player of the Season' in 1997/98 and ever-present in consecutive seasons, captaining Ipswich's 1999/2000 First Division play-off final triumph. He starred for his country in the 2002 World Cup. He moved to Charlton Athletic for £750,000 in June 2003.

MATTY HOLMES

Popular midfielder Matty Holmes featured in Cherries' 1991/92 FA Cup third round replay win at Newcastle United. A nephew of ex-Scottish international Bruce Rioch, the former Luton Town junior gained experience on loan at Poole Town prior to signing professional for AFC Bournemouth in August 1988 and was also loaned to Cardiff City. He made his Second Division debut in Cherries' 3-2 win at home to Barnsley in April 1989 and was later joined by his younger brother Danny at Dean Court, scoring eight goals in 114 League games before following Harry Redknapp to West Ham for £40,000 in August 1992. Playing alongside Ian Bishop in their 1992/93 promotion success and 1993/94 FA Cup run, he was sold to Blackburn Rovers for £1,200,000 in August 1995 but struggled to impress with the Premiership Champions and joined Charlton Athletic for £250,000 in July 1997. He featured in their 1997/98 promotion campaign but was plagued with injury and has since reunited with Mark Morris at Dorchester Town, leading them to the Dr. Marten's Division One title in 2002/03.

TREVOR HOWARD

Versatile midfielder Trevor Howard was AFC Bournemouth's leading marksman in 1974/75. Signing professional for Norwich City in July 1967, he made his League debut as substitute at home to Rotherham United seven months later and featured prominently as they won the Second Division title in 1971/72. He was a League Cup finalist at Wembley in 1972/73 and moved to Cherries in a £50,000 deal involving Tony Powell in August 1974, scoring 11 goals in 86 League games while at Dean Court. Cost-saving measures led to him joining Cambridge United on a free transfer in July 1976 and he was ever-present in their 1976/77 Fourth Division title triumph under Ron Atkinson. He also starred in Cambridge's 1977/78 promotion success but a serious knee injury at home to Leicester City in November 1978 ended his playing career and he then worked for the club as a lottery agent. Still living in Cambridge, he spent 17 years as a senior meter inspector for British Gas until February 1998 and is now a self-employed taxi driver.

JACK HOWARTH

Centre-forward Jack Howarth was an experienced member of John Benson's squad at Dean Court. Initially with Stanley United, he joined Chelsea in October 1963 but failed to impress at Stamford Bridge under Tommy Docherty and moved to Swindon Town on a free transfer in October 1964. He joined Aldershot in July 1965 and was leading marksman in five successive seasons before reuniting with Dick Connor at Rochdale for a record £10,000 in January 1972. Returning to Aldershot ten months later, he helped to clinch promotion for the first time in 1972/73 and netted a club record 171 League goals overall prior to joining AFC Bournemouth for £6,000 in January 1977. He partnered Derek Showers in Cherries' attack and scored six times in 42 Fourth Division games, loaned to Dorchester Town before moving to Southport in March 1978. Subsequently with Farnborough Town, Andover, Basingstoke Town, Salisbury and Romsey Town, he has since worked as a postman in Southampton and now lives in Romsey.

BOBBY HOWE

Left-back Bobby Howe was a versatile member of John Bond's squad at Dean Court. A former West Ham apprentice, he signed professional in January 1963 and played alongside Harry Redknapp as they won the FA Youth Cup that season. He made his League debut at home to Southampton in September 1966 and gained considerable top-flight experience before reuniting with John Bond at Bournemouth for £33,000 in January 1972. Partnering Mel Machin in defence as Cherries mounted successive promotion challenges, he scored six goals in 100 Third Division games until injury ended his career and then assisted his brother-in-law Trevor Hartley at Dean Court for a year until January 1975. He had a spell as Plymouth's youth coach, then linked up with Jimmy Gabriel's Seattle Sounders where he became coach. Subsequently director of coaching for Washington State, he has since been senior director of coaching and education for the USA Soccer Federation and head coach of Portland Timbers.

EDDIE HOWE

England U-21 international defender Eddie Howe was AFC Bournemouth's 'Player of the Season' in two consecutive seasons. A notable product of the club's successful youth policy, he made his League debut at right-back in place of the suspended Nell Young in the 2-0 win at home to Hull City seven months before signing professional at Dean Court in July 1996. He formed an excellent central defensive partnership with Ian Cox as Cherries played at Wembley in the 1998 Auto Windscreens Shield final. Capped by his country at U-21 level against South Africa and Argentina in that summer's Toulon tournament, he starred as Mel Machin's side narrowly missed the Second Division play-offs in successive seasons and scored the 1998/99 FA

Cup third round winner against West Brom. He overcame a knee injury and netted ten goals in 200 Second Division games before being sold to Portsmouth for £400,000 in March 2002. His half-brother Steve Lovell had moved from Cherries to Portsmouth for £250,000 in August 1999.

GARY HOWLETT

Former Republic of Ireland international midfielder Gary Howlett featured in AFC Bournemouth's 1986/87 Third Division title triumph. Initially with Home Farm in his native Dublin, he joined Coventry City in November 1980 but failed to make an impact at Highfield Road and moved to Brighton in August 1982. He scored on his First Division debut at home to Liverpool seven months later and played alongside Jimmy Case in the 1983 FA Cup final at Wembley, joining Cherries for £15,000 in December 1984. Netting seven goals in 60 League outings while at Dean Court, he was loaned to Aldershot and Chester City before being sold to York City for £8,000 in January 1988. He joined Shelbourne in February 1991 and starred in their 1991/92 FAI League Championship success, also representing the League of Ireland. After a loan spell with Crusaders, he moved to Malahide United as player-coach and has since coached at Shelbourne and Monaghan United while working for Aer Lingus at Dublin Airport.

HARRY HUGHES

Centre-half Harry Hughes skippered Cherries to the FA Cup sixth round in 1956/57. Impressing with Symingtons in the United Counties League, he joined Southport in August 1950 and moved to Chelsea in February 1951 after his demob from national service in the Army. He made his First Division debut at home to Liverpool in August 1951 but failed to displace John Harris at Stamford Bridge and Jack Bruton signed him in June 1952. Initially understudying the likes of Bob Hardy and Johnny Crosland at Bournemouth, he scored twice in 77 Third Division (South) games prior to joining Gillingham in July 1958. Ever-present in two consecutive seasons, he played under Freddie Cox again while at Priestfield Stadium and joined Guildford City in July 1963 but a broken leg ended his playing career the following season. Later manager of Woking and Guildford City, he still lives near Guildford and after managing the Tottenham Hotspur club shop for 11 years now devotes his time to the Christians in Sport organisation which he helped found.

RICHARD HUGHES

Versatile Scottish U-21 international midfielder Richard Hughes starred as Cherries narrowly failed to qualify for the Second Division play-offs in 2000/01. Born in Glasgow, he spent six years with Italian Serie A side Atalanta while his parents were living there and developed in the junior and youth sides. He played with stars like Dominic Morfeo and Fillipo Inzaghi prior to joining Arsenal in August 1997 on the recommendation of Highbury's director of youth development Liam Brady. Despite impressing in Arsenal's Avon Insurance Combination side, he failed to secure a first-team slot with Arsene Wenger's 'double' winners and joined AFC Bournemouth for £20,000 in July 1998. He made his League debut as Cherries kicked off the 1998/99 campaign with a 2-0 win at home to Lincoln City, starring as Mel Machin's side challenged for the Second Division play-offs that season. Scoring 14 goals in 131 League outings for Cherries, he followed Eddie Howe to Harry Redknapp's Portsmouth for £100,000 in July 2002.

RALPH HUNT

Young centre-forward Ralph Hunt played alongside Stan Newsham in Cherries' attack. A nephew of ex-Spurs star Doug Hunt, he signed professional for hometown Portsmouth in August 1950 and made his First Division debut at Middlesbrough in December 1952. Jack Bruton signed him in February 1954 and he displaced Frank Fidler at Dean Court, scoring seven times in 33 Third Division (South) games for Bournemouth before moving to Norwich City for £2,500 in July 1955. He netted a club record 31 League goals in 1955/56 and was sold to Derby County for £4,200 in August 1958, joining Grimsby

Town a year later and topping their goalscoring charts in 1959/60. Swapped for Swindon Town's Freddie Jones in July 1961, he moved to Port Vale for £3,200 in December 1961, then Newport County for £2,000 in July 1962. He was leading marksman in 1962/63 and joined Chesterfield in July 1964 but tragically died in a car crash five months later. His younger brother Dennis played over 300 games for Gillingham.

JOHN IMPEY

Central defender John Impey skippered AFC Bournemouth's 1981/82 promotion success. An England Schoolboy and Youth international, he signed professional for Cardiff City in August 1972 and made his Second Division debut at home to Portsmouth four months later. John Benson snapped him up on a free transfer in July 1975 and he partnered the likes of Roger Brown and Phil Brignull in the heart of Cherries' defence, scoring seven goals in 284 League games prior to joining Torquay United in August 1983. He moved to Exeter City in August 1985, then rejoined Torquay in July 1986 and helped them to reach the Fourth Division play-off final in 1987/88 before following Stuart Morgan to Weymouth in September 1988. Subsequently on Torquay's coaching staff, he succeeded Dave Smith as manager in May 1991 and plotted promotion via that month's Wembley play-off final. He remained in charge at Plainmoor until sacked in October 1991 and is now a self-employed builder/property developer in Torquay.

PETER JOHNSON

Winger Peter Johnson was a popular member of John Benson's squad at Dean Court. A former Arsenal and Tottenham Hotspur junior, he signed professional for Orient in August 1971 and made his League debut at Swindon Town eight months later. He was all set to join AEK Athens but the deal fell through after civil war broke out in Greece and he joined Malcolm Allison's Crystal Palace initially on trial in August 1974, then moved to AFC Bournemouth in an exchange deal involving Mark Nightingale in August 1976. He scored 11 goals in 107 Fourth Division games for Cherries before reuniting with Stuart Morgan at Weymouth in July

1979, starring as they were Alliance Premier League runners-up in 1979/80. Following a brief spell with Barnet, he rejoined Weymouth in November 1981 and played with several ex-Cherries prior to joining Parley Sports in June 1983. Subsequently with Poole Town, he still lives locally and is now a financial planning consultant for Allied Dunbar in Bournemouth.

ANDY JONES

Ex-Welsh international striker Andy Jones partnered Luther Blissett in AFC Bournemouth's attack. A former Wrexham apprentice, he starred for Rhyl prior to joining Port Vale for £3,000 in May 1985 and was leading marksman in their 1985/86 promotion success under John Rudge. Sold to Charlton Athletic for £350,000 in September 1987, he was capped six times by his country and rejoined Port Vale on loan in February 1989 to boost that season's promotion challenge. Also loaned to Bristol City, Harry Redknapp paid £80,000 for him in October 1990 and he scored eight goals in 40 Third Division games for Cherries before moving to Leyton Orient for £90,000 in October 1991. He starred in their 1991/92 FA Cup run but a knee injury ended his League career the following season and he then played for Poole Town, Havant Town and Ringwood Town. Still living in Ringwood, he became a product manager for Mizuno soccer boots and since November 1998 has been a network and service manager for British Telecom.

BRYN JONES

Hard-tackling left-back Bryn Jones was a key figure in Cherries' 1961/62 promotion near-miss. From a famous footballing family, he starred in the same Swansea Boys team as Len Allchurch, Mel Charles and Terry Medwin and signed professional for Swansea Town in September 1951. He played in midfield alongside his younger brother Cliff in their Second Division side before being sold to Newport County for £2,600 in June 1958 and joined Bournemouth for £5,000 in February 1960. Bill McGarry switched him to full-back with great success and he scored five goals in 118 Third Division games prior to joining Northampton Town for £7,000 in October 1963. Reunited with McGarry at Watford a month later, he was captain at Vicarage Road before moving to Chelmsford City in October 1966 and joined Folkestone as player-manager in July 1967. He spent 18 years as a sports teacher at Holloway Boys Comprehensive School until kidney illness forced early retirement in July 1989 and he died in October 1990.

DAVID JONES

Young central defender David Jones featured prominently in Cherries' 1970/71 promotion success. A former apprentice at Dean Court, he made a significant contribution as Bournemouth were FA Youth Cup semi-finalists in 1968/69 and signed professional in January 1970. John Bond gave him his Fourth Division debut in the 2-0 win at Newport County seven months later and he starred alongside Tony Powell in Cherries' 1971/72 promotion near-miss, scoring five times in 134 League outings before being sold to Nottingham Forest for £80,000 in August 1974. Reunited with John Bond and several ex-Cherries at Norwich City for £55,000 in September 1975, he was capped eight times by Wales until a knee injury ended his League career in June 1980. He then helped Wroxham to win the Anglian Combination title in successive seasons while employed at JH Culyer sports shop in Norwich. Now living in Highcliffe, he works for Perstorp Ltd printers and has coached at Cherries' School of Excellence, Brockenhurst and Lymington & New Milton.

ROGER JONES

England U-23 goalkeeper Roger Jones helped Cherries take Liverpool to an FA Cup third round replay in 1967/68. A former Portsmouth apprentice, he signed professional in November 1964 but was a victim of

economy cuts at Fratton Park and moved to Bournemouth in May 1965. He made his League debut at Oxford United six months later and succeeded David Best in goal early in the 1966/67 campaign, playing 160 Third Division games before being sold to Blackburn Rovers for £30,000 in January 1970. Ever-present in their 1974/75 Third Division title triumph, he followed Gordon Lee to Newcastle United for £100,000 in March 1976 and moved to Stoke City in February 1977. He starred in their 1978/79 promotion success, then joined Derby County for £25,000 in July 1980 and reunited with Denis Smith at York City in August 1982. Skippering their 1983/84 Fourth Division title triumph, he followed Smith to Sunderland as reserve team coach and is now a self-employed painter and decorator in Madeley, Staffs.

STEVE JONES

Popular striker Steve Jones was AFC Bournemouth's leading marksman in two consecutive seasons. He impressed with Billericay Town in the Diadora League prior to joining West Ham for £22,000 in November 1992 and scored on his home debut against Barnsley three months later, helping the Hammers to regain top-flight status at the first attempt in 1992/93. Mel Machin paid £150,000 for him in November 1994 after a loan spell and he starred alongside Steve Fletcher in that season's dramatic relegation escape. He netted 26 goals in 74 Second Division games before rejoining Harry Redknapp's West Ham in a cash and exchange deal involving Mark Watson in May 1996. Sold to Charlton Athletic for £400,000 in February 1997, he briefly returned to Dean Court on loan in December 1997 and scored a further four times in five League outings for Cherries. He featured in Charlton's epic 1997/98 First Division play-off final triumph at Wembley and has since played for Bristol City and Hornchurch, helping the latter to the Rymans Division One title in 2002/03.

CLAUS JORGENSEN

Hard-working Danish midfielder Claus Jorgensen was voted AFC Bournemouth's 'Player of the Year' in 1999/2000. He impressed with Danish Second Division outfit AC Horsens before moving to Dean Court in July 1999 and made his debut in Cherries' 2-1 victory at home to Cambridge United on the opening day of the season. Quickly adapting to the speed and physical side of the English game, he helped AFC Bournemouth to beat top-flight Charlton Athletic in the 1999/2000 Worthington Cup second round and proved to be a tremendous success. He missed just three matches as Cherries narrowly failed to qualify for the Second Division play-offs in 2000/01. Scoring 14 goals in 87 League games while at Dean Court, he joined Bradford City on a Bosman free transfer in July 2001. He was a regular during the closing weeks of 2001/02 when he showed good versatility at right-back in place of Norwegian international Gunnar Halle, but was released by the club in May 2003

ALBERT KEETLEY

Versatile full-back Albert Keetley was a popular member of Jack Bruton's squad at Dean Court. He represented England National Association of Boys Clubs and was an amateur with Keyworth United and Nottingham Forest before representing the Army during national service in Hong Kong. Signing professional for Bury in March 1950, he made his League debut at Birmingham City ten months later but failed to secure a regular first-team slot at Gigg Lane and joined Bournemouth for £1,000 in July 1952. He provided reliable defensive cover for the likes of Laurie Cunningham and Ian Drummond, making 86 Third Division (South) appearances for Cherries before a knee injury ended his playing career and he moved to Weymouth as trainer-coach in July 1959. Also serving Bradford City and Exeter City in a similar capacity until November 1965, he then worked as a house parent for Dr Barnardo's in Exeter. He spent 23 years with various branches of Bournemouth Social Services until June 1993 and still lives locally in retirement.

DICK KEITH

Ex-Northern Ireland international full-back Dick Keith featured in Cherries' 1963/64 promotion near-miss. Born in Belfast, he starred as Linfield won the Northern Irish Cup in 1952/53 and the Northern Irish League title in three successive seasons. He was Northern Ireland 'Player of the Year' in 1955/56 and moved to Newcastle United for £9,000 in September 1956, forming an outstanding defensive partnership with Alf McMichael for club and country. Capped 23 times by Northern Ireland including the 1958 World Cup, he had a spell as Newcastle's skipper prior to joining Bournemouth for £3,300 in February 1964. Playing alongside the likes of Brian Farmer and John Compton at Dean Court, he made 47 Third Division appearances prior to joining Weymouth in August 1966 as Terry Gulliver moved in the opposite direction. He was subsequently employed as a warehouse supervisor at Kennedy's builder merchants in Bournemouth until his tragic death from head injuries suffered in an accident at work in February 1967.

EDDIE KELLY

Former Scottish U-23 midfielder Eddie Kelly featured in AFC Bournemouth's 1981/82 promotion campaign. Initially with Possilpark YMCA in his native Glasgow, he signed professional for Arsenal in February 1968 and made his First Division debut at home to Sheffield Wednesday in September 1969. He starred in their 1969/70 Fairs Cup final triumph and 1970/71 'double' success, scoring in that season's FA Cup final. Sold to QPR for £60,000 in September 1976, he followed Frank McLintock to Leicester City for £50,000 in July 1977 and skippered their 1979/80 Second Division title triumph. He joined Notts County in July 1980 and inspired their 1980/81 promotion success, then reunited with David Webb at Dean Court in August 1981. Making 13 Fourth Division appearances for Cherries, he rejoined Leicester in November 1981 and helped them regain top-flight status in 1982/83. He briefly linked up with Webb again at Torquay United in October 1984. Settling in Torquay, he has since been a publican and worked in double-glazing.

JOHN KING

Fearless wing-half John King was a popular member of Don Welsh's squad at Dean Court. A former Everton junior, he signed professional in March 1956 and made his First Division debut at Preston North End in October 1957. He was displaced by Jimmy Gabriel and moved to Bournemouth in July 1960, scoring his solitary goal in 21 Third Division games in Cherries' 2-1 win at home to Tranmere Rovers in January 1961. Sold to Tranmere for £2,000 a month later, he helped them to win promotion in 1966/67 and joined Port Vale in July 1968. He starred in their 1969/70 promotion success, then had a spell with Wigan Athletic before returning to Tranmere as a coach. Appointed manager in May 1975, he plotted promotion in 1975/76 and subsequently achieved managerial success at Northwich Victoria and Caernarfon Town. He rejoined Tranmere as manager in April 1987 and guided them from the Fourth Division to First Division play-offs as well as Leyland/DAF Cup success before becoming director of football in April 1995.

TOM KING

Hard-tackling right-back Tom King partnered George Bellis in Cherries' defence. Initially with Woolsthorpe-by-Belvoir, he impressed with Sneinton prior to joining Notts County in August 1934 and made his League debut at home to Bradford Park Avenue seven months later. He was an early Bob Crompton signing for Bournemouth in August 1935 and helped to strengthen a suspect defence, featuring in that season's 8-1 FA Cup first round replay win over Walthamstow Avenue. Making 66 Third Division (South) appearances while at Dean Court, he joined Luton Town in February 1937 and helped them to clinch the Third Division (South) title in 1936/37. A knee injury ended his playing career during the war and he worked as a lathe operator for George Kent Ltd engineering firm in Luton until rejoining Luton Town as groundsman for 10 years in July 1954. Subsequently employed by Hydrosteer Engineering in Luton until retiring in June 1974, he then lived near his sister-in-law in Scarborough until his death in June 1993.

HARRY KINGHORN

One of Cherries' finest servants, Harry Kinghorn had two spells as manager during 24 years at Dean Court. A former goalkeeper, he played for Arniston Rovers, Alloa and Leith Athletic prior to joining Sheffield Wednesday in January 1909. He made his First Division debut at Preston NE a month later and provided reliable cover for Teddy Davison during three seasons at Hilisborough. Subsequently a scout for Arsenal, he joined Bournemouth as trainer-manager in June 1923 and signed record goalscorer Ron Eyre before becoming trainer on Leslie Knighton's arrival as manager in July 1925. He became Cherries' oldest League player at 48 when he made an emergency appearance in the 0-0 draw at Brentford in March 1929. Serving under Knighton, Frank Richards, Billy Birrell, Bob Crompton and Charlie Bell until taking charge again in June 1939, he managed the 1945/46 Third Division (South) Cup final triumph. After leaving the club in May 1947, he returned to Scotland and scouted for Portsmouth until his death in Montrose in April 1955.

BILL KITCHENER

Versatile left-back Bill Kitchener featured prominently in Cherries' 1971/72 promotion near-miss. A former West Ham apprentice, he played alongside Harry Redknapp and Bobby Howe in their 1962/63 FA Youth Cup final triumph and signed professional in November 1963. He gained top-flight experience prior to reuniting with John Bond at Torquay United for £10,000 in December 1967 after a loan spell. Starring in successive promotion challenges, he followed Bond and the likes of Tony Scott and John Benson to Dean Court for £15,000 in July 1971. Partnering Mel Machin in AFC Bournemouth's defence, he featured in the record 11-0 FA Cup first round win at home to Margate in November 1971 and scored twice in 36 Third Division outings for Cherries until injury curtailed his League career in February 1973. Subsequently playing for Cambridge City, Wealdstone, Christchurch and New Milton, since August 1978 he has been a police constable stationed at Lymington, New Milton, Ringwood, Burley, Lyndhurst and now Southampton.

LESLIE KNIGHTON

Manager Leslie Knighton plotted successive FA Cup runs while in charge at Dean Court. Born near Burton-on-Trent, he had his playing career cut short by an ankle injury and became manager of Castleford Town at the age of 20 in July 1904. He joined Huddersfield Town as assistant in August 1909, then moved to Manchester City in a similar capacity three years later. Appointed Arsenal's manager in May 1919, he made several shrewd signings but was sacked in June 1925 after clashing with chairman Sir Henry Norris and became Bournemouth's manager the following month. He brought George Collin and Arthur Roe with him and Cherries took eventual winners Bolton Wanderers to an FA Cup fourth round replay in 1925/26, then Liverpool to a third round replay in 1926/27. Leaving to take charge of Birmingham in July 1928, he guided them to the 1931 FA Cup final before managing Chelsea for six years until April 1939. He was subsequently Shrewsbury Town's manager until December 1948, then retired to Bournemouth and was secretary of Northbourne Golf Club until his death in May 1959.

EDDIE LAWRENCE

Ex-Welsh international left-half Eddie Lawrence starred as Cherries finished in their highest pre-war position in 1936/37. Joining Wrexham from local side Druids in February 1926, he made his League debut at home to Durham City two months later but failed to secure a regular first-team slot at the Racecourse and moved to Clapton Orient in August 1928. He toured Canada with the Welsh FA in 1929 and joined newly-promoted Notts County in May 1931. He was capped twice before Charlie Bell brought him to Dean Court in August 1936. A member of Bournemouth's side that visited Everton in that season's FA Cup third round, his solitary goal in 39 Third Division (South) games clinched Cherries' 2-1 win at home to Reading in April 1937 and he rejoined Clapton Orient the following month. He served in the RAF in North Africa during the Second World War and then settled in Nottingham, working for the John Player cigarette company. Subsequently a scout for Notts County until May 1979, he died in July 1989.

GEORGE LAWRENCE

Popular winger George Lawrence helped AFC Bournemouth to reach the FA Cup fourth round in 1990/91. A former Southampton apprentice, 'Chicken George' signed professional in September 1980 and made his First Division debut at home to Notts County in October 1981. He moved to Oxford United for £45,000 in November 1982 after a loan spell and starred in their 1983/84 Third Division title triumph, also featuring in their 1984/85 Second Division title campaign until rejoining Southampton in January 1985. An FA Cup semi-finalist in 1985/86, he was sold to Millwall for £160,000 in July 1987 and helped them to win the Second Division title in 1987/88. Harry Redknapp paid £100,000 for him in August 1989 and he netted five times in 75 League outings while at Dean Court prior to joining Finnish side Mikkelin Pallo in June 1992. He briefly moved via Weymouth to Portsmouth in February 1993 and then played for Hibernians in Malta as well as spells at Hednesford Town and Rushden & Diamonds.

CHRIS LEADBITTER

Strong midfielder Chris Leadbitter was a versatile member of Tony Pulis' squad at Dean Court. An ex-Grimsby Town apprentice he signed professional in September 1985 but failed to make an impact at Blundell Park and moved to Hereford United in August 1986. He joined Cambridge United in August 1988 and was an influential figure in their meteoric rise from the Fourth Division to Second under John Beck, also helping them to reach the FA Cup sixth round in successive seasons. Tony Pulis paid £25,000 for him in August 1993 and he featured in AFC Bournemouth's 1994/95 relegation escape under Mel Machin, scoring three goals in 54 Second Division games for Cherries prior to joining Plymouth Argyle in July 1995. He starred in their 1995/96 Third Division play-off final triumph at Wembley, then moved via Dorchester Town to Torquay United in November 1997. Featuring in the 1997/98 Third Division play-off final, he has since played for Plymouth Argyle and Guisborough Town.

DEREK LEAVER

Inside-forward Derek Leaver partnered Stan Newsham and Ollie Norris in Cherries' attack. He represented England National Association of Boys' Clubs and gained Lancashire Youth honours while an amateur with Burnley before representing the RAF during national service based in Kirkham. He signed professional for Blackburn Rovers in May 1949 and scored on his Second Division debut in their 4-1 win at home to Manchester City in November 1950, featuring in consecutive promotion challenges prior to reuniting with Jack Bruton at Dean Court in July 1955. Scoring five goals in 29 Third Division (South) games for Bournemouth, he joined Crewe Alexandra in March 1956 after seeking a return north. He moved to Macclesfield Town in July 1957, then played for Wigan Athletic before his career was ended by a knee injury and spent 35 years running the family firm D&C Leaver bakers and confectioners in Blackburn until retiring in November 1995. The business is now managed by his son David and supplies Blackburn Rovers.

IAN LEIGH

Young goalkeeper Ian Leigh starred in AFC Bournemouth's 1981/82 promotion success. He impressed with Swaythling before Alec Stock signed him in October 1979 and he made his League debut as cover for the injured Kenny Allen in Cherries' 1-0 defeat at Peterborough United in October 1981. Retaining his first-team place for the rest of that season, he was a key figure in AFC Bournemouth's 1983/84 FA Cup third round win at home to holders Manchester United and Associate Members' Cup final triumph. He later contested Cherries' goalkeeping slot with John Smeulders and had loan spells at Bristol City and Torquay United. Making 123 League appearances while at Dean Court prior to joining Hamrun Spartans in May 1986, he starred in two Maltese League and Cup 'double' successes and also played for Poole Town, Bashley and Salisbury in the Southern League. He spent five years with Les Parodi's company Clean Ahead and has since worked as a salesman in insurance and now double-glazing based in Southampton.

DAVE LENNARD

Midfielder Dave Lennard was an experienced member of John Benson's squad at Dean Court. A former Bolton Wanderers junior, he signed professional in December 1961 and made his First Division debut against Birmingham City in April 1963. He joined Halifax Town with ex-England star Freddie Hill in July 1969 and was ever-present in their 1970/71 promotion near-miss, then played for Blackpool and Cambridge United before moving to Chester in September 1974. A key figure as they won promotion and reached the League Cup semi-finals in 1974/75, he joined Stockport County in July 1976 and John Benson signed him in September 1977. He scored four goals in 59 Fourth Division games for AFC Bournemouth prior to joining Salisbury as player-manager in July 1979, then had a spell with Basingstoke Town before rejoining Cherries as youth team boss and managed Bashley to the Wessex League title in 1986/87. He spent 15 years as a science teacher at Homefield School, Arnewood School and Kingsleigh School until July 1998 and is now a part-time postman in Bournemouth.

ROY LITTLEJOHN

Outside-right Roy Littlejohn gained England Amateur international honours while at Dean Court. Born locally, he attended Bournemouth Grammar School and progressed through the ranks at Dean Court to make his League debut in Bournemouth's 2-1 win at Swindon Town in September 1952. He contested a first-team slot with Derek Stroud and had a spell with Oxford City while studying at Oxford School of Architecture, scoring twice in 22 Third Division (South) games for Cherries before moving to Portsmouth in July 1956. Joining Woking a year later, he featured in their 1958 Amateur Cup final triumph at Wembley and moved to Poole Town in October 1959. He starred in the 1961/62 promotion success and joined Salisbury in May 1963, then played for Bridport and Christchurch. Still living in Bournemouth, he spent 33 years with Leslie Jones Architects in Poole - designing local shopping centres such as the Arndale Centre (Poole), Saxon Square (Christchurch), The Maltings (Salisbury) and Sovereign Centre (Boscombe) - and was senior partner when he retired in June 1992.

DENNIS LONGHORN

Young midfielder Dennis Longhorn featured in Cherries' 1970/71 promotion success under John Bond. A former Bournemouth apprentice, he made his League debut in the 1-1 draw at home to Torquay United five months before signing professional in August 1968 and scored once in 30 League outings prior to joining Mansfield Town for £5,000 in December 1971. He moved to Sunderland in exchange for John Lathan plus £20,000 in February 1974 and was a member of their 1975/76 Second Division title squad, gaining top-flight experience before being sold to Sheffield United for £25,000 in October 1976. Joining Aldershot for £20,000 in February 1978, he featured in their 1978/79 FA Cup run and moved to Colchester United in May 1980. He was an influential figure in consecutive promotion challenges, then joined Chelmsford City in July 1983 and starred as they were Southern League runners-up in 1985/86. Subsequently manager/coach of Halstead Town, Wivenhoe Town and Braintree Town, he is now football coach at Center Parcs in Thetford.

BRIAN LOUGHNANE

Winger Brian Loughnane was a popular member of Freddie Cox's squad at Dean Court. A former Manchester City amateur, he was a PTI in the RASC during national service based at Oakham and had a spell with Witton Albion in the Cheshire League prior to signing professional for Leeds United in August 1952. He failed to make an impact at Elland Road and moved to Shrewsbury Town on a free transfer in July 1953, playing alongside Ray Weigh before Freddie Cox paid £1,500 for him in July 1956. Unlucky not to feature in Bournemouth's big FA Cup ties against Wolves, Spurs and Manchester United that season as Nelson Stiffle kept him out of the side, he scored six goals in 43 League games for Cherries before moving to Wellington Town in July 1959. He then played for GKN Sankey where he worked as a metal finisher. Now living in Shrewsbury, he spent 23 years as a maintenance worker at Rolls Royce until retiring after a heart-attack in October 1984. His son Peter also played for Shrewsbury Town.

HARRY LOWE

Manager Harry Lowe guided Cherries to the Third Division (South) runners-up slot in 1947/48. He impressed as an inside-forward with St Andrews United in Scottish junior soccer prior to joining Watford in March 1929 and made his League debut at home to Southend United nine months later. Ever-present in 1931/32, he featured in the 1934/35 Third Division (South) Cup final and joined QPR in exchange for Ted Goodier in June 1935. He was ever-present in 1938/39 and guested for several clubs during the war, then scouted for Chelsea prior to becoming Guildford City manager in July 1945. Succeeding Harry Kinghorn as Bournemouth's manager in July 1947, he made several shrewd signings and plotted consecutive promotion challenges. He was dismissed in February 1950, then recruited several ex-Cherries during two years as Yeovil Town's boss before scouting for Watford and managing Cheshunt. Subsequently director of a lampshade business in Pewsey, he remained in Wiltshire until his death in October 1988.

BILLY LUNN

Popular Inside-left Billy Lunn featured in Cherries' 1947/48 promotion near-miss. A former Northern Ireland Schoolboy international, he had spells with Distillery and Glenavon before moving to West Brom in February 1946 and made his League debut in place of Billy Elliott against Chesterfield in April 1947. Harry Lowe signed him in February 1948 and he displaced Fred Rowell in Bournemouth's attack, featuring in that season's title decider against QPR watched by a then record 25,495 crowd at Dean Court. Scoring 19 goals in 47 Third Division (South) games for Cherries, he moved to Newport County in July 1950 and reunited with Harry Lowe at Yeovil Town in June 1952. He was leading marksman in two consecutive seasons, then featured in their 1954/55 Southern League and Cup 'double' triumph and was joined at Huish by his younger brother Harry. Settling in Bournemouth, he worked as a sales rep for household goods until retiring in May 1988 and suffered from Alzheimer's disease before his death in January 2000.

MIKE LYONS

Hard-tackling right-back Mike Lyons helped Cherries to reach the FA Cup sixth round in 1956/57. Initially a centre-forward, he turned professional for Bristol City in

June 1950 and was given his League debut at Torquay United ten months later. He moved to Bristol Rovers in July 1953, spending national service in the Army Medical Corps before switching to a defensive role and Freddie Cox signed him in July 1956. Forming an effective full-back partnership with Arnold Woollard at Dean Court, he made 105 League appearances for Bournemouth prior to joining Swindon Town to £1,000 in October 1959 and then featured in Yeovil Town's 1960/61 Southern League Cup success. Subsequently reserve team trainer/physio at Bristol Rovers for 17 years while a self-employed insurance broker, he then assisted Stuart Taylor and Bobby Jones at Bath City before following the latter to Forest Green Rovers and was briefly Almondsbury Town chairman. He now owns several properties in Bristol and is godfather to Tony Pulis' eldest son.

JACK McDONALD

Goalscoring outside-left Jack McDonald was ever-present in Cherries' 1947/48 promotion near-miss. A former Wolverhampton Wanderers junior, he signed professional in September 1938 and made his First Division debut at home to Chelsea seven months later. He followed the well-worn trail to Dean Court in May 1939 and was a wartime guest for several clubs, featuring in Bournemouth's 1945/46 Third Division (South) Cup final success. Leading marksman in 1946/47, he scored 35 goals in 80 League outings for Cherries before being sold to Fulham for £12,000 in June 1948. He starred in their 1948/49 Second Division title triumph and moved to Southampton for £5,000 in August 1952, then joined Southend United in May 1953. Subsequently with Weymouth and Poole Town while a PE teacher at Homefield School, he was then licensee of the Royal Oak in Bere Regis and Tatnum Hotel in Poole. He spent 18 years as a sales rep for Pearl Assurance in Wimborne until retiring in November 1983, then moved to Burghead near Elgin and now lives in Ryde (IOW).

MARTIN MACDONALD

Versatile right-half Martin Macdonald was a popular member of Jack Bruton's squad at Dean Court. A former Portsmouth junior, he signed professional as a winger in November 1948 but failed to secure a first-team slot at Fratton Park as Pompey were League Champions in two consecutive seasons. He joined Bournemouth in November 1951 and his solitary goal in 51 Third Division (South) games came in Cherries' 3-1 victory at Norwich City in December 1953, moving to Weymouth in July 1956. Reunited with Ken Bird at Dorchester Town in June 1957, he starred alongside Denis Cheney, Laurie Cunningham and Derek Stroud in their 1957/58 FA Cup run and briefly moved to Western League rivals Portland United in July 1963. He worked in the packing department of Joe Caslake's engineering firm, then spent 14 years as caretaker at the Convent of the Cross in Bournemouth. Still living locally, he was subsequently a machinist at Wellworthy/AE Goetze in Ringwood for 20 years until retiring in September 1996.

TED MacDOUGALL

Ace marksman Ted MacDougall was voted AFC Bournemouth's all-time favourite player. Signing professional for Liverpool in January 1966, he moved to York City for £3,000 in July 1967 and joined Cherries for £10,000 in June 1969. He was top scorer in three successive seasons including the 1970/71 promotion triumph under John Bond, netting a record nine goals against Margate in the 1971/72 FA Cup first round. Sold to Manchester United for a record £220,000 in September 1972, he moved via West Ham to John Bond's Norwich City for £140,000 in December 1973 and played in the 1975 League Cup final. Capped seven times by Scotland, he linked up with Phil Boyer again at Southampton for £50,000 in September 1976 and starred in their 1977/78 promotion success. He rejoined Cherries in November 1978 and netted 119 goals in 198 League games overall before moving to Blackpool as player-coach in March 1980. Settling in Canada, he later reunited with Alan Ball as Portsmouth's chief scout and has since returned to the United States.

MIKE McELHATTON

Young, versatile midfielder Mike McElhatton featured in AFC Bournemouth's 1994/95 relegation escape. A Republic of Ireland Schoolboy international, he made his League debut as a trainee in Cherries' 0-0 draw at home to Wigan Athletic two months before signing professional under Tony Pulis in July 1993. He provided reliable defensive cover for the likes of Mark Morris and Neil Young, regularly featuring as a substitute and overcoming injury problems to score twice in 42 Second Division games while at Dean Court prior to joining Scarborough for £15,000 in October 1996 after a loan spell. Reunited with Gareth Williams at the McCain Stadium, he donned the goalkeeper's jersey in their 2-2 draw at home to Rochdale in February 1997 and starred as Scarborough qualified for the Third Division play-offs in 1997/98. He joined Rushden & Diamonds in June 1998 and helped take Leeds United to an FA Cup third round replay in 1998/99, then win the Conference title in 2000/01. He was awarded a testimonial in late 2002, before injury ended his career.

BILL McGARRY

Hard-tackling former England international right-half Bill McGarry had a successful spell as Cherries' player-manager. Initially with Northwood Mission, he joined Port Vale in June 1945 and was ever-present in 1949/50. He moved to Huddersfield Town for £12,000 in March 1951 and was ever present in their 1952/53 promotion success. Also starring in their 1954/55 FA Cup run, he was capped four times prior to joining Bournemouth as player-boss in March 1961 and plotted the 1961/62 promotion near-miss. A strong disciplinarian, he scored twice in 78 Third Division games before leaving to manage Watford in July 1963. He took charge of Ipswich Town in October 1964 and guided them to the Second Division title in 1967/68, then became Wolves' manager in November 1968 and plotted their 1974 League Cup final triumph. After coaching in Saudi Arabia, he managed Newcastle United for three years until August 1980, then coached in Zambia and briefly rejoined Wolves as manager in September 1985. He now lives in Stoke-on-Trent in retirement.

DOUG McGIBBON

Centre-forward Doug McGibbon was Cherries' leading marksman in three successive seasons. The son of former Southampton forward Charlie McGibbon, he played for Air Service Training (Hamble) prior to signing professional for Saints in December 1938 and made his League debut at Plymouth Argyle five months later. He guested for Swindon Town during the war and netted six goals for Saints against Chelsea in 1945/46, moving to Fulham for £4,250 in January 1947. Harry Lowe paid £5,000 for him in September 1948 and he netted 65 goals in 103 Third Division (South) games for Bournemouth prior to joining Lovell's Athletic in August 1951. His playing career was ended by a serious head injury soon after and he worked for Lovell's as a sales rep, then managed their Brixton depot before returning to Air Service Training (Hamble) as sports officer in August 1955. He spent 24 years as an engineer with Sperry/Honeywells aircraft instruments in Brentford until retiring in February 1984 and died in Aylesbury in October 2002.

BRIAN McGORRY

Hard-working midfielder Brian McGorry was AFC Bournemouth's leading goalscorer in 1992/93. He impressed in non-League soccer with Weymouth before Harry Redknapp paid £30,000 for him in August 1991 and made his Third Division debut in Cherries' 0-0 draw at Reading two months later. Scoring 11 goals in 61 League outings while at Dean Court, he moved to Peterborough United for £60,000 in February 1994 but was unable to prevent relegation that season and joined Wycombe Wanderers in August 1995. He was sidelined by injury while at Adams Park and had a loan spell at Cardiff City prior to joining Hereford United in March 1997, featuring in their relegation decider at home to Brighton two months later which ended with their loss of Football League status. Starring in Hereford's 1997/98 FA Cup run, he was reunited with Alex Watson at Torquay United in July 1998 and moved to Telford United in July 1999. He skippered their 1999/2000 FA Trophy run, then was an FA Trophy finalist and Dr. Marten's Premier Division winners with Tamworth in 2002/03.

MEL MACHIN

Mel Machin achieved success as both a player and manager at AFC Bournemouth. A former Port Vale junior, he signed professional in July 1962 and made his League debut at Carlisle United three months later. He moved to Gillingham in July 1966 and reunited with John Bond at Dean Court for £9,000 in December 1970. Starring at right-back in Bournemouth's 1970/71 promotion success, he netted seven goals in 110 League games before following Bond to Norwich City in December 1973. Featuring in the 1975 League Cup final, he became Norwich's chief coach after injury ended his playing career in September 1977, then joined Manchester City as manager in May 1987 and plotted their 1988/89 promotion success. Subsequently managing Barnsley, he scouted for West Ham, Spurs and Liverpool prior to rejoining Cherries as manager in August 1994 and guided them to the 1998 Auto Windscreens Shield final at Wembley. He was director of football for two years until August 2002, then Huddersfield Town's caretaker-boss in the latter part of 2002/03, but failed to save them from relegation.

TOM McINALLY

Ex-Scotland international inside-forward Tom McInally was one of Cherries' most notable inter-war signings. He impressed with St Anthony's prior to joining Celtic in May 1919 and was twice leading marksman, starring in their 1921/22 Scottish League title triumph. Moving to Third Lanark in September 1922, he topped their goalscoring charts in three successive seasons and rejoined Celtic in May 1925. He was a key figure as they won the Scottish League title in 1925/26 and Scottish Cup in 1926/27, and also gained two caps in 1926. After a disagreement with manager Willie Maley, he joined Sunderland in May 1928 and skippered their 1928/29 League Championship challenge before Frank Richards lured him to Dean Court in November 1929. His solitary goal in 10 Third Division (South) games came in Bournemouth's 5-1 win at Gillingham on Christmas Day 1929 and he joined Morton in May 1930. Later with Derry City, Armadale and Nithsdale Wanderers, he then scouted for Celtic until his death in September 1955.

JOHNNY MacKENZIE

Popular outside-right Johnny MacKenzie was an influential figure in Cherries' 1947/48 promotion near-miss. Born in Glasgow, he joined Partick Thistle in November 1944 and was serving with Jim Stirling in the Scots Guards at Victoria Barracks, Windsor, when Harry Lowe signed him on loan in August 1947. He created numerous goalscoring chances for Dudley Milligan as Bournemouth were Third Division (South) runners-up that season, netting nine goals in 38 League games prior to rejoining Partick in July 1948. Starring as the Jags were Scottish League Cup finalists in 1953/54, 1956/57 and 1958/59, he gained a then club record nine Scottish caps before moving to Dumbarton in July 1960 and then spent three seasons in Irish soccer with Derry City. He worked for Hugh Smith engineers in Glasgow, then took a Hoover sales service franchise and was subsequently a sales rep for Dowly Hydraulics/Dunlop in East Kilbride until retiring in September 1990. He now lives on the remote Isle of Tiree in the Hebrides.

BILL McKINNEY

Tough-tackling right-back Bill McKinney was an experienced member of Freddie Cox's squad at Dean Court. He impressed with Wallsend Rising Sun and Wallsend St Lukes while employed as a panel beater in Newcastle Docks, then joined Newcastle United in May 1956 and represented the Army during national service as a PTI at Catterick. He was given his First Division debut at Tottenham Hotspur in December 1957 and captained his hometown club under Joe Harvey, featuring in their 1964/65 Second Division title campaign before following Dick Keith to Bournemouth for £2,750 in August 1965. Making 17 Third Division appearances for Cherries prior to joining Mansfield Town in June 1966 after a disagreement with Freddie Cox, he starred alongside Phil Ferns (Snr) in their 1966/67 FA Cup run. He joined Wellington Town in July 1968 but an Achilles tendon injury ended his career the following season. Now living near his son and daughter in Telford, he spent 26 years as a panel beater with GKN Sankey until retiring in August 1997.

PETER McSEVICH

Popular goalkeeper Peter McSevich was ever-present for Cherries in 1930/31. A Scottish junior international, he impressed with Shieldmuir prior to joining Celtic in August 1924 and moved to Aberdeen a year later. He contested their goalkeeper slot with Harry Blackwell and joined Bournemouth in July 1928, starring as Cherries took West Ham to an FA Cup fifth round replay in 1928/29. Scoring in the 4-1 defeat at Brighton in October 1931 when switched to outside-right after being injured in the match, he made 142 Third Division (South) appearances prior to joining Coventry City in February 1932. He moved to FA Cup giantkillers Walsall in June 1933 and played in the 1934/35 Third Division (North) Cup final, then briefly joined Wellington Town in July 1936. Subsequently serving Walsall over a lengthy period as dressing-room attendant and part-time coach, he spent 28 years as caretaker at Walsall Library until retiring in May 1967 and remained in Walsall until his death in January 1979.

HARRY MARDON

Popular centre forward Harry Mardon was Cherries' leading goalscorer in 1937/38. Born in Cardiff, he grew up in Bristol and developed in local soccer with Victoria Albion. He had a spell with Hereford United in the Birmingham League prior to joining Notts County in July 1936 and made his League debut at home to QPR two months later. Featuring alongside legendary former Scottish international Hughie Gallacher as County finished Third Division (South) runners-up in 1936/37, he moved to Dean Court in an exchange deal involving Joe Riley in December 1937. He scored four goals in Bournemouth's then record 7-1 win at home to Southend United on New Year's Day 1938, netting 14 times in 25 Third Division (South) games for Cherries prior to joining Bristol City in September 1938. Settling in Bristol, he spent 30 years as a boilermaker at Charles Hill Shipyard in Hotwells until made redundant in June 1975 and suffered a fatal heart-attack in July 1981. His grandson Paul Mardon was a Welsh international.

FRED MARSDEN

Long-serving right-back Fred Marsden was ever-present in Cherries' 1947/48 promotion near-miss. A former Blackburn Rovers junior, he had spells with Clitheroe and Manchester Central before signing professional for Accrington Stanley in October 1934 and made his League debut in a 6-0 defeat at Walsall two months later. He moved to Wolverhampton Wanderers in January 1935 and gained top-flight experience prior to joining Bournemouth in July 1936, one of many Buckley Babes who made a similar move to Dean Court during Charlie Bell's reign. He skippered Cherries' 1945/46 Third Division (South) Cup final triumph and formed a memorable defensive quartet with Ken Bird, Joe Sanaghan and Fred Wilson, scoring once in 194 League games before following Paddy Gallacher to Weymouth in June 1949. An experienced figure in their 1949/50 FA Cup run, he returned to Dean Court as 'A' team player-coach in June 1951 and later ran a motor delivery services business. He remained local until his death in November 1989.

CLIFF MARSH

Popular inside-forward Cliff Marsh partnered Doug McGibbon and Jack Cross in Cherries' attack. Initially with Tyldesley United, he impressed with Winsford United in the Cheshire League and rejected terms from Grimsby Town prior to joining Leeds United in September 1948. He scored on his League debut at home to West Brom a month later but failed to secure a regular first-team slot at Elland Road and Harry Lowe signed him in May 1949. Netting twice in 39 Third Division (South) games for Bournemouth, he moved to Worcester City with centre-half Bill Gripton in June 1952. He was reunited with the likes of Billy Lunn, Mick Reid and Bob Hardy after joining Yeovil Town in June 1953 and starred in their 1954/55 Southern League and Cup double triumph. Subsequently manager of the fencing department of Vigar & Co timber merchants in Winton until ill health forced his retirement in December 1983, he remained local until his sudden death at Queen's Park Golf Club on Christmas Eve 1990.

STEVE MASSEY

Fast, skilful striker Steve Massey played alongside Mick Butler in AFC Bournemouth's attack. A former Stockport County apprentice, he made his League debut as a 16 year-old, scoring against Darlington five months before signing professional in July 1975. Featuring alongside ex-England star Mike Summerbee while at Edgeley Park, John Benson paid £5,000 for him in July 1978 and he netted 19 goals in 97 Fourth Division games for Cherries prior to joining Peterborough United with Geoff Butler in August 1981. He joined Northampton Town in February 1982 and topped their goalscoring charts in 1982/83, then was sold to Hull City for £20,000 in July 1983. Starring in their 1984/85 promotion success, he moved via Cambridge United to Wrexham in July 1986 and gained ECWC experience before an ankle injury ended his League career. He was Truro City's player-manager while running Mullion Holiday Park in Helston and now runs Landscove Holiday Park in Brixham as well as Devon Valley Holiday Village in Shaldon.

NEIL MASTERS

Versatile left-back Neil Masters was a young member of Tony Pulis' squad at AFC Bournemouth. A Northern Ireland Youth international, he signed professional at Dean Court under Harry Redknapp in August 1990 and made his League debut in Cherries' 0-0 draw at Wigan Athletic in October 1992. He displaced long-serving Paul Morrell in defence alongside Adrian Pennock and featured in that season's FA Cup third round tie at Premiership high-fliers Blackburn Rovers. Scoring twice in 38 Second Division games for AFC Bournemouth, his impressive displays tempted Wolverhampton Wanderers to pay £300,000 for him in December 1993 and he helped them to qualify for the First Division play-offs in 1994/95 but successive injuries hindered his progress at Molineux. He reunited with Tony Pulis at Gillingham in March 1997 and briefly rekindled his defensive partnership with Adrian Pennock until a knee injury led to him being released in March 1999, then had a spell with Norwegian side Moss.

RON MEADOWS

Goalkeeper Ron Meadows provided reliable cover for Ken Bird while at Dean Court. Born in Lancaster, he developed in local soccer with Glasson Dock and had a spell with Morecambe before representing the RAF during wartime service as a Spitfire pilot in the Middle East. He had a trial with Preston North End prior to signing professional for Burnley in September 1946 but was unable to secure a First Division slot at Turf Moor as Jimmy Strong made a club record 220 consecutive appearances and moved to Bournemouth with inside-forward Gordon Haigh in April 1950. Given his League debut at home to Southend United on Boxing Day 1950, after Cherries' 6-1 Christmas Day defeat at Southend, he played 16 Third Division (South) games prior to joining Accrington Stanley in July 1952. He joined Lancaster City as player-coach in July 1953, then had a spell as Morecambe's assistant-boss. Still living near Lancaster, he became senior manager during 27 years with Storey Bros plastics firm until early retirement in December 1981.

SCOTT MEAN

Stylish midfielder Scott Mean had two spells at AFC Bournemouth. A former trainee at Dean Court, he signed professional for Cherries in August 1992 and made his League debut in that month's 1-1 draw at Preston North End. He was an influential figure in AFC Bournemouth's 1994/95 relegation escape, impressing with his accurate passing and penetrating runs. Loaned to Harry Redknapp's West Ham in March 1996 with a view to a £750,000 transfer, the move was put on ice until he proved his fitness after a knee injury. He eventually joined the Hammers in a £100,000 deal four months later but failed to start a Premiership match while at Upton Park and was loaned to John Rudge's Port Vale in August 1998. Unlucky to suffer a cruciate ligament injury on his debut at home to West Brom, he was sidelined for the rest of that season and returned to AFC Bournemouth on a free transfer from West Ham in July 1999. He scored 12 goals in 106 Second Division games overall for Cherries prior to joining Crawley Town in June 2000.

DICK MELLORS

Giant goalkeeper Dick Mellors was ever-present for Cherries in 1936/37. A former amateur with Chesterfield and Mansfield Town, he signed professional for Sheffield Wednesday in December 1925 and made his First Division debut at Huddersfield Town in February 1927. He understudied England international John Brown at Hillsborough and was a member of Wednesday's squad that won the League Championship in two consecutive seasons. Moving to Reading in July 1931, he starred as they were Third Division (South) runners-up in 1931/32. Billy Birrell signed him in June 1934 and he featured in Bournemouth's 8-1 FA Cup first round replay win at home to Walthamstow Avenue in 1936/37, making 117 Third Division (South) appearances before moving to Queen of the South in December 1937. He rejoined Cherries as trainer after the war until the appointment of Arthur Cunliffe in June 1950, later following his daughter Peggy and her husband (former secretary Tommy Locks) to Australia where he died in Sydney in October 1960.

LES MELVILLE

Left-half Les Melville was a popular member of Freddie Cox's squad at Dean Court. An England Youth international, he signed professional for Everton in April 1950 but failed to secure a First Division slot at Goodison Park behind the likes of Peter Farrell and Cyril Lello. He joined Bournemouth for £1,000 in July 1956 and made his League debut in Cherries' 3-0 defeat at Southampton a month later. Unlucky not to feature in that season's big FA Cup ties as Joe Brown kept him out of the side, he made 25 Third Division (South) appearances prior to joining Oldham Athletic in March 1958. He moved to Worcester City four months later and starred alongside ex-Welsh international skipper Roy Paul in their epic 1958/59 FA Cup third round defeat of Liverpool, then joined Macclesfield Town in July 1960. Now living in Stockport, he spent 25 years as a design engineer for heating-ventilation firms Henry Simons and Hall & Kay, then was a sales rep for Barber Coleman air conditioners until retiring in November 1995.

JOHN MEREDITH

Experienced winger John Meredith was ever-present for Cherries in 1969/70. Signing professional for Doncaster Rovers in January 1958, he made his League debut at Plymouth Argyle eight months later and was sold to Sheffield Wednesday for £11,000 in February 1961. He failed to secure a regular First Division slot at Hillsborough before joining Chesterfield in July 1962, then moved to Freddie Cox's Gillingham for £4,500 in March 1964 and was ever-present in three consecutive seasons. Reunited with Cox at Dean Court in an exchange deal involving Ken Pound in August 1969, he helped Bournemouth to beat Sheffield Wednesday in that season's League Cup second round replay and also featured in the 1970/71 promotion campaign until a broken leg ended his League career. He scored once in 51 League games for Cherries prior to joining Hastings United as player-manager in August 1972. Now living in York, he has spent the past 29 years as a divisional administrator for Combined Insurance Company of America.

KEITH MILLER

Versatile midfielder Keith Miller was ever-present in Cherries' 1970/71 promotion success. Initially with Walthamstow Avenue, he joined West Ham in September 1965 and made his First Division debut at Ipswich Town in November 1968. He reunited with John Bond at Bournemouth for £10,000 in July 1970 and was also ever-present in the 1971/72 promotion near-miss, featuring in that season's record 11-0 FA Cup first round win over Margate. Appointed captain at Dean Court, he scored 19 goals in 383 League games for Cherries and had a testimonial against Spurs in May 1980 shortly before joining Dorchester Town. He starred as they took AFC Bournemouth to a FA Cup second round replay in 1981/82 and became player-manager, plotting their 1986/87 promotion triumph and 1989/90 FA Cup run. Later managing Fareham Town and Poole Town, he still lives locally and for the past 23 years has held various sales and marketing posts in publishing. Now sales manager of Compass Publications.

PAUL MILLER

Hard-tackling central defender Paul Miller was an experienced member of Harry Redknapp's squad at Dean Court. A former Tottenham Hotspur apprentice, 'Max' signed professional in May 1977 and made his First Division debut in the local derby at Arsenal in April 1979. He starred alongside Graham Roberts in two consecutive FA Cup final successes at Wembley and scored in their 1984 UEFA Cup final triumph. Sold to Charlton Athletic for £130,000 in February 1987, he featured prominently in successive relegation escapes and joined Watford for £85,000 in October 1988. Harry Redknapp paid £50,000 for him in August 1989 but he was unable to prevent relegation that season and had a loan spell at Brentford. Netting his solitary goal in 47 League games in AFC Bournemouth's 2-2 draw at home to Leyton Orient in December 1990, he moved to Swansea City in January 1991 but a knee injury ended his career soon after. He has since worked for the merchant bank Kleinwort Benson in the City and been a director of FIFA licensed agents PML.

RALPH MILLER

Versatile defender Ralph Miller featured in Cherries' 1968/69 promotion challenge under Freddie Cox. Starting with Slough Town, he joined Charlton Athletic in September 1963 and made his League debut at Rotherham United a year later. He moved to Gillingham with David Stocks in May 1965 and played alongside several one-time Cherries before following Stocks to Bournemouth in July 1968. Missing just one match in his first season at Dean Court, his solitary goal in 72 League outings came in Cherries' 2-1 defeat at Southport in December 1968 and he joined Weymouth initially on loan in November 1970. He was a Southern League Cup finalist in 1970/71, then featured prominently alongside Roy Gater as they won the Southern League Cup for the first time in 1972/73. Reuniting with Tony Nelson at Poole Town in May 1976, he joined Tony Priscott's Ringwood Town a year later. Still living in East Howe, he was a building labourer and for the past 15 years has been a self-employed painter and decorator.

DUDLEY MILLIGAN

Bustling centre-forward Dudley Milligan was leading marksman as Cherries were Third Division (South) runners-up in 1947/48. Born in Johannesburg, he was capped three times for South Africa while with Johannesburg Rangers and had a trial with Dundee prior to joining Clyde in December 1937. He moved to Chesterfield in November 1938 and scored on his international debut for Northern Ireland against Wales four months later. Top scorer in the first two seasons of war-time soccer before guesting for Irish clubs Linfield, Larne and Distillery, he was suspended by the FA for a spell in October 1942. An early Harry Lowe signing in August 1947, he was as hard as nails with a fiery temperament and partnered Jack McDonald in Bournemouth's attack. He scored in the FA Cup third round tie at home to Wolves in 1947/48 and netted 26 goals in 45 Third Division (South) games while at Dean Court prior to joining Walsall in October 1948. He subsequently worked as a welder in Belfast before returning to his native South Africa.

TOMMY MITCHINSON

Stylish midfielder Tommy Mitchinson featured in Cherries' 1971/72 promotion near-miss under John Bond. Signing professional for Sunderland in December 1960, he was a member of their 1963/64 promotion squad and gained top-flight experience prior to joining Mansfield Town for £10,000 in January 1966. He was ever-present alongside ex-Cherries Bill McKinney and Phil Ferns (Snr) in 1966/67 and followed Tommy Cummings to Aston Villa for £18,000 in August 1967, then joined Torquay United for £8,000 in May 1969. Reunited with the likes of Tony Scott, John Benson, Bill Kitchener and Mickey Cave at AFC Bournemouth for £23,000 in December 1971, his solitary goal in 32 Third Division games came in that season's 3-0 win at home to Bradford City. He contracted meningitis soon after and considers himself fortunate to have survived the illness which ended his playing career. For the past 30 years he has been a self-employed milkman in his native Sunderland.

PETER MONAGHAN

Scottish left-half Peter Monaghan was a young member of Charlie Bell's squad at Dean Court. Initially with St John's Boys Guild in his native Stevenston, he impressed with Ardeer Recreation before moving to Bournemouth in June 1937 and was given his League debut in the 1-1 draw at home to QPR three months later. He formed an effective half-back line with Willie Smith and Fred Pincott while at Dean Court, playing in the 1938/39 FA Cup third round tie at First Division Leeds United. His sole goal in 63 Third Division (South) games came in Cherries' 5-2 win at home to Bristol Rovers in March 1939 and he featured in Bournemouth's remarkable 10-0 victory at home to Northampton Town in September 1939, expunged from official records on the outbreak of the Second World War. He was tragically killed in action in the Netherlands as the Allied Forces advanced into Germany. The club held a benefit match for his widow and daughter against Southampton in May 1946.

DEAN MOONEY

Much-travelled striker Dean Mooney was AFC Bournemouth's joint leading goalscorer in 1980/81. A former Orient apprentice, he signed professional in July 1974 and made his Second Division debut at home to Bristol Rovers seven months later. He joined SK Haugar in July 1976 and scored in the 1979 Norwegian Cup final, also playing for Dulwich Hamlet, Walthamstow Avenue, Oxford City and Swedish side GAIS before moving to Dean Court for £15,000 in December 1980. Partnering Trevor Morgan in Cherries' attack, he featured in the 1981/82 promotion campaign and netted 10 goals in 27 Fourth Division games. He had spells with Vasalund and Trowbridge Town before helping Road Sea Southampton to win promotion in 1983/84, then briefly reunited with David Webb at Torquay United in August 1984. Later rejoining Road Sea Southampton, he gave Bournemouth Electric lengthy service as a player, coach and manager and has since been joint boss of Parley Sports and now Poole Town while a self-employed taxi driver.

BILL MORALEE

Long-serving left-half Bill Moralee was ever-present for Cherries in 1931/32. Initially an inside-forward with Crook Town, he impressed in the Northern League prior to joining Huddersfield Town in July 1927. He was unable to secure a first-team place as they were League Championship runners-up and FA Cup finalists in 1927/28, moving to Dean Court with his left-wing partner Tommy Duff in June 1928. Given his League debut in Bournemouth's 2-1 win at home to Coventry City three months later, he starred as Frank Richards' side took West Ham to an FA Cup fifth round replay in 1928/29. He formed an effective half-back line with Cliff Halliwell and Jack Coxford, scoring six goals in 189 Third Division (South) games for Cherries before following Billy Birrell to OPR in June 1936. Featuring in their 1937/38 promotion challenge, he settled in Bournemouth after the Second World War and worked as a bookmaker until suffering a fatal heart-attack in August 1967. His widow Grace still lives in Ensbury Park.

JON MOORE

Left-back Jon Moore was a versatile member of Alec Stock's squad at AFC Bournemouth. A Welsh Schoolboy and Youth international, he signed professional for Bristol Rovers in November 1973 but failed to secure a Second Division slot before being sold to Millwall for £20,000 in December 1974. He made his League debut at Sunderland that month and was an influential figure in the Lions' 1975/76 promotion success and 1977/78 FA Cup run. Alec Stock snapped him up on a free transfer in May 1979 and he scored twice in 36 Fourth Division games for Cherries prior to joining Poole Town in March 1981. He moved to Maidstone United five months later and starred alongside Mark Newson in their 1983/84 Alliance Premier League title triumph, then returned from a spell at Gravesend & Northfleet to help them win the Bob Lord Trophy in 1984/85. Rejoining Gravesend for two seasons in July 1985, he now lives in nearby Hartley and has spent the past 21 years as a foreign exchange broker for Tullett & Tokyo in the City.

STUART MORGAN

Central defender Stuart Morgan was an early John Benson signing for AFC Bournemouth. A former West Ham junior, he signed professional in March 1967 and made his League debut on loan to Torquay United in February 1969. He moved to Reading in November 1969, then joined Colchester United in August 1972 and helped to win promotion in 1973/74. Reunited with John Benson at Dean Court for £3,500 in March 1975, he netted five goals in 81 League outings for Cherries prior to joining Weymouth in June 1977 and became their manager in November 1978. He rejoined AFC Bournemouth as Harry Redknapp's assistant from November 1983 until leaving in September 1985 to manage Torquay United. Rejoining Weymouth as manager in June 1987, he later returned to Dean Court as youth development officer until July 1992. He assisted David Webb at Brentford prior to managing Dorchester Town for six years until sacked in September 1999 and has since scouted for Harry Redknapp at West Ham and Portsmouth.

TREVOR MORGAN

Much-travelled striker Trevor Morgan was AFC Bournemouth's leading marksman in two consecutive seasons. He impressed with Tonbridge, Dartford and Leytonstone/Iford prior to joining Cherries for £3,000 in September 1980, making his League debut in that month's 1-1 draw at Bradford City. Sold to Mansfield Town for £10,000 in November 1981, he returned to Dean Court for a cut-price £4,000 four months later and helped to clinch promotion in 1981/82. He also featured in Cherries' 1983/84 FA Cup third round defeat of holders Manchester United, scoring 46 goals in 141 League games overall before moving to Bristol City in March 1984. Following spells with Exeter City and Bristol Rovers, he rejoined Bristol City in January 1987. He moved to Bolton Wanderers five months later, starring in their 1987/88 promotion success and 1988/89 Sherpa Van Trophy final triumph before joining Colchester United in October 1989. Later assisting Terry Cooper at Exeter and Birmingham, he has since coached in Australia.

PAUL MORRELL

Long-serving left-back Paul Morrell was a key figure in AFC Bournemouth's 1986/87 Third Division title triumph. Initially with Poole Town, he joined Bath City for £3,000 in February 1980 and moved to Stuart Morgan's Weymouth for £5,000 in July 1981. He starred in their 1982 Bob Lord Trophy final success and 1982/83 FA Cup run before moving to Dean Court in June 1983. Scoring in Cherries' 1984 Associate Members Cup final triumph, he helped Harry Redknapp's side take Manchester United to an FA Cup fifth round replay in 1988/89. He netted eight goals in 343 League games until released by Tony Pulis shortly after his testimonial against Southampton in May 1993. Following spells with Leyton Orient, Bashley and Hong Kong side Sing Tao, he joined Geoff Butler's Salisbury City in December 1994 and featured in that season's promotion success. He then played for Bournemouth 'Poppies', Sturminster Marshall, Poole Borough and is now joint boss of Poole Town with Dean Mooney, working locally as a probation service officer.

MARK MORRIS

Central defender Mark Morris was AFC Bournemouth's 'Player of the Season' in 1992/93. Signing professional for Wimbledon in September 1980, he made his League debut at home to Exeter City in October 1981 and featured in their meteoric rise from the Fourth Division to First. He had a loan spell at Aldershot before following Dave Bassett to Watford for £35,000 in July 1987, then reunited with Bassett and several ex-Dons at Sheffield United for £175,000 in July 1989. An influential figure in their 1989/90 promotion triumph, Harry Redknapp paid £95,000 for him in July 1991 and he starred in Cherries' 1991/92 FA Cup third round replay win at Newcastle

United. He became captain at Dean Court and scored eight goals in 194 League games, loaned to Tony Pulis' Gillingham prior to reuniting with Jimmy Case at Brighton in October 1996. Moving to Hastings Town in December 1997, he joined Dorchester Town in February 1999 and managed them to Dr Marten's League Cup success in 2001/02 and the Eastern Division title in 2002/03.

NEIL MOSS

Goalkeeper Neil Moss starred in AFC Bournemouth's 2002/03 Third Division play-off final triumph. Born locally, he attended Twynham School in Christchurch and signed professional at Dean Court in January 1993. He made his League debut in Cherries' 2-1 defeat at Swansea City three months later and was the club's first substitute keeper when he replaced Vince Bartram during the 3-3 draw at Brighton in January 1994. Starting the 1994/95 campaign as first choice, he kept seven consecutive clean sheets as Ian Andrews' deputy in 1995/96 and moved to Southampton for an initial £250,000 in December 1995. He gained Premiership experience as understudy to Dave Beasant and Paul Jones and was loaned to Gillingham, rejoining Cherries on loan in September 2002. Returning on a permanent basis in February 2003, he has made 55 League appearances overall for his favourite club. His parents Chris and Jenny are both very keen Cherries fans, while his late grandfather Percy was a season-ticket holder for over 60 years.

PAUL MOULDEN

Striker Paul Moulden partnered Luther Blissett in AFC Bournemouth's attack. The son of former Rochdale winger Tony Moulden, he earned a place in the Guinness Book of Records with his incredible 289 goals for Bolton Lads' Club in 1981/82. He gained England Schoolboy and Youth international honours before signing professional for Manchester City in September 1984 and starred in their 1986 FA Youth Cup final triumph, then was leading marksman as they regained top-flight status under Mel Machin in 1988/89. Moving to Dean Court as part of the £465,000 deal involving Ian Bishop in July 1989, he scored 13 times in 32 Second Division games for Cherries prior to joining Oldham Athletic for £225,000 in March 1990. He featured in their 1990/91 Second Division title triumph and was loaned to Brighton before being sold to Birmingham City for £150,000 in March 1993. Joining Huddersfield Town in March 1995, he has since played for Rochdale, Accrington Stanley, Bacup Borough and Castleton Gabriels while running a fish and chip shop in Bolton.

DENNY MUNDEE

Utility player Denny Mundee featured in Cherries' 1991/92 FA Cup third round replay win at Newcastle United. A former QPR apprentice, he turned professional with Swindon Town in August 1986 but failed to make an impact at the County Ground and impressed as a striker with Geoff Butler's Salisbury before Harry Redknapp signed him in May 1988. He was given his

League debut in AFC Bournemouth's 2-0 defeat at Oldham Athletic five months later and returned from a loan spell at Torquay United to score six goals in 100 League games for Cherries prior to joining David Webb's Brentford in August 1993. Starring as they qualified for the Second Division play-offs in 1994/95, he moved to Brighton in October 1995 and briefly played for Dorchester Town and Salisbury again before joining Bath City in February 1998 but a back injury ended his career soon after. He settled in Throop and became a wallcoating specialist for Mastex Coatings with his older brother Brian who briefly played for Cherries during the 1982/83 campaign.

ROB MURRAY

Versatile central defender Rob Murray was an influential figure in AFC Bournemouth's 1994/95 relegation escape. A former trainee at Dean Court, he was given his League debut in Cherries' 2-0 defeat at Blackpool four months before signing professional under Tony Pulis in January 1993 and gained Scotland U-21 international recognition against Iceland in March 1993. He secured a regular place in AFC Bournemouth's starting line-up after Mel Machin converted him to a defensive role, displacing Alex Watson midway through the 1994/95 campaign. Partnering Mark Morris in the heart of defence, he impressed with his aerial ability and showed fine distribution. He briefly returned to attack as replacement for the injured Steve Fletcher during the 1996/97 season and scored 12 goals in 147 Second Division games for Cherries prior to being released in May 1998. After a spell in the United States with Colin Clarke's Richmond Kickers, he played for Dorchester Town until sidelined by injury and is now living in Kidderminster.

TOMMY NAYLOR

Versatile defender Tommy Naylor helped Cherries take Liverpool to an FA Cup third round replay in 1967/68. A former apprentice at Dean Court, he signed professional under Reg Flewin in October 1963 and made his League debut in Bournemouth's 4-3 defeat at Colchester United in October 1964. He featured in the 1968/69 promotion challenge and was a member of John Bond's 1970/71 promotion squad, scoring three goals in 142 League games before moving to new-boys Hereford United in August 1972. An influential figure in their 1972/73 promotion success, he scored in Hereford's 1973/74 FA Cup third round replay win at home to West Ham and joined Ronnie Bolton's Dorchester Town in November 1974. He briefly linked up again with Tony Priscott and Rod Taylor at Ringwood Town while employed as a driver for a frozen foods company, then became a taxi driver. Now living in Strouden Park, he is a keen member of Burley Golf Club and a night support worker for the Hesley Group.

GORDON NEAVE

Popular Scottish left-half Gordon Neave was ever-present for Cherries in 1952/53. The son of former Kilmarnock star Bobby Neave, he impressed with Pollok Juniors prior to joining Portsmouth in March 1947 but failed to secure a First Division slot as the great half-back line of Jimmy Scoular, Reg Flewin and Jimmy Dickinson inspired their 1948/49 League Championship triumph. Harry Lowe signed him and defensive partner Ian Drummond in June 1949 and he made his League debut in Bournemouth's 2-0 defeat at Leyton Orient in January 1951, playing alongside the likes of Dai Woodward and Bob Hardy while at Dean Court. He made 85 Third Division (South) appearances for Cherries before joining Aldershot in July 1955. Returning to Portsmouth as youth team coach under Freddie Cox in September 1958, he was Pompey's trainer, physio and kit man with two testimonial matches during a remarkable 41-year period at Fratton Park. He was their longest serving member of staff when he retired at 74 in May 1999 and still lives in Copnor.

TONY NELSON

Tony Nelson gave Cherries fine service in various capacities during 19 years at Dean Court. The son of former Scottish international Jimmy Nelson, he joined Newport County as a centre-forward in August 1950 and gained Welsh Amateur international honours. He moved to Bristol City in May 1954 but failed to secure a first-team slot and was an early Freddie Cox signing in June 1956. Converted to a central defensive role, he starred in Bournemouth's 1961/62 promotion near-miss under Bill McGarry as well as that season's League Cup third round win over Cardiff City. He scored once in 195 League games prior to assisting Freddie Cox at Dean Court, then was chief scout and caretaker-manager until John Benson took charge in January 1975. Later manager of Poole Town, Bournemouth 'Poppies' and the Dorset FA side, he still lives locally and was Winton branch manager of Morris Dibben estate agents until April 1997. He was then part-time property manager for Smith Robinson chartered surveyors in Poole until retiring in April 2000.

STAN NEWSHAM

Fast inside-forward Stan Newsham was Cherries' leading marksman in three consecutive seasons. Born in Farnworth, he played locally for Daubhill Athletic and joined Bolton Wanderers as an amateur after national service in the Royal Engineers. Jack Bruton signed him in June 1952 and he made his League debut in Bournemouth's 5-1 win at home to Walsall ten months later. He partnered the likes of Ollie Norris and Brian Bedford in Cherries' attack, starring in the 1956/57 FA Cup run and scoring 74 goals in 142 Third Division (South) games while at Dean Court before being sold to Notts County for £10,000 in August 1957. Top scorer in their 1959/60 promotion success, he briefly played for Wellington Town and Burton Albion prior to managing Ringwood Town for two seasons while running a fruiterers in Pokesdown. He subsequently ran the Good Companion pub in Portsmouth, then the Fisherman's Rest in Titchfield until retiring in May 1991 and resided in Portsmouth until his death in May 2001.

MARK NEWSON

Influential right-back Mark Newson skippered AFC Bournemouth's 1986/87 Third Division title triumph. A former Charlton Athletic apprentice, he signed professional in December 1978 but failed to make an impact at The Valley and moved to Maidstone United in February 1980. He gained England Semi-Pro honours and starred in their 1980/81 FA Cup run, 1983/84 Alliance

Premier League title triumph and 1985 Bob Lord Trophy final success. Harry Redknapp signed him in May 1985 and he was ever-present in his first two seasons at Dean Court, starring alongside Paul Morrell as Cherries took Manchester United to an FA Cup fifth round replay in 1988/89. He scored 23 goals in 177 League games before being sold to Fulham for £125,000 in February 1990, then played for Barnet, Aylesbury United, Gravesend & Northfleet, Fisher Athletic and Romford. Now project manager of West Ham's football in the community scheme and a part-time analyst for the Press Association.

GRAHAM NEWTON

Popular wing-half Graham Newton helped Cherries take Burnley to an FA Cup third round replay in 1965/66. A former Wolverhampton Wanderers amateur, 'Sammy' signed professional for Blackpool in August 1961 and moved to Walsall in February 1962. He joined Coventry City for £8,000 in January 1964, helping to clinch the Third Division title that season and Reg Flewin paid £4,750 for him in December 1964. Scoring three goals in 28 Third Division games for Bournemouth, he moved to Atlanta Chiefs in April 1967 and starred in their 1968 NASL Soccer Bowl triumph. He had spells with Port Vale, Reading and Hednesford Town prior to joining Worcester City in November 1970, then played for Stourbridge before assisting Nobby Clark as Worcester won the Southern League in 1978/79. After managing Willenhall Town's 1983/84 promotion success, he briefly rejoined Stourbridge as manager. Now living in Pattingham, he runs International Soccer Camps UK as well as coaching for Ralph Lundy Soccer Camps in the United States.

MARK NIGHTINGALE

Versatile defender Mark Nightingale was a member of AFC Bournemouth's 1984 Associate Members Cup winning side. An England Youth international, he signed professional at Dean Court in July 1974 and made his League debut in Cherries' 1-0 win at Tranmere Rovers a month later. He starred in the 1975/76 promotion challenge and was swapped for Crystal Palace's Peter Johnson in July 1976. Reuniting with John Bond at Norwich City in July 1977, he helped to regain top-flight status in 1981/82 and had a spell with Hong Kong side Bulova prior to rejoining AFC Bournemouth in August 1982. He also featured in the 1983/84 FA Cup third round win at home to holders Manchester United and was twice ever-present, scoring eight goals in 199 League games overall for Cherries before moving to Peterborough United in July 1986. Joining Kettering Town in August 1988, he starred in their 1988/89 FA Cup run and then played for King's Lynn, Wisbech Town and Warboys Town. He is now a production operator for Hotpoint in Peterborough.

OLLIE NORRIS

olourful Irish inside-forward Ollie Norris starred as Cherries reached the FA Cup sixth round in 1956/57. Signing professional for Middlesbrough in July 1948, he made his First Division debut at Newcastle United in April 1952 and played alongside England star Wilf Mannion. He had a spell with Worcester City before reuniting with Joe Brown at Bournemouth in July 1955, partnering the likes of Stan Newsham and Brian Bedford in attack and making headlines for his jack-in-the-box antics during Cherries' record Cup run under Freddie Cox. Scoring 34 goals in 96 League games while at Dean Court, he moved to Northampton Town in September 1958 and then had spells with Gloucester City (P/M), Ashford Town, Rochdale and Sligo Rovers before emigrating to Australia in January 1962. He was player-coach of Melbourne sides Wilhelmina, Croatia, Hakoah and Just, then a PE teacher at various Melbourne colleges until December 1983. Now living in the Moorool Bark suburb, he runs his own party fun-bags business in semi-retirement.

PETER NORTON

Right-back Peter Norton was a young member of Freddie Cox's squad at Dean Court. The son-in-law of former Cherries favourite Laurie Cunningham, he attended Portchester School and progressed through the ranks to sign professional for Bournemouth in November 1966. Given his League debut as substitute in Cherries' 3-1 defeat at Middlesbrough four months later, he contested a first-team slot with Terry Gulliver and his solitary goal in 19 Third Division games came in that season's 2-2 draw at home to Reading. He moved to Ernie Tagg's newly-promoted Crewe Alexandra in July 1968 but failed to secure a first-team slot behind record appearance holder Tommy Lowry. Reunited with Billy Coxon at Parley Sports in July 1969, he featured in successive Dorset Combination title and Dorset Senior Cup final triumphs over the next 19 seasons. Now living in Creekmoor, he became a sergeant during 30 years with Dorset Police until retiring in June 1999 and gained British Police representative honours.

RALPH NORTON

Versatile forward Ralph Norton played alongside the likes of John Hold and Chris Weller while at Dean Court. Signing professional for Reading in October 1959, he made his League debut at Notts County eleven months later and featured prominently as they took top-flight Burnley to an FA Cup fourth round replay in 1964/65. Freddie Cox snapped him up on a free transfer in July 1966 and he scored four goals in 48 Third Division games for Bournemouth before following Rodney Taylor to Poole Town in July 1968, starring with Irvin Brown in that season's relegation escape. He joined Southern League Cup finalists Cheltenham Town in July 1969 and was their leading marksman in 1969/70, then briefly linked up with ex-Cherries Derek Burns and Bob Walker at Salisbury in July 1970. Later playing for Cheltenham again and Welton Rovers, he studied for an HND in mathematics with the Open University. Now living in Keynsham, he has spent the past 32 years with Rolls Royce at Filton and is a senior buyer for engine components.

GARRETH O'CONNOR

Irish midfielder Garreth O'Connor scored a memorable individual goal in AFC Bournemouth's 2002/03 Third Division play-off final triumph. He impressed alongside Shaun Maher with Bohemians prior to joining Cherries in June 2000 and made his League debut as a substitute in the 3-1 defeat at Colchester United three months later. At one stage during the 2001/02 campaign he was on the verge of reuniting with Roddy Collins on loan to Carlisle United and it looked as though his days at AFC Bournemouth were numbered. He was recalled to the first-team in the fine 3-1 victory at home to high-flying Stoke City in February 2002 and earned an extended run in the side until injury ruled him out of the closing stages of the season. Returning to his best form during the 2002/03 promotion campaign, he scored numerous vital goals, including two late penalties in the 3-0 win over Swansea City in February 2003. He has netted nine goals in 91 League games for Cherries.

MARK O'CONNOR

Hard-working midfielder Mark O'Connor featured in AFC Bournemouth's 1986/87 Third Division title triumph. A former QPR apprentice, he signed professional in June 1980 and made his League debut against Chelsea on Boxing Day 1981. The Eire U-21 international was a member of Terry Venables' 1982/83 Second Division title squad and reunited with Gerry Francis on loan to Exeter City in October 1983, then joined Bristol Rovers for £20,000 in August 1984. Harry Redknapp paid £25,000 for him in March 1986 and he helped Cherries take Manchester United to an FA Cup fifth round replay in 1988/89. He followed Tony Pulis to Gillingham for £70,000 in December 1989, then reunited with him at AFC Bournemouth in July 1993 and scored 15 goals in 186 League games overall for Cherries before following Pulis back to Gillingham in August 1995. Featuring in the 1995/96 promotion campaign, he ran their School of Excellence and also worked under Pulis at Bristol City and Portsmouth where he is now youth team manager.

SEAN O'DRISCOLL

Former Republic of Ireland international midfielder Sean O'Driscoll holds AFC Bournemouth's appearance record. He impressed with Alvechurch prior to joining Fulham for £12,000 in November 1979 and made his League debut at Preston North End two months later. An influential figure as Fulham won promotion in 1981/82 and so nearly reached the top-flight in 1982/83, 'Noisy' was capped three times during the tour of South America in May 1982. He followed John Beck and Roger Brown to Dean Court initially on loan in February 1984 before a £6,000 transfer that summer, starring in Cherries' 1984 Associate Members Cup final success and 1986/87 Third Division title triumph. Twice ever-present, he also helped take Manchester United to an FA Cup fifth round replay in 1988/89 and scored 19 goals in a record 423 League games for AFC Bournemouth. He had a spell as player-physio, then became youth team manager in December 1994, first-team coach in January 1999 and has been manager since August 2000, plotting the 2002/03 promotion success.

KEN OLIVER

Centre-forward Ken Oliver was an experienced member of Freddie Cox's squad at Dean Court. Initially with Lumley Juniors, he had spells with Sunderland and South Shields prior to joining Barnsley in February 1960 and starred as they took Leicester City to an FA Cup sixth round replay in 1960/61. He moved to Watford for £5,000 in July 1963 and featured in their 1963/64 promotion near-miss, then was swapped for Workington's Dave Carr in March 1965. Freddie Cox paid £3,500 for him in January 1967 and he starred in Bournemouth's relegation battle, scoring four goals in 14 Third Division games before a knee injury ended his playing career in January 1968. He coached at Bradford City and Newcastle United until May 1974, then managed Crook Town prior to coaching at Birmingham City, Walsall and Tottenham Hotspur as well as in Qatar and Saudi Arabia. After a period as Walsall's physio, he has been a consultant for FIFA licensed KAM Sports

International since October 1987 and is also a self-employed taxi driver in Tamworth.

ALAN O'NEILL

Inside-forward Alan O'Neill played alongside the likes of Denis Coughlin and Ken Hodgson in Cherries' attack. Signing professional for Sunderland in February 1955, he made his First Division debut at Cardiff City in November 1956 and was leading marksman in 1957/58. He moved to Aston Villa for £22,000 in October 1960 and scored in their 1961 League Cup final triumph, then joined Plymouth Argyle for £10,000 in November 1962. Sold to Bournemouth for £5,275 in February 1964, he featured in that season's promotion near-miss and scored eight goals in 37 Third Division games before joining Cambridge United in June 1966. He played for Southern Suburbs, Chelmsford City, Drumcondra, Toronto Hellas, New York Cosmos and Vancouver Whitecaps prior to becoming South Shields' manager. Plotting their 1973/74 FA Trophy run, he also achieved managerial success with Blyth Spartans. He later ran Pine Crest Guest House in Southbourne, then Ashlands Hotel/Rest Home until March 1999 and is a keen member of Dudsbury Golf Club.

JON O'NEILL

Utility player Jon O'Neill appeared for AFC Bournemouth in the 1998 Auto Windscreens Shield final at Wembley. Born in Glasgow, he joined Queen's Park in July 1991 and scored on his Scottish League debut at home to East Stirlingshire a month later. He was leading marksman in 1993/94 and followed his former work colleague Malky Mackay to Celtic in May 1994 but failed to secure a regular first-team slot despite featuring in Mark Hughes' testimonial at Old Trafford. Mel Machin signed him initially on loan in March 1996 and the move became permanent that summer. He was top scorer for Cherries' reserves in 1996/97 and regularly featured as a substitute, impressing with his versatility. Making a significant contribution as AFC Bournemouth narrowly missed the promotion play-offs in two consecutive seasons, he scored 10 goals in 124 Second Division games prior to joining Ross County in October 2000. He moved to Queen of the South in January 2001 and starred in their 2001/02 Scottish League Second Division title triumph.

JOHN O'ROURKE

Former England U-23 striker John O'Rourke was an early Trevor Hartley signing for AFC Bournemouth. An ex-Arsenal junior, he moved via Chelsea to Luton Town in December 1963 and topped their goalscoring charts in three consecutive seasons. He joined Middlesbrough for £20,000 in July 1966 and was leading marksman in their 1966/67 promotion success, then moved to Ipswich Town for £30,000 in February 1968. Helping to clinch the Second Division title that season, he was sold to Coventry City for £80,000 in November 1969 and was a key figure as they qualified for the Fairs Cup in 1969/70. He joined QPR for £70,000 in October 1971 and featured in the 1972/73 promotion campaign, moving to AFC Bournemouth for £35,000 in January 1974. Scoring four goals in 22 League outings, he was controversially sacked for disciplinary reasons and joined Poole Town in October 1975. He then had spells with Johannesburg Rangers, Weymouth, Dorchester Town and Poole again and now runs Lakewood News in Highcliffe.

MARK OVENDALE

Popular goalkeeper Mark Ovendale was ever-present for AFC Bournemouth in 1998/99. He impressed with Wisbech Town in the Eastern Counties League and had a trial with Stoke City prior to joining Northampton Town in August 1994. Given his Third Division debut at Preston NE three months later, he failed to secure a regular first team slot at Sixfields Stadium and moved to Barry Town on a free transfer in July 1995. He established a League of Wales record by going 1,072 minutes without conceding a goal in 1995/96, starring as Barry won the title in three consecutive seasons and Welsh Cup final in 1996/97. Also gaining European experience with the Linnets, Mel Machin paid £30,000 for him in May 1998 and he proved to be an excellent shot stopper who commanded the penalty area. He was a key figure as Cherries narrowly failed to qualify for the play-offs in 1998/99, making 89 Second Division appearances before being sold to Luton Town for £425,000 in August 2000 and helping them to win promotion in 2001/02 before being released in May 2003.

JOE PARKINSON

Versatile midfielder Joe Parkinson was an influential member of Tony Pulis' squad at Dean Court. A former Wigan Athletic trainee, 'Parky' scored on his full League debut at Mansfield Town two months before signing professional in March 1989 and helped them take Coventry City to a FA Cup third round replay in 1990/91. He moved to AFC Bournemouth for an initial £35,000 set by transfer tribunal in July 1993 and quickly impressed as a tireless ball-winner with excellent passing ability. His solitary goal in 30 Second Division games clinched Cherries' 1-1 draw at Hartlepool United a month later and he followed assistant manager David Williams to Everton for £250,000 rising to £800,000 after subsequent appearances in March 1994. He starred in their 1995 FA Cup final triumph and was also a Wembley winner in that year's Charity Shield but a serious knee injury ended his playing career in November 1999 and he became full-time Fans Liaison Officer at Goodison Park.

LES PARODI

Young left-back Les Parodi partnered Clive Payne in AFC Bournemouth's defence. A former Charlton Athletic junior, he impressed with Staines Town in the Athenian League before John Bond signed him in September 1972 and featured in the 1973/74 Football Combination title triumph. He made his League debut as substitute in Cherries' 1-1 draw at Tranmere Rovers in February 1974 and quickly established a regular first-team slot in place of Bobby Howe, scoring twice in 49 Third Division games until a pelvic injury curtailed his League career in April 1975. He then had spells with Christchurch, Southampton reserves, AP Leamington, Salisbury, Poole Town, Dorchester Town, Oxford City and Dagenham as well as playing for Seattle Sounders and Columbus Magic in the United States before running a sports promotion company with Glenn Hoddle. Still living in Bournemouth, he has forged a successful business career with his Clean Ahead corporate sign company, Tager Inns group in East Anglia and local property interests.

EDDIE PARRIS

Former Welsh international outside-left Eddie Parris played under three different managers while at Dean Court. Born in Pwllmeyric of West Indian parents, he impressed with Chepstow Town prior to joining Bradford Park Avenue in August 1928 and made his Second Division debut at Tottenham Hotspur six months later. He was leading marksman as they reached the FA Cup fifth round for the fourth consecutive season in 1931/32, also starring in successive promotion challenges and capped by his country against Northern Ireland in December 1931. Billy Birrell signed him in June 1934 and he featured in Bournemouth's 8-1 FA Cup first round replay win at home to Walthamstow Avenue in 1935/36. He netted 23 times in 104 Third Division (South) games for Cherries before moving to Luton Town in February 1937 and helped to clinch the Third Division (South) title that season, then joined Northampton Town in November 1937. Later playing for Cheltenham Town, he resided in Gloucester until his death in February 1971.

TOMMY PATERSON

Striker Tommy Paterson was a popular member of John Benson's squad at Dean Court. A former Leicester City apprentice, he joined Middlesbrough in September 1974 and Jack Charlton gave him his First Division debut at home to Birmingham City three months later. John Benson paid £2,000 for him in April 1976 and he partnered the likes of Kevin Reeves and Jack Howarth in AFC Bournemouth's attack, scoring ten goals in 57 Fourth Division games before returning to his native North-East with Darlington in June 1978. He reunited with Stuart Morgan at Weymouth in June 1979 and was leading marksman as they were Alliance Premier League runners-up in 1979/80, then played for Poole Town, Dorchester Town and Geoff Butler's Salisbury prior to coaching Wimborne Town and Boscombe Albion. Still living in Bournemouth, he has run his own industrial cleaning business for the past 23 years and is a keen member of Dudsbury Golf Club. His father-in-law Ken 'Nimbus' Sullivan gave Cherries lengthy back-room service.

TOMMY PATON

Scottish inside-forward Tommy Paton played for Cherries either side of the Second World War. Initially with Ardeer Recreation, he joined Wolverhampton Wanderers in June 1937 but failed to secure a first-team slot and moved to Swansea Town in October 1938. Charlie Bell signed him in February 1939 and he scored in Bournemouth's 10-0 win at home to Northampton town seven months later, then guested for several clubs during the Second World War. As a wartime officer in Bomber Command he was taken prisoner after being shot down near Heidelberg but returned to feature in Cherries' 1945/46 Third Division (South) Cup final triumph, scoring eight goals in 46 League games overall before being sold to Watford for £1,000 in January 1948. He switched to wing-half and became captain, then joined Folkestone in August 1952 and starred in their 1952/53 Kent League title triumph. Later a clerk with HM Customs & Excise at the local docks until retiring in December 1978, he resided in Folkestone until his death in December 1991.

CLIVE PAYNE

Right-back Clive Payne featured prominently in AFC Bournemouth's 1975/76 promotion challenge. Initially a centre-forward, he represented Norfolk Schoolboys and signed professional for Norwich City in March 1968. He made his League debut at home to Sheffield United six months later and was ever-present in their 1971/72 Second Division title triumph, then played alongside Geoff Butler in the 1973 League Cup final at Wembley. Also featuring in that year's Texaco Cup final, he moved to Dean Court in a multi-player exchange deal involving Mel Machin, John Benson and Fred Davies in December 1973. He scored three goals in 101 League games for Cherries until a recurring ankle injury curtailed his League career in April 1976. Subsequently player-manager of Aylsham, he ran a sports shop for five years and then was a sales rep for Everest and Yeoman Windows in Norwich. Still living in his native Aylsham, he now runs Aylsham Windows and plays cricket for Cromer in the Norfolk Alliance League.

GAVIN PEACOCK

Ex-England Youth international midfielder Gavin Peacock remains AFC Bournemouth's most expensive signing. The son of former Charlton Athletic favourite Keith Peacock, he signed professional for QPR in November 1984 and made his First Division debut at home to Sheffield Wednesday two years later. His father paid £40,000 to sign him for Gillingham in October 1987 and he impressed at Priestfield Stadium before Harry Redknapp splashed out a record £250,000 for him in August 1969. He netted eight goals in 56 League games for Cherries prior to joining Newcastle United in exchange for Wayne Fereday plus £150,000 in November 1990. Ever-present and top scorer in 1991/92, he was a key figure in their 1992/93 First Division title triumph and moved to Chelsea for £1,250,000 in August 1993. He played alongside Mark Stein in the 1994 FA Cup final at Wembley, rejoining QPR in a joint £3,500,000 deal with John Spencer in November 1996 and subsequently loaned to Charlton. Now a match summariser for Radio Five Live, he had a testimonial in May 2003 when QPR hosted Chelsea.

ADRIAN PENNOCK

Versatile defender Adrian Pennock was an early Tony Pulis signing for AFC Bournemouth. A former Norwich City trainee, he signed professional in July 1989 and was given his First Division debut at Southampton seven months later but failed to make any further appearances in the top-flight while at Carrow Road. Tony Pulis paid £30,000 for him in August 1992 and he partnered the likes of Neil Masters and Alex Watson in AFC Bournemouth's defence. Starring in the 1994/95 relegation escape under Mel Machin, he netted nine goals in 131 Second Division games for Cherries and overcame a serious knee injury before reuniting with Pulis at Gillingham for £30,000 in October 1996. He featured in the dramatic 1998/99 Second Division play-off final defeat against Manchester City and was a Wembley winner a year later as they beat John Benson's Wigan Athletic in the play-off final to reach the First Division for the first time. Released after recurring injury problems, he joined Gravesend & Northfleet in January 2003.

JACK PERCIVAL

Left-half Jack Percival was an experienced figure as Cherries were Third Division (South) runners-up in 1947/48. Initially with Low Pittington, he moved via Durham City to Manchester City in October 1932 and made his First Division debut as Matt Busby's understudy at home to Aston Villa a year later. He was ever-present skipper as they won the League Championship for the first time in 1936/37, also featuring in their 1946/47 Second Division title campaign. An early Harry Lowe signing in May 1947, he played in Bournemouth's 1947/48 title decider at home to QPR and his sole goal in 52 Third Division (South) games clinched Cherries' 2-1 win at Newport County in August 1948. He returned to his native North-East as Murton's player-manager in June 1949, then became Shotton CW player-coach before rejoining Durham City as manager. Settling in West Rainton, he worked at Lambton Colliery and then was a HGV driver for Golightly & Sons until his tragic death in a motor accident near Rochdale in January 1976.

LOU PETERS

Ex-England Youth international winger Lou Peters was a popular member of Freddie Cox's squad at Dean Court. Real name Roger, he signed professional for Bristol City in March 1961 and made his League debut at home to Brentford a month later. He starred alongside former England international John Atyeo and future Cherries striker Brian Clark in City's 1964/65 promotion triumph, also featuring in their 1965/66 promotion near-miss and successive FA Cup runs. Leading marksman in 1966/67, Freddie Cox paid £5,000 for him in June 1968 and he made a significant contribution to Bournemouth's 1968/69 promotion challenge. Creating numerous goalscoring chances for the likes of Keith East and Ken Pound while at Dean Court, he netted three times in 37 Third Division games for Cherries before following Tommy Taylor to Bath City in January 1970 after being displaced by John Meredith. He became a senior consultant during 30 years with Sun Life of Canada and is now an independent financial adviser based in Weston-in-Gordano.

GERRY PEYTON

Republic of Ireland international goalkeeper Gerry Peyton was 'Player of the Season' in Cherries' 1986/87 Third Division title triumph. Initially with Atherstone Town, he moved to Burnley in May 1975 and gained top-flight experience prior to joining Fulham for £35,000 in December 1976. He was a key figure as they won promotion in 1981/82 and so nearly reached the First Division in 1982/83, then was loaned to Southend United before Harry Redknapp snapped him up on a free transfer in July 1986. Also starring as AFC Bournemouth took Manchester United to an FA Cup fifth round replay in 1988/89, he made 202 League appearances and gained a club record seven caps while at Dean Court before following Jimmy Gabriel to Everton in July 1991. He had loan spells at Bolton Wanderers, Brentford and Chelsea prior to briefly rejoining Brentford in March 1993, then reunited with Harry Redknapp at West Ham. Subsequently coaching in Japan and Sweden, he has since been a goalkeeping coach at clubs like Southampton, West Brom and Fulham.

FRED PINCOTT

Big centre-half Fred Pincott was ever-present for Cherries in 1937/38. Starting with Bristol Royal Victoria, he joined Wolverhampton Wanderers in November 1931 and was given his First Division debut as George Bellis' understudy in the 7-1 defeat at home to Arsenal a year later. Billy Birrell signed him in May 1934 and he featured alongside the likes of Willie Smith and Peter Monaghan while at Dean Court, playing 196 Third Division (South) games prior to joining Dartford in June 1939. A wartime guest for Bournemouth, Bristol City and Chester, he joined Gravesend & Northfleet in June 1946 and returned to Football League action with Newport County in July 1947. He moved to Bideford as player-coach a year later and became a driver for Devon Creameries, then worked for a tyre company in Avonmouth. Subsequently settling in Eastleigh near his eldest daughter, he was a labourer for Pirelli Group and the local council until retiring in March 1978. He remained in Eastleigh until his death in February 2000.

KEN POUND

Winger Ken Pound starred as Cherries took Liverpool to an FA Cup third round replay in 1967/68. Initially an amateur with hometown Portsmouth, he followed Basil Hayward to Yeovil Town in July 1963 and featured in their 1963/64 Southern League title triumph before moving to Swansea Town in July 1964. Freddie Cox signed him in exchange for Denis Coughlin in August 1966 and he scored 24 goals in 102 Third Division games for Bournemouth prior to being swapped for Gillingham's John Meredith in July 1969. Moving to Weymouth in July 1971, he starred as they won the Southern League Cup in 1972/73. He became their reserve team coach, then worked in the commercial departments of Bath City, Maidstone United and Southampton prior to rejoining Cherries as promotions officer until Brian Tiler's arrival in March 1983. Subsequently a regional manager for the Children Nationwide charity, he had a spell as Brighton and Hove Albion's commercial manager and has since been a financial adviser for Britannic Assurance in Southampton.

TONY POWELL

Versatile central defender Tony Powell was a key figure in Cherries' 1970/71 promotion success. Initially a striker, he represented Bristol Boys at soccer and boxing and impressed with Bath City before Freddie Cox paid £1,000 for him in April 1968. 'Knocker' established a regular first-team slot during the 1969/70 campaign after being switched to a defensive role and scored 10 goals in 219 League games for AFC Bournemouth before following John Bond to Norwich City in an exchange deal involving Trevor Howard in August 1974. Starring alongside several other one-time Cherries as Norwich won promotion and were League Cup finalists in 1974/75, he was ever-present in three consecutive

seasons before reuniting with Jimmy Gabriel at San Jose Earthquakes in March 1981. Subsequently with Seattle Sounders, he has since led a colourful lifestyle in the United States and is now a receptionist at a hotel in Hollywood. He was the subject of a feature in the 'Mail on Sunday' on 20th October 2002.

TONY PRISCOTT

Slightly-built winger Tony Priscott was Cherries' joint leading marksman in 1966/67. A former Portsmouth junior, he signed professional in July 1959 and Freddie Cox gave him his League debut in Pompey's 6-1 defeat at Charlton Athletic nine months later. He featured in their 1961/62 Third Division title campaign and moved to Aldershot in August 1962, starring in the 1963/64 FA Cup run. Top scorer in 1964/65, he played under Cox again after joining Bournemouth for £5,000 in January 1966 and netted six goals in 61 League games prior to rejoining Aldershot for £3,000 in August 1967. He created numerous chances for record goalscorer Jack Howarth before moving to Poole Town in July 1971. He joined Ringwood Town as player-manager in June 1973 and ran a building company with his team-mate Rod Taylor until August 1982. He claims life began at 40 when he discovered God and after studying at Moorlands College in Sopley, is now full time joint pastor at King's Church in Ringwood.

JACK PROCTOR

Hard-tackling right-back Jack Proctor was a popular member of Billy Birrell's squad at Dean Court. Starting with New Delaval Villa, he joined Huddersfield Town in November 1930 but failed to secure a First Division slot behind England international Roy Goodall and moved to Bournemouth in May 1932. He was given his League debut in Cherries' 3-0 defeat at Cardiff City three months later, displacing long-serving Jack Hayward in defence and playing alongside the likes of Jack Whitehouse, Reg Parker and Jackie Randle while at Dean Court. Making 53 Third Division (South) appearances for Bournemouth, he was unable to prevent Billy Birrell's side having to seek re-election in 1933/34 and moved to Hartlepool United in July 1934. He featured prominently as they took top-flight Grimsby Town to an FA Cup third round replay in 1935/36 and joined Blyth Spartans in August 1938. Subsequently employed as a labourer in a local timber yard until retiring in August 1975, he remained in his native New Delaval until his death in April 1978.

DAVID PUCKETT

Striker David Puckett made a significant contribution to AFC Bournemouth's 1986/87 Third Division title triumph. A former Southampton apprentice, he signed professional in November 1978 and made his First Division debut alongside Kevin Keegan against Everton in March 1981. He helped Saints to finish as League Championship runners-up in 1983/84, moving to Dean Court with Mark Whitlock in July 1986 as part of the record deal for Colin Clarke. A knee injury suffered in Cherries' 3-0 Boxing Day 1986 win at Bristol Rovers sidelined him for almost a year and he was loaned to Stoke City and Swansea City before joining Aldershot in January 1989. He was top scorer in four consecutive seasons and rejoined AFC Bournemouth when Aldershot folded in March 1992. Netting 14 goals in 39 League games overall for Cherries, he moved to Woking in August 1992 and featured in their 1994 FA Trophy final triumph. He has since played for Weymouth, Newport (IOW), Salisbury City, Havant Town, Wokingham, Bashley, Eastleigh and BAT.

TONY PULIS

Hard-tackling midfielder Tony Pulis was an influential figure in Cherries' 1986/87 Third Division title success. A former Bristol Rovers apprentice, he made his League debut at Bristol City shortly before signing professional under Don Megson in September 1975. He played alongside David Williams in midfield and spent a year with Hong Kong side Happy Valley prior to rejoining Rovers as player-coach in June 1982, then moved to hometown Newport County for £8,000 in July 1984. Harry Redknapp signed him in August 1986 and he impressed with his versatility before being sold to Gillingham for £10,000 in July 1989. He returned to AFC Bournemouth as player-coach in August 1990 and scored four goals in 90 League games overall prior to succeeding Redknapp as manager from June 1992 until dismissed in August 1994. Rejoining Gillingham as manager in June 1995, he guided them to promotion in 1995/96 and the Second Division play-off final in 1998/99. He has since managed Bristol City, Portsmouth and now Stoke City.

STEPHEN PURCHES

Versatile favourite Stephen Purches scored a spectacular goal in AFC Bournemouth's 2002/03 Third Division play-off final triumph. A former West Ham trainee midfielder, he signed professional at Upton Park in July 1998 and appeared for Cherries as a triallist in the 1999 Avon Insurance Combination Cup final when he starred in a superb 3-1 win over Ipswich Town. He joined AFC Bournemouth on a free transfer in July 2000 and made his League debut in the 1-1 draw at Bristol Rovers on the opening day of the season, quickly establishing himself as the regular left-back as Cherries challenged for the Second Division play-offs in 2000/01. Scoring his first goal in the 3-1 victory over Stoke City in February 2002, he was subsequently joined at Dean Court by his younger brother John. An influential figure as Sean O'Driscoll's side regained Second Division status at the first attempt in 2002/03, he has netted five goals in 118 League outings for Cherries.

JIMMY QUINN

Northern Ireland international striker Jimmy Quinn was AFC Bournemouth's leading marksman in 1991/92. He developed with Congleton Town, Whitchurch Alport and Oswestry Town prior to joining Swindon Town for £10,000 in December 1981 and moved to Blackburn Rovers for £32,000 in August 1984. Rejoining Swindon for £50,000 in December 1986, he helped to win promotion that season and was top scorer in 1987/88. He joined Leicester City for £210,000 in June 1988, then moved via Bradford City to West Ham for £320,000 in December 1989. A promotion winner in 1990/91, Harry Redknapp paid £40,000 for him to replace Luther Blissett in August 1991 and he netted 19 goals in 43 Third Division games for Cherries prior to joining Reading for £55,000 in July 1992. Leading marksman in their 1993/94 Second Division title triumph, he scored in the 1994/95 First Division play-off final and was joint player-boss until May 1997. He became Peterborough United's player-coach, managed Swindon Town and Northwich Victoria, then took charge at Shrewsbury Town in June 2003.

BILLY RAFFERTY

Much-travelled striker Billy Rafferty was AFC Bournemouth's leading goalscorer in 1984/85. Starting with Port Glasgow Rovers, he joined Coventry City in September 1969 and gained top-flight experience before moving to Blackpool in October 1972 as part of the deal for Tommy Hutchison. He joined Plymouth Argyle for £25,000 in March 1974 and was top scorer in their 1974/75 promotion success, netting in that season's 7-3 win at Dean Court. Sold to Carlisle United for £25,000 in May 1976, he twice topped their goalscoring charts and joined Wolves for £125,000 in March 1978. He moved to Newcastle United for £175,000 in October 1979, then joined Portsmouth for £80,000 in December 1980 and starred in their 1982/83 Third Division title triumph. Harry Redknapp paid £4,000 for him in February 1984 and he netted 19 goals in 58 League outings for Cherries prior to joining Farense in July 1985, then played for Portuguese rivals Loultanos. He now runs Shapers Health & Beauty Salon in Carlisle.

DENNIS RAMPLING

Outside-right Dennis Rampling was a popular member of Harry Lowe's squad at Dean Court. Initially an apprentice engine fitter for D Napier & Sons in Acton, he impressed with their works team in local soccer and joined Fulham in November 1942. He gained representative honours during national service in the RAF and made his League debut at home to Coventry City in April 1948, moving to Bournemouth as part of the deal that took Jack McDonald to Craven Cottage two months later. Contesting a first-team slot with Arnold Stephens, he helped Cherries' reserves to win the 1949 Combination Cup and scored four goals in 24 Third Division (South) games prior to joining Brentford in May 1949. He later played for Weymouth and Ashford Town, then was a referee in the Athenian League. Employed as a fitter for EMI and Fairey Aviation in Hayes, he was then a publican in Aldershot and Chobham until early retirement in August 1977. He subsequently settled in Worthing before moving back to Woking.

MARK RAWLINSON

Versatile midfielder Mark Rawlinson was an early Mel Machin signing for AFC Bournemouth. A former Manchester United trainee, he featured in the same youth team as Nicky Butt, Paul Scholes, Keith Gillespie, David Beckham and the Neville brothers and signed professional at Old Trafford in July 1993. He secured a regular slot in United's reserve team that won the Pontins League title in 1993/94 but failed to gain a Premiership chance and Mel Machin snapped him up on a free transfer in July 1995. Given his League debut as a substitute in Cherries' 2-1 win at Wycombe Wanderers a month later, he impressed as a determined tackler with good passing ability. He gained a regular place in the starting line-up midway through the 1996/97 campaign, taking over the central midfield role after Matt Holland switched to defence and scoring twice in 79 Second

Division games for AFC Bournemouth before moving to Exeter City in July 2000. Joining Weymouth in July 2001, he runs his own personal training business.

JOE READMAN

Versatile forward Joe Readman played alongside record goalscorer Ron Eyre while at Dean Court. Born in Hartlepool, he developed with Wheatley Hill Alliance prior to joining Bolton Wanderers in February 1923 but failed to gain a First Division slot with the FA Cup winners and moved to Bournemouth in May 1924. Given his League debut in Cherries' 2-0 defeat at Plymouth Argyle five months later, he made a significant contribution to the upturn in the club's fortunes under Leslie Knighton and netted 20 goals in 49 Third Division (South) games prior to joining Brighton in August 1927. He was a prolific goalscorer for their reserves but had limited first-team opportunities and moved to newly-promoted Millwall in July 1928, then joined Mansfield Town in July 1931. Scoring their first-ever goal in the Football League at home to Swindon Town a month later, he moved to Ramsgate in August 1933 and subsequently played for his works team Ramsgate Press Wanderers. He resided in Ramsgate until his death in January 1973.

BOB REDFERN

Outside-right Bob Redfern played for Cherries either side of the Second World War. Initially with Tow Law Juniors, he joined Wolverhampton Wanderers in May 1936 and had a spell with their nursery side Cradley Heath before following the well-worn trail to Dean Court with Jack Rowley in February 1937. He made his League debut in that month's 1-1 draw at Walsall and netted twice in Bournemouth's 10-0 win at home to Northampton Town in September 1939, then guested for Luton Town, York City, Crystal Palace and Fulham during wartime service in the RAF. Scoring five goals in 89 Third Division (South) games for Cherries, he joined Brighton in August 1947 and briefly reunited with Paddy Gallacher at Weymouth in August 1948 while studying to become a schoolteacher. He then served Bournemouth 'Poppies' over 20 years as player-coach, secretary and manager, teaching at St James CE Primary School, South Kinson Juniors and Stourfield Junior School until retiring in April 1978. He remained local until his death in July 2002.

HARRY REDKNAPP

Harry Redknapp managed AFC Bournemouth to the Third Division title in 1986/87. An England Youth international winger, he signed professional for West Ham in March 1964 and played alongside World Cup trio Bobby Moore, Geoff Hurst and Martin Peters. He reunited with John Bond at Dean Court for £31,000 in August 1972 and scored five goals in 101 League games for Cherries prior to joining Brentford in September 1976. Also playing for Seattle Sounders, he assisted Bobby Moore at Oxford City before returning to AFC Bournemouth as player-coach. After a spell as caretaker-boss, he became manager in November 1983 and plotted that season's FA Cup third round defeat of holders Manchester United and Associate Members Cup final success. He remained in charge at Dean Court until resigning in June 1992, then assisted Billy Bonds before succeeding him as West Ham's manager, for seven years, in August 1994. After a spell as Portsmouth's director of football, he became manager in March 2002 and plotted Pompey's 2002/03 First Division title triumph.

JAMIE REDKNAPP

Outstanding midfielder Jamie Redknapp gained 17 England caps after leaving AFC Bournemouth. The youngest son of Harry Redknapp, he attended Twynham School in Christchurch and gained England Schoolboy honours prior to joining Cherries as a trainee under his father's management after a spell on Tottenham Hotspur's books. He made his Second Division debut as a 16 year-old in the 4-1 win at Hull City five months before signing professional in June 1990 and played 13 League games for AFC Bournemouth prior to joining Liverpool for £350,000 in January 1991, with Alex Watson moving in the opposite direction. Just nine months later he became the youngest player to represent Liverpool in Europe and gained a record 19 England U-21 caps. He was an influential figure in their 1995 Coca-Cola Cup final triumph, then returned to Wembley in the 1996 FA Cup final and became captain at Anfield. His progress was hindered by successive injuries and he moved to Tottenham Hotspur in April 2002. He is married to pop star Louise.

DEREK REEVES

Experienced centre-forward Derek Reeves featured in Cherries' 1962/63 promotion challenge. He represented Poole and Dorset Schools and had a spell with Bournemouth Gasworks before moving to Southampton in December 1954. Scoring on his League debut to clinch a 1-1 draw at Dean Court four months later, he was Saints' leading marksman in four consecutive seasons. He netted a record 39 goals in the 1959/60 Third Division title campaign, also starring in their 1960/61 League Cup run with a record five goals in the fourth round win against Leeds United. Bill McGarry paid £8,000 for him in November 1962 to replace Dickie Dowsett in Bournemouth's attack and he played alongside the likes of Charlie Woods and Jimmy Singer. Scoring eight times in 35 Third Division games while at Dean Court before moving to Worcester City in June 1965, his playing career was ended by injury soon after. He became a representative for a Bournemouth building firm, then was a driver for Dorset Social Services until his death from cancer in May 1995.

KEVIN REEVES

Brilliant young striker Kevin Reeves was AFC Bournemouth's leading goalscorer in 1975/76. Born in Burley, he attended Twynham School in Christchurch and progressed through the ranks to sign professional at Dean Court in July 1975. The England Youth international was given his full League debut in Cherries' 0-0 draw at Stockport County two months later and forged an exciting teenage partnership with Howard Goddard, netting 20 goals in 63 League games before joining John Bond's Norwich City for £50,000 in February 1977. Gaining the first of two England caps against Bulgaria in November 1979, he was an early £1 million transfer to Manchester City in March 1980 and scored in the 1981 FA Cup final replay. He was twice leading marksman and followed John Bond to Burnley for £100,000 in August 1983 but an arthritic hip ended his League career at 26. Briefly with Barrow and Yeovil Town, he reunited with Bond as Birmingham City's youth coach and since November 1989 has assisted Brian Flynn at Wrexham and Swansea City.

CARL RICHARDS

Big Jamaican striker Carl Richards was leading marksman in AFC Bournemouth's 1986/87 Third Division title triumph. Initially with Dulwich Hamlet, he topped their goalscoring charts in 1983/84 and moved to Enfield in July 1984. He was leading scorer in the 1985/86 Gola League title triumph and gained England Semi-Pro recognition shortly before Harry Redknapp paid £10,000 for him in July 1986. Partnering Trevor Aylott in Cherries' attack, he netted 16 goals in 71 League games prior to joining Birmingham City for £70,000 in October 1988. He was sold to Peterborough United for £37,000 in July 1989, then joined Blackpool for £60,000 in January 1990 and helped them qualify for the Fourth Division play-offs in 1990/91. Following a loan spell at Maidstone United, he rejoined Enfield in December 1991 and featured in two consecutive Diadora League Cup finals. He then played for Bromley and Tooting & Mitcham until injury ended his career. He is now a house husband with two children in Brockley, SE London.

DEREK RICKARD

Striker Derek Rickard was one of several experienced players signed during Trevor Hartley's reign at Dean Court. He represented Plymouth and Devon Schools, then appeared for Torpoint Athletic and St Austell while employed as a joiner at Devonport dockyard. Moving to Plymouth Argyle initially as a part-timer in July 1969, he made his League debut at Halifax Town five months later. He was top scorer in 1971/72 and helped Argyle to reach the League Cup semi-finals in 1973/74, then moved to AFC Bournemouth with Neil Hague for a joint £15,000 fee in July 1974. Unable to prevent Cherries' relegation in 1974/75, he netted six goals in 32 League games before joining Falmouth Town in June 1976. He starred as they won the Western League title in successive seasons, then moved to Saltash United and was later player-coach and chairman of Weston Mill Oak Villa. Still living in his native Plymouth, he ran the newsagents in Weston Mill for 22 years until August 1998 and is now a driver for the Evening Herald newspaper.

HUGHEN RILEY

Midfielder Hughen Riley was an experienced member of John Benson's squad at AFC Bournemouth. Signing professional for Rochdale in December 1966, he made his League debut at Newport County eight months later and was a member of their 1968/69 promotion squad. He also helped Rochdale to finish in their highest-ever League position in 1969/70 and beat top-flight Coventry City in the 1970/71 FA Cup third round. Joining Crewe Alexandra in December 1971, he was sold to Bury for £5,000 in November 1974 and John Benson signed him in April 1976. He netted seven goals in 72 Fourth Division outings for Cherries prior to joining David Best's Dorchester Town in July 1978, then reunited with Stuart Morgan at Weymouth. He has since been a licensee at The Greyhound Inn at Winterbourne Kingston, Swan Inn in Sherborne, The Mariners at Hythe, World's End near Wimborne, The Shirehorse in Blandford, Whincroft at Ferndown, The Lion in Pagham, The Hen & Chicken Inn in Alton and now The Five Bells in Buriton.

JOE RILEY

Centre-forward Joe Riley was Cherries' leading marksman in two consecutive seasons. Initially with Conisbrough Welfare, he developed with Denaby United and Goldthorpe United prior to joining Bristol Rovers in May 1931. He scored a hat-trick on his League debut in their 4-1 win at home to Bournemouth eight months later but had limited opportunities behind England internationals Tommy Cook and Viv Gibbins and moved to rivals Bristol City in May 1933. Top scorer as they won the Welsh Cup in 1933/34, he netted all five goals in that season's 5-0 victory at home to Brighton and joined Bournemouth for £2,000 in June 1935. He inspired Cherries' 1936/37 promotion challenge under Charlie Bell and scored an impressive 57 goals in 93 Third Division (South) games while at Dean Court before moving to Notts County in an exchange deal involving Harry Mardon in December 1937. Joining Gloucester City in July 1938, he subsequently became a Bristol City scout based in Cheltenham.

ALEX RITCHIE

Diminutive Scottish outside-right Alex Ritchie was Cherries' joint leading goalscorer in 1934/35. Starting with Fauldhouse United, he joined Airdrie in September 1922 and had spells with Armadale, St Bernards, Raith Rovers, Peebles Rovers and Dunfermline Athletic prior to rejoining Raith in May 1926. He featured in their 1926/27 promotion campaign and moved to Blackpool in July 1928, making a significant contribution to their 1929/30 Second Division title triumph. Sold to Reading for £1,000 in March 1931, he was an influential figure in their 1931/32 promotion near-miss. He joined Watford in a joint deal with Frank McPherson in June 1933 and moved to Bournemouth in June 1934, scoring 11 goals in 33 Third Division (South) games while at Dean Court before returning to Scotland with newly-promoted Third Lanark in June 1935. Helping them to reach the Scottish Cup final in 1935/36, he joined Hibernian in August 1936 and then played for Albion Rovers. Subsequently a scout for Reading, he died in Mossend in July 1954.

LES ROBERTS

Inside-right Les Roberts starred as Cherries took Bolton Wanderers to an FA Cup fourth round replay in 1925/26. A former Aston Villa amateur, he turned professional with Chesterfield in May 1922 and scored on his League debut at Tranmere Rovers seven months later. He moved to Sheffield Wednesday in June 1923, then joined Merthyr Town in August 1924 and Harry Kinghorn brought him and right-wing partner Pat Clifford to Dean Court in December 1924. Making a significant contribution to Bournemouth's improved form, he scored 11 goals in 51 Third Division (South) games prior to joining Bolton Wanderers for £1,500 after the FA Cup replay in February 1926. He joined Swindon Town in June 1927, then had spells with Brentford, Manchester City, Exeter City, Crystal Palace, Chester, Rotherham United, Scunthorpe United and New Brighton. The first player to appear in the Football League for 12 different clubs, he spent 18 years in business locally after the war and resided in Christchurch until his death in May 1980.

WALTER ROBERTS

Welsh left-half Walter Roberts played alongside Dal Woodward and Jim Stirling while at Dean Court. Born in Wrexham, he signed professional for his hometown club in August 1938 and made his League debut at Doncaster Rovers four months later. He served in the Royal Artillery during the Second World War and was rescued from Dunkirk before fighting in the Middle East. Securing a regular first-team slot at Wrexham during the 1946/47 season, he lost his place after injury and Harry Lowe swapped Fred Rowell for him in August 1948. He contested Bournemouth's left half position with the likes of Jack Percival, Dennis Martin and Jack Lewis, helping the reserves to win the Combination Cup in 1949 and making 14 Third Division (South) appearances for Cherries prior to joining Ellesmere Port in July 1950. Later with Winsford United and Blaenau Ffestiniog, he was briefly Wrexham's reserve team coach. He still lives in Wrexham and spent 25 years as a shop assistant at a fishmongers until early retirement in December 1977.

STEVE ROBINSON

Northern Ireland international midfielder Steve Robinson was capped five times while at Dean Court. A former Tottenham Hotspur trainee striker, he signed professional in January 1993 and made his Premiership debut at Blackburn Rovers nine months later. He was loaned to Leyton Orient before following Neil Young to AFC Bournemouth on a free transfer in October 1994. Impressing with his versatility, he excelled as an attacking midfielder in Cherries' 1994/95 relegation escape and became the club's regular penalty-taker. He was capped by his country at five different levels and played at Wembley in the 1998 Auto Windscreens Shield final, starring as Mel Machin's side narrowly failed to qualify for the promotion play-offs in two consecutive seasons. Selected for the 1998/99 PFA Second Division team along with Mark Stein and Jamie Vincent, he scored 51 goals in 240 League games for AFC Bournemouth prior to joining Preston NE for £375,000 in May 2000 and moved to Luton Town for £50,000 in July 2002.

JOCK ROBSON

Scottish goalkeeper Jock Robson starred as Cherries took Liverpool to an FA Cup third round replay in 1926/27. He served in France with the 6th Seaforth Highlanders during the First World War and impressed with hometown Vale of Leithen prior to joining Arsenal in

November 1921. Given his First Division debut in the 5-0 win at home to Bolton Wanderers on Boxing Day 1922, he kept his place for the remainder of that season and was ever-present in 1923/24. He was displaced by internationals Bill Harper and Dan Lewis at Highbury and followed Leslie Knighton to Bournemouth in August 1926. Contesting Cherries' goalkeeping slot with Vic Crumley, he played 42 Third Division (South) games while at Dean Court before returning to Scotland with Montrose in August 1928. He coached Leithen Rovers for many seasons while employed as a labourer by Innerleithen Borough Council, then spent 27 years as caretaker of Innerleithen Memorial Hall until retiring in March 1967 and resided in Innerleithen until his death in September 1995.

FRED ROWELL

Popular inside-left Fred Rowell starred in Cherries' 1945/46 Third Division (South) Cup final triumph. Born in Seaham, he developed in Durham junior soccer before signing professional for Bournemouth in September 1941 and played wartime football that season until the club suspended matches for the remainder of the Second World War. He scored twice on his League debut in the 6-1 win at Norwich City on Boxing Day 1946 and featured alongside Jack McDonald and Dudley Milligan in Cherries' 1947/48 promotion near-miss. Netting 11 goals in 31 Third Division (South) games while at Dean Court, he joined Wrexham in exchange for Walter Roberts in July 1948. A Welsh Cup finalist in 1950, he moved to Aldershot in August 1950 and reunited with Fred Wilson at Weymouth in June 1951. Helping to reach the Southern League Cup final in 1952/53, he then played for Portland United and was Bournemouth Gasworks' trainer. He became clerk of works in the housing department of Poole Corporation and died in Poole in March 1988.

KEITH ROWLAND

Versatile left-back Keith Rowland was capped 19 times by Northern Ireland after leaving AFC Bournemouth. A Northern Ireland Youth international, he signed professional at Dean Court in October 1989 and made his League debut as a substitute in Cherries' 2-1 defeat at home to Darlington in August 1991. He quickly secured a regular first-team slot alongside skipper Kevin Bond and featured in that season's FA Cup third round replay win at Newcastle United. Scoring twice in 72 League games, he was loaned to Coventry City before following Harry Redknapp to West Ham for £110,000 in August 1993. Reunited with Matty Holmes at Upton Park, he provided reliable cover for Julian Dicks in the top-flight and helped West Ham to reach the FA Cup sixth round in 1993/94. He also featured in a midfield role for the Hammers and moved to QPR with fellow Irish international Iain Dowie as part of the deal involving Trevor Sinclair in January 1998. After a loan spell at Luton Town, he joined Chesterfield in August 2001 and moved to Barnet in December 2002.

EDDIE ROWLES

Young striker Eddie Rowles featured in Cherries' 1970/71 promotion campaign under John Bond. A former apprentice at Dean Court, he made his Third Division debut as a 16 year-old in the 4-0 defeat at Bury six months before signing professional under Freddie Cox in March 1968. He also helped Bournemouth take Bill Shankly's Liverpool to an FA Cup third round replay in 1967/68, reach the FA Youth Cup semi-finals in 1968/69 and beat Sheffield Wednesday in the 1969/70 League Cup second round. Scoring 12 goals in 67 League games for Cherries, he joined York City in exchange for Ian Davidson in July 1971 and moved to Torquay United for £6,000 in June 1973. He was leading marksman in 1973/74, then joined Darlington in August 1975 and topped their goalscoring charts in 1976/77. Sold to Colchester United for £15,000 in December 1977, he featured in successive promotion challenges until a knee injury ended his career in May 1982. He still lives in Colchester and is now a self-employed painter and decorator.

JACK ROWLEY

Ace marksman Jack Rowley was capped six times by England after leaving Dean Court. A former Wolverhampton Wanderers junior, he signed professional as an outside-left in November 1935 and had a spell with their nursery side Cradley Heath before following the well-worn trail to Bournemouth with Bob Redfern in February 1937. He made his League debut in that month's 1-1 draw at Walsall and scored 12 goals in 22 Third Division (South) games for Cherries prior to joining Manchester United for £3,000 in October 1937. Helping them to regain top-flight status that season, 'The Gunner' netted twice in United's 1948 FA Cup final success and was top scorer six times including their 1951/52 League Championship triumph. Joining Plymouth Argyle as player-boss, for five years, in February 1955, he then managed Oldham Athletic (twice), Ajax, Wrexham and Bradford PA. He later ran a newsagents and sub-post office in Shaw and died in June 1998. His younger brother Arthur holds the Football League's all-time goalscoring record.

JOHN RUDGE

Experienced striker John Rudge was an early John Benson signing for Cherries. Signing professional for Huddersfield Town in November 1961, he made his League debut against Swansea in May 1963 and moved to Carlisle United in December 1966. He helped them win at Newcastle United in the 1967/68 FA Cup third round and joined Torquay United in January 1969. Moving to Bristol Rovers in exchange for Plainmoor idol Robin Stubbs in February 1972, he featured in their 1973/74 promotion success alongside the Bruce Bannister and Alan Warboys 'Smash and Grab' partnership and reunited with John Benson at Dean Court for £6,000 in March 1975. He scored twice in 21 League outings for Cherries until injury ended his career, then rejoined

Torquay as Mike Green's assistant in May 1977. Appointed as Port Vale's manager in December 1983, he guided them to promotion three times and the Autoglass Trophy final in 1993. He was controversially sacked in January 1999 and became Stoke City's director of football.

ALAN RULE

Versatile right-half Alan Rule played alongside Joe Brown and Harry Hughes while at Dean Court. Starting with Swaythling Youth Club, he developed with Pirelli General, Thornycrofts, Basingstoke Town and Winchester City and represented Hampshire before signing professional for Chelsea in November 1952. He helped their reserves to win the Football Combination title in 1954/55 but was unable to force his way into their League Championship side and moved to Norwich City in September 1956. Given his League debut alongside record appearance holder Ron Ashman at Millwall a month later, Freddie Cox signed him in June 1957 and he made 25 Third Division (South) appearances for Cherries. Appointed youth team coach for a season after a knee injury ended his career in June 1959, he coached Swaythling Athletic while employed as a wireman by Plessey in Southampton. He then worked for Thorns Lighting, Vosper Thornycrofts, Safeways and Circle K until early retirement in January 1989 and still lives in Sholing.

PETER RUSHWORTH

Right-half Peter Rushworth was a popular member of Jack Bruton's squad at Dean Court. Initially with Cheltenham works team Rotal Air Screws (Dowty Group), he joined Cheltenham Town where his father Keith was chairman and president during 50 years service. He moved to Leicester City for £1,350 in November 1951 but failed to gain a first-team place at Filbert Street. Jack Bruton signed him in June 1953 and he made his League debut in Bournemouth's 3-1 defeat at Crystal Palace four months later. He scored once in 88 Third Division (South) games for Cherries prior to joining Salisbury with Ian Allen in July 1957. Ever-present in two consecutive seasons, he starred in their 1957/58 and 1960/61 Western League title triumphs and then coached Bournemouth 'Poppies', Poole Town and Christchurch. He was a design draughtsman with Vickers Armstrong/BAC at Hurn, then spent 20 years on the PE staff at Homefield School with ex-Cherries Sid Miles and Eric Wilkinson until retiring in July 1992 and still lives in Christchurch.

COLIN RUSSELL

Much-travelled striker Colin Russell played alongside Colin Clarke in AFC Bournemouth's attack. A former Liverpool apprentice, he signed professional in April 1978 and made his First Division debut at home to Sunderland three years later. He was unable to secure a regular first-team place at Anfield behind the likes of Kenny Dalglish and Ian Rush and moved to Huddersfield Town for £15,000 in September 1982, starring in their 1982/83 promotion campaign. Loaned to struggling Stoke City in March 1984, he helped them retain top-flight status that season. Harry Redknapp paid £15,000 for him in August 1984 and he played for Cherries at Manchester United in the 1984/85 FA Cup third round, then scored against Everton in the 1985/86 Milk Cup second round. Netting 14 goals in 68 Third Division games, he was sold to Doncaster Rovers for £5,000 in July 1986 and joined Scarborough in October 1987. He later played for Wigan Athletic, Colne Dynamoes, Bangor City, Morecambe, Droylsden and Warrington Town, settling back on Merseyside.

JACK RUSSELL

Flying outside-left Jack Russell was Cherries leading marksman in two consecutive seasons. Starting with Northfield, he developed with Bournville and Bromsgrove Rovers prior to joining Birmingham February 1924. He was given his First Division debut at Manchester City two months later but struggled to make an impact and moved to Bristol Rovers in June 1927, then Worcester City in July 1928. Starring as they won the Birmingham League title in two successive years, he joined Bournemouth in May 1930 and netted four goals at home to both Clapton Orient and Bristol City in January 1933. Scoring 42 times in 138 Third Division (South) games overall while at Dean Court, he moved to Luton Town in June 1934. Joining Norwich City four months later, he played in their first ever match at Carrow Road in August 1935 and returned to Worcester in May 1936. He became Shirley Town's player-manager, then had a spell with Solihull Town. Settling in back in Northfield after the war, he died in Bromsgrove in December 1995.

KEVIN RUSSELL

Much-travelled striker Kevin Russell was one of Tony Pulis' last signings for AFC Bournemouth. Initially a Brighton junior, 'Rooster' turned professional with Portsmouth in October 1984 and made his League debut at home to Bradford City in May 1986. The England Youth international featured in Pompey's 1986/87 promotion campaign and moved to Wrexham for £10,000 in July 1987, finishing top scorer as they reached the Fourth Division play-off final in 1988/89. Joining Leicester City for £175,000 in June 1989, he featured in the 1991/92 Second Division play-off final. He joined Stoke for £95,000 in July 1992 and starred alongside Mark Stein in their 1992/93 Second Division title triumph, then moved to Burnley for £150,000 in June 1993. Tony Pulis paid £125,000 for him in March 1994 and his solitary goal in 30 Second Division games clinched Cherries' 1-1 draw at Hull City the following month. Sold to Notts County for £60,000 in February 1995, he returned to Wrexham five months later where he is now assisting Denis Smith.

JOHN SAINTY

Versatile striker John Sainty was AFC Bournemouth's leading goalscorer in 1973/74. An England Schoolboy international, he signed professional for Tottenham Hotspur in July 1963 and moved to Reading in August 1967. He scored twice on his League debut at home to

Stockport County that month and played alongside Denis Allen before Freddie Cox paid £5,000 for him in February 1970. Starring in Cherries' 1970/71 promotion success, he netted 21 goals in 118 League outings and was loaned to Mansfield Town before joining Aldershot in August 1974. He helped them to retain Third Division status at AFC Bournemouth's expense in 1974/75, then reunited with John Bond as a coach at Norwich City and Manchester City. Appointed as Chester's manager for a year in November 1982, he became Burnley's youth team coach under Bond and then managed Glossop and Mossley. He assisted Danny Bergara and Dave Jones at Stockport before following the latter to Southampton in June 1997 and became their Academy director.

JOE SANAGHAN

Fearless left-back Joe Sanaghan featured prominently in Cherries' 1947/48 promotion near-miss. Born in Motherwell, he signed professional for Bradford PA in August 1935 and gained early Second Division experience. Charlie Bell snapped him up on a free transfer in June 1937 and he formed a memorable defensive quartet with Ken Bird, Fred Marsden and Fred Wilson either side of the Second World War. He helped Bournemouth to win the Third Division (South) Cup in 1945/46 and was ever-present in 1946/47, playing in the big FA Cup third round ties against Derby County, Wolves and Manchester United in consecutive seasons. Given a benefit match at home to Notts County on Good Friday 1949, he made 170 Third Division (South) appearances prior to joining Stockport County in August 1949. He starred in the 1949/50 FA Cup run and played in front of their record attendance in the fifth round tie at home to Liverpool. Briefly a licensee in Stockport, he returned to Ireland where he tragically died at just 36 in November 1951.

BOBBY SAVAGE

Popular midfielder Bobby Savage starred in AFC Bournemouth's 1984 Associate Members Cup final triumph. Signing professional for Liverpool in January 1978, he was unable to gain a place in Bob Paisley's all-conquering side and joined Wrexham on an extended loan in October 1982. He scored on his League debut that month and was 'Player of the Season' as they were Welsh Cup finalists in 1982/83. Sold to Stoke City for £10,000 in July 1983, he sampled top-flight football before Harry Redknapp paid £15,000 for him five months later. He inspired Cherries' 1983/84 FA Cup third round win over holders Manchester United but a broken leg sidelined him for the 1985/86 season. Featuring in the 1986/87 Third Division title campaign, he scored 18 times in 82 League games before being sold to Bradford City for £35,000 in December 1986. He joined Bolton Wanderers in September 1987 and helped to win promotion in 1987/88 as well as the Sherpa Van Trophy final in 1989. Another broken leg ended his career soon after and he has since coached Knowsley United, Liverpool Schools U-15 side and at Tranmere Rovers School of Excellence.

EDGAR SAXTON

Hard-tackling right-back Edgar Sexton was an influential figure during Cherries' early Football League days. Starting with Carlton Victoria, he joined Barnsley in May 1917 and made his Second Division debut at Bury on New Year's Day 1920. He failed to secure a regular first-team slot at Oakwell behind Jack Tindall and joined Boscombe in July 1921. Featuring prominently in consecutive FA Cup runs, he formed an effective defensive partnership with Billy Lamb as Cherries were Southern League runners-up in 1922/23. He helped the club to consolidate higher status after Bournemouth gained election to the Football League in 1923 and made 77 Third Division (South) appearances prior to becoming assistant-trainer at Dean Court in July 1928, then was head trainer until the Second World War. Later an outside rep for Hunt & Co engineers until retirement in July 1963, he resided locally until returning to his native Carlton in ill-health. He spent the last months of his life being cared for by his niece Clara and died in March 1966.

MARK SCHIAVI

Popular midfielder Mark Schiavi was a young member of Harry Redknapp's squad at Dean Court. An England Youth international, he signed professional for West Ham in November 1981 but failed to make an impact at Upton Park and Don Megson signed him on loan in September 1983. He was given his League debut in Cherries' 3-0 defeat at Lincoln City the following month and Harry Redknapp brought him back to AFC Bournemouth on a free transfer in July 1984, making 29 Third Division appearances overall. Moving to Northampton Town in July 1985, he reunited with John Beck at Cambridge United in September 1986 and joined Kettering Town in July 1987. He then played for Enfield, Brixworth, Irthlingborough Diamonds and Bourne Town before linking up with Mark Nightingale again at Warboys Town. Now living in Rippingale, he was a senior computer programmer for Hotpoint and has since run his own Vigence computer consultancy firm which has a major contract with the Royal Mail in Chesterfield.

HARRY SCOTT

Versatile inside-forward Harry Scott partnered record goalscorer Ron Eyre in Cherries' attack. Initially a miner at Stainforth Colliery, he impressed in the same Doncaster-based Pilkington Recs side as his younger brother Jack (later with Norwich City and Southampton) before Frank Richards signed him in June 1929. He scored on his League debut in Bournemouth's 3-0 win at home to Exeter City three months later and netted 35 goals in 81 Third Division (South) games while at Dean Court prior to joining Swindon Town on a free transfer in June 1932. Also playing alongside their record goalscorer Harry Morris, he moved to Doncaster Rovers in June 1933 and rejoined Pilkington Recs in June 1934. He skippered their team to Doncaster Challenge Cup final glory in 1935/36 and was leading marksman in successive seasons until wartime service in the Royal Engineers. Settling in Edenthorpe, he spent a total of 30 years as a pipe-fitter for the Pilkington division of Rockware Glass in Doncaster until October 1971. He died in February 1989.

JOEY SCOTT

Striker Joey Scott played alongside Ted MacDougall during his second spell at AFC Bournemouth. He captained the Plymouth Schoolboys side including Trevor Francis and was briefly an amateur with Plymouth Argyle while employed as a painter in Plymouth dockyard. Joining Falmouth Town in July 1972, he starred as they won the Western League title in four successive seasons and John Benson paid £1,000 for him in June 1978. He scored twice in Cherries' 7-1 win at home to Doncaster Rovers eight months later and four goals in 21 Fourth Division games overall before following Trevor Finnigan to Yeovil Town for £5,500 in December 1979. Moving to Hungerford Town for £4,000 in August 1980, he then played for Barnstaple Town and Derek Rickard's Weston Mill Oak Villa before managing Kitto YMCA. He spent 11 years as foreman of painters back at Plymouth dockyard and since June 1995 has been a social worker in Plymouth, also assisting Leigh Cooper at Holsworthy.

TONY SCOTT

Experienced winger Tony Scott starred in Cherries' 1970/71 promotion success. An England Youth international, he turned professional with West Ham in May 1958 and gained top-flight experience before following Phil Woosnam to Aston Villa for £25,000 in October 1965. Reunited with John Bond at Torquay United for £7,000 in September 1967, he featured in their 1967/68 promotion near-miss and linked up with Bond again at Dean Court for £4,000 in July 1970. He created numerous goalscoring chances for Ted MacDougall and Phil Boyer, playing in Bournemouth's record 11-0 FA Cup first round win over Margate in 1971/72 and netting six times in 61 League games prior to joining Exeter City in June 1972. Injury ended his playing career two years later and he ran a butchers shop in Exeter, then coached soccer in Kuwait before reuniting with Bond as Manchester City's youth team coach. He emigrated to Australia after discovering God and has since worked for a lift manufacturer and run an ice cream parlour in Perth.

TERRY SHANAHAN

Versatile striker Terry Shanahan was a popular member of John Benson's squad at Dean Court. Initially a Tottenham Hotspur apprentice, he signed professional for Ipswich Town in July 1969 and made his First Division debut at home to Southampton in April 1971. He was loaned to Blackburn Rovers before following Frank Brogan to Halifax Town for £8,000 in November 1971 and topped their goalscoring charts in 1973/74. Swapped for Chesterfield's Ray McHale in October 1974, he moved to Millwall for £10,000 in April 1976 and starred in their 1976/77 League Cup run. John Benson signed him in July 1977 and his solitary goal in 18 Fourth Division games came in Cherries' 4-2 win at home to Newport County eight months later. He joined Aldershot in July 1978, then played for Phoenix Firebirds and managed Swanage T&H. Rejoining AFC Bournemouth as youth team manager under Harry Redknapp, he was assistant-boss for two years until July 1992, then coached under Redknapp at West Ham and now runs County News in Winchester.

DAVID SHEARER

Scottish striker David Shearer briefly partnered Trevor Aylott in AFC Bournemouth's attack. Starting with Inverness Clachnacuddin in the Highland League, he joined Middlesbrough for £5,000 in January 1978, and scored twice on his First Division debut at home to Chelsea three months later. He was a prolific goalscorer during a loan spell at Wigan Athletic and secured a regular top-flight slot on his return to Boro, featuring in their 1980/81 FA Cup run. Moving to Grimsby Town in August 1983, he joined Gillingham in August 1984 and starred alongside Tony Cascarino as they mounted successive promotion challenges. Harry Redknapp paid £15,000 for him in October 1987 and he displaced Carl Richards, scoring three goals in 11 Second Division games for Cherries prior to joining Scunthorpe United in February 1988. He reunited with David Booth at Darlington ten months later, then played for Billingham Synthonia and settled back in Fort William as a labourer but is now a house-husband unable to work due to an arthritic hip.

PETER SHEARER

Versatile midfielder Peter Shearer skippered Cherries during Tony Pulis' reign at Dean Court. A former Birmingham City apprentice, he made his League debut at home to Shrewsbury Town three months prior to signing professional in February 1985. He moved via Nuneaton Borough to Cheltenham Town for £3,000 in July 1988 and gained England Semi-Pro recognition before Harry Redknapp paid £18,000 for him in March 1989. Unable to prevent AFC Bournemouth's relegation in 1989/90, he was linked with a big money move to Dundee until sidelined by injury and scored ten goals in 85 League games while at Dean Court prior to rejoining Birmingham for £75,000 in January 1994. He featured prominently in their 1994/95 Second Division title and Auto Windscreens Shield 'double' triumph but an Achilles tendon injury ended his playing career shortly after following Barry Fry to Peterborough United in

August 1997. Now living in Sutton Coldfield, he has since coached at Birmingham City's Academy.

DEREK SHOWERS

Ex-Welsh international striker Derek Showers was AFC Bournemouth's leading marksman in 1977/78. Signing professional for Cardiff City in August 1970, he made his League debut at Oxford United four months later and was a member of their 1975/76 promotion and Welsh Cup 'double' squad. Capped twice by his country, John Benson paid £5,000 for him in July 1977 and he netted 19 goals in 60 Fourth Division games for Cherries before being sold to Portsmouth for £12,000 in February 1979. He missed much of their 1979/80 promotion campaign with a knee injury and moved to Hereford United in December 1980. A Welsh Cup finalist again in 1980/81, he reunited with Terry Shanahan at Swanage T&H in July 1983 and then played for Dorchester Town and AFC Lymington while working at Bournemouth post office. He returned to his native Merthyr Tydfil as a postman and continued his playing career with Barry Town, Brecon and Hoover Sports before managing Treharris. Now a driver for Castle Howell.

BRIAN SIDDALL

Small, constructive inside-right Brian Siddall played alongside Stan Newsham in Cherries' attack. Initially a winger with Witton Albion, he joined Wolverhampton Wanderers in July 1947 and represented the RAF during national service. He failed to make an impact at Molineux and had spells with Witton again and Northwich Victoria before moving to Stoke City for £2,500 in February 1951. Joining Bournemouth in January 1954, he scored in the record 7-0 win at home to Swindon Town in September 1956. He netted 14 times in 86 Third Division (South) games prior to joining Ipswich Town in May 1957, and was a member of Alf Ramsey's 1960/61 Second Division title squad. A groin injury ended his League career and he joined Haverhill Rovers as player-boss in May 1961, then spent a period with Clacton Town. He became an estate agent in Ipswich, then worked at Felixstowe docks for 17 years until the onset of Alzheimer's disease forced his early retirement in December 1989 and is now living in Castle Douglas, Scotland.

JIMMY SINGER

Versatile inside-left Jimmy Singer was leading marksman in Cherries' 1962/63 promotion challenge. A former Newport County amateur, he turned professional at Somerton Park in May 1956 and returned from national service in Malaya to make his League debut at home to Brentford in March 1958. He impressed in the same Newport side as Bryn Jones before being sold to Birmingham City for £6,000 in September 1960 and featured in the 1960/61 Fairs Cup final second-leg against Italian giants AS Roma. Following right-back Brian Farmer to Bournemouth for £7,000 in September 1962, he played alongside fellow newcomers Charlie Woods and Derek Reeves as Bill McGarry rebuilt his attack after the 1961/62 promotion near-miss. He netted 22 goals in 59 Third Division games while at Dean Court prior to rejoining Newport in July 1964, but knee trouble soon ended his playing career. After running a fish and chip shop in Caerleon, he moved to Guernsey 23 years ago and has since run a restaurant/ night-club in St Peter Port.

JOHN SMEULDERS

Former England Youth goalkeeper John Smeulders had three spells at Dean Court. Signing professional for Orient in July 1974, he failed to secure a Second Division slot behind John Jackson and joined AFC Bournemouth in July 1979. He made his League debut at Newport County six months later and contested the goalkeeper slot with Kenny Allen before moving to Trowbridge Town in January 1981. Rejoining Cherries from Weymouth for £4,000 in January 1984, he displaced Ian Leigh and set a club record seven consecutive clean-sheets during the 1984/85 campaign. He followed Stuart Morgan to Torquay United in July 1986, then had spells with Peterborough United and Poole Town before returning to Dean Court as non-contract cover for Gerry Peyton in August 1987. Making 98 League appearances overall for AFC Bournemouth, he also played for Brentford, Weymouth and Farnborough Town until a knee injury ended his career in May 1989. He now lives in Corfe Mullen and is a driver for Allied Bakeries.

BERTIE SMITH

Centre-half Bertie Smith was an experienced member of Cherries' 1928/29 FA Cup run squad. He impressed with Nunhead in the Isthmian League prior to joining Huddersfield Town in April 1922 and was given his First Division debut at Preston North End ten months later. Providing reliable cover for England international Tom Wilson as Herbert Chapman's star-studded side won the League Championship in three consecutive years, he moved to Bradford City in September 1926 and joined FA Cup giant-killers Rhyl in July 1927. He moved to Bangor City five months later and helped to clinch the Welsh League title that season, then was an early Frank Richards signing for Bournemouth in July 1928. Playing alongside the likes of Jack Bradford and Cliff Halliwell, he made 28 Third Division (South) appearances prior to joining the coaching staff at Dean Court for the 1929/30 campaign and later played local soccer for Streatham Town back in south London. Subsequently a Surrey County AFA coach, he died in Wandsworth in July 1957.

BRIAN SMITH

Ex-England Youth midfielder Brian Smith featured in AFC Bournemouth's 1981/82 promotion campaign. Signing professional for Bolton Wanderers in September 1973, he made his League debut at York City in October 1974 and helped to reach the League Cup semi-finals in 1976/77. He was a member of Bolton's 1977/78 Second Division title squad and had loan spells at Bradford City and Tulsa Roughnecks prior to joining Blackpool in August 1979. David Webb snapped him up on a free transfer in December 1980 and he inspired Cherries' run of 14 unbeaten matches during the latter half of that season. He scored twice in 40 Fourth Division games while at Dean Court before moving to Bury in March

1982, then joined Parley Sports four months later and subsequently played for Salisbury. Now living back in Atherton, he scouted for Bolton Wanderers and had a mobile video round before setting up his own Fizeek sportswear company. He has since coached at Atherton Collieries, Daisy Hill and Ashton Town.

JACK SMITH

Ex-England international inside-right Jack Smith played alongside Joe Riley in Cherries' attack. He developed with Whitburn and North Shields Athletic prior to joining South Shields in June 1919 and made his Second Division debut at Tottenham Hotspur three months later. Top scorer on three occasions, he was ever-present in 1925/26 and starred as they reached the FA Cup fifth round in two consecutive seasons. He moved to Portsmouth in December 1927 and was an important figure as they were FA Cup finalists in 1928/29 and 1933/34. Twice leading marksman while at Fratton Park, he was capped three times and gained considerable top-flight experience before Bob Crompton signed him in May 1935. He featured in Bournemouth's 8-1 FA Cup first round replay win at home to Walthamstow Avenue in 1935/36 and scored twice in 41 Third Division (South) games for Cherries before moving to Clapton Orient in October 1936. Injury ended his playing career soon after and he later resided in Stockton until his death in January 1977.

RON SMITH

Outside-left Ron Smith was a young member of Don Welsh's squad at Dean Court. A former Stoke City amateur, he signed professional for Liverpool in December 1957, but failed to secure a first-team place at Anfield and followed Don Welsh to Bournemouth in May 1959. He was given his League debut in Cherries' 2-1 win at Colchester United five months later and scored six times in 36 Third Division games before moving to Crewe Alexandra in July 1961. Featuring prominently as they won promotion for the first time in 1962/63, he joined Port Vale in October 1963 and reunited with Billy Bingham at Southport in July 1965. He was ever-present as they reached the FA Cup fifth round in 1965/66, then starred in their 1966/67 promotion campaign and subsequently played for Altrincham, Netherfield, Formby and Fleetwood Hesketh while employed at Liverpool Docks. He still lives in Formby and managed his local club before assisting Alan Kershaw at Hesketh Bank and Everton's Football in the Community residential courses.

WILLIE SMITH

Scottish right-half Willie Smith was an influential figure in Cherries' 1936/37 promotion challenge. Born in Cellardyke, he played for Anstruther Amateurs, St Monans Swifts and St Andrews Athletic prior to joining Bournemouth on the recommendation of manager Billy Birrell's father who was a local baker. He made his League debut in Cherries' 2-1 defeat at Cardiff City in October 1934 and formed an effective half-back line with Fred Pincott and Peter Monaghan. Featuring in the 10-0 annihilation of Northampton Town in September 1939, he scored six goals in 154 Third Division (South) games while at Dean Court. He was a wartime guest for Dunfermline Athletic, then played for Dundee United before coaching Rosyth Recreation for several seasons. Subsequently chief draughtsman at the British Aluminium works in Burntisland for 30 years until retiring in June 1978, he still lives in Burntisland and is now Cherries' oldest surviving first-team player. His son Alex played for Dunfermline Athletic, Glasgow Rangers and Aberdeen.

TOMMY SOUTHREN

Fast outside-right Tommy Southren was an experienced member of Don Welsh's squad at Dean Court. Born in Sunderland, he grew up in Welwyn Garden City and impressed with Peartree Old Boys prior to joining West Ham in December 1949. He made his League debut at home to QPR ten months later and helped West Ham's reserves to win the Combination League and Cup 'double' in 1953/54. Sold to Aston Villa for £12,000 in December 1954, he was unlucky not to feature in their 1957 FA Cup final triumph after being displaced by the arrival of Leslie Smith. He joined Cherries for £4,000 in October 1958 and created numerous goalscoring chances for the likes of Mike Burgess and Dickie Dowsett, netting 11 times in 64 Third Division games for Cherries until a knee injury ended his playing career in May 1960. Settling back in Welwyn Garden City, he was briefly a sheet metal worker for Welwyn Metal Products and spent 30 years as a fitter with Nabisco (Shredded Wheat) until early retirement in February 1991.

NIGEL SPACKMAN

Versatile young midfielder Nigel Spackman starred in AFC Bournemouth's 1981/82 promotion success. He developed with Basingstoke Town and Andover before Alec Stock signed him in May 1980, making his League debut in Cherries' 4-0 defeat at York City three months later. Scoring ten goals in 119 League games while at Dean Court, he joined Chelsea for £40,000 in June 1983 and was an influential figure in their 1983/84 Second

Division title triumph. He was ever-present as they reached the Milk Cup semi-finals in 1984/85, then featured in their 1986 Full Members Cup final success. Sold to Liverpool for £400,000 in February 1987, he was a League Championship winner and FA Cup finalist in 1987/88 and joined QPR for £500,000 in February 1989. He moved to Glasgow Rangers in November 1989 and starred in three consecutive Scottish League title triumphs, then played for Chelsea again and Sheffield United. After coaching England U-18's, he managed Barnsley until October 2001 and has since worked in the media.

RON SPELMAN

Outside-right Ron Spelman featured in Cherries' 1961/62 promotion near-miss under Bill McGarry. He gained Norfolk Youth honours before signing professional for Norwich City in July 1956 and made his League debut at home to Aldershot in April 1958. A member of Norwich's 1959/60 promotion squad, he had limited opportunities and moved to Northampton Town in November 1960. He helped to win promotion that season and joined Bournemouth in exchange for Arnold Woollard in March 1962. Also featuring in Cherries' 1962/63 promotion challenge, he scored four goals in 28 Third Division games before following Bill McGarry to Watford for £2,000 in September 1963 and starred in their 1963/64 promotion near-miss. He joined Oxford United in May 1965 and later played for Wisbech Town. After 12 years as a heating engineer, he ran the Little John pub in Norwich and was then a driver for Fyffes until early retirement in May 1992. He still lives in Norwich and looks after his son, Mark, who has multiple sclerosis.

TOMMY STANDLEY

Versatile left-half Tommy Standley was an influential figure in Cherries' 1961/62 promotion near-miss. Initially a centre-forward with Basildon United while employed in a garage in Leyton High Road, he turned professional for QPR in May 1957 and made his League debut at Brentford seven months later. He joined Bournemouth in an exchange deal involving Tommy Anderson in November 1958 and starred alongside John Arnott and Tony Nelson as Cherries beat top-flight Cardiff City in the 1961/62 League Cup third round, also featuring in successive promotion challenges. He netted five goals in 159 Third Division outings while at Dean Court and quit soccer after being released in May 1965, rejecting an offer to join Gillingham that summer to become a chaser for Harris Legus furniture manufacturers in London. For the past 37 years he has lived in Great Cornard and was a machine mechanic for Gainsborough Knitting Mills in nearby Bures until closure in July 1973, then worked as a printer for Lucas until retiring in July 1997.

MARK STEIN

Experienced striker Mark Stein was AFC Bournemouth's leading marksman in two consecutive seasons. An England Youth international, he signed professional for Luton Town in January 1984 and played alongside older

brother Brian in their 1988 Littlewoods Cup final triumph as well as that season's Simod Cup final. Sold to QPR for £300,000 in August 1988, he was swapped for Oxford United's David Bardsley in September 1989 and joined Stoke City for £100,000 in September 1991. He scored their winner in the 1992 Autoglass Trophy final, then was leading marksman in their 1992/93 Second Division title triumph and moved to Chelsea for £1,400,000 in October 1993. Top scorer as they were FA Cup finalists in 1994, he was loaned to Stoke and Ipswich Town before Mel Machin signed him initially on loan in March 1998. He played for Cherries in that season's Auto Windscreens Shield final at Wembley and netted 30 goals in 90 Second Division games prior to rejoining Luton in July 2000, then moved to Dagenham & Redbridge in July 2001, leading their attack in successive promotion near-misses.

ARNOLD STEPHENS

Young outside-right Arnold Stephens was a popular member of Harry Lowe's squad at Dean Court. A former Wolverhampton Wanderers junior, 'Steve' signed professional in April 1945 but failed to secure a first team slot at Molineux and followed the well-worn trail to Bournemouth in December 1948. He made his League debut in Cherries' 2-0 defeat at Swansea Town on New Year's Day 1949 and featured in the Golden Jubilee match at home to Nottingham Forest in November 1949. Struck down by a serious illness in the summer of 1950, he spent many months in bed and was told by specialists that he would never play football again. He refused to accept their advice, however, and began a long, dedicated fight for fitness. Regaining his first-team place early in the 1953/54 season, he helped Bournemouth to beat local rivals Southampton in the FA Cup first round replay and scored 12 goals in 70 Third Division (South) games overall until he was forced to return to hospital in April 1955. He tragically died the following month.

GARETH STEWART

Ex-England Schoolboy and Youth international goalkeeper Gareth Stewart starred as AFC Bournemouth narrowly failed to reach the Second Division play-offs in 2000/01. Initially a Blackburn Rovers trainee, he signed professional at Ewood Park in February 1997 and joined Cherries in July 1999. He made his League debut in place of Mark Ovendale in the 3-1 defeat at Wigan Athletic four months later and began the 2000/01 campaign as second choice to Michael Menetrier, finally making his breakthrough in October 2000. A fine shot stopper, he missed just one match as Cherries battled to avoid relegation in 2001/02 but sustained an ankle injury before the start of the 2002/03 campaign and was sidelined for almost three months. When Neil Moss returned to Southampton he broke his leg against Southend United in the FA Cup and then badly cut his thumb in a domestic accident.

NELSON STIFFLE

Skilful little outside-right Nelson Stiffle starred as Cherries reached the FA Cup sixth round in 1956/57. Born in India, he learned the game playing barefoot and came to England as a 21 year-old. He impressed with Ashton United and joined Chester in December 1951, making his League debut at home to Mansfield Town three months later. Following a period back in non-League soccer with Altrincham, he moved to Chesterfield in March 1954 and was an influential figure in their 1954/55 promotion challenge. Jack Bruton signed him in May 1955 and he contested Bournemouth's right wing slot with the likes of Roy Littlejohn and Brian Loughnane, playing in the big FA Cup ties against Wolves, Spurs and Manchester United in 1956/57. He scored seven goals in 35 League games while at Dean Court prior to joining Exeter City in March 1958, then moved to Coventry City in July 1960. He emigrated to Australia in July 1961 and played for Bankstown in New South Wales, then coached various sides and now lives in retirement near Brisbane.

JIM STIRLING

Big, tough-tackling centre-half Jim Stirling succeeded Fred Wilson in the heart of Cherries defence. Born in Airdrie, he played for Coltness United and was serving with Johnny MacKenzie in the Scots Guards at Victoria Barracks, Windsor, when Harry Lowe signed him in July 1947. He made his League debut in Bournemouth's 1-0 win at home to Swindon Town seven months later and featured in successive promotion challenges, scoring his solitary goal in 73 Third Division (South) games in the 2-1 victory at home to Reading on Boxing Day 1949. Also helping Cherries to win at Second Division Bradford Park Avenue in that season's FA Cup third round, he moved to Birmingham City for £10,500 in June 1950 but failed to make an impact and joined Southend United in December 1950. He starred in their 1956/57 FA Cup third round triumph at home to Liverpool and was ever present in 1957/58, then played for Poole Town. He subsequently ran a newsagents in Charminster until December 1995 and still lives locally in retirement.

ALEC STOCK

Vastly experienced manager Alec Stock succeeded John Benson in charge of AFC Bournemouth. Initially a forward with Redhill, he had a spell with Charlton Athletic prior to joining QPR in February 1938 and scored on his League debut at home to Reading that month. He was a Major in the Royal Armoured Corps during the Second World War and became Yeovil Town's player-manager in June 1946, plotting their epic 1948/49 FA Cup run. Taking charge of Leyton Orient in May 1949, he managed them to the Third Division (South) title in 1955/56 between spells at Arsenal and Roma. Returning to QPR as manager in August 1959, he guided them to a Third Division title and League Cup 'double' in 1966/67 and to the top-flight in 1967/68. He then managed Luton Town to promotion in 1969/70 and Fulham to the FA Cup final in 1974/75. After a spell as a QPR director, he became Cherries manager for two years in January 1979, then was general manager and a director at Dean Court. He remained local until his death in April 2001.

BRIAN STOCK

Welsh U-21 international midfielder Brian Stock wrote his name in the history books by scoring the first-ever goal at the Fitness First Stadium. A product of Cherries' youth set up, he made his League debut as a substitute in the 3-1 defeat at Colchester United in January 2000 and started four consecutive games during the closing weeks of that season. But he struggled to make an impact until the 2001/02 campaign and scored his first senior goal with a stunning last-gasp winner over Bury at Dorchester's Avenue Stadium in September 2001. His opening strike in the 3-0 victory at home to Wrexham two months later was the first goal scored at the Fitness First Stadium. He made his Welsh U-21 debut in Finland in September 2002 and climaxed a memorable season by coming on as a substitute in AFC Bournemouth's 5-2 win over Lincoln City in the 2002/03 Third Division play-off final. He has netted four goals in 59 League games for the club.

DAVID STOCKS

Hard-tackling, versatile defender David Stocks was ever-present for Cherries in two consecutive seasons. A former Charlton Athletic junior, he signed professional in January 1962 and made his League debut at Liverpool three months later. He moved to Gillingham with Ralph Miller in May 1965 and played alongside several other one-time Cherries before following Freddie Cox to Dean Court in an exchange deal involving Charlie Crickmore in June 1966. He starred as Bournemouth took Liverpool to an FA Cup third round replay in 1967/68 and won promotion under John Bond in 1970/71. Scoring twice in 220 League games for Cherries, he moved to Torquay United for £3,500 in January 1972 and was ever-present in 1974/75. Injury ended his League career and he then played for Parley Sports and Wimborne Town, also captaining Moordown cricket club for many years. He has built a successful career in financial services with Hambro Life Assurance, Coleman Group and now as managing director of Stocks Financial Management.

DEREK STROUD

Popular outside-right Derek Stroud was a young member of Jack Bruton's squad at Dean Court. Initially with hometown Wimborne, he joined Poole Town in July 1948 and starred as they were Western League runners-up in 1949/50. Jack Bruton signed him in August 1950 and he scored the winner on his home debut for Bournemouth against Northampton Town four months later. He netted 17 times in 78 Third Division (South) games prior to joining Grimsby Town in June 1953. Securing a regular Second Division slot under Bill Shankly, he reunited with Ken Bird at Dorchester Town in July 1955 and starred in successive FA Cup runs. He was an experienced figure as Dorchester were Western League runners-up in 1960/61 and moved to Portland United in July 1963, then Ringwood Town a year later where he briefly succeeded Stan Newsham as player-manager. Still living in Wimborne, he spent 38 years as a despatch manager for Keith Spicer Ltd until retiring in December 1993 and is a keen supporter of Wimborne Town.

CHRIS SULLEY

Popular left-back Chris Sulley was ever-present for AFC Bournemouth in three consecutive seasons. A former Chelsea apprentice, he turned professional in August 1978 and David Webb signed him in March 1981. He was given his League debut in Cherries' 3-3 draw at home to Darlington that month and starred alongside Tom Heffernan in the 1981/82 promotion success, then helped to beat holders Manchester United in the 1983/84 FA Cup third round as well as winning the Associate Members' Cup. Scoring three goals in 206 League games while at Dean Court, he joined Dundee United in June 1986 and moved to Blackburn in March 1987. He featured in that season's Full Members' Cup final triumph and helped Blackburn to qualify for the Second Division play-offs in four consecutive years, then joined John Rudge's Port Vale in July 1992. Reunited with John Beck at Preston North End in July 1993, he became their youth team manager and then returned to Blackburn as YDO until January 1998. He is now academy director at Bolton Wanderers.

ALAN SUMMERHILL

Young defender Alan Summerhill featured in Cherries' 1969/70 League Cup second round replay win over Sheffield Wednesday. A former apprentice at Dean Court, he signed professional under Freddie Cox in July 1968 and helped Bournemouth to reach the FA Youth Cup semi-finals in 1968/69. He made his League debut in the 1-1 draw at Brighton in August 1969 and played 28 Third Division games before moving to Crewe Alexandra in September 1970. Reunited with Roy Gater and Keith East while at Gresty Road, he joined Wimbledon in August 1972 and moved to their Southern League rivals Guildford City in July 1973. He was ever-present in 1974/75 and when that club folded in December 1976, he joined Liss as player-manager. Subsequently licensee of the George & Dragon in Petersfield, the Cheshire Cheese in Shavington and Royal Oak in Worleston, he then became a warehouse supervisor for Wincanton Logistics in Winsford and has recently gained a Sport & Health Studies degree at Manchester Metropolitan University.

JACK SURTEES

Versatile inside-forward Jack Surtees played alongside Jack Russell in Cherries' attack. The younger brother of former Aston Villa player Albert Surtees, he developed with Percy Main Amateurs in the Tyneside League prior to joining Middlesbrough in March 1930 and made his First Division debut alongside record goalscorer George Camsell at Chelsea in January 1932. He joined Portsmouth in June 1932 but again failed to secure a regular first-team slot and Billy Birrell signed him in June 1933. Scoring four goals in 21 Third Division (South) games for Bournemouth, he joined Northampton Town in May 1934 and moved to Sheffield Wednesday seven months later. He established a First Division place alongside England star Ellis Rimmer and climaxed a remarkable season by featuring in Wednesday's 1935 FA Cup final triumph at Wembley. Moving to Nottingham Forest in October 1936, the Second World War ended his playing career and he subsequently settled back in his native North-East. He died in North Shields in July 1992.

ERNIE TAGG

Influential right-half Ernie Tagg starred in Cherries' 1947/48 promotion near-miss. Signing professional for Crewe Alexandra in October 1937, he made his League debut at Oldham Athletic three months later and was sold to Wolverhampton Wanderers for £1,200 in May 1938. He gained top-flight experience with the 1939 FA Cup finalists before following the well-worn trail to Dean Court in May 1939, guesting for Crewe during the Second World War and helping Bournemouth to win the Third Division (South) Cup in 1945/46. Scoring eight times in 80 Third Division (South) games for Cherries prior to joining Carlisle United in November 1948, he returned to Crewe as part-time trainer while working as a milkman, then was assistant-boss before becoming manager at Gresty Road from November 1964 until June 1971. Also serving Crewe as secretary for a spell, he was caretaker-boss during the 1974/75 campaign and then a director for seven years until May 1983. He still lives in his native Crewe and is a life member of Crewe Alexandra.

RODNEY TAYLOR

Versatile left-half Rodney Taylor was a popular member of Freddie Cox's squad at Dean Court. Signing professional forms for Portsmouth in May 1961, he skippered them to the FA Youth Cup semi-finals in 1961/62 but failed to gain a first-team place at Fratton Park and followed Freddie Cox to Gillingham in July 1963. He made his League debut at Oxford United four months later and was a member of Gills' 1963/64 Fourth Division title squad. Reunited with Cox at Bournemouth in February 1966, he made 30 Fourth Division appearances for Cherries prior to joining Poole Town in August 1967. He was an influential figure in successive relegation battles and moved to Andover in July 1971, then linked up with Tony Priscott again at Ringwood Town in July 1973. They were partners in a building company until August 1982, then Rod ran a nursing home with his wife for a period and has since returned to the building trade. He now lives in Moor Crichel and his son Spencer is the golf professional at Ashley Wood Golf Club.

TOMMY TAYLOR

Versatile inside forward Tommy Taylor was Cherries' joint leading marksman in 1966/67. A former Tottenham Hotspur junior, he signed professional for Portsmouth in April 1964 but failed to secure a first team slot and moved to Gillingham in May 1965. He made his League debut at Oxford United six months later and joined Bournemouth with David Stocks in an exchange deal involving Charlie Crickmore in June 1966. Scoring eight goals in 26 Third Division games while at Dean Court, he moved to Bath City in May 1968. He featured in their 1968/69 promotion success and was reunited with Ronnie Bolton at Poole Town in July 1971, then linked up with Chris Weller again at Salisbury. After a spell at Minehead, he rejoined Poole in February 1975 and later played for Swanage T&H, Poole again and Flight Refuelling before managing Bournemouth 'Poppies' (twice) and Wimborne Town. He has spent 25 years in the aircraft industry and is now logistics quality supervisor for FR Aviation (Cobham Group) at Hurn Airport.

SHAUN TEALE

Commanding central defender Shaun Teale was AFC Bournemouth's 'Player of the Year' in two consecutive seasons. A former Everton apprentice, he had spells with Burscough, Ellesmere Port, Southport and Northwich Victoria prior to joining Stuart Morgan's Weymouth for £20,000 in August 1987. He starred alongside Paul Compton and gained England Semi-Pro recognition before Harry Redknapp paid £50,000 for him in January 1989. Given his Second Division debut in Cherries' 2-1 win at home to West Brom a month later, he was ever-present in 1990/91 and scored four goals in 100 League outings before being sold to Aston Villa for £300,000 in July 1991. Ever present in 1991/92, he was an influential figure as Villa were Premier League runners-up in 1992/93 and won the Coca-Cola Cup final at Wembley in 1994. He joined Tranmere Rovers for £450,000 in August 1995 and then had spells at Preston NE, Motherwell, Carlisle United and Southport before rejoining Burscough as player-boss, plotting their 2003 FA Trophy triumph.

REES THOMAS

Versatile full-back Rees Thomas played alongside Mike Lyons in Cherries' defence. Initially on Brighton's groundstaff, the Welsh Schoolboy international turned professional with Cardiff City in January 1951 but failed to secure a first-team place at Ninian Park. He was one of several Cardiff players loaned to Torquay United during this period and made his League debut for the Gulls at Swindon Town in March 1954. Rejoining Brighton in September 1956, he featured in their 1957/58 Third Division (South) title campaign. Freddie Cox signed him in January 1958 and he helped Cherries to qualify for the newly-formed Third Division that season, making 48 League appearances before following Cox to Portsmouth with Jimmy White in July 1959. He joined Aldershot in July 1961 and moved to Hereford United in July 1964, helping to win the Southern League First Division title in 1964/65. After working as a postman in Aldershot, he has lived in his native Aberdare for the past 33 years but was unable to keep steady employment due to serious back trouble.

BILL THOMPSON

Scottish left-back Bill Thompson was a versatile member of Jack Bruton's squad at Dean Court. Born in Glasgow, he played for Carnoustie prior to joining Portsmouth in March 1946 and helped Pompey retain the League Championship in 1949/50. He failed to establish a regular first-team place at Fratton Park and Jack Bruton signed him in January 1953. Displacing Jack Fisher in Cherries' defence, he played 45 Third Division (South) games for Bournemouth prior to joining Guildford City in July 1954. Appointed player-manager in November 1955, he plotted Guildford's 1955/56 Southern League title triumph and became Exeter City's manager in May 1957. He left to take charge of Worcester City in January 1958, then returned to Portsmouth as caretaker manager in February 1961. Subsequently coaching Sparta Rotterdam to Dutch Cup final success in 1966 and Ismaili to the Egyptian League title in 1967, he settled back in Portsmouth and was involved with local soccer courses until his sudden death on Boxing Day 1988.

IAN THOMPSON

Striker Ian Thompson scored in Cherries' 1983/84 FA Cup third round win at home to holders Manchester United. Initially with Welling United, 'Thommo' had spells with BAT and Andover prior to joining Poole Town in August 1980. He was ever-present as they reached the Anglo-Italian Tournament final in 1980/81, then joined Salisbury for £1,000 in August 1981 and was twice leading marksman before Don Megson paid £16,000 for him in July 1982. Also featuring in AFC Bournemouth's 1984 Associate Members' Cup final triumph, he netted 30 goals in 121 League games while at Dean Court until a pelvic injury ended his League career and he rejoined Salisbury as player-coach in August 1986. Following a teaching appointment in South Wales, he briefly reunited with Max Thompson and Phil Brignull at struggling Newport County before helping Merthyr Tydfil win the Southern League title in 1988/89. He then played for Haverfordwest and Inter-Cardiff and is now deputy head of Morriston Comprehensive School in Swansea.

PETER THOMPSON

Ex-England Amateur international centre-forward Peter Thompson featured in Cherries' 1961/62 promotion near-miss. Starting with Blackhall CW, he was a PT instructor in the RAF and joined Wrexham in November 1955. He scored twice on his League debut against Crewe Alexandra a month later and played in the 1956/57 FA Cup fourth round tie against Manchester United. Joining Hartlepool United in July 1957, he moved to Derby County in November 1958 and topped their goalscoring charts in 1959/60. Bill McGarry paid £5,000 for him in January 1962 and he netted 14 goals in 39 League games for Bournemouth before returning to Hartlepool in September 1963. He was twice leading marksman prior to joining Boston United in July 1966 and had a spell with Scarborough while training to become a youth social worker and teacher. After gaining an MA in philosophy, he lectured Secondary Teacher Training at Sunderland Polytechnic and was then licensee of the Seagull Inn in his native Blackhall where he now lives in retirement.

JASON TINDALL

Central defender Jason Tindall was a versatile member of AFC Bournemouth's 2002/03 promotion squad. A former Charlton Athletic trainee, he signed professional in July 1996 and starred as their reserves won the Avon Insurance Combination title in 1997/98. Despite this success, he was unable to secure a first-team slot at The Valley and Mel Machin snapped him up on a free transfer in July 1998. He netted a penalty on his full League debut in AFC Bournemouth's 3-0 win at home to Millwall a month later and helped Cherries to beat Wolverhampton Wanderers in the 1998/99 Worthington Cup second round. Overcoming successive injury problems, he skippered Cherries reserves to Avon Insurance Combination Cup final glory in 1999/2000 and regained a regular first-team slot in the heart of defence alongside the likes of Karl Broadhurst and Carl Fletcher. He was unlucky to miss the 2002/03 Third Division play-off final triumph through injury and has scored six goals in 141 League outings for Cherries.

TOMMY TIPPETT

Popular outside-left Tommy Tippett created numerous chances for Jack Cross while at Dean Court. The son of the former West Ham winger of the same name, he played for Ilford Youth Association while an apprentice electrician with the local council and guested for West Ham, Southend United and Plymouth Argyle during Second World War service in the Royal Navy. He signed professional for Southend in May 1946 and made his League debut at home to Ipswich Town four months later, featuring in their 1949/50 promotion near-miss. Jack Bruton paid £3,000 for him in September 1951 and he impressed with his long throw-ins, netting 10 goals in 37 Third Division (South) games for Bournemouth prior to joining Dartford in July 1953 after an ankle injury. He later played for Gravesend & Northfleet, Canterbury City and Jimmy Blair's Ramsgate Athletic. Now living in Romford, he was a keen member of Hainault Golf Club and spent 40 years as a self-employed electrician until retiring after a stroke in December 1995.

DAVID TOWN

Quick, lively striker David Town was a young member of Mel Machin's squad at AFC Bournemouth. Born locally, he was a prolific goalscorer in Cherries' youth and reserve sides and still a trainee when Tony Pulis gave him his League debut as a substitute in the 2-1 victory at home to Reading in May 1994. He signed professional under Machin in April 1995 and made his full League debut in Cherries' 3-1 defeat at York City eleven months later, securing a regular first-team slot alongside Steve Fletcher during the second half of the 1996/97 campaign. Loaned to Dorchester Town, he had limited chances after the arrival of Mark Stein and scored twice in 56 Second Division games while at Dean Court before joining Rushden & Diamonds for £30,000 in June 1999, helping them take Sheffield United to an FA Cup third round replay in 1999/2000. He joined Boston United in March 2001 and featured in their 2001/02 Conference title triumph, moving to Havant & Waterlooville in May 2003.

NEIL TOWNSEND

Ex-England youth central defender Neil Townsend played alongside John Impey while at AFC Bournemouth. Signing professional for Northampton Town in September 1968, he made his League debut at Mansfield Town two months later but struggled to establish a regular first-team slot and moved to Bedford Town in July 1972. He starred in their 1972/73 FA Trophy run and was sold to Southend United for £6,000 in July 1973, featuring prominently as they reached the FA Cup fifth round in 1975/76 and won promotion in 1977/78. Joining Stuart Morgan's Weymouth for £2,000 in November 1978, he helped them reach the Southern League Cup semi-finals in 1978/79 and Alec Stock paid £15,000 for him in July 1979. He contested a first-team place with the likes of Jeff Bryant and Jon Moore, scoring twice in 34 Fourth Division games while at Dean Court until an Achilles tendon injury ended his career in May 1981. Now living back in Northampton, he ran Kingfisher Health Studio, then Derngate Gym and now works for Securicor.

REG TRIM

Talented young full-back Reg Trim was one of Cherries' finest discoveries during the inter-war era. A former England Schoolboys captain, he signed professional at Dean Court in April 1931 and made his League debut in Bournemouth's 3-0 defeat at QPR a month later. He quickly impressed alongside Jack Hayward and made 20 Third Division (South) appearances for Cherries before being sold to Arsenal for £1,000 in April 1933. Understudy to England international Eddie Hapgood as they were League Champions in three consecutive seasons, he gained top-flight experience and helped Arsenal reserves to win the London Combination title three times. He moved to Nottingham Forest in July 1937, then became a wartime hero as a squadron leader in the RAF and played for Swindon Town prior to becoming Leyton Orient's trainer. Rejoining the RAF as a flight controller, he then had a spell with Hurn-based Flight Refuelling before working for the Bournemouth Water Company until retirement in October 1978. He died in June 1997.

BILL TUNNICLIFFE

Popular outside-left Bill Tunnicliffe played for Cherries either side of the Second World War. A former Port Vale junior, he made his League debut at home to Rotherham United eleven months before turning professional in January 1937. He moved to Dean Court in July 1938 and featured in Bournemouth's 10-0 win at home to Northampton Town in September 1939, then guested for several clubs during wartime service in the RASC. Scoring seven goals in 49 Third Division (South) games for Cherries, he moved to Wrexham for £1,000 in June 1947. He was leading marksman in 1947/48 and ever-present in his first two seasons at the Racecourse Ground, featuring in the 1950 Welsh Cup final. Joining Bradford City in January 1953, he then moved to Stafford Rangers in August 1955 and Cheshire League rivals Congleton Town a year later. He was subsequently manager-coach of his local side Queen Street Boys and remained in his native Potteries until his death at Bradwell Hall Nursing Home in Newcastle-under-Lyme in March 1997.

JAMIE VINCENT

Attacking left-back Jamie Vincent played for AFC Bournemouth in the 1998 Auto Windscreens Shield final at Wembley. A former Crystal Palace trainee, he signed professional in July 1993 and Mel Machin brought him to Dean Court on loan in November 1994. He made his League debut in that month's 2-0 defeat at Oxford United and helped to lift Cherries off the bottom of the table before returning to Selhurst Park. Deputising for Dean Gordon as Palace qualified for the First Division play-offs in 1995/96, he rejoined AFC Bournemouth in a deal rising up to £65,000 plus 15 per cent of any future profit in August 1996. He starred as Cherries narrowly missed the Second Division play-offs in two consecutive seasons and was selected for the PFA Second Division side together with Mark Stein and Steve Robinson in 1998/99. Scoring five goals in 113 League games overall before being controversially sold to Huddersfield Town for £550,000 on the transfer deadline in March 1999, he moved to Portsmouth for £800,000 in February 2001.

BILL VOISEY

Tenacious half-back Bill Voisey was an experienced figure in Cherries first Football League campaign. He developed in local soccer on the Isle of Dogs prior to joining Millwall in July 1908 and was a Kent Senior Shield Winner in 1912/13. A sergeant in the Royal Artillery during the Great War, he was highly decorated for his bravery and played for England in the Victory international against Wales in October 1919. He went on the FA tour of South Africa shortly before scoring Millwall's first-ever goal in the Football League at home to Bristol Rovers in August 1920. Moving to Bournemouth in July 1923, he featured in Cherries first-ever Football League game at Swindon Town a month later and netted twice in 26 Third Division (South) games prior to joining Leytonstone as coach in July 1924. Subsequently assistant-trainer and trainer at Fulham, he rejoined Millwall as trainer in July 1939 and managed them during the Second World War. He then scouted for the Lions until retiring in May 1962. He died in Worcester in October 1964.

CHRISTER WARREN

Versatile left-sided player Christer Warren played for Cherries at Wembley in the 1998 Auto Windscreens Shield final. He attended Ferndown Upper School and joined Cheltenham Town as a trainee striker in July 1991, scoring their equaliser at home to AFC Bournemouth in the 1992/93 FA Cup second round. Moving to Southampton for £60,000 in March 1995, he made his Premiership debut at Arsenal six months later but failed to secure a regular first-team slot at The Dell. He was loaned to Brighton and Fulham on loan before Mel Machin paid £50,000 for him in October 1997 and he netted AFC Bournemouth's winner at Preston on his debut. Featuring prominently as Cherries beat West Brom in the 1998/99 FA Cup third round and narrowly failed to qualify for the Second Division play-offs in two consecutive seasons, he switched to a left-back role after Jamie Vincent's departure. He scored 13 goals in 103 Second Division games while at Dean Court before moving to QPR in June 2000 and has since played for Bristol Rovers and Eastleigh.

ALEX WATSON

Ex-England Youth central defender Alex Watson was ever-present for AFC Bournemouth in 1992/93. The younger brother of Everton stalwart Dave Watson, he signed professional for Liverpool in May 1985 and made his First Division debut for Kenny Dalglish's title-chasers at QPR in March 1988. He featured in Liverpool's 1988 Charity Shield triumph at Wembley and had a loan spell with Derby County prior to joining Cherries for £100,000 in January 1991 as Jamie Redknapp moved in the opposite direction. Partnering the likes of Shaun Teale and Mark Morris in the heart of AFC Bournemouth's defence, he had a spell as captain and scored five goals in 151 League outings while at Dean Court. He briefly reunited with Tony Pulis on loan at Gillingham before being sold to Torquay United for £50,000 in November 1995. Ever-present in two consecutive seasons, he starred as they beat Cherries in the 1997/98 Coca-Cola Cup first round and reached the Third Division play-off final. He moved to Exeter City in July 2001 and was released in May 2003 after they lost Football League status.

BILLY WAUGH

Scottish winger Billy Waugh was an experienced member of Jack Bruton's squad at Dean Court. Initially with Rosewell Rosedale, he was also an amateur with Hearts and Bathgate Thistle prior to joining Luton Town in September 1944 while a PT instructor in the RAF stationed at Bicester. He scored in Luton's first post-war League match and was an influential figure as they reached the FA Cup fifth round in three successive seasons, moving to QPR for £5,000 in July 1950. Unable to prevent relegation in 1951/52, he joined Bournemouth in July 1953 and contested a first-team slot with the likes of Peter Harrison, Arnold Stephens and Billy Hughes. He netted three goals in 18 Third Division (South) games for Cherries prior to briefly joining Chelmsford City in July 1954, then played for Bedford Town, Ashford Town and March Town before managing Electrolux and Langford. Still living in Luton, he spent 30 years as recreation club manager of Electrolux until retiring in December 1985 and is now president of South Midlands League side Langford.

DAVID WEBB

Colourful young manager David Webb plotted AFC Bournemouth's 1981/82 promotion success. A former West Ham amateur, he signed professional for Leyton Orient in May 1963 and was swapped for Southampton's George O'Brien in March 1966, starring in defence as Saints clinched top-flight status that season. Moving to Chelsea in exchange for Joe Kirkup in February 1968, he scored their 1970 FA Cup final replay winner and starred in Chelsea's 1971 ECWC final triumph as well as playing in the 1972 League Cup final. He followed Dave Sexton to QPR for £120,000 in July 1974 and helped them to finish League Championship runners-up in 1975/76, then played for Leicester City and Derby County prior to joining Cherries as player-coach in May 1980. Appointed player-manager seven months later, he made 11 League appearances until dismissed in December 1982 and later took charge of Torquay United. He became Southend United's boss in June 1986 and guided them to the First Division, then managed Chelsea, Brentford, Yeovil Town and Southend again.

RAY WEIGH

Versatile outside-left Ray Weigh created numerous goalscoring chances for Doug McGibbon while at Dean Court. He was an Army Cup finalist with the Royal Engineers stationed in Liss and Harry Lowe signed him in March 1949. Scoring on his League debut in Bournemouth's 2-1 win at Ipswich Town five months later, he also netted in Cherries' Golden Jubilee match at home to Nottingham Forest in November 1949 and managed eight goals in 28 Third Division (South) games before moving to Stockport County in July 1951. He joined Shrewsbury Town in June 1954, then played for Aldershot and Dorchester Town prior to becoming Christchurch's player-coach in July 1959. He was later secretary-manager of Pokesdown Old Boys and spent 15 years as a sales re-merchandiser for Brooke Bond Tea, then was caretaker at Beaufort School. Still living locally, he ran a private hire car business until retiring in June 1994 and is a Cherries season-ticket holder. His nephews, Tony and Gren Millington, were both notable goalkeepers.

CHRIS WELLER

Inside-forward Chris Weller was a popular figure during two spells at Dean Court. Initially with Thornycrofts, he had a spell with Reading prior to joining Bournemouth in August 1959. He made his League debut in Cherries' 3-2 defeat at Notts County a year later and featured in the 1961/62 promotion near-miss under Bill McGarry, moving to Bristol Rovers in June 1965. Rejoining Bournemouth in January 1966, he scored 26 goals in 111 Third Division games overall before moving to Yeovil Town in June 1967. He was leading marksman in 1967/68 and starred in their 1970/71 Southern League title triumph, also helping Yeovil to win at Dean Court in that season's FA Cup second round. Moving to Salisbury in May 1973, he joined Poole Town in June 1975 and reunited with Tony Priscott at Ringwood Town in July 1976. He became Holt United's player-boss in July 1978 and has since been manager/coach of Shaftesbury, Holt again, Wimborne Town, Brockenhurst and Bournemouth 'Poppies' while a self-employed plumber and heating engineer in Verwood.

ALAN WELSH

Scottish striker Alan Welsh was an early Trevor Hartley signing for AFC Bournemouth. Starting with Bonnyrigg Rose, he joined Millwall in July 1965 and made his League debut against Scunthorpe United two months later. He was a member of their 1965/66 promotion squad but struggled to make an impact and moved to Torquay United in November 1967. Leading marksman in 1971/72, he joined Plymouth Argyle for £15,000 in July 1972 and topped their goalscoring charts in 1972/73. He starred as Plymouth reached the League Cup semi-finals in 1973/74 and moved to Dean Court for £25,000 in February 1974. Netting three goals in 35 Third Division games for Cherries, he rejoined Millwall in August 1975 and featured in their 1975/76 promotion campaign prior to playing for Maidstone United and South African side Cape Town City. Now a keen squash player living in Forest Hill, he helped his brother-in-law Billy Neil in Millwall's commercial department before working in the print trade and has since been employed in the building trade.

DON WELSH

Former England international left-half Don Welsh succeeded Freddie Cox as manager at Dean Court. He served in the Royal Navy at Devonport prior to joining Torquay United in January 1933 and starred as they were Third Division (South) Cup finalists in 1933/34, moving to Charlton Athletic for £3,250 in February 1935. He skippered them from the Third Division to First Division and to League Championship runners-up in 1936/37. Capped three times, he also starred as Charlton reached two Wembley Cup finals during the Second World War and captained their 1947 FA Cup final triumph after being a losing finalist the previous season. He became Brighton's manager in November 1947 and took charge of Liverpool for five years in March 1951. Appointed Bournemouth's manager in July 1958, he remained in charge at Dean Court until sacked in February 1961. He then ran a youth centre in Camberwell and managed Wycombe Wanderers prior to joining Charlton's administration staff, living in Cheam until his death in February 1990.

ALFIE WHITE

Inside-forward Alfie White was a popular member of Billy Birrell's squad at Dean Court. Starting with Spennymoor United, he quickly impressed in the North-Eastern League and joined Derby County on the same day as ex-Cherries' left-back George Collin in November 1927. He made his First Division debut as an 18-year-old at Leicester City two months later and was a young member of Derby's squad that finished League Championship runners-up in 1929/30. Unable to secure a regular first-team slot behind England internationals Harry Bedford and Jack Bowers, he reunited with Jack Whitehouse at Bournemouth in October 1931. He helped Cherries to reach the FA Cup fourth round in 1931/32 and scored 35 goals in 125 Third Division (South) games while at Dean Court before moving to Wrexham in May 1936. Rejoining Spennymoor in July 1937, he was leading marksman in two consecutive seasons. He settled back in his hometown and was a storeman for Siemens until retiring in May 1974, remaining in Spennymoor until his death.

JIMMY WHITE

Ex-England Youth central defender Jimmy White was ever-present for Cherries in 1967/68. Born in Parkstone, he attended Kemp Welch School and became Bournemouth's youngest League debutant at 15 years 321 days in the 3-1 win at home to Port Vale in April 1958. He followed Freddie Cox to Portsmouth that summer and featured in their 1961/62 Third Division title campaign. Reunited with Cox at Gillingham in June 1963, he helped to win the Fourth Division title in 1963/64 and followed Cox back to Bournemouth for £5,000 in July 1966. He starred as Cherries took Liverpool to an FA Cup third round replay in 1967/68 and beat Sheffield Wednesday in the 1969/70 League Cup second round. Scoring seven goals in 177 Third Division games overall, he joined Cambridge United as player-coach in December 1970 and was later manager/coach of King's Lynn, Cambridge City, Chatteris Town, Histon and Finnish side TP Sienejuki. Now living in Over, he is an operating theatre attendant at Addenbrooke's Hospital in Cambridge.

KEVIN WHITE

Young midfielder Kevin White helped Cherries take Liverpool to a FA Cup third round replay in 1967/68. A former apprentice at Dean Court, he signed professional under Freddie Cox in August 1966 and made his League debut in Bournemouth's 1-0 win at Scunthorpe United a month later. He secured a regular first-team slot the following season but was displaced by new signings like Lou Peters and John Meredith. Confined to the reserves as John Bond plotted promotion in 1970/71, he scored four goals in 48 Third Division games for Cherries before moving to Bath City in June 1971. Unable to prevent relegation in 1971/72, he had a spell with hometown Poole prior to joining Salisbury in August 1973. He played alongside his former Cherries team-mates Tommy Taylor and Chris Weller in their Southern League side, then reunited with Peter Norton at Parley Sports. Subsequently with New Milton, he settled in Parkstone as a self-employed plumber and heating engineer and has since worked for John Hickman (Heating) Ltd.

JACK WHITEHOUSE

Experienced inside-forward Jack Whitehouse played alongside Ron Eyre and Jack Russell in Cherries' attack. Initially with Smethwick Hall, he had a spell with Redditch prior to joining Birmingham in August 1916 and guested for Derby County and Chelsea during the Great War. He starred in Birmingham's 1920/21 Second Division title triumph and moved to Derby County in May 1923. An influential figure in consecutive promotion near-misses, he helped the Rams to regain top-flight status in 1925/26 and was sold to Sheffield Wednesday for £5,000 in February 1929. He was a member of their squad that won the League Championship in two consecutive seasons and joined Bournemouth in August 1930, successfully switching to left-back during the 1931/32 campaign. Netting 17 goals in 105 League games while at Dean Court, he moved to Folkestone in May 1933 and featured in their 1933/34 Kent Senior Cup and Shield 'double' triumph. He had a spell as Worcester City's player-manager, then scouted for Derby and died in Halesowen in January 1948.

MARK WHITLOCK

Central defender Mark Whitlock featured prominently in AFC Bournemouth's 1986/87 Third Division title triumph. A former Southampton apprentice, he signed professional in March 1979 and made his First Division debut at home to Wolves in September 1981. He was loaned to Grimsby Town and Aldershot before helping Saints to finish League Championship runners-up in 1983/84 and moved to AFC Bournemouth with David Puckett as part of the Colin Clarke deal in July 1986. Partnering John Williams in the heart of Cherries' defence, he helped to beat Southampton in the 1987/88 Littlewoods Cup second round and scored once in 99 League games while at Dean Court before moving to Reading in December 1988. He was an experienced figure in their 1989/90 FA Cup run and reunited with David Puckett and Adrian Randall at Aldershot in August 1990, featuring in their fateful 1991/92 campaign. Subsequently with Aerostructures, he has since worked as a security officer notably at Ocean Village in Southampton.

ERNIE WHITTAM

Stocky inside-right Ernie Whittam was a popular member of Charlie Bell's squad at Dean Court. Initially an amateur with Huddersfield Town whilst employed at a local bakery, he signed professional in November 1928 and made his First Division debut at Grimsby Town ten months later. He was unable to secure a regular first-team place with the 1930 FA Cup finalists and moved to Chester in May 1933, featuring in their 1934/35 Third Division (North) title challenge. Joining Mansfield Town in May 1935, he moved to Wolverhampton Wanderers in February 1936 and gained further top-flight experience before following the well-worn trail to Bournemouth in May 1936. He formed an effective right-wing triangle with Willie Smith and Bob Redfern while at Dean Court, netting 28 goals in 107 Third Division (South) games for Cherries prior to joining Reading in June 1939. His football career was ended by the Second World War and he subsequently settled back in Huddersfield until his untimely death from cancer.

JOHN WILLIAMS

Tall central defender John Williams was an influential figure in Cherries' 1986/87 Third Division title triumph.

A former Tranmere Rovers junior, the popular Scouser made his League debut at Swindon Town seven months before signing professional in October 1979 and featured in their 1981/82 League Cup run. 'Willo' joined Port Vale for £12,000 in July 1985 and starred in their 1985/86 promotion success under John Rudge, moving to Dean Court for £30,000 in December 1986. Featuring prominently as Cherries beat Southampton in the 1987/88 Littlewoods Cup second round and took Manchester United to an FA Cup fifth round replay in 1988/89, he scored nine goals in 117 League games until sold to Cardiff City for £15,000 in December 1991. Returning to AFC Bournemouth in July 1993, he was youth team boss prior to assisting Mel Machin and had a testimonial against Southampton in July 1998. He was dismissed in February 2000 and subsequently worked in the licensed trade. Now a match summariser for Radio Solent.

KEITH WILLIAMS

Versatile midfielder Keith Williams starred in AFC Bournemouth's 1981/82 promotion success. Signing professional for Aston Villa in April 1975, he failed to secure a First Division slot and moved to Northampton Town in February 1977. He made his League debut in that month's 5-3 win at home to Shrewsbury Town and was 'Player of the Season' in 1980/81. David Webb snapped him up on a free transfer in August 1981 and he became Cherries' player-coach after recurring injury problems restricted his appearances. A member of AFC Bournemouth's 1986/87 Third Division title squad, he scored once in 102 League games while at Dean Court and briefly played for Bath City prior to reuniting with Roger Brown at Colchester United in December 1987. He then played for Swanage T&H before spells with Salisbury, Poole Town and Bournemouth 'Poppies'. After linking up with Shaun Brooks again at Ringwood Town, he is now managing Bournemouth 'Poppies' and works as despatch manager for Bezier Corporate Print in Poole.

LEN WILLIAMS

Young Welsh winger Len Williams created numerous goalscoring chances for Ron Eyre while at Dean Court. His older brothers Frank and Jesse both played for Wrexham and he joined Bournemouth from Wrexham amateur soccer, initially on trial, in December 1929. He made his League debut in Cherries' 0-0 draw at home to Southend United a month later and scored 15 goals in 90 Third Division (South) games before moving to Portsmouth in an exchange deal involving Jack Friar and Jack Surtees in August 1933. Gaining top-flight experience with Pompey, he joined Aldershot in August 1934 and was joint leading marksman in 1935/36. He moved to Charlton Athletic in June 1936, then rejoined Aldershot in July 1938 and skippered Worcester City in wartime soccer. Subsequently Poole Town's coach while working as an insurance agent, he ran Sterte sub Post Office for 21 years until retiring in May 1973 and remained in Poole until his death in June 1990. His son Bryan was founder-chairman of Dexter Sports and now runs Rossmore sub Post Office.

FRED WILSON

Commanding centre-half Fred Wilson was a key figure in Cherries' 1947/48 promotion near-miss. A former Wolverhampton Wanderers junior, he turned professional in May 1936 and was one of several 'Buckley Babes' who moved to Dean Court in May 1937. He was given his League debut in Bournemouth's 0-0 draw at home to Clapton Orient in March 1939 when the famous defensive quartet of Ken Bird, Fred Marsden, Joe Sanaghan and Fred Wilson made their first appearance together in the League team. After Second World War service in the Hampshire Regiment, he featured in Cherries' 1945/46 Third Division (South) Cup final triumph and was ever-present in 1946/47. He succeeded Fred Marsden as skipper and made 98 League appearances before moving to Weymouth in July 1951. A partner of Bailey & Wilson bookmakers in Bennett Road until December 1961, he was subsequently a security guard at BDH Chemicals in Poole until retiring in November 1983 and remained local until suffering a fatal heart-attack in December 1993.

GEORGE WILSON

Much-travelled Irish goalkeeper George Wilson was a key figure in Cherries' 1925/26 FA Cup run. Initially with Dublin Amateurs, he joined Bohemians in July 1922 and briefly played for Holyhead and Clapton Orient before Harry Kinghorn signed him in June 1924. He took over from Alec Heron in Bournemouth's goal and made his League debut in the 3-1 defeat at Millwall two months later, missing just one game during his first season at Dean Court as Cherries narrowly avoided having to seek re-election for the second consecutive year. Starring as Bournemouth took eventual winners Bolton Wanderers to an FA Cup fourth round replay in 1925/26, he was displaced by the arrival of Jock Robson from Arsenal and made 81 Third Division (South) appearances prior to joining Cheshire League side Witton Albion in August 1926. He then had spells with Connah's Quay, New Brighton, Notts County, Mold Town and Llanelli before settling back in his native Ireland, playing for Waterford, Bray Unknowns, Belfast Celtic and Larne until retiring.

JOHN WINGATE

Versatile midfielder John Wingate was a member of Trevor Hartley's squad at AFC Bournemouth. A former Exeter City junior, he had spells with Torquay United and Newton Abbot Spurs prior to joining Budleigh Salterton and topped their goalscoring charts in 1967/68. He joined Dawlish Town in July 1968 and made his League debut as an amateur for Plymouth Argyle at home to Gillingham five months later, leaving Dawlish to sign professional for Exeter City in February 1969. Starring in their 1973/74 League Cup run, he moved to Dean Court in exchange for John Rutter in July 1974. He deputised in goal for the injured Kevin Chariton during Cherries' 1974/75 FA Cup second round replay defeat at home to Wycombe Wanderers and netted three goals in 33 Third Division games prior to rejoining Exeter in July 1975. Later with Bideford and Falmouth Town, he became a partner in his family's Cornish Candy confectionery business. He now lives in Colaton Raleigh and is a full-time tennis coach at East Devon Tennis Centre in Exmouth.

PAUL WOOD

Skilful, versatile winger Paul Wood scored in Cherries' 1991/92 FA Cup third round replay win at Newcastle United. A former Portsmouth apprentice, he signed professional in November 1982 and made his League debut at Middlesbrough in January 1984. He helped Pompey to regain top-flight status in 1986/87 after two near misses, but a pelvic injury restricted his appearances and he was sold to Brighton for £80,000 in August 1987. Starring in their 1987/88 promotion success, he joined Sheffield United for £90,000 in February 1990 and helped them to clinch promotion that season. He reunited with Mark Morris at AFC Bournemouth for £40,000 in October 1991 after a lengthy loan spell and netted 18 times in 99 League outings while at Dean Court before returning to Portsmouth for £40,000 in February 1994. Moving to Happy Valley in June 1997, he briefly played for Andover prior to joining Havant & Waterlooville in September 1998, featuring in their 1998/99 Dr Martens League Southern Division title triumph and 2002/03 FA Trophy run.

CHARLIE WOODS

Young inside-right Charlie Woods partnered the likes of Jimmy Singer and Denis Coughlin in Cherries' attack. Initially with Cleator Moor Celtic he joined Newcastle United in May 1959 and scored on his First Division debut at Fulham in August 1960. He moved to Bournemouth for £5,000 in November 1962 and starred in successive promotion challenges, netting 26 goals in 70 Third Division games prior to joining Crystal Palace in November 1964. Reunited with Bill McGarry at Ipswich Town in July 1966, he featured in their 1967/68 Second Division title campaign and moved to Watford for £10,000 with Ron Wigg in June 1970. Following Ken Furphy to Blackburn Rovers as youth team coach, he rejoined Ipswich in a similar capacity in March 1973 and plotted FA Youth Cup success. He was subsequently reserve team coach, then assistant-manager and chief scout at Portman Road until joining Spurs as chief scout in May 1998, linking up with Bobby Robson again as Newcastle United's chief scout in July 2000.

DAI WOODWARD

Welsh wing-half Dai Woodward gave Cherries marvellous service in various capacities over 25 years at Dean Court. Real name Laurie, he signed professional for Wolverhampton Wanderers in May 1938 and was loaned to Walsall, helping them to reach the FA Cup fifth round in 1938/39. Following several other 'Buckley Babes' to Dean Court in May 1939, he served with his cousin Viv Woodward (who played for Fulham) in the Welch Regiment during the Second World War. He made a significant contribution as Bournemouth won the Third Division (South) Cup in 1945/46 and narrowly missed promotion in 1947/48, also featuring in Cherries' 1948/49 FA Cup third round tie at Manchester United. Scoring seven goals in 275 Third Division (South) games, he later

coached the 'A' team, then was reserve team trainer and assistant-trainer until June 1964 and had a testimonial against Arsenal. He was subsequently a self-employed painter and decorator until retiring in July 1988 and remained local until his death in December 1997.

ARNOLD WOOLLARD

Cultured left-back Arnold Woollard featured prominently as Cherries reached the FA Cup sixth round in 1956/57. Born in Bermuda, he played in that country for Hamilton and Bermuda AA prior to joining Northampton Town in August 1949. He struggled to make an impact and joined Peterborough United in June 1952, starring in their 1952/53 FA Cup run. Sold to Newcastle United for £5,000 in December 1952, he gained top-flight experience before Freddie Cox paid £2,000 for him in June 1956. He formed an effective defensive partnership with Mike Lyons as Bournemouth defeated Wolves and Spurs en-route to an epic FA Cup sixth round clash at home to Manchester United in 1956/57, also featuring in Cherries' 1961/62 promotion challenge. Making 161 League appearances while at Dean Court, he rejoined Northampton in exchange for Ron Spelman in March 1962 and was a member of their 1962/63 Third Division title squad. He later worked in government service in Bermuda and since August 1988 has lived near Newport Pagnell in retirement.

REG WRIGHT

Popular left-back Reg Wright played alongside long-serving Jack Hayward in Cherries' defence. Signing professional for Sheffield Wednesday in July 1921, he moved to Worksop Town in July 1924 and impressed in the Midland League. He had a trial with Mansfield Town prior to joining Blackpool in May 1925 and Frank Richards brought him to Dean Court in June 1928. A member of Bournemouth's 1928/29 FA Cup run squad, he contested a first-team slot with the likes of Harry Isherwood and Sam Brown. He played 31 Third Division (South) games for Cherries prior to reuniting with Teddy Davison at newly-promoted Chesterfield in June 1931, then had spells with Frickley Colliery, Worksop Town, Buxton and Mosborough Trinity before linking up with Teddy Davison again as Sheffield United's trainer in July 1936. Subsequently assistant-trainer back at Sheffield Wednesday, he then rejoined Davison as trainer to Chesterfield's juniors. A Methodist lay-preacher, he resided in Chesterfield until his death in January 1973.

NEIL YOUNG

Attacking right-back Neil Young played for AFC Bournemouth in the 1998 Auto Windscreens Shield final at Wembley. A former Tottenham Hotspur trainee, he signed professional in August 1991 but failed to secure a Premiership slot at White Hart Lane and Mel Machin snapped him up on a free transfer in October 1994. He made his League debut in Cherries' 1-0 defeat at home to Brentford that month and was an influential figure in the 1994/95 relegation escape, quickly impressing as an excellent tackler able to provide good crosses and support to the front players. Partnering the likes of Russell Beardsmore and Jamie Vincent in defence, he was a consistent performer as AFC Bournemouth narrowly failed to qualify for the Second Division play-offs in two consecutive seasons. He featured in exciting Cup wins over West Brom, Wolverhampton Wanderers and Charlton Athletic and overcame a long-term knee problem to help Sean O'Driscoll's side triumph in the 2002/03 Third Division play-off final.

CHERRIES MISCELLANY

DEAN COURT

Dean Court has been the Cherries' ground for the past 93 years and is named after the club's benefactor, who became club president. When JE Cooper-Dean JP let the wasteland to Boscombe FC at a peppercorn rent, voluntary labour prepared a pitch and built a stand for 300 spectators under the supervision of Wilf Hayward. The ground was officially opened on 31st December 1910 with the first match being against Southampton Reserves. The Main Stand was erected with the steel framework of the restaurant of the British Empire Exhibition at Wembley bought for £12,000 and declared open on 27th August 1927 for a game against Swindon Town. The South End covered terrace was also opened before a Swindon match, on 5th September 1936. The New Stand was built after the club's epic 1956/57 FA Cup run and refurbished in the summer of 1964. The Brighton Beach End was sarcastically named because it used to be a stony bank! From March 2001 onwards, the ground was redeveloped with the pitch turned through 90 degrees. The Fitness First Stadium, built at a cost of £6.5M, was opened in November 2001.

INTERNATIONALS

Seven players have gained full international honours whilst at Dean Court. Goalkeeper Tommy Godwin was the first Cherries player to represent his country in a full international when he starred in the Republic of Ireland's 4-1 win against the Netherlands in May 1956, gaining the last four of his 13 caps while at Bournemouth. Striker Colin Clarke made his full international debut in Northern Ireland's 0-0 draw against France in February 1986 and starred in the 1986 Mexico World Cup. He won six of his 38 caps with Cherries and holds his country's goalscoring record. Goalkeeper Gerry Peyton gained a club record seven caps for the Republic of Ireland and was a non-playing member of his country's 1990 World Cup squad, capped 33 times overall. Northern Ireland international striker Jimmy Quinn gained one of his 46 caps while at Dean Court, featuring in the 2-2 draw against Lithuania in April 1992. Midfielder Steve Robinson was been capped five times by Northern Ireland, while former skipper Ian Cox played for Trinidad & Tobago. Striker Warren Feeney made his debut for Northern Ireland against Liechtenstein in March 2002.

PLAYER OF THE SEASON

The Mickey Cave/Daily Echo trophy for the club's Player of the Season has been won by 15 different players. Named after the former Cherries favourite who tragically died in November 1985, the award was first won by Eire international goalkeeper Gerry Peyton in 1987 after he was ever-present in that year's Third Division title triumph. Two players - Shaun Teale and Eddie Howe - have won the award in two consecutive seasons. Several players have won the award in their first season at Dean Court, among them Claus Jorgensen, Gerry Peyton, Luther Blissett and Steve Cotterill. The overall list of winners in the competition's history is: Gerry Peyton (1987), Paul Morrell (1988), Luther Blissett (1989), Shaun Teale (1990 and 1991), Kevin Bond (1992), Mark Morris (1993), Steve Cotterill (1994), Steve Fletcher (1995), Matt Holland (1996), Ian Cox (1997), Eddie Howe (1998 and 1999), Claus Jorgensen (2000), Wade Elliott (2001), Warren Feeney (2002) and Carl Fletcher (2003). The AFC Bournemouth Exiles Club also vote for their Player of the Season. The winners since 1988 are: Trevor Aylott (1988), Ian Bishop (1989), Shaun Teale (1990 and 1991), Kevin Bond (1992), Mark Morris (1993), Alex Watson (1994), Neil Young (1995), Matt Holland (1996), Ian Cox (1997), Eddie Howe (1998 and 1999), Claus Jorgensen (2000), Jason Tindall (2001), Warren Feeney (2002) and Carl Fletcher (2003).

SECRETARIES

AFC Bournemouth has been well served by six different club secretaries since the Second World War. Prior to this, the role of secretary and manager was usually combined and Cherries' first secretary of the modern style was Tommy Locks. Appointed in July 1939, having spent three years as assistant secretary, he held the post until July 1949, when he emigrated to Australia after marrying Dick Mellor's daughter, Peggy. He was replaced as secretary by Harry Stace who remained at Dean Court for a record 27 years until retiring in May 1976, ably assisted by Ron Miller for much of that period. Accountant Graham Mackrell was then secretary until leaving to join Luton Town in a similar capacity in November 1981, and became secretary of Sheffield Wednesday and West Ham. He was succeeded by Cynthia Dowsett, the wife of former Cherries' player and commercial manager Dickie Dowsett, then ex-Aston Villa star Brian Tiler was managing director and secretary for six years until resigning shortly before his tragic death in July 1990. The post has since been held by his assistant Keith MacAlister who first joined the club's fund-raising department 33 years ago.

TRAINERS

Trainers Arthur Cunliff and John Kirk gave Cherries outstanding service and both had a testimonial at Dean Court. Former outside-left Arthur Cunliffe joined Blackburn Rovers from Chorley in January 1928 and was capped twice by England before moving to Aston Villa with Ronnie Dix in May 1933. He then played for Middlesbrough, Burnley and Hull City prior to joining Rochdale in August 1945 and became their trainer. Reunited with Jack Bruton at Dean Court as trainer-physio from June 1950 until retiring in May 1974, he remained local until his death in August 1986 and his widow Betty is a Cherries season-ticket holder. Ex-goalkeeper John Kirk represented the National Association of Boys' Clubs and was briefly with Arthur Cunliffe as a Rochdale amateur in 1945/46. He played for Peterborough United during RAF service and then turned professional with Bolton Wanderers. After a serious knee injury, he moved via Dartford to Poole Town in August 1952 and became their trainer in July 1960. He was also assistant groundsman at Dean Park prior to becoming Cherries' assistant-trainer in September 1964 then was

trainer and kitman until retiring in May 1993. His son of the same name is one of Cherries' keenest supporters.

TRANSFERS

AFC Bournemouth's record incoming and outgoing transfers are Gavin Peacock and Matt Holland respectively. Ex-England Youth midfielder Gavin Peacock joined Cherries from Gillingham for a record £250,000 in August 1989. The club's first five-figure signing was Ted MacDougall from York City for £10,000 in July 1969 and Phil Boyer followed him to Dean Court for a then record £20,000 in December 1970. The £70,000 paid for Cardiff City's Brian Clark in October 1972 remained a record until Shaun Close arrived from Spurs for £90,000 in February 1988, while Cherries' first six-figure signing was Bobby Barnes from Swindon Town for £100,000 in March 1989. For outgoing transfers, the £220,000 sale of ace marksman MacDougall to Manchester United in September 1972 was a record until Colin Clarke's £400,000 transfer to Southampton in June 1986. Ian Bishop was sold to Manchester City for £465,000 in August 1989 before Efan Ekoku joined Norwich City for £765,000 in March 1993. Midfielder Joe Parkinson joined Everton in March 1994 in a deal rising to a similar amount Current Eire international Matt Holland was sold to Ipswich Town for a record £800,000 in July 1997.

YOUTH DEVELOPMENT

Many fine young players have progressed through the ranks at AFC Bournemouth. Notable post-war graduates from Dean Court include England internationals Kevin Reeves and Jamie Redknapp who both attended Twynham Comprehensive School in Christchurch, as did current goalkeeper Neil Moss. The Cherries were FA Youth Cup semi-finalists in 1968/69 and Freddie Cox did much to promote youth development, with the likes of John Hold, Eddie Rowles, Dennis Longhorn and David Jones gaining early first-team chances. Ace talent spotter Reg Tyrrell discovered starlets such as Ian Cunningham, Mark Nightingale, Howard Goddard and Kevin Reeves. The successful youth policy was then scrapped as an economy measure and managers like David Webb and Harry Redknapp tended to recruit older players. Mel Machin and current boss Sean O'Driscoll have both been keen to promote young talent including England U-21 star Eddie Howe, while the likes of England international Rio Ferdinand, and current hot-shot Jermain Defoe have gained valuable experience on loan to Cherries from West Ham.

Cartoons such as these from the Bournemouth Echo were a regular feature of the sports pages for much of the first half of the 20th century

INTRODUCTION TO THE STATISTICS PAGES

The season-by-season grids show the results of games in all major competitions, including the Football League, F.A. Cup, Football League Cup, Third Division (South) Cup, the Full Members' Cup and the Associate Members' Cup. The latter competition has been played under a number of sponsor's names and is currently the LDV Vans Trophy. Boscombe's three post-World War One seasons in the Southern League are included.

Home games are identified by the opponent's name in upper case, away games by the use of lower case. Bournemouth's score is always given first. Attendances for League games are taken from the official Football League records for seasons 1925/26 to 2000/01; for other seasons attendances based on newspaper reports have been used.

Substitutes, from season 1965/66 onwards, have the numbers 12, 13 and 14. Number 12 is used if only one substitute was used (no matter what number was on the player's shirt). The players replaced are underlined.

A full player list is provided for every player who has made a Football League appearance. Date and place of birth are shown, where known, and the year of death. Players with the same name are given a (1) or (2) after their name to avoid confusion. The next two columns, "seasons played", act as an index to the season-by-season grids. The years shown are the "first year" of the season; for example, 1971 is season 1971/72. The two columns show the season in which the player made his first team debut; and the final season that he played. However, if he only played in one season, the second column is blank. An entry of "2002" in the second column does not imply that the player has left the club, but means that he appeared in the "final season" (2002/03) of the book.

Note that some players also made F.A. Cup appearances before 1920/21 and in 1945/46. If a player also made a League appearance his F.A. Cup appearances from these seasons are included in the list. Previous and next clubs show where he was transferred from, and the club he moved to. Non-league club information is included when known.

The appearance columns have separate totals for the League, F.A. Cup, Football League Cup and the other minor tournaments. "Goals scored" are also shown under the four headings. If a player has had more than one spell at the club playing first team football, a consolidated set of appearance and goals are shown on the first line. Subsequent lines show the seasons involved on his return to the club, and his new pair of previous and next clubs.

A full record of meetings against all other League clubs (in the Football League) is included. Some clubs have played under different names, but the totals are consolidated under the present day name in this table. Final League tables are also included.

BOSCOMBE'S F.A. CUP RECORD TO 1919/20

1909/10

Rd	Month	Day	Opponent	Score	Scorers	Att	1	2	3	4	5	6	7	8	9	10	11
PR	Sep	18	B'mouth Gas Works	0-0		800	Bennett P	Edney A	Adams	New JP	Cassidy W	Taylor P	Marsh C	Parsley G	Penton B	Bleathman J	Lean T
rep		22	B'mouth Gas Works	2-1	Penton 2	1000	Bennett P	Lean T	Giles PS	New JP	Cassidy W	Taylor P	Marsh C	Parsley G	Penton B	Bleathman J	Manns E
Q1	Oct	2	Poole	2-3	Penton 2	1000	Bennett P	Lean T	Adams	Cassidy W	Small JC	Taylor P	Marsh C	Parsley G	Penton B	Kitcher V	Manns E

Boscombe's ground of insufficient standard for the FA Cup - all matches played away

1910/11

Rd	Month	Day	Opponent	Score	Scorers	Att	1	2	3	4	5	6	7	8	9	10	11
Q1	Oct	1	Weymouth	4-3	Penton 3, Whiterow	500	Bennett P	Lean T	Giles PS	New JP	Small JC	Cassidy W	Marsh C	Parsley G	Penton B	Whiterow F	Manns E
Q2		15	Poole	0-0		700	Bennett P	Lean T	Giles PS	New JP	Small JC	Parsley G	Marsh C	Dorey M	Parsley C	Whiterow F	Manns E
rep		19	Poole	4-1	Penton 2, Wellstead, Marsh	300	Bennett P	Lean T	Giles PS	Cassidy W	Small JC	Parsley G	Marsh C	Wellstead C	Penton B	Smith GE	Manns E
Q3	Nov	5	Torquay Town	0-1		2000	Bennett P	Lean T	Giles PS	New JP	Small JC	Parsley G	Marsh C	Bleathman J	Penton B	Whiterow F	Manns E

Boscombe's ground of insufficient standard for the FA Cup - all matches played away

1911/12

Did not enter

1912/13

Rd	Month	Day	Opponent	Score	Scorers	Att	1	2	3	4	5	6	7	8	9	10	11
PR	Sep	28	PORTLAND	6-0	Smith 2 (1p), Whiterow 2, Tarrant 2	2000	Clarkson W	Parsley G	Giles PS	New JP	Small JC	Taylor P	Blanchard P	Smith GE	Tarrant B	Whiterow F	Bleathman J
Q1	Oct	12	Gosport United	1-1	Tarrant	1000	Clarkson W	Parsley G	Giles PS	New JP	Small JC	Taylor P	Blanchard P	Smith GE	Tarrant B	Whiterow F	Bleathman J
rep		16	GOSPORT UNITED	7-1	Blanchard 3, Whiterow 2, Tarrant 2	2000	Clarkson W	Parsley G	Giles PS	New JP	Small JC	Taylor P	Blanchard P	Smith GE	Tarrant B	Whiterow F	Bleathman J
Q2	Nov	2	BASINGSTOKE	3-1	Small, Smith, Whiterow	2000	Clarkson W	Parsley G	Giles PS	New JP	Small JC	Taylor P	Bleathman J	Tarrant B	Smith GE	Whiterow F	Manns E
Q3		16	1st KINGS RR CORPS	0-0		2000	Clarkson W	Parsley G	Giles PS	Tarrant B	Small JC	Taylor P	Bleathman J	Smith GE	Gill A	Whiterow F	Manns E
rep		20	Ist Kings RR Corps	0-1		1000	Clarkson W	Parsley G	Giles PS	Tarrant B	Small JC	Taylor P	Bleathman J	Smith GE	Newell	Whiterow F	Manns E

PR drawn away but switched to Boscombe by arrangement. 1st King's Royal Rifle Corps played at Eggar's Hill, Aldershot

1913/14

Rd	Month	Day	Opponent	Score	Scorers	Att	1	2	3	4	5	6	7	8	9	10	11
PR	Sep	27	Royal Engineers, Aldershot	2-1	Penton, Smith	1000	Clarkson W	Parsley G	Giles PS	Colbourne W	Small JC	Taylor P	Blanchard P	Smith GE	Penton B	Whiterow F	Phillips HC
Q1	Oct	11	Cowes	3-2	Smith, Penton 2	1000	Clarkson W	Parsley G	Giles PS	New JP	Small JC	Taylor P	Blanchard P	Smith GE	Penton B	Whiterow F	Phillips HC
Q2	Nov	1	BOURNEMOUTH	0-1		2000	Clarkson W	Parsley G	Giles PS	New JP	Small JC	Taylor P	Blanchard P	Smith GE	Penton B	Whiterow F	Phillips HC

1914/15

Rd	Month	Day	Opponent	Score	Scorers	Att	1	2	3	4	5	6	7	8	9	10	11
PR	Sep	26	RGA WEYMOUTH		walkover												
Q1	Oct	10	B'MOUTH TRAMWAYS		walkover												
Q2		24	Thornycrofts Athletic	6-1	Smith 2, Prince, Powell 2, Peel	1000	Kitchen GW	Parsley G	Glover HV	Peel AW	Small JC	Whiterow F	Mouncher S	Smith GE	Prince P	Powell H	Shaw F
Q3	Nov	7	Cowes	1-0	Smith	1000	Kitchen GW	Parsley G	Glover HV	Peel AW	Small JC	Whiterow F	Mouncher S	Smith GE	Prince P	Powell H	Shaw F
Q4		21	WELTON ROVERS	2-1	Powell 2	2000	Kitchen GW	Parsley G	Glover HV	Peel AW	Campbell AK	Whiterow F	Charlton D	Powell H	Prince P	Smith GE	Dempsey T
Q5	Dec	5	BRENTFORD	0-0		4000	Kitchen GW	Peel AW	Glover HV	Taylor P	Campbell AK	Whiterow F	Shaw F	Charlton D	Prince P	Powell H	Dempsey T
rep		9	Brentford	1-0	Powell	2000	Kitchen GW	Peel AW	Glover HV	Taylor P	Campbell AK	Whiterow F	Shaw F	Charlton D	Prince P	Powell H	Dempsey T
Q6		19	Bristol Rovers	0-3		3000	Kitchen GW	Peel AW	Glover HV	Taylor P	Campbell AK	Whiterow F	Shaw F	Prince P	Smith GE	Powell H	Dempsey T

"RGA" is Royal Garrison Artillery. PR game drawn away, switched to Dean Court, but RGA then scratched.

Thornycrofts Athletic based in Basingstoke

Q4 drawn away but switched to Dean Court for a financial consideration

1919/20

Rd	Month	Day	Opponent	Score	Scorers	Att	1	2	3	4	5	6	7	8	9	10	11
PR	Sep	27	POOLE ST MARY'S	9-0	* see below	2000	Heron AA	Parsley G	Perrett F	Colbourne WR	White H	Welsted	Blanchard	Dunford ER	Clapson	New J	Chalcraft
Q1	Oct	11	Basingstoke	0-1		1500	Heron AA	Parsley G	Perrett F	Colbourne WR	White H	Whiterow F	Watts	Dunford ER	Clapson	New J	Chalcraft

Scorers in PR: Dunford 3, New, Chalcraft 2, Clapson, White, Blanchard

Boscombe 1920/21

5th in the Southern League

						Barnes F	Brighton HG	Cherrett PAM	Colbourne WR	Dempsey	Diaper	Dunford ER	Ferguson CF	Garrett A	Heron AA	Lamb JF	Lawson MB	Leavey HJ	Marshall E	Marshall G	Marshall KC	Martland R	Meyer HJ	New JP	Parsley G	Ramsay EE	Sharp	Smith G	Wakeley F	Whitcher	White H	Wilson
1	Sep 4	THORNYCROFTS	1-0	Whitcher	3000				4	11		8	5		1	3		6							2		9		10	7		
2	11	LUTON TOWN RES.	2-1	Dempsey, Wakeley	3000				4	11		8	5		1	3		6							2		10		9	7		
3	18	Luton Town Res.	0-0						4	11		8	5		1	3		6							2		10		9	7		
4	25	Gillingham Res.	1-6	Dunford					4			8	5		1	3	11	6					10		2				9	7		
5	Oct 2	MILLWALL RES.	2-3	Dunford, Leavey	3000				4			8	5			3	11	10			1				2				9	7	6	
6	16	GILLINGHAM RES.	5-2	Wakeley, Dunford, Smith 3	2000				2			8	5		1	3	11	6							4			10	9	7		
7	Nov 6	SOUTHAMPTON RES.	2-0	Martland 2	4000				4		5	8			1	3	11	6				9			2			10		7		
8	Dec 11	Thornycrofts (Woolston)	1-1	Leavey (p)					4		6	8			1	3		11				5			2			10	9	7		
9	18	PORTSMOUTH RES.	1-0	Leavey	3000			9	4		6	8		11	1	3		10				5			2				7			
10	Jan 1	Brighton & HA Res.	0-7				7	9	4		6			11	1	3		10				5			2				8			
11	8	READING RES.	3-0	* See below	4000	8		9	4		6			11		3		10			1	5			2				7			
12	22	BRIGHTON & HA RES.	3-2	Cherrett, Smith, Leavey	3000			9	2		6				1	3	11	8				5		4				10	7			
13	Feb 12	Southampton Res.	0-0					9	4					11	1	3		8				5		6	2			10	7			
14	19	CHARLTON ATH. RES.	1-0	Cherrett	3000			9	4					11	1	3		8				5		6	2			10	7			
15	23	Portsmouth Res.	0-0			7		9	4					11	1	3		8				5		6	2			10				
16	26	Reading Res.	0-1			7		9	4						1	3		8				5		6	2			10	11			
17	Mar 5	Chatham	0-2					9	4						1	3	11	8				5		6	2			10	7			
18	12	CHATHAM	1-0	Garrett	3000		7		4			8		11	1	3						5		6	2			10	9			
19	19	Watford Res.	0-4						4			8		11	1	3						5		6	2			10	7			
20	Apr 9	NORWICH C RES.	1-0	Brighton	3000		8								1	3			6			5				2		10		7		9
21	16	WATFORD RES.	0-0		2000		8								1	3			6			5						10		7		9
22	23	Charlton Ath. Res.	1-5	Smith					4			8			1	3			6	11		5			2			10	7			9
23	25	Millwall Res.	0-6						4			8				3			6	11	1	5			2			10	7			9
24	30	Norwich C Res.	0-0						4		6	8								11	1	5	10		2	3		9	7			
					Apps	3	4	9	22	3	7	14	6	8	20	23	6	17	4	3	4	18	2	8	21	2	3	16	20	10	1	4
					Goals		1	3		1		3		1				5				3						5	2	1		

Scorers in game 11: Cherrett, Martland (p), Leavey
Played in one game; W Heron (21, at 2), Hillier (19, 9),
Cornick played at 11 in games 20 and 21
G Manson played at 4 in games 20 and 21.

F.A. Cup

						Barnes F	Brighton HG	Cherrett PAM	Colbourne WR	Dempsey	Diaper	Dunford ER	Ferguson CF	Garrett A	Heron AA	Lamb JF	Lawson MB	Leavey HJ	Marshall E	Marshall G	Marshall KC	Martland R	Meyer HJ	New JP	Parsley G	Ramsay EE	Sharp	Smith G	Wakeley F	Whitcher	White H	Wilson
Q1	Oct 9	BLANDFORD	1-1	Parsley (p)	3000				4			8	5			3		10			1		11		2				9	7	6	
rep	13	Blandford	1-2	Parsley (p)	2000							8	6		1			11				5		4	2			10	9	7		

Played at 3 in replay: F Perrett

		P	W	D	L	F	A	Pts
1	Brighton & Hove A. Res	24	16	3	5	65	29	35
2	Portsmouth Res	24	13	7	4	44	20	33
3	Millwall Res	24	12	4	8	46	24	28
4	Southampton Res	24	10	7	7	53	35	27
5	BOSCOMBE	24	10	6	8	25	40	26
6	Reading Res	24	11	3	10	41	34	25
7	Luton Town Res	24	8	8	8	38	35	24
8	Charlton Ath. Res	24	8	8	8	41	41	24
9	Watford Res	24	9	4	11	43	45	22
10	Norwich City Res	24	7	7	10	31	39	21
11	Gillingham Res	24	6	5	13	32	47	17
12	Chatham	24	5	6	13	24	49	16
13	Thornycrofts	24	4	6	14	29	74	14

Boscombe 1921/22

7th in the Southern League

No	Date	Opponent	Score	Scorers	Att	Bailey WG	Brighton HG	Cartmell JR	Cobb HG	Colbourne WR	Frost HV	Harrison HF	Heron AA	Lamb JF	Leavey HJ	Lewry WG	Manson G	Marshall KC	Matthews VE	Mavin FJ	Meader E	Meyer HJ	New JP	Noble AH	Parsley G	Ramsay EE	Saxton E	Smith G	Wakeley F	Watts AG	White H	Wingham HC	Young W
1	Aug 27	Portsmouth Res.	1-0	Bailey		10		11		4	6		1	3	8	9							5	7			2						
2	Sep 3	PORTSMOUTH RES.	0-1		4000	8		11		4	6			3	10	9		1					5	7			2						
3	7	LUTON TOWN RES.	1-0	Noble	2000			11		4	6			3	8	9		1				10	5	7			2						
4	10	NORWICH CITY RES.	2-1	Leavey, Bailey	4000	9		11		4	6			3	8			1				10	5	7			2						
5	17	Norwich City Res.	2-1	Lewry, Mavin		8		11		4				3		9		1		5		10	6	7			2						
6	21	READING RES.	1-0	Leavey	2000	10		11		4				3	8	9		1		5			6	7			2						
7	Oct 15	Luton Town Res.	0-4			10		11		4			1	3	8	9							6	7			2				5		
8	19	CHARLTON ATH. RES.	1-1	Meyer	2000			11		4			1	3	8	9				5		10	6	7			2						
9	24	Millwall Res.	0-3					11					1	3	4	9				5		10	6	7			2		8				
10	29	GUILDFORD UNITED	2-0	Meader, Meyer	4000			11		4			1	3	8		6				9	10		7			2				5		
11	Nov 12	GILLINGHAM RES.	2-5	Colbourne (p), Cartmell	3000			11		4			1	3	8	9			5			10		7			2					6	
12	19	Watford Res.	0-6				4											1			9				2	3		10	8	6			7
13	26	WATFORD RES.	1-0	Bailey	3000	9		11					1	3	5				6		8	10		7			2					4	
14	Dec 10	SOUTHEND UTD. RES.	3-1	Meyer, Cartmell, Bailey	1700	8		11		4			1	3	6				5		9	10		7			2						
15	24	BATH CITY	2-0	Bailey, Noble	3000	8		11		4			1	3	6				5		9	10		7			2						
16	26	Southampton Res.	0-2			8		11		4			1	3	6				5		9	10		7			2						
17	27	SOUTHAMPTON RES.	2-0	Bailey, Meader	5000	8		11		4			1	3					5		9	10		7			2					6	
18	Jan 4	Southend Utd. Res.	1-1	Cartmell		8		11		4			1	3		6			5		9	10					2		7				
19	7	MILLWALL RES.	2-0	Meader, Meyer	2000	8		11		4			1	3					5		9	10					2		7			6	
20	21	Plymouth Argyle Res.	0-4			8		11		4			1	3					5		9	10					2		7			6	
21	28	PLYMOUTH ARG. RES.	0-3		2000	8				4			1	3	11				5		9	10					2		7			6	
22	Feb 4	Bristol City Res.	2-3	Bailey, Smith		9		11		4			1	3					5			10					2	8	7			6	
23	8	Reading Res.	2-0	Meyer, Matthews		9		11		4			1	3					5			10					2	8	7			6	
24	11	BRISTOL CITY RES.	1-1	Bailey	2000	9		11		4			1	3					5			10					2	8	7			6	
25	18	Exeter City Res.	0-1			9		11		4			1	3					5			10					2	8	7			6	
26	25	Bath City	0-3			9		11					1	3		4	2		5			10						8	7			6	
27	Mar 4	BRIGHTON &HA RES.	0-0		2300	8		11		4			1	2					5		9	10				3			7			6	
28	11	Brighton & HA Res,	0-0			8		11		4			1	3	6				5		9	10		7								2	
29	18	SWINDON TOWN RES.	1-0	Cartmell	2000			9	11	4			1	3	8		6		5			10		7			2						
30	25	Swindon Town Res.	2-1	Meader, Matthews				11		4		9	1	3	10				5		8			7			2					6	
31	Apr 1	Guildford United	1-5	Harrison				11		4		9	1	3	10	6			5		8			7								2	
32	3	Charlton Ath. Res.	0-2					9	11	4			1	3	10				5		8			7	2							6	
33	15	Bristol Rovers Res.	2-0	Smith, Wingham					11				1	3	4	9			5		8			7			2	10				6	
34	17	EXETER CITY RES.	2-0	Noble (p), Smith	2000				11			9	1	3	4				5		8			7			2	10				6	
35	22	BRISTOL ROVERS RES.	2-1	Meader, Noble	2000				11			9	1	3	4				5		8			7	2			10				6	
36	29	Gillingham Res.	0-5						11			9	1	3	4				5		8			7	2			10				6	
					Apps	22	1	30	6	28	4	5	30	35	24	13	3	6	25	4	20	24	9	25	4	2	28	10	12	1	2	20	1
					Goals	8		4		1		1			2	1			2	1	5	5		4				3				1	

Fielded the reserve team on Nov 19 (first team in FA Cup action)
Played in this game: E Marshall (5), H Phillips (11).

F.A. Cup

Rd	Date	Opponent	Score	Scorers	Att	Bailey WG	Brighton HG	Cartmell JR	Cobb HG	Colbourne WR	Frost HV	Harrison HF	Heron AA	Lamb JF	Leavey HJ	Lewry WG	Manson G	Marshall KC	Matthews VE	Mavin FJ	Meader E	Meyer HJ	New JP	Noble AH	Parsley G	Ramsay EE	Saxton E	Smith G	Wakeley F	Watts AG	White H	Wingham HC	Young W
PR	Sep 24	ROYAL GARRISON ART.	2-0	Meyer, New	3000			11		4				3	8	9		1				10	6	7			2				5		
Q1	Oct 8	Bournemouth	0-0		4000	10		11		4			1	3	8	9				5			6	7			2						
rep	12	BOURNEMOUTH	6-0	* See below	3000	10		11		4			1	3	8	9							6	7			2				5		
Q2	22	THORNYCROFTS	1-0	Saxton (p)	2000			11		4			1	3	8							10	6	7			2		9		5		
Q3	Nov 5	Harland & Wolff	3-2	Lewry, Colbourne, Meyer	2000			11		4				3	8	9		1				10	6	7			2				5		
Q4	19	Torquay United	1-0	Meyer	4000	9		11		4			1	3	8							10	6	7			2				5		
Q5	Dec 3	Swansea Town	0-4		10795	9		11		4			1	3	6							10	8	7			2				5		

Scorers in Q1 replay: Leavey, Bailey 3, Lewry, Breaker (og)

Boscombe were drawn away to the 1st Reserve Brigade, Royal Garrison Artillery (of Farnham) in the PR.
The Brigade had left Farnham for Woolwich, which was outside the geographical area for Boscombe's division of the Cup.
The Brigade withdrew from the Hampshire League, but remained in the Cup; the venue was switched.

Thornycrofts is Thornycrofts (Woolston)

		P	W	D	L	F	A	Pts
1	Plymouth Argyle Res	36	22	5	9	91	38	49
2	Bristol City Res	36	18	8	10	73	50	44
3	Portsmouth Res	36	17	10	9	63	41	44
4	Southampton Res	36	19	5	12	70	47	43
5	Gillingham Res	36	17	9	10	65	47	43
6	Charlton Ath. Res	36	18	6	12	69	54	42
7	BOSCOMBE	36	17	5	14	38	55	39
8	Luton Town Res	36	17	4	15	50	54	38
9	Watford Res	36	15	7	14	65	53	37
10	Brighton & Hove A Res	36	12	13	11	60	52	37
11	Bath City	36	16	5	15	55	53	37
12	Swindon Town Res	36	14	7	15	59	46	35
13	Bristol Rovers Res	36	13	7	16	50	82	33
14	Millwall Res	36	13	4	19	49	53	30
15	Reading Res	36	11	7	18	46	59	29
16	Exeter City Res	36	10	9	17	42	63	29
17	Guildford United	36	11	6	19	44	56	28
18	Norwich City Res	36	10	6	20	47	88	26
19	Southend United Res	36	9	3	24	47	92	21

Boscombe 1922/23

2nd in the Southern League

							Armstrong JW	Brown EA	Budden WL	Butt LG	Davey HH	Duff D	Harrison HF	Heron AA	James WE	Kelsall A	Lamb JF	Marshall KC	Matthews VE	Meyer HJ	New JP	Parsley G	Phillips H	Saxton E	Smith CF	Smith G	Turner F	Wakeley F	Watts AG	Wingham HC	Young W
1	Aug	26	Torquay United	1-0	Kelsall									1	11	10	3		5			2						7		6	
2	Sep	2	COVENTRY CITY RES.	0-0		3700				4	9			1	11	10	3		5	8		2						7		6	
3		9	Southend United Res	2-1	Davey 2					4	9			1	11	10	3		5	8		2						7	6		
4		13	Exeter City Res	1-2	Matthews					4	9			1	11		3		5	8		2						7		6	
5		16	SWINDON TOWN RES.	1-1	Devey	4000		11		4	9			1	10		3		5	8		2						7		6	
6		30	YEOVIL & PETTERS UTD.	4-0	Meyer 2, James 2	3000				4	9			1	10		3		5	8			11	2				7		6	
7	Oct	11	EXETER CITY RES.	2-1	Davey, James	2000				4	9		8	1	11		3		5	10				2				7		6	
8		14	Reading Res.	3-0	James, Meyer, Davey					4	9			1	10		3		5	8			11	2				7		6	
9		28	BATH CITY	0-0		2000				4	9	10		1	11		3		5	8				2				7		6	
10	Nov	13	Millwall Res.	3-1	Davey 3					4	9			1	10		3		5	8			11	2				7		6	
11		25	BRISTOL ROVERS RES.	2-2	Meyer, Turner	1500				4				1	10		3		5	8		2				11	9	7		6	
12	Dec	2	PORTSMOUTH RES.	0-1		4000	10							1	11		3		5	8	4			2		9		7		6	
13		9	Portsmouth Res.	3-2	Turner 2, Watts		8							1	10		3		5					2		11	9	7	6	4	
14		16	READING RES.	2-0	Armstrong, Wingham	3000	8							1	10		3		5					2		11	9	7	6	4	
15		25	Southampton Res.	0-1			8				9			1	11		3		5					2			10	7	6	4	
16		26	SOUTHAMPTON RES.	2-0	Davey, James	5000	10				9			1	11		3		5	8				2				7	6	4	
17	Jan	6	BRISTOL CITY RES.	3-2	Meyer 2, Davey	4000	10			5	9			1	11		3			8				2				7	6	4	
18		13	Bristol Rovers Res.	0-1						4	9			1	10		3		5	8				2		11				6	7
19		20	SOUTHEND UTD. RES.	2-0	Meyer 2	2500				4	9			1	10		3		5	8			11	2				7		6	
20		27	Coventry City Res	1-0	Meyer					4	9			1	10		3			8			11	2	5			7		6	
21	Feb	10	PLYMOUTH ARG. RES.	1-1	Davey	3000	10			4	9			1	11		3			8				2	5			7		6	
22		17	BRIHGTON & HA RES.	4-1	James 2 (1p), Meyer, Armstrong	2000	10			4	9				11			1		8				2	5			7	6	3	
23		24	Brighton & HA Res.	0-3			10			4	9				11		3	1		8				2	5			7		6	
24	Mar	3	Watford Res.	4-1	James, Meyer, C Smith, Davey		10			4	9				11		3			8				1	5			7	6	2	
25		10	WATFORD RES.	5-0	Davey, Meyer 2, Armstrong, James	3000	10			4	9				11		3			8				1	5			7	6	2	
26		21	Swindon Town Res	3-1	Budden, Wakeley, James		8		10	4	9			1	11		3							2				7	6	5	
27		24	LUTON TOWN RES.	2-0	Armstrong, Davey	3000	8		10	4	9			1	11		3							2	5			7		6	
28		30	GUILDFORD UNITED	2-0	Davey, James	4000	10		8	4	9			1	11		3							2	5			7		6	
29	Apr	2	Guildford United	1-2	James (p)		10		8	4	9			1	11		3							2	5			7		6	
30		7	TORQUAY UNITED	0-0		3000	10		8	4	9			1	11		3							2				7	6	5	
31		11	Plymouth Argyle Res.	0-3			10		8	4	9			1	11		3							2	5			7	6		
32		14	NORWICH CITY RES.	2-1	Davey, C Smith	3000	10		8	4	9			1	11		3							2	5			7		6	
33		18	Bristol City Res.	2-3	Wakeley, Davey		8			4	9			1	11		3						10	2	5			7		6	
34		21	Norwich City Res.	2-1	Armstrong, Davey		10		8	7	9			1	11		3							2	5				6	4	
35		25	Luton Town Res.	0-0			10		8	4	9			1	11		3							2	5			7		6	
36		28	Bath City	1-2	Davey		10		8		9			1	11		3							2	5			7	6	4	
37	May	2	MILLWALL RES.	3-0	Davey 2, Armstrong	2000	10		8	4	9			1	11		3							2	5			7		6	
38		5	Yeovil & Petters United	3-0	Butt, Davey 2				10	8	9			1	11		3							2	5			7	6	4	
						Apps	23	1	12	31	33	1	1	34	38	3	37	2	18	21	1	6	6	32	17	5	4	36	15	36	1
						Goals	6		1	1	23				12	1			1	13					2		3	2	1	1	

Played in game one only: Drinkwater (9), J Green (8), M Guy (4)
Kirkpatrick played at 10 in game 4

F.A. Cup

							Armstrong JW	Brown EA	Budden WL	Butt LG	Davey HH	Duff D	Harrison HF	Heron AA	James WE	Kelsall A	Lamb JF	Marshall KC	Matthews VE	Meyer HJ	New JP	Parsley G	Phillips H	Saxton E	Smith CF	Smith G	Turner F	Wakeley F	Watts AG	Wingham HC	Young W
PR	Sep	23	BLANDFORD	3-0	Phillips, Meyer, Davey	2000				4	9			1	10		3		5	8		2	11					7		6	
Q1	Oct	7	B'mouth Tramways	2-1	Meyer, Wakeley	4300				4	9			1	11		3		5	8				2		10		7		6	
Q2		21	SHOLING ATHLETIC	2-1	James 2	3000				4	9	10		1	11		3		5	8				2				7		6	
Q3	Nov	4	GOSPORT ATHLETIC	4-0	James 3, Davey	2000				4	9			1	10		3		5	8				2				7		6	
Q4		18	Exeter City	0-0		5900				4	9			1	10		3		5	8			11	2				7		6	
rep		22	EXETER CITY	1-3	G Smith	5000				4	9			1	10		3		5	8				2		11		7		6	

DW Hayward played at 11 in Q3

		P	W	D	L	F	A	Pts
1	Bristol City Res	38	24	5	9	84	39	53
2	BOSCOMBE	38	22	7	9	67	34	51
3	Portsmouth Res	38	23	3	12	93	51	49
4	Bristol Rovers Res	38	20	8	10	59	41	48
5	Plymouth Argyle Res	38	20	7	11	74	41	47
6	Torquay United	38	18	8	12	63	38	44
7	Brighton & Hove A Res	38	20	3	15	95	60	43
8	Luton Town Res	38	16	11	11	67	56	43
9	Southend United Res	38	18	6	14	69	68	42
10	Southampton Res	38	18	5	15	65	54	41
11	Reading Res	38	15	10	13	61	55	40
12	Millwall Res	38	15	8	15	56	61	38
13	Coventry City Res	38	15	7	16	65	59	37
14	Guildford United	38	13	6	19	54	73	32
15	Swindon Town Res	38	10	8	20	44	71	28
16	Bath City	38	11	6	21	34	79	28
17	Watford Res	38	10	6	22	56	104	26
18	Yeovil & Petters Utd.	38	9	7	22	42	68	25
19	Norwich City Res	38	10	5	23	43	81	25
20	Exeter City Res	38	7	6	25	37	95	20

1923/24

21st in Division Three (South)

			Opponent	Score	Scorers	Att	Armstrong JW	Budden WL	Butt LG	Davey HH	Donowa GW	Harrison HF	Heron AA	Lamb JF	Leitch W	Lister JS	Lock H	Marshall KC	Miller J (Jimmy)	Robinson F	Saxton E	Simpson A	Smith CF	Tait J	Voisey WT	Walker JH	Whelpton JI	Wingham HC
1	Aug	25	Swindon Town	1-3	Lister	9545			4	9			1	3		8			7	11		10	5		6			2
2	Sep	1	SWINDON TOWN	0-0		6614	10		4	9				3		8			7	11			5		6		1	2
3		5	Watford	0-0		5561	10		4	9			1	3		8			7	11			5		6			2
4		8	Exeter City	2-0	Davey, Lister	6500	10		4	9			1	3		8			7	11			5		6			2
5		15	EXETER CITY	1-0	Davey	6000	10		4	9			1	3		8			7	11			5		6			2
6		19	WATFORD	1-1	Davey (p)	4000	10		4	9			1	3	6	8			7	11					5			2
7		22	Aberdare Athletic	0-1		5000	10		4	9			1	3		8			7	11			5		6			2
8		29	ABERDARE ATHLETIC	0-1		5000	10		4	9			1	3		8			7	11			5		6			2
9	Oct	6	Norwich City	1-1	Davey (p)	11000	10		8	9			1	3		4			7	11			5		6			2
10		13	NORWICH CITY	1-2	Davey (p)	5000	10		4	8			1	3		9			7	11			5		6			2
11		20	MILLWALL	2-0	Davey, Lister	6000	10		4	9			1	3	5	8			7	11					6			2
12		27	Millwall	2-4	Lister, Davey	18000	10		4	9			1	3	5	8			7	11					6			2
13	Nov	3	Southend United	1-1	Armstrong	7000	10		4				1	3	5	8			7	11				9	6			2
14		10	SOUTHEND UNITED	0-1		5000	10		4	9			1	3	5	8			7	11					6			2
15		17	Reading	2-1	Armstrong, Davey	8000	10		4	9			1	3	6				7	11	2	8	5					
16		24	READING	0-0		4000	10		4	9			1	3	6				7	11	2		5		8			
17	Dec	1	Luton Town	2-6	Davey 2	7000	10		4	9			1	3	6				7	11	2		5		8			
18		8	LUTON TOWN	2-3	Davey, Voisey	3000	10		4	9			1	3	6				7	11	2		5		8			
19		15	BRIGHTON & HOVE ALB	1-0	Davey	5000			4	9			1	3	6				7	11	2	10	5		8			
20		22	Brighton & Hove Albion	0-5		6500			4	9			1	3	6	7				11	2	10	5		8			
21		25	BRENTFORD	2-4	Voisey, Davey	5000	10		4	9			1	3	6				7	11	2		5		8			
22		26	Brentford	0-2		8000			4					3	6	9			7	11	1	10	5		8			2
23		29	BRISTOL ROVERS	0-1		4000			4					3	6	9			7	11	1		5	10	8			2
24	Jan	5	Bristol Rovers	4-3	Lister 2, Davey, Robinson	8000	10		4	8				3	6	9	1		7	11	2		5					
25		19	SWANSEA TOWN	0-0		4500	10		4					3	6	9	1		7	11	2		5		8			
26		26	Swansea Town	0-1		15300	10	8	4					3	6	9	1		7	11	2		5					
27	Feb	2	Northampton Town	1-3	Simpson	7663	11	8	4					3	6	9	1		7		2	10	5					
28		9	NORTHAMPTON T	2-1	Lister, Simpson	5000	10	11	4					3	6	9	1		7		2	8	5					
29		16	Gillingham	0-1		5000	10	11	4					3	6	9	1		7		2	8	5					
30		23	GILLINGHAM	0-0		3000			4	11				3	6	9	1		7		2	8	5	10				
31	Mar	1	Queen's Park Rangers	1-0	Davey	8000		11	4	9				3	6		1		7		2	8	5	10				
32		8	QUEEN'S PARK RANGERS	3-1	Davey, Tait, Simpson	5000			4	9	11			3	6			1	7		2	8	5	10				
33		15	PLYMOUTH ARGYLE	0-0		6300			4	9				3	6			1	7	11	2	8	5	10				
34		22	Plymouth Argyle	0-4		9000			4	9				3	6	11	1		7		2		5	10		8		
35		29	Newport County	0-2		8000	10		4	9		7		3	6		1			11	2		5	8				
36	Apr	5	NEWPORT COUNTY	0-1		4000	10	8	4	9			1	3	6				7	11	2		5					
37		12	MERTHYR TOWN	3-3	Budden, Davey 2 (1p)	2221	10	11	4	8		7		3	6	9	1				2		5					
38		18	Portsmouth	0-3		20000	10	11	4	8			1	3	6	9			7		2		5					
39		19	Merthyr Town	2-4	Davey 2 (1p)	5000	8		4	9			1	3	6	11			7		2		5	10				
40		21	PORTSMOUTH	0-0		8926			8	9			1	3	6				7	11			5	10	4			2
41		26	CHARLTON ATHLETIC	1-0	Tait	3000			8	9		11		3	6		1		7				5	10	4			2
42	May	3	Charlton Athletic	2-1	Tait 2	1000			8	9		7		3	6		1			11	2		5	10	4			
						Apps	29	8	42	34	1	4	24	42	33	28	13	2	38	31	26	12	37	12	26	1	1	18
						Goals	2	1		20						7				1		3		4	2			

Average home attendance reported as 4697

F.A. Cup

Scratched from preliminary quailifying round when drawn away against Portsea Island Gas Company.
Draw made before the club were elected to the Football League.

		P	W	D	L	F	A	W	D	L	F	A	Pts
1	Portsmouth	42	15	3	3	57	11	9	8	4	30	19	59
2	Plymouth Argyle	42	13	6	2	46	15	10	3	8	24	19	55
3	Millwall	42	17	3	1	45	11	5	7	9	19	27	54
4	Swansea Town	42	18	2	1	39	10	4	6	11	21	38	52
5	Brighton & Hove Albion	42	16	4	1	56	12	5	5	11	12	25	51
6	Swindon Town	42	14	5	2	38	11	3	8	10	20	33	47
7	Luton Town	42	11	7	3	35	19	5	7	9	15	25	46
8	Northampton Town	42	14	3	4	40	15	3	8	10	24	32	45
9	Bristol Rovers	42	11	7	3	34	15	4	6	11	18	31	43
10	Newport County	42	15	4	2	39	15	2	5	14	17	49	43
11	Norwich City	42	13	5	3	45	18	3	3	15	15	41	40
12	Aberdare Athletic	42	9	9	3	35	18	3	5	13	10	40	38
13	Merthyr Town	42	11	8	2	33	19	0	8	13	12	46	38
14	Charlton Athletic	42	8	7	6	26	20	3	8	10	12	25	37
15	Gillingham	42	11	6	4	27	15	1	7	13	16	43	37
16	Exeter City	42	14	3	4	33	17	1	4	16	4	35	37
17	Brentford	42	9	8	4	33	21	5	0	16	21	50	36
18	Reading	42	12	2	7	35	20	1	7	13	16	37	35
19	Southend United	42	11	7	3	35	19	1	3	17	18	65	34
20	Watford	42	8	8	5	35	18	1	7	13	10	36	33
21	BOURNEMOUTH	42	6	8	7	19	19	5	3	13	21	46	33
22	Queen's Park Rangers	42	9	6	6	28	26	2	3	16	9	51	31

1924/25

20th in Division Three (South)

No	Date	Opponent	Score	Scorers	Att	Buchanan J	Budden WL	Butt LG	Charleston T	Clifford P	Davey HH	Eyre CR	Hayward DW	Heron AA	Lamb JF	Leitch W	Lowson EB	Maidment HW	Marshall GH	McCulloch MJ	McCulloch RG	Meyer HJ	Miles WP	Rattray HW	Readman JA	Richardson GWR	Roberts CL	Saxton E	Smith CF	Wilson GR
1	Aug 30	Millwall	1-3	Davey	25000	7		4			9				3	6					11		10	8				2	5	1
2	Sep 3	NORWICH CITY	0-0		6000	7		4			9				3	6					11		10	8				2	5	1
3	6	LUTON TOWN	2-1	Miles, Davey	6000	7		4	2		9				3	6					11		10	8					5	1
4	13	Gillingham	0-0		5000	7		4			9				3	6					11		10	8				2	5	1
5	20	SOUTHEND UNITED	1-0	Rattray	5000	7		4	2		9				3	6					11		10	8					5	1
6	27	BRIGHTON & HOVE ALB	0-0		6000	7		4	2		9				3	6					11		10	8					5	1
7	Oct 4	Plymouth Argyle	0-2		13000	7		4	2						3	6					11		10	8	9				5	1
8	9	Norwich City	3-6	Readman 2, Buchanan	4500	7	8	4	2						3	6		11					10		9				5	1
9	11	BRISTOL CITY	1-3	Miles	5000	7		4	2						3	6		11					10	8	9				5	1
10	18	Swindon Town	0-4		8000	7		8	2		9				3	6					11		10			4			5	1
11	22	BRENTFORD	2-0	Leitch, Readman	3000	7		4							3	8					11		10		9	6		2	5	1
12	25	Watford	1-2	Buchanan	5000	7		4							3	8					11		10		9	6		2	5	1
13	Nov 1	NORTHAMPTON T	1-2	Readman	1546	7		4							3	8							10	11	9	6		2	5	1
14	8	Charlton Athletic	2-2	Readman 2 (1p)	6000	7		4								8	3				11			10	9	6		2	5	1
15	22	Merthyr Town	1-3	Smith	5000										3	4		7			11	8		10	9	6		2	5	1
16	Dec 6	Swansea Town	0-1		15500			4			9				3	6		7			11		10		8			2	5	1
17	20	Bristol Rovers	0-1		8000			4		7	9				3	6					11		10				8	2	5	1
18	25	NEWPORT COUNTY	0-0		6000			4		7					3	6					11		10		9		8	2	5	1
19	26	Newport County	0-2		8000			4		7					3	6					11		10		9		8	2	5	1
20	Jan 3	Luton Town	2-0	Roberts, Eyre	5000			4		7		9			3	6	2				11		10				8		5	1
21	10	READING	0-0		6000			4		7		9			3	6	2				11		10				8		5	1
22	17	GILLINGHAM	3-0	Eyre 2 (1p), Miles	6000			4		7		9				6			3		11		10				8	2	5	1
23	24	Southend United	0-3		8000			4		7		9				6			3		11		10				8	2	5	1
24	Feb 7	PLYMOUTH ARGYLE	0-1		6878			4		7		9				6			3		11				10		8	2	5	1
25	11	MILLWALL	0-1		3000			4		7		9				6			3		11				10		8	2	5	1
26	14	Bristol City	1-2	R McCulloch	8000			4		7		9				5			3		11	10				6	8	2		1
27	21	SWINDON TOWN	0-0		5000		10	4		7		9				6			3		11						8	2	5	1
28	28	WATFORD	2-1	R McCulloch, Roberts	5000			4		7		9				6			3		11				10		8	2	5	1
29	Mar 7	Northampton Town	0-3		5000			4		7		9				6			3	10	11						8	2	5	1
30	11	Brighton & Hove Albion	1-0	Eyre	2000			4		7		9		1					3	10	11					6	8	2	5	
31	14	CHARLTON ATHLETIC	2-1	Roberts, Smith	5000			4		7		9				6			3	10	11						8	2	5	1
32	21	Queen's Park Rangers	2-0	Eyre, Roberts	7000			4		7		9				6			3	10	11						8	2	5	1
33	25	EXETER CITY	1-1	Smith	4000			4		7		9				6			3	10	11						8	2	5	1
34	28	MERTHYR TOWN	2-0	Roberts, Eyre	4000			4		7		9				6			3	10	11						8	2	5	1
35	Apr 4	Reading	1-0	R McCulloch	5000			4		7		9				6			3	10	11						8	2	5	1
36	10	ABERDARE ATHLETIC	3-1	Eyre, M McCulloch, R McCulloch	6000			4		7		9				6			3	10	11						8	2	5	1
37	11	SWANSEA TOWN	0-2		8158			4		7		9				6			3	10	11						8	2	5	1
38	13	Aberdare Athletic	2-4	Eyre 2	4000			4		7		9							3	10	11					6	8	2	5	1
39	18	Exeter City	1-2	Roberts	6000	10		4		7		9				6			3		11						8	2	5	1
40	22	QUEEN'S PARK RANGERS	0-2		3500	10		4		7		9				6			3		11						8	2	5	1
41	25	BRISTOL ROVERS	0-1		4000	10		4		7		9	11			6			3								8	2	5	1
42	May 2	Brentford	2-1	Eyre 2	4000	10		4		7		9			3	6					11						8	2	5	1
					Apps	18	2	41	7	26	9	23	1	1	21	40	3	4	20	10	38	2	21	11	14	9	26	33	41	41
					Goals	2					2	11				1				1	4		3	1	6		6		3	

Average home attendance reported as 4973

F.A. Cup

Rd	Date	Opponent	Score	Scorers	Att	Buchanan J	Budden WL	Butt LG	Charleston T	Clifford P	Davey HH	Eyre CR	Hayward DW	Heron AA	Lamb JF	Leitch W	Lowson EB	Maidment HW	Marshall GH	McCulloch MJ	McCulloch RG	Meyer HJ	Miles WP	Rattray HW	Readman JA	Richardson GWR	Roberts CL	Saxton E	Smith CF	Wilson GR
Q4	Nov 15	Yeovil & Petter's Utd.	2-3	Rattray, R McCulloch	6000	7		4								8	3				11			10	9	6		2	5	1

		P	W	D	L	F	A	W	D	L	F	A	Pts
1	Swansea Town	42	17	4	0	51	12	6	7	8	17	23	57
2	Plymouth Argyle	42	17	3	1	55	12	6	7	8	22	26	56
3	Bristol City	42	14	5	2	40	10	8	4	9	20	31	53
4	Swindon Town	42	17	2	2	51	13	3	9	9	15	25	51
5	Millwall	42	12	5	4	35	14	6	8	7	23	24	49
6	Newport County	42	13	6	2	35	12	7	3	11	27	30	49
7	Exeter City	42	13	4	4	37	19	6	5	10	22	29	47
8	Brighton & Hove Albion	42	14	3	4	43	17	5	5	11	16	28	46
9	Northampton Town	42	12	3	6	34	18	8	3	10	17	26	46
10	Southend United	42	14	1	6	34	18	5	4	12	17	43	43
11	Watford	42	12	3	6	22	20	5	6	10	16	27	43
12	Norwich City	42	10	8	3	39	18	4	5	12	14	33	41
13	Gillingham	42	11	8	2	25	11	2	6	13	10	33	40
14	Reading	42	9	6	6	28	15	5	4	12	9	23	38
15	Charlton Athletic	42	12	6	3	31	13	1	6	14	15	35	38
16	Luton Town	42	9	10	2	34	15	1	7	13	15	42	37
17	Bristol Rovers	42	10	5	6	26	13	2	8	11	16	36	37
18	Aberdare Athletic	42	13	4	4	40	21	1	5	15	14	46	37
19	Queen's Park Rangers	42	10	6	5	28	19	4	2	15	14	44	36
20	BOURNEMOUTH	42	8	6	7	20	17	5	2	14	20	41	34
21	Brentford	42	8	7	6	28	26	1	0	20	10	65	25
22	Merthyr Town	42	8	3	10	24	27	0	2	19	11	50	21

1925/26

8th in Division Three (South)

						Armstrong JD	Bliss H	Bow WJ	Buchanan J	Butt LG	Clifford P	Collin G	Davies T	Eyre CR	Foster CL	Hayward JW	Heron AA	Leitch W	Lowson EB	Maidment HW	Miles WP	Readman JA	Roberts CL	Roe A	Saxton E	Smith CF	Stringfellow JF	Wilson GR
1	Aug 29	SWINDON TOWN	2-0	Eyre 2	9006		10			4	7	3		9				6		11			8		2	5		1
2	31	Luton Town	1-4	Eyre	7880		10			4	7	3		9				6		11			8		2	5		1
3	Sep 5	Exeter City	1-0	Eyre	7973		10				7	3		9				6		11			8	4	2	5		1
4	9	LUTON TOWN	2-2	Roberts, Eyre	5612		10				7	3		9				6		11			8	4	2	5		1
5	12	READING	1-1	Maidment	7087					4	7	3		9						11	10		8	6	2	5		1
6	19	Norwich City	1-3	Maidment	7366					4	7	3		9						11	10		8	6	2	5		1
7	23	NEWPORT COUNTY	0-2		4137	2	10			4	7	3		9						11			8	6		5		1
8	26	Charlton Athletic	0-5		7593		10			4	7	3		9		2				11			8	6		5		1
9	Oct 1	Newport County	2-1	Maidment, Wetherby (og)	5092					4	7	3		9		2		6		11			10			5	8	1
10	3	GILLINGHAM	1-2	Stringfellow	5794					4	7	3		9		2		6		11			10			5	8	1
11	10	Merthyr Town	2-0	Roberts, Eyre	8327					4	7	3		9		2				11			10	6		5	8	1
12	17	SOUTHEND UNITED	1-2	Smith	5725					4	7	3		9		2				11			10	6		5	8	1
13	24	Plymouth Argyle	2-7	Eyre, Stringfellow	10593					4	7	3		9		2				11			10	6		5	8	1
14	31	Northampton Town	1-1	Roberts	6495					4	7	3	6	9		2				11			10	5			8	1
15	Nov 7	Millwall	1-0	Stringfellow	10551					4	7	3	6	9		2				11			10	5			8	1
16	14	BRENTFORD	3-2	Noble (og), Roe, Eyre	4530					4	7	3	6	9		2				11			10	5			8	1
17	21	Watford	0-0		5909					4	7	3	6	9		2				11			10	5			8	1
18	Dec 5	Aberdare Athletic	3-3	Eyre 3	3422	3			8	4	7		6	9		2				11			10	5				1
19	19	Crystal Palace	1-3	Smith	10682				7	4		3		9		2	1			11			10	5		6	8	
20	25	BRISTOL ROVERS	2-0	Hayward, Butt	6107				7	4		3		9		2				11			10	5		6	8	1
21	26	Bristol Rovers	2-7	Eyre 2	11856				7			3		9		2			4	11			10	5		6	8	1
22	Jan 2	Swindon Town	2-8	Roberts, Stringfellow	5625			1	7			3		9		2		4		11			10	5		6	8	
23	13	BRISTOL CITY	1-1	Clifford	3251				8		7	3		9		2				11			10	5		6	4	1
24	16	EXETER CITY	2-1	Roberts, Readman	3636				8		11	3		9		2						7	10	5		6	4	1
25	23	Reading	2-5	Readman, Buchanan	8842				7	4	11	3				2						9	10	5		6	8	1
26	Feb 6	CHARLTON ATHLETIC	4-1	Hayward, Eyre 2, Butt	4328				10	4	7			9	11	2		5							3	6	8	1
27	13	Gillingham	2-1	Clifford, Stringfellow	6075				10	4	7			9	11	2								5	3	6	8	1
28	20	MERTHYR TOWN	2-1	Eyre 2	5125				10	4	7			9	11	2								5	3	6	8	1
29	24	BRIGHTON & HOVE ALB	0-3		4181				10	4	7			9	11	2								5	3	6	8	1
30	27	Southend United	0-3		6417				10	4	7	3		9		2				11				5		6	8	1
31	Mar 6	PLYMOUTH ARGYLE	1-2	Roe	7427				10	4	7	3		9		2				11				5		6	8	1
32	13	NORTHAMPTON T	4-2	Readman 3, Stringfellow	5376				7	4		3		8		2				11		9		5		6	10	1
33	20	MILLWALL	0-0		5637				7	4		3		8		2				11		9		5		6	10	1
34	27	Brentford	2-0	Buchanan 2	7687				7	4		3		8		2				11		9		5		6	10	1
35	Apr 2	Queen's Park Rangers	2-2	Eyre, Readman	7065				7	4		3		8		2				11		9		5		6	10	1
36	3	WATFORD	3-4	Maidment, Readman 2	5748				7	4		3		9		2				11		8		5		6	10	1
37	5	QUEEN'S PARK RANGERS	4-1	Eyre 3, Maidment	5576				7	4		3		9		2				11		8		5		6	10	1
38	10	Brighton & Hove Albion	4-3	Clifford, Eyre 3	6403	2			10	4	7	3		9						11				5		6	8	1
39	17	ABERDARE ATHLETIC	3-0	Stringfellow, Readman, Maidment	4683	2			7	4		3		8						11		9		5		6	10	1
40	21	NORWICH CITY	2-2	Buchanan, Eyre (p)	4128	2			7	4		3		8						11		9		5		6	10	1
41	24	Bristol City	0-5		5559	2			10	4	7	3		9						11				5		6	8	1
42	May 1	CRYSTAL PALACE	6-1	Eyre 2, Stringfellow, Maidment 2, Buchanan	6051				8	4	7	3		9		2				11				5		6	10	1
					Apps	6	6	1	25	36	30	37	5	41	4	31	1	8	1	36	2	10	25	37	10	37	33	40
					Goals				5	2	3			27		2				8		9	5	2		2	8	

Two own goals

F.A. Cup

						Armstrong JD	Bliss H	Bow WJ	Buchanan J	Butt LG	Clifford P	Collin G	Davies T	Eyre CR	Foster CL	Hayward JW	Heron AA	Leitch W	Lowson EB	Maidment HW	Miles WP	Readman JA	Roberts CL	Roe A	Saxton E	Smith CF	Stringfellow JF	Wilson GR
R1	Nov 28	MERTHYR TOWN	3-0	Eyre, Maidment, Roberts	6000					4	7	3	6	9		2				11			10	5			8	1
R2	Dec 12	Brentford	2-1	Stringfellow, Eyre	9000				7	4		3		9		2				11			10	5		6	8	1
R3	Jan 9	READING	2-0	Eyre 2	12190				8		7	3		9		2				11			10	5		6	4	1
R4	30	BOLTON WANDERERS	2-2	Stringfellow, Roberts	10165				7	4	11	3		9		2							10	5		6	8	1
rep	Feb 3	Bolton Wanderers	2-6	Butt, Eyre	24798				7	4	11	3		9		2							10	5		6	8	1

		P	W	D	L	F	A	W	D	L	F	A	Pts
1	Reading	42	16	5	0	49	16	7	6	8	28	36	57
2	Plymouth Argyle	42	16	2	3	71	33	8	6	7	36	34	56
3	Millwall	42	14	6	1	52	12	7	5	9	21	27	53
4	Bristol City	42	14	3	4	42	15	7	6	8	30	36	51
5	Brighton & Hove Albion	42	12	4	5	47	33	7	5	9	37	40	47
6	Swindon Town	42	16	2	3	48	22	4	4	13	21	42	46
7	Luton Town	42	16	4	1	60	25	2	3	16	20	50	43
8	BOURNEMOUTH	42	10	5	6	44	30	7	4	10	31	61	43
9	Aberdare Athletic	42	11	6	4	50	24	6	2	13	24	42	42
10	Gillingham	42	11	4	6	36	19	6	4	11	17	30	42
11	Southend United	42	13	2	6	50	20	6	2	13	28	53	42
12	Northampton Town	42	13	3	5	47	26	4	4	13	35	54	41
13	Crystal Palace	42	16	1	4	50	21	3	2	16	25	58	41
14	Merthyr Town	42	13	3	5	51	25	1	8	12	18	50	39
15	Watford	42	12	5	4	47	26	3	4	14	26	63	39
16	Norwich City	42	11	5	5	35	26	4	4	13	23	47	39
17	Newport County	42	11	5	5	39	27	3	5	13	25	47	38
18	Brentford	42	12	4	5	44	32	4	2	15	25	62	38
19	Bristol Rovers	42	9	4	8	44	28	6	2	13	22	41	36
20	Exeter City	42	13	2	6	54	25	2	3	16	18	45	35
21	Charlton Athletic	42	9	7	5	32	23	2	6	13	16	45	35
22	Queen's Park Rangers	42	5	7	9	23	32	1	2	18	14	52	21

1926/27

7th in Division Three (South)

	Date		Opponent	Score	Scorers	Att	Armstrong JD	Blair J	Buchanan J	Butt LG	Clifford P	Collin G	Craig FG	Crumley JB	Eyre CR	Halliwell JC	Hayward JW	Maidment HW	Miles WP	Readman JA	Robson JH	Roe A	Saxton E	Smith CF	Stringfellow JF	Taylor FE	Thomson D	Walker RG	Wood J
1	Aug	28	Aberdare Athletic	1-2	Maidment	3679			7	4		3			9		2	11			1	5		6	8	10			
2	Sep	4	GILLINGHAM	4-2	Buchanan, Taylor 2, Maidment	6791			7	4		3		1	9		2	11				5		6	8	10			
3		8	Plymouth Argyle	1-1	Readman	8796			7	4		3		1			2	11		9		5		6	8	10			
4		11	Watford	2-1	Stringfellow, Maidment	8968			7	4		3		1			2	11		9		5		6	8	10			
5		13	Swindon Town	0-2		7578				4		3		1			2	11		9		5		6	8	10			7
6		18	CRYSTAL PALACE	1-1	Eyre	7504			10	4		3		1	9		2	11				5		6	8				7
7		22	SWINDON TOWN	1-2	Buchanan	5647	2		10	4				1	9			11				5		6	8			3	7
8		25	Coventry City	2-6	Craig, Eyre	5951	2		7	4			10	1	9			11				5		6	8			3	
9	Oct	2	QUEEN'S PARK RANGERS	6-2	* see below	6342	2			4				1	9		3	11				5		6	8	10			7
10		9	Charlton Athletic	3-1	Readman 3	6563			10	4				1			2	11	3	9		5		6	8				7
11		16	MERTHYR TOWN	1-1	Stringfellow	6043			10	4	7	2		1				11	3	9		5		6	8				
12		23	Exeter City	0-4		6710			7	4		3		1	9							5	2	6	10	8	11		
13		30	BRISTOL ROVERS	0-1		5062			7	4		3								9	1	5	2	6	10	8	11		
14	Nov	6	Millwall	1-1	Clifford	11986			7		11	3	10			4	2		5	9	1			6	8				
15		20	Northampton Town	2-2	Eyre 2	4165			7		11	3	10		9	4	2		5		1			6	8				
16	Dec	4	Norwich City	1-4	Eyre	5619							10		9	4			5	7	1		2	6		8	11	3	
17		18	Southend United	3-0	Eyre 2, Beaumont (og)	6058								1	9	4	2		5	7				6	10	8	11	3	
18		25	Newport County	1-2	Eyre	6359		3							9	4	2		5	7	1			6	10	8	11		
19		27	NEWPORT COUNTY	2-1	Eyre 2	8916		3							9	4	2		5	7	1			6	10	8	11		
20	Jan	1	PLYMOUTH ARGYLE	6-2	* see below	7188		3	7						9	4	2		5		1			6	10	8	11		
21		15	ABERDARE ATHLETIC	3-0	Taylor 2, Eyre	4799		3	7						9	4	2		5		1			6	10	8	11		
22		22	Gillingham	0-1		1740		3	7						9	4	2		5		1			6	10	8	11		
23		26	LUTON TOWN	2-0	Stringfellow, Eyre	1833		3							9	4	2		5	7	1			6	10	8	11		
24		29	WATFORD	6-0	Taylor 2, Stringfellow 2, Eyre 2	3864		3							9	4	2		5	7	1			6	10	8	11		
25	Feb	5	Crystal Palace	2-2	Eyre, Taylor	11474		3							9	4	2		5	7	1			6	10	8	11		
26		12	COVENTRY CITY	1-2	Stringfellow	4312		3							9	4	2		5	7	1			6	10	8	11		
27		19	Queen's Park Rangers	1-1	Eyre	6678		3							9	4	2		5	7	1			6	10	8	11		
28		26	CHARLTON ATHLETIC	0-3		2254		3							9	4	2		5	7	1			6	10	8	11		
29	Mar	2	BRIGHTON & HOVE ALB	1-0	Eyre	3153		3			7				9	4	2		5	8	1			6	10		11		
30		5	Merthyr Town	6-4	Eyre 3, Clifford 2, Stringfellow	1529		3			7				9	4	2		5	8	1			6	10		11		
31		12	EXETER CITY	4-3	Stringfellow 2, Ditchburn (og), Clifford	5518		3			7				9	4			5	8	1		2	6	10		11		
32		16	BRENTFORD	3-1	Stringfellow, Eyre, Miles	3195		3			7				9	4			5	8	1		2	6	10		11		
33		19	Bristol Rovers	1-2	Thomson	6140		3			7				9	4			5	8	1		2	6	10		11		
34		26	MILLWALL	0-1		5152		3			7				9	4		11	5	8	1		2	6	10				
35	Apr	2	Brentford	0-0		6766	2	3			7		8		9	4		11	5		1			6	10				
36		9	NORTHAMPTON T	3-1	Eyre 3	3579	2	3			7		10		9	4		11	5		1			6	8				
37		15	Bristol City	0-2		24644	2	3			7		10			4		11	5		1			6	8	9			
38		16	Brighton & Hove Albion	2-0	Taylor, Readman	8567	2	3			7					4		11	5	9	1			6	10	8			
39		18	BRISTOL CITY	2-0	Eyre, Taylor	12839		3			11				9	4	2		5		1			6	10	8			7
40		23	NORWICH CITY	0-1		4253	2				11				9	4	3		5		1			6	10	8			7
41		30	Luton Town	0-4		6709	2				7				9	4	3	11	5		1			6	10	8			
42	May	7	SOUTHEND UNITED	3-0	Maidment 2, Stringfellow	3269		3			7				9	4	2	11	5		1			6	10	8			
						Apps	9	23	16	13	17	11	7	12	33	29	28	18	31	24	30	13	7	42	41	27	20	4	7
						Goals			3		4		1		28			6	1	5				1	13	11	2		1

Scorers in game 9: Stringfellow, Eyre 2 (1p), Wood, Maidment, Taylor

Scorers in game 20: Buchanan, Thomson, Smith, Eyre, Taylor, Stringfellow

Two own goals

F.A. Cup

	Date		Opponent	Score	Scorers	Att	Armstrong JD	Blair J	Buchanan J	Butt LG	Clifford P	Collin G	Craig FG	Crumley JB	Eyre CR	Halliwell JC	Hayward JW	Maidment HW	Miles WP	Readman JA	Robson JH	Roe A	Saxton E	Smith CF	Stringfellow JF	Taylor FE	Thomson D	Walker RG	Wood J
R1	Nov	27	SWINDON TOWN	1-1	Hayward	9417					7	3	10		9	4	2	11	5		1			6	8				
rep		29	Swindon Town	4-3	Eyre 2, Taylor 2	7120						3			9	4			5	7	1		2	6	10	8	11		
R2	Dec	11	Bristol City	1-1	Stringfellow	20297			7			3			9	4	2		5		1			6	10	8	11		
rep		15	BRISTOL CITY	2-0	Eyre 2	8849			7						9	4	2		5		1		3	6	10	8	11		
R3	Jan	8	LIVERPOOL	1-1	Taylor	13409		3	7						9	4	2		5		1			6	10	8	11		
rep		12	Liverpool	1-4	Eyre	36800		3	7						9	4	2		5		1			6	10	8	11		

		P	W	D	L	F	A	W	D	L	F	A	Pts
1	Bristol City	42	19	1	1	71	24	8	7	6	33	30	62
2	Plymouth Argyle	42	17	4	0	52	14	8	6	7	43	47	60
3	Millwall	42	16	2	3	55	19	7	8	6	34	32	56
4	Brighton & Hove Albion	42	15	4	2	61	24	6	7	8	18	26	53
5	Swindon Town	42	16	3	2	64	31	5	6	10	36	54	51
6	Crystal Palace	42	12	6	3	57	33	6	3	12	27	48	45
7	BOURNEMOUTH	42	13	2	6	49	24	5	6	10	29	42	44
8	Luton Town	42	12	9	0	48	19	3	5	13	20	47	44
9	Newport County	42	15	4	2	40	20	4	2	15	17	51	44
10	Bristol Rovers	42	12	4	5	46	28	4	5	12	32	52	41
11	Brentford	42	10	9	2	46	20	3	5	13	24	41	40
12	Exeter City	42	14	4	3	46	18	1	6	14	30	55	40
13	Charlton Athletic	42	13	5	3	44	22	3	3	15	16	39	40
14	Queen's Park Rangers	42	9	8	4	41	27	6	1	14	24	44	39
15	Coventry City	42	11	4	6	44	33	4	3	14	27	53	37
16	Norwich City	42	10	5	6	41	25	2	6	13	18	46	35
17	Merthyr Town	42	11	5	5	42	25	2	4	15	21	55	35
18	Northampton Town	42	13	4	4	36	23	2	1	18	23	64	35
19	Southend United	42	12	3	6	44	25	2	3	16	20	52	34
20	Gillingham	42	10	5	6	36	26	1	5	15	18	46	32
21	Watford	42	9	6	6	36	27	3	2	16	21	60	32
22	Aberdare Athletic	42	8	2	11	38	48	1	5	15	24	53	25

1927/28

14th in Division Three (South)

	Date	Opponent	Score	Scorers	Att	Baynham DM	Blair J	Bradford J	Buchanan J	Butt LG	Clifford P	Crumley JB	Crump LV	Drummond RC	Eyre CR	Halliwell JC	Hayward JW	Jones E	Maidment HW	McKay N	Miles WP	Pike TE	Robson JH	Saxton E	Smith CF	Stringfellow JF	Taylor FE	Threlfall W	Tyler W	Walker RG	Young A
1	Aug 27	SWINDON TOWN	2-0	Clifford, Eyre	10208		3				7		11		9	4	2				5		1		6	10	8				
2	31	SOUTHEND UNITED	2-3	Eyre, Taylor	5874		3				7		11		9	4	2				5		1		6	10	8				
3	Sep 3	Brentford	1-2	Stringfellow	11108		3				7		11		9	4	2				5		1		6	10	8				
4	7	Southend United	0-3		5631		3				7				9	4	2		11				1		6	10	8				5
5	10	LUTON TOWN	2-2	Eyre 2	6040	3					7				9	4	2		11		5		1		6	10	8				
6	17	Millwall	0-2		14371		3				7				9	4	2				5	11	1		6	10	8				
7	21	QUEEN'S PARK RANGERS	1-2	Pike	4440		3				7				9	4	2				5	11	1		6	10	8				
8	24	CRYSTAL PALACE	2-2	Eyre, Stringfellow	5933		3				7	1	11		9	4	2								6	10	8				5
9	Oct 1	Exeter City	1-4	Eyre	6136		3				7	1		8	9	4	2				5	11			6	10					
10	8	TORQUAY UNITED	1-1	Taylor	5781		3				7	1		8	9	4	2					11				10	5		6		
11	15	Norwich City	3-3	Stringfellow, Eyre, Campbell(og)	9675		3			4	7	1			9	6	2				10	11				8	5				
12	22	GILLINGHAM	3-0	Eyre, Miles, Pickering (og)	4119		3			4	7	1			9	6	2				10	11				8	5				
13	29	Coventry City	2-3	Miles, Eyre	10933		3	6		4	7	1			9		2				10	11				8	5				
14	Nov 5	NEWPORT COUNTY	0-0		5324		3	6			7	1			9	4	2				10	11				8	5				
15	12	Walsall	3-2	Eyre, Taylor 2	3917		3	6			7	1			9	4	2					11			5	8	10				
16	19	MERTHYR TOWN	2-1	Eyre 2	2077		3	6			7	1			9	4	2				5	11				8	10				
17	Dec 3	BRISTOL ROVERS	4-3	Eyre 2, Clifford, Pike	4414	3				4	7	1			9	6	2				5	11					8				
18	17	WATFORD	1-0	Eyre	3798		3	6			7	1			9	4	2				5	11				8	10				
19	24	Queen's Park Rangers	0-2		6260		3	6			7	1			9	4	2				5	11				8	10				
20	26	BRIGHTON & HOVE ALB	3-1	Maidment, Halliwell, Eyre	2288	2	3	6			7	1			9	4			11		5					8	10				
21	27	Brighton & Hove Albion	2-3	Stringfellow, Eyre	6380	2	3	6			7	1			9	4			11		5					8	10				
22	Jan 7	BRENTFORD	1-0	Taylor	4796	3		6			7	1			9	4				8	5	11		2			10				
23	21	Luton Town	3-3	Taylor, Maidment, Miles	6453		3	6				1			9	4	2		7		5	11				8	10				
24	28	MILLWALL	5-0	Miles 2, Taylor, Pike, Eyre	4695		3	6			7	1			9	4	2				5	11				8	10				
25	Feb 4	Crystal Palace	1-6	Eyre	10862		3	6			7	1			9	4	2				5					8	10	11			
26	11	EXETER CITY	2-0	Taylor 2	5863		3	6			7	1			9	4	2				5					8	10	11			
27	18	Torquay United	2-2	Eyre, Taylor	4236		3	6			7	1			9	4	2	8			5						10	11			
28	25	NORWICH CITY	2-1	Eyre, Hayward (p)	6041		3	6			7	1			9	4	2	8	11		5						10				
29	Mar 3	Gillingham	1-2	Hayward	6817		3	6			7	1			9	4	2	8	11		5						10				
30	10	COVENTRY CITY	2-3	Jones, Eyre	4493		3	6			7	1			9	4	2	8	11		5					10					
31	17	Newport County	3-4	Jones, Stringfellow, Eyre	3754		3	6			7	1			9	4	2	8	11		5					10					
32	21	Swindon Town	2-3	Stringfellow, Eyre	2685		3	6			7	1			9	4	2	8	11		5					10					
33	24	WALSALL	3-1	Eyre, Miles, Hayward (p)	4549		3	6			7	1			9	4	2		11		5					8	10				
34	31	Merthyr Town	1-1	Clifford	1039	2	3	6			7	1			9	4			11						5	8	10				
35	Apr 7	CHARLTON ATHLETIC	3-1	Stringfellow, Eyre 2	5764		3	6			7	1			9	4	2		11		5					8	10				
36	9	NORTHAMPTON T	1-1	Stringfellow	9099		3	6			7	1		11	9	4	2				5					8	10				
37	10	Northampton Town	1-1	Stringfellow	11693		3		8		7			11	9	4	2				5		1		6	10					
38	14	Bristol Rovers	0-3		5681		3	6	10		7			11	9	4	2						1		5	8					
39	16	Charlton Athletic	1-1	Drummond	1227			6	10		7			11	9	4	2				5		1			8				3	
40	21	PLYMOUTH ARGYLE	2-2	Eyre 2 (1p)	5495		3	6	10		7	1		11	9	4					2					8	5				
41	25	Plymouth Argyle	1-3	Eyre	5519		3	6	10		11				9	4					5		1			8				2	
42	28	Watford	0-2		5102	2	3	6	10		11				9	4							1		5	8	7				

Played in one game: W Chivers (17, at 10), TC Johnstone (41, 7)

	Baynham DM	Blair J	Bradford J	Buchanan J	Butt LG	Clifford P	Crumley JB	Crump LV	Drummond RC	Eyre CR	Halliwell JC	Hayward JW	Jones E	Maidment HW	McKay N	Miles WP	Pike TE	Robson JH	Saxton E	Smith CF	Stringfellow JF	Taylor FE	Threlfall W	Tyler W	Walker RG	Young A
Apps	7	38	28	6	4	41	30	4	7	42	41	35	6	13	1	35	16	12	1	14	37	34	3	1	2	2
Goals						3			1	30	1	3	2	2		6	3				9	10				

Two own goals

F.A. Cup

	Date	Opponent	Score	Scorers	Att	Baynham DM	Blair J	Bradford J	Buchanan J	Butt LG	Clifford P	Crumley JB	Crump LV	Drummond RC	Eyre CR	Halliwell JC	Hayward JW	Jones E	Maidment HW	McKay N	Miles WP	Pike TE	Robson JH	Saxton E	Smith CF	Stringfellow JF	Taylor FE	Threlfall W	Tyler W	Walker RG	Young A
R1	Nov 26	Coventry City	2-2	Pike 2	13627		3	6			7	1			9	4	2				5	11				8	10				
rep	30	COVENTRY CITY	2-0	Pike, Eyre	5566		3	6			7	1			9	4	2				5	11				8	10				
R2	Dec 10	BRISTOL ROVERS	6-1	Taylor 2, Clifford 2, Miles, Eyre	9098		3	6			7	1			9	4	2				5	11				8	10				
R3	Jan 14	Sheffield Wednesday	0-3		26297		3	6	7			1			9	4	2				5	11				8	10				

		P	W	D	L	F	A	W	D	L	F	A	Pts
1	Millwall	42	19	2	0	87	15	11	3	7	40	35	65
2	Northampton Town	42	17	3	1	67	23	6	6	9	35	41	55
3	Plymouth Argyle	42	17	2	2	60	19	6	5	10	25	35	53
4	Brighton & Hove Albion	42	14	4	3	51	24	5	6	10	30	45	48
5	Crystal Palace	42	15	3	3	46	23	3	9	9	33	49	48
6	Swindon Town	42	12	6	3	60	26	7	3	11	30	43	47
7	Southend United	42	14	2	5	48	19	6	4	11	32	45	46
8	Exeter City	42	11	6	4	49	27	6	6	9	21	33	46
9	Newport County	42	12	5	4	52	38	6	4	11	29	46	45
10	Queen's Park Rangers	42	8	5	8	37	35	9	4	8	35	36	43
11	Charlton Athletic	42	12	5	4	34	27	3	8	10	26	43	43
12	Brentford	42	12	4	5	49	30	4	4	13	27	44	40
13	Luton Town	42	13	5	3	56	27	3	2	16	38	60	39
14	BOURNEMOUTH	42	12	6	3	44	24	1	6	14	28	55	38
15	Watford	42	10	5	6	42	34	4	5	12	26	44	38
16	Gillingham	42	10	3	8	33	26	3	8	10	29	55	37
17	Norwich City	42	9	8	4	41	26	1	8	12	25	44	36
18	Walsall	42	9	6	6	52	35	3	3	15	23	66	33
19	Bristol Rovers	42	11	3	7	41	36	3	1	17	26	57	32
20	Coventry City	42	5	8	8	40	36	6	1	14	27	60	31
21	Merthyr Town	42	7	6	8	38	40	2	7	12	15	51	31
22	Torquay United	42	4	10	7	27	36	4	4	13	26	67	30

1928/29

9th in Division Three (South)

							Bradford J	Bryce RS	Cherrett PAM	Clifford P	Crumley JB	Dixon CH	Dudley SM	Duff TE	Eyre CR	Graham GK	Halliwell JC	Hayward JW	Isherwood H	Johnson JC	Kinghorn HMcG	McSevich P	Miles WP	Moralee WE	Murphy VJ	Nichol WB	Smith AWT	Smith CF	Stringfellow JF	Walker RG	Wright R
1	Aug	25	SOUTHEND UNITED	2-2	Robinson (og), Cherrett	9042	6		8	7	1				9		4	2	3				5		11	10					
2		27	Norwich City	1-5	Cherrett	8060	6		8	7	1				9		4	2	3				5		11	10					
3	Sep	1	Merthyr Town	0-1		6719			9	7					8		4	2	3			1			11		5	6	10		
4		5	NORWICH CITY	2-0	Cherrett, Eyre	3902			9	7					8		4	2	3			1			11		5	6	10		
5		8	FULHAM	1-0	Cherrett	8031			8	7		4			9		6					1			11		5		10	3	2
6		15	BRENTFORD	1-1	Cherrett	7573			8	7		4			9		6					1			11		5		10	3	2
7		22	Luton Town	1-2	Eyre	10675			8			5		11	9		4	2		7		1		10			6			3	
8		29	COVENTRY CITY	2-1	Eyre, Hayward	7087			8			5		11	9		4	2		7		1		10			6			3	
9	Oct	6	Northampton Town	0-2		8519			8			5		11	9		4	2		7		1		10			6			3	
10		13	CHARLTON ATHLETIC	4-2	Johnson, Eyre 2, Hayward (p)	6678	6		8	11		5			9		4	2		7		1					10			3	
11		20	Queen's Park Rangers	0-0		11815			8	11		5			9		4	2		7		1					6		10	3	
12		27	BRISTOL ROVERS	6-2	Eyre 3, Johnson, Hayward, Cherrett	5066	6	11	8			5			9		4	2		7		1					10			3	
13	Nov	3	Watford	3-0	Eyre 3	9570	6	11	8			5			9		4	2		7		1					10			3	
14		10	WALSALL	1-2	Cherrett	5570	6	11	8			5			9		4	2		7		1					10			3	
15		17	Newport County	2-0	Bryce, Clifford	3309	6	11	8	7	1	5			9		4	2									10			3	
16	Dec	1	Swindon Town	3-3	Eyre 2, Bryce	6031	6	11	8	7	1	5			9		4	2	3								10				
17		15	Gillingham	2-2	Eyre, Graham	3202	6	11	8	7		5			9	10	4	2	3			1									
18		22	PLYMOUTH ARGYLE	4-1	Cherrett, Eyre 2, Hayward (p)	5936	6	11	8	7		5			9	10	4	2	3			1									
19		25	EXETER CITY	3-1	Eyre 2, Lowton (og)	7994	6	11	8	7		5			9	10	4	2	3			1									
20		26	Exeter City	3-6	Eyre 2, Johnson	9240	6			7		5	11		9	10	4	2	3	8		1									
21		29	Southend United	4-4	Cherrett 2, Eyre, Moralee	5432	6		8	7		5	11		9	10		2	3			1		4							
22	Jan	5	MERTHYR TOWN	3-0	Bryce, Cherrett 2	4566	6	11	8	7		5			9	10	4	2	3			1									
23		19	Fulham	0-3		17356	6	11	8		1	5			9	10	4	2	3	7											
24	Feb	2	LUTON TOWN	3-3	Bryce 2, Eyre	3726	6	11	8	7		5			9	10		2	3			1		4							
25		6	TORQUAY UNITED	4-3	Eyre (p), Graham, Cherrett, Bryce (p)	2903	6	11	8	7		5			9	10			3			1		4							2
26		9	Coventry City	2-1	Cherrett, Bryce	11403	6	11	9	7						10	4	2	3			1	5	8							
27		23	Charlton Athletic	2-6	Johnson, Moralee	12629	6	11		7		5				10		2	3	9		1	4	8							
28	Mar	2	QUEEN'S PARK RANGERS	2-3	Bryce, Eyre	5045	6	11		7		5			9	10		2	3			1		8							4
29		9	Bristol Rovers	2-1	Cherrett, Eyre	7658	6	11	8	7					9	10	4	2				1	3				5				
30		13	Brentford	0-0		3366	2	8		7					9	10	4				11	1		6			5			3	
31		16	WATFORD	3-3	Eyre 2 (1p), Cherrett	4326	6	11	8	7					9	10	4		2			1					5			3	
32		20	NORTHAMPTON T	2-0	Bryce, Eyre	3196	6	11	8	7					9		4	2				1		10			5				3
33		23	Walsall	1-2	Bryce	4729	6	11	8	7	1	5			9	10	4										3				2
34		29	Brighton & Hove Albion	0-1		9494	6	11	8	7	1	5			9		4							10			3				2
35		30	NEWPORT COUNTY	0-1		5190	6	11		7	1				9		4							10			5		8	3	2
36	Apr	1	BRIGHTON & HOVE ALB	3-2	Bryce, Eyre, Cherrett	6247	6	11	8	7	1				9		4							10			5			3	2
37		6	Crystal Palace	3-1	Bryce 2, Clifford	20792	6	11	8	7					9		4	2				1		10			5				3
38		13	SWINDON TOWN	2-1	Hayward, Cherrett	5176	6	11	8	7					9		4	2				1		10			5				3
39		20	Torquay United	1-4	Cherrett	4170	6	11	8	7					9		4	2				1		10			5				3
40		24	CRYSTAL PALACE	2-0	Bryce, Eyre	5005	6	11	8	7					9		4	2				1		10			5				3
41		27	GILLINGHAM	4-3	Bryce, Eyre 2, Moralee	4370	6	11	8	7					9		4	2				1		10			5				3
42	May	4	Plymouth Argyle	0-2		8657	6	11		7					9	8	4	2				1		10			5				3

FL home attendances have not had 280 season tickets added to them for games 25 to 41, except for games 31 and 32

	Bradford J	Bryce RS	Cherrett PAM	Clifford P	Crumley JB	Dixon CH	Dudley SM	Duff TE	Eyre CR	Graham GK	Halliwell JC	Hayward JW	Isherwood H	Johnson JC	Kinghorn HMcG	McSevich P	Miles WP	Moralee WE	Murphy VJ	Nichol WB	Smith AWT	Smith CF	Stringfellow JF	Walker RG	Wright R
Apps	34	29	36	35	9	25	2	3	40	17	37	33	18	11	1	33	5	20	6	2	28	2	6	15	15
Goals		15	19	2					32	2		5		4				3							

Two own goals

F.A. Cup

							Bradford J	Bryce RS	Cherrett PAM	Clifford P	Crumley JB	Dixon CH	Dudley SM	Duff TE	Eyre CR	Graham GK	Halliwell JC	Hayward JW	Isherwood H	Johnson JC	Kinghorn HMcG	McSevich P	Miles WP	Moralee WE	Murphy VJ	Nichol WB	Smith AWT	Smith CF	Stringfellow JF	Walker RG	Wright R
R1	Nov	24	Poole	4-1	Clifford, Eyre 2, Cherrett	6139	6	11	8	7	1	5			9		4	2									10			3	
R2	Dec	8	Guildford City	5-1	Hayward (p), Eyre 3, Clifford	5000	6	11	8	7		5			9		4	2	3			1							10		
R3	Jan	12	Accrington Stanley	1-1	Clifford	8027	6	11	8	7		5			9	10	4	2	3			1									
rep		16	ACCRINGTON STANLEY	2-0	Clifford, Bryce	10486	6	11	8	7		5			9	10	4	2	3			1									
R4		26	WATFORD	6-4	Bryce, Cherrett, Eyre 3, Clifford	13311	6	11	8	7	1	5			9	10	4	2	3												
R5	Feb	16	WEST HAM UNITED	1-1	Graham	11301	6	11	9	7		5				10	4	2	3			1		8							
rep		20	West Ham United	1-3	Hayward (p)	30217	6	11	8	7		5			9	10	4	2	3			1									

		P	W	D	L	F	A	W	D	L	F	A	Pts
1	Charlton Athletic	42	14	5	2	51	22	9	3	9	35	38	54
2	Crystal Palace	42	14	2	5	40	25	9	6	6	41	42	54
3	Northampton Town	42	14	6	1	68	23	6	6	9	28	34	52
4	Plymouth Argyle	42	14	6	1	51	13	6	6	9	32	38	52
5	Fulham	42	14	3	4	60	31	7	7	7	41	40	52
6	Queen's Park Rangers	42	13	7	1	50	22	6	7	8	32	39	52
7	Luton Town	42	16	3	2	64	28	3	8	10	25	45	49
8	Watford	42	15	3	3	55	31	4	7	10	24	43	48
9	BOURNEMOUTH	42	14	4	3	54	31	5	5	11	30	46	47
10	Swindon Town	42	12	5	4	48	27	3	8	10	27	45	43
11	Coventry City	42	9	6	6	35	23	5	8	8	27	34	42
12	Southend United	42	10	7	4	44	27	5	4	12	36	48	41
13	Brentford	42	11	4	6	34	21	3	6	12	22	39	38
14	Walsall	42	11	7	3	47	25	2	5	14	26	54	38
15	Brighton & Hove Albion	42	14	2	5	39	28	2	4	15	19	48	38
16	Newport County	42	8	6	7	37	28	5	3	13	32	58	35
17	Norwich City	42	12	3	6	49	29	2	3	16	20	52	34
18	Torquay United	42	10	3	8	46	36	4	3	14	20	48	34
19	Bristol Rovers	42	9	6	6	39	28	4	1	16	21	51	33
20	Merthyr Town	42	11	6	4	42	28	0	2	19	13	75	30
21	Exeter City	42	7	6	8	49	40	2	5	14	18	48	29
22	Gillingham	42	7	8	6	22	24	3	1	17	21	59	29

1929/30

10th in Division Three (South)

No	Month	Day	Opponent	Score	Scorers	Att	Beswick SMA	Birch J	Bradford J	Brown S	Bryce RS	Clifford P	Crawford GW	Eyre CR	Forbes AS	Green RE	Halliwell JC	Hayward JW	Johnson JC	Kirkpatrick E	Lampard AJ	Lumsden JB	McInally TB	McSevich P	Moralee WE	Robinson SH	Scott WH	Williams LS	Wright R
1	Aug	31	Northampton Town	0-2		14397	10		6		11	7	5	9			4	2				8		1					3
2	Sep	2	Fulham	3-3	Beswick, Eyre, Bryce	12993	10		6		11	7	5	9			4	2				8		1					3
3		7	EXETER CITY	3-0	Eyre, Bryce, Scott	6885	10		6		11	7	5	9			4	2						1			8		3
4		11	FULHAM	5-0	Clifford, Beswick, Bryce, Eyre 2	6842	10		6		11	7		9	5		4	2						1			8		3
5		14	Southend United	1-4	Clifford	9577	10		6		11	7		9	5		4	2						1			8		3
6		18	CRYSTAL PALACE	2-1	Beswick, Scott	6635	10		6		11	7		9	5		4	2						1			8		3
7		21	LUTON TOWN	5-1	Hayward (p), Eyre 2, Clifford, Bryce	7268	10		6		11	7		9	5		4	2						1			8		3
8		28	Coventry City	2-0	Eyre 2	18323	10		6	3	11	7		9	5		4	2						1			8		
9	Oct	5	Walsall	2-2	Scott, Bryce	7818	10		6	3	11	7		9	5		4	2						1			8		
10		12	QUEEN'S PARK RANGERS	0-0		8371	10		6	3	11	7		9	5		4	2						1			8		
11		19	WATFORD	3-2	Eyre, Beswick, Clifford	8040	10		6	3	11	7		9	5			2		4				1			8		
12		26	Newport County	1-1	Scott	3640			6	3	11	7		9	5			2		4				1	10		8		
13	Nov	2	TORQUAY UNITED	4-1	Halliwell, Bryce, Beswick, Scott	6770	10		6	3	11	7		9	5		4	2						1			8		
14		9	Merthyr Town	1-0	Scott	2990	10		6	3	11	7		9	5		4	2						1			8		
15		16	PLYMOUTH ARGYLE	1-1	Scott	13667	10		6	3	11	7		9	5		4	2						1			8		
16		23	Swindon Town	1-1	Eyre	6007	10		6	3	11	7		9	5		4	2						1			8		
17	Dec	21	Clapton Orient	0-0		4872	10		6	3	11	7		9	5		4	2					8	1					
18		25	Gillingham	5-1	Eyre 2, McInally, Beswick, Hayward	3954	10		6	3	11	7		9	5		4	2					8	1					
19		26	GILLINGHAM	1-2	Bryce	11481	10		6	3	11	7		9	5		4	2					8	1					
20	Jan	4	Exeter City	2-1	Scott 2	6568			6	3	11	7		9	5		4	2					10	1			8		
21		18	SOUTHEND UNITED	0-0		5623	10	5	6	3		7		9			4							1			8	11	2
22		25	Luton Town	0-1		6971	10	2	6	3	7			9			4						8	1				11	5
23	Feb	1	COVENTRY CITY	1-0	Eyre	4708		2	6	3		7		9			4						10	1			8	11	5
24		8	WALSALL	1-1	Groves (og)	4916	8		6	3		7		9			4	2					10	1				11	5
25		15	Queen's Park Rangers	1-3	Scott	9464			6	3			5	9			4	2	7				10	1			8	11	
26		22	Watford	0-0		5380		2	6	3	11	7		9			4						10	1		5	8		
27		26	NORTHAMPTON T	3-1	Scott, Beswick, Eyre	3889	10	2	6			7		9			4							1		5	8	11	3
28	Mar	1	NEWPORT COUNTY	1-1	Williams	5509	10	2	6			7		9			4							1		5	8	11	3
29		8	Torquay United	0-7		3443	8		6		11	7		9			4	2					10	1		5			3
30		12	BRIGHTON & HOVE ALB	1-1	Eyre	3476	10	2	6	3		7		9			4				1					5	8	11	
31		15	MERTHYR TOWN	4-2	Moralee, Beswick, Bradford, Eyre	3748	8	2	6	3		7		9			4				1				10	5		11	
32		22	Plymouth Argyle	1-2	Eyre	14226	10	2	6	3	11	7		9			4							1		5	8		
33		26	BRENTFORD	1-2	Robinson	5494	10	2	6	3	11	7		9			4							1		5	8		
34		29	SWINDON TOWN	1-3	Moralee	4753	8	2	6	3	11	7		9			4							1	10	5			
35	Apr	5	Brighton & Hove Albion	3-4	Eyre 2, Bryce	6753	10		6	3	11	7		9			4	2						1		5	8		
36		9	Bristol Rovers	1-2	Eyre	1500	10		6	3	11	7		9	5		4	2						1			8		
37		12	BRISTOL ROVERS	3-1	Forbes, Scott, Beswick	3392	10		6	3	11	7		9	5		4	2						1			8		
38		19	Brentford	0-1		7694	10		6	3	11	7		9	5		4	2						1			8		
39		21	NORWICH CITY	2-3	Hayward (p), Bryce	6576	10		6	3	11	7		9	5		4	2						1			8		
40		22	Norwich City	0-1		10439			6	3	11	7		9	5	10	4	2						1			8		
41		26	CLAPTON ORIENT	5-1	Hayward 2 (1p), Eyre 3	3649			6	3	11	7		9	5	10	4	2						1			8		
42	May	3	Crystal Palace	1-1	Scott	10678			6	3	11	7		9	5	10	4	2						1			8		
						Apps	34	11	42	32	34	40	4	42	24	3	40	31	1	2	2	2	10	40	3	10	32	9	14
						Goals	9		1		9	4		23	1		1	5					1		2	1	13	1	

One own goal

F.A. Cup

Round	Month	Day	Opponent	Score	Scorers	Att	Beswick SMA	Birch J	Bradford J	Brown S	Bryce RS	Clifford P	Crawford GW	Eyre CR	Forbes AS	Green RE	Halliwell JC	Hayward JW	Johnson JC	Kirkpatrick E	Lampard AJ	Lumsden JB	McInally TB	McSevich P	Moralee WE	Robinson SH	Scott WH	Williams LS	Wright R
R1	Nov	30	TORQUAY UNITED	2-0	Beswick, Eyre	8497	10		6	3	11	7		9	5		4	2						1			8		
R2	Dec	14	Caernarvon Athletic	1-1	Beswick	6080	10		6	3	11	7		9	5		4	2					8	1					
rep		18	CAERNARVON ATHLETIC	5-2	Edwards (og), Eyre 2, Beswick, Bryce	7117	10		6	3	11	7		9	5		4	2					8	1					
R3	Jan	11	Fulham	1-1	Eyre	21806	8		6	3	11	7		9	5		4	2					10	1					
rep		15	FULHAM	0-2		12121		2	6	3	11	7		9	5		4						10	1			8		

	Team	P	W	D	L	F	A	W	D	L	F	A	Pts
1	Plymouth Argyle	42	18	3	0	63	12	12	5	4	35	26	68
2	Brentford	42	21	0	0	66	12	7	5	9	28	32	61
3	Queen's Park Rangers	42	13	5	3	46	26	8	4	9	34	42	51
4	Northampton Town	42	14	6	1	53	20	7	2	12	29	38	50
5	Brighton & Hove Albion	42	16	2	3	54	20	5	6	10	33	43	50
6	Coventry City	42	14	3	4	54	25	5	6	10	34	48	47
7	Fulham	42	12	6	3	54	33	6	5	10	33	50	47
8	Norwich City	42	14	4	3	55	28	4	6	11	33	49	46
9	Crystal Palace	42	14	5	2	56	26	3	7	11	25	48	46
10	BOURNEMOUTH	42	11	6	4	47	24	4	7	10	25	37	43
11	Southend United	42	11	6	4	41	19	4	7	10	28	40	43
12	Clapton Orient	42	10	8	3	38	21	4	5	12	17	41	41
13	Luton Town	42	13	4	4	42	25	1	8	12	22	53	40
14	Swindon Town	42	10	7	4	42	25	3	5	13	31	58	38
15	Watford	42	10	4	7	37	30	5	4	12	23	43	38
16	Exeter City	42	10	6	5	45	29	2	5	14	22	44	35
17	Walsall	42	10	4	7	45	24	3	4	14	26	54	34
18	Newport County	42	9	9	3	48	29	3	1	17	26	56	34
19	Torquay United	42	9	6	6	50	38	1	5	15	14	56	31
20	Bristol Rovers	42	11	3	7	45	31	0	5	16	22	62	30
21	Gillingham	42	9	5	7	38	28	2	3	16	13	52	30
22	Merthyr Town	42	5	6	10	39	49	1	3	17	21	86	21

1930/31

10th in Division Three (South)

			Opponent	Res	Scorers	Att	Beswick SMA	Birch J	Bradford J	Brown S	Coxford J	Eyre CR	Forbes AS	Green RE	Halliwell JC	Hayward JW	Hutchinson W	McSevich P	Moralee WE	Morgan MBB	Peed F	Robinson SH	Russell CJ	Scott WH	Sherman FH	Trim RF	Turner HL	Webb WG	Whitehouse JC	Williams LS	Wright R
1	Aug	30	Swindon Town	1-4	Webb	6903			6	3	5	9			4	2		1		7			10					11	8		
2	Sep	3	QUEEN'S PARK RANGERS	2-0	Eyre, Hayward (p)	6665			6	3	5	9			4	2		1		7			10					11	8		
3		6	SOUTHEND UNITED	0-0		7719			6	3		9	5		4	2	11	1		7			10						8		
4		8	Walsall	3-3	Eyre 3	5363			6	3		9	5		4	2		1		7			10						8	11	
5		13	WATFORD	1-1	Whitehouse	6055			6	3		9	5		4	2	11	1		7			10						8		
6		17	WALSALL	0-2		3329				3	5			10	4	2		1	6	7	9								8	11	
7		20	Notts County	0-2		9579	7		6	3			5		4	2		1			9		11	8					10		
8		27	CLAPTON ORIENT	1-1	Whitehouse	5928	7		6	3		9	5		4	2		1					11	8					10		
9	Oct	4	Thames	4-1	Eyre 2, Scott 2	2861	7		6	3		9	5		4	2		1					11	8					10		
10		11	NORWICH CITY	4-1	Beswick, Eyre, Scott, Whitehouse	6044	7		6	3		9	5		4	2		1					11	8					10		
11		18	Luton Town	3-2	Scott 2, Eyre	7367	7			3		9	5		4	2		1	6				11	8					10		
12		25	BRISTOL ROVERS	4-0	Eyre, Scott 2, Russell	6167	7			3		9	5		4	2		1	6				11	8					10		
13	Nov	1	Newport County	3-7	Whitehouse, Russell 2	2827	7			3		9	5		4	2		1	6				11	8					10		
14		8	GILLINGHAM	2-1	Whitehouse 2	5490				3		9	5		4	2		1	6				11	8				7	10		
15		15	Exeter City	1-4	Eyre	5184	7			3		9	5		4	2		1	6					8				11	10		
16		22	BRIGHTON & HOVE ALB	1-2	Webb	4934		2		3		9	5		4			1	6			8		10	7			11			
17	Dec	6	NORTHAMPTON T	1-3	Sherman	4850	8			3		9	5		4	2		1	6						7			11	10		
18		13	Southend United	0-4		4635						9	5		4	2		1	6				10		7			11	8		3
19		18	Brentford	2-1	Scott, Williams	2306						9	5		4	2		1	6				10	8				11		7	3
20		20	CRYSTAL PALACE	0-0		5077		3			5	9			4	2		1	6				10		7			11	8		
21		25	Coventry City	3-3	Whitehouse 2, Hayward	18724		3			5	9			4	2		1	6				11	10	7				8		
22		26	COVENTRY CITY	2-0	Whitehouse, Scott	8176		3			5	9			4	2		1	6				11	10	7				8		
23		27	SWINDON TOWN	4-1	Whitehouse, Sherman, Scott, Eyre	6284		3			5	9			4	2		1	6				11	10	7				8		
24	Jan	17	Watford	0-2		6790		3			5	9			4	2		1	6				11	10	7				8		
25		21	Torquay United	4-4	Eyre 2, Scott, Williams	1745		3				9	5		4	2		1	6				11	10					8	7	
26		28	NOTTS COUNTY	2-1	Eyre 2	4778		3				9	5		4	2		1					11	10	7		6		8		
27		31	Clapton Orient	0-0		5039		3				9	5		4	2		1					11	10	7		6		8		
28	Feb	7	THAMES	3-3	Eyre, Russell, Whitehouse	4890		3				9	5		4	2		1	6				11	10	7				8		
29		14	Norwich City	1-2	Williams	5347	9			3	5				4	2		1	6				11	8					10	7	
30		21	LUTON TOWN	0-0		4439				3	5	9			4	2		1	6				11	8	7			10			
31		28	Bristol Rovers	5-2	Russell, Eyre 3, Moralee	6707				3	5	9				2		1	6				11	8	7		4	10			
32	Mar	7	NEWPORT COUNTY	4-2	Webb, Scott, Eyre, Hayward (p)	3091				3	5	9				2		1	6				11	8	7		4	10			
33		14	Gillingham	0-0		5023				3	5	9				2		1	6				11	8	7		4	10			
34		21	EXETER CITY	3-1	Scott, Eyre, Webb	5337				3	5	9				2		1	6				11	8	7		4	10			
35		28	Brighton & Hove Albion	1-3	Eyre	5524				3	5	9				2		1	6				11	8	7		4	10			
36	Apr	3	Fulham	0-1		7375				3	5	9			4	2		1	6				11	8	7			10			
37		4	TORQUAY UNITED	2-2	Sherman, Eyre	5381				3	5	9			4	2		1					11	8	7		6	10			
38		6	FULHAM	2-1	Eyre, Scott	4573	10	3			5	9			4	2		1					11	8	7		6				
39		11	Northampton Town	2-2	Sherman, Scott	4830		3			5	9			4	2		1	6				11	8	7			10			
40		18	BRENTFORD	1-0	Scott	3662		3			5	9			4	2		1	6				11	8	7			10			
41		25	Crystal Palace	0-1		7754				3	5	9		10	4	2		1	6				11	8						7	
42	May	2	Queen's Park Rangers	0-3		6193					5	9		10	4	2		1	6				11	8		3				7	
						Apps	11	13	9	27	22	39	20	3	37	41	2	42	29	6	2	1	38	33	22	1	9	19	27	7	2
						Goals	1					24				3			1				5	16	4			4	11	3	

F.A. Cup

			Opponent	Res	Scorers	Att	Beswick SMA	Birch J	Bradford J	Brown S	Coxford J	Eyre CR	Forbes AS	Green RE	Halliwell JC	Hayward JW	Hutchinson W	McSevich P	Moralee WE	Morgan MBB	Peed F	Robinson SH	Russell CJ	Scott WH	Sherman FH	Trim RF	Turner HL	Webb WG	Whitehouse JC	Williams LS	Wright R
R1	Nov	29	Walsall	0-1		4113				3		9	5		4	2		1	6				11	8				7	10		

		P	*W*	*D*	*L*	*F*	*A*	*W*	*D*	*L*	*F*	*A*	*Pts*
1	Notts County	42	16	4	1	58	13	8	7	6	39	33	59
2	Crystal Palace	42	17	2	2	71	20	5	5	11	36	51	51
3	Brentford	42	14	3	4	62	30	8	3	10	28	34	50
4	Brighton & Hove Albion	42	13	5	3	45	20	4	10	7	23	33	49
5	Southend United	42	16	0	5	53	26	6	5	10	23	34	49
6	Northampton Town	42	10	6	5	37	20	8	6	7	40	39	48
7	Luton Town	42	15	3	3	61	17	4	5	12	15	34	46
8	Queen's Park Rangers	42	15	0	6	57	23	5	3	13	25	52	43
9	Fulham	42	15	3	3	49	21	3	4	14	28	54	43
10	BOURNEMOUTH	42	11	7	3	39	22	4	6	11	33	51	43
11	Torquay United	42	13	5	3	56	26	4	4	13	24	58	43
12	Swindon Town	42	15	5	1	68	29	3	1	17	21	65	42
13	Exeter City	42	12	6	3	55	35	5	2	14	29	55	42
14	Coventry City	42	11	4	6	55	28	5	5	11	20	37	41
15	Bristol Rovers	42	12	3	6	49	36	4	5	12	26	56	40
16	Gillingham	42	10	6	5	40	29	4	4	13	21	47	38
17	Walsall	42	9	5	7	44	38	5	4	12	34	57	37
18	Watford	42	9	4	8	41	29	5	3	13	31	46	35
19	Clapton Orient	42	12	3	6	47	33	2	4	15	16	58	35
20	Thames	42	12	5	4	34	20	1	3	17	20	73	34
21	Newport County	42	10	5	6	45	31	1	1	19	24	80	28
22	Norwich City	42	10	7	4	37	20	0	1	20	10	56	28

1931/32

15th in Division Three (South)

						Beswick SMA	Birch J	Coxford J	Eyre CR	Forbes AS	Gold W	Halliwell JC	Hayward JW	McSevich P	Miller J	Moralee WE	Nicholson S	Parker RW	Russell CJ	Scott WH	Sherman FH	Thain AC	Trim RF	Webb WG	Webster E	White A	Whitehouse JC	Williams E	Williams LS
1	Aug 29	BRISTOL ROVERS	2-2	Thain, Russell	8178		3	5	9			4	2	1		6			11			10					8		7
2	Sep 2	Torquay United	1-1	Eyre	4485		3	5	9			4	2	1		6			11			10					8		7
3	5	Queen's Park Rangers	3-0	Eyre 2, Russell	18938			5	9			4	2	1		6			11			10	3				8		7
4	9	NORWICH CITY	1-0	Whitehouse	6182			5	9			4	2	1		6			11			10	3				8		7
5	12	EXETER CITY	5-2	Eyre 3, Russell, Hayward	6560			5	9			4	2	1		6			11			10	3				8		7
6	14	Norwich City	2-1	Thain, L Williams	8736			5	9			4	2	1		6			11			10	3				8		7
7	19	CRYSTAL PALACE	4-1	Whitehouse 2, Eyre 2	9638			5	9			4	2	1		6			11			10	3				8		7
8	26	Watford	2-4	Eyre 2	11008			5	9			4	2	1		6			11			10	3				8		7
9	Oct 3	MANSFIELD TOWN	3-2	L Williams, Hayward (p), Thain	7674			5	9			4	2	1		6			11			10	3				8		7
10	10	Brighton & Hove Albion	1-4	McSevich	9134			5	9			4	2	1		6			11			10	3				8		7
11	17	Coventry City	1-6	Hayward (p)	12847			5	9			4	2	1		6			11			10	3				8		7
12	24	GILLINGHAM	0-2		5365			5	9				2	1		6			11		7	10	3		4		8		
13	31	Luton Town	0-1		7231			5	9				2	1		6			11			10		7	4	8	3		
14	Nov 7	CARDIFF CITY	3-0	Hayward (p), Thain, White	6562			5	9				2	1		6			11			10		7	4	8	3		
15	14	Northampton Town	1-1	Thain	6161			5	9				2	1		6						11		10	4	8	3		7
16	21	READING	2-2	Richardson (og), Eyre	6209			5	9					1		6						11	3	10	4	8	2		7
17	Dec 5	FULHAM	0-3		5576	9		5		2		4		1		6			11				3	7		8	10		
18	14	Thames	2-4	Thain, Coxford	827	9		5				4	2	1		6						10	3	11		8			7
19	19	BRENTFORD	1-3	Hayward	5003			5				4	2	1		6				8		10	3	11		9			7
20	25	Clapton Orient	2-1	White, Scott	7366			5				4	2	1		6				8		10		11		9	3		7
21	26	CLAPTON ORIENT	0-1		10255	7		5	9			4	2	1		6				8		10					3		11
22	Jan 2	Bristol Rovers	1-4	Scott	4798	7		5	9			4	2	1		6				8						10	3		11
23	13	Southend United	3-1	Eyre 2, Scott	4227	7		5	9			4	2	1		6				8						10	3		11
24	16	QUEEN'S PARK RANGERS	2-2	Scott, White	5641	7		5				4	2	1		6				8						10	3	9	11
25	27	Exeter City	0-1		3101					5		4	2	1		6			11	10						8	3	9	7
26	30	Crystal Palace	1-1	E Williams	12493								2	1		6	5		11	10					4	8	3	9	7
27	Feb 6	WATFORD	3-3	Eyre, White, Scott	5083				9			4	2	1		6	5		11	10						8	3		7
28	13	Mansfield Town	1-2	Scott	5479				9		1	4	2			6	5		11	10						8	3		7
29	20	BRIGHTON & HOVE ALB	1-2	White	4597						1	4	2			6	5			8	7					10	3	9	11
30	27	COVENTRY CITY	2-2	Hayward (p), Coxford	4408			5			1	4	2			6				8	7					10	3	9	11
31	Mar 5	Gillingham	4-1	Russell, L Williams, Eyre, Webb	5087			5	9		1	4	2			6			11					10		8	3		7
32	12	LUTON TOWN	1-1	L Williams	4277			5	9		1	4	2			6			11					10		8	3		7
33	19	Cardiff City	0-0		6863			5			1	4	2			6		3	11					10		8	9		7
34	25	Swindon Town	0-3		5631			5			1	4	2			6		3	11					10		9	8		7
35	26	NORTHAMPTON T	1-1	E Williams	3272			5			1	4	2			6			11					10		8	3	9	7
36	28	SWINDON TOWN	2-1	White, Hayward (p)	6245			5			1	4	2			6			11	8				10		9	3		7
37	Apr 2	Reading	1-3	Scott	9350			5			1		2		4	6			11	8				10		9	3		7
38	9	SOUTHEND UNITED	0-0		3549			5			1		2		4	6			11	8				10		9	3		7
39	16	Fulham	0-3		14544			5			1		2		4	6			11	8				10		9	3		7
40	23	THAMES	4-2	White, Eyre, L Williams 2	2950			5	9	4	1		2			6			11				3	10		8			7
41	30	Brentford	2-4	Eyre, Russell	5906			5	9		1	4	2			6			11					10		8	3		7
42	May 7	TORQUAY UNITED	5-0	Eyre 2, Russell, L Williams, Hayward(p)	3474			5	9		1	4	2			6			11					10		8	3		7
					Apps	6	2	37	26	3	15	32	40	27	3	42	4	2	31	16	3	20	15	20	6	29	39	6	38
					Goals			2	19				8	1					6	7		6		1		7	3	2	7

One own goal

F.A. Cup

						Beswick SMA	Birch J	Coxford J	Eyre CR	Forbes AS	Gold W	Halliwell JC	Hayward JW	McSevich P	Miller J	Moralee WE	Nicholson S	Parker RW	Russell CJ	Scott WH	Sherman FH	Thain AC	Trim RF	Webb WG	Webster E	White A	Whitehouse JC	Williams E	Williams LS
R1	Nov 28	NORTHFLEET UNITED	1-1	White	6213			5	9					1		6			11			10	3	7	4	8	2		
rep	Dec 2	Northfleet United	1-0	Webb	4253	9		5				4	2	1		6			11				3	7		8	10		
R2	12	BLYTH SPARTANS	1-0	Hayward (p)	7268	9		5				4	2	1		6							3	11		8	10		7
R3	Jan 9	Halifax Town	3-1	Beswick 2, Eyre	18388	7		5	9			4	2	1		6				8						10	3		11
R4	23	Sheffield Wednesday	0-7		32000	7			9	5		4	2	1		6				8						10	3		11

		P	W	D	L	F	A	W	D	L	F	A	Pts
1	Fulham	42	15	3	3	72	27	9	6	6	39	35	57
2	Reading	42	19	1	1	65	21	4	8	9	32	46	55
3	Southend United	42	12	5	4	41	18	9	6	6	36	35	53
4	Crystal Palace	42	14	7	0	48	12	6	4	11	26	51	51
5	Brentford	42	11	6	4	40	22	8	4	9	28	30	48
6	Luton Town	42	16	1	4	62	25	4	6	11	33	45	47
7	Exeter City	42	16	3	2	53	16	4	4	13	24	46	47
8	Brighton & Hove Albion	42	12	4	5	42	21	5	8	8	31	37	46
9	Cardiff City	42	14	2	5	62	29	5	6	10	25	44	46
10	Norwich City	42	12	7	2	51	22	5	5	11	25	45	46
11	Watford	42	14	4	3	49	27	5	4	12	32	52	46
12	Coventry City	42	17	2	2	74	28	1	6	14	34	69	44
13	Queen's Park Rangers	42	11	6	4	50	30	4	6	11	29	43	42
14	Northampton Town	42	12	3	6	48	26	4	4	13	21	43	39
15	BOURNEMOUTH	42	8	8	5	42	32	5	4	12	28	46	38
16	Clapton Orient	42	7	8	6	41	35	5	3	13	36	55	35
17	Swindon Town	42	12	2	7	47	31	2	4	15	23	53	34
18	Bristol Rovers	42	11	6	4	46	30	2	2	17	19	62	34
19	Torquay United	42	9	6	6	49	39	3	3	15	23	67	33
20	Mansfield Town	42	11	5	5	54	45	0	5	16	21	63	32
21	Gillingham	42	8	6	7	26	26	2	2	17	14	56	28
22	Thames	42	6	7	8	35	35	1	2	18	18	74	23

1932/33

18th in Division Three (South)

	Date		Opponent	Score	Scorers	Att	Beswick SMA	Chalmers WR	Coen JL	Coxford J	Eyre CR	Gold W	Hayward JW	Ledwidge J	McGowan R	McPhail DD	Miller J	Moralee WE	Nicholson S	Parker RW	Proctor JR	Richmond WC	Russell CJ	Stevens G	Trim RF	Webb WG	White A	Whitehouse JC	Whitelaw R	Williams LS
1	Aug	27	SWINDON TOWN	5-1	Webb, Eyre, Williams, Russell, White	6364				5	9	1	2				4	6					11			10	8	3		7
2		29	Cardiff City	0-3		8351				5	9	1					4	6			2		11			10	8	3		7
3	Sep	3	Clapton Orient	1-1	Williams	7525				5	9	1					4				2		11			10	8	3	6	7
4		7	CARDIFF CITY	3-2	Whitelaw, Russell 2	6264				5	9	1					4				2		11			10	8	3	6	7
5		10	NORTHAMPTON T	1-1	Eyre	6623				5	9	1					4				2		11			10	8	3	6	7
6		17	Bristol City	1-1	Ledwidge	9009				5	9	1		8			4				2		11			10		3	6	7
7		24	COVENTRY CITY	3-1	Ledwidge, Russell, Eyre	6441				5	9	1		8			4				2		11				10	3	6	7
8	Oct	1	Brentford	1-1	Eyre	12963				5	9	1		8			4	6			2		11				10	3		7
9		8	TORQUAY UNITED	1-2	Eyre	6124				5	9	1		8			4	6			2		11				10	3		7
10		15	Exeter City	3-2	Ledwidge 2, Williams	6641					9	1		8			4	5			2		11				10	3	6	7
11		22	Reading	2-6	Eyre, Ledwidge	7855					9	1		8			4	5			2		11				10	3	6	7
12		29	NORWICH CITY	1-1	Eyre	3823				5	9	1		8			4	6			2		11				10	3		7
13	Nov	5	Brighton & Hove Albion	0-3		4767				5	9	1	2				4	6					11			8	10	3		7
14		12	BRISTOL ROVERS	2-2	Ledwidge, Eyre	4566				5	9	1	2	8			4	6					11				10	3		7
15		19	Aldershot	1-1	Williams	3727				5		1	2	8	9		4	6					11				10	3		7
16	Dec	3	Southend United	1-2	McGowan	6014				5		1	2		9	7					3	6	11			8	10		4	
17		10	CRYSTAL PALACE	3-2	Russell 3	2862				5	9	1				7	4	6			2		10				8	3		11
18		17	Gillingham	0-4		4843		11		5	9	1				7	4				2	6	10				8	3		
19		24	WATFORD	2-2	Russell 2 (2p)	4038				5	9	1		8		7	4	6			2		10	11				3		
20		26	LUTON TOWN	0-2		7342	7			5	9	1		8		11	4	6			2		10					3		
21		27	Luton Town	2-1	White, Beswick	10428	7			5		1			9	11	4	6			2		10				8	3		
22		31	Swindon Town	0-2		4512	9			5		1	11								2	6	10				8	3	4	7
23	Jan	7	CLAPTON ORIENT	4-2	Russell 4	4006				5		1				7	4			3	2	6	9				8	10		11
24		14	Newport County	1-1	Williams	2237				5		1				7	4	6		3	2		9				8	10		11
25		18	QUEEN'S PARK RANGERS	3-0	Russell 2, Whitehouse	2645				5		1				7	4	6		3	2		9				8	10		11
26		21	Northampton Town	0-6		5018						1				11	4	6	5	3	2		9				8	10		7
27		28	BRISTOL CITY	6-1	White, Whitehouse, Russell 4 (1p)	3581			1								4	6	5	3	2		9			11	8	10		7
28	Feb	4	Coventry City	0-3		11080			1								4	6	5	3	2		9			11	8	10		7
29		11	BRENTFORD	1-1	Whitehouse	6853			1	5							4	6		3			9		2	11	8	10		7
30		18	Torquay United	1-2	White	2904			1	5							4			3		6	9		2	11	8	10		7
31		25	EXETER CITY	1-1	Russell	3588			1	5					7		4			3		6	9		2	11	8	10		
32	Mar	4	READING	0-3		5599			1	5							4			3		6	9		2	11	8	10		7
33		11	Norwich City	0-6		11955			1	5							4			3		6	9		2	11	8	10		7
34		18	BRIGHTON & HOVE ALB	1-1	Williams	4209			1	5				7	9		4			3		6			2		8	10		11
35		25	Bristol Rovers	0-1		8046			1	5				7	9		4			3	2	6					8	10		11
36	Apr	1	ALDERSHOT	1-0	Ledwidge	3538			1	5				8		7	4		9	3	2	6					10			11
37		8	Queen's Park Rangers	1-3	Whitelaw (p)	4176			1	5				8		7	4			3	2	6					9		10	11
38		15	SOUTHEND UNITED	4-0	White 3, Williams	4549				5		1	2	8		7	4			3		6					9	10		11
39		17	NEWPORT COUNTY	1-2	White	5540				5		1	2	8		7	4			3		6					9	10		11
40		22	Crystal Palace	0-3		7885		7		5		1					4			3	2	6				8	9	10		11
41		29	GILLINGHAM	1-0	Chalmers	2710		7		5		1					4			3	2	6				8	9	10		11
42	May	6	Watford	1-2	White	3938		7		5		1					4			3	2	6				8	9	10		11
						Apps	3	4	11	37	18	31	8	17	6	14	40	20	4	20	30	17	33	1	6	18	39	39	10	36
						Goals	1	1			8			7	1								20			1	9	3	2	7

F.A. Cup

	Date		Opponent	Score	Scorers	Att	Beswick SMA	Chalmers WR	Coen JL	Coxford J	Eyre CR	Gold W	Hayward JW	Ledwidge J	McGowan R	McPhail DD	Miller J	Moralee WE	Nicholson S	Parker RW	Proctor JR	Richmond WC	Russell CJ	Stevens G	Trim RF	Webb WG	White A	Whitehouse JC	Whitelaw R	Williams LS
R1	Nov	26	Torquay United	0-0		6000				5	9	1		8			4	6			2		11				10	3		7
rep		30	TORQUAY UNITED	2-2	(aet) Eyre 2	4965				5	9	1	2	8			4	6			3		11				10			7
rep2	Dec	5	Torquay United	2-3	Tennant (og), Russell	2500				5	9	1					4	6			2		11			8	10	3		7

Replay 2 at Ashton Gate, Bristol

		P	*W*	*D*	*L*	*F*	*A*	*W*	*D*	*L*	*F*	*A*	*Pts*
1	Brentford	42	15	4	2	45	19	11	6	4	45	30	62
2	Exeter City	42	17	2	2	57	13	7	8	6	31	35	58
3	Norwich City	42	16	3	2	49	17	6	10	5	39	38	57
4	Reading	42	14	5	2	68	30	5	8	8	35	41	51
5	Crystal Palace	42	14	4	3	51	21	5	4	12	27	43	46
6	Coventry City	42	16	1	4	75	24	3	5	13	31	53	44
7	Gillingham	42	14	4	3	54	24	4	4	13	18	37	44
8	Northampton Town	42	16	5	0	54	11	2	3	16	22	55	44
9	Bristol Rovers	42	13	5	3	38	22	2	9	10	23	34	44
10	Torquay United	42	12	7	2	51	26	4	5	12	21	41	44
11	Watford	42	11	8	2	37	22	5	4	12	29	41	44
12	Brighton & Hove Albion	42	13	3	5	42	20	4	5	12	24	45	42
13	Southend United	42	11	5	5	39	27	4	6	11	26	55	41
14	Luton Town	42	12	8	1	60	32	1	5	15	18	46	39
15	Bristol City	42	11	5	5	59	37	1	8	12	24	53	37
16	Queen's Park Rangers	42	9	8	4	48	32	4	3	14	24	55	37
17	Aldershot	42	11	6	4	37	21	2	4	15	24	51	36
18	BOURNEMOUTH	42	10	7	4	44	27	2	5	14	16	54	36
19	Cardiff City	42	12	4	5	48	30	0	3	18	21	69	31
20	Clapton Orient	42	7	8	6	39	35	1	5	15	20	58	29
21	Newport County	42	9	4	8	42	42	2	3	16	19	63	29
22	Swindon Town	42	7	9	5	36	29	2	2	17	24	76	29

1933/34

21st in Division Three (South)

	Date		Opponent	Score	Scorers	Att	Berry WG	Chalmers WR	Coen JL	Coxford J	Dumbrell G	Farrow GH	Fletcher J	Friar J	Gold W	Lax G	Littlewood SC	Miller J	Moralee WE	Parker RW	Proctor JR	Randle J	Richmond WC	Russell CJ	Surtees JW	Trevisone R	Tunstall W	White A	Wilson CH	Wilson FW
1	Aug	26	Charlton Athletic	3-4	White, Friar, Berry	11003	11			5				7	1		9	4		3			6	10				8	2	
2		30	WATFORD	3-2	White 3	6772	11			5				7	1		9	4		3			6	10				8	2	
3	Sep	2	NORTHAMPTON T	4-0	Friar 2, White, Littlewood	7925				5				7	1		9	4		3			6	11				10	2	8
4		6	Watford	2-1	Friar, Littlewood	5913				5				7	1		9	4		3			6	11				10	2	8
5		9	CARDIFF CITY	1-3	F Wilson (p)	9315				5				7	1		9	4		3			6	11				10	2	8
6		16	Exeter City	0-4		7053	11			5		6		7	1		9	4			3				8			10	2	
7		23	GILLINGHAM	1-1	Friar	4874	11			5		6		7	1		9	4			2	3			8			10		
8		30	Crystal Palace	1-4	Tunstall	13502				5		6		7	1			4			2	3		11	8		9	10		
9	Oct	7	BRISTOL ROVERS	2-0	Russell (p), Friar	5885			1	5		6		7				4			3			11	8		9	10	2	
10		14	Southend United	2-1	Surtees, White	4809			1	5		6		7				4			3			11	8		9	10	2	
11		21	Torquay United	0-1		3557			1	5		6		7		2		4			3			11	8		9	10		
12		28	QUEEN'S PARK RANGERS	3-2	Russell (p), Coxford, Tunstall	6324			1	5		6		7		2		4				3		11	8		9	10		
13	Nov	4	Newport County	1-1	Friar	7079			1	5		6		7				4			2	3		11	8		9	10		
14		11	NORWICH CITY	2-4	White, Russell	8241			1	5		6		7				4			2	3		11	8		9	10		
15		18	Bristol City	1-3	Russell (p)	10070		10	1	5		6		7		4						3		11	9			8	2	
16	Dec	2	Swindon Town	2-3	Russell 2	6969	7	10	1	5	2	6						4				3		11	8			9		
17		16	Aldershot	0-0		2790	11	10	1	5	2	6						4				3		9	7			8		
18		23	LUTON TOWN	4-3	Dumbrell 2, Russell, Surtees	4081		10		5	9	6			1			4			2	3		11	7			8		
19		25	READING	1-1	Surtees	8133		10		5	9	6			1			4			2	3		11	7			8		
20		26	Reading	0-4		17323		10		5	9	6			1			4			2	3		11	7			8		
21		30	CHARLTON ATHLETIC	1-2	Fletcher	5847				5	9	6	8		1			4			2	3		11	7		10			
22	Jan	6	Northampton Town	1-4	Berry	11978	11	7	1	5		6	8					4			3	2		9	10					
23		17	CLAPTON ORIENT	2-0	Fletcher, Surtees	2398		7	1	5	9	6	8					4			2	3		11	10					
24		20	Cardiff City	2-4	Friar 2	4261	11	10	1	5		6	8	7		3	9	4			2									
25		27	EXETER CITY	1-3	Littlewood	5515		10	1	5		6	8	7			9	4			2	3		11						
26	Feb	3	Gillingham	1-5	Chalmers	2633		10	1			6	8	7			9	4			2	3	5	11						
27		10	CRYSTAL PALACE	1-1	Littlewood	4852		10		5		6	8	7	1		9	4			2	3		11						
28		17	Bristol Rovers	0-3		9753		10		5		6	8	7	1		9	4			2			11					3	
29		24	SOUTHEND UNITED	1-4	Friar	4145		10		5	9		8	7				4	6		2	3		11		1				
30	Mar	3	TORQUAY UNITED	3-4	Littlewood, Russell 2	3613			1	5		6	8	7		3	9	4			2			11				10		
31		10	Queen's Park Rangers	0-1		7149		10		5	9	4		7	1				6			3		11	8			2		
32		17	NEWPORT COUNTY	0-0		3402		10			9	4		7	1				6			3	5	11	8			2		
33		24	Norwich City	1-6	Littlewood	11855	11	10	1			4		7			9		6			3	5		8			2		
34		31	BRISTOL CITY	5-0	Littlewood 3, Chalmers, Birks (og)	5029		10	1	5		4	8	7			9		6			3		11				2		
35	Apr	2	COVENTRY CITY	3-3	Littlewood, Friar, Russell (p)	6762		10	1	5		4	8	7			9		6			3		11				2		
36		3	Coventry City	1-4	Lax	14484	11	10	1	5		4	8	7		6	9					3						2		
37		7	Clapton Orient	1-4	Littlewood	11231		10	1	5		4	8	7			9		6			3		11				2		
38		14	SWINDON TOWN	1-1	Chalmers	3596		10	1	5	9	6	8	7				4				3		11				2		
39		18	BRIGHTON & HOVE ALB	1-1	Russell	2148	11	10	1	5		6	8	7				4				3		9				2		
40		21	Brighton & Hove Albion	0-6		4291	11	10	1	5	9		8	7		6		4				3							2	
41		28	ALDERSHOT	1-2	Russell	2554	11	10	1			4	8	7					6		3		5	9				2		
42	May	5	Luton Town	0-2		5614		10	1	5	9	4	8	7					6		3			11				2		
						Apps	13	26	25	38	13	35	19	34	16	7	18	32	9	5	23	28	9	36	21	1	8	32	11	3
						Goals	2	3		1	2		2	11		1	11							12	4		2	7		1

One own goal

F.A. Cup

	Date		Opponent	Score	Scorers	Att	Berry WG	Chalmers WR	Coen JL	Coxford J	Dumbrell G	Farrow GH	Fletcher J	Friar J	Gold W	Lax G	Littlewood SC	Miller J	Moralee WE	Parker RW	Proctor JR	Randle J	Richmond WC	Russell CJ	Surtees JW	Trevisone R	Tunstall W	White A	Wilson CH	Wilson FW
R1	Nov	25	HAYES	3-0	Surtees, White 2	6356		10	1	5		6		7				4			2	3		11	8			9		
R2	Dec	9	TRANMERE ROVERS	2-4	Russell 2	7704	11	10	1	5	2	6		7				4				3		9	8					

Division 3 (South) Cup

	Date		Opponent	Score	Scorers	Att	Berry WG	Chalmers WR	Coen JL	Coxford J	Dumbrell G	Farrow GH	Fletcher J	Friar J	Gold W	Lax G	Littlewood SC	Miller J	Moralee WE	Parker RW	Proctor JR	Randle J	Richmond WC	Russell CJ	Surtees JW	Trevisone R	Tunstall W	White A	Wilson CH	Wilson FW
R1	Jan	24	BRISTOL CITY	7-1	* see below	2000		10	1	5		6	8	7			9	4			2	3		11						
R2	Mar	7	NORTHAMPTON TOWN	1-2	Surtees	2000		10		5		4		7	1		9		6			3		11	8			2		

Scorers in R1: Chalmers, Friar 2, Fletcher, Littlewood 2, Russell

		P	W	D	L	F	A	W	D	L	F	A	Pts
1	Norwich City	42	16	4	1	55	19	9	7	5	33	30	61
2	Coventry City	42	16	3	2	70	22	5	9	7	30	32	54
3	Reading	42	17	4	0	60	13	4	8	9	22	37	54
4	Queen's Park Rangers	42	17	2	2	42	12	7	4	10	28	39	54
5	Charlton Athletic	42	14	5	2	53	27	8	3	10	30	29	52
6	Luton Town	42	14	3	4	55	28	7	7	7	28	33	52
7	Bristol Rovers	42	14	4	3	49	21	6	7	8	28	26	51
8	Swindon Town	42	13	5	3	42	25	4	6	11	22	43	45
9	Exeter City	42	12	5	4	43	19	4	6	11	25	38	43
10	Brighton & Hove Albion	42	12	7	2	47	18	3	6	12	21	42	43
11	Clapton Orient	42	14	4	3	60	25	2	6	13	15	44	42
12	Crystal Palace	42	11	6	4	40	25	5	3	13	31	42	41
13	Northampton Town	42	10	6	5	45	32	4	6	11	26	46	40
14	Aldershot	42	8	6	7	28	27	5	6	10	24	44	38
15	Watford	42	12	4	5	43	16	3	3	15	28	47	37
16	Southend United	42	9	6	6	32	27	3	4	14	19	47	34
17	Gillingham	42	8	8	5	49	41	3	3	15	26	55	33
18	Newport County	42	6	9	6	25	23	2	8	11	24	47	33
19	Bristol City	42	7	8	6	33	22	3	5	13	25	63	33
20	Torquay United	42	10	4	7	32	28	3	3	15	21	65	33
21	BOURNEMOUTH	42	7	7	7	41	37	2	2	17	19	65	27
22	Cardiff City	42	6	4	11	32	43	3	2	16	25	62	24

1934/35

17th in Division Three (South)

No	Date		Opponent	Score	Scorers	Att	Cameron WT	Chalmers WR	Curwood A	Farrow GH	Fletcher J	Gold W	Lawson HT	Mellors RD	Messer AT	Moore TD	Moralee WE	Mortimer R	Parker RW	Parris JE	Pincott FC	Richardson, Jack	Richardson J (John)	Richmond WC	Ritchie AW	Smith G	Smith JW	Smith W	Tait T	Turner JT	Twiss R	White A
1	Aug	27	Newport County	1-6	Chalmers	7651		10		4		1					6			11	5		2		7				9	3		8
2	Sep	1	COVENTRY CITY	0-2		7737		10		4		1			5		6			11			2		7				9	3		8
3		5	NEWPORT COUNTY	3-1	Farrow (p), Ritchie, Tait	5722		10		4		1			5		6		3	11					7				9	2		8
4		8	Clapton Orient	1-0	Tait	10304		10		4		1			5		6		3	11					7				9	2		8
5		10	Millwall	0-2		6195	8	10		4		1			5		6		3	11		9			7					2		
6		15	GILLINGHAM	1-1	Mortimer	6208		10		4	8	1			5		6	7	3	11									9	2		
7		22	Reading	1-4	Chalmers	6734		10		4	8	1			5		6	7	3	11									9	2		
8		29	NORTHAMPTON T	0-1		4410		8		4		1				10	6	7	3	11	5								9	2		
9	Oct	6	Cardiff City	1-2	Farrow	5053				8		1				10	6	7	3	11	5							4	9	2		
10		13	Watford	1-3	Tait	6999				8		1				10	6	7	3	11	5							4	9	2		
11		20	ALDERSHOT	4-1	Parris 2, Moore, Mortimer	4921				8				1		10	6	7		11	5		3			2		4	9			
12		27	Swindon Town	2-0	Tait 2	7645				10	8			1			6	7		11	5		3			2		4	9			
13	Nov	3	LUTON TOWN	1-3	Fletcher	5939				10	8			1			6	7		11	5		3			2		4	9			
14		10	Brighton & Hove Albion	0-2		2728				10	8		9	1			6	7	3	11	5							4		2		
15		17	CRYSTAL PALACE	1-1	Farrow (p)	4828				10	8		9	1			6		3	11	5				7			4		2		
16	Dec	1	BRISTOL ROVERS	3-0	Ritchie, Farrow 2	3748		11		10	8			1			6		3		5				7			4		2		9
17		15	TORQUAY UNITED	1-2	Farrow	3171		11		8		1					6		3		5				7			4		2	10	9
18		22	Queen's Park Rangers	1-2	W Smith	4300			9	8		1					6		3	11	5				7			4		2		10
19		25	EXETER CITY	3-2	Parris, Ritchie, White	6414			9	8		1					6			11	5		3		7			4		2		10
20		26	Exeter City	1-4	Farrow	7653		10	9	8				1						11	5		3		7			4		2		6
21		29	MILLWALL	3-1	Moore, Ritchie, Farrow (p)	5038			9	8				1		10			3	11	5				7			4		2		6
22	Jan	5	Coventry City	1-4	Ritchie	14226			9	8				1		10			3	11	5				7			4		2		6
23		12	Charlton Athletic	1-0	Ritchie	10944		10	9					1			6		3	11	5				7			4		2		8
24		19	CLAPTON ORIENT	1-0	Ritchie	4307		10	9					1			6		3	11	5				7			4		2		8
25		26	Gillingham	1-3	Ritchie	2672		10						1			6	9	3	11	5				7			4		2		8
26	Feb	2	READING	4-1	Mortimer, Ritchie 2, Parris	5611		10		8				1			6	9	3	11	5				7			4		2		
27		9	Northampton Town	1-0	Ritchie	3641		10		8				1			6	9	3	11	5				7			4		2		
28		16	CARDIFF CITY	3-1	Ritchie, Parris, Farrow	4764		10		8				1			6	9	3	11	5				7			4		2		
29		23	WATFORD	1-2	Farrow	6768		10		8				1			6	9	3	11	5				7			4		2		
30	Mar	2	Aldershot	1-1	Farrow	3396		10		8				1			6	9		11	5				7	3		4		2		
31		9	SWINDON TOWN	1-1	Parris	3493		10		8				1			6	9		11	5				7	3		4		2		
32		16	Luton Town	0-4		8497		10		8			9	1			6			11				5	7	3		4		2		
33		23	BRIGHTON & HOVE ALB	1-0	Turner	4503		10		8				1	5		6	9		11					7	3		4		2		
34		30	Crystal Palace	0-1		8029		10		8				1	5		6	9		11					7	3		4		2		
35	Apr	6	CHARLTON ATHLETIC	2-2	White 2	6598		10		8				1	5		6			11					7	3		4		2		9
36		10	Southend United	0-0		3479		10		9				1			6			11	5				7	3		4		2		8
37		13	Bristol Rovers	1-4	White	5192		10		8				1			6			11	5				7	3		4		2		9
38		19	Bristol City	1-2	White	8916		10		8				1			6			11	5				7	3		4		2		9
39		20	SOUTHEND UNITED	2-1	White 2	5192		10		8				1			6			11	5				7	3		4		2		9
40		22	BRISTOL CITY	1-1	White	8539		10		8				1			6			11	5				7	3		4		2		9
41		27	Torquay United	2-1	White, Chalmers	2623		10		8				1			6			11	5				7	3		4		2		9
42	May	4	QUEEN'S PARK RANGERS	0-2		4970		10		4				1			6			11	5				7	3	8			2		9
						Apps	1	31	7	39	7	13	3	29	9	6	39	18	22	40	32	1	7	1	33	16	1	33	12	39	1	22
						Goals		3		11	1					2		3		6					12			1	5	1		9

F.A. Cup

Rd	Date		Opponent	Score	Scorers	Att	Cameron WT	Chalmers WR	Curwood A	Farrow GH	Fletcher J	Gold W	Lawson HT	Mellors RD	Messer AT	Moore TD	Moralee WE	Mortimer R	Parker RW	Parris JE	Pincott FC	Richardson, Jack	Richardson J (John)	Richmond WC	Ritchie AW	Smith G	Smith JW	Smith W	Tait T	Turner JT	Twiss R	White A
R1	Nov	24	Aldershot	0-4		5111				10	8		9	1			6		3	11	5				7			4		2		

Division 3 (South) Cup

Rd	Date		Opponent	Score	Scorers	Att	Cameron WT	Chalmers WR	Curwood A	Farrow GH	Fletcher J	Gold W	Lawson HT	Mellors RD	Messer AT	Moore TD	Moralee WE	Mortimer R	Parker RW	Parris JE	Pincott FC	Richardson, Jack	Richardson J (John)	Richmond WC	Ritchie AW	Smith G	Smith JW	Smith W	Tait T	Turner JT	Twiss R	White A
R1	Sep	26	SWINDON TOWN	3-0	Farrow 2 (1p), Tait	2292		8		4				1		10	6	7		11	5					3			9	2		
R2	Oct	17	COVENTRY CITY	2-5	Townsend, Tait	1000				6	8	1						7		11	5		3			2		4	10			

Played at 9 in R2: EE Townsend

		P	W	D	L	F	A	W	D	L	F	A	Pts
1	Charlton Athletic	42	17	2	2	62	20	10	5	6	41	32	61
2	Reading	42	16	5	0	59	23	5	6	10	30	42	53
3	Coventry City	42	14	5	2	56	14	7	4	10	30	36	51
4	Luton Town	42	12	7	2	60	23	7	5	9	32	37	50
5	Crystal Palace	42	15	3	3	51	14	4	7	10	35	50	48
6	Watford	42	14	2	5	53	19	5	7	9	23	30	47
7	Northampton Town	42	14	4	3	40	21	5	4	12	25	46	46
8	Bristol Rovers	42	14	6	1	54	27	3	4	14	19	50	44
9	Brighton & Hove Albion	42	15	4	2	51	16	2	5	14	18	46	43
10	Torquay United	42	15	2	4	60	22	3	4	14	21	53	42
11	Exeter City	42	11	5	5	48	29	5	4	12	22	46	41
12	Millwall	42	11	4	6	33	26	6	3	12	24	36	41
13	Queen's Park Rangers	42	14	6	1	49	22	2	3	16	14	50	41
14	Clapton Orient	42	13	3	5	47	21	2	7	12	18	44	40
15	Bristol City	42	14	3	4	37	18	1	6	14	15	50	39
16	Swindon Town	42	11	7	3	45	22	2	5	14	22	56	38
17	BOURNEMOUTH	42	10	5	6	36	26	5	2	14	18	45	37
18	Aldershot	42	12	6	3	35	20	1	4	16	15	55	36
19	Cardiff City	42	11	6	4	42	27	2	3	16	20	55	35
20	Gillingham	42	10	7	4	36	25	1	6	14	19	50	35
21	Southend United	42	10	4	7	40	29	1	5	15	25	49	31
22	Newport County	42	7	4	10	36	40	3	1	17	18	72	25

1935/36

8th in Division Three (South)

			Opponent	Score	Scorers	Att	Akers WWG	Barrow WH	Bellis GA	Blezzard RJ	Bucknall W	Burgin M	Chalmers WR	Farrow GH	Flaherty J	Gold W	Hooton A	King TP	Mellors RD	Messer AT	Moralee WE	Morgan R	Parris JE	Pincott FC	Riley J	Smith JW	Smith W	Thompson C	Turner JT	Twiss R	White A
1	Aug	31	Southend United	3-3	Parris, Riley 2 (1p)	11487		7	3		2		10						1		6		11	5	9	8	4				
2	Sep	4	LUTON TOWN	2-1	Riley 2	9018		7	3		2		10						1		6		11	5	9	8	4				
3		7	NORTHAMPTON T	4-0	Riley 2, Chalmers, Parris	9547		7	3				10					2	1		6		11	5	9	8	4				
4		9	Luton Town	0-0		9350		7	3				10					2	1		6		11	5	9	8	4				
5		14	Crystal Palace	0-2		15651		7	3				10					2	1		6		11	5	9	8	4				
6		18	Notts County	3-1	Riley, Chalmers, Parris	7735		7	3				10	4				2	1		6		11	5	9	8					
7		21	READING	4-1	Parris 2, Riley, Barrow	13016		7	3				10	4				2	1		6		11	5	9	8					
8		28	Cardiff City	1-1	Chalmers	11844		7	3				10					2	1		6		11	5	9	8	4				
9	Oct	5	GILLINGHAM	1-2	Riley	9186		7	3				10	4				2	1		6		11	5	9	8					
10		12	Brighton & Hove Albion	1-0	Riley (p)	8482		7	3				10	4				2	1		6		11	5	9	8					
11		19	EXETER CITY	1-1	Riley	7763		7	3				10	4				2	1		6		11	5	9	8					
12		26	Newport County	0-0		6320		7	3				10					2	1		6		11	5	9	8					4
13	Nov	2	COVENTRY CITY	1-1	Riley	10309		7	3				10	4				2	1		6		11	5	9	8					
14		9	Queen's Park Rangers	0-2		10042		7	3				10	4				2	1		6		11	5	9	8					
15		16	ALDERSHOT	0-0		7221		7	3			9	10	4				2	1		6		11	5		8					
16		23	Torquay United	2-0	Parris, Burgin	4313		7	3			9	10	4				2	1	5	6		11			8					
17	Dec	7	Bristol City	0-1		7223		7	3			9	10	4				2	1		6		11	5		8					
18		21	Swindon Town	3-2	Riley, Parris, Barrow	3733		7	3					10				2	1		6		11	5	9	8	4				
19		25	Bristol Rovers	1-2	Parris	11231		7	3					10				2	1		6		11	5	9	8	4				
20		26	BRISTOL ROVERS	2-1	Riley, Farrow	12257		7	3					10				2	1				11	5	9	8	4			6	
21		28	SOUTHEND UNITED	2-1	Parris, W Smith	7768		7	3					10				2	1				11	5	9	8	4			6	
22	Jan	4	Northampton Town	1-2	Riley	6167		7	3					10				2	1			8	11	5	9		4			6	
23		18	CRYSTAL PALACE	2-5	Barrow, Chalmers	6926		7	3				10	4				2	1		6		11	5	9	8					
24		22	MILLWALL	1-2	Parris	2354			3	11			10	4				2	1		6		7	5	9	8					
25		25	Reading	2-0	Riley 2 (1p)	7737		7	3				10	4				2	1		6		11	5	9	8					
26	Feb	1	CARDIFF CITY	4-4	Riley 2, Parris 2	7058		7	3				10					2	1		6		11	5	9	8	4				
27		8	Gillingham	2-1	Parris, Riley	6342	7		3				10					2	1		6		11	5	9	8	4				
28		15	BRIGHTON & HOVE ALB	1-2	Riley	5689	7		3				10	4				2	1		6		11	5	9	8					
29		22	Exeter City	3-1	Riley 2, Akers	3513	7		3				10	4				2	1		6		11	5	9	8					
30		29	QUEEN'S PARK RANGERS	0-1		6138	7		5		3		10	6				2	1				11		9	8	4				
31	Mar	7	Watford	1-4	White	6541	7		3					6	10		4	2	1				11	5		8					9
32		14	NEWPORT COUNTY	2-0	Parris, Akers	5396	7		3					6			4	2	1				11	5	9	8		10			
33		21	Aldershot	0-2		4054	7		3					4				2	1		6		11	5	9	8		10			
34		28	TORQUAY UNITED	1-1	Thompson	5227	7		3					6				2	1				11	5	9	8	4	10			
35	Apr	4	Millwall	0-3		7086	7		3					6			4		1				11	5	9	8		10	2		
36		10	Clapton Orient	1-1	Morgan	8325	7		3					6			4	2	1			10	11	5	9			8			
37		11	BRISTOL CITY	3-0	Riley 2, J Smith	6637	7		3				10	6				2	1				11	5	9	8	4				
38		13	CLAPTON ORIENT	2-0	Barrow, Akers	7905	7	11	3				10	6		1		2						5	9	8	4				
39		18	Coventry City	0-2		20985	7		3				10	6				2	1				11	5	9	8	4				
40		22	WATFORD	2-2	Chalmers, J Smith	3630			3			7	10	6				2	1				11	5	9	8	4				
41		25	SWINDON TOWN	1-0	Akers	3951	7		3			9	10	6				2	1				11	5		8	4				
42	May	2	NOTTS COUNTY	0-1		4872	7		3		2		10	6		1							11	5	9	8	4				

	Akers WWG	Barrow WH	Bellis GA	Blezzard RJ	Bucknall W	Burgin M	Chalmers WR	Farrow GH	Flaherty J	Gold W	Hooton A	King TP	Mellors RD	Messer AT	Moralee WE	Morgan R	Parris JE	Pincott FC	Riley J	Smith JW	Smith W	Thompson C	Turner JT	Twiss R	White A
Apps	15	26	42	1	4	5	31	33	1	2	4	38	40	1	27	2	41	40	37	40	21	5	1	3	2
Goals	4	4				1	5	1								1	14		25	2	1	1			1

F.A. Cup

			Opponent	Score	Scorers	Att	Akers WWG	Barrow WH	Bellis GA	Blezzard RJ	Bucknall W	Burgin M	Chalmers WR	Farrow GH	Flaherty J	Gold W	Hooton A	King TP	Mellors RD	Messer AT	Moralee WE	Morgan R	Parris JE	Pincott FC	Riley J	Smith JW	Smith W	Thompson C	Turner JT	Twiss R	White A
R1	Nov	30	Walthamstow Avenue	1-1	Parris	6288		7	3			9	10	4				2	1		6		11	5		8					
rep	Dec	4	WALTHAMSTOW AVENUE	8-1	Chalmers 3, Barrow, Parris 3, Burgin	6321		7	3			9	10	4				2	1		6		11	5		8					
R2		14	BARROW	5-2	Parris 3, Barrow, Riley	11679		7	3					10				2	1		6		11	5	9	8	4				
R3	Jan	11	Bradford City	0-1		15856		7	3				10	4				2	1		6		11	5	9	8					

Division 3 (South) Cup

			Opponent	Score	Scorers	Att	Akers WWG	Barrow WH	Bellis GA	Blezzard RJ	Bucknall W	Burgin M	Chalmers WR	Farrow GH	Flaherty J	Gold W	Hooton A	King TP	Mellors RD	Messer AT	Moralee WE	Morgan R	Parris JE	Pincott FC	Riley J	Smith JW	Smith W	Thompson C	Turner JT	Twiss R	White A
R1	Sep	26	Clapton Orient	1-1	Barrow	1000		7	3				10	4				2	1		6	11		5	9						8
rep	Oct	9	CLAPTON ORIENT	6-2	Chalmers, Riley 2, Barrow, Parris 2	2300		7	3				10	4				2	1		6		11	5	9	8					
R2		30	BRISTOL CITY	1-0	Burgin	2261		7	3			9	10					2	1		6		11	5						4	
R3	Nov	7	Coventry City	2-3	Morgan, Parris	2000			3				10	4				2	1		6	8	11	5	9						

Played at 8 in R2: CR Adkins. Played at 7 in R3: H Pearson

		P	W	D	L	F	A	W	D	L	F	A	Pts
1	Coventry City	42	19	1	1	75	12	5	8	8	27	33	57
2	Luton Town	42	13	6	2	56	20	9	6	6	25	25	56
3	Reading	42	18	0	3	52	20	8	2	11	35	42	54
4	Queen's Park Rangers	42	14	4	3	55	19	8	5	8	29	34	53
5	Watford	42	12	3	6	47	29	8	6	7	33	25	49
6	Crystal Palace	42	15	4	2	64	20	7	1	13	32	54	49
7	Brighton & Hove Albion	42	13	4	4	48	25	5	4	12	22	38	44
8	BOURNEMOUTH	42	9	6	6	36	26	7	5	9	24	30	43
9	Notts County	42	10	5	6	40	25	5	7	9	20	32	42
10	Torquay United	42	14	4	3	41	27	2	5	14	21	35	41
11	Aldershot	42	9	6	6	29	21	5	6	10	24	40	40
12	Millwall	42	9	8	4	33	21	5	4	12	25	50	40
13	Bristol City	42	11	5	5	32	21	4	5	12	16	38	40
14	Clapton Orient	42	13	2	6	34	15	3	4	14	21	46	38
15	Northampton Town	42	12	5	4	38	24	3	3	15	24	66	38
16	Gillingham	42	9	5	7	34	25	5	4	12	32	52	37
17	Bristol Rovers	42	11	6	4	48	31	3	3	15	21	64	37
18	Southend United	42	8	7	6	38	21	5	3	13	23	41	36
19	Swindon Town	42	10	5	6	43	33	4	3	14	21	40	36
20	Cardiff City	42	11	5	5	37	23	2	5	14	23	50	36
21	Newport County	42	8	4	9	36	44	3	5	13	24	67	31
22	Exeter City	42	7	5	9	38	41	1	6	14	21	52	27

1936/37

6th in Division Three (South)

							Bellis GA	Bucknall W	Burns R	Chalmers WR	Cooke TV	Davis E	Gilmore HP	Hutchison D	Keating RE	Kilcar SP	King TP	Lawrence E	Marsden F	Mellors RD	O'Brien W	Parker ESH	Parris JE	Picton HV	Pincott FC	Redfern R	Riley J	Rowley JF	Smith W	Tarrant H	Whittam EA
1	Aug	29	Aldershot	3-1	Smith, Hutchinson, Riley	5655	3		7	10				11			2	6		1					5		9		4		8
2	Sep	2	GILLINGHAM	1-0	Whittam	7034	3		7	10				11			2	6		1					5		9		4		8
3		5	SWINDON TOWN	5-2	* see below	9913	3		7	10		9					2	6		1			11		5				4		8
4		9	Gillingham	0-1		4421	3		7	10		9					2	6		1			11		5				4		8
5		12	Millwall	2-0	Riley, Burns	18534	3		7	10							2	6		1			11		5		9		4		8
6		19	BRISTOL ROVERS	3-0	Riley 3	13113	3		7	10							2	6		1			11		5		9		4		8
7		23	Watford	0-4		3768	3		7	10							2	6		1			11		5		9		4		8
8		26	Northampton Town	0-0		9764	3		7	10							2	6		1			11		5		9		4		8
9	Oct	3	NOTTS COUNTY	1-0	Riley	11974	3		7	10							2	6		1			11		5		9		4		8
10		10	BRIGHTON & HOVE ALB	1-0	Riley	9630	4	3	7	10							2	6		1			11		5		9				8
11		17	Clapton Orient	1-2	Parris	7842	3			10							2	6		1		11	7		5		9		4		8
12		24	WALSALL	3-2	Chalmers, Whittam (p), Riley	8742	3		7	10							2	6		1			11		5		9		4		8
13		31	Luton Town	0-1		11581	3		7	10							2	6		1			11		5		9		4		8
14	Nov	7	CARDIFF CITY	0-2		9231	3		7	10							2	6		1		11			5		9		4		8
15		14	Crystal Palace	2-2	Whittam, Riley	14108			7	10							2	6	3	1			11		5		9		4		8
16		21	EXETER CITY	0-0		7042			7	10							2	6	3	1			11		5		9		4		8
17	Dec	5	QUEEN'S PARK RANGERS	3-1	Riley 2, Parris	7120				10			4		7	8	2	6	3	1			11		5		9				
18		19	TORQUAY UNITED	3-3	Riley 3	6219				10			4		7	8	2	6	3	1			11		5		9				
19		25	Southend United	0-0		10550				10			4		7	8	2	6	3	1			11		5		9				
20		26	ALDERSHOT	2-1	Keating, Riley	12866				10			4		7		2	6	3	1		11			5		9				8
21		28	SOUTHEND UNITED	1-0	Keating	5905				10			4		7		2	6	3	1		11			5		9				8
22	Jan	2	Swindon Town	1-3	Riley	7408				10	2		4		7			6	3	1		11			5		9				8
23		9	MILLWALL	2-1	Keating, Parris	8498			7	10			4		8		2	6	3	1			11		5		9				
24		20	Reading	2-3	Riley (p), Keating	4218				10			4		7	8	2	6	3	1			11		5		9				
25		23	Bristol Rovers	0-4		5229				10			4		7	8	2	6	3	1			11		5		9				
26		27	Bristol City	1-4	Riley	3785				10			4				2	6	3	1			11		5		9			7	8
27	Feb	6	Notts County	3-4	Burns, Keating, Riley	17695			7	10			4		8		2	6	3	1			11		5		9				
28		13	Brighton & Hove Albion	0-1		10778				10			4		7	8	2	6	3	1			11		5		9				
29		20	CLAPTON ORIENT	2-1	Riley 2 (1p)	5576			7	10			4				2	6	3	1		11			5		9				8
30		27	Walsall	1-1	Whittam	2760				10	3							6	2	1					5	7	9	11	4		8
31	Mar	6	LUTON TOWN	2-1	Rowley, Whittam	9432				10	3							6	2	1					5	7	9	11	4		8
32		13	Cardiff City	1-2	Rowley	8582				10	3							6	2	1					5	7	9	11	4		8
33		20	CRYSTAL PALACE	3-1	Rowley 2, Whittam	5047				10	3							6	2	1					5	7	9	11	4		8
34		26	Newport County	0-4		10007				10	3							6	2	1					5	7	9	11	4		8
35		27	Exeter City	1-1	Rowley	6117				10	3							6	2	1					5	7	9	11	4		8
36		29	NEWPORT COUNTY	5-0	Riley 3, Whittam, Chalmers	9373				10	3							6	2	1					5	7	9	11	4		8
37	Apr	3	READING	2-1	Rowley, Lawrence	7061				10	3							6	2	1	5					7	9	11	4		8
38		10	Queen's Park Rangers	2-1	Rowley 2	6002				10	3							6	2	1					5	7	9	11	4		8
39		17	BRISTOL CITY	0-0		6183				10	3							6	2	1					5	7	9	11	4		8
40		21	NORTHAMPTON T	3-2	Whittam 2, Riley	3684				10	3								2	1				6	5	7	9	11	4		8
41		24	Torquay United	0-0		3062				10	3								2	1		11		6	5	7	9		4		8
42	May	1	WATFORD	3-2	Chalmers, Riley, Rowley	5110				10	3								2	1				6	5	7	9	11	4		8
						Apps	14	1	18	42	14	2	13	2	11	6	28	39	28	42	1	7	22	3	41	13	40	12	28	1	34
						Goals			3	4				1	5			1					3				26	9	2		11

Scorers in game 3: Smith, Chalmers, Whittam 2 (1p), Burns

F.A. Cup

							Bellis GA	Bucknall W	Burns R	Chalmers WR	Cooke TV	Davis E	Gilmore HP	Hutchison D	Keating RE	Kilcar SP	King TP	Lawrence E	Marsden F	Mellors RD	O'Brien W	Parker ESH	Parris JE	Picton HV	Pincott FC	Redfern R	Riley J	Rowley JF	Smith W	Tarrant H	Whittam EA
R1	Nov	28	HARWICH & PARKESTON	5-1	Marsden 2, Parris, Riley, Kilcar	8505			7	10						8	2	6	3	1			11		5		9		4		
R2	Dec	12	Mansfield Town	3-0	Parris 2, Riley	11200				10			4		7	8	2	6	3	1			11		5		9				
R3	Jan	16	Everton	0-5		35468			7	10			4		8		2	6	3	1			11		5		9				

Division 3 (South) Cup

							Bellis GA	Bucknall W	Burns R	Chalmers WR	Cooke TV	Davis E	Gilmore HP	Hutchison D	Keating RE	Kilcar SP	King TP	Lawrence E	Marsden F	Mellors RD	O'Brien W	Parker ESH	Parris JE	Picton HV	Pincott FC	Redfern R	Riley J	Rowley JF	Smith W	Tarrant H	Whittam EA
R1	Sep	30	Luton Town	1-3	Parris	2527			7	10						8	2	6	3				11		5		9		4		

Played at 1: W Gold

		P	W	D	L	F	A	W	D	L	F	A	Pts
1	Luton Town	42	19	1	1	69	16	8	3	10	34	37	58
2	Notts County	42	15	3	3	44	23	8	7	6	30	29	56
3	Brighton & Hove Albion	42	15	5	1	49	16	9	0	12	25	27	53
4	Watford	42	14	4	3	53	21	5	7	9	32	39	49
5	Reading	42	14	5	2	53	23	5	6	10	23	37	49
6	BOURNEMOUTH	42	17	3	1	45	20	3	6	12	20	39	49
7	Northampton Town	42	15	4	2	56	22	5	2	14	29	46	46
8	Millwall	42	12	4	5	43	24	6	6	9	21	30	46
9	Queen's Park Rangers	42	12	2	7	51	24	6	7	8	22	28	45
10	Southend United	42	10	8	3	49	23	7	3	11	29	44	45
11	Gillingham	42	14	5	2	36	18	4	3	14	16	48	44
12	Clapton Orient	42	10	8	3	29	17	4	7	10	23	35	43
13	Swindon Town	42	12	4	5	52	24	2	7	12	23	49	39
14	Crystal Palace	42	11	7	3	45	20	2	5	14	17	41	38
15	Bristol Rovers	42	14	3	4	49	20	2	1	18	22	60	36
16	Bristol City	42	13	3	5	42	20	2	3	16	16	50	36
17	Walsall	42	11	3	7	38	34	2	7	12	25	51	36
18	Cardiff City	42	10	5	6	35	24	4	2	15	19	63	35
19	Newport County	42	7	7	7	37	28	5	3	13	30	70	34
20	Torquay United	42	9	5	7	42	32	2	5	14	15	48	32
21	Exeter City	42	9	5	7	36	37	1	7	13	23	51	32
22	Aldershot	42	5	6	10	29	29	2	3	16	21	60	23

1937/38

13th in Division Three (South)

No	Month	Day	Opponent	Result	Scorers	Att	Brooks LW	Brown BR	Chalmers WR	Coley WE	Cooke TV	Harvey J	Keeley A	Lovery JB	Mardon HJ	Marsden F	Mellors RD	Millar NH	Milne AS	Monaghan P	O'Brien W	Picton HV	Pincott FC	Redfern R	Rhodes A	Riley J	Rowley JF	Sanaghan J	Sellars W	Sibley ES	Smith W	Taylor E	Whittam EA
1	Aug	28	Southend United	0-1		10830		7	10		3					2	1					6	5			9	11				4		8
2	Sep	1	CLAPTON ORIENT	2-1	Riley, Smith	6852		7	10		3					2	1					6	5			9	11				4		8
3		4	QUEEN'S PARK RANGERS	1-1	Riley	8882			10		3					2	1			6			5	7		9	11				4		8
4		9	Clapton Orient	0-3		2805			10		3					2	1			6			5	7		9	11				4		8
5		11	Brighton & Hove Albion	1-3	Whittam	9483			10	6	3					2	1						5	7		9	11				4		8
6		14	Bristol Rovers	1-2	Rowley	4443	1		10	6						3							5	7		9	11			2	4		8
7		18	CRYSTAL PALACE	1-0	Riley	8520	1									3			10	6			5	7		9	11			2	4		8
8		25	CARDIFF CITY	3-0	Whittam, Riley 2	10320	1									3			10	6			5	7		9	11			2	4		8
9	Oct	2	Walsall	0-2		5938	1									3			10	6			5	7		9	11			2	4		8
10		9	NORTHAMPTON T	0-0		7417	1		10							3				6			5	7		9	11			2	4		8
11		16	Notts County	2-1	Rowley, Smith	15218	1		10							3				6			5	7		9	11			2	4		8
12		23	NEWPORT COUNTY	1-1	Riley	4741	1		10			11				3				6			5	7		9				2	4		8
13		30	Bristol City	1-2	Whittam	10371	1		10					11		3		2		6			5	7		9					4		8
14	Nov	6	WATFORD	0-0		6412	1		10					11		3		2		6			5	7		9					4		8
15		13	Gillingham	2-0	Riley, Lovery	4648	1		10					11		3		2		6			5	7		9					4	8	
16		20	EXETER CITY	2-2	Taylor, Chalmers	6610	1		10					11		3		2		6			5	7		9					4	8	
17	Dec	4	ALDERSHOT	3-0	Whittam 2, Millar	4298	1		10					11		2		9		6			5	7				3			4		8
18		18	READING	1-1	Taylor	5477	1							11		2		9		6			5	7				3			4	10	8
19		25	TORQUAY UNITED	0-0		6842	1		10					11	9	2				6			5	7				3			4		8
20		27	Torquay United	0-0		5054	1		11						9	2				6			5		8			3			4	7	10
21	Jan	1	SOUTHEND UNITED	7-1	* See below	5726	1			6				11	9	2							5	7	8			3			4		10
22		15	Queen's Park Rangers	2-1	Mardon, Whittam	12846	1			6				11	9	2							5	7	8			3			4		10
23		22	BRIGHTON & HOVE ALB	0-0		7698	1			6				11	9	2							5	7	8			3			4		10
24		26	Swindon Town	0-1		2332	1			6				11	9	2							5	7	8			3			4		10
25		29	Crystal Palace	1-0	Lovery	10485	1			6				11	9	2							5	7	8			3			4		10
26	Feb	5	Cardiff City	0-3		17563	1		10					11	9	3		2		6			5	7							4		8
27		12	WALSALL	5-0	O'Brien 2, Mardon, Lovery 2	5296	1							11	9	3		2		6	10		5	7							4		8
28		19	Northampton Town	3-1	Lovery, O'Brien, Mardon	5337	1						7	11	9	3		2		6	10		5								4		8
29		26	NOTTS COUNTY	1-1	Whittam	8599	1						7	11	9	3		2		6	10		5								4		8
30	Mar	5	Newport County	1-1	Lovery	8285	1							11	9	3		2		6	10		5	7							4		8
31		12	BRISTOL CITY	0-0		11578	1							11	9	3		2		6	10		5	7							4		8
32		19	Watford	2-0	Redfern, Whittam	10294	1							11	9	3		2		6	10		5	7							4		8
33		26	GILLINGHAM	2-0	O'Brien, Smith	6559	1							11	9	3		2		6	10		5	7							4		8
34	Apr	2	Exeter City	1-3	Rhodes	4956	1			4				11		3		2			10	6	5	7	9								8
35		9	SWINDON TOWN	1-2	Mardon	5843			11	4					9			2		6	10		5	7				3	1				8
36		15	MANSFIELD TOWN	5-4	Mardon 4, Whittam	8616				4				11	9	3		2		6	10		5	7					1				8
37		16	Aldershot	0-2		5254				4				11	9	3		2		6	10		5	7					1				8
38		18	Mansfield Town	2-3	O'Brien, Lovery	7198				4				11	9	3		2		6	10		5	7					1				8
39		23	MILLWALL	0-3		9099	1							11	9	3		2		6	10		5	7							4		8
40		25	Millwall	0-4		23021	1		10					11	9	2				6			5	7				3			4		8
41		30	Reading	1-4	Rhodes	3874		7		4				11	9	3		2		6	10		5		8				1				
42	May	7	BRISTOL ROVERS	1-3	Mardon	4118	1							11	9	2				6	10	4	5	7				3					8
						Apps	32	3	19	13	5	1	2	28	23	41	5	21	3	32	15	4	42	36	8	16	11	12	5	7	35	4	39
						Goals			1					8	13			1			5			1	3	7	2				3	2	10

Scorers in game 21: Mardon 4, Lovery, Rhodes, Whittam

F.A. Cup

Rd	Month	Day	Opponent	Result	Scorers	Att	Brooks LW	Brown BR	Chalmers WR	Coley WE	Cooke TV	Harvey J	Keeley A	Lovery JB	Mardon HJ	Marsden F	Mellors RD	Millar NH	Milne AS	Monaghan P	O'Brien W	Picton HV	Pincott FC	Redfern R	Rhodes A	Riley J	Rowley JF	Sanaghan J	Sellars W	Sibley ES	Smith W	Taylor E	Whittam EA
R1	Nov	27	DARTFORD	0-0		6446	1		10					11		3		2		6			5	7		9					4	8	
rep	Dec	1	Dartford	6-0	* see below	3000	1		10					11		3		9		6			5			7		2			4		8
R2		11	Newport County	1-2	Millar	10500	1							11		2		9		6			5	7				3			4	10	8

Scorers in R1 replay: Millar, Chalmers 2, Collins (og), Whittam 2 (1p)

Division 3 (South) Cup

Rd	Month	Day	Opponent	Result	Scorers	Att	Brooks LW	Brown BR	Chalmers WR	Coley WE	Cooke TV	Harvey J	Keeley A	Lovery JB	Mardon HJ	Marsden F	Mellors RD	Millar NH	Milne AS	Monaghan P	O'Brien W	Picton HV	Pincott FC	Redfern R	Rhodes A	Riley J	Rowley JF	Sanaghan J	Sellars W	Sibley ES	Smith W	Taylor E	Whittam EA
R1	Oct	6	READING	1-2	Riley	2000	1				2	11				3		8		6			5	7		9	10				4		

		P	*W*	*D*	*L*	*F*	*A*	*W*	*D*	*L*	*F*	*A*	*Pts*
1	Millwall	42	15	3	3	53	15	8	7	6	30	22	56
2	Bristol City	42	14	6	1	37	13	7	7	7	31	27	55
3	Queen's Park Rangers	42	15	3	3	44	17	7	6	8	36	30	53
4	Watford	42	14	4	3	50	15	7	7	7	23	28	53
5	Brighton & Hove Albion	42	15	3	3	40	16	6	6	9	24	28	51
6	Reading	42	17	2	2	44	21	3	9	9	27	42	51
7	Crystal Palace	42	14	4	3	45	17	4	8	9	22	30	48
8	Swindon Town	42	12	4	5	33	19	5	6	10	16	30	44
9	Northampton Town	42	12	4	5	30	19	5	5	11	21	38	43
10	Cardiff City	42	13	7	1	57	22	2	5	14	10	32	42
11	Notts County	42	10	6	5	29	17	6	3	12	21	33	41
12	Southend United	42	12	5	4	43	23	3	5	13	27	45	40
13	BOURNEMOUTH	42	8	10	3	36	20	6	2	13	20	37	40
14	Mansfield Town	42	12	5	4	46	26	3	4	14	16	41	39
15	Bristol Rovers	42	10	7	4	28	20	3	6	12	18	41	39
16	Newport County	42	9	10	2	31	15	2	6	13	12	37	38
17	Exeter City	42	10	4	7	37	32	3	8	10	20	38	38
18	Aldershot	42	11	4	6	23	14	4	1	16	16	45	35
19	Clapton Orient	42	10	7	4	27	19	3	0	18	15	42	33
20	Torquay United	42	7	5	9	22	28	2	7	12	16	45	30
21	Walsall	42	10	4	7	34	37	1	3	17	18	51	29
22	Gillingham	42	9	5	7	25	25	1	1	19	11	52	26

1938/39

15th in Division Three (South)

							Bird KB	Brooks LW	Elliott WB	Fletcher AF	Gallacher P	Jones JL	Kirkham RJ	Langley WE	Lovery JB	Mardon HJ	Marsden F	Millar NH	Monaghan P	Paton TG	Pincott FC	Ranson R	Redfern R	Sanaghan J	Sellars W	Shaw TF	Smith W	Tunnicliffe WF	Whittam EA	Wilson FC
1	Aug	27	CRYSTAL PALACE	1-1	Whittam (p)	9078		1			10	6		9			2				5		7	3			4	11	8	
2		31	READING	0-0		6901		1			10	6		9			2				5		7	3			4	11	8	
3	Sep	3	Walsall	2-1	Langley, Tunnicliffe	11522		1				6		9			2				5		7	3		10	4	11	8	
4		7	Ipswich Town	2-0	Langley 2	12550		1				6		9			2				5		7	3		10	4	11	8	
5		10	MANSFIELD TOWN	1-1	Tunnicliffe	9414		1				6		9			2				5		7	3		10	4	11	8	
6		17	Queen's Park Rangers	0-2		12157		1	7			6		9			2				5			3		10	4	11	8	
7		24	SOUTHEND UNITED	0-4		7975		1				6		9			2				5		7	3		10	4	11	8	
8	Oct	1	Exeter City	0-0		6887					10			9	11		2		6		5		7	3	1		4		8	
9		8	CARDIFF CITY	0-0		7211			7		10			9			2		6		5			3	1		4	11	8	
10		15	BRISTOL CITY	4-0	Marsden (p), Mardon, Elliott, Shaw	6888			7							9	2		6		5			3	1	10	4	11	8	
11		22	Watford	0-1		8818			7							9	2		6		5			3	1	10	4	11	8	
12		29	NOTTS COUNTY	3-2	Langley 2, Whittam	7585			7					9			2		6		5			3	1	10	4	11	8	
13	Nov	5	Northampton Town	0-2		8645			7					9			2		6		5			3	1	10	4	11	8	
14		12	NEWPORT COUNTY	0-1		7857			7				9	10			2		6		5			3	1		4	11	8	
15		19	Clapton Orient	1-1	Whittam	9832			7				9	10			2		6		5			3	1		4	11	8	
16	Dec	3	Swindon Town	2-4	Langley 2	8704			7	10				9			2		6		5			3	1		4	11	8	
17		17	Aldershot	1-2	Tunnicliffe	3609			7	10				9			2		6		5			3	1		4	11	8	
18		24	Crystal Palace	0-3		4404				10				9			2		6		5		7	3	1		4	11	8	
19		27	Bristol Rovers	0-1		11316				10			2	9					6		5		7	3	1		4	11	8	
20		31	WALSALL	3-1	Kirkham 2, Whittam	5331					10	6	9					2			5		7	3	1		4	11	8	
21	Jan	14	Mansfield Town	0-2		3098				10	8		9				2		6		5		7	3	1		4	11		
22		18	TORQUAY UNITED	2-5	Jones, Lovery	2270					8	6	9		11		2				5	3	7		1	10	4			
23		21	QUEEN'S PARK RANGERS	4-2	Langley 3, Smith	5206				10			3	9			2		6		5		7		1		4	11	8	
24		28	Southend United	2-2	Langley 2	5845	1			10			3	9			2		6		5		7				4	11	8	
25	Feb	4	EXETER CITY	2-0	Whittam, Redfern	5692	1			10			3	9			2		6		5		7				4	11	8	
26		11	Cardiff City	0-5		12309	1						3	9			2		6	10	5		7				4	11	8	
27		18	Bristol City	0-2		10131	1			6				9			2			10	5		7	3			4	11	8	
28		25	WATFORD	1-1	Kirkham	3677	1			6			9				2			10	5		7	3			4	11	8	
29	Mar	4	Notts County	1-0	Tunnicliffe	8539	1						9				2		6	10	5		7	3			4	11	8	
30		11	NORTHAMPTON T	3-1	Kirkham, Redfern 2	4983	1			10			9				2		6	8	5		7	3			4	11		
31		15	PORT VALE	1-1	Paton	3243	1			10			9				2		6	8	5		7	3			4	11		
32		18	Newport County	2-2	Kirkham 2	11637	1						9				2		6	8	5		7	3			4	11	10	
33		25	CLAPTON ORIENT	0-0		4641	1						9				2		6	8			7	3			4	11	10	5
34		29	BRISTOL ROVERS	5-2	* see below	2601	1						9				2		6	8	5		7	3			4	11	10	
35	Apr	1	Torquay United	0-2		3566	1					4	9				2		6	8	5		7	3				11	10	
36		7	Brighton & Hove Albion	1-1	Kirkham	10320	1				10		9				2		6	8	5		7	3			4	11		
37		8	SWINDON TOWN	2-0	Kirkham 2	7325	1				10		9				2		6	8	5		7	3			4	11		
38		10	BRIGHTON & HOVE ALB	2-0	Gallacher, Kirkham	7528	1				10	4	9				2		6	8	5		7	3				11		
39		15	Port Vale	0-2		3902	1				10	4	9				2		6	8	5		7	3				11		
40		22	ALDERSHOT	4-0	Kirkham 3, Whittam	4504	1				10		9				2		6	4	5		7	3				11	8	
41		29	Reading	0-1		2705					10		9				2		6	4	5		7	3	1			11	8	
42	May	6	IPSWICH TOWN	0-0		4736					10		9				2		6	8	5		7	3	1		4	11		
						Apps	17	7	10	12	14	12	25	22	2	2	40	1	31	17	41	1	32	37	18	10	37	40	33	1
						Goals			1		1	1	14	12	1	1	1		1	2			3			1	1	6	6	

Scorers in game 34: Tunnicliffe 2, Paton, Kirkham, Monaghan

F.A. Cup

							Bird KB	Brooks LW	Elliott WB	Fletcher AF	Gallacher P	Jones JL	Kirkham RJ	Langley WE	Lovery JB	Mardon HJ	Marsden F	Millar NH	Monaghan P	Paton TG	Pincott FC	Ranson R	Redfern R	Sanaghan J	Sellars W	Shaw TF	Smith W	Tunnicliffe WF	Whittam EA	Wilson FC
R1	Nov	26	BRISTOL CITY	2-1	Elliott, Langley	10207			7				9	10			2		6		5			3	1		4	11	8	
R2	Dec	10	Bristol Rovers	3-0	Elliott, Langley 2	11982			7	10				9			2		6		5			3	1		4	11	8	
R3	Jan	11	Leeds United	1-3	Fletcher	10114				10			9				2		6		5		7	3	1		4	11	8	

Division 3 (South) Cup

							Bird KB	Brooks LW	Elliott WB	Fletcher AF	Gallacher P	Jones JL	Kirkham RJ	Langley WE	Lovery JB	Mardon HJ	Marsden F	Millar NH	Monaghan P	Paton TG	Pincott FC	Ranson R	Redfern R	Sanaghan J	Sellars W	Shaw TF	Smith W	Tunnicliffe WF	Whittam EA	Wilson FC
R2	Feb	1	Exeter City	2-1	Shaw, Jones	1000	1					9			11		2						7	3		10				5
R3		20	Queen's Park Rangers	2-3	Paton 2	2000	1					9	10					2	6	8		3	7					11		5

Played in R2: WH Cooke (4), R Twiss (6), PW Bright (8)

Played in R3: WH Cooke (4)

		P	W	D	L	F	A	W	D	L	F	A	Pts
1	Newport County	42	15	4	2	37	16	7	7	7	21	29	55
2	Crystal Palace	42	15	4	2	49	18	5	8	8	22	34	52
3	Brighton & Hove Albion	42	14	5	2	43	14	5	6	10	25	35	49
4	Watford	42	14	6	1	44	15	3	6	12	18	36	46
5	Reading	42	12	6	3	46	23	4	8	9	23	36	46
6	Queen's Park Rangers	42	10	8	3	44	15	5	6	10	24	34	44
7	Ipswich Town	42	14	3	4	46	21	2	9	10	16	31	44
8	Bristol City	42	14	5	2	42	19	2	7	12	19	44	44
9	Swindon Town	42	15	4	2	53	25	3	4	14	19	52	44
10	Aldershot	42	13	6	2	31	15	3	6	12	22	51	44
11	Notts County	42	12	6	3	36	16	5	3	13	23	38	43
12	Southend United	42	14	5	2	38	13	2	4	15	23	51	41
13	Cardiff City	42	12	1	8	40	28	3	10	8	21	37	41
14	Exeter City	42	9	9	3	40	32	4	5	12	25	50	40
15	BOURNEMOUTH	42	10	8	3	38	22	3	5	13	14	36	39
16	Mansfield Town	42	10	8	3	33	19	2	7	12	11	43	39
17	Northampton Town	42	13	5	3	41	20	2	3	16	10	38	38
18	Port Vale	42	10	5	6	36	23	4	4	13	16	35	37
19	Torquay United	42	7	5	9	27	28	7	4	10	27	42	37
20	Clapton Orient	42	10	9	2	40	16	1	4	16	13	39	35
21	Walsall	42	9	6	6	47	23	2	5	14	21	46	33
22	Bristol Rovers	42	8	8	5	30	17	2	5	14	25	44	33

1939/40

Football League Division Three (South): Season abandoned on outbreak of War.

1	Aug	26	Notts County	1-2	Kirkham	10772	Sellars W	Marsden F	Sanaghan J	Smith W	Pincott F	Monaghan P	Redfern R	Paton TG	Kirkham J	Gallacher P	Tunnicliffe WF
2		30	QUEEN'S PARK RANGERS	2-2	Monaghan, Redfern	4512	Sellars W	Marsden F	Wilkinson EC	Smith W	Pincott F	Monaghan P	Redfern R	Paton TG	Kirkham J	Gallacher P	Tunnicliffe WF
3	Sep	2	NORTHAMPTON T	10-0	* see below	2916	Sellars W	Marsden F	Sanaghan J	Smith W	Pincott F	Monaghan P	Redfern R	Paton TG	Kirkham J	Gallacher P	Tunnicliffe WF

Scorers in game 3: Gallacher 2, Kirkham 3, Redfern 2, Marsden, Tunnicliffe, Paton

Regional League South B Division

1	Oct	21	Southampton	2-1	Paton, Langley	3000	Stone JSG	Marsden F	Sanaghan J	Burke C	Wilson FC	Twiss R	Redfern R	Paton TG	Kirkham J	Gallacher P	Langley WE
2		28	BRIGHTON & HOVE ALB	6-1	Kirkham 2, Gallacher, Redfern, Paton, Twiss	1737	Stone JSG	Marsden F	Sanaghan J	Burke C	Wilson FC	Twiss R	Redfern R	Paton TG	Kirkham J	Gallacher P	McDonald JC
3	Nov	4	Reading	3-6	Gallacher, Redfern 2	4000	Stone JSG	Marsden F	Sanaghan J	Burke C	Wilson FC	Twiss R	Redfern R	Lovery JB	Kirkham J	Gallacher P	McDonald JC
4		11	FULHAM	2-1	Paton, Langley	2796	Bird KB	Marsden F	Sanaghan J	Burke C	Wilson FC	Twiss R	Redfern R	Paton TG	Langley WE	Gallacher P	McDonald JC
5		18	Portsmouth	5-3	Kirkham 2, McDonald, Paton, Redfern	3000	Bird KB	Marsden F	Sanaghan J	Burke C	Wilson FC	Twiss R	Redfern R	Paton TG	Kirkham J	Gallacher P	McDonald JC
6		25	QUEEN'S PARK RANGERS	3-0	Paton, Gallacher, McDonald	3050	Bird KB	Marsden F	Sanaghan J	Burke C	Wilson FC	Twiss R	Redfern R	Paton TG	Kirkham J	Gallacher P	McDonald JC
7	Dec	2	Aldershot	4-1	Gallacher, Paton, Kirkham, Redfern	5000	Bird KB	Marsden F	Sanaghan J	Burke C	Wilson FC	Twiss R	Redfern R	Paton TG	Kirkham J	Gallacher P	McDonald JC
8		9	Brentford	2-5	Burke, Kirkham (p)	4680	Bird KB	Marsden F	Sanaghan J	Burke C	Wilson FC	Twiss R	Redfern R	Paton TG	Kirkham J	Gallacher P	McDonald JC
9		16	CHELSEA	2-2	McDonald, Kirkham	4000	Bird KB	Marsden F	Sanaghan J	Burke C	Wilson FC	Twiss R	Redfern R	Paton TG	Kirkham J	Gallacher P	McDonald JC
10		23	SOUTHAMPTON	3-2	Paton, Gallacher, Kirkham (p)	2500	Schofield A	Marsden F	Sanaghan J	Burke C	Wilson FC	Twiss R	Redfern R	Paton TG	Kirkham J	Gallacher P	McDonald JC
11		25	Brighton & Hove Albion	3-1	Paton, Redfern, Gallacher (p)	3500	Bird KB	Marsden F	Sanaghan J	Burke C	Wilson FC	Twiss R	Redfern R	Paton TG	Langley WE	Gallacher P	McDonald JC
12		26	READING	2-1	Kirkham 2	7000	Bird KB	Marsden F	Sanaghan J	Burke C	Wilson FC	Twiss R	Redfern R	Paton TG	Kirkham J	Gallacher P	McDonald JC
13		30	Fulham	2-5	Paton, Bacuzzi (og)	2629	Bird KB	Marsden F	Sanaghan J	Burke C	Wilson FC	Twiss R	Lovery JB	Paton TG	Kirkham J	McDonald JC	Langley WE
14	Jan	6	PORTSMOUTH	5-0	Redfern, Paton 2, Gallacher, Kirkham	5000	Bird KB	Marsden F	Sanaghan J	Burke C	Wilson FC	Twiss R	Redfern R	Paton TG	Kirkham J	Gallacher P	McDonald JC
15		13	Queen's Park Rangers	1-2	Paton	8136	Bird KB	Marsden F	Sanaghan J	Burke C	Wilson FC	Twiss R	Redfern R	Paton TG	Kirkham J	Gallacher P	McDonald JC
16		20	ALDERSHOT	2-0	Paton, Gallacher	2000	Bird KB	Marsden F	Sanaghan J	Burke C	Wilson FC	Twiss R	Redfern R	Paton TG	Kirkham J	Gallacher P	McDonald JC
17		27	BRENTFORD	2-2	Kirkham (p), McDonald	3000	Bird KB	Marsden F	Sanaghan J	Burke C	Wilson FC	Twiss R	Redfern R	Paton TG	Kirkham J	Gallacher P	McDonald JC
18	Feb	22	Chelsea	3-4	McDonald, Kirkham, Redfern	3500	Bird KB	Marsden F	Sanaghan J	Burke C	Wilson FC	Rowe T	Redfern R	Paton TG	Kirkham J	Gallacher P	McDonald JC

Regional League South D Division

1	Feb	10	Reading	4-1	Langley, Paton 2, McDonald	1500	Bird KB	Marsden F	Sanaghan J	Burke C	Rowe T	Twiss R	Redfern R	Paton TG	Langley WE	Gallacher P	McDonald JC
2		24	Norwich City	3-4	McDonald, Paton, Marsden (p)	2816	Bird KB	Marsden F	Sanaghan J	Burke C	Rowe T	Twiss R	Redfern R	Paton TG	Millar NH	Gallacher P	McDonald JC
3	Mar	2	WATFORD	1-1	Langley	3000	Bird KB	Marsden F	Sanaghan J	Burke C	Rowe T	Wilson FC	Redfern R	Paton TG	Langley WE	Gallacher P	McDonald JC
4		9	Aldershot	2-3	McDonald, Burke	3000	Bird KB	Marsden F	Sanaghan J	Twiss R	Rowe T	Wilson FC	Redfern R	McDonald JC	Burke C	Gallacher P	Banks R
5		16	CLAPTON ORIENT	4-0	Burke 3, Paton	3000	Bird KB	Marsden F	Sanaghan J	Twiss R	Rowe T	Wilson FC	McDonald JC	Paton TG	Kirkham J	Gallacher P	Banks R
6		22	Southend United	1-2	Marsden (p)	4000	Bird KB	Marsden F	Sanaghan J	Burke C	Wilson FC	Twiss R	McDonald JC	Paton TG	Langley WE	Gallacher P	Banks R
7		23	BRIGHTON & HOVE ALB.	5-0	Paton 3, Marsden (p), Banks	5000	Bird KB	Marsden F	Sanaghan J	Twiss R	Rowe T	Wilson FC	Banks R	Paton TG	Burke C	Gallacher P	McDonald JC
8		25	SOUTHEND UNITED	6-1	McDonald, Marsden (p), Paton, Burke 2, Gallacher	5000	Bird KB	Marsden F	Sanaghan J	Twiss R	Rowe T	Wilson FC	Banks R	Paton TG	Burke C	Gallacher P	McDonald JC
9		30	CRYSTAL PALACE	2-3	Paton 2	5000	Bird KB	Marsden F	Sanaghan J	Twiss R	Rowe T	Wilson FC	Banks R	Paton TG	Burke C	Gallacher P	McDonald JC
10	Apr	3	QUEEN'S PARK RANGERS	1-0	Gallacher	3000	Bird KB	Marsden F	Sanaghan J	Twiss R	Rowe T	Wilson FC	McDonald JC	Paton TG	Burke C	Gallacher P	Edrich WJ
11		6	READING	3-1	Paton 2, Kirkham	3000	Bird KB	Marsden F	Sanaghan J	Burke C	Rowe T	Wilson FC	Redfern R	Paton TG	Kirkham J	McDonald JC	Banks R
12		11	Clapton Orient	0-2		1000	Bird KB	Marsden F	Sanaghan J	Burke C	Swinfen R	Tennant C	Banks R	Foss F	Millar NH	Bigg R	McDonald JC
13		17	Brighton & Hove Albion	3-3	Banks 2, Millar	100	Schofield A	Marsden F	Sanaghan J	Burke C	Hitchmough HR	Twiss R	Banks R	Lovery JB	Kirkham J	Gardiner C	McDonald JC
14	May	18	Crystal Palace	0-6		4223	Coles G	Marsden F	Millar NH	Burke C	Hitchmough HR	Rowe T	Cowan SA	Bright PW	Langley WE	McDonald JC	Banks R
15		25	Watford	1-7	Redfern	1230	Coles G	Marsden F	Millar NH	Hitchmough HR	Rowe T	Burke C	Redfern R	Paton TG	Langley WE	McDonald JC	Banks R
16	Jun	1	Queen's Park Rangers	0-5		2000	Schofield A	Marsden F	Kelly JE	Hitchmough HR	Rowe T	Twiss R	Cowan SA	Burke C	Langley WE	McDonald JC	Banks R
17		8	ALDERSHOT	2-1	Kirkham 2	300	Schofield A	Marsden F	Sanaghan J	Millar NH	Burke C	Malton A	Cowan SA	McDonald JC	Kirkham J	Brewer N	Bungay E

Home game with Norwich City scheduled for June 5th but not played

League Cup

1	Apr	13	BRISTOL CITY	5-1	McDonald 2, Paton, Gallacher, Marsden (p)	4851	Bird KB	Marsden F	Sanaghan J	Burke C	Rowe T	Wilson FC	Redfern R	Paton TG	Kirkham J	Gallacher P	McDonald JC
2		20	Plymouth Argyle	1-0	Redfern	6404	Bird KB	Marsden F	Sanaghan J	Burke C	Rowe T	Wilson FC	Redfern R	Paton TG	Kirkham J	Gallacher P	McDonald JC
3		27	PLYMOUTH ARGYLE	4-1	Gallacher, Kirkham 3	6831	Bird KB	Marsden F	Sanaghan J	Burke C	Rowe T	Wilson FC	Redfern R	Paton TG	Kirkham J	Gallacher P	McDonald JC
4	May	4	WEST BROMWICH ALB.	1-2	Kirkham	9665	Bird KB	Marsden F	Sanaghan J	Burke C	Rowe T	Wilson FC	Banks R	Paton TG	Kirkham J	Gallacher P	McDonald JC
5		11	West Bromwich Albion	1-3	McDonald	7615	Schofield A	Marsden F	Millar NH	Burke C	Wilson FC	Twiss R	Cowan SA	Paton TG	Langley WE	Bright PW	McDonald JC

Guest players included JB Lovery (Bradford City) and T Rowe (Portsmouth)

1940/41

League

No.	Month	Date	Opponent	Score	Scorers	Att.	1	2	3	4	5	6	7	8	9	10	11
1	Aug	31	ALDERSHOT	3-4	Mathews, McDonald, Cowan	1239	Levitt GR	Millar NH	Dixon S	Burke C	Hitchmough HR	Stuttard JE	Cowan SA	Burke G	Mathews RJ	Barrowman W	McDonald JC
2	Sep	7	BRISTOL CITY	5-2	Reid, Mathews 3, Bungay	1271	Levitt GR	Sibley ES	Dixon S	Burke C	Hitchmough HR	Stuttard JE	Cowan SA	Mannion W	Mathews RJ	Reid EJ	Bungay E
3		14	Southampton	1-6	Mathews	1000	Levitt GR	Burke C	Dixon S	Reid EJ	Hitchmough HR	Stuttard JE	Cowan SA	Mannion W	Mathews RJ	McDonald JC	Bungay E
4	Oct	12	READING	1-1	C Burke	2000	Levitt GR	Brunton H	Dixon S	Hitchmough HR	Dann S	Stuttard JE	Cowan SA	Burke C	Mathews RJ	Smith W	McDonald JC
5		19	Reading	1-5	Barrowman	2000	Levitt GR	Brunton H	Kelly JE	Hitchmough HR	Wilson FC	McDonald JC	Cowan SA	Smith W	Burke C	Barrowman W	King AE
6	Nov	2	CRYSTAL PALACE	3-2	Kirkham 2, C Burke	2000	Levitt GR	Dixon S	Kelly JE	Burke C	Brunton H	Stuttard JE	Cowan SA	Watson W	Kirkham J	Smith W	McDonald JC
7		9	Portsmouth	2-4	C Burke (p), McDonald	500	Levitt GR	Dixon S	Kelly JE	Hitchmough HR	Brunton H	Stuttard JE	Cowan SA	Gray H	Burke C	Smith W	McDonald JC
8		16	PORTSMOUTH	4-3	Mathews 2, McDonald 2	1000	Levitt GR	Dixon S	Kelly JE	Hitchmough HR	Dann S	Stuttard JE	Cowan SA	Burke C	Mathews RJ	Smith W	McDonald JC
9		23	Aldershot	2-5	McDonald, Clarke	2000	Levitt GR	Millar NH	Young RG	Burke C	Hitchmough HR	Smith W	Cowan SA	Raynor G	Clarke C	Watson W	McDonald JC
10		30	SOUTHAMPTON	1-1	McDonald	1000	Levitt GR	Kelly JE	Young RG	Hitchmough HR	Brunton H	Burke C	Cowan SA	Watson W	Millar NH	Smith W	McDonald JC
11	Dec	7	Crystal Palace	0-6		1200	Levitt GR	Kelly JE	Young RG	Burke C	Hitchmough HR	Malton A	Cowan SA	Day	Newman' (1)	Watson W	McDonald JC
12		14	Bristol City	0-3		500	Levitt GR	Millar NH	Kelly JE	Hitchmough HR	Brunton H	Burke C	Cowan SA	Newman' (1)	Johnson	Smith W	McDonald JC
13		21	CARDIFF CITY	2-5	C Burke, Cowan	800	Levitt GR	Millar NH	Young RG	Hitchmough HR	Wilson FC	Smith W	Cowan SA	Watson W	Burke C	Newman' (1)	Knight
14		25	BRISTOL CITY	7-1	Smith, C Burke, Mathews 3, Cowan, Spencer	600	Flint HG	Burns L	Trim RF	Burke C	Robinson TW	Wilson FC	Cowan SA	Watson W	Mathews RJ	Smith W	Spencer DH
15		28	Cardiff City	1-5	Spencer	3500	Levitt GR	Burns L	Lomas	Syddall	Robinson TW	Freeman	Cowan SA	Burke C	Dando	McDonald JC	Spencer DH
16	Jan	11	SOUTHAMPTON	5-3	C Burke, Mathews 2, Cowan 2	2841	Wright	Burns L	Young RG	Priestley M	Robinson TW	Burke C	Cowan SA	Watson W	Mathews RJ	Smith W	McDonald JC
17		18	WATFORD	2-5	Cowan, Mathews	300	Green LF	Burns L	Young RG	Priestley M	Robinson TW	McDonald JC	Cowan SA	Watson W	Mathews RJ	Smith W	Okin F
18		25	Portsmouth	2-10	Smith, McDonald	1500	Green LF	Burns L	Young RG	Priestley M	Robinson TW	Syddall	Cowan SA	Watson W	Tebbutt	Smith W	McDonald JC
19	Feb	1	Brighton & Hove Alb.	1-2	C Burke	1000	Dent	Gale	Young RG	Syddall	Robinson TW	Ashall	Cowan SA	Watson W	Burke C	Smith W	McDonald JC
20		8	SOUTHEND UNITED	3-0	Mathews, McDonald, Gray	800	Burke C	Trim RF	Young RG	Cooke WH	Robinson TW	Smith W	Cowan SA	Gray H	Mathews RJ	Rowell JF	McDonald JC
21	Mar	1	SOUTHAMPTON	3-3	Tunnicliffe, Cowan 2	1000	Archibald	Millar NH	Young RG	Priestley M	Jourdan	McDonald JC	Cowan SA	Brunton H	Whittingham A	Chapman	Tunnicliffe WF
22		15	BRIGHTON & HOVE ALB.	1-3	Cowan	1000	Whitelaw DL	Phipps H	Young RG	Brunton H	Robinson TW	Wilson FC	Cowan SA	Smith W	Whittingham A	Mason J	McDonald JC
23		22	PORTSMOUTH	3-0	Brunton, McDonald, Cowan	3000	Bartram S	Dixon S	Trim RF	Newman' (2)	Robinson TW	Wilson FC	Cowan SA	Brunton H	Whittingham A	Smith W	McDonald JC
24		29	Watford	0-5		1200	Bartram S	Westlake FA	Dixon S	Priestley M	Blackadder F	Young RG	Cowan SA	Watson W	Whittingham A	Smith W	McDonald JC
25	Apr	12	SOUTHAMPTON	4-2	Whittingham 3, Brunton	1000	Bartram S	Dixon S	Young RG	Rothery H	Robinson TW	Longdon C	Cowan SA	Brunton H	Whittingham A	Watson W	McDonald JC
26		26	LUTON TOWN	2-1	Chew (og), Whittingham	2000	Bartram S	Dixon S	Young RG	Rothery H	Robinson TW	Longdon C	Cowan SA	Watson W	Whittingham A	Smith W	McDonald JC
27	May	10	Portsmouth	0-5		2000	Bartram S	Dixon S	Young RG	Priestley M	Robinson TW	Whittingham A	Cowan SA	Gray H	Mathews RJ	Smith W	Jefferies

League Cup

Month	Date	Opponent	Score	Scorers	Att.	1	2	3	4	5	6	7	8	9	10	11
Feb	15	Tottenham Hotspur	1-4	Sibley (p)	3413	Burke C	Sibley ES	Trim RF	Smith W	Robinson TW	Wilson FC	Cowan SA	Paton TG	Mathews RJ	Watson W	McDonald JC
	22	TOTTENHAM H.	1-6	Gray	2000	Flint HG	Burke C	Kelly JE	Smith W	Robinson TW	Wilson FC	Cowan SA	Gray H	Mathews RJ	Watson W	McDonald JC

Hants Combination Cup

Month	Date	Opponent	Score	Scorers	Att.	1	2	3	4	5	6	7	8	9	10	11
Apr	5	SOUTHAMPTON	1-1	Whittingham (p)	2000	Whitelaw DL	Westlake FA	Dixon S	Rothery H	Robinson TW	Young RG	Cowan SA	Brunton H	Whittingham A	Watson W	McDonald JC
May	3	SOUTHAMPTON	2-3	Whittingham 2 (1p)	2000	Bartram S	Westlake FA	Dixon S	Rothery H	Oakes, James	Longdon C	Cowan SA	Watson W	Whittingham A	Smith W	McDonald JC

Portsmouth beat Aldershot and then Southampton to win the Cup

Guest Players:

Archibald (Army)
Ashall (Army)
W Barrowman (Scots junior club)
S Bartram (Charlton Ath.)
F Blackadder (Carlisle United)
H Brunton (Manchester City)
E Bungay (Bournemouth Gasworks)
G Burke (Gateshead)
L Burns (ex Cardiff City)
C Clarke (Luton Town)

SA Cowan (Bournemouth Gasworks)
S Dann (Newcastle United)
Dent (Army)
S Dixon (Plymouth Argyle)
HG Flint (Army)
Gale (Army)
H Gray (Barnsley)
LF Green (Christchurch)
JE Kelly (York City)
C Longdon (Brighton & Hove Alb.)

A Malton (Bournemouth Gasworks)
W Mannion (Middlesbrough)
RJ Mathews (Walthamstow Ave)
J Oakes (Charlton Ath.)
F Okin (Kingstonian)
G Raynor (Aldershot)
EJ Reid (Norwich City)
TW Robinson (Barnsley)
H Rothery (Sheff. United)
ES Sibley (Blackpool)

DH Spencer (Army amateur)
JE Stuttard (Plymouth Argyle)
Tebbutt (Army)
RF Trim (Nottingham Forest)
W Watson (Huddersfield Town)
FA Westlake (Sheff. Wednesday)
DL Whitelaw (ex Southend United)
A Whittingham (Bradford City)

1941/42

Football League (Southern Section)

1	Sep	13	BRISTOL CITY	2-1	Rowell, Gray	2943	Holland	Dixon S	Young RG	Rothery H	Cawthorne W	Whittingham A	Cowan SA	Smith W	Tarrant	Rowell JF	Young G
2		20	Bristol City	1-2	H Griffiths	4500	Weare AJ	Marsden F	Dixon S	Cawthorne W	Robinson TW	Young RG	Cowan SA	Griffiths H	Morrison JA	Whittingham A	Smith W
3		27	Luton Town	1-3	Whittingham	1500	Weare AJ	Marsden F	Dixon S	Young RG	Robinson TW	Smith W	Cowan SA	Gallacher P	Whittingham A	Rowell JF	Rose NJ
4	Oct	4	LUTON TOWN	1-0	Whittingham (p)	3000	Rigg T	Westlake FA	Dixon S	Rothery H	Robinson TW	Smith W	Cowan SA	Watson W	Whittingham A	Hinchliffe T	Rose NJ
5		11	SOUTHAMPTON	6-1	Hinchliffe 2, Morrison 2, Tidman 2	3500	Rigg T	Westlake FA	Dixon S	Brook L	Robinson TW	Whittingham A	Cowan SA	Watson W	Morrison JA	Hinchliffe T	Tidman O
6		18	Southampton	3-4	Brook, Whittingham (p), Rowell	1600	Rigg T	Marsden F	Dixon S	Cawthorne W	Robinson TW	Whittingham A	Tidman O	Brook L	Morrison JA	Watson W	Rowell JF
7		25	Cardiff City	2-0	Morrison, Brook	5000	Weare AJ	Westlake FA	Marsden F	Cawthorne W	Robinson TW	Whittingham A	Cowan SA	Brook L	Morrison JA	Watson W	Rowell JF
8	Nov	1	CARDIFF CITY	3-2	Brook, H Griffiths, Cawthorne	4000	Weare AJ	Marsden F	Young RG	Cawthorne W	Robinson TW	Whittingham A	Cowan SA	Griffiths H	Brook L	Watson W	McDonald JC
9		22	Southampton	2-5	Deakin, Watson	2500	Weare AJ	Westlake FA	Young RG	Cawthorne W	Robinson TW	Whittingham A	Cowan SA	Watson W	Morrison JA	Rowell JF	Deakin G
10		29	SOUTHAMPTON	5-0	Whittingham, Rowell 3, Morrison	2500	Weare AJ	Dixon S	Simpson J	Woodward L	Riches W	Young RG	Cowan SA	Whittingham A	Morrison JA	Veal W	Rowell JF

League War Cup Qualifying Matches

1	Jan	10	Bristol City	0-5		4000	Rigg T	Marsden F	Dixon S	Cawthorne W	Riches W	Woodward L	Cowan SA	Sweeney	Ray CH	Whittingham A	McDonald JC
2		17	BRISTOL CITY	2-2	Whittingham 2	2000	Rigg T	Marsden F	Dixon S	Cawthorne W	Riches W	Woodward L	Cowan SA	Watson W	Whittingham A	Griffiths H	Rowell JF
3		31	SOUTHAMPTON	3-4	Whittingham, McCulloch 2	2500	Whitehead GK	Dixon S	Simpson J	Waller H	Wilson FC	Woodward L	Whittingham A	Watson W	McCulloch D	Rowell JF	Griffiths MW
4	Feb	7	CARDIFF CITY	2-1	Whittingham, Cowan	1500	Bartram S	Dixon S	Young RG	Cawthorne W	Waller H	Simpson J	Cowan SA	Whittingham A	McCulloch D	Rowell JF	Delaney
5		14	Cardiff City	0-6		5500	Tweedy GJ	Young RG	Simpson J	Cawthorne W	Lindley WM	Picton H	Cowan SA	Halliday T	Whittingham A	Layton WH	Spencer
6		21	Southampton	2-2	Whittingham, Cowan	2000	Tweedy GJ	Dixon S	Young RG	Cawthorne W	Riches W	Woodward L	Cowan SA	Watson W	Whittingham A	Rowell JF	Griffiths MW
7		28	SOUTHAMPTON	2-0	M Griffiths, Cowan	2000	Platt EH	Dixon S	Young RG	Gunn GD	Riches W	Woodward L	Cowan SA	Watson W	Whittingham A	Veal W	Griffiths MW
8	Mar	7	Southampton	0-1		2000	Bartram S	Dixon S	Young RG	Cawthorne W	Westlake FA	Woodward L	Cowan SA	Stapleton	Whittingham A	Tarrant	Rowell JF

Guest players:

S Bartram (Charlton Ath.)
L Brook (Huddersfield Town)
G Deakin (Chester)
S Dixon (Plymouth Argyle)
H Griffiths (Tranmere Rovers)
M Griffiths (Leicester City)
T Halliday (Exeter City)
T Hinchliffe (Derby County)
WH Layton (Reading)
W Lindley (Everton)
D McCulloch (Derby County)
J Morrison (Tottenham Hotspur)
H Picton (Crewe Alex.)
C Ray (Aldershot)

W Riches (Hull City)
T Rigg (Middlesbrough)
TW Robinson (Barnsley)
J Simpson (Huddersfield Town)
Stapleton - may be Albert, of Southport
Tarrant (Sutton United)
G Tweedy (Grimsby Town)
O Tidman (Chelmsford City)
H Waller (Arsenal)
W Watson (Huddersfield Town)
F Westlake (Sheffield Wed.)
G Whitehead (Bolton Wan.)
A Whittingham (Bradford City)

1945/46

Winners of Division Three (South) League Cup

Division Three South: Southern Section

No	Month	Date	Opponent	Score	Scorers	Att	1	2	3	4	5	6	7	8	9	10	11
1	Aug	25	Cardiff City	3-9	Burke 2, Thomas (p)	8856	Bird KB	Marsden F	Dixon S	Taylor J	Pincott F	Simpson J	Redfern R	Paton TG	Thomas JE	Bretherton T	King AE
2	Sep	1	CARDIFF CITY	1-5	Dixon	6150	Bird KB	Marsden F	Dixon S	Taylor J	Cothliff HJ	Simpson J	Redfern R	Paton TG	Jones NG	Stocker TM	McDonald JC
3		8	ALDERSHOT	7-0	Thomas 3, Paton, Busby, McDonald, Finch	5775	Bird KB	Marsden F	Simpson J	Robinson J	Wilson FC	Cothliff HJ	Finch LC	Paton TG	Thomas JE	Busby M	McDonald JC
4		12	Torquay United	2-3	Redfern, Mayes	1836	Mallen RH	Paton TG	Dixon S	Robinson J	Darling HL	Raybould ME	Mayes TB	Thomas SE	Thomas JE	Jones NG	Redfern R
5		15	Aldershot	2-2	Finch, Paton	4052	Bird KB	Marsden F	Simpson J	Robinson J	Wilson FC	Dixon S	Finch LC	Paton TG	Thomas JE	Fielding WA	McDonald JC
6		22	BRISTOL CITY	8-1	Paton, Thomas 3, Finch 2, Fielding, McDonald	6969	Bird KB	Marsden F	Simpson J	Busby M	Wilson FC	Summerbee GC	Finch LC	Paton TG	Thomas JE	Fielding WA	McDonald JC
7		29	Bristol City	1-1	McDonald	11162	Bird KB	Marsden F	Simpson J	Robinson J	Dixon S	Preece JC	Redfern R	Paton TG	Jones NG	Cothliff HJ	McDonald JC
8	Oct	6	Brighton & Hove Alb.	2-4	McDonald, Thomas	7243	Bird KB	Marsden F	Simpson J	Robinson J	Dixon S	Summerbee GC	Burke C	Paton TG	Thomas JE	Cothliff HJ	McDonald JC
9		13	BRIGHTON & HOVE ALB.	3-0	McDonald, Kirkham, Paton	7361	Bird KB	Marsden F	Simpson J	Burke C	Dixon S	Summerbee GC	Mayes TB	Paton TG	Kirkham J	Cothliff HJ	McDonald JC
10		20	EXETER CITY	3-1	Thomas 2, Cothliff	6051	Bird KB	Marsden F	Simpson J	Burke C	Troke FJ	Summerbee GC	Mayes TB	Paton TG	Thomas JE	Cothliff HJ	Ross
11		24	SWINDON TOWN	2-4	Thomas, Cothliff	2630	Bird KB	Trim RF	Simpson J	Burke C	Troke FJ	Tagg E	Mayes TB	Paton TG	Thomas JE	Cothliff HJ	King AE
12		27	Exeter City	3-0	Paton, McDonald, Summerbee	6376	Bird KB	Marsden F	Simpson J	Burke C	Troke FJ	Summerbee GC	Mayes TB	Paton TG	Thomas JE	Cothliff HJ	McDonald JC
13	Nov	7	Swindon Town	1-2	Thomas	4612	Bird KB	Dixon S	Simpson J	Burke C	Troke FJ	Cothliff HJ	Mayes TB	Paton TG	Thomas JE	Finch LC	McDonald JC
14	Dec	1	Reading	2-3	Paton, McDonald (p)	5179	Bird KB	Marsden F	Young RG	Burke C	Tootill GA	Cothliff HJ	Squires A	Paton TG	Troke FJ	Gallacher P	McDonald JC
15		8	READING	4-1	Thomas 2, McDonald 2	4433	Bird KB	Paton TG	Young RG	Burke C	Tootill GA	Squires A	Olver WE	Bretherton T	Thomas JE	Gallacher P	McDonald JC
16		22	Bristol Rovers	2-2	McDonald, Burke	7229	Bird KB	Marsden F	Young RG	Squires A	Troke FJ	Cothliff HJ	Redfern R	Paton TG	Burke C	Gallacher P	McDonald JC
17		25	Crystal Palace	1-4	McDonald (p)	10455	Bird KB	Marsden F	Young RG	Squires A	Troke FJ	Cothliff HJ	Redfern R	Paton TG	Burke C	Gallacher P	McDonald JC
18		26	CRYSTAL PALACE	2-1	Burke, Dawes (og)	10052	Bird KB	Marsden F	Young RG	Squires A	Troke FJ	Cothliff HJ	Finch LC	Paton TG	Burke C	Gallacher P	McDonald JC
19		29	TORQUAY UNITED	0-2		5831	Bird KB	Marsden F	Summerbee GC	Burke C	Troke FJ	Robinson J	Liddle TB	Paton TG	Thomas JE	Gallacher P	McDonald JC
20	Jan	5	BRISTOL ROVERS	3-5	McDonald 2, Paton	5942	Bird KB	Marsden F	Martin E	Burke C	Troke FJ	Cothliff HJ	Olver WE	Paton TG	Taylor (RAF)	Gallacher P	McDonald JC

Division Three (South) Cup

No	Month	Date	Opponent	Score	Scorers	Att	1	2	3	4	5	6	7	8	9	10	11
1	Jan	12	ALDERSHOT	3-0	McDonald, Mayes, Burke	6048	Mallen RH	Marsden F	Sanaghan J	Paton TG	Troke FJ	Cothliff HJ	Mayes TB	Rose JW	Burke C	Gallacher P	McDonald JC
2		19	Aldershot	1-2	Gallacher	3456	Bird KB	Marsden F	Young RG	Tagg E	Burke C	Sanaghan J	Redfern R	Paton TG	Wilkinson E	Gallacher P	McDonald JC
3	Feb	2	Brighton & Hove Alb.	4-1	Paton, McDonald, Thomas 2	4000	Bird KB	Marsden F	Sanaghan J	Burke C	Wilson FC	Tagg E	Redfern R	Paton TG	Thomas JE	Gallacher P	McDonald JC
4		9	Swindon Town	0-0		9149	Bird KB	Marsden F	Sanaghan J	Salter RJ	Burke C	Tagg E	Redfern R	Paton TG	Thomas JE	Gallacher P	McDonald JC
5		16	SWINDON TOWN	6-1	Thomas 2, McDonald 3, Paton	7169	Bird KB	Marsden F	Sanaghan J	Summerbee GC	Burke C	Tagg E	Redfern R	Paton TG	Thomas JE	Gallacher P	McDonald JC
6		23	Crystal Palace	1-2	Kirkham	10862	Bird KB	Marsden F	Sanaghan J	Gallacher P	Burke C	Tagg E	Salter RJ	Paton TG	Kirkham J	McDonald JC	Grant
7	Mar	2	CRYSTAL PALACE	4-0	Thomas 2, Paton, Redfern	9869	Bird KB	Marsden F	Sanaghan J	Gallacher P	Burke C	Tagg E	Redfern R	Paton TG	Thomas JE	Kirkham J	McDonald JC
8		9	BRISTOL ROVERS	3-3	Paton, Thomas 2	10019	Bird KB	Marsden F	Sanaghan J	Gallacher P	Burke C	Tagg E	Redfern R	Paton TG	Thomas JE	Kirkham J	McDonald JC
9		16	Bristol Rovers	2-1	Kirkham, Paton	9000	Bird KB	Marsden F	Sanaghan J	Gallacher P	Burke C	Tagg E	Rose JW	Paton TG	Thomas JE	Kirkham J	McDonald JC
10		23	Reading	1-1	Thomas	10790	Bird KB	Marsden F	Sanaghan J	Gallacher P	Burke C	Tagg E	Currie JE	Paton TG	Thomas JE	Kirkham J	McDonald JC
11		30	READING	3-2	Currie, Kirkham, McDonald	12487	Bird KB	Marsden F	Sanaghan J	Woodward L	Burke C	Tagg E	Currie JE	Paton TG	Kirkham J	Gallacher P	McDonald JC
12	Apr	6	EXETER CITY	1-1	Thomas	9755	Bird KB	Marsden F	Sanaghan J	Gallacher P	Burke C	Tagg E	Currie JE	Paton TG	Thomas JE	Kirkham J	McDonald JC
13		13	Exeter City	1-3	McDonald	8000	Bird KB	Marsden F	Sanaghan J	Burke C	Wilson FC	Gallacher P	Currie JE	Paton TG	Thomas JE	Kirkham J	McDonald JC
14		19	BRIGHTON & HOVE ALB.	4-0	Thomas, Kirkham, Currie, McDonald	9419	Bird KB	Marsden F	Sanaghan J	Burke C	Wilson FC	Gallacher P	Currie JE	Paton TG	Thomas JE	Kirkham J	McDonald JC
15		20	BRISTOL CITY	3-2	Thomas 2, Kirkham	12863	Bird KB	Marsden F	Sanaghan J	Burke C	Wilson FC	Gallacher P	Currie JE	Paton TG	Thomas JE	Kirkham J	McDonald JC
16		22	Bristol City	0-1		11632	Bird KB	Marsden F	Sanaghan J	Burke C	Wilson FC	Gallacher P	Currie JE	Paton TG	Thomas JE	Kirkham J	McDonald JC
SF		27	QUEEN'S PARK RANGERS	1-1	Tagg	12762	Bird KB	Marsden F	Sanaghan J	Burke C	Wilson FC	Gallacher P	Currie JE	Paton TG	Kirkham J	Tagg E	McDonald JC
SFr	May	1	Queen's Park Rangers	1-0	(aet) Kirkham	18065	Bird KB	Marsden F	Sanaghan J	Woodward L	Wilson FC	Gallacher P	Currie JE	Paton TG	Kirkham J	Tagg E	McDonald JC
F		4	Walsall	1-0	McDonald	19175	Bird KB	Marsden F	Sanaghan J	Woodward L	Wilson FC	Gallacher P	Currie JE	Paton TG	Kirkham J	Tagg E	McDonald JC

SF replay played to a finish: Kirkham scored after 136 minutes. Final at Stamford Bridge.

F.A. Cup (played over two legs)

Round	Month	Date	Opponent	Score	Scorers	Att	1	2	3	4	5	6	7	8	9	10	11
R1/1	Nov	17	Lovell's Athletic	1-4	Thomas	4000	Bird KB	Marsden F	Cooke WH	Burke C	Troke FJ	Tagg E	Mayes TB	Paton TG	Thomas JE	Smart L	McDonald JC
R1/2		24	LOVELL'S ATHLETIC	3-2	Paton, Thomas 2	8894	Bird KB	Marsden F	Cooke WH	Burke C	Troke FJ	Thomas DJ	Mayes TB	Paton TG	Thomas JE	Gallacher P	McDonald JC

Guest players in League matches were limited to five per team (August 25th) and three per team from November 7th onwards. Guest players were not allowed in the F.A. Cup but an exception was made for JE Thomas, an amateur registered with West Brom. Other guest players:

T Bretherton (RAF)
Matt Busby (Liverpool)
H Cothliff (Torqyau United)
L Darling (Brighton & Hove Alb.)
S Dixon (Plymouth Argyle)
W Fielding (Everton)
LC Finch (Barnet)

Grant (RAF amateur, recruited 15 mins before kick-off)
NG Jones (Wrexham)
A King (Bournemouth Gasworks)
Liddle (RAF)
T Martin (Brighton & Hove Alb.)
TB Mayes (Royal Engereers amateur)
RH Mallen (RAF amateur)

J Preece (Southport, but guesting for Bristol City)
ME Raybould (Cardiff City)
J Robinson (Norwich City)
Ross (RAF, last minute recruit)
J Simpson (Huddersfield Town)
Squires (RAF)
TM Stocker (Hitchin)

G Sumemrbee (Aldershot)
J Taylor (Huddersfield Town)
Taylor (RAF, last minute recruit at Eastville)
SE Thomas (RAF)
G Toothill (Sheffield United)
RF Trim (Derby County)
F Troke (Gosport Boro Ath. amateur)

TABLES 1939/40 to 1945/46

1939/40

SOUTH 'B'

	p	w	d	l	f	a	pts
Queen's Park Rangers	18	12	2	4	49	26	26
BOURNEMOUTH	18	11	2	5	52	37	24
Chelsea	18	9	5	4	43	37	23
Reading	18	10	2	6	47	42	22
Brentford	18	8	2	8	42	41	18
Fulham	18	7	4	7	50	51	18
Portsmouth	18	7	2	9	37	42	16
Aldershot	18	5	4	9	38	49	14
Brighton & Hove Albion	18	5	1	12	42	53	11
Southampton	18	4	0	14	41	63	8

SOUTH 'D'

	p	w	d	l	f	a	pts
Crystal Palace	18	13	1	4	62	30	27
Queen's Park Rangers	18	10	3	5	38	28	23
Watford	18	7	7	4	41	29	21
Southend	18	8	3	7	41	37	19
Aldershot	18	7	3	8	38	36	17
Clapton Orient	18	7	3	8	33	45	17
Norwich City	17	6	4	7	31	31	16
BOURNEMOUTH	17	7	2	8	38	40	16
Reading	18	6	2	10	31	42	14
Brighton & Hove Albion	18	2	4	12	30	65	8

Bournemouth v Norwich City not played

1940/41

There were 34 clubs in the 'South' Division, with positions decided on 'goal average'. Bournemouth finished in 29th place with a goal average of 0.641 and this record:

p	w	d	l	f	a
27	9	3	15	59	92

1941/42

SOUTH DIVISION

	p	w	d	l	f	a	pts	av.
Leceister City	17	11	3	3	40	17	25	26.40
West Bromwich Albion	13	9	1	3	62	26	19	26.30
Cardiff City	15	9	1	5	43	28	19	22.80
Norwich City	8	4	2	2	20	13	10	22.50
BOURNEMOUTH	10	6	0	4	26	18	12	21.60
Bristol City	15	9	0	6	46	45	18	21.60
Walsall	18	9	1	8	49	45	19	19.00
Northampton Town	16	7	2	7	39	38	16	18.00
Wolverhampton Wan.	16	6	2	8	27	36	14	15.75
Southampton	10	4	0	6	27	32	8	14.40
Luton Town	18	5	1	12	34	73	11	11.00
Nottingham Forest	13	2	1	10	18	39	5	6.90
Swansea Town	9	1	0	8	18	39	2	4.00

Positions were calculated on 'average points' assuming each club had played 18 matches

LEAGUE CUP QUALIFYING COMPETITION

There were 51 clubs in the competition, of which 32 qualified for the rounds proper. Bournemouth finished in 40th place and did not qualify.
Their record was:

p	w	d	l	f	a	pts
8	2	2	4	11	21	6

1942/43 to 1944/45

Did not compete

1945/46

THIRD DIVISION SOUTH (SOUTH REGION)

	p	w	d	l	f	a	pts
Crystal Palace	20	13	3	4	55	31	29
Cardiff City	20	13	2	5	69	31	28
Bristol City	20	11	2	7	51	40	24
Brighton & Hove Albion	20	10	1	9	49	50	21
Bristol Rovers	20	7	6	7	44	44	20
Swindon Town	20	8	3	9	35	47	19
BOURNEMOUTH	20	7	3	10	52	50	17
Aldershot	20	6	5	9	38	56	17
Exeter City	20	6	4	10	33	41	16
Reading	20	5	5	10	43	49	15
Torquay United	20	5	4	11	22	52	14

THIRD DIVISION SOUTH (SOUTH) CUP: QUALIFYING COMPETITION

	p	w	d	l	f	a	pts
BOURNEMOUTH	16	8	4	4	37	20	20
Bristol Rovers	16	8	3	5	27	19	19
Reading	16	8	2	6	46	29	18
Crystal Palace	16	7	4	5	37	30	18
Cardiff City	16	8	1	7	39	22	17
Bristol City	16	7	3	6	30	27	17
Torquay United	16	6	4	6	19	30	16
Exeter City	16	5	4	7	22	28	14
Swindon Town	16	5	4	7	21	35	14
Aldershot	16	3	4	9	23	48	10
Brighton & Hove Albion	16	1	6	9	23	45	8

Some games played against clubs in the South (North) group, therefore the table does not balance.

1946/47

7th in Division Three (South)

			Opponent	Score	Scorers	Att	Bird KB	Burke C	Currie JE	Dickie MM	Gallacher P	Gray H	Hutchinson JA	Kirkham RJ	Longdon CW	Marsden F	McDonald JC	Paton TG	Redfern R	Rose JW	Rowell JF	Sanaghan J	Sille LT	Tagg E	Tunnicliffe WF	Walker RW	Wilson FC	Woodward L
1	Aug	31	Notts County	0-1		26779	1	4			6		10	9		2	11	8	7			3					5	
2	Sep	4	QUEEN'S PARK RANGERS	1-1	Hutchinson	5738	1	4			6		10	9	7	2		8				3			11		5	
3		7	NORTHAMPTON T	2-1	Hutchinson (p), Burke	13461	1	4			6		10	9	7	2		8				3			11		5	
4		9	Cardiff City	0-2		19239	1	4			6		10	9		2		8	7			3			11		5	
5		14	Aldershot	1-2	Kirkham	5183	1	4			6		10	9		2	11	8	7			3					5	
6		18	CARDIFF CITY	2-0	Kirkham (p), Hutchinson	8926	1	7			6		8	9		2	11	10				3					5	4
7		21	BRIGHTON & HOVE ALB	1-0	Kirkham	12569	1	7			6		8	9		2	11	10				3					5	4
8		25	Queen's Park Rangers	0-3		17207	1	4					8	9		2	11	7				3		10			5	6
9		28	Exeter City	1-4	Paton	9874	1	4						9		2	11	8	7			3		10			5	6
10	Oct	5	PORT VALE	3-0	Tagg, Kirkham 2	11642	1		7		4			9		2	11	8				3		10			5	6
11		12	Bristol City	0-1		22336	1		7		4			9		2	11	8				3		10			5	6
12		19	SOUTHEND UNITED	3-1	Kirkham, McDonald, Currie	9621	1		7		4			9		2	11	8				3		10			5	6
13		26	Bristol Rovers	2-0	Kirkham 2	11260	1		7		4			9		2	11	8				3		10			5	6
14	Nov	2	MANSFIELD TOWN	3-1	McDonald 2, Paton	12562	1		7		4			9		2	11	8				3		10			5	6
15		9	Torquay United	2-2	Tagg, Kirkham 2	6352	1				4			9		2	7	8				3		10	11		5	6
16		16	CRYSTAL PALACE	4-0	Guthrie (og), Tunnicliffe, Paton, Kirkham (p)	13383	1				4			9		2	11	8				3		10	7		5	6
17		23	Reading	2-3	Kirkham, Paton	11514	1		7		4			9		2	11	8				3		10			5	6
18	Dec	7	Watford	2-0	Kirkham, McDonald	5981	1				4			9		2	11	8				3		10	7		5	6
19		25	NORWICH CITY	0-1		10071	1	4						9		2	11	8		7		3		10			5	6
20		26	Norwich City	6-1	Tagg 2, McDonald 2, Rowell 2	23404	1	4						9		2	11		7		10	3		8			5	6
21		28	NOTTS COUNTY	1-2	Kirkham (p)	13491	1	4						9		2	11		7		10	3		8			5	6
22	Jan	1	IPSWICH TOWN	1-1	McDonald	9124	1	4				8		9		2	11		7			3		10			5	6
23		4	Northampton Town	1-2	McDonald	9176	1				4	8		9		2	11		7			3		10			5	6
24		15	WALSALL	2-3	Walker 2	5990	1	4				8				2	11					3		10	7	9	5	6
25		18	ALDERSHOT	2-2	McDonald, Gray	11294	1	4				8				2	11					3		10	7	9	5	6
26		25	Brighton & Hove Albion	1-1	Tagg	7725	1	4				8			9	2	11					3		10	7		5	6
27	Feb	15	BRISTOL CITY	0-0		10159	1	4	9	7		8				2	11					3		10			5	6
28	Mar	1	BRISTOL ROVERS	1-3	Burke	12006	1	9		7	4	8				2						3		10	11		5	6
29		10	Port Vale	0-1		4928	1	9		7		8				2	11				10	3		4			5	6
30		15	TORQUAY UNITED	5-0	Rowell 2, Dickie, Burke 2	5910	1	9		7		8				2	11				10	3		4			5	6
31		22	Crystal Palace	1-0	McDomald	11825	1	9		7		8				2	11				10	3		4			5	6
32		29	READING	1-0	Gray	10925	1	9		7		8				2	11				10	3		4			5	6
33	Apr	4	SWINDON TOWN	5-2	McDonald 2, Burke 2, Rowell	14056	1	9		7		8				2	11				10	3		4			5	6
34		5	Walsall	0-3		9666	1	9		7		8				2	11				10	3		4			5	6
35		7	Swindon Town	3-1	Burke, Gray, McDonald	20051	1	9		7		8				2	11				10	3		4			5	6
36		12	WATFORD	0-1		11452	1			7		8				2	9				10	3	11	4			5	6
37		19	Ipswich Town	1-2	McDonald	11063	1			7		8			9	2	11				10	3		4			5	6
38		26	LEYTON ORIENT	2-0	Longdon, Woodward	7780	1			7		8			9	2	11				10	3		4			5	6
39	May	3	Mansfield Town	1-1	Rowell	5042	1			7		8			9	2	11				10	3		4			5	6
40		10	EXETER CITY	4-1	Gray, Rowell, Blood (og), McDonald	9083	1			7		8			9	2	11				10	3		4			5	6
41		17	Southend United	2-2	Russell, Woodward	6952	1			7		8			9	2	11				10	3		4			5	6
42		24	Leyton Orient	3-2	McDonald 2, Rowell	9937	1			7		8			9	2	11				10	3		4			5	6
						Apps	42	25	7	16	18	21	8	23	9	42	38	19	8	1	16	42	1	35	10	2	42	37
						Goals		7	1	1		4	3	13	1		17	4			9			5	1	2		2

Two own goals

F.A. Cup

			Opponent	Score	Scorers	Att	Bird KB	Burke C	Currie JE	Dickie MM	Gallacher P	Gray H	Hutchinson JA	Kirkham RJ	Longdon CW	Marsden F	McDonald JC	Paton TG	Redfern R	Rose JW	Rowell JF	Sanaghan J	Sille LT	Tagg E	Tunnicliffe WF	Walker RW	Wilson FC	Woodward L
R1	Nov	30	Exeter City	4-2	Gallacher, Tunnicliffe, Kirkham (p), Paton	16168	1				4			9		2	11	8				3		10	7		5	6
R2	Dec	14	Aldershot	4-2	Tagg, Kirkham 2, McDonald	16384	1				4			9		2	11	8				3		10	7		5	6
R3	Jan	11	Derby County	0-2		18438	1	4				8				2	11					3		10	7	9	5	6

		P	W	D	L	F	A	W	D	L	F	A	Pts
1	Cardiff City	42	18	3	0	60	11	12	3	6	33	19	66
2	Queen's Park Rangers	42	15	2	4	42	15	8	9	4	32	25	57
3	Bristol City	42	13	4	4	56	20	7	7	7	38	36	51
4	Swindon Town	42	15	4	2	56	25	4	7	10	28	48	49
5	Walsall	42	11	6	4	42	25	6	6	9	32	34	46
6	Ipswich Town	42	11	5	5	33	21	5	9	7	28	32	46
7	BOURNEMOUTH	42	12	4	5	43	20	6	4	11	29	34	44
8	Southend United	42	9	7	5	38	22	8	3	10	33	38	44
9	Reading	42	11	6	4	53	30	5	5	11	30	44	43
10	Port Vale	42	14	4	3	51	28	3	5	13	17	35	43
11	Torquay United	42	11	5	5	33	23	4	7	10	19	38	42
12	Notts County	42	11	4	6	35	19	4	6	11	28	44	40
13	Northampton Town	42	11	5	5	46	33	4	5	12	26	42	40
14	Bristol Rovers	42	9	6	6	34	26	7	2	12	25	43	40
15	Exeter City	42	11	6	4	37	27	4	3	14	23	42	39
16	Watford	42	11	4	6	39	27	6	1	14	22	49	39
17	Brighton & Hove Albion	42	8	7	6	31	35	5	5	11	23	37	38
18	Crystal Palace	42	9	7	5	29	19	4	4	13	20	43	37
19	Leyton Orient	42	10	5	6	40	28	2	3	16	14	47	32
20	Aldershot	42	6	7	8	25	26	4	5	12	23	52	32
21	Norwich City	42	6	3	12	38	48	4	5	12	26	52	28
22	Mansfield Town	42	8	5	8	31	38	1	5	15	17	58	28

1947/48

Second in Division Three (South)

							Barclay JM	Bird KB	Blair JA	Blizzard LWB	Cross J	Dickie MM	Gallacher P	Gray H	Liddle TB	Lunn WJ	Marsden F	McDonald JC	McKenzie JA	Milligan D	Paton TG	Percival J	Rowell JF	Sanaghan J	Stanners W	Stirling JR	Tagg E	Wilson FC	Woodward L	Young RG
1	Aug	23	SWANSEA TOWN	1-0	Paton	17474		1			9						2	11	7		10	8		3			4	5	6	
2		28	Notts County	2-1	McDonald, Milligan	14065		1									2	11	7	9	10	8		3			4	5	6	
3		30	Brighton & Hove Albion	2-0	McKenzie 2	9525		1									2	11	7	9	8		10	3			4	5	6	
4	Sep	3	NOTTS COUNTY	2-0	Tagg, McDonald	16885		1									2	11	7	9	8		10	3			4	5	6	
5		6	Ipswich Town	1-1	Milligan	15835		1									2	11	7	9	8		10	3			4	5	6	
6		11	Newport County	2-2	Gray, Milligan	13977		1						8			2	11	7	9	10			3			4	5	6	
7		13	BRISTOL CITY	2-0	Milligan, Gray	19059		1						8			2	11	7	9	10			3			4	5	6	
8		17	NEWPORT COUNTY	5-0	McDonald 2 (1p), Milligan, Gray, Paton	17391		1						8			2	11	7	9	10						4	5	6	3
9		20	Reading	0-3		14614		1						8	3		2	11	7	9		10					4	5	6	
10		27	WALSALL	1-1	Milligan	19587		1						8			2	11	7	9	10			3			4	5	6	
11	Oct	4	Leyton Orient	0-2		11704		1						8			2	11	7	9	10			3			4	5	6	
12		11	WATFORD	1-1	Milligan	18541		1	10					8			2	11	7	9				3			4	5	6	
13		18	Queen's Park Rangers	0-1		21639		1	10			7		8			2	11		9				3			4	5	6	
14		25	PORT VALE	3-0	McKenzie, Milligan, Rowell	17025		1	8								2	11	7	9			10	3			4	5	6	
15	Nov	1	Swindon Town	1-0	McDonald	17386		1	8								2	11	7	9			10	3			4	5	6	
16		8	TORQUAY UNITED	6-2	McDonald 4, Milligan 2	17477		1	8								2	11	7	9			10	3			4	5	6	
17		15	Crystal Palace	0-2		14244		1	8								2	11	7	9			10	3			4	5	6	
18		22	ALDERSHOT	1-1	McKenzie	12727		1	8								2	11	7	9			10	3			4	5	6	
19	Dec	6	BRISTOL ROVERS	3-0	McDonald, Milligan 2	12340		1	8								2	11	7	9			10	3			4	5	6	
20		20	Swansea Town	2-3	Gallacher, McDonald	18546		1	8				9				2	11	7			6	10	3			4	5		
21		26	Southend United	2-0	Gallacher, Barclay	15091	9	1	8				10				2	11	7			6		3			4	5		
22		27	SOUTHEND UNITED	0-1		15985	9	1	8				10				2	11	7			6		3			4	5		
23	Jan	3	BRIGHTON & HOVE ALB	4-1	Tagg 2, Blair, Rowell	13354		1	8								2	11	7	9		6	10	3			4	5		
24		17	IPSWICH TOWN	4-0	Milligan 2, Blair, McDonald	15168		1	8								2	11	7	9		6	10	3			4	5		
25		24	Norwich City	1-0	Milligan	18581		1	8								2	11	7	9		6	10	3			4	5		
26		31	Bristol City	4-0	McKenzie, Milligan 3	23287		1	8								2	11	7	9		6	10	3			4	5		
27	Feb	7	READING	2-0	McKenzie, McDonald (p)	18049		1	8								2	11	7	9		6	10	3			4	5		
28		14	Walsall	0-0		18153		1	8								2	11	7	9		6		3			10	5	4	
29		21	LEYTON ORIENT	1-1	McKenzie	13371		1	8							10	2	11	7	9		6		3			4	5		
30		28	Watford	3-0	Milligan 2, Lunn	15778		1	8							10	2	11	7	9		6		3			4	5		
31	Mar	13	Port Vale	1-2	Milligan	15221		1	8							10	2	11	7	9		6		3			4	5		
32		20	SWINDON TOWN	1-0	McDonald	17267		1	8							10	2	11	7	9		6		3		5	4			
33		26	Exeter City	1-1	Milligan	15861		1	8							10	2	11	7	9		6		3			4	5		
34		27	Torquay United	1-0	McDonald (p)	9818		1	8							10	2	11	7	9		6		3			4	5		
35		29	EXETER CITY	2-1	Milligan, McKenzie	23099		1	8							10	2	11	7	9		6		3			4	5		
36	Apr	3	CRYSTAL PALACE	0-0		16597		1	8							10	2	11	7	9		6		3			4	5		
37		10	Aldershot	3-0	McDonald 2, McKenzie	8456		1	8							10	2	11	7	9		6		3			4	5		
38		14	QUEEN'S PARK RANGERS	0-1		25495		1	8							10	2	11	7	9		6		3			4	5		
39		17	NORTHAMPTON T	2-0	McDonald (p), Barclay	14818	9	1	8	4	7					10	2	11				6		3				5		
40		24	Bristol Rovers	2-1	Lunn 2	15206			8							10	2	11	7	9		6		3	1		4	5		
41		29	Northampton Town	6-3	Cross, Milligan 2, McDonald, Blair, Lunn	6674			8		7					10	2	11		9		6		3	1		4	5		
42	May	1	NORWICH CITY	1-3	Lunn	12216					7			8		10	2	11		9		6		3	1		4	5		
						Apps	3	39	30	1	4	1	3	9	1	14	42	42	38	37	10	26	15	40	3	1	41	41	20	1
						Goals	2		3		1		2	3		5		19	9	25	2		2				3			

F.A. Cup

							Barclay JM	Bird KB	Blair JA	Blizzard LWB	Cross J	Dickie MM	Gallacher P	Gray H	Liddle TB	Lunn WJ	Marsden F	McDonald JC	McKenzie JA	Milligan D	Paton TG	Percival J	Rowell JF	Sanaghan J	Stanners W	Stirling JR	Tagg E	Wilson FC	Woodward L	Young RG
R1	Nov	29	GUILDFORD CITY	2-0	Milligan, McDonald	14324		1	8								2	11	7	9			10	3			4	5	6	
R2	Dec	13	BRADFORD CITY	1-0	Blair	18537		1	8								2	11	7	9		6	10	3			4	5		
R3	Jan	10	WOLVERHAMPTON WAN.	1-2	Milligan	23782		1	8								2	11	7	9		6	10	3			4	5		

		P	*W*	*D*	*L*	*F*	*A*	*W*	*D*	*L*	*F*	*A*	*Pts*
1	Queen's Park Rangers	42	16	3	2	44	17	10	6	5	30	20	61
2	BOURNEMOUTH	42	13	5	3	42	13	11	4	6	34	22	57
3	Walsall	42	13	5	3	37	12	8	4	9	33	28	51
4	Ipswich Town	42	16	1	4	42	18	7	2	12	25	43	49
5	Swansea Town	42	14	6	1	48	14	4	6	11	22	38	48
6	Notts County	42	12	4	5	44	27	7	4	10	24	32	46
7	Bristol City	42	11	4	6	47	26	7	3	11	30	39	43
8	Port Vale	42	14	4	3	48	18	2	7	12	15	36	43
9	Southend United	42	11	8	2	32	16	4	5	12	19	42	43
10	Reading	42	10	5	6	37	28	5	6	10	19	30	41
11	Exeter City	42	11	6	4	34	22	4	5	12	21	41	41
12	Newport County	42	9	8	4	38	28	5	5	11	23	45	41
13	Crystal Palace	42	12	5	4	32	14	1	8	12	17	35	39
14	Northampton Town	42	10	5	6	35	28	4	6	11	23	44	39
15	Watford	42	6	6	9	31	37	8	4	9	26	42	38
16	Swindon Town	42	6	10	5	21	20	4	6	11	20	26	36
17	Leyton Orient	42	8	5	8	31	32	5	5	11	20	41	36
18	Torquay United	42	7	6	8	40	29	4	7	10	23	33	35
19	Aldershot	42	5	10	6	22	26	5	5	11	23	41	35
20	Bristol Rovers	42	7	3	11	39	34	6	5	10	32	41	34
21	Norwich City	42	8	3	10	33	34	5	5	11	28	42	34
22	Brighton & Hove Albion	42	8	4	9	26	31	3	8	10	17	42	34

1948/49

3rd in Division Three (South)

No	Date	Opponent	Score	Scorers	Att	Barclay JM	Bennett KE	Bird KB	Blair JA	Blakeman AG	Cheney D	Cross J	Cunningham L	Hanlon W	Holland KA	Jones G	Lunn WJ	Martin DV	McGibbon D	Milligan D	Percival J	Rampling DW	Reid MJ	Roberts WE	Sanaghan J	Stephens AE	Stirling JR	Tagg E	Wilson FC	Woodward L	Young CR
1	Aug 21	Newport County	2-1	Blair, Percival	11015		10	1	8				2	11						9	6	7			3			4	5		
2	25	BRISTOL ROVERS	1-0	Hanlon	18381		10	1	8				2	11						9	6	7			3			4	5		
3	28	SWANSEA TOWN	1-1	Lunn	20150	9	10	1	8				2				11				6	7			3			4	5		
4	30	Bristol Rovers	0-4		14623	9	10	1	8				2				11				6	7			3			4	5		
5	Sep 4	Reading	2-4	Jones, Lunn	14795			1	8			7	2			11	10			9	6				3				5	4	
6	8	WALSALL	2-0	Lunn 2	14585			1	8				2			11	10			9	6	7			3		5			4	
7	11	CRYSTAL PALACE	2-0	Lunn, Jones	17517			1	8				2			11	10			9	6	7			3		5			4	
8	16	Walsall	0-0		13631		8	1					2			11	10			9	6	7			3		5			4	
9	18	Watford	1-0	Lunn	12895			1					2		8	11	10			9	6	7			3		5			4	
10	22	EXETER CITY	1-0	Hanlon	14933			1					2	11	8		10			9	6	7			3		5			4	
11	25	BRIGHTON & HOVE ALB	0-1		17777			1	8			9	2	11	10						6	7			3		5			4	
12	29	ALDERSHOT	1-0	Hanlon	14260		10	1	8				2	11					9		6	7			3		5			4	
13	Oct 2	IPSWICH TOWN	4-2	Rampling, McGibbon 2, Bennett	19378		10	1	8				2	11					9		6	7			3		5			4	
14	9	Southend United	0-0		11970		10	1	8				2	11					9		6	7			3		5			4	
15	16	NORTHAMPTON T	5-2	McGibbon 2, Rampling, Blair 2	16803		10	1	8		11		2						9		6	7			3		5			4	
16	23	Leyton Orient	2-1	Blair, McGibbon	18880		10	1	8		11		2						9		6	7			3		5			4	
17	30	PORT VALE	2-0	Blair, Cheney	18436		10	1	8		11		2						9		6	7			3		5			4	
18	Nov 6	Bristol City	1-2	McGibbon	21414		10	1	8		11		2						9		6	7			3		5			4	
19	13	SWINDON TOWN	3-0	Rampling, Jones, McGibbon	19495		10	1	8				2			11			9		6	7			3		5			4	
20	20	Norwich City	1-1	Rampling	28349		10	1	8				2			11			9		6	7			3		5			4	
21	Dec 4	Millwall	0-4		23163		10	1	8				2			11			9		6	7			3				5	4	
22	18	NEWPORT COUNTY	1-2	McGibbon	13188			1	8		7		2			11	10		9		4				3		5			6	
23	25	TORQUAY UNITED	5-0	McGibbon 4, Cheney	12463		10	1	8		11		2						9			7		3			5			6	4
24	27	Torquay United	1-1	McGibbon	10174		10	1	8		11		2						9			7		3			5			6	4
25	Jan 1	Swansea Town	0-2		19412		10	1	8		11		2						9					3		7	5			6	4
26	15	READING	1-3	McGibbon (p)	15888			1	8				3				10		9			7				11	6		5	4	
27	22	Crystal Palace	1-2	McGibbon	13862		10	1	8				2	11					9					6	3	7	5			4	
28	Feb 5	WATFORD	2-1	Reid, McGibbon	13030			1		10			2	11					9				8	6	3	7	5			4	
29	19	Brighton & Hove Albion	6-1	* see below	20859			1		10			2	11					9		6		8		3	7	5			4	
30	26	Ipswich Town	0-1		13289			1		10			2	11					9		6		8		3	7	5			4	
31	Mar 5	SOUTHEND UNITED	3-2	McGibbon 3 (1p)	12158			1		10			2	11					9		6		8		3	7	5			4	
32	12	Northampton Town	0-1		8473			1		10			2	11					9		6		8		3	7	5			4	
33	19	LEYTON ORIENT	3-0	McGibbon, Stephens, Walton(og)	13716			1	8	10			2	11					9						3	7			5	6	4
34	26	Port Vale	2-0	McGibbon, Stephens	8560			1		8			2	11			10		9						3	7			5	6	4
35	Apr 2	BRISTOL CITY	0-0		14004			1		8			2	11			10		9						3	7			5	6	4
36	9	Swindon Town	2-2	Blakeman 2	14154			1	8	10			2	11					9						3	7	5			6	4
37	15	NOTTS COUNTY	2-1	Blakeman, McGibbon (p)	24141			1	8	10			2	11				6	9						3	7			5		4
38	16	NORWICH CITY	1-2	McGibbon	13044			1	8	10	11		2					6	9						3	7			5		4
39	18	Notts County	3-2	McGibbon 2 (2p), Blakeman	28161			1	8	10	11		2					6	9			7			3		5				4
40	23	Exeter City	3-2	Stephens 2, McGibbon (p)	8979			1		8	10		2	11				6	9						3	7	5				4
41	30	MILLWALL	2-0	McGibbon 2 (1p)	12124			1	8	10	11		2					6	9						3	7	5				4
42	May 7	Aldershot	0-0		6923			1	8	10	11		2					6	9						3	7	5				4
					Apps	2	19	42	31	15	13	2	42	19	3	9	12	6	31	8	26	24	5	5	38	17	31	4	12	32	13
					Goals		1		5	6	2			3		3	6		30		1	4	2			5					

Scorers in game 29: McGibbon 2, Stephens, Blakeman 2, Reid

F Marsden played at 2 in game 26

One own goal

F.A. Cup

Rd	Date	Opponent	Score	Att	Barclay JM	Bennett KE	Bird KB	Blair JA	Blakeman AG	Cheney D	Cross J	Cunningham L	Hanlon W	Holland KA	Jones G	Lunn WJ	Martin DV	McGibbon D	Milligan D	Percival J	Rampling DW	Reid MJ	Roberts WE	Sanaghan J	Stephens AE	Stirling JR	Tagg E	Wilson FC	Woodward L	Young CR
R3	Jan 8	Manchester United	0-6	55012		10	1	8		11		2						9		6	7			3		5			4	

		P	W	D	L	F	A	W	D	L	F	A	Pts
1	Swansea Town	42	20	1	0	60	11	7	7	7	27	23	62
2	Reading	42	17	1	3	48	18	8	4	9	29	32	55
3	BOURNEMOUTH	42	15	2	4	42	17	7	6	8	27	31	52
4	Swindon Town	42	11	9	1	38	20	7	6	8	26	36	51
5	Bristol Rovers	42	13	5	3	42	23	6	5	10	19	28	48
6	Brighton & Hove Albion	42	11	5	5	32	26	4	13	4	23	29	48
7	Ipswich Town	42	14	3	4	53	30	4	6	11	25	47	45
8	Millwall	42	12	7	2	42	23	5	4	12	21	41	45
9	Torquay United	42	12	5	4	45	26	5	6	10	20	44	45
10	Norwich City	42	11	6	4	32	10	5	6	10	35	39	44
11	Notts County	42	15	3	3	68	19	4	2	15	34	49	43
12	Exeter City	42	12	5	4	45	26	3	5	13	18	50	40
13	Port Vale	42	11	3	7	32	21	3	8	10	19	33	39
14	Walsall	42	9	5	7	34	28	6	3	12	22	36	38
15	Newport County	42	8	6	7	41	35	6	3	12	27	57	37
16	Bristol City	42	8	9	4	28	24	3	5	13	16	38	36
17	Watford	42	6	9	6	24	21	4	6	11	17	33	35
18	Southend United	42	5	10	6	18	18	4	6	11	23	28	34
19	Leyton Orient	42	9	6	6	36	29	2	6	13	22	51	34
20	Northampton Town	42	9	6	6	33	20	3	3	15	18	42	33
21	Aldershot	42	6	5	10	26	29	5	6	10	22	30	33
22	Crystal Palace	42	7	8	6	27	27	1	3	17	11	49	27

1949/50

12th in Division Three (South)

	Date	Opponent	Score	Scorers	Att	Bird KB	Blair JA	Blakeman AG	Buchanan CC	Cheney D	Cross J	Cunningham L	Drummond IP	Duke GE	Fisher JA	Haigh G	Lewis J	Lunn WJ	Marsh C	Martin DV	McGibbon D	Roberts WE	Stephens AE	Stirling JR	Weigh RE	Wilson FC	Woodward L	Young CR
1	Aug 20	Ipswich Town	2-1	Wright, McGibbon	15148	1		10				2	3						8	6	9		7	5	11		4	
2	24	EXETER CITY	2-0	McGibbon 2	18807	1	10				8	2	3							6	9		7	5	11		4	
3	27	PORT VALE	2-2	McGibbon (p), Weigh	19101	1	10				8	2	3							6	9		7	5	11		4	
4	31	Exeter City	2-1	McGibbon (p), Stephens	12055	1	10					2	3						8	6	9		7	5	11			4
5	Sep 3	Notts County	0-2		34606	1	10					2	3						8	6	9		7	5	11			4
6	7	WATFORD	0-0		16172	1	8			10		2	3							6	9		7	5	11			4
7	10	SOUTHEND UNITED	3-0	McGibbon 2, Cheney	17181	1	8			11		2	3					10		6	9		7	5			4	
8	15	Watford	1-4	Lunn	7564	1	8			11		2	3					10		6	9		7	5			4	
9	17	Bristol Rovers	0-0		18640		8			11		2	3	1				10		6	9		7	5			4	
10	21	BRISTOL CITY	3-1	Cheney, Lunn, McGibbon	8899		8			11		2	3	1				10		6	9		7	5			4	
11	24	BRIGHTON & HOVE ALB	2-2	Lunn 2	17391		8			11		2	3	1				10		6	9		7			5	4	
12	Oct 1	CRYSTAL PALACE	2-0	McGibbon 2	16738		8			11		2	3	1				10			9	6	7	5			4	
13	8	Walsall	1-1	Cross	10714		8			11	7	2	3	1				10			9	6		5			4	
14	15	MILLWALL	1-0	Cross	17524		8			11	7	2	3	1				10			9	6		5			4	
15	22	Swindon Town	1-3	McGibbon (p)	15084		8			11	7	2	3	1				10			9	6		5			4	
16	29	TORQUAY UNITED	1-2	Woodward	16276		8			11	7	2	3	1				10			9	6		5			4	
17	Nov 5	Aldershot	1-0	Weigh	4254	1	10	9				2	3									6	7	5	11		4	8
18	12	NOTTM. FOREST	1-2	Weigh	18452	1	10	9				2	3				6						7	5	11		4	8
19	19	Northampton Town	3-2	Lunn 2, Cross	15103		8				9	2	3	1			6	10					7	5	11		4	
20	Dec 3	Newport County	0-5		10560		8	10			9	2	3	1			6						7	5	11		4	
21	17	IPSWICH TOWN	4-0	Cross 2 (1p), Weigh, Lunn	10196	1			8		9	2	3				6	10					7	5	11		4	
22	24	Port Vale	1-1	Cross	13092	1			8		9	2	3				6	10					7	5	11		4	
23	26	READING	2-1	Stirling, Lewis	17639	1			8		9		3		2		6	10					7	5	11		4	
24	27	Reading	1-2	Cross	22248	1			8		9		3		2		6	10					7	5	11		4	
25	31	NOTTS COUNTY	3-0	Blakeman, Cross 2	22651	1		8			9		3		2		6	10					7	5	11		4	
26	Jan 14	Southend United	0-1		11973	1		8			9		3		2			10				6	7	5	11		4	
27	21	BRISTOL ROVERS	0-2		12277	1		8			9		3		2		6	10					7	5	11		4	
28	Feb 4	Brighton & Hove Albion	1-1	Cheney	14512	1				10	9	2			3		6				8		7	5	11		4	
29	18	Crystal Palace	0-1		22322	1				10	9	2			3		6				8		7	5	11		4	
30	25	WALSALL	1-1	McGibbon	11877	1				10	7	2			3		6		8		9			5	11		4	
31	Mar 4	Millwall	0-1		20087	1				7		2			3		6	10	8		9			5	11		4	
32	11	SWINDON TOWN	1-1	Lunn	11216	1				11		2			3		6	10	8		9		7	5			4	
33	18	Torquay United	1-3	McGibbon	6955	1			8	11		2			3		6	10			9		7	5			4	
34	25	ALDERSHOT	2-1	Stephens, Blakeman	9381	1		10	8	11		2			3		6				9		7	5			4	
35	Apr 1	Nottingham Forest	0-3		16777	1		10	8	11		2			3		6				9		7	5			4	
36	7	Leyton Orient	1-2	Cross	13925	1		10		11	9	2			3		6				8		7	5			4	
37	8	NORTHAMPTON T	1-2	McGibbon	12540	1				11	9	2			3				10		8	6	7	5			4	
38	10	LEYTON ORIENT	4-1	McGibbon, Stephens 2, Cheney	9832	1				11	9	2			3				10		8	6	7	5			4	
39	15	Norwich City	1-0	Cheney	18355	1				11	9	2			3	10					8	6	7	5			4	
40	22	NEWPORT COUNTY	1-1	McGibbon	10842	1				11	9	2			3		6		10		8		7	5			4	
41	29	Bristol City	2-3	Cross, Woodward	11350	1				11	9	2			3	10	6				8		7	5			4	
42	May 6	NORWICH CITY	2-0	McGibbon 2	10748	1				11	9	2			3	10	6				8		7	5			4	
					Apps	32	19	10	7	26	25	37	27	10	20	3	21	21	9	11	31	10	36	41	21	1	39	5
					Goals			2		5	11						1	8			18		4	1	5		2	

F.A. Cup

	Date	Opponent	Score	Scorers	Att	Bird KB	Blair JA	Blakeman AG	Buchanan CC	Cheney D	Cross J	Cunningham L	Drummond IP	Duke GE	Fisher JA	Haigh G	Lewis J	Lunn WJ	Marsh C	Martin DV	McGibbon D	Roberts WE	Stephens AE	Stirling JR	Weigh RE	Wilson FC	Woodward L	Young CR
R3	Jan 7	Bradford Park Avenue	1-0	Cross	19709	1		8			9		3		2			10				6	7	5	11		4	
R4	28	NORTHAMPTON TOWN	1-1	Weigh	22360	1		8			9		3		2		6	10					7	5	11		4	
rep	Feb 2	Northampton Town	1-2	Cross	22574	1					9	2	3				6	10			8		7	5	11		4	

		P	W	D	L	F	A	W	D	L	F	A	Pts
1	Notts County	42	17	3	1	60	12	8	5	8	35	38	58
2	Northampton Town	42	12	6	3	43	21	8	5	8	29	29	51
3	Southend United	42	15	4	2	43	15	4	9	8	23	33	51
4	Nottingham Forest	42	13	0	8	37	15	7	9	5	30	24	49
5	Torquay United	42	13	6	2	40	23	6	4	11	26	40	48
6	Watford	42	10	6	5	26	13	6	7	8	19	22	45
7	Crystal Palace	42	12	5	4	35	21	3	9	9	20	33	44
8	Brighton & Hove Albion	42	9	8	4	32	24	7	4	10	25	45	44
9	Bristol Rovers	42	12	5	4	34	18	7	0	14	17	33	43
10	Reading	42	15	2	4	48	21	2	6	13	22	43	42
11	Norwich City	42	11	5	5	44	21	5	5	11	21	42	42
12	BOURNEMOUTH	42	11	6	4	38	19	5	4	12	19	37	42
13	Port Vale	42	12	6	3	33	13	3	5	13	14	29	41
14	Swindon Town	42	9	7	5	41	30	6	4	11	18	32	41
15	Bristol City	42	12	4	5	38	19	3	6	12	22	42	40
16	Exeter City	42	9	8	4	37	27	5	3	13	26	48	39
17	Ipswich Town	42	9	6	6	36	36	3	5	13	21	50	35
18	Leyton Orient	42	10	6	5	33	30	2	5	14	20	55	35
19	Walsall	42	8	8	5	37	25	1	8	12	24	37	34
20	Aldershot	42	10	5	6	30	16	3	3	15	18	44	34
21	Newport County	42	11	5	5	50	34	2	3	16	17	64	34
22	Millwall	42	11	1	9	39	29	3	3	15	16	34	32

1950/51

9th in Division Three (South)

						Barry PP	Bird KB	Boxshall D	Buchanan CC	Casey T	Cheney D	Collins AD	Cross J	Cunningham L	Drummond IP	Evans H	Fisher JA	Gripton EW	Haigh G	Lewis J	Marsh C	McGibbon D	Meadows JR	Neave IJG	Stroud DNL	Weigh RE	Wilkinson DL	Wilson FC	Woodward L
1	Aug 19	BRISTOL CITY	1-0	Evans	21398		1	7		6	11			2		10	3	5	8			9							4
2	23	GILLINGHAM	3-1	Weigh, Evans, McGibbon	16070		1	7		6				2		10	3	5	8			9				11			4
3	26	Millwall	0-3		26095		1	7		6				2		10	3	5	8			9				11			4
4	30	Gillingham	2-2	Weigh, Collins	15397		1			6		7		2		10	3	5	8			9				11			4
5	Sep 2	WATFORD	3-3	Weigh, Evans, Haigh	15899		1	7		6			9	2		10	3	5	8							11			4
6	7	Colchester United	1-4	Evans	14199		1	7		6				2		10	3	5	8			9				11			4
7	9	Walsall	1-0	Evans	8787		1	7		6				2	3	10		5	8			9				11			4
8	13	COLCHESTER UNITED	2-0	McGibbon, Haigh	18452		1	7		6	11			2	3	10		5	8			9							4
9	16	LEYTON ORIENT	5-0	McGibbon 4 (1p), Boxshall	15775	3	1	7		6	11			2		10		5	8			9							4
10	23	Ipswich Town	0-1		12331	3	1	7		6	11			2		10		5	8			9							4
11	30	PLYMOUTH ARGYLE	0-2		14742	3	1	7		6	11			2		10		5	8			9							4
12	Oct 7	Bristol Rovers	0-2		17998	3	1			6	11	7		2		10		5	8			9							4
13	14	CRYSTAL PALACE	5-0	* see below	14187		1	9		6	11	7		2	3	10		5				8							4
14	21	Brighton & Hove Albion	1-2	McGibbon	13053		1	9		6	11	7		2	3	10		5				8							4
15	28	NEWPORT COUNTY	2-0	Cheney, McGibbon	13466		1			6	11	7	9	2	3	10				5		8							4
16	Nov 4	Norwich City	0-3		23160		1	9		6	11			2	3	10				5		8			7				4
17	11	NORTHAMPTON T	1-0	Stroud	13004		1	9		6	11			2	3				10	5		8			7				4
18	18	Port Vale	1-3	Haigh	8153		1	9		6	11			2	3				10	5		8			7				4
19	Dec 2	Torquay United	2-0	Stroud, Evans	7989		1	9	8	6				2	3	10				5					7	11			4
20	16	Bristol City	0-2		15438		1	11	10	6			9	2	3					5		8			7				4
21	23	MILLWALL	1-0	Stroud	9502		1	11	10	6			9	2	3					5		8			7				4
22	25	Southend United	1-6	Stroud	8885		1	11	10	6			9	2	3							8			7			5	4
23	26	SOUTHEND UNITED	3-1	Cross. McGibbon, Evans	14132			11		6			9	2	3	10		5				8	1		7				4
24	30	Watford	1-2	Cross	9616			11		6			9	2	3	10		5				8	1		7				4
25	Jan 6	Swindon Town	1-2	Cross	6971					6	11		9	2	3			5		4	8		1		7		10		
26	13	WALSALL	3-1	Stroud, Marshall, Boxshall	9943			9		6	11			2	3			5		4	10	8	1		7				
27	20	Leyton Orient	0-2		9813			9		6				2	3	11		5			10	8	1	4	7				
28	27	SWINDON TOWN	2-1	McGibbon, Cross	10034			11		6			9	2	3			5			10	8	1		7				4
29	Feb 3	IPSWICH TOWN	2-1	McGibbon (p), Stroud	9383			11		6			9	2	3			5			10	8	1		7				4
30	10	NOTTM. FOREST	3-2	McGibbon, Boxshall 2	15882			11		6			9	2	3			5			10	8	1		7				4
31	17	Plymouth Argyle	1-3	McGibbon	13324			11		6			9	2	3			5			10	8	1		7				4
32	Mar 3	Crystal Palace	1-0	Cross	13323			11					9	2	3			5		6	10	8	1		7				4
33	10	BRIGHTON & HOVE ALB	2-2	Cross, Stroud	9391			11					9	2	3			5		6	10	8	1		7				4
34	14	BRISTOL ROVERS	2-0	McGibbon, Cross	8943			11					9	2	3			5		6	10	8	1		7				4
35	23	EXETER CITY	1-1	McGibbon	11017			11					9	2	3			5		6	10	8	1		7				4
36	24	NORWICH CITY	0-0		14165			11					9	2	3			5		6	10	8	1		7				4
37	26	Exeter City	1-2	Cheney	9913			11			9			2	3			5		6	10	8	1		7				4
38	31	Northampton Town	1-0	Boxshall	6260		1	11			9		7	2	3			5		6	10	8							4
39	Apr 7	PORT VALE	3-1	McGibbon, Cheney 2	8742		1	11			9		7	2	3			5		6	10	8							4
40	14	Nottingham Forest	0-1		22428		1	11			9		7	2	3			5		6	10	8							4
41	18	Reading	0-0		13025		1	11	9				7	2	3			5		6	10	8							4
42	21	TORQUAY UNITED	0-0		10594		1	11			9		7	2	3			5		6	10	8							4
43	25	ALDERSHOT	4-0	Cheney 3, Boxshall	7640		1	11			9			2	3	10		5		6	8				7				4
44	28	Aldershot	1-0	Stroud	3744		1	11			9			2	3	10		5		6	8				7				4
45	30	Newport County	0-1		5563		1	11			9			2			3	5		6	8	10			7				4
46	May 5	READING	1-0	Cheney	10424		1	11			9			2			3	5		6	8	10			7				4
					Apps	4	31	42	5	31	23	5	22	46	34	22	8	38	14	24	22	41	15	1	26	7	1	1	43
					Goals			7			9	1	7			8			3		1	17			8	3			

Scorers in game 13: Whittaker (og), Boxshall, Cheney, Evans, McGibbon

One own goal

F.A. Cup

						Barry PP	Bird KB	Boxshall D	Buchanan CC	Casey T	Cheney D	Collins AD	Cross J	Cunningham L	Drummond IP	Evans H	Fisher JA	Gripton EW	Haigh G	Lewis J	Marsh C	McGibbon D	Meadows JR	Neave IJG	Stroud DNL	Weigh RE	Wilkinson DL	Wilson FC	Woodward L
R1	Nov 25	COLCHESTER UNITED	1-0	Boxshall	15359		1	9		6				2	3				10	5		8			7	11			4
R2	Dec 9	Aldershot	0-3		10500		1	9	8	6	11			2	3	10				5					7				4

		P	W	D	L	F	A	W	D	L	F	A	Pts
1	Nottingham Forest	46	16	6	1	57	17	14	4	5	53	23	70
2	Norwich City	46	16	6	1	42	14	9	8	6	40	31	64
3	Reading	46	15	6	2	57	17	6	9	8	31	36	57
4	Plymouth Argyle	46	16	5	2	54	19	8	4	11	31	36	57
5	Millwall	46	15	6	2	52	23	8	4	11	28	34	56
6	Bristol Rovers	46	15	7	1	46	18	5	8	10	18	24	55
7	Southend United	46	15	4	4	64	27	6	6	11	28	42	52
8	Ipswich Town	46	15	4	4	48	24	8	2	13	21	34	52
9	BOURNEMOUTH	46	17	5	1	49	16	5	2	16	16	41	51
10	Bristol City	46	15	4	4	41	25	5	7	11	23	34	51
11	Newport County	46	13	4	6	48	25	6	5	12	29	45	47
12	Port Vale	46	13	6	4	35	24	3	7	13	25	41	45
13	Brighton & Hove Albion	46	11	8	4	51	31	2	9	12	20	48	43
14	Exeter City	46	11	4	8	33	30	7	2	14	29	55	42
15	Walsall	46	12	4	7	32	20	3	6	14	20	42	40
16	Colchester United	46	12	5	6	43	25	2	7	14	20	51	40
17	Swindon Town	46	15	4	4	38	17	3	0	20	17	50	40
18	Aldershot	46	11	8	4	37	20	4	2	17	19	68	40
19	Leyton Orient	46	13	2	8	36	28	2	6	15	17	47	38
20	Torquay United	46	13	2	8	47	39	1	7	15	17	42	37
21	Northampton Town	46	8	9	6	39	30	2	7	14	16	37	36
22	Gillingham	46	10	7	6	41	30	3	2	18	28	71	35
23	Watford	46	8	5	10	29	28	1	6	16	25	60	29
24	Crystal Palace	46	6	5	12	18	39	2	6	15	15	45	27

1951/52

14th in Division Three (South)

			Opponent	Score	Scorers	Att	Bird KB	Boxshall D	Buchanan CC	Casey T	Cheney D	Cross J	Cunningham L	Drummond IP	Eyre EL	Fisher JA	Gaynor LA	Girling HM	Gripton EW	Hardy GD	Marsh C	Meadows JR	Neave IJG	Stroud DNL	Tippett TJ	Wilkinson DL	Woodward L
1	Aug	18	Torquay United	2-2	Cheney, Marsh	11556	1			6	9		2	3			10	11	5		8			7			4
2		22	BRISTOL CITY	0-0		16659	1	11		6	9		2	3			10		5		8			7			4
3		25	GILLINGHAM	3-3	Cheney 2, Gaynor	12573	1			6	9		2	3			10	11	5		8			7			4
4		28	Bristol City	0-1		19750	1	11		10	9		2	3					5		8		6	7			4
5	Sep	1	Brighton & Hove Albion	1-0	Cheney	14255	1	11		10	9		2	3					5		8		6	7			4
6		5	PORT VALE	0-1		11455	1	11		10	9		2	3					5		8		6	7			4
7		8	MILLWALL	0-2		12457	1		8	6	11	9	2	3					5		10		4	7			
8		10	Port Vale	2-2	Cross, Boxshall	12601	1	7	8		11	9	2	3			10		5				6				4
9		15	SWINDON TOWN	4-1	Cheney, Cross 2, May (og)	9622	1	7	8		11	9	2	3			10		5				6				4
10		22	Southend United	0-1		8850	1	7	8		11	9	2	3			10		5				6				4
11		29	NEWPORT COUNTY	5-1	Buchanan, Cheney, Coss, Tippett, Drummond	12719	1		8		10	9	2	3					5				6	7	11		4
12	Oct	6	Walsall	2-2	Buchanan, Stroud	8242	1		8		10	9	2	3					5				6	7	11		4
13		13	SHREWSBURY TOWN	2-0	Cross 2	12807	1		8		10	9	2	3					5				6	7	11		4
14		20	Aldershot	3-1	Wilkinson 2, Cross	8413	1		8			9	2	3					5				6	7	11	10	4
15		27	WATFORD	0-0		11615	1		8			9	2	3					5				6	7	11	10	4
16	Nov	3	Bristol Rovers	2-1	Tippett, Stroud	17293	1		8			9	2	3					5				6	7	11	10	4
17		10	PLYMOUTH ARGYLE	1-2	Cross	18624	1		8			9	2	3	10				5				6	7	11		4
18		17	Norwich City	0-2		20902	1	7	8			9	2	3	10				5				6		11		4
19	Dec	1	Colchester United	1-1	Wilkinson	8902	1			6	8	9	2	3					5				4	7	11	10	
20		8	CRYSTAL PALACE	1-2	Cross	7153	1			6	8	9	2	3					5				4	7	11	10	
21		22	Gillingham	2-0	Cross, Stroud	10296	1			6	8	9	2	3	10				5					7	11		4
22		25	LEYTON ORIENT	3-2	Eyre, Stroud, Tippett	10739	1			6	8	9	2	3	10				5					7	11		4
23		26	Leyton Orient	0-1		13606	1			6	8	9	2	3	10				5					7	11		4
24		29	BRIGHTON & HOVE ALB	3-1	Stroud, Tippett, Cross	12847	1			6	8	9	2	3	10				5					7	11		4
25	Jan	5	Millwall	1-3	Cross	19517	1			6	8	9	2	3	10				5					7	11		4
26		12	TORQUAY UNITED	3-1	Cheney, Tippett, Eyre	10668	1			6	8	9	2	3	10				5					7	11		4
27		16	READING	1-2	Eyre	8269	1			6	8	9	2	3	10				5					7	11		4
28		19	Swindon Town	0-2		16516	1	7	8	6		9	2		10	3			5						11		4
29		26	SOUTHEND UNITED	2-1	Cross, Casey	10024	1		8	6		9	2	3				11	5						7	10	4
30	Feb	2	Ipswich Town	1-3	Buchanan	11663	1		9	6			2	3	10				5					7	11	8	4
31		9	Newport County	0-2		11148	1			6		9	2	3	10		8		5					7	11		4
32		16	WALSALL	2-1	Cross, Tippett	8749				6		9	2	3	10		8		5			1		7	11		4
33		23	IPSWICH TOWN	2-2	Eyre 2	9974	1			6	9	7	2	3	10		8		5						11		4
34	Mar	1	Shrewsbury Town	0-2		10705	1			6	9	7	2	3	10		8		5				4		11		
35		8	ALDERSHOT	0-2		8969	1			6	9		2	3	10				5		8			7	11		4
36		15	Watford	2-1	Eyre 2	7207	1		7	6	10	9	2	3	8					5					11		4
37		22	BRISTOL ROVERS	1-0	Eyre	10243	1		7	6		9	2	3	8		10		5						11		4
38		29	Plymouth Argyle	1-4	Tippett	12024	1		7	6		9	2	3	8		10		5						11		4
39	Apr	5	NORWICH CITY	1-2	Woodward	7108	1		7	6		9	2	3	8		10						5		11		4
40		12	Exeter City	2-2	Cross, Gaynor	7890	1		7	6		9	2	3	8		10	11	5								4
41		14	NORTHAMPTON T	3-0	Eyre 2, Cross	9933	1			6		9	2	3	8		10		5					7	11		4
42		15	Northampton Town	3-5	Gaynor, Cheney, Cross	9524	1			6	8	9	2	3			10						5	7	11		4
43		19	COLCHESTER UNITED	5-0	Cross (p), Cheney, Tippett 2, Woodward	8612	1			6	8	9	2	3			10			5				7	11		4
44		23	EXETER CITY	0-4		8247	1			6	8	9	2	3			10			5				7	11		4
45		26	Crystal Palace	2-2	Tippett, Gaynor	10765	1			6		9	2	3	8		10		5					7	11		4
46	May	3	Reading	0-5		7910	1			6		9	2	3	8		10		5					7	11		4
						Apps	45	9	20	35	29	38	46	45	24	1	20	4	41	3	8	1	20	33	35	7	42
						Goals		1	3	1	9	18		1	10		4				1			5	10	3	2

One own goal

F.A. Cup

			Opponent	Score	Scorers	Att	Bird KB	Boxshall D	Buchanan CC	Casey T	Cheney D	Cross J	Cunningham L	Drummond IP	Eyre EL	Fisher JA	Gaynor LA	Girling HM	Gripton EW	Hardy GD	Marsh C	Meadows JR	Neave IJG	Stroud DNL	Tippett TJ	Wilkinson DL	Woodward L
R1	Nov	24	Southend United	1-6	Stroud	12000	1		8			9	2	3	10				5				6	7	11		4

		P	W	D	L	F	A	W	D	L	F	A	Pts
1	Plymouth Argyle	46	19	3	1	70	19	10	5	8	37	34	66
2	Reading	46	19	2	2	73	23	10	1	12	39	37	61
3	Norwich City	46	18	1	4	55	15	8	8	7	34	35	61
4	Millwall	46	16	5	2	46	21	7	7	9	28	32	58
5	Brighton & Hove Albion	46	15	4	4	57	24	9	6	8	30	39	58
6	Newport County	46	13	7	3	45	26	8	5	10	32	50	54
7	Bristol Rovers	46	14	5	4	60	20	6	7	10	29	33	52
8	Northampton Town	46	17	1	5	65	31	5	4	14	28	43	49
9	Southend United	46	16	6	1	56	17	3	4	16	19	49	48
10	Colchester United	46	12	7	4	32	22	5	5	13	24	55	46
11	Torquay United	46	10	3	10	53	42	7	7	9	33	56	44
12	Aldershot	46	11	4	8	40	27	7	4	12	38	62	44
13	Port Vale	46	11	11	1	33	16	3	4	16	17	50	43
14	BOURNEMOUTH	46	11	4	8	42	30	5	6	12	27	45	42
15	Bristol City	46	13	6	4	44	26	2	6	15	14	43	42
16	Swindon Town	46	9	9	5	29	22	5	5	13	22	46	42
17	Ipswich Town	46	12	4	7	45	31	4	5	14	18	43	41
18	Leyton Orient	46	12	5	6	39	26	4	4	15	16	42	41
19	Crystal Palace	46	9	7	7	32	28	6	2	15	29	52	39
20	Shrewsbury Town	46	11	3	9	35	29	2	7	14	27	57	36
21	Watford	46	7	7	9	34	37	6	3	14	23	44	36
22	Gillingham	46	10	7	6	47	31	1	6	16	24	50	35
23	Exeter City	46	10	4	9	40	36	3	5	15	25	50	35
24	Walsall	46	11	3	9	38	31	2	2	19	17	63	31

1952/53

9th in Division Three (South)

						Bird KB	Buchanan CC	Cheney D	Cross J	Cunningham L	Drummond IP	Eyre EL	Fidler F	Fisher JA	Gaynor LA	Godwin TF	Haddington RW	Hardy GD	Harrison P	Hughes HJ	Littlejohn RD	MacDonald M	Neave IJG	Newsham S	Stroud DNL	Thompson WG	Tippett TJ	Woodward L
1	Aug 23	NORTHAMPTON T	0-1		14771			9		2	3	10				1	8		7	5			6				11	4
2	27	Aldershot	0-1		7520				9	2	3	10				1	8		7	5			6				11	4
3	30	Leyton Orient	2-2	Harrrison, Stroud	11273				9	2	3	10			8	1			11	5			6		7			4
4	Sep 3	ALDERSHOT	0-3		9878				9	2	3	10			8	1			11	5			6		7			4
5	6	IPSWICH TOWN	2-1	Harrison, Buchanan	10709		8	10	9		2			3		1			11	5			6		7			4
6	11	Newport County	1-2	Harrison	9127		8	10	9		2			3		1		5	11				6		7			4
7	13	Reading	3-1	Cheney, Cross, Buchanan	16635		8	10	9		2			3		1		5	11				6		7			4
8	17	NEWPORT COUNTY	1-2	Cross	10370		8	10	9		2			3		1		5	11				6		7			4
9	20	Swindon Town	2-1	Cross, Cheney	11220		8	10	9		2			3		1		5	11		7		6					4
10	24	GILLINGHAM	4-2	Cheney, Buchanan 2, Harrison	8062		8	10	9		2			3		1		5	11		7		6					4
11	27	SOUTHEND UNITED	5-1	Cheney, Buchanan 3, Harrison	12821		8	10	9		2			3		1		5	11		7		6					4
12	Oct 1	BRIGHTON & HOVE ALB	2-1	Cheney, Cross (p)	9023		8	10	9		2			3		1		5	11		7		6					4
13	4	Watford	0-3		15389		8	10	9		2			3		1		5	11		7		6					4
14	11	COLCHESTER UNITED	1-0	Cross	11728		8	10	9		2			3		1		5	11		7		6					4
15	18	Norwich City	1-1	Cheney	26071		8	10	9		2			3		1		5	11		7		6					4
16	25	COVENTRY CITY	3-0	Harrison, Cheney 2	13777		8	10	9		2	11		3		1		5	7				6					4
17	Nov 1	Exeter City	1-5	Cheney	10078		8	10	9		2	11		3		1		5	7				6					4
18	8	BRISTOL ROVERS	1-2	Cross	18638		8	10	9	2		11		3		1		5	7				6					4
19	15	Millwall	1-3	Buchanan	15235		8	10	9	2				3		1		5	11		7		6					4
20	Dec 13	Queen's Park Rangers	1-2	Gaynor (p)	8015			10			2	8	9	3	4	1			11	5	7		6					
21	20	Northampton Town	1-5	Fidler	8649			10			2	8	9	3	4	1			11	5			6		7			
22	26	Torquay United	1-5	Harrison (p)	9600			10			2	8	9	3		1			11	5		4	6		7			
23	27	TORQUAY UNITED	0-1		11176			10			2	8	9	3		1		5	11				6		7			4
24	Jan 3	LEYTON ORIENT	4-1	Fidler 2, Buchanan, Cheney	8380		7	10			2	8	9	3		1		5	11				6					4
25	10	Crystal Palace	0-1		12394		7	10			2	8	9	3		1		5	11				6					4
26	17	Ipswich Town	1-2	Cross	9629	1	7	10	9		2	8		3				5	11				6					4
27	24	READING	2-0	Stroud, Harrison	9021		8		9		2			3	10	1		5	11				6		7			4
28	31	CRYSTAL PALACE	4-2	Cross 3, Buchanan	7724		8		9		2				10	1		5	11				6		7	3		4
29	Feb 7	SWINDON TOWN	1-1	Fidler	8799		8				2		9		10	1		5	11				6		7	3		4
30	14	Southend United	0-0		5445		8		9		2				10	1		5	11				6		7	3		4
31	21	WATFORD	4-1	Stroud 2, Cross, Harrison	9323		8	10	9		2					1		5	11				6		7	3		4
32	28	Colchester United	1-1	Harrison	7858		8	10	9		2					1		5	11				6		7	3		4
33	Mar 7	NORWICH CITY	0-0		11154		8	10	9		2					1		5	11				6		7	3		4
34	14	Coventry City	3-2	Cross, Harrison, Buchanan	13274		8	10	9		2					1		5	11				6		7	3		4
35	21	EXETER CITY	2-1	Harrison, Cross	10340		8	10	9		2					1		5	11				6		7	3		4
36	28	Bristol Rovers	1-2	Cross	16092		8	10	9		2					1		5	11				6		7	3		4
37	Apr 3	Bristol City	1-1	Cross	25403		8	10	9		2					1		5	11				6		7	3		4
38	4	MILLWALL	1-1	Cross	13704		8	10	9		2				7	1		5	11				6			3		4
39	6	BRISTOL CITY	4-1	Buchanan, Cross, Cheney 2	13892		8	10	9		2				7	1		5	11				6			3		4
40	11	Gillingham	2-1	Harrison, Cheney	10448		8	10	9		2				7	1		5	11				6			3		4
41	15	SHREWSBURY TOWN	2-0	Harrison, Cheney	7626		8	10	9		2				7	1			11	5			6			3		4
42	18	WALSALL	5-1	Fidler 4, Cheney	8462		8	10			2		9			1		5	11				6	7		3		4
43	22	Brighton & Hove Albion	0-2		11889		8	10			2		9			1			11	5			6	7		3		4
44	25	Shrewsbury Town	0-1		7411		8	10			2		9			1			11	5			6	7		3		4
45	30	Walsall	2-2	Fidler, Cross	3887		8		9		2		10			1			11	5		4	6	7		3		
46	May 2	QUEEN'S PARK RANGERS	1-0	Hughes	8276		8		9	2	3		10			1			11	5			6	7				4
					Apps	1	38	37	35	7	44	14	12	23	12	45	2	33	46	13	9	2	46	5	20	18	2	42
					Goals		12	15	18				9		1				14	1					4			

F.A. Cup

						Bird KB	Buchanan CC	Cheney D	Cross J	Cunningham L	Drummond IP	Eyre EL	Fidler F	Fisher JA	Gaynor LA	Godwin TF	Haddington RW	Hardy GD	Harrison P	Hughes HJ	Littlejohn RD	MacDonald M	Neave IJG	Newsham S	Stroud DNL	Thompson WG	Tippett TJ	Woodward L
R1	Nov 22	Ipswich Town	2-2	Cheney, Harrison	10337		8	10	9	2				3		1		5	11		7		6					4
rep	26	IPSWICH TOWN	2-2	Rees (og), Cross (p)	7294		8	10	9	2				3		1		5	11		7		6					4
rep2	Dec 1	Ipswich Town	2-3	Eyre 2	5000		8	9		2		10		3		1			11	5	7		6					4

R1 replay and replay 2 a.e.t. Replay 2 at Highbury.

		P	W	D	L	F	A	W	D	L	F	A	Pts
1	Bristol Rovers	46	17	4	2	55	19	9	8	6	37	27	64
2	Millwall	46	14	7	2	46	16	10	7	6	36	28	62
3	Northampton Town	46	18	4	1	75	30	8	6	9	34	40	62
4	Norwich City	46	16	6	1	56	17	9	4	10	43	38	60
5	Bristol City	46	13	8	2	62	28	9	7	7	33	33	59
6	Coventry City	46	15	5	3	52	22	4	7	12	25	40	50
7	Brighton & Hove Albion	46	12	6	5	48	30	7	6	10	33	45	50
8	Southend United	46	15	5	3	41	21	3	8	12	28	53	49
9	BOURNEMOUTH	46	15	3	5	49	23	4	6	13	25	46	47
10	Watford	46	12	8	3	39	21	3	9	11	23	42	47
11	Reading	46	17	3	3	53	18	2	5	16	16	46	46
12	Torquay United	46	15	4	4	61	28	3	5	15	26	60	45
13	Crystal Palace	46	12	7	4	40	26	3	6	14	26	56	43
14	Leyton Orient	46	12	7	4	52	28	4	3	16	16	45	42
15	Newport County	46	12	4	7	43	34	4	6	13	27	48	42
16	Ipswich Town	46	10	7	6	34	28	3	8	12	26	41	41
17	Exeter City	46	11	8	4	40	24	2	6	15	21	47	40
18	Swindon Town	46	9	5	9	38	33	5	7	11	26	46	40
19	Aldershot	46	8	8	7	36	29	4	7	12	25	48	39
20	Queen's Park Rangers	46	9	9	5	37	34	3	6	14	24	48	39
21	Gillingham	46	10	7	6	30	26	2	8	13	25	48	39
22	Colchester United	46	9	9	5	40	29	3	5	15	19	47	38
23	Shrewsbury Town	46	11	5	7	38	35	1	7	15	30	56	36
24	Walsall	46	5	9	9	35	46	2	1	20	21	72	24

1953/54

19th in Division Three (South)

			Opponent	Score	Scorers	Att	Buchanan CC	Cheney D	Cross J	Cunningham L	Drummond IP	Fidler F	Gaynor LA	Godwin TF	Hardy GD	Harrison P	Hobbs JE	Hughes HJ	Hughes W	Hunt RAR	Keetley AE	MacDonald M	Martin DV	Murray T	Neave IJG	Newsham S	Rushworth PT	Siddall AB	Stephens AE	Thompson WG	Waugh WL	Woodward L
1	Aug	19	Swindon Town	1-2	Cross	14571	8	10	9	2	3			1		11		5							6						7	4
2		22	MILLWALL	4-1	Buchanan, Cross 2 (1p), Cheney	15047	8	10	9	2	3			1		11									6					5	7	4
3		26	NORTHAMPTON T	2-1	Cross 2	14409	8	10	9	2	3			1		11			7						6					5		4
4		29	Leyton Orient	0-5		11320	8	10	9	2	3			1		11			7						6					5		4
5	Sep	3	Northampton Town	1-2	Cross	12618	8	10	9		2			1	5	11									6					3	7	4
6		5	READING	1-1	Cross	13148	8	10	9		2			1	5	11									6					3	7	4
7		9	COVENTRY CITY	1-0	Gaynor	11003		10	9				8	1	5	11					2				6					3	7	4
8		12	Southend United	1-2	Cheney	9112		10	9				8	1	5	11					2				6					3	7	4
9		14	Coventry City	0-2		10581		10			2	9	8	1	5	11									6				7	3		4
10		19	BRIGHTON & HOVE ALB	1-1	Cheney	13541		10			2	9		1	5	11									6	8			7	3		4
11		23	Ipswich Town	1-2	Cheney	10028		10			2	9		1	5	11									6	8			7	3		4
12		26	Watford	3-2	Woodward, Fidler, Gaynor	17233		10			2	9	8	1	5	11									6				7	3		4
13		30	IPSWICH TOWN	2-3	Fiddler, Harrison	8192		10			2	9	8	1	5	11									6				7	3		4
14	Oct	3	TORQUAY UNITED	1-2	Cheney	10853		10				9	8	1	5	11					2				6				7	3		4
15		10	Crystal Palace	1-3	Fidler	15756		10	9		3	8		1	5	11					2						6		7			4
16		17	BRISTOL CITY	5-2	Guy (og), Fidler, Cross 2, Williams (og)	10066		10	9		3	8		1	5	11					2	4					6		7			
17		24	Aldershot	2-1	Fidler, Waugh	5923		10			3	9	8	1	5						2	4					6		7		11	
18		31	SWINDON TOWN	4-0	Stephens, Cheney 2, Waugh	7625		10			3	9	8	1	5						2	4					6		7		11	
19	Nov	7	Walsall	0-1		7613		10			3		8	1	5	11	9				2	4					6		7			
20		14	SHREWSBURY TOWN	2-1	Harrison, Gaynor	8622		9			3		8	1	5	11					2	4					6		7		10	
21		28	NEWPORT COUNTY	1-1	Fidler	9189		10			3	9	8	1	5	11					2	4					6		7			
22	Dec	5	Norwich City	3-1	Stephens, MacDonald, Gaynor	16246		10			3	9	8	1	5	11					2	4							7	6		
23		19	Millwall	1-2	Stephens	7573		10			3	9	8	1	5	11					2	4							7	6		
24		25	SOUTHAMPTON	3-1	Drummond, Fidler, Ganor	11900		10			3	9	8	1	5	11					2	4							7	6		
25		26	Southampton	1-2	Fidler	18493		10			3	9	8	1	5	7					2	4								6	11	
26	Jan	2	LEYTON ORIENT	1-2	Gaynor	9014		10			3	9	8	1	5	7					2	4								6	11	
27		9	GILLINGHAM	4-1	Evans (og), Waugh, Siddall 2	9215		10			3	9		1	5	11					2	4						8		6	7	
28		16	Reading	1-0	Fidler	10205					3	9	10	1	5	11					2	4						8		6	7	
29		23	SOUTHEND UNITED	0-1		9363					3	9	10	1	5	11					2	4						8		6	7	
30		30	Gillingham	0-1		4207		9			3			1	5	11					2					10		8		6	7	4
31	Feb	6	Brighton & Hove Albion	0-3		13177		9			3			1	5	11					2					10		8		6	7	4
32		13	WATFORD	1-3	Fidler	8508					3	9		1	5				7		2				4	10	6	8			11	
33		20	Torquay United	0-2		6387		10			3			1	5				7	9	2				4	8	6				11	
34		27	CRYSTAL PALACE	2-0	Hunt, Siddall	8740	10			2				1	5	11			7	9	3						4	8		6		
35	Mar	6	Bristol City	1-1	Gaynor	16821	10			2			8	1	5	11			7	9	3						4			6		
36		13	EXETER CITY	4-1	* see below	8268	10			2				1	5	11			7	9	3						4	8		6		
37		20	Newport County	0-4		10421				2				1	5	11			7	9	3			10			4	8		6		
38		27	WALSALL	1-1	Harrison	7565				2				1	5	11			7	9	3			10			4	8		6		
39	Apr	3	Shrewsbury Town	1-1	Murray	6905				2				1	5	11			7	9	3	4	6	10				8				
40		7	QUEEN'S PARK RANGERS	0-1		5721				2				1	5	11			7	9	3	4	6	10				8				
41		10	NORWICH CITY	2-0	Siddall, Buchanan	8524	10			2		9		1	5	11			7		3	4	6					8				
42		16	Colchester United	1-1	Harrison	8223	10			2		9		1	5	11			7		3	4	6					8				
43		17	Queen's Park Rangers	1-2	Wood (og)	10007	10			2		9		1	5	11			7		3	4	6					8				
44		19	COLCHESTER UNITED	4-2	Fidler 2, Siddall, Harrison	7778				2		9		1	5	11			7		3	4	6	10				8				
45		24	ALDERSHOT	1-1	Fidler	7439				2		9		1		11		5	7		3	4		10	6			8				
46		28	Exeter City	0-1		5357				2		9		1		11		5			3	4		10	6			8	7			
						Apps	12	30	10	17	30	26	19	46	40	42	1	3	16	8	35	22	6	7	18	6	14	18	17	28	18	17
						Goals	3	7	9		1	13	7			6			1	1		1		1				6	3		3	1

Scorers in game 36: Siddall, W Hughes, Buchanan, Harrison (p)

Four own goals

F.A. Cup

			Opponent	Score	Scorers	Att	Buchanan CC	Cheney D	Cross J	Cunningham L	Drummond IP	Fidler F	Gaynor LA	Godwin TF	Hardy GD	Harrison P	Hobbs JE	Hughes HJ	Hughes W	Hunt RAR	Keetley AE	MacDonald M	Martin DV	Murray T	Neave IJG	Newsham S	Rushworth PT	Siddall AB	Stephens AE	Thompson WG	Waugh WL	Woodward L
R1	Nov	21	Southampton	1-1	Fidler	22101		10			3	9	8	1	5	11					2	4							7	6		
rep		25	SOUTHAMPTON	3-1	Fidler, Stephens, Cheney	13579		10			3	9	8	1	5	11					2	4							7	6		
R2	Dec	12	Scunthorpe United	0-1		12005		10			3	9	8	1	5	11					2	4							7	6		

		P	*W*	*D*	*L*	*F*	*A*	*W*	*D*	*L*	*F*	*A*	*Pts*
1	Ipswich Town	46	15	5	3	47	19	12	5	6	35	32	64
2	Brighton & Hove Albion	46	17	3	3	57	31	9	6	8	29	30	61
3	Bristol City	46	18	3	2	59	18	7	3	13	29	48	56
4	Watford	46	16	3	4	52	23	5	7	11	33	46	52
5	Northampton Town	46	18	4	1	63	18	2	7	14	19	37	51
6	Southampton	46	17	5	1	51	22	5	2	16	25	41	51
7	Norwich City	46	13	5	5	43	28	7	6	10	30	38	51
8	Reading	46	14	3	6	57	33	6	6	11	29	40	49
9	Exeter City	46	12	2	9	39	22	8	6	9	29	36	48
10	Gillingham	46	14	3	6	37	22	5	7	11	24	44	48
11	Leyton Orient	46	14	5	4	48	26	4	6	13	31	47	47
12	Millwall	46	15	3	5	44	24	4	6	13	30	53	47
13	Torquay United	46	10	10	3	48	33	7	2	14	33	55	46
14	Coventry City	46	14	5	4	36	15	4	4	15	25	41	45
15	Newport County	46	14	4	5	42	28	5	2	16	19	53	44
16	Southend United	46	15	2	6	46	22	3	5	15	23	49	43
17	Aldershot	46	11	5	7	45	31	6	4	13	29	55	43
18	Queen's Park Rangers	46	10	5	8	32	25	6	5	12	28	43	42
19	BOURNEMOUTH	46	12	5	6	47	27	4	3	16	20	43	40
19	Swindon Town	46	13	5	5	48	21	2	5	16	19	49	40
21	Shrewsbury Town	46	12	8	3	48	34	2	4	17	17	42	40
22	Crystal Palace	46	11	7	5	41	30	3	5	15	19	56	40
23	Colchester United	46	7	7	9	35	29	3	3	17	15	49	30
24	Walsall	46	8	5	10	22	27	1	3	19	18	60	26

1954/55

17th in Division Three (South)

						Att.	Allen JC	Brown J	Buchanan CC	Crosland JR	Cunningham L	Drummond IP	Fidler F	Godwin TF	Gunn AR	Harrison P	Hobbs JE	Hunt RAR	Keetley AE	MacDonald M	Murray T	Newsham S	Rushworth PT	Siddall AB
1	Aug	21	Coventry City	0-1		19571	11	6		5		2	9	1	7				3			10	4	8
2		25	ALDERSHOT	4-0	Newsham, Siddall, Fidler 2	13186	11	6		5		2	9	1	7				3			10	4	8
3		28	QUEEN'S PARK RANGERS	2-2	Fidler, Newsham	13665	11	6		5		2	9	1	7				3			10	4	8
4	Sep	1	Aldershot	1-1	Allen	5803	11	6		5		2	9	1	7				3			10	4	8
5		4	Newport County	1-1	Rushworth	9589	11	6		5		2	9	1	7				3			10	4	8
6		8	SWINDON TOWN	1-1	Fidler	11454	11	6		5		2	9	1	7				3			10	4	8
7		11	EXETER CITY	2-0	Gunn 2	11398	11	6		5		2	9	1	7				3			10	4	8
8		15	Swindon Town	2-0	Newsham (p), Siddall	7996	11	6		5		2	9	1	7				3			10	4	8
9		18	Colchester United	3-3	Newsham 2, Fidler	7801	11	6		5		2	9	1	7				3			10	4	8
10		22	CRYSTAL PALACE	4-1	Newsham 2, Fidler, Allen	10486	11	6		5		2	9	1	7				3			10	4	8
11		25	NORWICH CITY	1-3	Fidler	16389	11	6		5		2	9	1	7				3			10	4	8
12		29	Crystal Palace	1-2	Allen	6165	11	6		5		2	9	1	7				3			10	4	8
13	Oct	2	Southend United	2-2	Allen, Newsham	8905	11	6		5		2	9	1	7				3			10	4	8
14		9	MILLWALL	0-1		13315	11	6		5		2	9	1	7				3			10	4	8
15		16	Leyton Orient	1-3	Fidler	15115	11	6		5		2	9	1	7				3			10	4	8
16		23	GILLINGHAM	1-2	Newsham	10047	11	6		5		2	9	1		7			3			10	4	8
17		30	Brentford	3-1	Hunt, Dargie (og), Coote (og)	12037	11	6		5		3		1		7		10	2			9	4	8
18	Nov	6	SHREWSBURY TOWN	3-1	Newsham 2, Siddall	9528	11	6		5		3		1		7		10	2			9	4	8
19		13	Walsall	1-6	Newsham (p)	10152	11			5		3		1		7		10	2	6		9	4	8
20		27	Torquay United	1-0	Newsham	3644	11	6		5	2	3	9	1		7		10				8	4	
21	Dec	4	BRIGHTON & HOVE ALB	1-1	Newsham	8778	11	6		5	2	3	9	1		7		10				8	4	
22		18	COVENTRY CITY	2-1	Newsham, Hunt	8505	11	6		5	2	3		1		7		9				10	4	8
23		25	WATFORD	1-1	Newsham	9988	11	6		5	2	3		1		7		9				10	4	8
24		27	Watford	0-1		15202		6		5	2	3		1	7	11		9				10	4	8
25	Jan	1	Queen's Park Rangers	1-1	Newsham	9031		6		5	2	3		1	7	11		9				10	4	8
26		15	NEWPORT COUNTY	3-3	Siddall, Harrison, Hunt	5931		6		5	2	3		1	7	11		9				10	4	8
27		22	Exeter City	1-1	Newsham	7476		6		5	2	3		1	7	11		9				10	4	8
28		29	Southampton	0-0		18638		6		5	2	3		1	7	11		9				10	4	8
29	Feb	5	COLCHESTER UNITED	2-0	Hunt, Siddall	7508		6		5	2	3		1	7	11		9				10	4	8
30		12	Norwich City	1-0	Hunt	11432		6		5	2	3		1	7	11		9				10	4	8
31		19	SOUTHEND UNITED	2-1	Hunt, Newsham	7086		6		5	2	3		1	7	11		9				10	4	8
32		26	Millwall	1-1	Newsham (p)	10141		6		5	2	3		1	7	11		9				10	4	8
33	Mar	5	LEYTON ORIENT	0-3		12881		6		5	2	3		1	7	11		9				10	4	8
34		12	Gillingham	2-0	Newsham, Harrison	8236		6		5	2	3		1	7	11		9		4		10		8
35		19	BRENTFORD	1-2	Newsham (p)	8241		6		5	2	3		1	7	11		9		4		10		8
36		30	Reading	0-1		2342		6		5	2	3		1		11		9		4	7	10		8
37	Apr	2	WALSALL	1-1	Newsham	6444		6		5	2	3		1		11	9			4	7	10		8
38		9	Bristol City	2-2	Siddall, Hobbs	33302		6		5	2	3		1		11	9				7	10	4	8
39		11	NORTHAMPTON T	0-1		8759		6		5	2	3		1		11	9				7	10	4	8
40		12	Northampton Town	0-5		6618		6		5	2	3	8	1		11	9				7	10	4	
41		16	TORQUAY UNITED	0-2		6516		6		5	2	3	9	1		11					7	10	4	8
42		20	SOUTHAMPTON	1-1	Fidler	9786		6		5	2	3	9	1		11		10		4		8		7
43		23	Brighton & Hove Albion	1-1	Newsham (p)	10454	11	6		5	2	3	9	1				10		4		8		7
44		25	Shrewsbury Town	0-3		6862	11	6		5	2	3	9	1				10		4		8		7
45		27	BRISTOL CITY	0-1		9679	11	6		5	2	3		1			9	10		4		8		7
46		30	READING	0-0		6049	11	6	8	5	2	3		1				10		4		9		7
						Apps	27	45	1	46	27	46	23	46	27	27	5	25	19	10	6	46	37	43
						Goals	4						9		2	2	1	6				24	1	6

Two own goals

F.A. Cup

						Att.	Allen JC	Brown J	Buchanan CC	Crosland JR	Cunningham L	Drummond IP	Fidler F	Godwin TF	Gunn AR	Harrison P	Hobbs JE	Hunt RAR	Keetley AE	MacDonald M	Murray T	Newsham S	Rushworth PT	Siddall AB
R1	Nov	20	Barnstaple Town	4-1	Hurt, Harrison, Newsham, Siddall	7000	11	6		5	2	3		1		7		10				9	4	8
R2	Dec	11	OLDHAM ATHLETIC	1-0	Allen	13402	11	6		5	2	3		1		7		9				10	4	8
R3	Jan	8	WEST BROMWICH ALBION	0-1		22794		6		5	2	3		1	7	11		9				10	4	8

		P	W	D	L	F	A	W	D	L	F	A	Pts
1	Bristol City	46	17	4	2	62	22	13	6	4	39	25	70
2	Leyton Orient	46	16	2	5	48	20	10	7	6	41	27	61
3	Southampton	46	16	6	1	49	19	8	5	10	26	32	59
4	Gillingham	46	12	8	3	41	28	8	7	8	36	38	55
5	Millwall	46	14	6	3	44	25	6	5	12	28	43	51
6	Brighton & Hove Albion	46	14	4	5	47	27	6	6	11	29	36	50
7	Watford	46	11	9	3	45	26	7	5	11	26	36	50
8	Torquay United	46	12	6	5	51	39	6	6	11	31	43	48
9	Coventry City	46	15	5	3	50	26	3	6	14	17	33	47
10	Southend United	46	13	5	5	48	28	4	7	12	35	52	46
11	Brentford	46	11	6	6	44	36	5	8	10	38	46	46
11	Norwich City	46	13	5	5	40	23	5	5	13	20	37	46
13	Northampton Town	46	13	5	5	47	27	6	3	14	26	54	46
14	Aldershot	46	12	6	5	44	23	4	7	12	31	48	45
15	Queen's Park Rangers	46	13	7	3	46	25	2	7	14	23	50	44
16	Shrewsbury Town	46	14	5	4	49	24	2	5	16	21	54	42
17	BOURNEMOUTH	46	7	8	8	32	29	5	10	8	25	36	42
18	Reading	46	7	10	6	32	26	6	5	12	33	47	41
19	Newport County	46	8	8	7	32	29	3	8	12	28	44	38
20	Crystal Palace	46	9	11	3	32	24	2	5	16	20	56	38
21	Swindon Town	46	10	8	5	30	19	1	7	15	16	45	37
22	Exeter City	46	9	7	7	30	31	2	8	13	17	42	37
23	Walsall	46	9	6	8	49	36	1	8	14	26	50	34
24	Colchester United	46	7	6	10	33	40	2	7	14	20	51	31

1955/56

9th in Division Three (South)

							Allen JC	Brown J	Clayton L	Crosland JR	Cunningham L	Drummond IP	Godwin TF	Harrison P	Keetley AE	Leaver D	Littlejohn RD	MacDonald M	Newsham S	Norris OP	Rushworth PT	Siddall AB	Stiffle NE	Whiteside EK	Wilkinson E
1	Aug	20	Coventry City	1-3	Norris	24338		6		5	2	3	1	11		8		4	10	9			7		
2		24	COLCHESTER UNITED	3-1	Harrison, Norris, Newsham (p)	9074		6		5	2	3	1	11		8		4	10	9			7		
3		27	BRENTFORD	0-0		10451		6		5	2	3	1	11		8		4	10	9			7		
4	Sep	1	Colchester United	0-1		6964		6		5	2	3	1	11		8		4	10	9			7		
5		3	Watford	2-0	Norris, Littlejohn	12684		6		5	2	3	1	11		8	7	4	10	9					
6		7	SOUTHEND UNITED	4-1	Norris 2, Newsham (p), Leaver	9047		6		5	2	3	1	11		8	7	4	10	9					
7		10	READING	2-1	Newsham 2 (1p)	10252		6		5	2	3	1	11		8	7	4	10	9					
8		14	Southend United	1-4	Newsham	7359		6		5	2	3	1	11		8	7	4	10	9					
9		17	Millwall	0-4		11271		6		5	2	3	1	11		8	7	4	10	9					
10		22	Leyton Orient	0-3		9744		6		5	2	3	1	11		8	7	4	10	9					
11		24	GILLINGHAM	1-2	Newsham	8350		6		5	2	3	1	11		8	7	4	10	9					
12		28	NORWICH CITY	0-1		6233		6		5	2	3	1	11		8	7	4	10	9					
13	Oct	1	SOUTHAMPTON	1-3	Harrison	10561		6		5	2	3	1	11			8	4	10	9			7		
14		8	Ipswich Town	0-1		17084		6		5	2	3	1	11		10	7		8		4			9	
15		15	WALSALL	2-0	Harrison, Norris	7161	11	6		5	2	3	1	7		10			8	9	4				
16		22	Torquay United	0-0		6347	11	6		5	2	3	1	7		10			8	9	4				
17		29	NEWPORT COUNTY	0-0		7458		6		5	2	3	1	11		10	7		8	9	4				
18	Nov	5	Swindon Town	2-2	Littlejohn, Siddall	7814		6		5	2	3	1	11		9	7		10		4	8			
19		12	QUEEN'S PARK RANGERS	1-0	Allen	6934	11	6		5	2	3	1	7		10			8	9	4				
20		26	ALDERSHOT	2-2	Newsham, Leaver	6371	11	6		5	2	3	1	7		9			8		4				10
21	Dec	3	Crystal Palace	3-1	Leaver 2, Allen	9047	11	6		5	2	3	1	7		9			8		4				10
22		17	COVENTRY CITY	0-1		5029	10	6	4	5	2	3	1	7		8		11					9		
23		24	Brentford	1-2	Allen	8592	10	6	4	5	2	3	1	7		8		11					9		
24		26	EXETER CITY	0-0		8342	10	6	4	5	2	3	1	7		9		11	8						
25		27	Exeter City	0-2		10707	10	6	4	5	2	3	1	7		8		11		9					
26		31	WATFORD	4-0	Newsham 2, Norris, Leaver	6290		6	4	5	2	3	1	11		8	7		10	9					
27	Jan	14	Reading	2-0	Norris, Newsham	7519		6	4	5	2	3	1	11		8			10	9		7			
28		21	MILLWALL	4-0	Harrison 2, Newsham 2 (1p)	5645		6	4	5	2	3	1	11		8			10	9		7			
29		28	BRIGHTON & HOVE ALB	2-0	Newsham, Norris	10734		6	4	5	2	3	1	11		8			10	9		7			
30	Feb	11	Southampton	2-3	Newsham, Clayton	9185		6	4	5	2	3	1	11		8			10	9		7			
31		18	IPSWICH TOWN	1-1	Norris	8514	7	6	4	5	2	3	1	11					10	9		8			
32		25	Walsall	0-0		9090	7	6	4	5	2	3	1	11					10	9		8			
33	Mar	3	TORQUAY UNITED	2-0	Harrison, Newsham	7891	7	6	4	5	2	3	1	11					10	9		8			
34		10	Newport County	0-1		6668	7	6	4	5	2	3	1	11					10	9		8			
35		17	SWINDON TOWN	4-0	Newsham 2, Siddall, Harrison	6648	7	6	4	5	2	3	1	11					10	9		8			
36		24	Queen's Park Rangers	1-0	Newsham	5832	11	6	4	5	2	3	1						10	9		8	7		
37		30	SHREWSBURY TOWN	2-0	Allen, Siddall	8206	7	6	4	5	2	3	1	11					10	9		8			
38		31	NORTHAMPTON T	0-0		9010	7	6	4	5	2	3	1	11					10	9		8			
39	Apr	2	Shrewsbury Town	1-1	Norris	9802	7	6	4	5	2	3	1	11					10	9		8			
40		7	Aldershot	3-1	Newsham 2, Norris	4421	7	6		5	2		1	11	3				10	9	4	8			
41		12	Northampton Town	1-2	Allen	4179	11	6		5	2		1		3				10	9	4	8			7
42		14	CRYSTAL PALACE	1-0	Allen	5981	7	6		5	2		1	11	3				10	9	4				8
43		21	Brighton & Hove Albion	1-4	Norris	15348	8	6		5	2		1	11	3				10	9	4		7		
44		25	Norwich City	2-0	Harrison, Norris	12769	8	6		5	2		1	11	3				10	9	4		7		
45		28	LEYTON ORIENT	3-1	Norris, Allen, Stiffle	10615	8	6		5	2		1	11	3				10	9	4		7		
46	May	2	Gillingham	1-2	Stiffle	5214	8	6		5	2		1	11	3				10	9	4		7		
						Apps	25	46	18	46	46	39	46	44	7	29	13	17	43	39	15	16	12	1	4
						Goals	7		1					8		5	2		20	15		3	2		

F.A. Cup

							Allen JC	Brown J	Clayton L	Crosland JR	Cunningham L	Drummond IP	Godwin TF	Harrison P	Keetley AE	Leaver D	Littlejohn RD	MacDonald M	Newsham S	Norris OP	Rushworth PT	Siddall AB	Stiffle NE	Whiteside EK	Wilkinson E
R1	Nov	19	Reading	0-1		11113	11	6		5	2	3	1	7		10			8	9	4				

		P	W	D	L	F	A	W	D	L	F	A	Pts
1	Leyton Orient	46	18	3	2	76	20	11	5	7	30	29	66
2	Brighton & Hove Albion	46	20	2	1	73	16	9	5	9	39	34	65
3	Ipswich Town	46	16	6	1	59	28	9	8	6	47	32	64
4	Southend United	46	16	4	3	58	25	5	7	11	30	55	53
5	Torquay United	46	11	10	2	48	21	9	2	12	38	42	52
6	Brentford	46	11	8	4	40	30	8	6	9	29	36	52
7	Norwich City	46	15	4	4	56	31	4	9	10	30	51	51
8	Coventry City	46	16	4	3	54	20	4	5	14	19	40	49
9	BOURNEMOUTH	46	13	6	4	39	14	6	4	13	24	37	48
10	Gillingham	46	12	3	8	38	28	7	7	9	31	43	48
11	Northampton Town	46	14	3	6	44	27	6	4	13	23	44	47
12	Colchester United	46	14	4	5	56	37	4	7	12	20	44	47
13	Shrewsbury Town	46	12	9	2	47	21	5	3	15	22	45	46
14	Southampton	46	13	6	4	60	30	5	2	16	31	51	44
15	Aldershot	46	9	9	5	36	33	3	7	13	34	57	40
16	Exeter City	46	10	6	7	39	30	5	4	14	19	47	40
17	Reading	46	10	2	11	40	37	5	7	11	30	42	39
18	Queen's Park Rangers	46	10	7	6	44	32	4	4	15	20	54	39
19	Newport County	46	12	2	9	32	26	3	7	13	26	53	39
20	Walsall	46	13	5	5	43	28	2	3	18	25	56	38
21	Watford	46	8	5	10	31	39	5	6	12	21	46	37
22	Millwall	46	13	4	6	56	31	2	2	19	27	69	36
23	Crystal Palace	46	7	3	13	27	32	5	7	11	27	51	34
24	Swindon Town	46	4	10	9	18	22	4	4	15	16	56	30

1956/57

5th in Division Three (South)

	Date	Opponent	Score	Scorers	Att	Arnott JH	Bedford NB	Brown J	Clayton L	Crosland JR	Cunningham L	Cutler RV	Ellaway W	Godwin TF	Harrison P	Heath WHM	Hughes HJ	Keetley AE	Loughnane JB	Lyons MC	Melville L	Nelson JA	Newsham S	Norris OP	Rushworth PT	Siddall AB	Stiffle NE	Woollard AJ
1	Aug 18	Southampton	0-3		18121	9		4		5		11		1					7	3	6		10			8		2
2	22	IPSWICH TOWN	1-0	Newsham (p)	12365	9			4	5		11		1				3	7		6		10	8				2
3	25	TORQUAY UNITED	0-0		11227	9			4	5		11		1	7			3			6		10	8				2
4	29	Ipswich Town	0-1		11651	9			4	5		11		1	7			3			6		10	8				2
5	Sep 1	Millwall	4-3	Arnott 2, Newsham, Norris	11229	9				5		11		1	7			3			6		10	8	4			2
6	5	SHREWSBURY TOWN	6-1	Newsham 3, Arnott, Norris 2	8084	9				5		11		1	7			3			6		10	8	4			2
7	8	BRIGHTON & HOVE ALB	1-1	Newsham	13917	9				5		11		1	7			3			6		10	8	4			2
8	10	Shrewsbury Town	0-0		8098	9				5		11		1	7			3			6		10	8	4			2
9	15	Gillingham	0-1		9646	9				5		11		1	7			3			6		10	8	4			2
10	19	WALSALL	2-2	Newsham 2	8895	9				5		11		1	7			3			6		10	8	4			2
11	22	SWINDON TOWN	7-0	* See below	10598	9			4	5	2	11		1				3					10	8	6	7		
12	27	Walsall	0-0		8769	9			4		2	11		1			5	3					10	8	6	7		
13	29	Brentford	2-2	Newsham, Norris	12604	9			4	5	2	11		1	7			3					10	8	6			
14	Oct 6	NORWICH CITY	1-1	Newsham (p)	12032	9			4	5	2	11		1				3					10	8	6	7		
15	13	Colchester United	0-3		9363	8	9		4	5	2	11		1				3						10	6	7		
16	20	NEWPORT COUNTY	2-1	Bedford, Harrison	10335		9					7		1	11		5	3		2	6		10	8	4			
17	27	Reading	4-0	Norris 2, Newsham, Harrison	8981		9					7		1	11		5	3		2	6		10	8	4			
18	Nov 3	PLYMOUTH ARGYLE	2-1	Newsham 2 (1p)	11587		9					7		1	11		5	3		2	6		10	8	4			
19	10	Queen's Park Rangers	1-2	Norris	8554		9					11		1			5	3	7	2	6		10	8	4			
20	24	Southend United	1-2	Harrison	7885		9		4			11		1	7		5	3		2	6			10			8	
21	Dec 1	CRYSTAL PALACE	2-2	Newsham, Harrison	9584		9								11	1	5	3		2	6		10	8	4		7	
22	15	SOUTHAMPTON	1-0	Cutler	13644		9	6				11		1			5			2			10	8	4		7	3
23	22	Torquay United	0-1		5686		8	6				11		1			5			2			10	9	4		7	3
24	24	ALDERSHOT	3-2	Stiffle, Newsham 2	6528		9	4				11		1			5			2	6		10	8			7	3
25	26	Aldershot	2-3	Newsham, Stiffle	3797		9	6	4			11	10	1			5			2			8				7	3
26	29	MILLWALL	6-1	Norris 2, Newsham, Cutler, Bedford 2	9120		9	6	4			11		1			5			2			8	10			7	3
27	Jan 12	Brighton & Hove Albion	2-2	Cutler, Norris	9027		9	6	4			11		1			5			2			10	8			7	3
28	19	GILLINGHAM	3-1	Stiffle, Norris, Newsham	10002		9	6	4			11		1			5			2			10	8			7	3
29	Feb 2	Swindon Town	1-2	Cutler	11338	8	9	6	4			11		1			5			2			10				7	3
30	9	BRENTFORD	3-0	Cutler 2, Bedford	10898	9	8	6	4			11		1			5			2			10				7	3
31	20	Norwich City	3-1	Bedford, Newsham (p), Arnott	14079	9	8	6				11				1	5			2			10		4		7	3
32	23	COLCHESTER UNITED	1-1	Bedford	21272		9	6	4			11		1			5			2			10	8			7	3
33	Mar 7	Newport County	3-5	Cutler, Bedford, Stiffle	8047	9	8	6	4			11				1	5			2			10				7	3
34	9	EXETER CITY	3-1	Bedford, Arnott, Newsham (p)	11257	9	8	6	4			11		1			5			2			10				7	3
35	16	Plymouth Argyle	0-2		11261	9	8	6	4			11		1			5			2			7	10				3
36	23	QUEEN'S PARK RANGERS	1-0	Cutler	12552		9	6	4			11				1	5		7	2			10	8				3
37	26	Watford	1-1	Bedford	7090	9	8	6				11				1	5		7	2				10	4			3
38	30	Northampton Town	2-2	Arnott 2	7549	9	8	6	4			11		1			5		7	2			10					3
39	Apr 6	SOUTHEND UNITED	1-1	Norris	10788	9	8	6	4			11		1			5		7	2				10				3
40	13	Crystal Palace	1-1	Newsham	8571			6				11		1			5		7	2			10	8	4	9		3
41	19	COVENTRY CITY	1-2	Loughnane	10772			6				11				1	5		7	2			10	8	4	9		3
42	20	READING	2-1	Loughnane, Brown	10461			4				11				1	5		7	2	6		10	8		9		3
43	23	Coventry City	2-4	Arnott, Newsham	12637	9		4				11				1	5		7	2	6		10	8				3
44	27	NORTHAMPTON T	4-1	Newsham 3 (1p), Loughnane	8392	9		4				11	8			1	5		7	2	6		10					3
45	May 1	Exeter City	2-1	Newsham 2	5708	9		4				11	8			1	5		7	2	6		10					3
46	3	WATFORD	4-0	Brown, Norris, Shipwright (og), Loughnane	7522	9		4				11				1			7	2	6	5	10	8				3
					Apps	28	25	26	22	14	5	45	3	35	14	11	31	20	14	32	22	1	42	36	22	8	15	35
					Goals	9	9	2				9			4				4				30	15		1	4	

Scorers in game 11: Cutler, Newsham 2, Norris 2, Arnott, Siddall

One own goal

F.A. Cup

	Date	Opponent	Score	Scorers	Att	Arnott JH	Bedford NB	Brown J	Clayton L	Crosland JR	Cunningham L	Cutler RV	Ellaway W	Godwin TF	Harrison P	Heath WHM	Hughes HJ	Keetley AE	Loughnane JB	Lyons MC	Melville L	Nelson JA	Newsham S	Norris OP	Rushworth PT	Siddall AB	Stiffle NE	Woollard AJ
R1	Nov 17	BURTON ALBION	8-0	* See below	13245		9					11		1			5	3		2	6		10	8	4		7	
R2	Dec 8	Swindon Town	1-0	Cutler	17410		10	6				11		1			5	3		2			8	9	4		7	
R3	Jan 5	ACCRINGTON STANLEY	2-0	Norris, Bedford	17212		8	6	4			11		1			5			2			10	9			7	3
R4	26	Wolverhampton Wan.	1-0	Cutler	42011		9	6	4			11		1			5			2			10	8			7	3
R5	Feb 16	TOTTENHAM HOTSPUR	3-1	Norris, Newsham, Stiffle	25892		9	6	4			11		1			5			2			10	8			7	3
R6	Mar 2	MANCHESTER UNITED	1-2	Bedford	28799		9	6	4			11		1			5			2			10	8			7	3

Scorers in R1: Norris 3, Newsham 2, Wright (og), Lyons, Bedford

		P	W	D	L	F	A	W	D	L	F	A	Pts
1	Ipswich Town	46	18	3	2	72	20	7	6	10	29	34	59
2	Torquay United	46	19	4	0	71	18	5	7	11	18	46	59
3	Colchester United	46	15	8	0	49	19	7	6	10	35	37	58
4	Southampton	46	15	4	4	48	20	7	6	10	28	32	54
5	BOURNEMOUTH	46	15	7	1	57	20	4	7	12	31	42	52
6	Brighton & Hove Albion	46	15	6	2	59	26	4	8	11	27	39	52
7	Southend United	46	14	3	6	42	20	4	9	10	31	45	48
8	Brentford	46	12	9	2	55	29	4	7	12	23	47	48
9	Shrewsbury Town	46	11	9	3	45	24	4	9	10	27	55	48
10	Queen's Park Rangers	46	12	7	4	42	21	6	4	13	19	39	47
11	Watford	46	11	6	6	44	32	7	4	12	28	43	46
12	Newport County	46	15	6	2	51	18	1	7	15	14	44	45
13	Reading	46	13	4	6	44	30	5	5	13	36	51	45
14	Northampton Town	46	15	5	3	49	22	3	4	16	17	51	45
15	Walsall	46	11	7	5	49	25	5	5	13	31	49	44
16	Coventry City	46	12	5	6	52	36	4	7	12	22	48	44
17	Millwall	46	13	7	3	46	29	3	5	15	18	55	44
18	Plymouth Argyle	46	10	8	5	38	31	6	3	14	30	42	43
19	Aldershot	46	11	5	7	43	35	4	7	12	36	57	42
20	Crystal Palace	46	7	10	6	31	28	4	8	11	31	47	40
21	Exeter City	46	8	8	7	37	29	4	5	14	24	50	37
22	Gillingham	46	7	8	8	29	29	5	5	13	25	56	37
23	Swindon Town	46	12	3	8	43	33	3	3	17	23	63	36
24	Norwich City	46	7	5	11	33	37	1	10	12	28	57	31

1957/58

9th in Division Three (South)

	Date		Opponent	Score	Scorers	Att	Arnott JH	Bedford NB	Brown J	Brown KJ (Ken)	Burgess MR	Bushby D	Cutler RV	Dowsett GJ	Gibbs BR	Godwin TF	Hampson RG	Heath WHM	Hughes HJ	Keetley AE	Loughnane JB	Lyons MC	Melville L	Nelson IA	Norris OP	Rule AH	Stiffle NE	Thomas R	Tyrrell JJ	Woollard AJ
1	Aug	24	WATFORD	2-1	Norris, Tyrrell	16567		9	4				11			1			5	3	7	2	6		8				10	
2		28	Brighton & Hove Albion	1-2	Norris	16627		9	4				11			1			5	3	7	2	6		10				8	
3		31	Crystal Palace	0-3		13752	9		6				11			1			5	3		2		4	8		7			
4	Sep	4	BRIGHTON & HOVE ALB	1-3	Cutler (p)	12875		8	6				11	9		1			5	3		2		4	10		7			
5		7	TORQUAY UNITED	2-0	Cutler. Dowsett	13895		9	6				11	8				1	5			2		4	10		7			3
6		9	Coventry City	3-0	Dowsett 2, Norris	10013		9	6				11	8				1	5			2		4	10		7			3
7		14	Brentford	2-4	Stiffle, Cutler (p)	13733	9		6				11	8				1	5			2		4	10		7			3
8		18	COVENTRY CITY	0-0		11365	9		6				11	8				1	5			2		4	10		7			3
9		21	COLCHESTER UNITED	1-1	Dowsett	12057	9		6				11	8				1	5			2		4	10		7			3
10		23	Shrewsbury Town	4-0	Arnott, Norris, K Brown, Cutler	5485	8		6	7			10	11				1	5			2		4	9					3
11		28	Norwich City	2-2	Dowset, Wilson (og)	22221	9		6	11			7	8				1	5			2		4	10					3
12	Oct	2	SHREWSBURY TOWN	3-1	Bannister (og), Dowsett, J Brown	7714	9		6	11			7	8				1	5			2		4	10					3
13		5	Southampton	0-7		22047		9	6	11			7	8				1	5			2		4	10					3
14		12	SOUTHEND UNITED	2-1	Dowsett, Hughes	12605		9	6	11			7	8				1	5			2			10	4				3
15		19	Queen's Park Rangers	0-3		9007		9	6	11			7	8				1	5			2			10	4				3
16		26	EXETER CITY	2-1	Bedford, Dowsett	11623		9	6				11	10				1	5		7	2			8	4				3
17	Nov	9	MILLWALL	4-0	Bedford 3, Burgess	11086		9	4		10		11	8				1	5		7	2	6							3
18		23	ALDERSHOT	5-1	Bedford, Burgess 3, Dowsett	11961		9	6		10		11	8				1	5		7	2				4				3
19		30	Plymouth Argyle	1-3	Dowsett	16956		9	6		10		11	8				1	5		7	2				4				3
20	Dec	14	Newport County	1-3	Dowsett	5467	7		6		9			10	8	1			5		11	2				4				3
21		21	Watford	1-1	Dowsett	5877	9		6		10	4	11	8		1			5		7	2								3
22		25	READING	4-1	Dowsett 2, Loughnane, Bedford	11162		10	6		9	4	11	8				1	5		7	2								3
23		26	Reading	0-2		13339		8	6			4	11	10				1	5		7	2					9			3
24		28	CRYSTAL PALACE	3-1	Dowsett 2, Bedford	13073		8	6		9	4	11	10				1			7	2		5						3
25	Jan	4	WALSALL	1-2	Dowsett	9866		9	6		8	4	11	10				1			7	2		5						3
26		11	Torquay United	1-3	Arnott	5739	9	8	6				11	10		1			5		7	2				4				3
27		18	BRENTFORD	1-0	Arnott	11090	9		6				11	10		1			5		7	2			8	4				3
28		25	Swindon Town	0-1		12437	9		6				11	10		1			5		7				8	4		2		3
29	Feb	1	Colchester United	2-3	Arnott, Dowsett	8091	9		6				11	10		1			5		7				8	4		2		3
30		8	NORWICH CITY	3-1	Arnott, Bedford 2	11419	9	8	6				11	10				1	5		7					4		2		3
31		15	SOUTHAMPTON	5-2	Bedford 2, Cutler 2 (1p), Hampson	21655	9	8	6				11	10			7	1	5							4		2		3
32		22	Southend United	0-2		11131	9	10	6				11	8			7	1				2				4				3
33	Mar	1	QUEEN'S PARK RANGERS	4-1	Bedford 2, Cutler (p), Arnott	12711	9	8	6		5		11	10			7	1								4		2		3
34		8	Exeter City	2-1	Bedford 2	8047	9	8	6		5		11	10		1	7									4		2		3
35		15	GILLINGHAM	2-1	Cutler, Boswell (og)	11451	9	8	6		5		11	10		1	7									4		2		3
36		22	Aldershot	0-0		4342	9	8	6		5		11	10		1	7									4		2		3
37		29	NEWPORT COUNTY	4-3	Hampson, Arnott, Dowsett 2	11296	9	8	4		5		11	10		1	7									6		2		3
38	Apr	4	NORTHAMPTON T	1-1	Arnott	15196	9	8	4		5		11	10		1	7									6		2		3
39		5	Millwall	2-0	Dowsett, Gibbs	5078	9		6		5		11	10	8	1	7									4		2		3
40		8	Northampton Town	0-4		9888	9		4		5		11	10	8	1	7									6		2		3
41		12	PLYMOUTH ARGYLE	0-0		16075	9		6		5	4	11	10	8	1	7											2		3
42		16	Gillingham	1-1	Dowsett	3469		9	6		5		11	10	8	1					7					4		2		3
43		19	Port Vale	3-2	Cutler, Bedford, Gibbs	8481		8	4		5		11	10	9	1					7					6		2		3
44		24	Walsall	1-3	Cutler	7203		8	4		9		11	10		1			5		7					6		2		3
45		26	SWINDON TOWN	1-1	Dowsett	12930		8	4		5		11	10	9	1					7					6		2		3
46		30	PORT VALE	3-1	Jones (og), Cutler (p), Bedford	10683		8	4		5		11	10		1				3	7							2		
						Apps	25	31	46	6	22	6	45	43	7	23	11	23	30	5	22	28	3	13	19	25	8	18	2	41
						Goals	8	17	1	1	4		11	23	2		2		1		1				4		1		1	

Played in one game: W Ellaway (3, at 10), PH Gledstone (46, 6), SG Miles (32, 5) and J White (46, 9)

Four own goals

F.A. Cup

	Date		Opponent	Score	Scorers	Att	Arnott JH	Bedford NB	Brown J	Brown KJ (Ken)	Burgess MR	Bushby D	Cutler RV	Dowsett GJ	Gibbs BR	Godwin TF	Hampson RG	Heath WHM	Hughes HJ	Keetley AE	Loughnane JB	Lyons MC	Melville L	Nelson IA	Norris OP	Rule AH	Stiffle NE	Thomas R	Tyrrell JJ	Woollard AJ
R1	Nov	16	Oswestry Town	5-1	Dowsett, Bedford 3, Burgess	5313		9	6		10		11	8				1	5		7	2				4				3
R2	Dec	7	Northampton Town	1-4	Norris	12791		9	4				11	8		1			5		7	2	6		10					3

		P	W	D	L	F	A	W	D	L	F	A	Pts
1	Brighton & Hove Albion	46	13	6	4	52	30	11	6	6	36	34	60
2	Brentford	46	15	5	3	52	24	9	5	9	30	32	58
3	Plymouth Argyle	46	17	4	2	43	17	8	4	11	24	31	58
4	Swindon Town	46	14	7	2	47	16	7	8	8	32	34	57
5	Reading	46	14	5	4	52	23	7	8	8	27	28	55
6	Southampton	46	16	3	4	78	31	6	7	10	34	41	54
7	Southend United	46	14	5	4	56	26	7	7	9	34	32	54
8	Norwich City	46	11	9	3	41	28	8	6	9	34	42	53
9	BOURNEMOUTH	46	16	5	2	54	24	5	4	14	27	50	51
10	Queen's Park Rangers	46	15	6	2	40	14	3	8	12	24	51	50
11	Newport County	46	12	6	5	40	24	5	8	10	33	43	48
12	Colchester United	46	13	5	5	45	27	4	8	11	32	52	47
13	Northampton Town	46	13	1	9	60	33	6	5	12	27	46	44
14	Crystal Palace	46	12	5	6	46	30	3	8	12	24	42	43
15	Port Vale	46	12	6	5	49	24	4	4	15	18	34	42
16	Watford	46	9	8	6	34	27	4	8	11	25	50	42
17	Shrewsbury Town	46	10	6	7	29	25	5	4	14	20	46	40
18	Aldershot	46	7	9	7	31	34	5	7	11	28	55	40
19	Coventry City	46	10	9	4	41	24	3	4	16	20	57	39
20	Walsall	46	10	7	6	37	24	4	2	17	24	51	37
21	Torquay United	46	9	7	7	33	34	2	6	15	16	40	35
22	Gillingham	46	12	5	6	33	24	1	4	18	19	57	35
23	Millwall	46	6	6	11	37	36	5	3	15	26	55	31
24	Exeter City	46	10	4	9	37	35	1	5	17	20	64	31

1958/59

12th in Division Three

	Date	Opponent	Score	Scorers	Att	Anderson TC	Arnott JH	Bedford NB	Bolton R	Brown I	Brown J	Bumstead RG	Burgess MR	Coxon WG	Cutler RV	Dowsett GJ	Flood JE	Gibbs BR	Gledstone PH	Godwin TF	Hampson RG	Loughnane JB	Lyons MC	McManus EJ	Nelson JA	Norris OP	Southren T	Standley TL	Thomas J	Thomas R	Woollard AJ
1	Aug 23	SOUTHEND UNITED	1-4	Flood	14219						4		5		11	8	7		6	1						9				2	3
2	27	HALIFAX TOWN	3-0	Cutler (p), Bedford, Dowsett	12218	8	4	9			6		5		11	10	7			1			2							3	
3	30	Bury	1-5	Bedford	12044		4	9			6		5		11	10	7			1			2			8				3	
4	Sep 1	Halifax Town	1-0	Gledstone	9520		7	9	8		6		5		11	10			4	1			2							3	
5	6	QUEEN'S PARK RANGERS	2-0	Bedford, Bolton	11890		7	9	8		6		5		11	10			4	1			2							3	
6	10	READING	0-1		11415		7	9	8		6		5		11	10			4	1			2							3	
7	13	Rochdale	1-2	J Brown	6361			9	10		6		5				7	8	4	1	11		2							3	
8	17	Reading	0-2		17841	8	4	9	11	5			10						6	1		7	2							3	
9	20	DONCASTER ROVERS	1-0	Burgess	11551	8	4	9	11	5			10						6	1		7	2							3	
10	24	NORWICH CITY	2-0	Bolton, Anderson	8407	8	4	9	11	5			10						6	1		7	2							3	
11	27	Plymouth Argyle	1-3	Dowsett	24757	9	4		11	5			10			8	7		6	1			2							3	
12	Oct 1	Norwich City	2-2	Bolton, Burgess	18161		4		11	5	10		9			8	7		6	1			2							3	
13	4	TRANMERE ROVERS	4-0	Bolton (p), Burgess, Dowsett 2	9033		4		11	5	9		10			8	7		6	1			2							3	
14	6	Stockport County	1-3	Bolton (p)	9640		4		11	5	9		10			8	7		6	1			2							3	
15	11	SOUTHAMPTON	2-1	Burgess 2	18448		4		8	5	9		10				7		6	1	11		2							3	
16	18	Wrexham	0-1		12429		4		8	5	9		10				7		6	1	11		2							3	
17	25	BRADFORD CITY	4-0	Dowsett, Flood, Burgess 2	11219		4		10	5			9			8	7		6	1	11		2							3	
18	Nov 1	Hull City	3-5	Bolton, Flood, Burgess	14400		4		10	5			9			8	11		6	1			2				7				3
19	8	BRENTFORD	0-0		11564		4		10	5			9			8	11		6	1			2				7			3	
20	22	CHESTERFIELD	2-1	Burgess 2	9079						4		9	11			7		6	1			2		5		10	8		3	
21	29	Notts County	3-4	Southren, Burgess, Coxon (p)	7463					3	4		9	11			7		6	1			2		5		10	8			
22	Dec 6	HULL CITY	1-0	Coxon	9869						4		9	11					6	1		7	2		5		10	8		3	
23	13	Newport County	1-4	Burgess	5392						4		9	11					6	1		7	2		5		10	8		3	
24	20	Southend United	0-2		10082				10		4		9	11					6	1			2		5		7	8		3	
25	26	Colchester United	1-3	Burgess	9182				10		4		9	11					6	1			2		5		7	8		3	
26	27	COLCHESTER UNITED	1-1	Burgess	12504		4	8					9	11		10			6	1			2		5		7			3	
27	Jan 3	BURY	2-0	Dowsett, Bedford	10344		4	8					9	11		10			6	1			2		5		7			3	
28	10	Swindon Town	1-0	Bedford	10778		4	8					9	11		10			6	1			2		5		7			3	
29	17	Queen's Park Rangers	4-0	Coxon (p), Burgess 2, Bedford	6041		4	8					9	11		10			6	1			2		5		7			3	
30	24	MANSFIELD TOWN	3-3	Arnott, Southren, Burgess	10338		4	8					9	11		10			6	1			2		5		7			3	
31	31	ROCHDALE	0-0		9945		4	8					9	11		10			6	1		7	2		5					3	
32	Feb 7	Doncaster Rovers	1-5	Southren	4457		4					8	9	11					6	1		7	2		5		10			3	
33	14	PLYMOUTH ARGYLE	1-1	Arnott	15108		4	9				8		11		10			6	1			2		5		7				3
34	21	Tranmere Rovers	0-4		7296		4	9				8		11					6	1			2	7	5		10				3
35	28	Southampton	0-0		16896		4	9	10	5			6	11			7	8		1			2								3
36	Mar 7	WREXHAM	0-0		8587		4	9					6	11			7	8		1			2		5		10				3
37	14	Bradford City	1-0	Dowsett	11151		4				6		10	11		9				1			2		5		7	8			3
38	26	Accrington Stanley	2-3	Southren, Dowsett	4174		4				6		10	11		9				1			2		5		7	8			3
39	28	Brentford	1-1	Burgess	15970		4				6		10	11		9				1			2		5		7	8			3
40	30	ACCRINGTON STANLEY	5-2	* See below	8465		4				6		10	11		9				1			2		5		7	8			3
41	Apr 4	SWINDON TOWN	3-3	Burgess 2, Dowsett	9546		4				6	11	10			9				1			2		5		7	8			3
42	11	Chesterfield	0-1		7400		4			5		8	10	11		9			6	1			2				7				3
43	18	NOTTS COUNTY	0-0		8130		4			5		7	10	11		9			6				2					8	1		3
44	22	STOCKPORT COUNTY	2-0	Burgess 2	6381		4				6	8	10	11		9							2		5		7		1		3
45	25	Mansfield Town	4-1	Dowsett 3, Burgess	3703						4	8	10	11		9			6				2		5		7		1		3
46	29	NEWPORT COUNTY	1-1	Coxon	7386						4	8	10	11		9			6				2		5		7		1		3
					Apps	5	36	19	19	16	26	9	44	26	6	30	17	3	36	42	4	7	45	1	24	2	26	12	4	30	16
					Goals	1	2	6	6		1		24	4	1	13	3		1								6	1			

Scorers in game 40: Burgess, Standley, Dowsett, Southren 2

JJ Tyrrell played in game 1 at 10

F.A. Cup

	Date	Opponent	Score	Scorers	Att	Anderson TC	Arnott JH	Bedford NB	Bolton R	Brown I	Brown J	Bumstead RG	Burgess MR	Coxon WG	Cutler RV	Dowsett GJ	Flood JE	Gibbs BR	Gledstone PH	Godwin TF	Hampson RG	Loughnane JB	Lyons MC	McManus EJ	Nelson JA	Norris OP	Southren T	Standley TL	Thomas J	Thomas R	Woollard AJ
R1	Nov 15	Tooting & Mitcham Utd.	1-3	Burgess	9797				10		4		9			8	11		6	1			2		7		5			3	

		P	W	D	L	F	A	W	D	L	F	A	Pts
1	Plymouth Argyle	46	14	7	2	55	27	9	9	5	34	32	62
2	Hull City	46	19	3	1	65	21	7	6	10	25	34	61
3	Brentford	46	15	5	3	49	22	6	10	7	27	27	57
4	Norwich City	46	13	6	4	51	29	9	7	7	38	33	57
5	Colchester United	46	15	2	6	46	31	6	8	9	25	36	52
6	Reading	46	16	4	3	51	21	5	4	14	27	42	50
7	Tranmere Rovers	46	15	3	5	53	22	6	5	12	29	45	50
8	Southend United	46	14	6	3	52	26	7	2	14	33	54	50
9	Halifax Town	46	14	5	4	48	25	7	3	13	32	52	50
10	Bury	46	12	9	2	51	24	5	5	13	18	34	48
11	Bradford City	46	13	4	6	47	25	5	7	11	37	51	47
12	BOURNEMOUTH	46	12	9	2	40	18	5	3	15	29	51	46
13	Queen's Park Rangers	46	14	6	3	49	28	5	2	16	25	49	46
14	Southampton	46	12	7	4	57	33	5	4	14	31	47	45
15	Swindon Town	46	13	4	6	39	25	3	9	11	20	32	45
16	Chesterfield	46	12	5	6	40	26	5	5	13	27	38	44
17	Newport County	46	15	2	6	43	24	2	7	14	26	44	43
18	Wrexham	46	12	6	5	40	30	2	8	13	23	47	42
19	Accrington Stanley	46	10	8	5	42	31	5	4	14	29	56	42
20	Mansfield Town	46	11	5	7	38	42	3	8	12	35	56	41
21	Stockport County	46	9	7	7	33	23	4	3	16	32	55	36
22	Doncaster Rovers	46	13	2	8	40	32	1	3	19	10	58	33
23	Notts County	46	5	9	9	33	39	3	4	16	22	57	29
24	Rochdale	46	8	7	8	21	26	0	5	18	16	53	28

1959/60

10th in Division Three

							Arnott JH	Bolton R	Brown I	Brown J	Bumstead RG	Burgess MR	Coxon WG	Dowsett GJ	Evans RP	Gibbs BR	Gledstone PH	Godwin TF	Gregory JL	Jones BR	Lynne MGA	Massey RW	McManus EJ	Nelson JA	Smith R	Southren T	Standley TL	Woollard AJ
1	Aug	22	Shrewsbury Town	0-0		9432	4			6	9		11	8		10	3	1	2					5		7		
2		24	Port Vale	0-1		18037	4			6	9		11	8		10	3	1	2					5		7		
3		29	TRANMERE ROVERS	2-1	Bumstead, Burgess	11960	4			6	9	10	11	8			3	1	2					5		7		
4	Sep	2	PORT VALE	3-0	Burgess 2, Dowsett	11689	4			6	9	10	11	8			3	1	2					5		7		
5		5	Wrexham	2-1	Dowsett, Burgess	13771	4			6	9	10	11	8			3	1	2					5		7		
6		7	Accrington Stanley	1-2	Standley	5877	4			6	9	10	11				3	1	2					5		7	8	
7		12	GRIMSBY TOWN	4-2	Standley, Nelson, Southren, Coxon	12282	4			6	9	10	11				3	1	2					5		7	8	
8		16	ACCRINGTON STANLEY	3-1	Standley, Burgess, Coxon	10385	4				9	10	11		6		3	1	2					5		7	8	
9		19	Queen's Park Rangers	0-3		11410	4			6	9	8	11				3	1	2					5		7	10	
10		23	NEWPORT COUNTY	4-1	Evans 2, Southren, Coxon	9322	4			6	9	8	11		10		3	1	2					5		7		
11		26	BRADFORD CITY	3-2	Evans 2, Burgess	12367	4			6	9	8	11		10			1	2					5		7		3
12		28	Newport County	2-5	Coxon, Burton (og)	8683	4		2		9	6	11	8	10						1		7	5				3
13	Oct	3	Coventry City	0-4		17907	4			6	9	8	11		10				2		1			5		7		3
14		7	YORK CITY	2-0	Gledstone, Evans	6734	4			6	9		11	8	10		3		2		1			5		7		
15		10	Norwich City	3-2	Coxon, Dowsett, Southren	25163	4			6	9		11	8	10		3		2		1			5		7		
16		12	York City	2-3	Bumstead, Coxon	8278	4			6	9	10	11	8			3		2		1			5		7		
17		17	BRENTFORD	1-2	Bumstead	12216	4			6	9		11	8	10		3	1	2					5		7		
18		24	Colchester United	2-1	Bumstead, Dowsett	8118	4		2	6	9		10	8			3	1						5	11	7		
19		31	READING	1-1	Dowsett	11615			2	4	9	6	10	8				1	3					5	11	7		
20	Nov	7	Mansfield Town	4-3	Dowsett, Bumstead, Coxon, Evans	6792	4		2	6	9		11	8	10		3	1						5		7		
21		21	Bury	2-0	Southren, Bumstead	11135	4		2	6	9		11	8	10			1						5		7		3
22		28	BARNSLEY	1-1	Bumstead	9709	4		2	6	9		11	8	10			1						5		7		3
23	Dec	12	SOUTHEND UNITED	0-0		9666	4		2	6	9		11	8	10			1						5		7		3
24		19	SHREWSBURY TOWN	2-2	Hobson (og), I Brown	6886	4		2	6	9		11	8	10			1						5		7		3
25		26	SWINDON TOWN	3-1	Dowsett 2, Smith	10969	4		2	6	9			8				1						5	11	7	10	3
26		28	Swindon Town	0-2		10335	4		2		9	6		8			3	1					7	5	11		10	
27	Jan	2	Tranmere Rovers	1-1	J Brown	8650	4		2	6	9	8			10			1						5	11	7		3
28		16	WREXHAM	1-3	Smith (p)	7954	4		2	6	9			8	10			1						5	11	7		3
29		23	Grimsby Town	1-1	I Brown	8078	4		9		8	6	11	10			3	1						5		7		2
30	Feb	6	QUEEN'S PARK RANGERS	1-1	Dowsett	9855	4		9		7	6	11	10		8	3	1						5				2
31		13	Bradford City	0-0		12754	4		2		9	6	11	10		8	3	1						5		7		
32		20	COVENTRY CITY	2-2	Coxon (p), Evans	9327	4		2		9	6	11	10	8		3	1						5		7		
33		24	Southampton	3-4	Bumstead, Southren, Smith (p)	20800	4		2		9	6		10	8		3	1						5	11	7		
34		27	NORWICH CITY	0-0		12806	4		2		9	6		10			3	1		8			7	5	11			
35	Mar	5	Brentford	0-1		9764	4		2		7	9			10		6	1		8				5	11			3
36		12	COLCHESTER UNITED	3-2	Jones, Dowsett, Coxon	9256	4		2	6	10		11	9				1		8				5		7		3
37		19	Barnsley	0-1		5621	4		2		10		11	9				1		8				5		7	6	3
38		26	MANSFIELD TOWN	6-0	Dowsett 2, Coxon (p), Bumstead 3	7080	4		2		10		11	9	8			1						5		7	6	3
39	Apr	2	Halifax Town	0-1		5442	4		2		10		11	9	8			1						5		7	6	3
40		9	BURY	2-1	Dowsett, Jones	10089	4		2		10		11	9	8			1		7				5			6	3
41		15	Chesterfield	0-4		8231	4		2		10		11	9	8			1		7				5			6	3
42		16	Reading	2-2	Bumstead, Bolton	10618		10	2		8	5	11			9	3	1				4				7	6	
43		18	CHESTERFIELD	1-1	Coxon (p)	9098		10	2		8	5	11			9	3	1				4				7	6	
44		23	SOUTHAMPTON	1-3	Bumstead	21660	4		2		10	9	11		8		3	1						5		7	6	
45		30	Southend United	0-3		9043	4		2		9	6	11	7	8		3	1		10				5				
46	May	4	HALIFAX TOWN	1-0	Jones	6349	4				10	6	11	9			3	1		8				5		7		2
						Apps	43	2	29	26	46	27	39	34	24	6	29	41	17	8	5	2	3	44	9	38	14	20
						Goals		1	2	1	13	6	11	13	7		1			3				1	3	5	3	

Two own goals

F.A. Cup

							Arnott JH	Bolton R	Brown I	Brown J	Bumstead RG	Burgess MR	Coxon WG	Dowsett GJ	Evans RP	Gibbs BR	Gledstone PH	Godwin TF	Gregory JL	Jones BR	Lynne MGA	Massey RW	McManus EJ	Nelson JA	Smith R	Southren T	Standley TL	Woollard AJ
R1	Nov	14	Walthamstow Avenue	3-2	Evans, I Brown, Bumstead	4462	4		2	6	9		11	8	10		3	1						5		7		
R2	Dec	5	Enfield	5-1	Bumstead 2, Dowsett 2, Arnott	6800	4		2	6	9		11	8	10			1						5		7		3
R3	Jan	9	YORK CITY	1-0	Southren	14749	4		2	6	9			8	10			1						5	11	7		3
R4		30	Bradford City	1-3	Lawlor (og)	19701	4		9		7	6	11	10		8	3	1						5				2

		P	*W*	*D*	*L*	*F*	*A*	*W*	*D*	*L*	*F*	*A*	*Pts*
1	Southampton	46	19	3	1	68	30	7	6	10	38	45	61
2	Norwich City	46	16	4	3	53	24	8	7	8	29	30	59
3	Shrewsbury Town	46	12	7	4	58	34	6	9	8	39	41	52
4	Grimsby Town	46	12	7	4	48	27	6	9	8	39	43	52
5	Coventry City	46	14	6	3	44	22	7	4	12	34	41	52
6	Brentford	46	13	6	4	46	24	8	3	12	32	37	51
7	Bury	46	13	4	6	36	23	8	5	10	28	28	51
8	Queen's Park Rangers	46	14	7	2	45	16	4	6	13	28	38	49
9	Colchester United	46	15	6	2	51	22	3	5	15	32	52	47
10	BOURNEMOUTH	46	12	8	3	47	27	5	5	13	25	45	47
11	Reading	46	13	3	7	49	34	5	7	11	35	43	46
12	Southend United	46	15	3	5	49	28	4	5	14	27	46	46
13	Newport County	46	15	2	6	59	36	5	4	14	21	43	46
13	Port Vale	46	16	4	3	51	19	3	4	16	29	60	46
15	Halifax Town	46	13	3	7	42	27	5	7	11	28	45	46
16	Swindon Town	46	12	6	5	39	30	7	2	14	30	48	46
17	Barnsley	46	13	6	4	45	25	2	8	13	20	41	44
18	Chesterfield	46	13	3	7	41	31	5	4	14	30	53	43
19	Bradford City	46	10	7	6	39	28	5	5	13	27	46	42
20	Tranmere Rovers	46	11	8	4	50	29	3	5	15	22	46	41
21	York City	46	11	5	7	38	26	2	7	14	19	47	38
22	Mansfield Town	46	11	4	8	55	48	4	2	17	26	64	36
23	Wrexham	46	12	5	6	39	30	2	3	18	29	71	36
24	Accrington Stanley	46	4	5	14	31	53	7	0	16	26	70	27

1960/61

19th in Division Three

							Arnott JH	Bennett DM	Best D	Bimpson JL	Bolton R	Brown I	Bumstead RG	Burgess MR	Coxon WG	Dowsett GJ	Evans RP	Gibbs BR	Gledstone PH	Godwin TF	Jones BR	King JA	Lovie JTH	Lynne MGA	Massey RW	McGarry WH	Nelson JA	Smith R	Standley TL	Weller CW	Woollard AJ
1	Aug	20	QUEEN'S PARK RANGERS	1-0	Dowsett	12222	4							5		10		8			9	6	7	1				11	2		3
2		23	Bristol City	0-1		14455	4							5		10		8			9	6	7	1				11	2		3
3		27	Notts County	2-3	Dowsett, Bumstead	12115	4						8	5		10					9	6		1				11	2	7	3
4		31	BRISTOL CITY	2-2	Dowsett, Evans	9642	4				10		7	5		8	9					6		1				11	2		3
5	Sep	3	Tranmere Rovers	3-4	Bolton 2, Gibbs	8029					10	2	7	5			9	8	3			6		1				11	4		
6		5	Hull City	0-2		8496					10	4	7		11		9	8	3			6		1			5		2		
7		10	BRADFORD CITY	2-2	Arnott, Bolton	7970	7				10		8	5	11			9	3		6	4		1					2		
8		12	HULL CITY	2-2	Evans, Gibbs	5315	7				10	5			11		8	9	3		6	4		1					2		
9		17	Barnsley	3-2	Gibss, Coxon, Arnott	6004	7				10	5			11		8	9	3	1	6	4							2		
10		19	Coventry City	0-1		9709	7				10	5			11		8	9	3	1	6	4							2		
11		24	NEWPORT COUNTY	2-2	Dowsett, Gibbs	8507	6				10	5			11	7	8	9	3	1		4							2		
12		28	COVENTRY CITY	2-1	Dowsett, Gibbs	4353	6				10				11	7	8	9	3	1		4					5				2
13	Oct	1	Colchester United	1-0	Coxon	4576	6				10				11	7	8	9	3	1	2	4					5				
14		5	GRIMSBY TOWN	2-1	Gibbs, Coxon (p)	5987	4				10	2			11	7	8	9	3	1	6						5				
15		8	BRENTFORD	0-1		5820	4				10	2			11	7		9	3	1	8	6					5				
16		15	Swindon Town	1-0	Bolton	12295	7				10	2	8			9			3	1	6	4					5	11			
17		22	TORQUAY UNITED	1-3	Bolton	8277	7				10	2	8			9			3	1	6	4					5	11			
18		29	Port Vale	0-3		7752							7	6	11	10	8	9		1	3	4					5		2		
19	Nov	12	Chesterfield	1-0	Bumstead	4390	4				10		7	6			8		3	1	9						5	11	2		
20		19	BURY	0-3		9283	4				10		7	6					3	1	9	8					5	11	2		
21	Dec	3	SHREWSBURY TOWN	2-2	Skeech (og), Bumstead	4978	4				10	5	7	6				9	3	1								11	2	8	
22		10	Halifax Town	1-2	Weller	4623	4				10	5	7	6				9	3	1								11	2	8	
23		17	Queen's Park Rangers	1-3	Smith	6952	4				10	5	7	6				9	3					1				11	2	8	
24		26	Reading	3-4	Weller, Gibbs 2	8576	4				10	5	7	6				9	3					1				11	2	8	
25		27	READING	2-0	Bumstead, Gibbs	9925	4				10	5	7	6				9	3					1				11	2	8	
26		31	NOTTS COUNTY	1-3	Smith	7974	4				10	5	7	6				9	3					1				11	2	8	
27	Jan	9	Walsall	0-2		6238	4				10		7			8			3	1	9	6					5	11			2
28		14	TRANMERE ROVERS	2-1	Dowsett, King	6905	4				10		7			8			3	1	9	6					5	11			2
29		28	SOUTHEND UNITED	3-2	Bolton, Jones 2	5508	4				10		7			8			3	1	9	6					5	11			2
30	Feb	4	BARNSLEY	1-2	Bolton	6425					10		7			8			3	1	9		6				5	11	4		2
31		11	Newport County	0-2		3790	4				10		8		7					1	9		6		2		5	11			3
32		14	Bradford City	1-3	Smith (p)	7895	4	7		9	10		8							1			6		2		5	11			3
33		18	COLCHESTER UNITED	4-4	Simpson, Bolton, Weller, Bumstead	6793				9	10		7						3	1	4		6		2		5	11		8	
34		25	Shrewsbury Town	1-2	Bolton	5946				9	10		7						3	1	4		6				5	11		8	2
35	Mar	4	SWINDON TOWN	2-1	Weller, Bolton	7862				9	10		7						3	1	4		6				5	11		8	2
36		11	Torquay United	1-0	Weller	5174				9	10		7						3	1	6					4	5	11		8	2
37		18	PORT VALE	1-1	Weller	8735				9	10		7						3	1	6					4	5	11		8	2
38		25	Southend United	0-0		7609				9			7			10			3	1	6					4	5	11		8	2
39		31	WATFORD	0-1		11424				9			7		11	10			3	1	6					4	5			8	2
40	Apr	1	CHESTERFIELD	1-0	Dowsett	7760	4						7		11	10		9	3	1							5		6	8	2
41		3	Watford	1-0	Coxon	8311	4		1	7			10		11			9	3								5		6	8	2
42		8	Bury	1-1	Coxon	12075	4		1	9			7	6	11			10	3								5			8	2
43		15	WALSALL	0-3		10535			1	9			7		11			8	3				6			4	5			10	2
44		22	Brentford	2-2	Bumstead, Weller	4415			1		10		7		11	9			3							4	5		6	8	2
45		25	Grimsby Town	1-0	Mills (og)	4678			1		10	5	7		11	9			3							4			6	8	2
46		29	HALIFAX TOWN	1-2	Weller	7394			1		10	5	7		11			9	3							4			6	8	2
						Apps	31	1	6	11	36	18	36	16	20	21	12	25	39	28	27	21	9	12	3	8	28	27	26	21	24
						Goals	2			1	10		6		5	7	2	9			2	1						3		8	

Two own goals

F.A. Cup

							Arnott JH	Bennett DM	Best D	Bimpson JL	Bolton R	Brown I	Bumstead RG	Burgess MR	Coxon WG	Dowsett GJ	Evans RP	Gibbs BR	Gledstone PH	Godwin TF	Jones BR	King JA	Lovie JTH	Lynne MGA	Massey RW	McGarry WH	Nelson JA	Smith R	Standley TL	Weller CW	Woollard AJ
R1	Nov	5	Exeter City	1-1	Bumstead	8000	4				10		7	6	11		8		3	1	9						5		2		
rep		9	EXETER CITY	3-1	Bolton, Bumstead, Evans	6382	4				10		7	6	11		8		3	1	9						5		2		
R2		26	YEOVIL TOWN	3-1	Bolton, Weller, Smith	15932	4				10	5	7	6				9	3	1								11	2	8	
R3	Jan	7	Burnley	0-1		24817	4				10		7			8			3	1	9	6					5	11			2

F.L. Cup

							Arnott JH	Bennett DM	Best D	Bimpson JL	Bolton R	Brown I	Bumstead RG	Burgess MR	Coxon WG	Dowsett GJ	Evans RP	Gibbs BR	Gledstone PH	Godwin TF	Jones BR	King JA	Lovie JTH	Lynne MGA	Massey RW	McGarry WH	Nelson JA	Smith R	Standley TL	Weller CW	Woollard AJ
R2	Oct	12	CREWE ALEXANDRA	1-1	Coxon	3208	7				10	2	8		11			9	3	1	6	4					5				
rep		19	Crewe Alexandra	0-2	(a.e.t.)	8129	7				10	2	8			9			3	1	6	4					5	11			

		P	W	D	L	F	A	W	D	L	F	A	Pts
1	Bury	46	18	3	2	62	17	12	5	6	46	28	68
2	Walsall	46	19	4	0	62	20	9	2	12	36	40	62
3	Queen's Park Rangers	46	18	4	1	58	23	7	6	10	35	37	60
4	Watford	46	12	7	4	52	27	8	5	10	33	45	52
5	Notts County	46	16	3	4	52	24	5	6	12	30	53	51
6	Grimsby Town	46	14	4	5	48	32	6	6	11	29	37	50
7	Port Vale	46	15	3	5	63	30	2	12	9	33	49	49
8	Barnsley	46	15	5	3	56	30	6	2	15	27	50	49
9	Halifax Town	46	14	7	2	42	22	2	10	11	29	56	49
10	Shrewsbury Town	46	13	7	3	54	26	2	9	12	29	49	46
11	Hull City	46	13	6	4	51	28	4	6	13	22	45	46
12	Torquay United	46	8	12	3	37	26	6	5	12	38	57	45
13	Newport County	46	12	7	4	51	30	5	4	14	30	60	45
14	Bristol City	46	15	4	4	50	19	2	6	15	20	49	44
15	Coventry City	46	14	6	3	54	25	2	6	15	26	58	44
16	Swindon Town	46	13	6	4	41	16	1	9	13	21	39	43
17	Brentford	46	10	9	4	41	28	3	8	12	15	42	43
18	Reading	46	13	5	5	48	29	1	7	15	24	54	40
19	BOURNEMOUTH	46	8	7	8	34	39	7	3	13	24	37	40
20	Southend United	46	10	8	5	38	26	4	3	16	22	50	39
21	Tranmere Rovers	46	11	5	7	53	50	4	3	16	26	65	38
22	Bradford City	46	8	8	7	37	36	3	6	14	28	51	36
23	Colchester United	46	8	5	10	40	44	3	6	14	28	57	33
24	Chesterfield	46	9	6	8	42	29	1	6	16	25	58	32

1961/62

3rd in Division Three

No	Month	Day	Opponent	Score	Scorers	Att	Archer J	Arnott JH	Bain AE	Bennett DM	Best D	Bolton R	Brown I	Bumstead RG	Coxon WG	Dowsett GJ	Farmer FBW	Gibbs BR	Gledstone PH	Godwin TF	Jones BR	McGarry WH	Nelson JA	Spelman RE	Standley TL	Thompson P	Weller CW	Woollard AJ
1	Aug	19	Lincoln City	2-0	Archer, Coxon	7597	10				1			7	11	9			3			4	5		6		8	2
2		23	SHREWSBURY TOWN	0-0		11040	10				1			7	11	9			3			4	5		6		8	2
3		26	TORQUAY UNITED	3-1	Dowsett 2, Archer	9924	10				1			7	11	9			3			4	5		6		8	2
4		30	Shrewsbury Town	2-2	Dowsett 2	9559	10				1			7	11	9			3			4	5		6		8	2
5	Sep	2	Swindon Town	1-1	Coxon	9825	10				1			7	11	9			3			4	5		6		8	2
6		6	HULL CITY	1-1	Archer	8370	10				1			7	11	9			3			4	5		6		8	2
7		9	HALIFAX TOWN	2-1	Weller, Archer	9672	10				1			7	11	9					3	4	5		6		8	2
8		16	Queen's Park Rangers	1-1	Coxon	13088	10				1			7	11	9					3	4	5		6		8	2
9		18	Northampton Town	3-0	Bumstead, Dowsett 2	14350	10				1			7	11	9					3	4	5		6		8	2
10		23	BARNSLEY	5-0	Dowsett 2, Archer 2, Weller	10441	10				1			7	11	9					3	4	5		6		8	2
11		27	NORTHAMPTON T	3-2	Weller, Coxon, Archer	14112	10				1			7	11	9					3	4	5		6		8	2
12		30	Portsmouth	1-1	Dowsett	22654	10				1			7	11	9					3	4	5		6		8	2
13	Oct	4	NOTTS COUNTY	2-1	Dowsett, Coxon	15610	10				1			7	11	9					3	4	5		6		8	2
14		7	Peterborough United	2-1	Weller, Bumstead	17258	10	4			1			7	11	9					3		5		6		8	2
15		12	Notts County	2-3	Dowsett 2	11859	10				1			7	11	9					3	4	5		6		8	2
16		14	PORT VALE	1-0	Bain	13675	10		9					7	11					1	3	4	5		6		8	2
17		21	Newport County	1-0	Bain	7392	10	2	9					7	11					1	3	4	5		6		8	
18		28	SOUTHEND UNITED	3-0	Bain, Archer 2	11572	10	2	9					7	11					1	3	4	5		6		8	
19	Nov	11	COVENTRY CITY	1-1	Coxon	9113	10	2	8					7	11	9				1	3	4	5		6			
20		18	Brentford	2-2	Standley, Bumstead	9681	10	4						7	11	9		8		1	3		5		6			2
21	Dec	2	Bristol City	1-2	Bumstead	14285	10				1		5	7	11	9		8			3	4			6			2
22		9	BRADFORD PARK AVE.	2-2	Bumstead, McGarry (p)	9401	10				1			7	11	9					3	4	5		6		8	2
23		16	LINCOLN CITY	0-0		8635		4			1	8		7		9		10	3		2		5		6		11	
24		22	Torquay United	1-2	Archer	3864	10				1	11		7		9			3		2	4	5		6		8	
25		26	Watford	0-0		9441	10		9		1			7	11	8					3	4	5		6			2
26		30	WATFORD	4-1	Bain, Dowsett 3	8383	10		9		1			7	11	8					3	4	5		6			2
27	Jan	6	Grimsby Town	0-3		5585	10		9		1			7	11	8					3	4	5		6			2
28		13	SWINDON TOWN	0-0		9113	10		9		1			7	11	8					3	4	5		6			2
29		20	Halifax Town	1-3	Dowsett	4453	10				1			7	11	8	2				3	4	5		6	9		
30		27	READING	1-0	Gibbs	10047	10	4		11	1			7			2	8			3		5		6	9		
31	Feb	3	QUEEN'S PARK RANGERS	3-1	Bumstead, Bennett, Dowsett	11645	10			11	1			7		9	2	8	3			4	5		6			
32		9	Barnsley	2-2	Thompson 2	10818	10			11	1			7		9	2		3			4	5		6	8		
33		17	PORTSMOUTH	2-0	Thompson, Archer	22940	10			11	1					9	2		3			4	5		6	8	7	
34		24	PETERBOROUGH UTD.	1-1	Weller	13219				7	1				11	9	2		3			4	5		6	10	8	
35	Mar	10	NEWPORT COUNTY	2-1	Archer, Spelman	10610	10			11	1						2				3	4	5	7	6	9	8	
36		17	Southend United	0-0		7250	10				1				11		2				3	4	5	7	6	9	8	
37		19	Port Vale	0-1		8993	10				1				11		2				3	4	5	7	6	9	8	
38		24	GRIMSBY TOWN	2-3	Dowsett, McGarry	12620	10				1				11	9	2				3	4	5	7	6	8		
39		30	Coventry City	1-0	Bennett	8654				11	1					9	2	10			3	4	5	7	6	8		
40	Apr	7	BRENTFORD	1-1	Dowsett	10736				11	1					9	2	10			3	4	5	7	6	8		
41		12	Hull City	1-2	Spelman	5289	8	4		11	1	10					2	9			3		5	7	6			
42		14	Reading	1-0	Dowsett	7268	10			11	1	6				9	2				3	4	5	7			8	
43		20	CRYSTAL PALACE	1-0	Dowsett	13499	10			11	1	6				9	2				3	4	5	7			8	
44		21	BRISTOL CITY	2-1	Weller, Etheridge (og)	12922	10	4			1	6			11	9	2				3		5	7			8	
45		23	Crystal Palace	0-0		11319	10	4			1	6			11	9	2				3		5	7			8	
46		28	Bradford Park Avenue	2-1	Archer, Spelman	8107	10				1	6			11	9	2				3		5	7	4		8	
						Apps	42	10	8	11	41	8	1	32	34	38	18	8	12	5	36	38	45	12	42	11	31	23
						Goals	13		4	2				6	6	21		1				2		3	1	3	6	

One own goal

F.A. Cup

Rd	Month	Day	Opponent	Score	Scorers	Att	Archer J	Arnott JH	Bain AE	Bennett DM	Best D	Bolton R	Brown I	Bumstead RG	Coxon WG	Dowsett GJ	Farmer FBW	Gibbs BR	Gledstone PH	Godwin TF	Jones BR	McGarry WH	Nelson JA	Spelman RE	Standley TL	Thompson P	Weller CW	Woollard AJ
R1	Nov	4	MARGATE	0-3		12405	10	2	9					7	11					1	3	4	5		6		8	

F.L. Cup

Rd	Month	Day	Opponent	Score	Scorers	Att	Archer J	Arnott JH	Bain AE	Bennett DM	Best D	Bolton R	Brown I	Bumstead RG	Coxon WG	Dowsett GJ	Farmer FBW	Gibbs BR	Gledstone PH	Godwin TF	Jones BR	McGarry WH	Nelson JA	Spelman RE	Standley TL	Thompson P	Weller CW	Woollard AJ
R1	Sep	13	TORQUAY UNITED	2-2	Dowsett, Weller	5332	10	4			1			7	11	9					3		5		6		8	2
rep		25	Torquay United	1-0	Bumstead	4686		4	9		1			7	11			10			3		5		6		8	2
R2	Oct	9	Shrewsbury Town	3-1	Gibbs 2, Bain	8486		4	8		1		5		11	9		10			3				6			2
R3	Nov	15	CARDIFF CITY	3-0	Bumstead, Coxon, Dowsett	12857	10	4						7	11	9		8		1	3		5		6			2
R4	Dec	13	York City	0-1		6709	10				1	11		7		9					3		5		6		8	2

Played at 7 in R2: P Hall. Played at 4 in R4: RL (Ray) Massey

		P	W	D	L	F	A	W	D	L	F	A	Pts
1	Portsmouth	46	15	6	2	48	23	12	5	6	39	24	65
2	Grimsby Town	46	18	3	2	49	18	10	3	10	31	38	62
3	BOURNEMOUTH	46	14	8	1	42	18	7	9	7	27	27	59
4	Queen's Park Rangers	46	15	3	5	65	31	9	8	6	46	42	59
5	Peterborough United	46	16	0	7	60	38	10	6	7	47	44	58
6	Bristol City	46	15	3	5	56	27	8	5	10	38	45	54
7	Reading	46	14	5	4	46	24	8	4	11	31	42	53
8	Northampton Town	46	12	6	5	52	24	8	5	10	33	33	51
9	Swindon Town	46	11	8	4	48	26	6	7	10	30	45	49
10	Hull City	46	15	2	6	43	20	5	6	12	24	34	48
11	Bradford Park Avenue	46	13	5	5	47	27	7	2	14	33	51	47
12	Port Vale	46	12	4	7	41	23	5	7	11	24	35	45
13	Notts County	46	14	5	4	44	23	3	4	16	23	51	43
14	Coventry City	46	11	6	6	38	26	5	5	13	26	45	43
15	Crystal Palace	46	8	8	7	50	41	6	6	11	33	39	42
16	Southend United	46	10	7	6	31	26	3	9	11	26	43	42
17	Watford	46	10	9	4	37	26	4	4	15	26	48	41
18	Halifax Town	46	9	5	9	34	35	6	5	12	28	49	40
19	Shrewsbury Town	46	8	7	8	46	37	5	5	13	27	47	38
20	Barnsley	46	9	6	8	45	41	4	6	13	26	54	38
21	Torquay United	46	9	4	10	48	44	6	2	15	28	56	36
22	Lincoln City	46	4	10	9	31	43	5	7	11	26	44	35
23	Brentford	46	11	3	9	34	29	2	5	16	19	64	34
24	Newport County	46	6	5	12	29	38	1	3	19	17	64	22

1962/63

5th in Division Three

					Att	Archer J	Best D	Bolton R	Brown I	Bumstead RG	Coughlin DM	Coxon WG	Crickmore CE	Dowsett GJ	Farmer FBW	Gater R	Gibbs BR	Gledstone PH	Jones BR	McGarry WH	Nelson JA	Reeves DB	Singer DJ	Spelman RE	Standley TL	Thompson P	Weller CW	Woods CMP
1	Aug 18	PETERBOROUGH UTD.	3-3	Thompson 3	13146	10	1	4					11		2		8		3		5			7	6	9		
2	22	BRADFORD PARK AVE.	2-2	Thompson, Gibbs	12132	10	1	4					11		2		8		3		5			7	6	9		
3	25	Notts County	0-2		6749	10	1	6				11			2		8		3	4	5			7		9		
4	29	Bradford Park Avenue	1-1	Gibbs	9808		1	6		8		11			2		10		3	4	5			7		9		
5	Sep 1	COLCHESTER UNITED	1-1	Spelman	8887		1	6		8		11			2		10		3	4	5			7		9		
6	5	BRISTOL CITY	1-1	Gibbs	11502		1	6		8		11			2		10		3	4	5			7		9		
7	8	Southend United	1-0	Thompson	13614	8	1			11					2		10		3	4	5			7	6	9		
8	11	Bristol City	0-1		13283	8	1			7			11		2		10		3	4	5				6	9		
9	15	MILLWALL	1-1	Thompson	10108	8	1			11					2	4	10		3		5			7	6	9		
10	19	WATFORD	1-0	Crickmore	11260	8	1			7			11		2				3	4	5		10		6	9		
11	22	Shrewsbury Town	1-2	Crickmore	8593	8	1			7			11		2				3	4	5		10		6	9		
12	25	Watford	1-0	Archer	16016	8	1			7			11		2				3	4	5		10		6	9		
13	29	PORT VALE	2-0	Singer, Archer	9715	8	1			7			11		2				3	4	5		10		6	9		
14	Oct 3	Reading	1-2	Walker (og)	7452	8	1			7			11		2	4			3		5		10		6	9		
15	6	Northampton Town	2-2	Dowsett, Singer	12199	8	1	4		7			11	9	2				3		5		10		6			
16	13	QUEEN'S PARK RANGERS	2-1	Singer 2	11410	8	1	4		7			11	9	2				3		5		10		6			
17	20	Hull City	1-1	Dowsett	8702	8	1	4		7			11	9	2				3		5		10		6			
18	27	CRYSTAL PALACE	3-0	Bumstead, Singer 2	10455	8	1	4		7		11			2				3		5		10		6	9		
19	Nov 10	HALIFAX TOWN	1-1	Singer	8804	8	1	4		7		11			2				3		5		10		6	9		
20	17	Bristol Rovers	2-1	Woods, Bumstead	7909		1	6		7		11			2	5			3	4		9	10					8
21	24	READING	1-0	Reeves	11322		1	6		7		11			2	5			3	4		9	10					8
22	30	Carlisle United	3-0	Woods, Singer, Reeves	6903		1	6		7		11			2	5			3	4		9	10					8
23	Dec 8	SWINDON TOWN	0-0		9295		1	6		7		11			2	5			3	4		9	10					8
24	15	Peterborough United	0-3		11706		1	6		7		11			2	5		3		4		9	10					8
25	22	NOTTS COUNTY	3-1	Bolton, Woods, Coxon	9629		1	6		7		11			2	5		3		4		9	10					8
26	Feb 23	NORTHAMPTON T	3-0	Reeves, Bolton, Coxon	10230		1	6		7		11			2	5			3	4		9	10					8
27	Mar 2	Queen's Park Rangers	0-1		8393		1	6		7		11			2	5			3	4		9	10					8
28	9	HULL CITY	3-0	Woods, Reeves, Coxon	6613		1	6				11			2	5			3	4		9	10	7				8
29	11	Millwall	0-1		9008	8	1	6				11			2					4	5	9	10	7	3			
30	16	Crystal Palace	0-1		16191		1	6	3	7		11			2	5				4		9	10					8
31	20	BARNSLEY	1-1	Bolton	8038		1	6				11			2	5				4		9	10		3	8		7
32	23	WREXHAM	3-1	Singer 3	8576		1	6					11		2	5		3		4		9	10			8		7
33	30	Halifax Town	1-3	Woods	1803		1	6					11		2	5		3		4		9	10			8		7
34	Apr 2	Barnsley	2-2	Thompson 2	7117		1	6		7			11		2	5		3					10		4	9		8
35	6	BRISTOL ROVERS	1-1	Woods	8819		1	6		7	8		11		2	5		3							4	9		10
36	12	COVENTRY CITY	1-1	Bolton (p)	15001		1	6		11					2	5			3	4			10			9	7	8
37	13	Brighton & Hove Albion	1-0	Weller	10240		1	6					11		2	5			3				10		4	9	7	8
38	16	Coventry City	2-1	Crickmore 2	30289		1	6					11		2	5			3	4			10			9	7	8
39	20	CARLISLE UNITED	5-1	Woods 2, Thompson 2, Bolton(p)	8602		1	6					11		2	5			3	4			10			9	7	8
40	27	Swindon Town	1-2	Thompson	16691		1	6					11		2	5			3	4			10			9	7	8
41	May 4	SHREWSBURY TOWN	0-0		8573		1	6			8		11		2	5			3	4				7		9		10
42	8	BRIGHTON & HOVE ALB	1-0	Coxon	5797		1	6			8	11			2	5			3	4				7		9		10
43	11	Colchester United	1-3	Singer	4366	8	1	6			9	11			2	5			3	4			10	7				
44	13	Port Vale	3-0	Archer 2, Coxon	7362	8	1	6		7	9	11				5		2	3				10		4			
45	15	Wrexham	0-1		6174	8	1	6		7		11				5		2	3	4			10					9
46	18	SOUTHEND UNITED	0-0		6624	8	1	6		7	9	11				5		2	3				10		4			
					Apps	21	46	38	1	31	6	23	20	3	43	28	9	9	37	32	20	14	34	13	22	28	5	23
					Goals	4		5		2		5	4	2			3					4	12	1		11	1	8

One own goal

F.A. Cup

					Att	Archer J	Best D	Bolton R	Brown I	Bumstead RG	Coughlin DM	Coxon WG	Crickmore CE	Dowsett GJ	Farmer FBW	Gater R	Gibbs BR	Gledstone PH	Jones BR	McGarry WH	Nelson JA	Reeves DB	Singer DJ	Spelman RE	Standley TL	Thompson P	Weller CW	Woods CMP
R1	Nov 3	Coventry City	0-1		14449	8	1	4		7			11	9	2				3	5			10		6			

F.L. Cup

					Att	Archer J	Best D	Bolton R	Brown I	Bumstead RG	Coughlin DM	Coxon WG	Crickmore CE	Dowsett GJ	Farmer FBW	Gater R	Gibbs BR	Gledstone PH	Jones BR	McGarry WH	Nelson JA	Reeves DB	Singer DJ	Spelman RE	Standley TL	Thompson P	Weller CW	Woods CMP
R2	Sep 26	Fulham	0-4		7022	8	1			11				9	2			4	3		5			7	6		10	

		P	W	D	L	F	A	W	D	L	F	A	Pts
1	Northampton Town	46	16	6	1	64	19	10	4	9	45	41	62
2	Swindon Town	46	18	2	3	60	22	4	12	7	27	34	58
3	Port Vale	46	16	4	3	47	25	7	4	12	25	33	54
4	Coventry City	46	14	6	3	54	28	4	11	8	29	41	53
5	BOURNEMOUTH	46	11	12	0	39	16	7	4	12	24	30	52
6	Peterborough United	46	11	5	7	48	33	9	6	8	45	42	51
7	Notts County	46	15	3	5	46	29	4	10	9	27	45	51
8	Southend United	46	11	7	5	38	24	8	5	10	37	53	50
9	Wrexham	46	14	6	3	54	27	6	3	14	30	56	49
10	Hull City	46	12	6	5	40	22	7	4	12	34	47	48
11	Crystal Palace	46	10	7	6	38	22	7	6	10	30	36	47
12	Colchester United	46	11	6	6	41	35	7	5	11	32	58	47
13	Queen's Park Rangers	46	9	6	8	44	36	8	5	10	41	40	45
14	Bristol City	46	10	9	4	54	38	6	4	13	46	54	45
15	Shrewsbury Town	46	13	4	6	57	41	3	8	12	26	40	44
16	Millwall	46	11	6	6	50	32	4	7	12	32	55	43
17	Watford	46	12	3	8	55	40	5	5	13	27	45	42
18	Barnsley	46	12	6	5	39	28	3	5	15	24	46	41
19	Bristol Rovers	46	11	8	4	45	29	4	3	16	25	59	41
20	Reading	46	13	4	6	51	30	3	4	16	23	48	40
21	Bradford Park Avenue	46	10	9	4	43	36	4	3	16	36	61	40
22	Brighton & Hove Albion	46	7	6	10	28	38	5	6	12	30	46	36
23	Carlisle United	46	12	4	7	41	37	1	5	17	20	52	35
24	Halifax Town	46	8	3	12	41	51	1	9	13	23	55	30

1963/64

4th in Division Three

	Date		Opponent	Score	Scorers	Att	Archer J	Best D	Bolton R	Brown KJ	Bumstead RG	Coughlin DM	Coxon WG	Crickmore CE	Farmer FBW	Gater R	Gledstone PH	Groves J	Jones BR	Keith RM	MacDonald R	Nelson JA	O'Neill A	Reeves DB	Singer DJ	Spelman RE	Standley TL	Weller CW	Woods CMP
1	Aug	24	Southend United	1-1	Singer	10257		1	6					11	2	5			3					9	10	7	4		8
2		28	OLDHAM ATHLETIC	1-0	Woods	11360		1	6					11	2	4			3			5		9	10	7			8
3		31	WATFORD	2-0	Singer, Bolton	10481		1	6					11	2	5			3					9	10	7	4		8
4	Sep	7	Colchester United	2-1	Reeves, Singer	4845		1	6		7			11	2	5			3					9	10		4		8
5		11	Oldham Athletic	4-2	Woods 2, Bumstead, Bolton	16471		1	6		7			11	2	5			3					9	10		4		8
6		14	MILLWALL	4-0	Bumstead, Reeves, Singer, Woods	10696		1	6		7			11	2	5			3					9	10		4		8
7		18	PETERBOROUGH UTD.	3-0	Bumstead, Singer, Woods	14847		1	6		7			11	2	5			3					9	10		4		8
8		21	Barnsley	1-2	Crickmore	5989		1	6		7			11	2	5			3					9	10		4		8
9		28	HULL CITY	1-0	Reeves	11175		1	6		7			11	2	5			3					9	10		4		8
10		30	Peterborough United	1-2	Woods	15138		1	6		7			11	2	5	3							9			4	10	8
11	Oct	5	MANSFIELD TOWN	0-0		10728		1	6		7			11	2	5	3							9			4	10	8
12		7	Queen's Park Rangers	0-1		10045		1	6		7			11	2	5			3					9	10		4		8
13		12	Luton Town	0-1		6361		1	6		7			11	2	5	3							9	10		4		8
14		16	QUEEN'S PARK RANGERS	4-2	Coughlin 2, Bolton 2 (1p)	8915	10	1	6		7	9		11	2	5	3										4		8
15		19	BRISTOL CITY	0-1		11272		1	6		7	9		11	2	5					3				10		4		8
16		23	Wrexham	4-3	Coughlin 2, Crickmore, Singer	8370		1	6		7	9		11	2	5		4							10		3		8
17		26	Port Vale	0-0		12402	8	1	6		7	9		11	2	5		4							10		3		
18		30	WREXHAM	2-0	Singer, Crickmore	6755	8	1	6		7	9		11	2	5		4							10		3		
19	Nov	2	NOTTS COUNTY	1-1	Coughlin	9762	8	1	6		7	9	3	11	2	5		4							10				
20		9	Crewe Alexandra	0-1		5697	10	1			7	9	3	11	2	5		4				6						8	
21		23	Walsall	2-0	Coughlin, Archer	6398	10	1	6		7	9	3	11		5		4				2		8					
22		30	READING	1-2	Reeves	8084	10	1	6	2	7	9	3	11		5		4						8					
23	Dec	14	SOUTHEND UNITED	1-0	Coughlin	6034		1	6		7	9		11	2	5		4						8	10		3		
24		21	Watford	0-3		7459		1	6		7	9		11	2	5		4						8	10		3		
25		28	BRENTFORD	2-0	Coughlin, Singer	7507		1	6		7	9		11	2	5		4							10		3		8
26	Jan	4	CRYSTAL PALACE	4-3	Coughlin, Woods 2, Singer	8491		1	6		7	9		11	2	5		4							10		3		8
27		11	COLCHESTER UNITED	2-2	Crickmore, Coughlin	7885		1	6		7	9		11	2	5	3	4							10				8
28		18	Millwall	0-3		8870		1	6		7	9		11	2	5		4							10		3		8
29		25	Shrewsbury Town	2-5	Bumstead, Coughlin	4663		1	6		7	9		11	2	5		4							10		3		8
30	Feb	1	BARNSLEY	4-1	Coughlin 3, Bumstead	8242		1	6		7	9	3	11	2	5							10				4		8
31		8	Hull City	4-3	Woods 2, Crickmore, Coughlin	11511		1	6		7	9		11	2	5				3			10				4		8
32		15	Mansfield Town	1-1	Coughlin	7959		1	6	2	7	9		11		5				3			10				4		8
33		22	LUTON TOWN	3-1	Coughlin, O'Neill 2	9298		1	6		7	9		11	2	5		4		3			10						8
34		29	Coventry City	2-2	Crickmore, Woods	24955		1	6		7	9		11	2	5		4		3			10						8
35	Mar	7	PORT VALE	3-0	Coughlin 3	7584		1	6		7	9		11	2	5		4		3			10						8
36		14	Notts County	3-1	Coughlin, Loxley (og), Bolton	2640		1	6		7	9		11	2	5		4		3			10						8
37		21	COVENTRY CITY	2-1	Bumstead 2	16085		1	6		7	9	11		2	5		4		3			10						8
38		27	BRISTOL ROVERS	1-0	Coughlin	16998		1	6	3	7	9		11	2	5							10				4		8
39		28	Crystal Palace	1-2	Coughlin	22175		1	6	3	7	9		11	2	5							10				4		8
40		31	Bristol Rovers	3-2	Singer, Coughlin 2	12939		1	6	3	7	9		11	2	5							8		10		4		
41	Apr	4	WALSALL	1-1	Coughlin	9854		1	6	3	7	9		11	2	5							8		10		4		
42		11	Reading	0-2		9696		1	6		7	9		11	2	5				3			10				4		8
43		13	Brentford	0-2		10029	10	1			7	9		11	2	5		4		3			8				6		
44		18	SHREWSBURY TOWN	2-0	Archer 2	7433	10	1	6		7	9		11	2	5				3			8				4		
45		22	CREWE ALEXANDRA	3-0	Bodell (og), Archer 2	6604	10	1	6		7	9		11	2	5		4		3									8
46		25	Bristol City	1-3	Coughlin	7787	10	1	6		7	9		11	2	5		4		3									8
						Apps	11	46	44	6	43	33	6	45	43	46	5	22	10	12	1	3	15	17	25	3	33	3	34
						Goals	5		5		7	27		6									2	4	10				11

Two own goals

F.A. Cup

	Date		Opponent	Score	Scorers	Att	Archer J	Best D	Bolton R	Brown KJ	Bumstead RG	Coughlin DM	Coxon WG	Crickmore CE	Farmer FBW	Gater R	Gledstone PH	Groves J	Jones BR	Keith RM	MacDonald R	Nelson JA	O'Neill A	Reeves DB	Singer DJ	Spelman RE	Standley TL	Weller CW	Woods CMP
R1	Nov	16	BRISTOL ROVERS	1-3	Crickmore	12354	10	1	6		7	9	3	11	2	5		4											8

F.L. Cup

	Date		Opponent	Score	Scorers	Att	Archer J	Best D	Bolton R	Brown KJ	Bumstead RG	Coughlin DM	Coxon WG	Crickmore CE	Farmer FBW	Gater R	Gledstone PH	Groves J	Jones BR	Keith RM	MacDonald R	Nelson JA	O'Neill A	Reeves DB	Singer DJ	Spelman RE	Standley TL	Weller CW	Woods CMP
R2	Sep	25	Brentford	0-0		10830		1	6		7			11	2	5	3							9	10		4		8
rep	Nov	4	BRENTFORD	2-0	Weller, Bumstead	8047	10	1	6		7	9	3	11	2	5		4										8	
R3		6	NEWCASTLE UNITED	2-1	Bolton, Bumstead	11735	10	1	6		7	9	3	11	2	5		4										8	
R4		27	Stoke City	1-2	Coughlin	9766	10	1	6	2	7	9	3	11		5		4						8					

		P	*W*	*D*	*L*	*F*	*A*	*W*	*D*	*L*	*F*	*A*	*Pts*
1	Coventry City	46	14	7	2	62	32	8	9	6	36	29	60
2	Crystal Palace	46	17	4	2	38	14	6	10	7	35	37	60
3	Watford	46	16	6	1	57	28	7	6	10	22	31	58
4	BOURNEMOUTH	46	17	4	2	47	15	7	4	12	32	43	56
5	Bristol City	46	13	7	3	52	24	7	8	8	32	40	55
6	Reading	46	15	5	3	49	26	6	5	12	30	36	52
7	Mansfield Town	46	15	8	0	51	20	5	3	15	25	42	51
8	Hull City	46	11	9	3	45	27	5	8	10	28	41	49
9	Oldham Athletic	46	13	3	7	44	35	7	5	11	29	35	48
10	Peterborough United	46	13	6	4	52	27	5	5	13	23	43	47
11	Shrewsbury Town	46	13	6	4	43	19	5	5	13	30	61	47
12	Bristol Rovers	46	9	6	8	52	34	10	2	11	39	45	46
13	Port Vale	46	13	6	4	35	13	3	8	12	18	36	46
14	Southend United	46	9	10	4	42	26	6	5	12	35	52	45
15	Queen's Park Rangers	46	13	4	6	47	34	5	5	13	29	44	45
16	Brentford	46	11	4	8	54	36	4	10	9	33	44	44
17	Colchester United	46	10	8	5	45	26	2	11	10	25	42	43
18	Luton Town	46	12	2	9	42	41	4	8	11	22	39	42
19	Walsall	46	7	9	7	34	35	6	5	12	25	41	40
20	Barnsley	46	9	9	5	34	29	3	6	14	34	65	39
21	Millwall	46	9	4	10	33	29	5	6	12	20	38	38
22	Crewe Alexandra	46	10	5	8	29	26	1	7	15	21	51	34
23	Wrexham	46	9	4	10	50	42	4	2	17	25	65	32
24	Notts County	46	7	8	8	29	26	2	1	20	16	66	27

1964/65

11th in Division Three

No.	Month	Day	Opponent	Score	Scorers	Att	Archer J	Best D	Bolton R	Brown KJ	Bumstead RG	Compton JF	Coughlin DM	Coxon WG	Crickmore CE	Farmer FBW	Gater R	Groves J	Hodgson K	Keith RM	Naylor TV	Nelson JA	Newton GW	O'Neill A	Reeves DB	Standley TL	Weller CW	Woods CMP
1	Aug	22	READING	3-2	Compton, Crickmore, Hodgson	10314		1	6			3			11				9	2		5		10		4	7	8
2		26	EXETER CITY	2-2	O'Neill, Woods	12122		1	6			3			11				9	2		5		10		4	7	8
3		29	Peterborough United	3-4	O'Neill, Woods, Hodgson	11813		1	6			3			11				9	2		5		10		4	7	8
4	Sep	5	GRIMSBY TOWN	1-2	Hodgson	8872		1	6			3			11	2			9			5		10		4	7	8
5		9	OLDHAM ATHLETIC	0-0		9535		1	6			3			11	2		4	7			5		10	9			8
6		12	Mansfield Town	0-0		7621	10	1	6			3		11	7	2		4				5			9			8
7		15	Oldham Athletic	1-1	Bolton	13366	10	1	6			3		11	7	2		4				5			9			8
8		19	LUTON TOWN	4-0	Coxon, McBain (og), Woods 2	8763	10	1	6			3		11	7	2		4				5			9			8
9		26	Carlisle United	4-3	Hodgson, Woods 2, Coxon	8708	10	1	6		7	3		11		2		4	9			5						8
10		30	BRISTOL ROVERS	1-1	Hodgson	11272	10	1	6		7	3		11		2		4	9			5						8
11	Oct	3	PORT VALE	3-0	Hodgson 2, Archer	8609	8	1	6		7	3		11		2		4	9			5		10				
12		6	Bristol Rovers	2-4	Hodgson, Bumstead	14003	8	1	6		7	3		11		2		4	9			5		10				
13		10	Barnsley	2-2	Archer, Hodgson	4804	8	1	6		7	3		11		2		4	9			5		10				
14		14	COLCHESTER UNITED	3-1	Archer 2, Coxon	7176	8	1	6		7	3		11		2		4	9			5		10				
15		17	SCUNTHORPE UNITED	2-1	Bumstead, O'Neill	8406	8	1	6		7	3		11		2			9			5		10		4		
16		19	Colchester United	3-4	Archer, Woods, Hodgson	3454	10	1			7	3		11		2			9		6	5				4		8
17		24	Walsall	1-0	O'Neill	6631	10	1	6		7	3			11	2	5	4	9					8				
18		28	SHREWSBURY TOWN	2-1	Archer, Hodgson	7998	8	1	6		7	3			11	2	5	4	9					10				
19		31	WATFORD	0-0		9443	10	1	6		7	3			11	2	5	4	9					8				
20	Nov	7	Workington	0-2		6711	10	1	6		7	3			11	2	5	4	9									8
21		21	Gillingham	1-1	Archer	9652	10	1	4		7	3		11		2	5		9		6							8
22		28	BRISTOL CITY	1-2	Archer	9016	8	1	4		7	3		11		2	5		9		6			10				
23	Dec	12	Reading	0-1		5924	10	1	6				9		11	2	5		7	3			8			4		
24		19	PETERBOROUGH UTD.	0-1		5679		1	6		7		9		11	2	5			3			10	8		4		
25		26	SOUTHEND UNITED	2-1	Hodgson, Coxon	6248	10	1	6		7			11		2	5	4	9	3							8	
26		28	Southend United	1-2	Coxon	6219	10	1	6		7	3		11		2	5	4	9								8	
27	Jan	2	Grimsby Town	2-2	Bumstead, Bolton	7228	10	1	6		7			11		2	5	4	9	3			8					
28		9	HULL CITY	2-3	Hodgson, Bolton	7515	10	1	6		7	2		11			5	4	9	3			8					
29		16	MANSFIELD TOWN	2-0	O'Neill, Archer	5248	8	1	6		7	2		11			5	4	9	3				10				
30		29	Queen's Park Rangers	1-1	Weller	3520	8	1	6			2		11			5	4	9	3				10			7	
31	Feb	6	CARLISLE UNITED	0-4		6613	8	1	6			2		11			5	4	9	3				10			7	
32		13	Port Vale	2-1	Coughlin, Crickmore	3071	10	1	6	2			9		11		5	4	7	3							8	
33		17	Luton Town	1-0	Crickmore	4554	10	1	6	2			9		11		5	4	7	3							8	
34		20	BARNSLEY	1-0	Archer	5377	10	1	6	2			9		11		5	4	7	3							8	
35		26	Scunthorpe United	1-3	Coughlin	5110	10	1	6	2			9		11		5	4	7	3							8	
36	Mar	6	QUEEN'S PARK RANGERS	2-0	Weller, Coughlin	5937	10	1	6	2			9		11		5	4	7	3							8	
37		13	Watford	0-2		6814	10	1		2			9		11		5	4	7	3						6	8	
38		20	WORKINGTON	4-0	Chapman(og), Hodgson 2, Coughlin	4663	10	1	6	2	7		9		11		5	4	8	3								
39		27	Hull City	1-2	Crickmore	18530	10	1	6	2	7		9		11		5	4	8	3								
40	Apr	3	GILLINGHAM	1-2	Bumstead	7508	10	1	6	2	7		9		11		5	4	8	3								
41		9	Bristol City	0-0		12861	10	1			7		9	3	11		5	4	8	2	6							
42		16	Brentford	1-2	Hawley (og)	10519	10	1			7		9	3	11		5	4	8	2	6							
43		17	WALSALL	4-0	Archer, Hodgson, Coughlin, Bumstead	5700	10	1	4		7		9	3	11	2	5		8		6							
44		19	BRENTFORD	0-1		6196	10	1	4		7		9	3	11	2	5		8		6							
45		24	Shrewsbury Town	2-1	Bumstead, Coughlin	3053	10	1	4		7		9	3	11	2	5		8		6							
46		28	Exeter City	3-1	Hodgson 2, Bumstead	4956	10	1	6		7		9	3	11	2	5		8							4		
						Apps	40	46	42	9	29	27	17	26	29	28	30	32	42	22	8	16	4	18	4	10	14	13
						Goals	11		3		7	1	6	5	4				18					5			2	7

Three own goals

F.A. Cup

Rd	Month	Day	Opponent	Score	Scorers	Att	Archer J	Best D	Bolton R	Brown KJ	Bumstead RG	Compton JF	Coughlin DM	Coxon WG	Crickmore CE	Farmer FBW	Gater R	Groves J	Hodgson K	Keith RM	Naylor TV	Nelson JA	Newton GW	O'Neill A	Reeves DB	Standley TL	Weller CW	Woods CMP
R1	Nov	14	GRAVESEND & N'FLEET	7-0	Hodgson 3, Bolton, Bumstead, Coxon, Groves	8141	10	1	6		7	3		11		2	5	4	9									8
R2	Dec	5	BRISTOL CITY	0-3		10635	8	1	6		7				11	2	5		9	3				10		4		

F.L. Cup

Rd	Month	Day	Opponent	Score	Scorers	Att	Archer J	Best D	Bolton R	Brown KJ	Bumstead RG	Compton JF	Coughlin DM	Coxon WG	Crickmore CE	Farmer FBW	Gater R	Groves J	Hodgson K	Keith RM	Naylor TV	Nelson JA	Newton GW	O'Neill A	Reeves DB	Standley TL	Weller CW	Woods CMP
R2	Sep	23	NORTHAMPTON T	0-2		8807	10	1	6		7	3		11		2		4				5			9			8

		P	W	D	L	F	A	W	D	L	F	A	Pts
1	Carlisle United	46	14	5	4	46	24	11	5	7	30	29	60
2	Bristol City	46	14	6	3	53	18	10	5	8	39	37	59
3	Mansfield Town	46	17	4	2	61	23	7	7	9	34	38	59
4	Hull City	46	14	6	3	51	25	9	6	8	40	32	58
5	Brentford	46	18	4	1	55	18	6	5	12	28	37	57
6	Bristol Rovers	46	14	7	2	52	21	6	8	9	30	37	55
7	Gillingham	46	16	5	2	45	13	7	4	12	25	37	55
8	Peterborough United	46	16	3	4	61	33	6	4	13	24	41	51
9	Watford	46	13	8	2	45	21	4	8	11	26	43	50
10	Grimsby Town	46	11	10	2	37	21	5	7	11	31	46	49
11	BOURNEMOUTH	46	12	4	7	40	24	6	7	10	32	39	47
12	Southend United	46	14	4	5	48	24	5	4	14	30	47	46
13	Reading	46	12	8	3	45	26	4	6	13	25	44	46
14	Queen's Park Rangers	46	15	5	3	48	23	2	7	14	24	57	46
15	Workington	46	11	7	5	30	22	6	5	12	28	47	46
16	Shrewsbury Town	46	10	6	7	42	38	5	6	12	34	46	42
17	Exeter City	46	8	7	8	33	27	4	10	9	18	25	41
18	Scunthorpe United	46	9	8	6	42	27	5	4	14	23	45	40
19	Walsall	46	9	4	10	34	36	6	3	14	21	44	37
20	Oldham Athletic	46	10	3	10	40	39	3	7	13	21	44	36
21	Luton Town	46	6	8	9	32	36	5	3	15	19	58	33
22	Port Vale	46	7	6	10	27	33	2	8	13	14	43	32
23	Colchester United	46	7	6	10	30	34	3	4	16	20	55	30
24	Barnsley	46	8	5	10	33	31	1	6	16	21	59	29

1965/66

18th in Division Three

No	Date	Opponent	Score	Scorers	Att	Archer J	Ashworth JM	Best D	Bolton R	Bumstead RG	Coughlin DM	Coxon WG	Crickmore CE	Ferns P	Gater R	George RS	Hodgson K	Hold JD	Jones R	Keith RM	McKinney WE	Naylor TV	Newton GW	O'Neill A	Priscott AJ	Saunders RC	Taylor RV	Walker R	Weller CW
1	Aug 21	WALSALL	0-1		8936	10		1	6	7	9		11	4	5		8			3	2								
2	24	SWANSEA TOWN	2-1	Bolton, Archer	6364	10		1	6	7	9		11	4	5		8			3	2								
3	28	Workington	2-2	Coughlin, Hodgson	3516	10		1	6	7	9		11	4	5		8			3	2								
4	Sep 4	Gillingham	0-2		7996	10		1	6	7	9	12	11	4	5					3	2			8					
5	11	SOUTHEND UNITED	0-0		5586	10		1	6	7	9		11	4	5					3	2			8					
6	14	OXFORD UNITED	1-1	Ashworth	6005	8	10	1	6	7		11		4	5		9			3	2								
7	18	Swindon Town	0-0		14119	8	10	1	6	7		3	11	4	5		9				2		12						
8	25	SHREWSBURY TOWN	2-0	Archer, Bumstead	4268	8	10	1	6	7		3	11	4	5		9				2								
9	Oct 2	Grimsby Town	0-2		5780	8	10	1	6	7	12	3	11	4	5		9				2								
10	9	PETERBOROUGH UTD.	2-3	Hodgson, Archer	6330	8	10	1	6	7		3		4	5	11	9				2								
11	16	Exeter City	0-1		5383	8	10	1		7		11		4	5		9			3	2	6							
12	23	READING	3-2	Coughlin, Hodgson, Crickmore	5421	10	6	1		7	9	3	11	4	5		8				2								
13	30	Hull City	0-3		12440	10	6	1		7	9	3	11	4	5		8				2					12			
14	Nov 3	Oxford United	1-2	O'Neill	9902					7	9	3	11	4	5		8		1	2		6		10					
15	6	MANSFIELD TOWN	2-2	Coxon (p), Coughlin	4807			1		7	9	3	11	4	5		8			2		6		10					
16	20	BRIGHTON & HOVE ALB	0-1		5132	10		1		7	9		11	4	5		8			3	2	6							
17	23	Swansea Town	0-5		4217	8		1		7	9			4	5	11	10				2	6						3	
18	27	Scunthorpe United	0-3		2766	8	4	1		11	9			2	5	12	10					6				7		3	
19	Dec 11	Oldham Athletic	2-2	Archer, Bumstead	4622	8		1		7	9	3	11	4	5		10				2	6							
20	17	EXETER CITY	0-1		4257	8		1		7	9	3	11	4	5		10				2	6							
21	27	Bristol Rovers	0-0		10031	8	6	1		7	9	3	11	2	5		10						4						
22	28	BRISTOL ROVERS	1-0	Hodgson	5826	10	6	1		7	9	3	11	2	5		8						4						
23	Jan 1	Peterborough United	0-1		7125	10	6	1		7	9	3	11	2	5		8						4						
24	8	QUEEN'S PARK RANGERS	1-1	Crickmore	7616	10	6	1		7	9	3	11	2	5		8					12	4						
25	29	Walsall	1-2	Priscott	10047		6	1		7	9			2	5		8			3			4		11				10
26	Feb 5	WORKINGTON	1-1	Weller	4754	10	6	1		7	9			2	5		8			3			4		11				12
27	12	York City	2-0	Weller, Coughlin	3693		6	1		7	9			2	5		8			3			4		11				10
28	19	GILLINGHAM	1-1	Bumstead	6565		6	1		7			10	4	2		9					3	5		11				8
29	26	Southend United	2-1	Coughlin, Crickmore	6335		6	1		7	9		10	4	2							3	5		11				8
30	Mar 5	YORK CITY	1-0	Newton (p)	5709		6	1		7	9		10	4	2							3	5		11				8
31	7	Reading	0-1		8583		6	1		7	9			4	2		10					3	5		11				8
32	12	SWINDON TOWN	1-0	Bumstead	7395		6	1		7	10	3	9	4	2								5		11				8
33	19	Shrewsbury Town	2-0	Weller 2	5333		6	1		7	9	3	10	4	2								5		11				8
34	26	GRIMSBY TOWN	1-0	Newton (p)	6703		6	1		7	9	3	10	4	2		12						5		11				8
35	Apr 8	MILLWALL	0-0		12540		6	1		7		3	10	4	2		9						5		11				8
36	9	WATFORD	2-0	Hodgson, Newton (p)	6987		6	1		7		3	10	4	2		9						5		11				8
37	12	Millwall	0-1		17578		6	1		7		3	10	4	2		9						5		11				8
38	16	Brighton & Hove Albion	2-1	Coughlin 2	9652		6	1		7	9	3	10	4	2								5		11				8
39	23	SCUNTHORPE UNITED	1-2	Hodgson	6161		6	1		7	9	3	10	4	2		8						5		11				
40	26	BRENTFORD	0-1		5408		6	1		7	9	3	10	4	2								5		11				8
41	30	Watford	0-1		4517	11	6	1		7			10	4	2			9				3			8		5		12
42	May 7	OLDHAM ATHLETIC	1-0	Bumstead	4932		6	1		7			10	4	2		9					3			11		5		8
43	10	HULL CITY	1-1	Weller	7861		6	1		7			10	4	2		9					3			11		5		8
44	17	Brentford	0-1		5132		6	1		7				4	2		9					3	10		11		5		8
45	21	Queen's Park Rangers	0-5		4732		6	1		7	12			4	2		9					3	10		11		5		8
46	23	Mansfield Town	0-1		6385	10				7				4	2				1			3			11	8	5	6	9
					Apps	25	34	44	10	46	32	26	34	46	46	3	36	1	2	13	17	19	23	4	22	3	6	3	21
					Goals	4	1		1	5	7	1	3				6						3	1	1				5

F.A. Cup

Rd	Date	Opponent	Score	Scorers	Att	Archer J	Ashworth JM	Best D	Bolton R	Bumstead RG	Coughlin DM	Coxon WG	Crickmore CE	Ferns P	Gater R	George RS	Hodgson K	Hold JD	Jones R	Keith RM	McKinney WE	Naylor TV	Newton GW	O'Neill A	Priscott AJ	Saunders RC	Taylor RV	Walker R	Weller CW
R1	Nov 13	WEYMOUTH	0-0		11034		10	1		7	9	3	11	4	5		8			2		6							
rep	17	Weymouth	4-1	Crickmore, Archer (p), Coughlin 2	7183	10		1		7	9	3	11	4	5		8			2		6							
R2	Dec 4	BATH CITY	5-3	Naylor, Coughlin 3, Hodgson	9022	8		1		7	9	3	11	4	5		10				2	6							
R3	Jan 22	BURNLEY	1-1	Archer	16082	10	6	1		7	9	3	11	2	5		8						4						
rep	25	Burnley	0-7		21745	10	6	1		7	9	3	11	2	5		8						4						

F.L. Cup

Rd	Date	Opponent	Score	Scorers	Att	Archer J	Ashworth JM	Best D	Bolton R	Bumstead RG	Coughlin DM	Coxon WG	Crickmore CE	Ferns P	Gater R	George RS	Hodgson K	Hold JD	Jones R	Keith RM	McKinney WE	Naylor TV	Newton GW	O'Neill A	Priscott AJ	Saunders RC	Taylor RV	Walker R	Weller CW
R1	Sep 1	ALDERSHOT	0-0		5028	10		1	6	7	9	3	11	4	5		8			2									
rep	8	Aldershot	1-2	Archer (p)	4903	10		1	6	7	9		11	4	5					3	2			8					

		P	W	D	L	F	A	W	D	L	F	A	Pts
1	Hull City	46	19	2	2	64	24	12	5	6	45	38	69
2	Millwall	46	19	4	0	47	13	8	7	8	29	30	65
3	Queen's Park Rangers	46	16	3	4	62	29	8	6	9	33	36	57
4	Scunthorpe United	46	9	8	6	44	34	12	3	8	36	33	53
5	Workington	46	13	6	4	38	18	6	8	9	29	39	52
6	Gillingham	46	14	4	5	33	19	8	4	11	29	35	52
7	Swindon Town	46	11	8	4	43	18	8	5	10	31	30	51
8	Reading	46	13	5	5	36	19	6	8	9	34	44	51
9	Walsall	46	13	7	3	48	21	7	3	13	29	43	50
10	Shrewsbury Town	46	13	7	3	48	22	6	4	13	25	42	49
11	Grimsby Town	46	15	6	2	47	25	2	7	14	21	37	47
12	Watford	46	12	4	7	33	19	5	9	9	22	32	47
13	Peterborough United	46	13	6	4	50	26	4	6	13	30	40	46
14	Oxford United	46	11	3	9	38	33	8	5	10	32	41	46
15	Brighton & Hove Albion	46	13	4	6	48	28	3	7	13	19	37	43
16	Bristol Rovers	46	11	10	2	38	15	3	4	16	26	49	42
17	Swansea Town	46	14	4	5	61	37	1	7	15	20	59	41
18	BOURNEMOUTH	46	9	8	6	24	19	4	4	15	14	37	38
19	Mansfield Town	46	10	5	8	31	36	5	3	15	28	53	38
20	Oldham Athletic	46	8	7	8	34	33	4	6	13	21	48	37
21	Southend United	46	15	1	7	43	28	1	3	19	11	55	36
22	Exeter City	46	9	6	8	36	28	3	5	15	17	51	35
23	Brentford	46	9	4	10	34	30	1	8	14	14	39	32
24	York City	46	5	7	11	30	44	4	2	17	23	62	27

1966/67

20th in Division Three

			Opponent	Score	Scorers	Att	Adams RL	Ashworth JM	Best D	Bumstead RG	Gater R	Gulliver TR	Hold JD	Jones R	McKechnie TS	Naylor TV	Newton GW	Norton P	Norton R	Oliver K	Pound JHK	Priscott AJ	Stocks DH	Taylor RV	Taylor TWJ	Walker R	Weller CW	White J	White KN
1	Aug	20	Oxford United	1-1	Priscott	5621		6	1	11		2	9				4					7	3	8	10			5	
2		27	OLDHAM ATHLETIC	2-1	McKechnie, Pound	5891		6		7	4	2		1	9						8	11	3		10			5	
3	Sep	3	Scunthorpe United	1-0	T Taylor	4278		6		7	4	2		1	9						8		3		10			5	11
4		7	Brighton & Hove Albion	3-0	T Taylor 3	11044		6		7	4	2		1	9						8	11	3		10			5	
5		10	WORKINGTON	0-2		6959		6		7	4	2		1	9						8	11	3		10			5	
6		17	Gillingham	0-0		7247		6		7	4	2		1							10	11	3	9			8	5	12
7		24	ORIENT	1-0	Pound	5803				7	4	2	9	1							8	11	3	6			10	5	
8		28	BRIGHTON & HOVE ALB	2-1	Priscott, Pound	6137				7	4	2	9	1					12		8	11	3	6			10	5	
9	Oct	1	TORQUAY UNITED	1-0	Bumstead	6484				7	4	2	9	1					10		8	11	3	5		6			
10		8	Darlington	2-1	R Norton, Hold	6121				7	4	2	9	1					8			11	3	5	10	6			
11		15	QUEEN'S PARK RANGERS	1-3	R Norton	12164				7	4	2		1					8		9	11	3	5	10	6			
12		19	Shrewsbury Town	1-4	R Norton	5632		6		7	4	2		1					8		9	11	3	5	10				
13		22	Watford	0-3		7718				7	4	2		1	8				10		9		3		11	6		5	
14		29	SWINDON TOWN	1-4	McKechnie	6071		6		7	4	2		1	9				8			11	3				10	5	
15	Nov	5	Reading	0-0		4262		4		7			10	1		11			8		9		3	6		2		5	
16		12	DONCASTER ROVERS	4-1	Hold 2, Priscott, T Taylor	4273		4		7			9	1							10	11	3	6	8	2		5	
17		16	SHREWSBURY TOWN	0-3		3890		4		7		2	9	1							8	11	3	6	10			5	
18		19	Mansfield Town	0-1		6681		4		7		2	9	1		11			8				3	6			10	5	
19	Dec	3	Walsall	0-3		6835		4		7		2	9	1		11			8			12	3	6			10	5	
20		10	PETERBOROUGH UTD.	1-1	T Taylor	4064		6		7		2		1	9						8	11	3	4	10			5	
21		17	OXFORD UNITED	0-0		3555				11	4	2		1	9						8	7	3	6	10			5	
22		26	COLCHESTER UNITED	1-1	Weller	5135					4	2		1	9	6			10			7	3		11		8	5	
23		27	Colchester United	0-2		6140		4					8	1	9	6			11				3	7		2	10	5	
24		31	Oldham Athletic	1-1	Weller	11135		4				2	10	1	9	6			11				3	7			8	5	
25	Jan	14	Workington	0-0		2096		4		11		2		1	9	6					8	7	3				10	5	
26		21	GILLINGHAM	1-0	Ashworth	4937		4		7		2		1	8	6				9		11	3	12			10	5	
27		28	SCUNTHORPE UNITED	0-0		3561		4		11		2		1		6				9	10	7	3				8	5	
28	Feb	4	Orient	0-1		5771		4		11		2		1	8					9		7	3	6			10	5	
29		11	Torquay United	2-3	Weller, Priscott	6256		4		7		2		1		6				9		11	3	8			10	5	
30		18	MIDDLESBROUGH	1-1	Bumstead	5193		4		7		2		1		6				9		11	3	10			8	5	
31		25	DARLINGTON	1-1	Bumstead	4242		4		7		2		1		6			12	9		11	3	10			8	5	
32	Mar	7	Queen's Park Rangers	0-4		21558		4		7		2		1		6						11	3	10	9		8	5	
33		11	Middlesbrough	1-3	Priscott	15644		4		7		2		1		6		12		9	8	11	3	10				5	
34		18	WATFORD	0-0		4930				7	4			1		6		2	10	9	8	11	3					5	
35		24	Bristol Rovers	1-1	Priscott	13924				7	4			1		6		2	10		8	11	3				9	5	
36		25	Swindon Town	0-1		14275				7	4	12		1		10		2	6		9		3		11		8	5	
37		27	BRISTOL ROVERS	0-0		7110					4			1		6		2	10	9	8	11	3					5	7
38	Apr	1	READING	2-2	P Norton, Oliver	4610				7	4			1		10		2	6	9	8	11	3					5	
39		4	Swansea Town	1-0	Oliver	8752				7	4			1		10		2	6	9	8	11	3					5	
40		8	Doncaster Rovers	1-1	Oliver	2918				7	4			1		10		2	6	9	8	11	3					5	
41		15	MANSFIELD TOWN	1-3	Oliver (p)	4831					4			1		10		2	6	9	11	7	3				8	5	
42		22	Grimsby Town	0-1		3668				7	4	2		1		10			6	9	8	11	3					5	
43		26	SWANSEA TOWN	1-0	Hold	5165					4	2	9	1		10			6		8	11	3					5	7
44		29	WALSALL	3-0	Hold, K White, Pound	4229					4	2	9	1		3		10	6		8	11						5	7
45	May	6	Peterborough United	0-2		5047					4	2	9	1		3		10	6		8	11						5	7
46		13	GRIMSBY TOWN	0-0		3411	11	10		2	4			1		3			6		9	8						5	7
						Apps	1	26	1	38	28	35	15	45	14	27	1	11	27	14	32	39	43	24	16	7	20	42	7
						Goals		1		3			5		2			1	3	4	4	6			6		3		1

F.A. Cup

			Opponent	Score	Scorers	Att	Adams RL	Ashworth JM	Best D	Bumstead RG	Gater R	Gulliver TR	Hold JD	Jones R	McKechnie TS	Naylor TV	Newton GW	Norton P	Norton R	Oliver K	Pound JHK	Priscott AJ	Stocks DH	Taylor RV	Taylor TWJ	Walker R	Weller CW	White J	White KN
R1	Nov	26	WELTON ROVERS	3-0	Weller 2, Hold	6582		4		7		2	9	1		11			8				3	6			10	5	
R2	Jan	7	Queen's Park Rangers	0-2		11402		4		7		2		1	9	6			10			11	3				8	5	

F.L. Cup

			Opponent	Score	Scorers	Att	Adams RL	Ashworth JM	Best D	Bumstead RG	Gater R	Gulliver TR	Hold JD	Jones R	McKechnie TS	Naylor TV	Newton GW	Norton P	Norton R	Oliver K	Pound JHK	Priscott AJ	Stocks DH	Taylor RV	Taylor TWJ	Walker R	Weller CW	White J	White KN
R1	Aug	24	Swindon Town	1-2	McKechnie	7769		6	1	11		2	9		8		4					7	3		10			5	

		P	W	D	L	F	A	W	D	L	F	A	Pts
1	Queen's Park Rangers	46	18	4	1	66	15	8	11	4	37	23	67
2	Middlesbrough	46	16	3	4	51	20	7	6	10	36	44	55
3	Watford	46	15	5	3	39	17	5	9	9	22	29	54
4	Reading	46	13	7	3	45	20	9	2	12	31	37	53
5	Bristol Rovers	46	13	8	2	47	28	7	5	11	29	39	53
6	Shrewsbury Town	46	15	5	3	48	24	5	7	11	29	38	52
7	Torquay United	46	17	3	3	57	20	4	6	13	16	34	51
8	Swindon Town	46	14	5	4	53	21	6	5	12	28	38	50
9	Mansfield Town	46	12	4	7	48	37	8	5	10	36	42	49
10	Oldham Athletic	46	15	4	4	51	16	4	6	13	29	47	48
11	Gillingham	46	11	9	3	36	18	4	7	12	22	44	46
12	Walsall	46	12	8	3	37	16	6	2	15	28	56	46
13	Colchester United	46	14	3	6	52	30	3	7	13	24	43	44
14	Orient	46	10	9	4	36	27	3	9	11	22	41	44
15	Peterborough United	46	12	4	7	40	31	2	11	10	26	40	43
16	Oxford United	46	10	8	5	41	29	5	5	13	20	37	43
17	Grimsby Town	46	13	5	5	46	23	4	4	15	15	45	43
18	Scunthorpe United	46	13	4	6	39	26	4	4	15	19	47	42
19	Brighton & Hove Albion	46	10	8	5	37	27	3	7	13	24	44	41
20	BOURNEMOUTH	46	8	10	5	24	24	4	7	12	15	33	41
21	Swansea Town	46	9	9	5	50	30	3	6	14	35	59	39
22	Darlington	46	8	7	8	26	28	5	4	14	21	53	37
23	Doncaster Rovers	46	11	6	6	40	40	1	2	20	18	77	32
24	Workington	46	9	3	11	35	35	3	4	16	20	54	31

1967/68

13th in Division Three

No	Month	Day	Opponent	Score	Scorers	Att	Adams RL	Bolton R	Book K	Bumstead RG	East KMG	Gater R	Gulliver TR	Hall RF	Hill JE	Hold JD	Jones R	Longhorn D	Naylor TV	Norton P	Norton R	Pound JHK	Rowles AEJ	Stocks DH	Taylor TWJ	White J	White KN
1	Aug	19	BRISTOL ROVERS	3-1	Williams (og), Hold, Pound	6638				11		4	2	8		9	1		6			10		3		5	7
2		26	Barrow	1-1	Gater	7066				11		4	2	8		9	1		6		12	10		3		5	7
3	Sep	2	OXFORD UNITED	2-1	Hold, Pound	5836				11		4	2	8		9	1		6			10		3		5	7
4		4	SCUNTHORPE UNITED	1-0	Hold	6302				11		4	2	8		9	1		6			10		3		5	7
5		9	Bury	0-4		5780				7		4	2	8			1			6	11	10	9	3		5	12
6		15	Stockport County	1-3	Bumstead	9153		10		11				4			1		6	2		8		3	9	5	7
7		23	COLCHESTER UNITED	1-2	Pound	5491		10		11				4		9	1		6	2		8		3		5	7
8		26	Scunthorpe United	1-1	Taylor	4926		10				4	2				1		6		11	8		3	9	5	7
9		30	Peterborough United	0-2		7041		10		12		4	2				1		6		9	8		3	11	5	7
10	Oct	4	SOUTHPORT	4-1	K White, Stocks, Bolton, Bumstead	4099	11	10		8		4	2	12			1		6			9		3		5	7
11		7	SHREWSBURY TOWN	1-1	Bolton	5434	11	10		8		4	2				1		6			9		3		5	7
12		14	Swindon Town	0-4		11307	7	10		8		4	2			9	1		6			11		3		5	
13		21	READING	2-0	Bolton (p), Pound	5219		10		8		4	2				1		6			9		3	11	5	7
14		23	Southport	1-1	Taylor	6548		10		8		4	2				1		6			9		3	11	5	7
15		28	Torquay United	1-2	Gater	5578		10		8		4	2			9	1		6			7		3	11	5	
16	Nov	4	GRIMSBY TOWN	1-0	Hold	4237		10		8		4	2			9	1		6			7		3	11	5	
17		11	Gillingham	0-0		7419		10		8		4	2	12		9	1		6			7		3	11	5	
18		15	Oxford United	2-3	Hold, Pound	7047		10		8		4	2	11		9	1		6			7		3		5	
19		18	WALSALL	1-1	Hold	5985		11		8	10	4	2			9	1		6			7		3		5	
20		25	Northampton Town	0-1		9042		11		8	10	4	2	12		9	1		6			7		3		5	
21	Dec	2	ORIENT	0-0		4990		4		8	10		2			9	1		6			7		3	11	5	
22		16	Bristol Rovers	0-2		7080				8	10	4	2			9	1		6			11		3		5	7
23		23	BARROW	3-0	J White, Pound 2	4595	8			11	9	6	2				1		4			10		5		3	7
24		26	WATFORD	0-1		6930	8			11	9	6	2				1		4			10		5		3	7
25		30	Watford	2-0	Naylor, East	9643	8			11	9	4	2				1		6			10	12	3		5	7
26	Jan	13	BURY	1-0	East	10387		11	1	6	9		2						4			10	8	5		3	7
27		20	STOCKPORT COUNTY	1-0	East	5932		11		6	9		2				1		4			10	8	5		3	7
28	Feb	3	Colchester United	1-0	Pound	4075	12			6	9		2				1		4		11	10	8	5		3	7
29		10	PETERBOROUGH UTD.	3-3	K White, Rowles, Adams	6337	8			6	9		2				1		4		11	10	12	5		3	7
30		17	Mansfield Town	1-1	Rowles	6093				6	9		2				1		4		11		10	3	8	5	7
31		24	Shrewsbury Town	0-1		4858		11		6	9		2				1		4			10	8	3		5	7
32	Mar	2	SWINDON TOWN	2-1	Adams, R Norton	7517	10			6	9				2		1		4		7		8	5		3	11
33		9	OLDHAM ATHLETIC	0-0		5867	10			6	9				2		1		4		7		8	5		3	11
34		12	Oldham Athletic	1-1	East	3500				6	9		2			10	1		4		7	8		5		3	11
35		16	Reading	0-1		5663				6	9		2		12	10	1		4		7	8		5		3	11
36		23	TORQUAY UNITED	1-1	A Smith (og)	7521				6	10		2			9	1	7	4		11	8		5		3	
37		30	Grimsby Town	1-2	Longhorn	2458				6	9				2		1	7	4		11	8	10	5		3	
38	Apr	6	GILLINGHAM	4-0	Hold 3, K White	4915	10	11		6	8		2			9	1		4					5		3	7
39		12	BRIGHTON & HOVE ALB	2-2	Bolton, East	8329	10	11		6	8		2			9	1		4					5		3	7
40		13	Walsall	1-1	Pound	6815		11		6	9						1		4	2	7	10	8	5		3	
41		15	Brighton & Hove Albion	3-2	East 2, Bolton	8957		11		6	9					10	1		4	2	7		8	5		3	
42		20	NORTHAMPTON T	0-2		6148		11		6	9					10	1		4	2	7		8	5		3	12
43		22	Tranmere Rovers	0-0		5560				6	9					10	1		4	2	11		8	5		3	7
44		27	Orient	0-1		5470	12			6	9					10	1		4	2	11		8	5		3	7
45	May	4	TRANMERE ROVERS	3-0	Gulliver, Adams, East	4527	8			6	9		2			10	1		4		11			5		3	7
46		11	MANSFIELD TOWN	3-0	Adams, Naylor, Hold	4363	8			6	9		2			10	1	12	4		11			5		3	7
						Apps	15	24	1	45	28	22	36	11	4	25	45	3	45	8	20	35	16	46	10	46	34
						Goals	4	5		2	8	2	1			10		1	2		1	9	2	1	2	1	3

Two own goals

F.A. Cup

Rd	Month	Day	Opponent	Score	Scorers	Att	Adams RL	Bolton R	Book K	Bumstead RG	East KMG	Gater R	Gulliver TR	Hall RF	Hill JE	Hold JD	Jones R	Longhorn D	Naylor TV	Norton P	Norton R	Pound JHK	Rowles AEJ	Stocks DH	Taylor TWJ	White J	White KN
R1	Dec	9	NORTHAMPTON T	2-0	Bolton (p), Hold	4998		11		4	9		2			10	1		6	8				3		5	7
R2	Jan	6	Walthamstow Avenue	3-1	K White, Pound 2	5402	12		1	11	9	4	2			8			6			10		3		5	7
R3		27	LIVERPOOL	0-0		24388		11		6	9		2			12	1		4			10	8	5		3	7
rep		30	Liverpool	1-4	Hughes (og)	54075				6	9		2	11		12	1		4			10	8	5		3	7

F.L. Cup

Rd	Month	Day	Opponent	Score	Scorers	Att	Adams RL	Bolton R	Book K	Bumstead RG	East KMG	Gater R	Gulliver TR	Hall RF	Hill JE	Hold JD	Jones R	Longhorn D	Naylor TV	Norton P	Norton R	Pound JHK	Rowles AEJ	Stocks DH	Taylor TWJ	White J	White KN
R1	Aug	22	WATFORD	1-1	Hold	6573				11		4	2	8		9	1		6			10		3		5	7
rep		29	Watford	0-0	(aet)	6502				11		4	2	8		9	1		6			10		3		5	7
rep2	Sep	6	Watford	1-2	Hold	2720				11		4	2	8		9	1			12	6	10		3		5	7

R1 replay 2 at Swindon Town

		P	W	D	L	F	A	W	D	L	F	A	Pts
1	Oxford United	46	18	3	2	49	20	4	10	9	20	27	57
2	Bury	46	19	3	1	64	24	5	5	13	27	42	56
3	Shrewsbury Town	46	14	6	3	42	17	6	9	8	19	32	55
4	Torquay United	46	15	6	2	40	17	6	5	12	20	39	53
5	Reading	46	15	5	3	43	17	6	4	13	27	43	51
6	Watford	46	15	3	5	59	20	6	5	12	15	30	50
7	Walsall	46	12	7	4	47	22	7	5	11	27	39	50
8	Barrow	46	14	6	3	43	13	7	2	14	22	41	50
9	Peterborough United	46	14	4	5	46	23	6	6	11	33	44	50
10	Swindon Town	46	13	8	2	51	16	3	9	11	23	35	49
11	Brighton & Hove Albion	46	11	8	4	31	14	5	8	10	26	41	48
12	Gillingham	46	13	6	4	35	19	5	6	12	24	44	48
13	BOURNEMOUTH	46	13	7	3	39	17	3	8	12	17	34	47
14	Stockport County	46	16	5	2	49	22	3	4	16	21	53	47
15	Southport	46	13	6	4	35	22	4	6	13	30	43	46
16	Bristol Rovers	46	14	3	6	42	25	3	6	14	30	53	43
17	Oldham Athletic	46	11	3	9	37	32	7	4	12	23	33	43
18	Northampton Town	46	10	8	5	40	25	4	5	14	18	47	41
19	Orient	46	10	6	7	27	24	2	11	10	19	38	41
20	Tranmere Rovers	46	10	7	6	39	28	4	5	14	23	46	40
21	Mansfield Town	46	8	7	8	32	31	4	6	13	19	36	37
22	Grimsby Town	46	10	7	6	33	21	4	2	17	19	48	37
23	Colchester United	46	6	8	9	29	40	3	7	13	21	47	33
24	Scunthorpe United	46	8	9	6	36	34	2	3	18	20	53	32

1968/69

4th in Division Three

	Date		Opponents	Score	Scorers	Att	Adams RL	Bolton R	Book K	Bumstead RG	Burns DG	East KMG	Foote CRT	Gater R	Gulliver TR	Hold JD	Jones R	Longhorn D	Miller RE	Naylor TV	Peters RD	Pound JHK	Powell A	Rowles AEJ	Simmons DJ	Stocks DH	White J	White KN
1	Aug	10	Hartlepool	1-1	East	6791				6		9			2	10	1		3	12	11	8				5	4	7
2		17	PLYMOUTH ARGYLE	0-1		8200	10	7		2	6					9	1			4	11	8				5	3	
3		24	Bristol Rovers	2-3	Bolton 2	6761		11		7				4	2		1	9	3	10	12	8				5	6	
4		28	CREWE ALEXANDRA	4-0	Peters 2, East, Pound	5979		10		7		9		6	2		1		3	4	11	8				5		
5		31	SHREWSBURY TOWN	2-0	East 2	7330		10		7		9		6	2		1		3	4	11	8				5		
6	Sep	7	Northampton Town	3-1	Peters, Pound, Bolton	7812		10		7		9		6	2		1		3		11	8	12			5	4	
7		14	STOCKPORT COUNTY	1-0	Bolton	8237		10		7		9		6	2		1		3		11	8				5	4	
8		18	SWINDON TOWN	2-0	Bumstead, East	12113		10		7		9		6	2		1		3		11	8				5	4	
9		21	Watford	0-1		7688		10		7		9		6	2		1		3		11	8	12			5	4	
10		28	WALSALL	1-0	Bolton (p)	8475		10		7		9		6	2		1		3		11	8				5	4	
11	Oct	5	BRIGHTON & HOVE ALB	2-0	Bolton, East	7678		10		7		9		6	2		1		3		11	8				5	4	
12		7	Crewe Alexandra	2-0	Pound, Gater	4827				7		9		6	2		1		3	11		8		10		5	4	
13		12	Mansfield Town	1-3	East	5093		12		7		9		6	2		1		3		11	8		10		5	4	
14		19	SOUTHPORT	2-1	Hold, East	7303		6		7		9			2	10	1		3	4	11	8				5		
15		26	Rotherham United	1-1	Pound	8941		6		7		9				10	1		3	4	11	8				5	2	
16	Nov	2	BARNSLEY	3-0	East, Pound, Bolton	7569		6		7		9				10	1		3	4	11	8				5	2	
17		6	TORQUAY UNITED	3-0	East, Pound, Hold	9721		6		7		9				10	1		3	4	11	8				5	2	
18		23	Luton Town	1-1	Bumstead	14150		11		7		9		6		10	1		3	4	12	8				5	2	
19		30	GILLINGHAM	2-0	Pound, Simmons	7655		6		7		10		4		12	1		3		11	8			9	5	2	
20	Dec	14	MANSFIELD TOWN	2-1	Powell Bumstead	6347		6		7				4			1		3			8	10		9	5	2	11
21		20	Southport	1-2	Miller	4126		11		7		10		6			1		3	4		8			9	5	2	
22		26	Brighton & Hove Albion	1-4	Pound	14912				7		10		6	2		1		3		11	8			9	5	4	
23		28	ROTHERHAM UNITED	1-0	Bolton (p)	8558		6		7		10			2	12	1		3		11	8			9	5	4	
24	Jan	4	TRANMERE ROVERS	3-4	Simmons 2, Pound	8096		12		7					2	10	1		3	6	11	8			9	5	4	
25		11	Barnsley	0-1		10768		10		6		9					1	7	3	4	11				8	5	2	
26		18	OLDHAM ATHLETIC	3-1	Lawson (og), East, Bolton	7144		10		7		9					1	6	3	4	11	8				5	2	
27		25	Torquay United	0-0		9760		10		7		9			2		1	6	3		11	8				5	4	
28	Feb	1	Barrow	2-0	Pound 2	3228		10		7		9			2		1	6	3		11	8				5	4	
29		8	LUTON TOWN	0-2		9253		10		7	12	9			2		1	6	3		11	8				5	4	
30	Mar	1	HARTLEPOOL	4-0	Naylor, East, Bumstead, Bolton	6246		10		7		9			2		1		3	6	11	8				5	4	
31		3	Tranmere Rovers	1-2	East	3328		10		7		9			2		1		3	6	11	8				5	4	
32		8	Plymouth Argyle	1-1	East	11961			1	4		9			2			8	5	6	11		10			3		7
33		15	BRISTOL ROVERS	0-0		6832				7		9			2		1		3	4	11	8	10			5	6	
34		17	Orient	0-1		4090		12		7	8	9			2		1		3	4	11		10			5	6	
35		22	Shrewsbury Town	0-1		3747		12		7	11	9			2		1	8	3	4			10			5	6	
36		25	Oldham Athletic	0-2		3114		4		7		9			2		1		3		11		10			5	6	8
37		29	NORTHAMPTON T	3-2	Hold, J White 2	5089		4		7		9			2	10	1		3		11					5	6	8
38	Apr	4	READING	1-1	Bolton (p)	7496		4		8		9			2	10	1		3		11					5	6	7
39		5	Walsall	0-0		4892		4					12		2	10	1	8	3		11		9			5	6	7
40		8	Swindon Town	0-3		22671		4		7			8		2	9	1	11	3				10			5	6	
41		12	WATFORD	1-3	Powell	10431		4		11			8		2	9	1		3	12			10			5	6	7
42		16	Reading	1-0	Bolton	4497		11				9	7		2		1		3	4		8	10			5	6	
43		18	Stockport County	1-0	East	4423		11		12		9	7		2		1		3	4		8	10			5	6	
44		22	Gillingham	0-0		6615		11		2		9	7			10	1		3	4		8	12			5	6	
45		25	ORIENT	0-1		4597		11		2		9	7			12	1		3	4		8	10			5	6	
46		28	BARROW	1-0	Powell	3621		11				9	7		2	10	1		3	4			8			5	6	
						Apps	1	41	1	43	4	39	8	16	34	18	45	10	45	27	35	35	16	2	7	46	42	8
						Goals		12		4		15		1		3			1	1	3	11	3		3			2

F.A. Cup

	Date		Opponents	Score	Scorers	Att	Adams RL	Bolton R	Book K	Bumstead RG	Burns DG	East KMG	Foote CRT	Gater R	Gulliver TR	Hold JD	Jones R	Longhorn D	Miller RE	Naylor TV	Peters RD	Pound JHK	Powell A	Rowles AEJ	Simmons DJ	Stocks DH	White J	White KN
R1	Nov	16	Bury Town	0-0		2730		6		7		9				10	1		3	4	11	8				5	2	
rep		20	BURY TOWN	3-0	Hold, East, Bolton	9773		6		7		9		12		10	1		3	4	11	8				5	2	
R2	Dec	7	BRISTOL ROVERS	0-0		11014		11		7		9		6		10	1		3			8	4			5	2	
rep		10	Bristol Rovers	0-1		11898		5		7		12		6		10	1		3			8	9			4	2	11

F.L. Cup

	Date		Opponents	Score	Scorers	Att	Adams RL	Bolton R	Book K	Bumstead RG	Burns DG	East KMG	Foote CRT	Gater R	Gulliver TR	Hold JD	Jones R	Longhorn D	Miller RE	Naylor TV	Peters RD	Pound JHK	Powell A	Rowles AEJ	Simmons DJ	Stocks DH	White J	White KN
R1	Aug	13	SOUTHEND UNITED	1-6	Hold	7182	12			6		9				8	1		2	4	11	10				5	3	7

		P	W	D	L	F	A	W	D	L	F	A	Pts
1	Watford	46	16	5	2	35	7	11	5	7	39	27	64
2	Swindon Town	46	18	4	1	38	7	9	6	8	33	28	64
3	Luton Town	46	20	3	0	57	14	5	8	10	17	24	61
4	BOURNEMOUTH	46	16	2	5	41	17	5	7	11	19	28	51
5	Plymouth Argyle	46	10	8	5	34	25	7	7	9	19	24	49
6	Torquay United	46	13	4	6	35	18	5	8	10	19	28	48
7	Tranmere Rovers	46	12	3	8	36	31	7	7	9	34	37	48
8	Southport	46	14	8	1	52	20	3	5	15	19	44	47
9	Stockport County	46	14	5	4	49	25	2	9	12	18	43	46
10	Barnsley	46	13	6	4	37	21	3	8	12	21	42	46
11	Rotherham United	46	12	6	5	40	21	4	7	12	16	29	45
12	Brighton & Hove Albion	46	12	7	4	49	21	4	6	13	23	44	45
13	Walsall	46	10	9	4	34	18	4	7	12	16	31	44
14	Reading	46	13	3	7	41	25	2	10	11	26	41	43
15	Mansfield Town	46	14	5	4	37	18	2	6	15	21	44	43
16	Bristol Rovers	46	12	6	5	41	27	4	5	14	22	44	43
17	Shrewsbury Town	46	11	8	4	28	17	5	3	15	23	50	43
18	Orient	46	10	8	5	31	19	4	6	13	20	39	42
19	Barrow	46	11	6	6	30	23	6	2	15	26	52	42
20	Gillingham	46	10	10	3	35	20	3	5	15	19	43	41
21	Northampton Town	46	9	8	6	37	30	5	4	14	17	31	40
22	Hartlepool	46	6	12	5	25	29	4	7	12	15	41	39
23	Crewe Alexandra	46	11	4	8	40	31	2	5	16	12	45	35
24	Oldham Athletic	46	9	6	8	33	27	4	3	16	17	56	35

1969/70

21st in Division Three: Relegated

No	Date	Opponent	Score	Scorers	Att	Baker KR	Bugg AA	Bumstead RG	East KMG	Foote CRT	Gulliver TR	Harman PR	Hartley TJ	Hold JD	Jones R	Longhorn D	MacDougall EJ	Meredith JF	Miller RE	Naylor TV	Peters RD	Powell A	Rowles AEJ	Sainty JA	Simmonds MR	Stocks DH	Summerhill A	Tilsed RW	White J
1	Aug 9	Barnsley	0-1		10393			6	10	3	2		7	8	1		9	11								5			4
2	16	LUTON TOWN	0-1		9578			6	8	3	2		7	10	1		9	11				12				5			4
3	23	Brighton & Hove Albion	1-1	MacDougall	14382			6		2			7	8	1	10	9	11					12			5	4		3
4	26	Bury	0-1		4832			6		2			7	10	1	8	9	11					12			5	4		3
5	30	ROTHERHAM UNITED	1-0	East	7095			6	8	2			7	10	1		9	11		4						5	3		
6	Sep 6	Tranmere Rovers	5-1	Hold 3, MacDougall, White	5488			7		3	2			10	1		9	11					8			5	4		6
7	13	TORQUAY UNITED	1-2	Stocks	8729			7		3	2			10	1		9	11					8			5	4		6
8	17	SHREWSBURY TOWN	3-3	Hold, MacDougall, East	5785			7	8	3	2			10	1		9	11					12			5	4		6
9	20	Reading	0-2		7117			7		6	2			10	1		9	11					8			5	4		3
10	27	HALIFAX TOWN	0-0		5588			7		6	2			10	1		9	11				8	12			5	4		3
11	29	ROCHDALE	0-3		4775						2		12	10	1			11	3	4	7	9	8			5			6
12	Oct 4	Southport	0-3		3014			12		6				10	1		9	11	3	4	7		8			5			2
13	7	Luton Town	0-0		18065					6			7	10	1		9	11	3	4			8			5			2
14	11	FULHAM	2-2	MacDougall, Hold	8429					6			7	10	1		9	11	3	4			8		12	5			2
15	18	Walsall	1-2	Rowles	5388						2		7	10	1		9	11	3				8		6	5			4
16	25	BRISTOL ROVERS	2-2	MacDougall 2	6751				8		2			10	1		9	11	4				7		6	5			3
17	Nov 1	Orient	0-3		9231	1				4	2			10			9	11				6	7		8	5			3
18	8	STOCKPORT COUNTY	1-0	White	4903	1				3	2		7	10			8	11				6				5	4		9
19	22	GILLINGHAM	2-1	East, MacDougall (p)	4772	1			10	3	2		7				8	11				6				5	4		9
20	26	DONCASTER ROVERS	3-1	East, White, MacDougall	3806				10	3	2		7		1		8	11				6				5	4		9
21	29	Plymouth Argyle	1-0	Meredith	6606				10	3	2		7		1		8	11				6				5	4		9
22	Dec 13	Torquay United	2-2	MacDougall, White	5856				8	3	2		7		1		10	11				6				5	4		9
23	20	TRANMERE ROVERS	2-2	MacDougall, Powell	3934				8	3	2		7	12	1		10	11				6				5	4		9
24	26	BRIGHTON & HOVE ALB	0-0		7541				10	3	2		7		1		8	11				6				5	4		9
25	27	Rotherham United	0-3		10997			6		3	2		7		1		8	11				4	10			5			9
26	Jan 10	READING	1-2	MacDougall	3852					2		9	7		1		8	11	3			6				5	4		10
27	17	Halifax Town	1-4	MacDougall	3093				12	3	2					7	8	11	4			10				5	6	1	9
28	24	Bradford City	1-8	Foote	9296					6				10		7	9	11	2			4			12	5	3	1	8
29	26	Rochdale	1-0	MacDougall	5286	1		7	10	8	2						9	11	4			6				5			3
30	31	SOUTHPORT	1-0	MacDougall	4219	1		7	8		2		10				9	11	3			6				5			4
31	Feb 6	Fulham	1-1	MacDougall	9713		1	7	8		2						10	11	4			6		9		5			3
32	14	BARNSLEY	3-1	MacDougall 3 (1p)	4202		1	7	8		2						10	11	4			6		9		5			3
33	21	Bristol Rovers	2-5	MacDougall, East	10095		1	7	8		2						10	11	4			6		9		5			3
34	28	ORIENT	0-2		5440		1		8	7	2						10	11	4			6		9		5			3
35	Mar 4	BARROW	0-0		2353	1			8	4	2						10	11				6		9	7	5			3
36	14	PLYMOUTH ARGYLE	1-3	MacDougall	4201	1			8	4	2		7				10	11	12			6		9		5			3
37	16	Mansfield Town	0-2		8223	1				10			7	9			8	11	4			6				5	2		3
38	21	Barrow	1-1	East	2837	1			8	7							10	11	3			6		9		5	2		4
39	27	WALSALL	2-2	MacDougall (p), East	4938	1			8	7							10	11	3			6		9		5	2		4
40	28	BRADFORD CITY	0-0		4878	1			8	9							10	11	3	5		4	7				2		6
41	30	Stockport County	2-0	East 2	2143	1			8	9							10	11	3	5		4	7				2		6
42	Apr 4	BURY	2-0	East, Foote	3983	1			8	9							10	11	3	5		4	7				2		6
43	7	Doncaster Rovers	1-2	East	3732	1			8	9							10	11	3	5		4	7				2		6
44	15	Shrewsbury Town	0-2		3350	1			8	9							10	11	3	5		4	7	12			2		6
45	18	MANSFIELD TOWN	1-0	Hartley	4673	1							7	8			10	11	3			4	6			5	2		9
46	25	Gillingham	0-0		8638	1							7				10	11	3	5		4	6	8			2		9
					Apps	17	4	17	27	37	28	1	23	22	23	4	45	46	26	11	2	33	22	10	6	40	28	2	45
					Goals				11	2			1	5			21	1				1	1			1			4

F.A. Cup

Rd	Date	Opponent	Score	Scorers	Att	Baker KR	Bugg AA	Bumstead RG	East KMG	Foote CRT	Gulliver TR	Harman PR	Hartley TJ	Hold JD	Jones R	Longhorn D	MacDougall EJ	Meredith JF	Miller RE	Naylor TV	Peters RD	Powell A	Rowles AEJ	Sainty JA	Simmonds MR	Stocks DH	Summerhill A	Tilsed RW	White J
R1	Nov 15	LUTON TOWN	1-1	Hartley	7362	1				3	2		7	10			8	11				6				5	4		9
rep	18	Luton Town	1-3	White	13384	1				3	2		7	10			8	11				6	12			5	4		9

FL Cup

Rd	Date	Opponent	Score	Scorers	Att	Baker KR	Bugg AA	Bumstead RG	East KMG	Foote CRT	Gulliver TR	Harman PR	Hartley TJ	Hold JD	Jones R	Longhorn D	MacDougall EJ	Meredith JF	Miller RE	Naylor TV	Peters RD	Powell A	Rowles AEJ	Sainty JA	Simmonds MR	Stocks DH	Summerhill A	Tilsed RW	White J
R1	Aug 13	BRISTOL ROVERS	3-0	Hold, MacDougall 2	7478			6	8	3	2		7	10	1		9	11								5			4
R2	Sep 3	Sheffield Wednesday	1-1	Ellis (og)	14614			6		3	2			10	1	7	9	11					8			5	4		
rep	9	SHEFFIELD WEDNESDAY	1-0	Hold	15891			7		3	2			10	1		9	11					8			5	4		6
R3	24	LEICESTER CITY	0-2		15860				9	6	2		7	10	1		12	11					8			5	4		3

		P	*W*	*D*	*L*	*F*	*A*	*W*	*D*	*L*	*F*	*A*	*Pts*
1	Orient	46	16	5	2	43	15	9	7	7	24	21	62
2	Luton Town	46	13	8	2	46	15	10	6	7	31	28	60
3	Bristol Rovers	46	15	5	3	51	26	5	11	7	29	33	56
4	Fulham	46	12	9	2	43	26	8	6	9	38	29	55
5	Brighton & Hove Albion	46	16	4	3	37	16	7	5	11	20	27	55
6	Mansfield Town	46	14	4	5	46	22	7	7	9	24	27	53
7	Barnsley	46	14	6	3	43	24	5	9	9	25	35	53
8	Reading	46	16	3	4	52	29	5	8	10	35	48	53
9	Rochdale	46	11	6	6	39	24	7	4	12	30	36	46
10	Bradford City	46	11	6	6	37	22	6	6	11	20	28	46
11	Doncaster Rovers	46	13	4	6	31	19	4	8	11	21	35	46
12	Walsall	46	11	4	8	33	31	6	8	9	21	36	46
13	Torquay United	46	9	9	5	36	22	5	8	10	26	37	45
14	Rotherham United	46	10	8	5	36	19	5	6	12	26	35	44
15	Shrewsbury Town	46	10	12	1	35	17	3	6	14	27	46	44
16	Tranmere Rovers	46	10	8	5	38	29	4	8	11	18	43	44
17	Plymouth Argyle	46	10	7	6	32	23	6	4	13	24	41	43
18	Halifax Town	46	10	9	4	31	25	4	6	13	16	38	43
19	Bury	46	13	4	6	47	29	2	7	14	28	51	41
20	Gillingham	46	7	6	10	28	33	6	7	10	24	31	39
21	BOURNEMOUTH	46	8	9	6	28	27	4	6	13	20	44	39
22	Southport	46	11	5	7	31	22	3	5	15	17	44	38
23	Barrow	46	7	9	7	28	27	1	5	17	18	54	30
24	Stockport County	46	4	7	12	17	30	2	4	17	10	41	23

1970/71

2nd in Division Four: Promoted

	Date	Opponent	Score	Scorers	Att	Allen DJ	Baker KR	Benson JH	Boyer PJ	Davies F	Gulliver TR	Hartley TJ	Hold JD	Holland PG	Jones DE	Longhorn D	MacDougall EJ	Machin M	Meredith JF	Miller KR	Miller RE	Naylor TV	Powell A	Rowles AEJ	Sainty JA	Scott AJE	Stocks DH
1	Aug 15	Aldershot	0-2		6126	6				1	2	8					9		10	4			3	12	7	11	5
2	22	GRIMSBY TOWN	2-1	Worthington (og), Allen	7029	7				1	2	12					8		10	6		4	5		9	11	3
3	29	Newport County	2-0	Allen, MacDougall	3090	7				1	2				5		8			10		4	6		9	11	3
4	31	PETERBOROUGH UTD.	1-0	MacDougall	7359	7				1	2				5		8			10		4	6		9	11	3
5	Sep 5	STOCKPORT COUNTY	2-0	MacDougall 2 (1p)	6098	4				1	2				5	11	9			10			6		8	7	3
6	11	Southend United	2-1	Sainty. Gulliver	7545	7				1	2				5		8		11	6		4		10	9		3
7	18	COLCHESTER UNITED	4-1	MacDougall 4	7769	7				1	2				5		8		11	6			4	10	9	12	3
8	23	WORKINGTON	1-0	MacDougall	8921	9				1	2	12			5		8		11	6		12	4	10		7	3
9	26	York City	1-1	Rowles	4131					1	2	12			5		8			10		6	4	7	9	11	3
10	30	SCUNTHORPE UNITED	0-2		8219	10				1	2	12			5		8			6			4	7	9	11	3
11	Oct 3	CAMBRIDGE UNITED	3-0	MacDougall 2, Hold	7166	7				1	2		10		5		8			6			4		9	11	3
12	10	Brentford	2-1	MacDougall, Allen	5965	7				1	2		10		5		8			6			4		9	11	3
13	17	ALDERSHOT	1-1	MacDougall	9262	7				1	2	12	10		5		8			6			4		9	11	3
14	20	Oldham Athletic	2-2	MacDougall, Scott	10274	7				1	2	12			6		8			10	5		4		9	11	3
15	24	Chester	2-4	Scott, MacDougall	5702	7		11		1	2		12		5		8			6			4		9	10	3
16	31	LINCOLN CITY	3-0	Rowles, MacDougall, Sainty	6477	7		4		1	2				5	12	8			6			3	11	9	10	
17	Nov 7	Darlington	0-1		2480	7		4		1	2				5	11	8			6			3	10	9		
18	10	Southport	1-0	MacDougall	2299	6		4		1	2				5	7	8			3				10	9	11	
19	14	HARTLEPOOL	3-0	Rowles 2, MacDougall	5801			4		1	2				5	7	9			6			3	10	8	11	
20	28	CREWE ALEXANDRA	2-2	Rowles 2	7351			4		1	2				5	7	9			6			3	10	8	11	
21	Dec 5	Notts County	1-2	MacDougall	11711			4		1	2				5	12	9	7		6			3	10	8	11	
22	19	Grimsby Town	0-1		3143			4		1					5	12	9	2		7			4	10	8	11	3
23	Jan 2	Barrow	2-1	MacDougall 2 (2p)	2817			4	10	1		7					9	2		6			5	11	8		3
24	9	Scunthorpe United	1-1	Rowles	4366				10	1	2	7					9	4		6			5	11	8		3
25	16	OLDHAM ATHLETIC	5-0	Rowles 2, Boyer 2, MacDougall	7451		1		8			7					9	2		6			5	10	4	11	3
26	23	NORTHAMPTON T	4-2	Clarke (og), Boyer, MacDougall 2 (1p)	8763		1		8			7					9	2		6			5	10	4	11	3
27	27	EXETER CITY	4-1	Sainty, MacDougall 2 (1p), Hartley	9184				9	1		10					8	2		6			5	7	4	11	3
28	30	Crewe Alexandra	3-3	Boyer, MacDougall 2	3532				9	1		10					8	2		6			5	7	4	11	3
29	Feb 6	NOTTS COUNTY	1-1	Boyer	15431			12	10	1		7					9	2		6			5	8	4	11	3
30	13	Northampton Town	3-2	MacDougall 2 (1p), Boyer	8854			4	11	1		8			12		9	2		6			5	7	10		3
31	20	SOUTHPORT	0-1		10339				10	1	12	7					9	2		6			5	8	4	11	3
32	27	Lincoln City	2-1	Sainty, MacDougall (p)	4988			6	10	1	2	11					9	4		7			5		8		3
33	Mar 6	CHESTER	3-1	Boyer 2, MacDougall	8691			4	10	1		7					9	2		6			5		8	11	3
34	10	Workington	0-1		2398				10	1		8			4		9	2		6			5		7	11	3
35	13	Hartlepool	1-2	Sainty	2111				10	1				7	4		9	2		6			5		8	11	3
36	17	BARROW	0-0		6329				9	1				7	4		8	2		6			5		10	11	3
37	20	DARLINGTON	1-0	MacDougall	8455					1		12		7	4	8	9	2		6			5		10	11	3
38	26	Stockport County	1-1	MacDougall	1732				9	1				7	4		8	2		6			5	11	10		3
39	Apr 3	NEWPORT COUNTY	2-2	MacDougall 2	8295				9	1				7	4		8	2		6			5	10		11	3
40	9	SOUTHEND UNITED	4-0	Boyer 2, Powell, MacDougall	11330			10	9	1					4		8	2		6			5		7	11	3
41	10	Exeter City	0-0		7918			10	9	1	2			11	4		8			6			5		7		3
42	13	Cambridge United	2-0	Scott. MacDougall	6027				9	1				7	4		8	2		6			5	12	10	11	3
43	17	BRENTFORD	1-0	Miller	11206			2	9	1				7	4		8			6			5	11	10		3
44	23	Colchester United	1-1	MacDougall	4168			2	9	1				7	4		8			5			6		10	11	3
45	28	Peterborough United	1-3	MacDougall (p)	3312			6	9	1	2			7	4		8			3			5		10	11	
46	May 1	YORK CITY	4-0	MacDougall 2 (1p), Scott, Boyer	12627			6	9	1					4		8	2		10			5		7	11	3
					Apps	17	2	19	23	44	26	20	4	10	34	9	46	22	5	46	1	6	44	26	44	37	39
					Goals	3			11		1	1	1				42			1			1	9	5	4	

F.A. Cup

	Date	Opponent	Score	Scorers	Att	Allen DJ	Baker KR	Benson JH	Boyer PJ	Davies F	Gulliver TR	Hartley TJ	Hold JD	Holland PG	Jones DE	Longhorn D	MacDougall EJ	Machin M	Meredith JF	Miller KR	Miller RE	Naylor TV	Powell A	Rowles AEJ	Sainty JA	Scott AJE	Stocks DH
R1	Nov 21	Oxford City	1-1	MacDougall	1800			4		1	2				5	7	8			6			3	10	9	11	
rep	25	OXFORD CITY	8-1	MacDougall 6, Longhorn, Rowles	8448			4		1	2	12			5	7	8			6			3	10	9	11	
R2	Dec 12	YEOVIL TOWN	0-1		11583	12		4		1	2				5	10	9			6			3	11	8		

Played at 7 in R2: A Green

F.L. Cup

	Date	Opponent	Score	Scorers	Att	Allen DJ	Baker KR	Benson JH	Boyer PJ	Davies F	Gulliver TR	Hartley TJ	Hold JD	Holland PG	Jones DE	Longhorn D	MacDougall EJ	Machin M	Meredith JF	Miller KR	Miller RE	Naylor TV	Powell A	Rowles AEJ	Sainty JA	Scott AJE	Stocks DH
R1	Aug 19	Torquay United	1-1	Sainty	5647					1	2						8		10	6		4	5		9	11	3
rep	26	TORQUAY UNITED	1-2	Allen	8534	10				1	2						8		12	6		4	5		9	11	3

Played at 7 in both games: J White

		P	W	D	L	F	A	W	D	L	F	A	Pts
1	Notts County	46	19	4	0	59	12	11	5	7	30	24	69
2	BOURNEMOUTH	46	16	5	2	51	15	8	7	8	30	31	60
3	Oldham Athletic	46	14	6	3	57	29	10	5	8	31	34	59
4	York City	46	16	6	1	45	14	7	4	12	33	40	56
5	Chester	46	17	2	4	42	18	7	5	11	27	37	55
6	Colchester United	46	14	6	3	44	19	7	6	10	26	35	54
7	Northampton Town	46	15	4	4	39	24	4	9	10	24	35	51
8	Southport	46	15	2	6	42	24	6	4	13	21	33	48
9	Exeter City	46	12	7	4	40	23	5	7	11	27	45	48
10	Workington	46	13	7	3	28	13	5	5	13	20	36	48
11	Stockport County	46	12	8	3	28	17	4	6	13	21	48	46
12	Darlington	46	15	3	5	42	22	2	8	13	16	35	45
13	Aldershot	46	8	10	5	32	23	6	7	10	34	48	45
14	Brentford	46	13	3	7	45	27	5	5	13	21	35	44
15	Crewe Alexandra	46	13	1	9	49	35	5	7	11	26	41	44
16	Peterborough United	46	14	3	6	46	23	4	4	15	24	48	43
17	Scunthorpe United	46	9	7	7	36	23	6	6	11	20	38	43
18	Southend United	46	8	11	4	32	24	6	4	13	21	42	43
19	Grimsby Town	46	13	4	6	37	26	5	3	15	20	45	43
20	Cambridge United	46	9	9	5	31	27	6	4	13	20	39	43
21	Lincoln City	46	11	4	8	45	33	2	9	12	25	38	39
22	Newport County	46	8	3	12	32	36	2	5	16	23	49	28
23	Hartlepool	46	6	10	7	28	27	2	2	19	6	47	28
24	Barrow	46	5	5	13	25	38	2	3	18	26	52	22

1971/72

3rd in Division Three

No	Month	Day	Opponent	Res	Scorers	Att	Benson JH	Boyer PJ	Cave MJ	Chadwick DE	Davidson I	Davies F	De Garis JF	Gulliver TR	Howe RJ	Jones DE	Kitchener WH	Longhorn D	MacDougall EJ	Machin M	Miller KR	Mitchinson TW	Powell A	Sainty JA	Scott AJE	Stocks DH
1	Aug	14	SHREWSBURY TOWN	3-1	Miller, Boyer, MacDougall	11295	2	9	7		4	1					5		8		10		6	12	11	3
2		21	Bolton Wanderers	0-0		9276	2	9	7		10	1				4	5		8		11		6	12		3
3		28	ROTHERHAM UNITED	3-1	MacDougall, Cave, Sainty (p)	11876	11	9	7		12	1		2			5		8		10		6	4		3
4		31	BLACKBURN ROVERS	1-0	Cave	13280		9	7			1				4	5		8	2	10		6	11		3
5	Sep	4	Halifax Town	0-1		4778	2	9	7		12	1				4	5		8		10		6	11		3
6		11	ROCHDALE	4-1	Boyer, MacDougall 3 (1p)	8856	4	9	7			1				2	5	12	8		10		6	11		3
7		18	Wrexham	3-1	Miller, Cave, Boyer	6667	4	9	7			1				2	3	6	8		10		5	11		
8		25	CHESTERFIELD	1-0	MacDougall (p)	10681	4	9	7			1				2	3	12	8		10		5	11	6	
9		29	Notts County	1-1	MacDougall	13342	4	9	7			1				5	3		8	2	10		6	12	11	
10	Oct	2	Plymouth Argyle	1-1	Scott	14959	4	9	7			1				5	3		8	2	10		6		11	
11		9	SWANSEA CITY	2-1	Cave, Miller	12057	3	9	7			1				5			8	2	10		4	6	11	
12		15	Shrewsbury Town	2-3	MacDougall 2	6181	4	9	7			1				5	3	12	8	2	10		6	11		
13		19	PORT VALE	3-2	Boyer, MacDougall (p), Cave	10404		9	7		4	1				5	3		8	2	10		6		11	
14		23	ASTON VILLA	3-0	Boyer, MacDougall, Powell	20305	4	9	7			1				5	3		8	2	10		6		11	
15		29	Mansfield Town	5-0	Boyer, Jones, MacDougall 3	6622	4	9	7			1				5	3		8	2	10		6		11	
16	Nov	6	TORQUAY UNITED	1-0	MacDougall	13609	4	9	7		11	1				5	3		8	2	10		6			
17		13	Bradford City	2-2	MacDougall 2	5962	4	9	7			1	10			5	3		8	2	11		6			
18		27	Barnsley	0-0		8548	4	9	7			1	11			5	3		8	2	10		6			
19	Dec	4	YORK CITY	2-2	MacDougall 2	11244	4	9	7			1	12			5	3		8	2	10		6		11	
20		18	HALIFAX TOWN	3-1	Scott, Kitchener, Jones	10853	4	9	7			1	10			12	5		8	2	3		6		11	
21		27	Brighton & Hove Albion	0-2		30538	4	9	7			1	12			5	3		8	2	10		6		11	
22	Jan	1	WREXHAM	4-0	Powell, Boyer 3	12035		9	12			1				4	5		8	2	3	10	6	7	11	
23		8	Rotherham United	0-0		10208		9	12			1		2	7		5		8	6	3	10	4		11	
24		22	NOTTS COUNTY	2-0	Boyer, MacDougall	21154	4	9				1				6	5		8	2	3	10	7		11	
25		29	Port Vale	1-1	Howe	4937	4	9				1			11	5	3		8	2	10	7	6			
26	Feb	5	PLYMOUTH ARGYLE	1-0	MacDougall	13805	4	9				1			10	5			8	2	3	7	6		11	
27		12	Aston Villa	1-2	MacDougall	48110		9	12			1			10	5	4		8	2	3	7	6		11	
28		19	MANSFIELD TOWN	1-1	Machin	13417	12	9				1			10	5	3		8	2	6	7	4		11	
29		23	WALSALL	0-0		10016	12	9	11			1			7	4	3		8	2	5	10	6			
30		26	Torquay United	2-0	MacDougall 2	9805		9		7		1			6		3		8	2	5	10	4		11	
31	Mar	4	BRADFORD CITY	3-0	Chadwick, MacDougall, Mitchinson	12119	2	9		7		1			4	5	3		8		6	10			11	
32		8	BRISTOL ROVERS	2-0	Boyer, MacDougall	9132	11	9		7		1	12		4	5	3		8	2	6	10				
33		11	Swansea City	2-1	Boyer, Kitchener	7714	11	9		7	10	1		2	4	5	3		8		6					
34		14	Walsall	1-1	MacDougall	10819	4	9		7	10	1		2	11	5	3		8		6			12		
35		18	BOLTON WANDERERS	1-2	MacDougall	15113	2	9		7	10	1			4	5	3		8		6	12			11	
36		21	Oldham Athletic	1-3	Chadwick	7728	12	9		7		1		2	4	5	3		8		6	10			11	
37		25	Rochdale	1-1	MacDougall	4437	11	9		7		1			4	5	3		8	2	6	10				
38	Apr	1	BRIGHTON & HOVE ALB	1-1	MacDougall	22550	11	9		7		1			4	5			8	2	3	10	6			
39		5	Chesterfield	0-0		8546	4	9	12	7		1			11	5			8	2	3	10	6			
40		7	Tranmere Rovers	2-1	MacDougall 2	4504	4	9		12		1			7	5			8	2	3	10	6		11	
41		15	BARNSLEY	0-0		13976	4	9		7		1			11		5		8	2	3	10	6			
42		18	Bristol Rovers	2-1	Chadwick, Boyer	11372		9	11	7		1			3				8	2	6	10	5	4		
43		22	York City	2-0	MacDougall, Boyer	6917		9	11	7		1			4				8	2	3	10	5	6		
44		26	Blackburn Rovers	1-2	MacDougall	8941		9	11	7		1			3				8	2	6	10	5	4	12	
45		29	OLDHAM ATHLETIC	2-0	Boyer, MacDougall	9748		9	12	7		1			4				8	2	3	10	5	6	11	
46	May	3	TRANMERE ROVERS	0-0		11260		9	12	7		1			3				8	2	6	10	5	4	11	
						Apps	35	46	31	17	9	46	6	5	23	36	36	4	46	34	46	23	39	18	25	6
						Goals		15	5	3					1	2	2		35	1	3	1	2	1	2	

F.A. Cup

Rd	Month	Day	Opponent	Res	Scorers	Att	Benson JH	Boyer PJ	Cave MJ	Chadwick DE	Davidson I	Davies F	De Garis JF	Gulliver TR	Howe RJ	Jones DE	Kitchener WH	Longhorn D	MacDougall EJ	Machin M	Miller KR	Mitchinson TW	Powell A	Sainty JA	Scott AJE	Stocks DH
R1	Nov	20	MARGATE	11-0	MacDougall 9 (1p), Cave, Machin	12079	4	9	7			1	12			5	3		8	2	10		6		11	
R2	Dec	11	SOUTHEND UNITED	2-0	Boyer, MacDougall	14634	4	9	7			1	10				5		8	2	3		6		11	
R3	Jan	15	Walsall	0-1		9185	4	9	7			1	12	11		6	5		8	2	3		10			

F.L. Cup

Rd	Month	Day	Opponent	Res	Scorers	Att	Benson JH	Boyer PJ	Cave MJ	Chadwick DE	Davidson I	Davies F	De Garis JF	Gulliver TR	Howe RJ	Jones DE	Kitchener WH	Longhorn D	MacDougall EJ	Machin M	Miller KR	Mitchinson TW	Powell A	Sainty JA	Scott AJE	Stocks DH
R1	Aug	17	PORTSMOUTH	2-1	MacDougall 2	15382	2	9	7		4	1					5		8		10		6		11	3
R2	Sep	8	BLACKPOOL	0-2		15649	4	9	7			1				5	12		8	2	10		6	11		3

		P	W	D	L	F	A	W	D	L	F	A	Pts
1	Aston Villa	46	20	1	2	45	10	12	5	6	40	22	70
2	Brighton & Hove Albion	46	15	5	3	39	18	12	6	5	43	29	65
3	BOURNEMOUTH	46	16	6	1	43	13	7	10	6	30	24	62
4	Notts County	46	16	3	4	42	19	9	9	5	32	25	62
5	Rotherham United	46	12	8	3	46	25	8	7	8	23	27	55
6	Bristol Rovers	46	17	2	4	54	26	4	10	9	21	30	54
7	Bolton Wanderers	46	11	8	4	25	13	6	8	9	26	28	50
8	Plymouth Argyle	46	13	6	4	43	26	7	4	12	31	38	50
9	Walsall	46	12	8	3	38	16	3	10	10	24	41	48
10	Blackburn Rovers	46	14	4	5	39	22	5	5	13	15	35	47
11	Oldham Athletic	46	11	4	8	37	35	6	7	10	22	28	45
12	Shrewsbury Town	46	13	5	5	50	29	4	5	14	23	36	44
13	Chesterfield	46	10	5	8	25	23	8	3	12	32	34	44
14	Swansea City	46	10	6	7	27	21	7	4	12	19	38	44
15	Port Vale	46	10	10	3	27	21	3	5	15	16	38	41
16	Wrexham	46	10	5	8	33	26	6	3	14	26	37	40
17	Halifax Town	46	11	6	6	31	22	2	6	15	17	39	38
18	Rochdale	46	11	7	5	35	26	1	6	16	22	57	37
19	York City	46	8	8	7	32	22	4	4	15	25	44	36
20	Tranmere Rovers	46	9	7	7	34	30	1	9	13	16	41	36
21	Mansfield Town	46	5	12	6	19	26	3	8	12	22	37	36
22	Barnsley	46	6	10	7	23	30	3	8	12	9	34	36
23	Torquay United	46	8	6	9	31	31	2	6	15	10	38	32
24	Bradford City	46	6	8	9	27	32	5	2	16	18	45	32

1972/73

7th in Division Three

No.	Date	Opponent	Score	Scorers	Att.	Aimson PE	Baker KR	Benson JH	Boyer PJ	Cave MJ	Chadwick DE	Clark BD	Davies F	De Garis JF	Feely PJ	Gabriel J	Gibson IS	Goddard HJ	Groves AJ	Howe RJ	Jones DE	MacDougall EJ	Machin M	Miller KR	Mitchinson TW	Parsons JS	Powell A	Redknapp HJ	Sainty JA
1	Aug 12	Bolton Wanderers	0-3		7425				9	11	7		1			4				3	12	8	2	6	10		5		
2	19	CHESTERFIELD	2-2	Boyer, Sainty	12803			6	11	9			1			4				3	5	8	2				10		7
3	26	Watford	2-3	MacDougall 2	8373				9		12		1			6				3	5	8	2	4	10		11	7	
4	29	HALIFAX TOWN	1-0	Machin	11456				9				1			4				3	5	8	2	6	10		11	7	
5	Sep 2	SCUNTHORPE UNITED	1-1	MacDougall	10034			11	9		12		1							3	5	8	2	4	10		6	7	
6	9	York City	0-0		3509				9		7		1			4				3	5	8	2	6			11		10
7	16	SOUTHEND UNITED	2-0	Miller 2	10311				9	11	7		1			4				3	5	8	2	6					10
8	23	Brentford	1-1	MacDougall	11100				9	11			1			4				3	5	8	2	6	10		12	7	
9	26	PORT VALE	4-0	Cave 2, Redknapp, MacDougall	12145				9	11			1			4				3	5	8	2		10		6	7	12
10	30	SHREWSBURY TOWN	2-0	Miller, Boyer	10833				9	11			1			4				2	5			6	10		3	7	8
11	Oct 2	Wrexham	1-1	Cave	6586			2	9	11			1			4					5			6	10		3	7	8
12	7	TRANMERE ROVERS	1-1	Cave	12769				9	11		8	1			4	12			2	5			6	10		3	7	
13	10	Rotherham United	7-2	Clark 4, Groves 2, Cave	5309				9	6		8	1			4	10		11		5			2			3	7	
14	14	Notts County	2-0	Clark, Boyer	11914			6	9			8	1			4	10		11		5			2			3	7	
15	21	PLYMOUTH ARGYLE	0-1		14024				9	10		8	1			6	4		11		5			2			3	7	
16	24	ROCHDALE	4-2	Boyer 2, Machin, Gabriel	11741				9	10		8	1			6	4		11		5		2	3				7	
17	28	Grimsby Town	1-0	Groves	12552			5	9			8	1			6	4		11	3			2	10				7	
18	Nov 4	Port Vale	1-2	Clark	6414			4	9			8	1			5	10		11	2				6			3	7	
19	11	WREXHAM	1-0	Miller	11824				9			8	1			6	10		11	3			2	4			5	7	
20	25	CHARLTON ATHLETIC	3-1	Howe, Clark, Miller	12194				9			8	1			4	7		11	3	5		2	10			6		
21	Dec 2	Oldham Athletic	1-1	Clark	8206			12	9			8	1			4	7		11	3	5		2	10			6		
22	16	BRISTOL ROVERS	0-0		11767			5	9	12		8	1			4	7		11	6			2	10			3		
23	23	Walsall	0-1		4601			4	9	10		8	1						11	3			2	6			5	7	
24	26	BRENTFORD	3-2	Boyer, Groves, Clark	14372			4	9	6		8	1						11	3	12		2	10			5	7	
25	30	Chesterfield	1-1	Miller	7411			4	9	6		8	1			2			11	3				10			5	7	
26	Jan 6	WATFORD	3-0	Clark 2, Miller	11841				9	4		8	1			6			11	3			2	10			5	7	
27	20	Scunthorpe United	1-1	Clark	3635			6	9	10		8	1			4			11	3			2				5	7	
28	27	YORK CITY	2-3	Machin, Miller	11964				9	6		8	1			4	10		11	3			2	12			5	7	
29	29	Rochdale	0-1		3575			12		10		8	1			4	9		11	3			2	6			5	7	
30	Feb 3	ROTHERHAM UNITED	4-0	Boyer 2, Cave, Machin (p)	11216				9	6		8	1			4			11	3			2	10			5	7	12
31	9	Southend United	2-2	Cave, Machin	9677				9	10		8	1			4			11	3			2	6			5	7	
32	17	BOLTON WANDERERS	2-0	Boyer, Cave	18374				9	10		8	1			4			11	3	12		2	6			5	7	
33	24	Bristol Rovers	0-2		18567			12	9	10			1		8	4			11	3			2	6			5	7	
34	Mar 2	Tranmere Rovers	0-0		11262				9	11		8	1			4				3	5		2	10			6	7	
35	6	Swansea City	0-1		5390				9	11		8	1			4			12	3	5		2	10			6	7	
36	10	NOTTS COUNTY	1-1	Boyer	14830				9	10		8	1			4			11	3	12		2	6			5	7	
37	17	Plymouth Argyle	0-1		20104	10			9	7		12	1			4			11	6	5		2	8			3		
38	20	BLACKBURN ROVERS	3-0	Gabriel, Cave, Boyer	12839	8			9	10			1			4			11	3	5		2				6		7
39	24	GRIMSBY TOWN	1-1	Aimson	11393	8			9	10		12	1			4			11		6		2	3			5		7
40	31	Charlton Athletic	1-1	Gabriel	6541		1	5	9			8				4	11			3			2	10			6	7	
41	Apr 7	OLDHAM ATHLETIC	2-0	Edwards (og), Boyer	14130	12	1	5	9			8				4	7		11	3			2	10			6		
42	14	Blackburn Rovers	1-2	Miller	15114	10	1	5	9			8		7		4				3			2	11			6	12	
43	20	WALSALL	0-1		10736	8	1	6	9							4			11	3	5		2	10				7	
44	21	SWANSEA CITY	2-0	Gabriel, Aimson	8579	8	1	6	9		10					4			11	3	5		2			12			7
45	24	Shrewsbury Town	0-0		3457	10	1	6	9		4				8				11	2	5						3	7	
46	28	Halifax Town	0-2		3380	12	1		9		8			10		4		11		2	5			6			3	7	
					Apps	9	7	20	45	29	8	29	39	2	2	42	15	1	30	40	30	9	36	40	9	1	41	34	10
					Goals	2			12	9		12				4			4	1		5	5	9				1	1

One own goal

F.A. Cup

Rd	Date	Opponent	Score	Scorers	Att.	Aimson PE	Baker KR	Benson JH	Boyer PJ	Cave MJ	Chadwick DE	Clark BD	Davies F	De Garis JF	Feely PJ	Gabriel J	Gibson IS	Goddard HJ	Groves AJ	Howe RJ	Jones DE	MacDougall EJ	Machin M	Miller KR	Mitchinson TW	Parsons JS	Powell A	Redknapp HJ	Sainty JA
R1	Nov 18	CAMBRIDGE UNITED	5-1	Clark 2, Gibson, Groves, Boyer	10034				9			8	1			4	7		11	3	5		2	10			6		
R2	Dec 9	COLCHESTER UNITED	0-0		11164				9			8	1			4	7		11	6	5		2	10			3		
R2	11	Colchester United	2-0	Clark, Boyer	7419			5	9	7		8	1			4			11	6			2	10			3		
R3	Jan 13	Newcastle United	0-2		33920			5	9	4		8	1			6	12		11	3			2	10				7	

F.L. Cup

Rd	Date	Opponent	Score	Scorers	Att.	Aimson PE	Baker KR	Benson JH	Boyer PJ	Cave MJ	Chadwick DE	Clark BD	Davies F	De Garis JF	Feely PJ	Gabriel J	Gibson IS	Goddard HJ	Groves AJ	Howe RJ	Jones DE	MacDougall EJ	Machin M	Miller KR	Mitchinson TW	Parsons JS	Powell A	Redknapp HJ	Sainty JA
R1	Aug 15	Plymouth Argyle	2-0	MacDougall 2	12523			2	9	12			1			6				3	5	8	4		10		11		7
R2	Sep 6	BLACKPOOL	0-0		10577				9	11	7		1			4				3		8	2	6			5		10
rep	11	Blackpool	1-1	(aet) Powell	8685			12	9				1			4				3	5	8	2	11			6	7	10
rep2	18	Blackpool	1-2	(aet) Barton (og)	2337			12	9				1			4				3	5	8	2	11			6	7	10

Replay 2 at Villa Park

Played at 12 in R2: WH Kitchener

		P	W	D	L	F	A	W	D	L	F	A	Pts
1	Bolton Wanderers	46	18	4	1	44	9	7	7	9	29	30	61
2	Notts County	46	17	4	2	40	12	6	7	10	27	35	57
3	Blackburn Rovers	46	12	8	3	34	16	8	7	8	23	31	55
4	Oldham Athletic	46	12	7	4	40	18	7	9	7	32	36	54
5	Bristol Rovers	46	17	4	2	55	20	3	9	11	22	36	53
6	Port Vale	46	15	6	2	41	21	6	5	12	15	48	53
7	BOURNEMOUTH	46	14	6	3	44	16	3	10	10	22	28	50
8	Plymouth Argyle	46	14	3	6	43	26	6	7	10	31	40	50
9	Grimsby Town	46	16	2	5	45	18	4	6	13	22	43	48
10	Tranmere Rovers	46	12	8	3	38	17	3	8	12	18	35	46
11	Charlton Athletic	46	12	7	4	46	24	5	4	14	23	43	45
12	Wrexham	46	11	9	3	39	23	3	8	12	16	31	45
13	Rochdale	46	8	8	7	22	26	6	9	8	26	28	45
14	Southend United	46	13	6	4	40	14	4	4	15	21	40	44
15	Shrewsbury Town	46	10	10	3	31	21	5	4	14	15	33	44
16	Chesterfield	46	13	4	6	37	22	4	5	14	20	39	43
17	Walsall	46	14	3	6	37	26	4	4	15	19	40	43
18	York City	46	8	10	5	24	14	5	5	13	18	32	41
19	Watford	46	11	8	4	32	23	1	9	13	11	25	41
20	Halifax Town	46	9	8	6	29	23	4	7	12	14	30	41
21	Rotherham United	46	12	4	7	34	27	5	3	15	17	38	41
22	Brentford	46	12	5	6	33	18	3	2	18	18	51	37
23	Swansea City	46	11	5	7	37	29	3	4	16	14	44	37
24	Scunthorpe United	46	8	7	8	18	25	2	3	18	15	47	30

1973/74

11th in Division Three

							Baker KR	Benson JH	Boyer PJ	Buttle SA	Cave MJ	Chadwick DE	Davies F	De Garis JF	Delaney JJ	Feely PJ	Gabriel J	Gibson IS	Goddard HJ	Greenhalgh BA	Groves AJ	Howe RJ	Jones DE	Machin M	Miller KR	O'Rourke J	Parodi LV	Payne CE	Powell A	Redknapp HJ	Sainty JA	Welsh A
1	Aug	25	BRISTOL ROVERS	0-3		11428	1	5	9		7				6		4				11	2			3				10			
2	Sep	1	Brighton & Hove Albion	2-0	Howe, Feely	9819		4		11	8		1	10		9	6					3		2					5	7		
3		8	CHESTERFIELD	0-1		8670		4	12	11	9		1	10		8	6					3		2					5	7		
4		12	ALDERSHOT	3-0	Redknapp 2, Sainty	8248		4	10	11	8		1									3	5	2					6	7	9	
5		15	Walsall	2-1	Boyer 2	5220		4	8	11	10		1									3	5	2					6	7	9	
6		17	Rochdale	3-3	Boyer, Machin, Cave	2108		4	10	11	8		1									3	5	2					6	7	9	
7		22	TRANMERE ROVERS	2-1	Sainty, Redknapp	10011	1	4	10	11	8											3	5	2					6	7	9	
8		29	Huddersfield Town	1-1	Sainty	5360	1	4	8	11	10	12										3	5	2					6	7	9	
9	Oct	3	ROCHDALE	2-0	Jones, Powell	8836	1	4	10	11	8	12										3	5	2					6	7	9	
10		6	SOUTHPORT	2-0	Buttle, Cave	9775	1	4	8	11	10											3	5	2					6	7	9	
11		13	Shrewsbury Town	1-1	Jones	2377	1	4	8	11	10											3	5	2					6	7	9	
12		20	Port Vale	0-0		4006	1	4	10	11	8											3	5	2					6	7	9	
13		24	Aldershot	3-1	Sainty 3	5949	1	4	8	11	10										12	3	5	2					6	7	9	
14		27	WATFORD	1-0	Sainty	11422	1	4	8	11	6										10	2	5						3	7	9	
15	Nov	3	Halifax Town	1-1	Howe	2351	1	4	10	11		8		12								3	5	2					6	7	9	
16		10	BLACKBURN ROVERS	1-2	Boyer	10559	1	4	10	11		8										3	5	2					6	7	9	
17		14	CHARLTON ATHLETIC	1-0	Jones	8395	1	4	10	11		8										3	5	2					6	7	9	
18		17	Grimsby Town	1-1	Powell	8381	1	4	10	11	8											3	5	2					6	7	9	
19	Dec	1	Wrexham	1-0	Boyer	4092	1		10	11	8											3	5	2	4				6	7	9	
20		8	CAMBRIDGE UNITED	1-0	Sainty (p)	8582	1		10	11	8											3	5	2	4				6	7	9	
21		22	HUDDERSFIELD T	1-0	Boyer	9141	1		10	11	8						4					3	5					2	6	7	9	
22		26	Hereford United	2-0	Sainty, Boyer	10909	1		10	11	8						4				12	3	5					2	6	7	9	
23		29	Chesterfield	1-2	Redknapp	6996	1		10	11							4	8			12	3	5					2	6	7	9	
24	Jan	1	BRIGHTON & HOVE ALB	0-0		17079	1			11						10	4	8				3	5					2	6	7	9	
25		12	WALSALL	1-0	Boyer	8647	1		10	11	8						4	12				3	5					2	6	7	9	
26		19	Bristol Rovers	0-3		21354	1		10	11	8						4					3	5					2	6	7	9	
27		25	SOUTHEND UNITED	1-3	Howe	9676	1		10	11	8						4	12				3	5					2	6	7	9	
28	Feb	2	OLDHAM ATHLETIC	0-3		9571	1		10					11			4	8			12	2	5			9		3	6	7		
29		10	Tranmere Rovers	1-1	O'Rourke	3400	1			11	8									9		3	5			10	12	2	6	7	4	
30		16	SHREWSBURY TOWN	1-0	Howe	8690	1			12	8									9		3	5			10		2	6	7	4	11
31		24	Southport	0-1		2719	1			12	8									9		3	5		7	10		2	6		4	11
32	Mar	2	HEREFORD UNITED	3-2	Sainty(p), Chadwick, Greenhalgh	8370	1			11		12								8		3	5		10			2	6	7	4	9
33		6	York City	1-4	Greenhalgh	10652	1			11	12	10								9			5		3			2	6	7	4	8
34		9	Watford	1-1	Greenhalgh	7616	1				10				5					9		3			11			2	6	7	4	8
35		16	PORT VALE	2-2	Sainty, Greenhalgh	7968	1				8	10			5					9					3			2	6	7	4	11
36		19	Oldham Athletic	2-4	Powell, Sainty (p)	13957	1				10	12								9					5		3	2	6	7	4	8
37		23	Blackburn Rovers	3-4	Greenhalgh, Sainty, Welsh	5929	1				10				5	12				9			4				3	2	6	7	11	8
38		27	YORK CITY	1-3	Welsh	7404	1				10	11								9			5				3	2	6	7	4	8
39	Apr	1	Southend United	2-2	Feely, Greenhalgh	6618					10				5	11				9					7		3	2	6			8
40		6	Charlton Athletic	0-0		3984					10				5	11				9					4		3	2	6	7		8
41		12	PLYMOUTH ARGYLE	0-0		7792				12	10	7			5	11									4		3	2	6		9	8
42		13	GRIMSBY TOWN	1-1	Parsons	6233				11	8				5							3			4			2	6	7		10
43		15	Plymouth Argyle	0-2		9431				3	10				5										4		12	2	6	7	9	8
44		20	Cambridge United	1-2	Cave	3398					7				5				9	10		4				11	3	2	6			8
45		24	HALIFAX TOWN	1-1	Goddard	4475					10								7	9		4	5		3	11		2	6			8
46		27	WREXHAM	0-1		5589				8	7								9	10		4	5		3	11		2	6			
						Apps	33	18	26	35	39	11	5	4	10	7	11	5	3	15	6	37	34	18	16	7	9	26	46	39	36	16
						Goals			8	1	3	1				2			1	6		4	3	1		1			3	4	13	2

BD Clark played in game 1 at 8. JS Parsons played in game 42 at 9 and 43 at 11.
GA Jones played in games 45 and 46 at 12
KP Charlton played in 8 games (39 to 46) at 1
JT Rutter played in games 34, 35 at 12, 36 at 11 (subbed) and 39 at 4

F.A. Cup

							Baker KR	Benson JH	Boyer PJ	Buttle SA	Cave MJ	Chadwick DE	Davies F	De Garis JF	Delaney JJ	Feely PJ	Gabriel J	Gibson IS	Goddard HJ	Greenhalgh BA	Groves AJ	Howe RJ	Jones DE	Machin M	Miller KR	O'Rourke J	Parodi LV	Payne CE	Powell A	Redknapp HJ	Sainty JA	Welsh A
R1	Nov	24	CHARLTON ATHLETIC	1-0	Boyer	9352	1	4	10	11	8											3	5	2					6	7	9	
R2	Dec	15	Watford	1-0	Cave	5844	1		10	11	8						4					2	5		3				6	7	9	
R3	Jan	5	Orient	1-2	Powell	9589	1			11						10	4	8				3	5					2	6	7	9	

F.L. Cup

							Baker KR	Benson JH	Boyer PJ	Buttle SA	Cave MJ	Chadwick DE	Davies F	De Garis JF	Delaney JJ	Feely PJ	Gabriel J	Gibson IS	Goddard HJ	Greenhalgh BA	Groves AJ	Howe RJ	Jones DE	Machin M	Miller KR	O'Rourke J	Parodi LV	Payne CE	Powell A	Redknapp HJ	Sainty JA	Welsh A
R1	Aug	29	BRISTOL ROVERS	1-0	Redknapp	7520	1	4		11	9			12	5	8	6					3		2					10	7		
R2	Oct	10	SHEFFIELD WEDNESDAY	0-0		11017	1	4	10	11	8											3	5	2	12				6	7	9	
rep		15	Sheffield Wednesday	2-2	(aet) Sainty (p), Springett (og)	5883	1	4	10	11	8											3	5	2					6	7	9	
rep2		29	Sheffield Wednesday	1-2	(aet) Sainty	8894	1	4	10	11	8											2	5				3		6	7	9	

		P	W	D	L	F	A	W	D	L	F	A	Pts
1	Oldham Athletic	46	13	6	4	50	23	12	6	5	33	24	62
2	Bristol Rovers	46	15	6	2	37	15	7	11	5	28	18	61
3	York City	46	13	8	2	37	15	8	11	4	30	23	61
4	Wrexham	46	15	6	2	44	15	7	6	10	19	28	56
5	Chesterfield	46	14	6	3	31	16	7	8	8	24	26	56
6	Grimsby Town	46	14	6	3	48	21	4	9	10	19	29	51
7	Watford	46	12	6	5	34	21	7	6	10	30	35	50
8	Aldershot	46	13	6	4	47	22	6	5	12	18	30	49
9	Halifax Town	46	9	11	3	23	15	5	10	8	25	36	49
10	Huddersfield Town	46	14	5	4	37	16	3	8	12	19	39	47
11	BOURNEMOUTH	46	11	5	7	25	23	5	10	8	29	35	47
12	Southend United	46	10	7	6	40	30	6	7	10	22	32	46
13	Blackburn Rovers	46	13	4	6	38	21	5	6	12	24	43	46
14	Charlton Athletic	46	13	5	5	43	29	6	3	14	23	44	46
15	Walsall	46	11	7	5	37	19	5	6	12	20	29	45
16	Tranmere Rovers	46	10	8	5	31	15	5	7	11	19	29	45
17	Plymouth Argyle	46	13	6	4	37	17	4	4	15	22	37	44
18	Hereford United	46	10	5	8	31	25	4	10	9	22	32	43
19	Brighton & Hove Albion	46	10	3	10	31	31	6	8	9	21	27	43
20	Port Vale	46	12	6	5	37	23	2	8	13	15	35	42
21	Cambridge United	46	11	7	5	36	27	2	2	19	12	54	35
22	Shrewsbury Town	46	7	7	9	24	24	3	4	16	17	38	31
23	Southport	46	4	14	5	19	20	2	2	19	16	62	28
24	Rochdale	46	1	12	10	24	38	1	5	17	14	56	21

1974/75

21st in Division Three: Relegated

No	Date	Opponent	Res	Scorers	Att	Baker KR	Benson JH	Buttle SA	Charlton KP	Delaney JJ	Falconer H	Goddard HJ	Greenhalgh BA	Hague N	Howard TE	Jones GA	Livermore DE	Merrick NG	Miller KR	Morgan SE	Nightingale MBD	O'Rourke J	Parodi LV	Parsons JS	Payne CE	Redknapp HJ	Rickard DBP	Rudge JR	Talkes WN	Welsh A	Wingate J
1	Aug 17	Tranmere Rovers	1-0	Wingate	3141	1		11		5		4		6	10				3		7		12		2		8				9
2	24	GILLINGHAM	2-0	Miller, Buttle	7252	1		11		5		4		6	10				8		7		3		2						9
3	31	Colchester United	0-1		4930	1		11		5		4		6	10				8		7		3		2						9
4	Sep 7	SOUTHEND UNITED	0-0		6582			11	1	5		4		6	10				8		7		3		2						9
5	14	Hereford United	1-0	Howard	7238	1		11		5		4		6	10				8		7		3		2						9
6	21	BRIGHTON & HOVE ALB	2-0	Wingate, Howard	7951	1		11		5				6	10				8		7		3		2		4				9
7	28	Preston North End	2-5	Buttle, Hague	10421	1		11		5				6	10			12	8		7		3		2		4				9
8	Oct 2	WREXHAM	0-2		5457	1		11		5				6	10	12			8		7		3		2		4				9
9	5	Blackburn Rovers	0-1		10671	1		11			12	4		6	10			5			7		3		2				8		9
10	12	CRYSTAL PALACE	4-0	Howard (p), Goddard 2, Payne	10307	1		11				4			10			5	6				3	7	2				8		9
11	16	Chesterfield	0-0		3257	1		11				4			10			5	6				3	7	2				8		9
12	19	Watford	0-1		7361	1		11				4			10			5	6		12		3	7	2				8		9
13	23	GRIMSBY TOWN	0-1		5088				1	5		4		6	10				11				3	7	2		12		8		9
14	26	CHARLTON ATHLETIC	1-2	Miller	6585			11	1			4		6	10			5	8		12		3		2		7				9
15	Nov 2	PORT VALE	1-2	Parodi	5143	1		11					10	6	4	7		5	8				3		2					12	9
16	9	Walsall	0-2		4219			11	1	5			10	4	8				6			7	3		2						9
17	16	BURY	2-1	Hague, O'Rourke	4977				1	5		8	9	6	4				10			11	3		2					7	
18	30	ALDERSHOT	1-0	Welsh	5210				1	5		9	10	6	4				3			7	11		2					8	12
19	Dec 3	Huddersfield Town	2-2	Greenhalgh, Goddard	3804				1	5		9	10	6	4				3			7	11		2					8	
20	7	Plymouth Argyle	0-1		9984				1	4		9	10	5	6				3			8	11		2					7	
21	21	Halifax Town	2-3	Payne, Downes (og)	1523			11	1		3	9		2	4			5	7						8		12				10
22	26	HEREFORD UNITED	2-1	O'Rourke, Buttle	5803			11	1		2			6	4			5	7		12	10	3							8	9
23	28	Swindon Town	1-2	Hague	10129			11	1		2	9		6	4			5			12	10	3							7	8
24	Jan 4	HUDDERSFIELD T	1-1	O'Rourke	5078			11	1		2	9		6	4			5				10	3							7	8
25	11	PLYMOUTH ARGYLE	3-7	Wingate, Green (og), Howard	7352			11	1			8	12	6	4			5	7			10	3		2						9
26	18	Aldershot	2-1	Howard, Goddard	4256	1		11			12	9		6	4			5				10	3		2	7					8
27	Feb 1	WALSALL	0-1		6075	1	5	11				9		6	4							10	3		2	7					8
28	8	Port Vale	0-0		3710	1	6	11			12	9		5	4							10	3		2	7					8
29	22	Bury	0-1		4410	1	5	11						6	4				3			10	12		2	7				9	8
30	25	CHESTERFIELD	0-0		4116	1	6	11						5					3			10			2	7	4			8	9
31	Mar 1	COLCHESTER UNITED	0-2		4678	1	6	11					10	5								12	3		2	7	4			8	9
32	8	Grimsby Town	0-0		5962	1	5	11					8	6	4								3		2	7		9		10	
33	15	PRESTON NORTH END	1-0	Parodi	7337	1	4	11						6	8					5			3		2	7		9		10	
34	18	TRANMERE ROVERS	0-0		4246	1	4	11						6	10					5			3		2	7		9		8	12
35	21	Southend United	0-0		4466	1		11						6	10				4	5			3		2	7	12			8	9
36	26	Brighton & Hove Albion	1-2	Howard	10279	1								4	6				11	5			3		2	7	10	9		8	12
37	29	HALIFAX TOWN	0-1		5247	1		11						6	4		8		3	5					2	7	10	9		12	
38	31	SWINDON TOWN	1-1	Howard (p)	6216	1		11				12		6	10		8		4	5			3		2	7	9				
39	Apr 5	Charlton Athletic	3-2	Miller, Rickard, Howard (p)	9603	1		11						6	8		10		4	5			3		2	7	9				
40	7	Wrexham	1-1	Buttle	2669	1		11				12		6	10		8		4	5			3		2	7	9				
41	12	BLACKBURN ROVERS	0-0		7282	1		11				9		6	10		4		8	5			3		2	7					
42	16	Peterborough United	0-3		4580	1		11						6	10		8		4	5			3		2	7		9			
43	19	Crystal Palace	1-4	Buttle	12835	1		11						6	10		8		4	5			3		2	7	12	9			
44	23	Gillingham	0-1		5725	1	3	11						6	10		8	12	4	5					2	7				9	
45	26	WATFORD	4-2	Howard,Rickard,How(og),Buttle	4867	1		11		5				6	10		8		3						2		7			9	4
46	May 5	PETERBOROUGH UTD.	2-1	Rickard 2	4869	1	3	11						6	10		8	5	9						2		7				4
					Apps	33	10	40	13	15	7	25	9	43	44	2	10	15	36	12	13	15	40	4	43	19	18	7	5	19	33
					Goals			6				4	1	3	9				3			3	2		2		4			1	3

I Cunningham played in game 21 at 6.
KP Reeves played in game 46 at 12

Three own goals

F.A. Cup

Rd	Date	Opponent	Res	Scorers	Att	Baker KR	Benson JH	Buttle SA	Charlton KP	Delaney JJ	Falconer H	Goddard HJ	Greenhalgh BA	Hague N	Howard TE	Jones GA	Livermore DE	Merrick NG	Miller KR	Morgan SE	Nightingale MBD	O'Rourke J	Parodi LV	Parsons JS	Payne CE	Redknapp HJ	Rickard DBP	Rudge JR	Talkes WN	Welsh A	Wingate J
R1	Nov 23	SOUTHWICK	5-0	Goddard 3,Greenhalgh,Hague	5443				1	5		9	10	6	4				3			7	11		2					8	
R2	Dec 14	Wycombe Wanderers	0-0		7400				1	5		9	10	6	4				3				11		2					8	7
rep	18	WYCOMBE WANDERERS	1-2	Goddard	5407			11	1			9	10	6	4			5	7				3		2					8	12

F.L. Cup

Rd	Date	Opponent	Res	Scorers	Att	Baker KR	Benson JH	Buttle SA	Charlton KP	Delaney JJ	Falconer H	Goddard HJ	Greenhalgh BA	Hague N	Howard TE	Jones GA	Livermore DE	Merrick NG	Miller KR	Morgan SE	Nightingale MBD	O'Rourke J	Parodi LV	Parsons JS	Payne CE	Redknapp HJ	Rickard DBP	Rudge JR	Talkes WN	Welsh A	Wingate J
R1	Aug 21	Gillingham	1-1	Goddard	6465	1		11		5		4		6	10				8		7		3		2						9
rep	28	GILLINGHAM	1-1	(aet) Goddard	5774	1		11		5		4		6	10				8		7		3		2				12		9
rep2	Sep 3	Gillingham	2-1	(aet) Goddard, Howard	1570			11	1	5		4		6	10				8		7		3		2						9
R2	11	HARTLEPOOL UNITED	1-1	Delaney	4971			11	1	5		4		6	10				8		7		3	12	2						9
rep	18	Hartlepool United	2-2	(aet) Rickard, Delaney	5160	1		11		5		4		6	10				8				3		2		7				9
rep2	23	HARTLEPOOL UNITED	1-1	(aet) Delaney	4498	1		11		5				6	10	12			8		7		3		2		4				9
rep3	26	Hartlepool United	0-1		6970	1		11				4		6		7		5					3		2		12		10	8	9

R1 replay 2 at Brentford

		P	W	D	L	F	A	W	D	L	F	A	Pts
1	Blackburn Rovers	46	15	7	1	40	16	7	9	7	28	29	60
2	Plymouth Argyle	46	16	5	2	38	19	8	6	9	41	39	59
3	Charlton Athletic	46	15	5	3	51	29	7	6	10	25	32	55
4	Swindon Town	46	18	3	2	43	17	3	8	12	21	41	53
5	Crystal Palace	46	14	8	1	48	22	4	7	12	18	35	51
6	Port Vale	46	15	6	2	37	19	3	9	11	24	35	51
7	Peterborough United	46	10	9	4	24	17	9	3	11	23	36	50
8	Walsall	46	15	5	3	46	13	3	8	12	21	39	49
9	Preston North End	46	16	5	2	42	19	3	6	14	21	37	49
10	Gillingham	46	14	6	3	43	23	3	8	12	22	37	48
11	Colchester United	46	13	7	3	45	22	4	6	13	25	41	47
12	Hereford United	46	14	6	3	42	21	2	8	13	22	45	46
13	Wrexham	46	10	8	5	41	23	5	7	11	24	32	45
14	Bury	46	13	6	4	38	17	3	6	14	15	33	44
15	Chesterfield	46	11	7	5	37	25	5	5	13	25	41	44
16	Grimsby Town	46	12	8	3	35	19	3	5	15	20	45	43
17	Halifax Town	46	11	10	2	33	20	2	7	14	16	45	43
18	Southend United	46	11	9	3	32	17	2	7	14	14	34	42
19	Brighton & Hove Albion	46	14	7	2	38	21	2	3	18	18	43	42
20	Aldershot	46	13	5	5	40	21	1	6	16	13	42	38
21	BOURNEMOUTH	46	9	6	8	27	25	4	6	13	17	33	38
22	Tranmere Rovers	46	12	4	7	39	21	2	5	16	16	36	37
23	Watford	46	9	7	7	30	31	1	10	12	22	44	37
24	Huddersfield Town	46	9	6	8	32	29	2	4	17	15	47	32

1975/76

6th in Division Four

#	Month	Day	Opponent	Score	Scorers	Att	Ashworth PA	Baker KR	Benson JH	Best D	Butler G	Buttle SA	Chalk SR	Cunningham I	Goddard HJ	Grapes SP	Hague N	Howard TE	Impey JE	Miller KR	Morgan SE	Nightingale MBD	Payne CE	Redknapp HJ	Reeves KP	Rickard DBP	Russo G	Steele WM
1	Aug	16	Hartlepool	1-1	Goddard	2228		1	3					7	9		6	8			5	11	4			10	2	
2		23	DARLINGTON	1-2	Goddard	4298		1	3			11		12	9		6	4		8	5	7	2			10		
3		30	Bradford City	1-0	Goddard	2210		1	3			11			9		6			4	5	8	2	7		10		
4	Sep	6	DONCASTER ROVERS	0-1		3511		1				11			9		6	4		3	5	10	2	7	12	8		
5		12	Stockport County	0-0		3605		1				11			9		6	4		3	5	10	2	7	8	12		
6		20	NEWPORT COUNTY	2-0	Morgan, Reeves	3993	10	1				11		2	9		6	4		3	5	7			8			
7		24	BRENTFORD	3-0	Hague, Reeves, Goddard	4113	10	1				11			9		6	4		3	5	7	2		8			
8		27	Reading	1-2	Reeves	7423	10	1				11			9		6	4		3	5	7	2		8			
9	Oct	4	BARNSLEY	1-1	Nightingale (p)	4408	10	1				11		12	9		6	4		3	5	7	2		8			
10		10	Southport	2-0	Nightingale (p), Goddard	1044	10	1				11			9		6	4		3	5	7	2		8			
11		18	TRANMERE ROVERS	4-2	Nightingale (p), Goddard 2, Hague	5226	10	1				11		12	9		6	4		3	5	7	2		8			
12		22	ROCHDALE	2-1	Cunningham, Morgan	4395	10	1				11		12	9		6	4		3	5	7	2		8			
13		25	Lincoln City	0-1		7431	10	1	9			11		12			6	4		3	5	7	2		8			
14	Nov	1	CAMBRIDGE UNITED	3-0	Ashworth, Nightingale, Reeves	4863	10	1				11		9			6	4		3	5	7	2	12	8			
15		5	Crewe Alexandra	0-1		2081	10	1				11			9		6	4		3	5	7	2		8			
16		8	Watford	1-1	Goddard	4714	10	1				11			9		5	4	6	3		7	2		8			
17		15	SCUNTHORPE UNITED	1-0	Reeves	4333	10			1		11			9		5	4		3	6	7	2		8			
18		29	NORTHAMPTON T	0-0		5891	10	1				11			9		6	4	5	3		7	2		8			
19	Dec	6	Workington	3-1	Hague, Goddard, Rickard	1219	10	1				11			9		6	4		3	5	7	2	8		12		
20		20	HUDDERSFIELD T	1-0	Goddard	4012	10	1				11			9		6	4		3	5	7	2		8			
21		27	SWANSEA CITY	2-0	Buttle, Ashworth	6714	10	1				11			9		6	4		3	5	7	2	12	8			
22		30	Torquay United	1-2	Howard	3463	10	1				11			9		6	4	2	3	5	7			8			
23	Jan	2	Exeter City	0-1		3031	10	1	2			11			9		6	4		3	5	7		12	8			
24		10	BRADFORD CITY	2-1	Buttle, Reeves	4553	9	1				11					6	4		3	5	8	2	7	10			
25		17	Newport County	1-3	Payne	1473	10	1				11		7			6	4		3	5		2	12	9			8
26		24	STOCKPORT COUNTY	2-0	Steele, Howard	3927	10			1		11		7			6	4		3	5		2		9			8
27	Feb	7	CREWE ALEXANDRA	1-0	Morgan	3933	10	1				11		2	7		6	4		3	5				9			8
28		10	Rochdale	2-2	Reeves, Hague	1392		1				11		7	10		6	4		3	5		2		9	12		8
29		14	WATFORD	4-1	Goddard, Buttle, Steele (p), Reeves	4897		1				11		7	10		6	4		3	5		2		9			8
30		21	Scunthorpe United	0-2		2209		1				11		6	9		5	4		3	7		2		10	12		8
31		23	Brentford	2-1	Goddard, Reeves	4585	12	1				11		7	10		6			3	5		2		9	4		8
32	Mar	6	Cambridge United	1-0	Rickard	2066		1				11		7	10		6	8		3	5		2		9	4		
33		9	Barnsley	0-2		2674		1				11		7	10		6	4	5	3			2		9	8		
34		13	SOUTHPORT	3-3	Reeves, Goddard, Miller	4433		1			3				9	7	4	6	5	11		12	2		10	8		
35		15	Tranmere Rovers	0-2		3660		1			3				10	11	6	2		8	5	7	4		9			
36		20	Northampton Town	0-6		6780		1			3	11			9	7	6	4		10	5		2		8			
37		27	WORKINGTON	1-0	Buttle	3524		1			2	11		10	9	7	6			3	5	4			8			
38		30	Huddersfield Town	0-0		5834		1	10		2	11		4		7	6			3	5	8			9			
39	Apr	3	HARTLEPOOL	4-2	Morgan 2, Reeves, Grapes	3102	9	1			3	11		2		7	6	4			5	10			8			
40		7	READING	0-1		5372	10	1			3	11		2		7	6	4	12		5	8			9			
41		10	Doncaster Rovers	1-1	Reeves	4097	10				2	11	1	8			6	4		3	5	7			9			
42		16	EXETER CITY	1-0	Cunningham	4638	10	1			2	11		7			6	4		3	5	8			9			
43		17	TORQUAY UNITED	0-0		4180	10	1			2	11		4			6	8	12	3	5	7			9			
44		20	Swansea City	1-1	Reeves	2354	10	1			2			7	11		6	4		3	5	8			9	12		
45		24	Darlington	0-2		2249	11	1			2			7	10		6	4	5	3		8			9	12		
46		26	LINCOLN CITY	1-1	Reeves	4284	10	1			2			7	11		6	4	5	3		8			9			
						Apps	31	43	6	2	13	40	1	27	35	7	46	42	9	43	40	36	32	9	42	14	1	7
						Goals	2					4		2	13	1	4	2		1	5	4	1		14	2		2

F.A. Cup

Rd	Month	Day	Opponent	Score	Scorers	Att	Ashworth PA	Baker KR	Benson JH	Best D	Butler G	Buttle SA	Chalk SR	Cunningham I	Goddard HJ	Grapes SP	Hague N	Howard TE	Impey JE	Miller KR	Morgan SE	Nightingale MBD	Payne CE	Redknapp HJ	Reeves KP	Rickard DBP	Russo G	Steele WM
R1	Nov	22	Sutton United	1-1	Ashworth	2921	10	1				11			9		6	4		3	5	7	2		8			
rep		26	SUTTON UNITED	1-0	Ashworth	4109	10	1				11			9		6	4	5	3		7	2		8			
R2	Dec	13	HEREFORD UNITED	2-2	Ashworth, Goddard	6181	10	1				11			9		6	4		3	5	7	2	8				
rep		17	Hereford United	0-2		6351	10	1	2			11		5	9			4	6	3		7		8	12			

F.L. Cup

Rd	Month	Day	Opponent	Score	Scorers	Att	Ashworth PA	Baker KR	Benson JH	Best D	Butler G	Buttle SA	Chalk SR	Cunningham I	Goddard HJ	Grapes SP	Hague N	Howard TE	Impey JE	Miller KR	Morgan SE	Nightingale MBD	Payne CE	Redknapp HJ	Reeves KP	Rickard DBP	Russo G	Steele WM
R1/1	Aug	19	Plymouth Argyle	0-2		10849		1	4					11	9		6	8			5	7	2			10	3	
R1/2		26	PLYMOUTH ARGYLE	1-2	Rickard	3203		1	4			11			9		6			3	5	10	2	7	12	8		

		P	W	D	L	F	A	W	D	L	F	A	Pts
1	Lincoln City	46	21	2	0	71	15	11	8	4	40	24	74
2	Northampton Town	46	18	5	0	62	20	11	5	7	25	20	68
3	Reading	46	19	3	1	42	9	5	9	9	28	42	60
4	Tranmere Rovers	46	18	3	2	61	16	6	7	10	28	39	58
5	Huddersfield Town	46	11	6	6	28	17	10	8	5	28	24	56
6	BOURNEMOUTH	46	15	5	3	39	16	5	7	11	18	32	52
7	Exeter City	46	13	7	3	37	17	5	7	11	19	30	50
8	Watford	46	16	4	3	38	18	6	2	15	24	44	50
9	Torquay United	46	12	6	5	31	24	6	8	9	24	39	50
10	Doncaster Rovers	46	10	6	7	42	31	9	5	9	33	38	49
11	Swansea City	46	14	8	1	51	21	2	7	14	15	36	47
12	Barnsley	46	12	8	3	34	16	2	8	13	18	32	44
13	Cambridge United	46	7	10	6	36	28	7	5	11	22	34	43
14	Hartlepool	46	10	6	7	37	29	6	4	13	25	49	42
15	Rochdale	46	7	11	5	27	23	5	7	11	13	31	42
16	Crewe Alexandra	46	10	7	6	36	21	3	8	12	22	36	41
17	Bradford City	46	9	7	7	35	26	3	10	10	28	39	41
18	Brentford	46	12	7	4	37	18	2	6	15	19	42	41
19	Scunthorpe United	46	11	3	9	31	24	3	7	13	19	35	38
20	Darlington	46	11	7	5	30	14	3	3	17	18	43	38
21	Stockport County	46	8	7	8	23	23	5	5	13	20	53	38
22	Newport County	46	8	7	8	35	33	5	2	16	22	57	35
23	Southport	46	6	6	11	27	31	2	4	17	14	46	26
24	Workington	46	5	4	14	19	43	2	3	18	11	44	21

1976/77

13th in Division Four

							Baker KR	Barton F	Benson JH	Butler G	Buttle SA	Cave MJ	Chalk SR	Cunningham I	Gritt SJ	Howarth J	Impey JE	Johnson PJ	McAlinden RJ	Miller KR	Morgan SE	Paterson T	Reeves KP	Riley HW	Rudge JR	Stuckey BG
1	Aug	21	Halifax Town	3-2	Riley, Paterson, Buttle	1715	1	6	4	2	11							8		3	5	9	10	7		
2		24	WORKINGTON	1-1	Barton	3818	1	6		2	11						4	7		3	5	8	9	10		
3		28	SOUTHEND UNITED	2-0	Paterson, Barton (p)	4688	1	6	4	2	11			12			5	7		3		8		10	9	
4	Sep	4	Hartlepool	1-0	Paterson	1548	1	6	4	2				11			5	7		3		9		8	10	
5		11	SCUNTHORPE UNITED	2-2	Barton 2	4297	1	6		2							4	7		3	5	10	11	8	9	
6		18	Cambridge United	0-2		3689	1	6	4	2				11			5	7		3		8	9	10		
7		25	COLCHESTER UNITED	0-0		3881	1	6	4	2							5	7	11	3	12	8	10	9		
8	Oct	2	Rochdale	0-0		1807	1	6	4	2					12		8	7		3	5		9	10	11	
9		9	EXETER CITY	2-0	Rudge, Barton (p)	4621	1	6	4	2	11						5	7		3			9	10	8	
10		16	Watford	1-1	Reeves	5697	1	6	4	2	11						5	7		3		12	9	10	8	
11		23	CREWE ALEXANDRA	0-0		3908		6		2	11		1				4	7		3	5	8	9	10		
12		25	Darlington	0-4		3412			4	2	11		1	6				7		3	5	8	9	10	12	
13		30	ALDERSHOT	4-1	Paterson, Barton, Reeves, Riley	4504		6	4	2	11		1		12			7		3	5	8	9	10		
14	Nov	2	NEWPORT COUNTY	1-0	Barton	3570		6	4	2	11		1				12	7		3	5	8	9	10		
15		6	Brentford	2-3	Barton (p), Paterson	4254		6	4	2	11		1					7		3	5	8	9	10		
16		13	SOUTHPORT	5-0	Reeves 3, Barton, Johnson	4096	1	6	4	2	11						12	7		3	5	8	9	10		
17		26	Stockport County	0-1		3221	1	6	4	2	11							7		3	5	8		10	9	
18	Dec	4	BRADFORD CITY	1-1	Riley	4241	1	6	4	2	11							7		3	5	9	12	10	8	
19		18	Doncaster Rovers	0-0		3485	1	6	4	2	11						8	7		3	5		9	10		
20		27	SWANSEA CITY	1-1	Impey	6329	1	6	4	2	11						8	7		3	5	12	9	10		
21	Jan	1	BRENTFORD	3-1	Barton 2 (2p), Johnson	4268	1	6	4	2	11						8	7		3	5		9	10		
22		3	Aldershot	0-1		4955	1	6	4	2	11						8	7		3	5		9	10	12	
23		8	HUDDERSFIELD T	1-0	Riley	4494	1	6	4	2	11					9	5	7		3			8	10		
24		22	HALIFAX TOWN	3-0	Paterson, Johnson, Barton (p)	3888	1	6		2	11					9	4	7		3	5	10		8		
25		29	Barnsley	1-3	Paterson	5558	1	6		2	11			12		9	4	7		3	5	10		8		
26	Feb	4	Southend United	2-2	Johnson, Paterson	6278	1	6		2	11					9	4	7		3	5	8		10		
27		12	HARTLEPOOL	2-0	Howarth, Johnson	4409	1	6		2	11	7				9	4	10		3	5			8		
28		16	Torquay United	1-2	Howarth	2495	1	6		2	11	8				9	4	7		3	5			10		
29		19	Scunthorpe United	0-0		2836	1	6	5	2	11	7				9	4			3		8		10		
30		26	CAMBRIDGE UNITED	0-1		5265	1	6	4	2		9				7	5	11		3		8		10		
31	Mar	4	Colchester United	0-1		4948	1		4	2		9		6		7	5	11		3		8		10		
32		9	Workington	1-1	Riley	941	1	6		2		9		8		7	5	11		3	4	12		10		
33		12	ROCHDALE	1-1	Howarth	3400	1	6		2		8		4		7	5	11		3		9				10
34		19	Exeter City	1-1	Gritt	4065	1	6		2		8		4	10	9	5	7		3					12	11
35		26	WATFORD	2-1	Gritt 2	4445	1	6						2	8	9	5	11		3	4				10	7
36	Apr	2	Crewe Alexandra	1-2	Howarth	1862	1			6				2	8	9	5	11		3	4				10	7
37		9	TORQUAY UNITED	1-1	Rudge (p)	4048	1			2		6		4	10	9	5	11		3				12	8	7
38		11	Swansea City	0-3		6920	1	6	4	2		8		7		9	5	11		3				10		
39		12	Newport County	0-1		2962	1	6		7		8		2		9	5	11		3	4			10		
40		16	DARLINGTON	0-1		2841	1	6		3		8		2		9	5	11		7	4	12		10		
41		19	BARNSLEY	1-0	Paterson	2247	1	6	5	2		8		7		9	4			3		11		10		
42		22	Southport	0-0		992	1	6	4	2		8		7		9	5			3		11		10		
43		30	STOCKPORT COUNTY	3-0	Cave 2, Miller	2573	1	6		3		8		2		9	5			7	4	11		10		
44	May	3	Huddersfield Town	0-0		2342	1	6		2		8		7		9	5			3	4	11		10		
45		7	Bradford City	1-1	Howarth	7228	1	6	4	2				7		9	5	8		3		11		10		
46		14	DONCASTER ROVERS	3-1	Riley, Johnson, Howarth	2981	1	8	5	3				2		9	6	4		7		11		10		
						Apps	41	42	28	45	24	16	5	21	6	24	40	41	1	46	29	32	20	42	14	5
						Goals		12			1	2			3	6	1	6		1		9	6	5	2	

F.A. Cup

R1	Nov	20	NEWPORT COUNTY	0-0		4801	1	6	4	2	11							7		3	5	8	9	10		
rep		23	Newport County	0-3		3807	1	6	4	2	11						12	7		3	5	8	9	10		

F.L. Cup

R1/1	Aug	14	TORQUAY UNITED	0-0		2687	1	6	4	2	11				8		5	7		3			9	10		
R1/2		17	Torquay United	0-1		3439	1	6	4	2	11				8		5	7		3			9	10		

		P	*W*	*D*	*L*	*F*	*A*	*W*	*D*	*L*	*F*	*A*	*Pts*
1	Cambridge United	46	16	5	2	57	18	10	8	5	30	22	65
2	Exeter City	46	17	5	1	40	13	8	7	8	30	33	62
3	Colchester United	46	19	2	2	51	14	6	7	10	26	29	59
4	Bradford City	46	16	7	0	51	18	7	6	10	27	33	59
5	Swansea City	46	18	3	2	60	30	7	5	11	32	38	58
6	Barnsley	46	16	5	2	45	18	7	4	12	17	21	55
7	Watford	46	15	7	1	46	13	3	8	12	21	37	51
8	Doncaster Rovers	46	16	2	5	47	25	5	7	11	24	40	51
9	Huddersfield Town	46	15	5	3	36	15	4	7	12	24	34	50
10	Southend United	46	11	9	3	35	19	4	10	9	17	26	49
11	Darlington	46	13	5	5	37	25	5	8	10	22	39	49
12	Crewe Alexandra	46	16	6	1	36	15	3	5	15	11	45	49
13	BOURNEMOUTH	46	13	8	2	39	13	2	10	11	15	31	48
14	Stockport County	46	10	10	3	29	19	3	9	11	24	38	45
15	Brentford	46	14	3	6	48	27	4	4	15	29	49	43
16	Torquay United	46	12	5	6	33	22	5	4	14	26	45	43
17	Aldershot	46	10	8	5	29	19	6	3	14	20	40	43
18	Rochdale	46	8	7	8	32	25	5	5	13	18	34	38
19	Newport County	46	11	6	6	33	21	3	4	16	9	37	38
20	Scunthorpe United	46	11	6	6	32	24	2	5	16	17	49	37
21	Halifax Town	46	11	6	6	36	18	0	8	15	11	40	36
22	Hartlepool	46	8	9	6	30	20	2	3	18	17	53	32
23	Southport	46	3	12	8	17	28	0	7	16	16	49	25
24	Workington	46	3	7	13	23	42	1	4	18	18	60	19

1977/78

17th in Division 4

			Opponents	Score	Scorers	Att	Baker KR	Barton F	Benson JH	Borthwick GM	Brown RW	Butler G	Cave MJ	Chalk SR	Cunningham I	Finnigan TT	Howarth J	Impey JE	Johnson PJ	Lennard DH	Miller KR	Paterson T	Phillipson-Masters	Riley HW	Shanahan TC	Showers D	Wallbridge T
1	Aug	20	Crewe Alexandra	1-3	Showers	1596		6	4			3		1	2		9	5	7		11			10		8	
2		26	Scunthorpe United	0-0		4255	1	6	4			3			2		9	5	7		11			10		8	
3	Sep	3	SOUTHEND UNITED	0-3		3688	1	6	4				11		2		9	5	7		3	12		10		8	
4		10	Brentford	1-1	Paterson	7702	1	6	4				11		2			5	7		3	9		10		8	
5		13	YORK CITY	2-1	Phillipson-Masters, Riley	2863	1	6					11		2		12	5	7		3	9	4	10		8	
6		17	HALIFAX TOWN	0-0		3282	1	6				3	10		2				7	11	4		5	8		9	
7		24	Torquay United	1-1	Showers	2647	1	6				2	11		4				7	9	3		5	10		8	
8		27	Watford	1-2	Phillipson-Masters	8191	1	6				2	11				10	4	7	9	3		5			8	
9	Oct	1	SOUTHPORT	3-1	Showers 2, Johnson	3077	1	6				8	7		2		9	4	3	11			5			10	
10		5	DONCASTER ROVERS	0-1		2632	1	6				2	11		3		12	5	7	10			4		9	8	
11		8	Hartlepool United	1-0	Showers	2601	1	6	2			3	11					5	7	10			4		8	9	
12		15	WIMBLEDON	1-2	Barton	4272	1	6				3			2			5	7	10	4	12		11	9	8	
13		22	Northampton Town	0-1		3479	1	6	3			2	11					5	7	10	4	9				8	
14		25	READING	1-0	Showers	3210	1	6	4			2	11				12	5	7	10	3	9				8	
15		29	Aldershot	0-2		4863	1	6	3						2			5	7	10	4	9		11	12	8	
16	Nov	5	STOCKPORT COUNTY	1-0	Lennard	2795	1	6	4			2	7				9	5	11	10	3				12	8	
17		12	Rochdale	1-1	Showers	962	1	6	4			2	11				9	5	7	10	3					8	
18		19	DARLINGTON	2-0	Showers 2	2958	1	6				2	11		4		9	5	7	10	3					8	
19	Dec	3	Grimsby Town	2-0	Showers, Lennard	4012	1	6				2	11		4		9	5	7	10	3			12		8	
20		10	HUDDERSFIELD T	1-0	Sidebottom (og)	3249	1	11				2	6		4		9	5	7	10	3					8	
21		26	Newport County	2-3	Impey 2	7629		11				2	6	1	4		9	5	7	10	3					8	
22		27	SWANSEA CITY	0-1		5529		11				2	6	1	4		9	5	7	10	3	12				8	
23		30	Stockport County	1-2	Cave	5241		11				2	6	1	4		9	5	7	10	3	8					
24	Jan	2	BARNSLEY	2-2	Johnson, Showers	3909		11				2	6	1	4		9	5	7	10	3	12				8	
25		7	Reading	0-0		5490	1					2	6		4		9	5	7	10	3	8		11			
26		14	CREWE ALEXANDRA	1-0	Finnigan	3166	1					2	6		4	9		5	7	10	3			11		8	
27		21	SCUNTHORPE UNITED	1-1	Showers	2869	1					2	8		5	11		6	7	10	3			4	12	9	
28		27	Southend United	1-5	Riley	5128	1		5			2	6		4	9			7		3			11	10	8	
29	Feb	4	BRENTFORD	3-2	Cunningham, Finnigan, Kruse (og)	3417	1				5		6		2	9		4		10	3	7		11	12	8	
30		25	Southport	0-0		1470	1				6	4	8		2	10		5			3	7		11		9	
31		28	Halifax Town	0-0		1632	1				5	6			2	9		4			3	7		11	10	8	12
32	Mar	4	HARTLEPOOL UNITED	1-0	Showers	2992	1				6	4			2			5		10	3	7		11	9	8	
33		7	York City	0-0		1744	1				5	6			2	7		4		10	3	12		11	9	8	
34		11	Wimbledon	1-3	Miller	2834	1			12	5				2	6		4		10	3	7		11	9	8	
35		14	TORQUAY UNITED	1-1	Butler	2326	1			6	5	2				9		4		10	3	7		11		8	
36		17	NORTHAMPTON T	1-1	Finnigan	2221	1			6	5	2				9		4	7	10	3	12		11		8	
37		24	ALDERSHOT	0-0		4470	1				5	2				9		4	7	10	3			6	11	8	
38		25	Swansea City	0-1		7619	1				5	2				9		4	7	10	3	12		6	11	8	
39		28	NEWPORT COUNTY	4-2	Shanahan, Showers 2, Finnigan	2479	1				5	2				9		4	7	10	3			6	11	8	
40		31	Barnsley	0-3		5387	1				5	2			12	9		4	7	10	3			6	11	8	
41	Apr	4	WATFORD	1-2	Impey	6532	1			12	5	2				9		4	7	10	3	11		6		8	
42		8	ROCHDALE	1-0	Showers	2549	1			6	5				2	9		4	7	10	3	12			11	8	
43		15	Darlington	0-1		1286	1			6	5	12			2	7		4		10	3	11			9	8	
44		22	GRIMSBY TOWN	1-0	Showers	2518	1			6	5	3			2	9		4	7	10		11		12		8	
45		25	Doncaster Rovers	0-0		1654	1				5	3			2	9		4	11	10		7		6		8	
46		29	Huddersfield Town	0-2		1638	1				5	6			2	9		4	7	10	3			11		8	
						Apps	41	24	11	7	18	39	26	5	34	20	18	43	38	38	41	25	7	30	18	44	1
						Goals		1				1	1		1	4		3	2	2	1	1	2	2	1	17	

F.A. Cup

			Opponents	Score	Scorers	Att	Baker KR	Barton F	Benson JH	Borthwick GM	Brown RW	Butler G	Cave MJ	Chalk SR	Cunningham I	Finnigan TT	Howarth J	Impey JE	Johnson PJ	Lennard DH	Miller KR	Paterson T	Phillipson-Masters	Riley HW	Shanahan TC	Showers D	Wallbridge T
R1	Nov	26	Colchester United	1-1	Howarth	4456	1	11				2	6		4		9	5	7	10	3			12		8	
rep		29	COLCHESTER UNITED	0-0	(aet)	3838	1					2	6		4		9	5	7	10	3			11		8	
rep2	Dec	5	Colchester United	1-4	Barton	2230	1	11				2	6		4		9	5	7	10	3	12				8	

Replay 2 at Watford

F.L. Cup

			Opponents	Score	Scorers	Att	Baker KR	Barton F	Benson JH	Borthwick GM	Brown RW	Butler G	Cave MJ	Chalk SR	Cunningham I	Finnigan TT	Howarth J	Impey JE	Johnson PJ	Lennard DH	Miller KR	Paterson T	Phillipson-Masters	Riley HW	Shanahan TC	Showers D	Wallbridge T
R1/1	Aug	13	Hereford United	0-2		3582	1	6	4			3			2		9	5	7		10	12			8	11	
R1/2		16	HEREFORD UNITED	4-2	Showers, Barton (p), Johnson, Howarth	2198	1	6	4			3			2		9	5	7		11	12		10		8	
rep		23	Hereford United	2-1	(aet) Paterson, Barton	3334	1	6	4			3			2		9	5	7		11	12		10		8	
R2		31	Queen's Park Rangers	0-2		10006	1	6	4			3			2		9	5	7		11	12		10		8	

		P	W	D	L	F	A	W	D	L	F	A	Pts
1	Watford	46	18	4	1	44	14	12	7	4	41	24	71
2	Southend United	46	15	5	3	46	18	10	5	8	20	21	60
3	Swansea City	46	16	5	2	54	17	7	5	11	33	30	56
4	Brentford	46	15	6	2	50	17	6	8	9	36	37	56
5	Aldershot	46	15	8	0	45	16	4	8	11	22	31	54
6	Grimsby Town	46	14	6	3	30	15	7	5	11	27	36	53
7	Barnsley	46	15	4	4	44	20	3	10	10	17	29	50
8	Reading	46	12	7	4	33	23	6	7	10	22	29	50
9	Torquay United	46	12	6	5	43	25	4	9	10	14	31	47
10	Northampton Town	46	9	8	6	32	30	8	5	10	31	38	47
11	Huddersfield Town	46	13	5	5	41	21	2	10	11	22	34	45
12	Doncaster Rovers	46	11	8	4	37	26	3	9	11	15	39	45
13	Wimbledon	46	8	11	4	39	26	6	5	12	27	41	44
14	Scunthorpe United	46	12	6	5	31	14	2	10	11	19	41	44
15	Crewe Alexandra	46	11	8	4	34	25	4	6	13	16	44	44
16	Newport County	46	14	6	3	43	22	2	5	16	22	51	43
17	BOURNEMOUTH	46	12	6	5	28	20	2	9	12	13	31	43
18	Stockport County	46	14	4	5	41	19	2	6	15	15	37	42
19	Darlington	46	10	8	5	31	22	4	5	14	21	37	41
20	Halifax Town	46	7	10	6	28	23	3	11	9	24	39	41
21	Hartlepool United	46	12	4	7	34	29	3	3	17	17	55	37
22	York City	46	8	7	8	27	31	4	5	14	23	38	36
23	Southport	46	5	13	5	30	32	1	6	16	22	44	31
24	Rochdale	46	8	6	9	29	28	0	2	21	14	57	24

1978/79

18th in Division Four

	Date	Opponent	Score	Scorers	Att	Allen KR	Barton F	Benjafield BJ	Benson JH	Borthwick GM	Brown KG	Brown RW	Butler G	Butler MA	Cunningham I	Ferns PD	Finnigan TT	Holder P	Impey JE	Johnson PJ	Lennard DH	MacDougall EJ	Massey S	Miller KR	Scott J	Showers D	Weeks GJ
1	Aug 19	NEWPORT COUNTY	3-1	Massey (p), Finnigan, Walker (og)	3083	1					7	5	6	9	2		12		4		11		10	3		8	
2	22	Scunthorpe United	0-1		2573	1					11	5	6	9	2				4	7			10	3		8	
3	26	Darlington	0-0		1890	1			12	6	11	5		9	2		8		4	7			10	3			
4	Sep 2	HARTLEPOOL UNITED	0-1		2658	1				6	11	5		9	2		8		4	7			10	3		12	
5	9	Crewe Alexandra	0-1		1693	1			6		11	5		9	2		8		4	7	10			3		12	
6	12	HUDDERSFIELD T	2-0	R Brown, Showers	2416	1				6	11	5		9	2				4		7		10	3		8	
7	16	ROCHDALE	3-1	Barton, Impey, Butler	2674	1	7			6	11	5		9	2				4				10	3		8	
8	23	Port Vale	2-1	Massey, M Butler	3140	1	6				11	5		9	2				4		7		10	3		8	
9	26	Doncaster Rovers	1-1	M Butler	2441	1	6			7	11	5		9	2				4	12			10	3		8	
10	29	PORTSMOUTH	3-1	M Butler, Showers, Massey	10058	1	6			7	11	5		9	2				4	12			10	3		8	
11	Oct 7	ALDERSHOT	0-1		4605	1	6			7	11	5		9	2				4	12			10	3		8	
12	14	Hereford United	0-0		3752	1	7			6	11	5		9	2				4				10	3		8	
13	16	Stockport County	0-1		4092	1	6			7	11	5		9	2		12		4				10	3		8	
14	21	GRIMSBY TOWN	0-0		3399	1	7			6	11	5		9	2				4	12			10	3		8	
15	28	Halifax Town	2-0	Massey 2	1184	1	6			7	11	5		9	2				4	8			10	3			
16	Nov 4	TORQUAY UNITED	1-0	M Butler	3747	1	6			7	11	5		9	2				4	8			10	3			
17	11	Hartlepool United	0-0		3239	1	6			7	11	5	2	9					4	10		8	12	3			
18	18	DARLINGTON	2-2	M Butler 2	6005	1	6			7	11	5	2	9					4		12	8	10	3			
19	Dec 9	YORK CITY	1-2	Walsh (og)	3423	1	6			7		5		9	2				4	12	11	8	10	3			
20	23	WIMBLEDON	1-2	Lennard	3922	1	6			7		5		9	2				4		11	8		3		10	
21	26	Reading	0-1		6946	1	6			7		5		9	2				4		11	8		3		10	
22	30	Bradford City	1-2	R Brown	4026	1	6			7	11	5			2				4			8	10	3	9		
23	Jan 13	CREWE ALEXANDRA	0-1		2855	1	7			6		5			2	3				11	10	8		4	12	9	
24	Feb 3	DONCASTER ROVERS	7-1	Scott 2, MacDougall 2, Lennard, Johnson, Barton	2986	1	6			7		5			2	3				11	10	8		4	9		
25	6	PORT VALE	3-1	Scott, R Brown, MacDougall	3416	1	6			7	12	5			2				4	11	10	8		3	9		
26	10	Portsmouth	1-1	Johnson	12172	1	6			7	10	5			2				4	11		8	12	3	9		
27	21	NORTHAMPTON T	0-0		3990	1	6			7		5			2				4	11		8	10	3	9		
28	24	HEREFORD UNITED	1-1	K Brown	4292	1	6			7	10	5			2				4	11		8	12	3	9		
29	Mar 3	Grimsby Town	0-1		5693	1				7		5			2	4			6		12	8	10	3	9		11
30	6	Barnsley	0-1		7599	1				7		5			2	3			4	12		8	11	6	9		10
31	10	HALIFAX TOWN	1-0	MacDougall	3079	1				6		5			2			7	4	11	10	8		3	9		
32	13	Huddersfield Town	1-2	Borthwick	2268	1				7		5			2			6	4	11	10	8	12	3	9		
33	17	Torquay United	1-0	MacDougall	2080	1				7		5		9		3		6	4		10	8	11	2	12		
34	20	Aldershot	0-1		5490	1				6		5		9		3		7	4		10	8	11	2	12		
35	24	SCUNTHORPE UNITED	0-0		3028	1				6			5	9	2	3		7		12	10	8	11	4			
36	31	Wigan Athletic	0-1		5527	1				6		5	2	9		3		7			10	8	11	4			
37	Apr 3	Rochdale	1-2	M Butler	1136	1		6		7		5		9	2	3				11	10	8	12	4			
38	7	BARNSLEY	0-2		3265	1		8		6		5		9	2	3		7			12		11	4	10		
39	10	Wimbledon	0-4		3205	1				7	12	5		9		3		6	4		10	8	11	2			
40	14	READING	0-0		5638	1				7	10	5			2	3		6				8	11	4	9		
41	16	Northampton Town	2-4	K Brown, MacDougall	2253	1				7	10	5				3		6		12		8	11	2	9		4
42	21	BRADFORD CITY	1-0	MacDougall	2565	1				7	10	5			2			6	4	11		8		3	9		
43	23	STOCKPORT COUNTY	3-1	MacDougall, K Brown 2	2285	1				7	10	5			2			6	4	11		8		3	9		
44	28	York City	1-2	Scott	2171	1				7	10	5			2	12		6	4	11		8		3	9		
45	May 1	Newport County	0-2		2235	1				7	11	5			2	3		6	4			8	12	10	9		
46	5	WIGAN ATHLETIC	2-1	Massey, Johnson	3063	1				7	10	5			2			6	4	11		8	12	3	9		
					Apps	46	22	2	2	42	30	45	6	28	39	15	5	15	38	28	21	29	36	46	21	16	3
					Goals		2			1	4	3		8			1		1	3	2	8	6		4	2	

F.A. Cup

	Date	Opponent	Score	Scorers	Att	Allen KR	Barton F	Benjafield BJ	Benson JH	Borthwick GM	Brown KG	Brown RW	Butler G	Butler MA	Cunningham I	Ferns PD	Finnigan TT	Holder P	Impey JE	Johnson PJ	Lennard DH	MacDougall EJ	Massey S	Miller KR	Scott J	Showers D	Weeks GJ
R1	Nov 25	HITCHIN TOWN	2-1	Massey (p), M Butler	5008	1	6			7	11	5	2	9					4		3	8	10				
R2	Dec 16	Wimbledon	1-1	MacDougall	3308	1	6			7		5		9	2				4		11	8		3		10	
rep	28	WIMBLEDON	1-2	(aet) MacDougall	7192	1	6			7		5		9	2				4		11	8	12	3		10	

F.L. Cup

	Date	Opponent	Score	Scorers	Att	Allen KR	Barton F	Benjafield BJ	Benson JH	Borthwick GM	Brown KG	Brown RW	Butler G	Butler MA	Cunningham I	Ferns PD	Finnigan TT	Holder P	Impey JE	Johnson PJ	Lennard DH	MacDougall EJ	Massey S	Miller KR	Scott J	Showers D	Weeks GJ
R1/1	Aug 12	EXETER CITY	0-1		3180						11	5	6	9	2				4	12			10	3		8	7
R1/2	15	Exeter City	1-1	K Brown	3865						11	5	6	9	2				4	7			10	3		8	

Played at 1 in both games: KR Baker

		P	W	D	L	F	A	W	D	L	F	A	Pts
1	Reading	46	19	3	1	49	8	7	10	6	27	27	65
2	Grimsby Town	46	15	5	3	51	23	11	4	8	31	26	61
3	Wimbledon	46	18	3	2	50	20	7	8	8	28	26	61
4	Barnsley	46	15	5	3	47	23	9	8	6	26	19	61
5	Aldershot	46	16	5	2	38	14	4	12	7	25	33	57
6	Wigan Athletic	46	14	5	4	40	24	7	8	8	23	24	55
7	Portsmouth	46	13	7	3	35	12	7	5	11	27	36	52
8	Newport County	46	12	5	6	39	28	9	5	9	27	27	52
9	Huddersfield Town	46	13	8	2	32	15	5	3	15	25	38	47
10	York City	46	11	6	6	33	24	7	5	11	18	31	47
11	Torquay United	46	14	4	5	38	24	5	4	14	20	41	46
12	Scunthorpe United	46	12	3	8	33	30	5	8	10	21	30	45
13	Hartlepool United	46	7	12	4	35	28	6	6	11	22	38	44
14	Hereford United	46	12	8	3	35	18	3	5	15	18	35	43
15	Bradford City	46	11	5	7	38	26	6	4	13	24	42	43
16	Port Vale	46	8	10	5	29	28	6	4	13	28	42	42
17	Stockport County	46	11	5	7	33	21	3	7	13	25	39	40
18	BOURNEMOUTH	46	11	6	6	34	19	3	5	15	13	29	39
19	Northampton Town	46	12	4	7	40	30	3	5	15	24	46	39
20	Rochdale	46	11	4	8	25	26	4	5	14	22	38	39
21	Darlington	46	8	8	7	25	21	3	7	13	24	45	37
22	Doncaster Rovers	46	8	8	7	25	22	5	3	15	25	51	37
23	Halifax Town	46	7	5	11	24	32	2	3	18	15	40	26
24	Crewe Alexandra	46	3	7	13	24	41	3	7	13	19	49	26

1979/80

11th in Division 4

	Date	Opponent	Res	Scorers	Att	Allen K	Allen KR	Borthwick GM	Brown KG	Bryant JS	Butler MA	Chambers BM	Cunningham I	Elliott MR	Evanson JM	Ferns PD	Givens DJ	Heffernan TP	Holder P	Impey JE	MacDougall EJ	Massey S	Miller KR	Moore J	Smeulders J	Thomas B	Townsend NR
1	Aug 18	Rochdale	2-0	Cunningham, Chambers (p)	2310		1			4		6	2		11	10		8	7	5		9		3			
2	21	WALSALL	1-1	Heffernan	4833		1			4		6	2		11	10		8	7			9	3				5
3	25	NEWPORT COUNTY	3-2	Massey, Chambers (p), Townsend	5428		1			6		11	4			3		8	7	2	10	9					5
4	Sep 1	Scunthorpe United	1-2	Bryant	1586		1	12		4			2		10	3		8	7	6	11	9		5			
5	8	WIGAN ATHLETIC	1-2	Hinnigan (og)	4390		1			4		6	2		11			8	7	10	9	12		3			5
6	14	Stockport County	1-1	Chambers	3146		1	12			9	6	2		11				7	4		10		3		8	5
7	18	Portsmouth	0-4		15524		1	12			9	6	2		11				7	4		10		3		8	5
8	22	HALIFAX TOWN	0-1		3233		1	9		2	12	6			11	3		10	7	4				5		8	
9	28	Tranmere Rovers	5-0	Borthwick 2, Butler 2, Bryant	2803		1	10		5	9	6	2		11	3			7	4		8					
10	Oct 2	PORTSMOUTH	0-1		14114		1	10		5	9	6	2		11	3			7	4		8					
11	6	HARTLEPOOL UNITED	2-1	Holder, Butler	3180		1	10		5	9	6	2		11	3			7	4		8					
12	9	Walsall	0-0		4895		1	10		5	9	6	2		11	3			7	4		8					
13	12	York City	1-1	Holder	2840		1	10		5	9	6	2		11	3			7	4		8					
14	20	HUDDERSFIELD T	1-3	Chambers	4895		1	6		4	9	11	2			3		8	7	5	12	10					
15	23	HEREFORD UNITED	2-2	Chambers, Butler	2838		1	12		5	9	6	2			3		10	7	4	8		11				
16	27	Bradford City	2-2	MacDougall, Chambers	5807		1	6			9	10	2			3			7	5	8		11				4
17	Nov 3	ROCHDALE	4-0	Holder, Chambers, Butler, MacDougall	3188		1	8			11	6	2			3			7	4	10		9				5
18	7	Hereford United	1-2	MacDougall	1996		1	10	12		9	6	2			3			7	5	8		11				4
19	10	Lincoln City	1-1	Holder	3548		1	10			9	6	2			3			7	4	8		11				5
20	17	DONCASTER ROVERS	0-0		3771		1	6			9	10	2		12	3			7	4	8		11				5
21	Dec 1	PETERBOROUGH UTD.	0-0		3234		1				9	6	2		10	3			7	4	8		11				5
22	7	Crewe Alexandra	0-0		1974		1				9	6	2		10	3			7	4	8		11				5
23	21	NORTHAMPTON T	2-2	Butler, MacDougall	2335		1	12			9	6	2		10	3			7	4	8		11				5
24	26	Aldershot	1-0	Butler	5217		1				9	6	2		10	3			7	4	8		11				5
25	29	DARLINGTON	1-0	Butler	3260		1				9	6	2		10	3			7	4	8		11				5
26	Jan 1	TORQUAY UNITED	1-2	MacDougall	5185		1				9	6	2		10	3			7	4	8	12	11				5
27	5	Port Vale	1-1	Evanson	2875		1				9	6	2	7	10	3				4	8		11				5
28	26	Newport County	0-0		4856					6	9		2		10	3			7	4	8		11		1		5
29	Feb 2	STOCKPORT COUNTY	2-0	Butler, MacDougall	3044						9		2	7	10	3			6	4	8	12	11		1		5
30	6	Wigan Athletic	1-2	MacDougall	5904					4	9	12	2		10	3		7	6		8		11	5	1		
31	9	Halifax Town	0-2		1939					2	9	4		11	10	3		7			8		6	5	1		
32	16	TRANMERE ROVERS	2-1	MacDougall, Heffernan	2807						9	6	2			3		7		4	8	10	11		1		5
33	23	YORK CITY	0-0		3001						9	12	2			3		7	4	5	8	10	11	6	1		
34	Mar 1	Huddersfield Town	0-2		7740	3		12			9		4		11			8	7	5		10	2	6	1		
35	8	BRADFORD CITY	1-1	Ferns	2901						9	11	2	7		3		8	4	5		10		6	1		
36	15	Hartlepool United	1-3	Givens	2201						9	11	2			3	8	7	6	4		10		5	1		
37	22	LINCOLN CITY	0-0		2674						9	6	2			3	8	11	7	4		10	12	5	1		
38	25	SCUNTHORPE UNITED	3-3	Massey 2, Butler	2675			6	11		9	8	2			3			7	4		10			1		5
39	29	Doncaster Rovers	0-1		2327			6			9		2			3	8		7	4		10	11		1		5
40	Apr 5	ALDERSHOT	3-1	Givens 3	3757		1				9	6			11	3	8		7	4		10		2			5
41	7	Torquay United	0-0		2250		1	10			9	6			11	3	8		7	4		12		2			5
42	8	Northampton Town	1-0	Borthwick	3175		1	8			9	6			11	3			7	4		10		2			5
43	12	PORT VALE	3-1	Townsend, Butler, Evanson	2863		1	8			9	6			11	3		12	7	4		10		2			5
44	19	Peterborough United	0-2		2641		1	8			9	6			11	3		12	7	4		10		2			5
45	26	CREWE ALEXANDRA	0-1		2645		1	8			9	6			11	3		10	7	4		12		2			5
46	May 3	Darlington	1-0	Massey	1813		1				9	6			11	3		8	7	4		10		2			5
					Apps	1	34	25	2	16	41	41	37	4	32	42	5	20	43	43	23	30	23	20	12	3	29
					Goals			3		2	11	7	1		2	1	4	2	4		8	4					2

F.A. Cup

	Date	Opponent	Res	Scorers	Att	Allen K	Allen KR	Borthwick GM	Brown KG	Bryant JS	Butler MA	Chambers BM	Cunningham I	Elliott MR	Evanson JM	Ferns PD	Givens DJ	Heffernan TP	Holder P	Impey JE	MacDougall EJ	Massey S	Miller KR	Moore J	Smeulders J	Thomas B	Townsend NR
R1	Nov 24	Peterborough United	2-1	Chard (og), Evanson	3777		1				9	6	2		10	3			7	4	8		11				5
R2	Dec 15	Colchester United	0-1		3693		1				9	6	2		10	3			7	4	8		11				5

F.L. Cup

	Date	Opponent	Res	Scorers	Att	Allen K	Allen KR	Borthwick GM	Brown KG	Bryant JS	Butler MA	Chambers BM	Cunningham I	Elliott MR	Evanson JM	Ferns PD	Givens DJ	Heffernan TP	Holder P	Impey JE	MacDougall EJ	Massey S	Miller KR	Moore J	Smeulders J	Thomas B	Townsend NR
R1/1	Aug 11	Swansea City	1-4	Chambers	13500		1			4	12	6	2		11			8	7			9		3		10	5
R1/2	14	SWANSEA CITY	0-0		5824		1	12		4	10	6	2		11	3		8	7					5			

Played at 9 (substituted) in R1/2: J Scott

		P	W	D	L	F	A	W	D	L	F	A	Pts
1	Huddersfield Town	46	16	5	2	61	18	11	7	5	40	30	66
2	Walsall	46	12	9	2	43	23	11	9	3	32	24	64
3	Newport County	46	16	5	2	47	22	11	2	10	36	28	61
4	Portsmouth	46	15	5	3	62	23	9	7	7	29	26	60
5	Bradford City	46	14	6	3	44	14	10	6	7	33	36	60
6	Wigan Athletic	46	13	5	5	42	26	8	8	7	34	35	55
7	Lincoln City	46	14	8	1	43	12	4	9	10	21	30	53
8	Peterborough United	46	14	3	6	39	22	7	7	9	19	25	52
9	Torquay United	46	13	7	3	47	25	2	10	11	23	44	47
10	Aldershot	46	10	7	6	35	23	6	6	11	27	30	45
11	BOURNEMOUTH	46	8	9	6	32	25	5	9	9	20	26	44
12	Doncaster Rovers	46	11	6	6	37	27	4	8	11	25	36	44
13	Northampton Town	46	14	5	4	33	16	2	7	14	18	50	44
14	Scunthorpe United	46	11	9	3	37	23	3	6	14	21	52	43
15	Tranmere Rovers	46	10	4	9	32	24	4	9	10	18	32	41
16	Stockport County	46	9	7	7	30	31	5	5	13	18	41	40
17	York City	46	9	6	8	35	34	5	5	13	30	48	39
18	Halifax Town	46	11	9	3	29	20	2	4	17	17	52	39
19	Hartlepool United	46	10	7	6	36	28	4	3	16	23	36	38
20	Port Vale	46	8	6	9	34	24	4	6	13	22	46	36
21	Hereford United	46	8	7	8	22	21	3	7	13	16	31	36
22	Darlington	46	7	11	5	33	26	2	6	15	17	48	35
23	Crewe Alexandra	46	10	6	7	25	27	1	7	15	10	41	35
24	Rochdale	46	6	7	10	20	28	1	6	16	13	51	27

1980/81

13th in Division Four

							Allen KR	Bailey DS	Butler G	Chambers BM	Compton PD	Cunningham I	Dawtry KA	Elliott W (1)	Evanson JM	Ferns PD	Heffernan TP	Impey JE	Massey S	McGrath ML	Mooney DF	Moore J	Morgan TJ	Prosser NA	Prudham CE	Pugh GK	Smeulders J	Smith B	Spackman NJ	Sulley CS	Townsend NR	Webb DJ	Whittle A
1	Aug	16	York City	0-4		2195	1					2		12	11	3	6	4	10	7					9				8		5		
2		19	HEREFORD UNITED	1-0	Elliott	2991	1					2		7	11	3	6	4	10	12				9					8		5		
3		23	NORTHAMPTON T	0-0		2875	1					2		8	11	3	6	4	10	9					12				7		5		
4		30	Torquay United	0-2		2640	1					2		8	11	3	6	4	10	9									7		5		
5	Sep	6	Bradford City	1-1	Heffernan	3389	1					2		12	11	3	6	4	10	8			9						7		5		
6		13	TRANMERE ROVERS	1-0	Massey	2644	1					2			11	3	5	4	10	8			9						7			6	
7		16	HARTLEPOOL UNITED	1-0	Massey	2413	1					2			11	3	5	4	10	8			9						7			6	
8		20	Peterborough United	0-1		3774	1					2			11	3	6	4	10	8			9						7			5	
9		27	ROCHDALE	2-1	Morgan, Massey	2557	1					2			11	3	5	4	10	8			9						7			6	
10		30	Hartlepool United	0-1		2419	1					2		12	11	3	5	4	10	8			9						7			6	
11	Oct	4	SCUNTHORPE UNITED	2-2	Massey, Heffernan	3079	1					2			11	3	5	4	10	8			9						7			6	
12		7	Aldershot	0-0		3780	1					2			11	3	5	4		8			9		10				7			6	
13		11	Darlington	2-1	Massey 2	2045	1					2			11	3	5	4	10	8			9		12				7			6	
14		18	MANSFIELD TOWN	0-1		3335						2			11		5	4	10	8		3	9				1		7			6	
15		21	CREWE ALEXANDRA	0-0		2632	1				5	2		12		11	6	4	10	8		3	9						7				
16		24	Stockport County	1-2	Massey	2012	1				5	2			11	7	6	4	10	8		3	9										
17		27	Port Vale	2-0	Massey, Morgan	3009	1				5	2			11	8	6	4	10			3	9						7				
18	Nov	1	WIGAN ATHLETIC	3-0	Moore, Massey, Ferns	2983	1				5	2			11	7	6	4	10			3	9						8				
19		4	ALDERSHOT	0-2		3477	1				5	2			11	8	6	4	10	12		3	9						7				
20		8	Bury	0-3		2202	1				5	2		11		8	6	4	10			3	9						7				
21		12	Hereford United	0-1		1640	1	12			5			11		7	6	4	10	2		3	9						8				
22		15	YORK CITY	1-1	Moore	2203	1				5				11	2	6	4	10			3	9						7			8	
23		29	Halifax Town	2-1	Morgan 2	922	1				5	2				11	6	4	10	8		3	9						7				
24	Dec	6	DONCASTER ROVERS	1-2	Spackman	2495	1				5	2			8	11	6	4	10	12		3	9						7				
25		20	Lincoln City	0-2		3458	1	8			5	2		11			6	4	10			3	9	12					7				
26		26	SOUTHEND UNITED	2-1	Cusack (og), Spackman	4381	1		3		5	2		12	11		6	4	10		8		9						7				
27		27	Wimbledon	0-2		2681	1		11		5	2					6	4	10	12	8	3	9						7				
28	Jan	3	STOCKPORT COUNTY	0-1		2822					5	2				11	6		10	12	8	3	9				1	4	7				
29		10	Crewe Alexandra	2-0	Mooney 2	3087	1				5	2				11	6		10		9	3	8					4	7				
30		17	HALIFAX TOWN	2-1	Morgan, Ferns	2413	1			12	5	2				11	6		10		9	3	8					4	7				
31		24	TORQUAY UNITED	1-1	Mooney	3256	1		3		5					11	6	2			9		8					4	7				10
32		31	Northampton Town	1-0	Smith	2140	1		3		5					11	6	2			9		8					4	7				10
33	Feb	6	Tranmere Rovers	1-0	Ferns	1750	1		3		5					11	6	2			9		8					4	7				10
34		14	BRADFORD CITY	4-0	* See below	3561	1		3		5					11	6	2			9		8					4	7				10
35		21	Rochdale	0-0		1846	1		3		5					11	6	2			9		8					4	7				10
36		28	PETERBOROUGH UTD.	4-1	Mooney, Morgan 2, Ferns	5200	1		3		5					11	6	2			9		8					4	7				10
37	Mar	6	Scunthorpe United	1-1	Mooney	2519	1		3		5					11	6	2			9		8					4	7				10
38		14	DARLINGTON	3-3	Mooney 2, Ferns	4955	1		3		5		7			11	6	2			9		8					4		12			10
39		21	Mansfield Town	1-1	Mooney	2596	1		3				7			5	6	2			9		8					4	10	11			12
40		28	PORT VALE	0-0		4665	1		3		5		7				6	2			9		8					4	10	11			
41	Apr	4	Wigan Athletic	1-0	Spackman	3750	1		3		5	2	7				6				9		8			12		4	10	11			
42		11	BURY	2-2	Morgan, Pugh	4204	1		2		5		7			3	6		11		9		8			12		4	10				
43		17	Southend United	1-2	Morgan	7660	1				5		7			3	6	2			9		8					4	10	11			
44		18	WIMBLEDON	0-1		5048	1		3		5		7				6	2			9		8			12		4	10	11			
45		25	LINCOLN CITY	0-1		3542	1				5		7			3	6	2			9		8					4	10	11			
46	May	2	Doncaster Rovers	1-2	Dawtry	11373	1		3		5		7				6	2	4		9		8						10	11			
						Apps	44	2	16	1	31	29	9	11	21	38	46	41	31	22	21	16	42	2	4	3	2	18	44	8	5	10	9
						Goals							1	1		5	2		9		10	2	10			1		1	3				

Scorers in game 34: Mooney 2, Hebditch (og), Morgan

Two own goals

F.A. Cup

							Allen KR	Bailey DS	Butler G	Chambers BM	Compton PD	Cunningham I	Dawtry KA	Elliott W (1)	Evanson JM	Ferns PD	Heffernan TP	Impey JE	Massey S	McGrath ML	Mooney DF	Moore J	Morgan TJ	Prosser NA	Prudham CE	Pugh GK	Smeulders J	Smith B	Spackman NJ	Sulley CS	Townsend NR	Webb DJ	Whittle A
R1	Nov	22	Wycombe Wanderers	3-0	Massey, Morgan 2	4768	1					2			11	7	5	4	10			3	9						8			6	
R2	Dec	13	Charlton Athletic	1-2	Webb	7226	1					2		11		8	5	4	10			3	9						7			6	

F.L. Cup

							Allen KR	Bailey DS	Butler G	Chambers BM	Compton PD	Cunningham I	Dawtry KA	Elliott W (1)	Evanson JM	Ferns PD	Heffernan TP	Impey JE	Massey S	McGrath ML	Mooney DF	Moore J	Morgan TJ	Prosser NA	Prudham CE	Pugh GK	Smeulders J	Smith B	Spackman NJ	Sulley CS	Townsend NR	Webb DJ	Whittle A
R1/1	Aug	9	SWINDON TOWN	1-1	Massey	5121	1					2			11	3	6	4	10	7					9				8		5		
R1/2		12	Swindon T	0-2		5814	1					2		12	11	3	6	4	10	7					9				8		5		

		P	*W*	*D*	*L*	*F*	*A*	*W*	*D*	*L*	*F*	*A*	*Pts*
1	Southend United	46	19	4	0	47	6	11	3	9	32	25	67
2	Lincoln City	46	15	7	1	44	11	10	8	5	22	14	65
3	Doncaster Rovers	46	15	4	4	36	20	7	8	8	23	29	56
4	Wimbledon	46	15	4	4	42	17	8	5	10	22	29	55
5	Peterborough United	46	11	8	4	37	21	6	10	7	31	33	52
6	Aldershot	46	12	9	2	28	11	6	5	12	15	30	50
7	Mansfield Town	46	13	5	5	36	15	7	4	12	22	29	49
8	Darlington	46	13	6	4	43	23	6	5	12	22	36	49
9	Hartlepool United	46	14	3	6	42	22	6	6	11	22	39	49
10	Northampton Town	46	11	7	5	42	26	7	6	10	23	41	49
11	Wigan Athletic	46	13	4	6	29	16	5	7	11	22	39	47
12	Bury	46	10	8	5	38	21	7	3	13	32	41	45
13	BOURNEMOUTH	46	9	8	6	30	21	7	5	11	17	27	45
14	Bradford City	46	9	9	5	30	24	5	7	11	23	36	44
15	Rochdale	46	11	6	6	33	25	3	9	11	27	45	43
16	Scunthorpe United	46	8	12	3	40	31	3	8	12	20	38	42
17	Torquay United	46	13	2	8	38	26	5	3	15	17	37	41
18	Crewe Alexandra	46	10	7	6	28	20	3	7	13	20	41	40
19	Port Vale	46	10	8	5	40	23	2	7	14	17	47	39
20	Stockport County	46	10	5	8	29	25	6	2	15	15	32	39
21	Tranmere Rovers	46	12	5	6	41	24	1	5	17	18	49	36
22	Hereford United	46	8	8	7	29	20	3	5	15	9	42	35
23	Halifax Town	46	9	3	11	28	32	2	9	12	16	39	34
24	York City	46	10	2	11	31	23	2	7	14	16	43	33

1981/82

4th in Division Four: Promoted

	Date	Opponent	Result	Scorers	Att	Allen KR	Brignull PA	Carter SC	Compton PD	Crawford A	Dawkins DA	Dawtry KA	Edmunds P	Funnell A	George FC	Goddard HJ	Graham MM	Heffernan TP	Impey JE	Kelly EP	Leigh IR	Mooney DF	Morgan TJ	O'Donnell BF	Smith B	Spackman NJ	Sulley CS	Williams KD
1	Aug 29	CREWE ALEXANDRA	2-0	Morgan, Dawtry	3244	1			5			8	7					2	6			9	10		4		3	11
2	Sep 5	Mansfield Town	1-0	Edmunds	2950	1			5			8	7					2	6			9	10		4		3	11
3	12	DARLINGTON	2-0	Smith, Morgan	3900	1	5					8	7					2	6			9	10		4		3	11
4	19	Halifax Town	1-1	Funnell	1588	1			5			8		12				2	6	7		9	10		4		3	11
5	22	York City	1-0	Dawtry	2249	1			5			8	7	9				2	6				10		4	12	3	11
6	26	ROCHDALE	1-0	Dawtry	5146	1			5			8		9				2	6	7			10		4		3	11
7	29	WIGAN ATHLETIC	0-0		4952	1			5			8		9				2	6	7			10		4	11	3	
8	Oct 3	Stockport County	2-1	Funnell 2	2718	1			5			8	11	9				2	6	7			10		4		3	
9	10	NORTHAMPTON T	1-1	Morgan	5241	1			5			8	12	9				2	6	7			10		4		3	11
10	17	Peterborough United	0-1		4673				5			8		9				2	6	7	1	11	10		4		3	12
11	20	Aldershot	0-2		3704				5			8		9				2	6	7	1	11	10		4		3	
12	24	BURY	3-2	Graham 2, Funnell	4894				5					9			8	2	6	7	1				4	10	3	11
13	31	Tranmere Rovers	1-0	Heffernan	1732		5					4		9			8	2	6	7	1					10	3	11
14	Nov 3	SCUNTHORPE UNITED	2-0	Spackman, Graham	5032		5							9			8	2	6	7	1				4	10	3	11
15	7	PORT VALE	1-1	Spackman	5798		5							9			8	2	6	7	1				4	10	3	11
16	14	Blackpool	3-0	Funnell, Crawford, Brignull	4665		5			8				9				2	6	7	1				4	10	3	11
17	28	SHEFFIELD UNITED	0-0		9855		5			8		12		9				2	6	7	1				4	10	3	11
18	Dec 5	Hartlepool United	1-1	Heffernan	1763		5			10		6		11				2	4		1				7	9	3	8
19	26	COLCHESTER UNITED	1-1	Goddard	8829		5			8	12	7		9		10		2	6		1				4		3	11
20	28	Torquay United	2-1	Heffernan, Brignull	2791		5			8	4			9		10		2	6		1					7	3	11
21	Jan 23	Crewe Alexandra	0-0		1597		5			8			10	9		12		2	6		1				4	7	3	11
22	30	HALIFAX TOWN	1-1	Funnell	4690		5			8	12	4		9		10		2	6		1					7	3	11
23	Feb 2	BRADFORD CITY	0-2		5084		5				4	12	10	9		8		2	6		1					7	3	11
24	6	Darlington	1-0	Crawford	2443				5	8		10	7	9				2	6		1					4	3	11
25	9	YORK CITY	5-1	Crawford 2, Williams (p), Funnell, Edmunds	4373				5	8		10	7	9		12		2	6		1					4	3	11
26	13	STOCKPORT COUNTY	1-0	Crawford	5628				5	8		10	7	9				2	6		1					4	3	11
27	20	Rochdale	1-0	Heffernan	1295				5	8		10	7	9				2	6		1			11		4	3	
28	23	MANSFIELD TOWN	1-0	Funnell	5725				5	8		10	7	9				2	6		1					4	3	11
29	27	Northampton Town	0-1		2125				5	8			7	9		12		2	6		1				10	4	3	11
30	Mar 6	PETERBOROUGH UTD.	1-1	Funnell	7351		5	12		8		11		9	7			2	6		1				10	4	3	
31	9	ALDERSHOT	2-2	Dawtry 2	5333		5			8		11		9	7			2	6		1		10			4	3	
32	13	Bury	2-2	Spackman, Carter	4077		6	8	5			7		9				2			1		10			4	3	11
33	16	Scunthorpe United	2-0	Morgan, Funnell	1441		6	7	5			11		9				2			1		10			4	3	8
34	20	TRANMERE ROVERS	1-1	Crawford	5302		5	7		12		11		9				2	6		1		10		8	4	3	
35	27	Port Vale	1-1	Morgan	3004		5	7		9		11		12				2	6		1		10			4	3	8
36	31	Hereford United	2-1	Morgan, Funnell	3145		5	7		9				11				2	6		1		10			4	3	8
37	Apr 3	BLACKPOOL	1-0	Funnell	5146		5	7		9				11				2	6		1		10	12		4	3	8
38	10	Colchester United	2-1	Funnell, Crawford	2662		5	7		9				11				2	6		1		10	12		4	3	8
39	13	TORQUAY UNITED	4-0	Morgan, Heffernan 2 (1p), Impey	6398		5	7		9				11				2	6		1		10			4	3	8
40	17	HARTLEPOOL UNITED	5-1	Funnell 2, Crawford 2, Impey	6567		5	7		9				11				2	6		1		10	12		4	3	8
41	24	Sheffield United	0-0		18593		5	7		9				11				2	6		1		10	8		4	3	
42	May 1	HULL CITY	1-0	Heffernan	8055		5	7		9				11				2	6		1		10			4	3	8
43	4	Wigan Athletic	0-0		9021		5	7		9				11				2	6		1		10	12		4	3	8
44	8	Bradford City	2-2	Crawford, Goddard	9768		5	7		9				11		10		2	6		1					4	3	8
45	11	Hull City	0-0		3735	1	5	7	6	9	2	4		12		10	8							11			3	
46	15	HEREFORD UNITED	1-1	Funnell	9925		5	7		9				11				2	6		1		10			4	3	8
					Apps	10	29	16	20	28	5	29	14	43	2	9	5	45	43	13	36	6	25	7	22	35	46	37
					Goals		2	1		10		5	2	16		2	3	7	2				7		1	3		1

F.A. Cup

	Date	Opponent	Result	Scorers	Att	Allen KR	Brignull PA	Carter SC	Compton PD	Crawford A	Dawkins DA	Dawtry KA	Edmunds P	Funnell A	George FC	Goddard HJ	Graham MM	Heffernan TP	Impey JE	Kelly EP	Leigh IR	Mooney DF	Morgan TJ	O'Donnell BF	Smith B	Spackman NJ	Sulley CS	Williams KD
R1	Nov 21	READING	1-0	Funnell	7376		5			8		7		9				2	6		1				4	10	3	11
R2	Dec 12	Dorchester Town	1-1	Funnell	5200				5	8		7		9				2	6		1				4	10	3	11
rep	15	DORCHESTER TOWN	2-1	(aet) Crawford, Williams	6766				5	8	12	7		9				2	6		1				4	10	3	11
R3	Jan 2	OXFORD UNITED	0-2		8989		5			8	4			9		10		2	6		1				12	7	3	11

F.L. Cup (Milk Cup)

	Date	Opponent	Result	Scorers	Att	Allen KR	Brignull PA	Carter SC	Compton PD	Crawford A	Dawkins DA	Dawtry KA	Edmunds P	Funnell A	George FC	Goddard HJ	Graham MM	Heffernan TP	Impey JE	Kelly EP	Leigh IR	Mooney DF	Morgan TJ	O'Donnell BF	Smith B	Spackman NJ	Sulley CS	Williams KD
R1/1	Sep 1	FULHAM	0-1		3935	1			5			8	7					2	6			9	10		4		3	11
R1/2	15	Fulham	0-2		3583	1			5			8						2	6	7		9	10		4		3	11

F.L. Group Cup

	Date	Opponent	Result	Scorers	Att	Allen KR	Brignull PA	Carter SC	Compton PD	Crawford A	Dawkins DA	Dawtry KA	Edmunds P	Funnell A	George FC	Goddard HJ	Graham MM	Heffernan TP	Impey JE	Kelly EP	Leigh IR	Mooney DF	Morgan TJ	O'Donnell BF	Smith B	Spackman NJ	Sulley CS	Williams KD
GpF	Aug 15	Plymouth Argyle	0-0		2727	1			5				7					2	6			9	10		4	8	3	11
GpF	18	TORQUAY UNITED	1-1	Heffernan	2519	1			5				7					2	6	8		9	10		4	12	3	11
GpF	22	NEWPORT COUNTY	0-0		2511	1			5			12	7				13	2	6	8		9	10		4		3	11

Did not qualify for quarter-finals

1982/83

14th in Division Three

No.	Date	Opponent	Score	Scorers	Att.	Allen KR	Beck JA	Best G	Brignull PA	Carter SC	Compton PD	Crawford A	Dawkins DA	Dawtry KA	Funnell A	Golac I	Graham MM	Heffernan TP	Impey JE	Lee TC	Leigh IR	Madden DJ	Morgan TJ	Mundee BG	Neighbour JE	Nightingale MB	O'Donnell BF	Redknapp HJ	Spackman NJ	Sulley CS	Williams KD
1	Aug 28	WALSALL	3-0	Funnell 2, Spackman	5330	1			5	7				11	10			2	6				9				12		4	3	8
2	Sep 4	Oxford United	0-2		4907	1			5	7		11			10		12	2	6				9				8		4	3	
3	8	Millwall	0-2		3012	1	8		5	9			12		10			2	4				11				7		6	3	
4	11	SHEFFIELD UNITED	0-0		6424	1			5	7	6				10			2					9	11			4			3	8
5	18	Wigan Athletic	2-1	Funnell 2	4888	1			5	7	6				10			2					9	11			4			3	8
6	25	EXETER CITY	2-0	Beck, Morgan	7547	1	11		5	7	6				10			2					9				4			3	8
7	28	SOUTHEND UNITED	0-2		4502	1	4		5	7	6		12		10			2					9				11			3	8
8	Oct 2	Wrexham	0-1		2046	1	4		5	7	6	10			12			2					9						11	3	8
9	9	CARDIFF CITY	3-1	Morgan, Graham 2	5818				5		6				10		11	2			1		9					7	4	3	8
10	16	Portsmouth	2-0	Funnell, Heffernan	10961				5	7	6				10		11	2			1		9						4	3	8
11	19	Plymouth Argyle	0-2		2525				5	7	6			12	10		11	2			1		9						4	3	8
12	23	GILLINGHAM	0-1		5528				5	7	6			12	10		11	2			1		9						4	3	8
13	30	Preston North End	1-0	Heffernan	3583				5	7	6			11	12		10	2			1		9						4	3	8
14	Nov 2	BRISTOL ROVERS	0-0		6257				5	7	6	10	8	11			12	2			1		9						4	3	
15	6	HUDDERSFIELD T	0-1		5194				5	7	6	10		11			12	2			1		9						4	3	
16	13	Newport County	1-5	Brignull	4071				5	7	6				10		11	2			1		9			12			4	3	
17	27	BRADFORD CITY	2-2	Morgan 2	4125	1			5	7				11		2			6	10			9			8			4	3	
18	30	Bristol Rovers	1-1	Dawtry	4758	1			5	7				11		2			6	10			9			8			4	3	
19	Dec 4	Chesterfield	0-0		2226	1			5	7				11		2	4		6	10			9			8				3	
20	18	Lincoln City	0-9		4138	1			5	7				11			4	2	6	10			9	12		8				3	
21	27	READING	1-1	Lee	6118	1			5	7							11	2	6	10			9			12			4	3	8
22	28	Orient	0-5		3718	1			5	7							11	2	6	10			9						4	3	8
23	Jan 1	BRENTFORD	4-3	Brignull, Spackman 2, Dawtry	5593	1			5					11	7			2		10			9			8			4	3	6
24	3	Doncaster Rovers	1-2	Morgan	3297	1			5						7		12	2		10			9	11		6			4	3	8
25	15	Walsall	1-3	Lee	2735	1			5						11			2	6	10		8	9		7				4	3	
26	22	MILLWALL	3-0	Heffernan 3 (1p)	4707				5					11	10	6		2			1	8	9		7				4	3	
27	29	Sheffield United	2-2	Funnell, Heffernan (p)	11614				5						10	6		2			1	8	9		7	11			4	3	
28	Feb 1	OXFORD UNITED	2-0	Morgan, Spackman	3776				5					11	10	6		2		12	1	8	9		7				4	3	
29	5	Exeter City	2-4	Morgan 2	3008				5						10	2		3		12	1	8	9		7	11			4	6	
30	12	WREXHAM	1-1	Heffernan (p)	3827	1			5	11						8	12	2	6	10			9		7				4	3	
31	19	Cardiff City	1-1	Heffernan	4878				5					7		8		2	6	12	1		9			11			4	3	
32	26	PORTSMOUTH	0-2		13506		8		5					7			10	2	6	12	1		9			11			4	3	
33	Mar 5	Gillingham	5-2	Lee 2, Dawtry 2, Beck	3485		8		5					7				2	6	10	1		9			11			4	3	
34	12	PRESTON NORTH END	4-0	Lee, Heffernan (p), Morgan 2	4400		8		5					7				2	6	10	1		9			11			4	3	
35	15	PLYMOUTH ARGYLE	1-0	Nightingale	4258		8		5	7							12	2	6	10	1		9			11			4	3	
36	19	Huddersfield Town	0-0		8630		8		5					7				2	6	10	1		9			11			4	3	
37	26	NEWPORT COUNTY	0-1		9121		8	7	5					11			12	2	6	9	1					10			4	3	
38	Apr 2	ORIENT	2-0	Morgan, Beck	7039		8		5					7				2	6	10	1		9			11			4	3	
39	4	Reading	1-2	Morgan	4664		8		5					7			12	2	6	10	1		9			11			4	3	
40	9	CHESTERFIELD	2-1	Morgan, Beck	5227		8	7	5					12				2	6	10	1		9			11			4	3	
41	16	Southend United	0-0		4608		8	7	5									2	6	10	1		9			11			4	3	
42	23	LINCOLN CITY	1-0	Morgan	5010		8	7	5									2	6	10	1		9			11			4	3	
43	30	Bradford City	3-2	Dawtry, Lee, Morgan	3455				5					7				2	6	10	1		9			11			4	3	8
44	May 2	DONCASTER ROVERS	2-2	Sulley, Heffernan (p)	3995				5			12		7				2	6	10	1		9			11			4	3	8
45	7	WIGAN ATHLETIC	2-2	Nightingale, Morgan	4523			7	5					12				2	6	10	1		9			11			4	3	
46	14	Brentford	1-2	Lee	6191				5					7				2	6	10	1		9			11			4	3	12
					Apps	18	15	5	46	23	13	5	3	26	21	9	19	43	27	28	28	5	45	4	6	26	7	1	40	46	18
					Goals		4		2					5	6		2	10		7			16			2			4	1	

Played in one game: PG Aitken (16, at 8), DJ Webb (15, at 8 - subbed)
CJ Shaw played in games 45 and 46 at 8 (subbed in 46)

F.A. Cup

Rd	Date	Opponent	Score	Scorers	Att.	Allen KR	Beck JA	Best G	Brignull PA	Carter SC	Compton PD	Crawford A	Dawkins DA	Dawtry KA	Funnell A	Golac I	Graham MM	Heffernan TP	Impey JE	Lee TC	Leigh IR	Madden DJ	Morgan TJ	Mundee BG	Neighbour JE	Nightingale MB	O'Donnell BF	Redknapp HJ	Spackman NJ	Sulley CS	Williams KD
R1	Nov 20	SOUTHEND UNITED	0-2		4835	1			5	7			6	11	10	2	12						9						4	3	8

F.L. Cup (Milk Cup)

Rd	Date	Opponent	Score	Scorers	Att.	Allen KR	Beck JA	Best G	Brignull PA	Carter SC	Compton PD	Crawford A	Dawkins DA	Dawtry KA	Funnell A	Golac I	Graham MM	Heffernan TP	Impey JE	Lee TC	Leigh IR	Madden DJ	Morgan TJ	Mundee BG	Neighbour JE	Nightingale MB	O'Donnell BF	Redknapp HJ	Spackman NJ	Sulley CS	Williams KD
R1/1	Aug 31	Plymouth Argyle	0-2		3103	1			5	7		10		11				2	6				9						4	3	8
R1/2	Sep 14	PLYMOUTH ARGYLE	3-0	(aet) Funnell, Brignull, Morgan	3353	1			5	7	6		12		10								9	11			4			3	8
R2/1	Oct 6	Manchester United	0-2		22091	1			5		6	11			10			2					9					7	4	3	8
R2/2	26	MANCHESTER UNITED	2-2	Compton, Morgan	13226				5	7	6			10	12		11	2			1		9						4	3	8

F.L. Trophy

Rd	Date	Opponent	Score	Scorers	Att.	Allen KR	Beck JA	Best G	Brignull PA	Carter SC	Compton PD	Crawford A	Dawkins DA	Dawtry KA	Funnell A	Golac I	Graham MM	Heffernan TP	Impey JE	Lee TC	Leigh IR	Madden DJ	Morgan TJ	Mundee BG	Neighbour JE	Nightingale MB	O'Donnell BF	Redknapp HJ	Spackman NJ	Sulley CS	Williams KD
GpC	Aug 14	ALDERSHOT	2-2	Dawtry, Spackman	2412				5	11	6		2	7	10			12			1						3		4		8
GpC	18	Reading	2-4	Graham, Dawtry	1136	1			5		6	11		7	9		10	2					12	3					4		8
GpC	21	OXFORD UNITED	3-0	Morgan, Spackman, Dawtry	2561	1			5			11		7	10			2	6				9				8		4	3	

Did not qualify for QF

Played at 9 on Aug. 14: HJ Goddard

1983/84

17th in Division Three: Associate Members Cup Winners

	Date	Opponent	Score	Scorers	Att	Beck JA	Brignull PA	Brown RW	Carter SC	Dawtry KA	Duffield MJ	Graham MM	La Ronde E	Lee TC	Leigh IR	Morgan TJ	Morrell PDP	Nightingale MB	O'Driscoll SM	Rafferty WH	Ramsbottom N	Savage RJ	Schiavi MA	Shaw CJ	Smeulders J	Sulley CS	Thompson IP	Thompson MS	Train R	Williams KD
1	Aug 27	PRESTON NORTH END	0-1		4163	6	4		11	12					1	9	3	2								8	10	5		7
2	Sep 3	Burnley	1-5	Duffield	5525	6	4				11			12		9	3	2			1					8	10	5		7
3	6	Wimbledon	2-3	Graham, Morgan (p)	2435	6					4	11		12		9	3	2			1					8	10	5		7
4	10	WIGAN ATHLETIC	0-1		3161	6	4				11	8				9		2			1			12		3	10	5		7
5	17	Millwall	1-3	Graham	4774	6	4		11		8	10	7			9		2			1					3	12	5		
6	24	GILLINGHAM	2-0	Beck 2	3045	6	5				7	10	2		1	9		4						12		3	11			8
7	27	BRISTOL ROVERS	0-1		3328	6	5				7	10	2		1	9	12	4						8		3	11			
8	Oct 1	Lincoln City	0-3		3528	6	5					10	2		1	9		4					7			3	11			8
9	8	PLYMOUTH ARGYLE	2-1	Morgan, I Thompson	3759	4	5					10	2		1	9		6					7			3	11			8
10	15	Sheffield United	0-2		8984	4	5					12	2		1	9	10	6					7			3	11			8
11	18	Walsall	1-3	Morgan	3782	4	5						2		1	9	10	6					7			3	11			8
12	22	OXFORD UNITED	2-1	I Thompson, Morgan	4758	4	5					10	2		1	9		6					7			3	11			8
13	29	Brentford	1-1	Morgan	4630	4	5						2	10	1	9		6					7			3	11			8
14	Nov 1	ROTHERHAM UNITED	4-2	Lee, Morgan, I Thompson	3495	4	5						2	10	1	9		6					7			3	11	8		
15	5	HULL CITY	2-3	Brignull, I Thompson	4644	4	5					12	2	10	1	9		6					7			3	11	8		
16	11	Southend United	0-0		3556	4	5						2	10	1	9		6					7			3	11			8
17	26	BOLTON WANDERERS	2-2	Morgan 2	3941	4	5					10		12	1	9	2	6					8			3	11		7	
18	Dec 3	Scunthorpe United	2-1	Morgan 2	2344	4	6	5				10			1	9	8	2								3	11		7	
19	17	Bradford City	2-5	I Thompson 2	2842	4	6	5	10						1	9	8	2								3	11		7	
20	26	NEWPORT COUNTY	1-1	Morgan	7220	4	6		10			12	2		1	9	8	5								3	11		7	
21	27	Orient	0-2		4077	4	6		12				2		1	9	8	5								3	11		7	10
22	31	EXETER CITY	3-1	Savage, Morgan, I Thompson	5133	4	6					10			1	9		5				8				3	11	2	7	
23	Jan 2	Port Vale	1-2	Tartt (og)	4008	4	6		12			10			1	9		5				8				3	11	2	7	
24	14	Preston North End	0-2		3512	7	6	5				10	2		1	9	12	8				4				3	11			
25	21	MILLWALL	1-1	I Thompson	4242	4	6	5				10	2		1	9		8				7				3	11			
26	Feb 4	LINCOLN CITY	3-0	Morgan, Brignull, Graham	3597	12	6	5				10			1	9	7	2				4				3	11			8
27	11	Gillingham	1-2	Savage (p)	4891	8	6	5				10				9	7	2				4			1	3	11			
28	18	BRENTFORD	0-3		4308	8	6					10	2		1	9	7	5	11			4				3	12			
29	25	Oxford United	2-3	Sulley, I Thompson	6750	4	6		12			10	2		1	9		5	8							3	11			7
30	Mar 3	WALSALL	3-0	Brignull, Rafferty 2	3913	4	6	5							1		10	2	7	9						3	11			8
31	6	Hull City	1-3	Swann (og)	6897	4	6	5							1		10	2	8	9		12				3	11			7
32	10	SOUTHEND UNITED	1-0	Savage (p)	3615	4	6	5				11			1		10	2	7	9		8				3				12
33	17	Plymouth Argyle	0-1		7235	4	6	5				11			1			2	7	9		8				3				10
34	20	Wigan Athletic	3-1	Brignull, Rafferty, I Thompson	2910	4	6	5				12			1			2	7	9		8				3	11			10
35	24	SHEFFIELD UNITED	0-1		4767		6	5				10			1			2	7	9		8				3	11			4
36	31	WIMBLEDON	2-3	I Thompson 2	3538	10	6	5				12			1			2	7	9		8				3	11			4
37	Apr 7	Bristol Rovers	3-1	Savage, Brignull, Beck	5006	10	6	5							1			2	7	9		8				3	11			4
38	9	BURNLEY	1-0	Brown	4113	10	6	5							1			2	7	9		8				3	11			4
39	14	SCUNTHORPE UNITED	1-1	Savage (p)	3501	10	6	5							1			2	7	9		8				3	11			4
40	17	Rotherham United	0-1		3937	10	6	5				12			1			2	7	9		8				3	11			4
41	21	Newport County	1-2	Graham	2356	4	6	5				10			1			2	7	9		8				3	11			
42	24	ORIENT	3-2	Sulley, Nightingale, Brignull	3736	4	6	5				10			1			2	7	9		8				3	11			
43	28	Bolton Wanderers	1-0	Rafferty	3045	4	6	5							1		10	2	7	9		8				3	11			
44	May 5	PORT VALE	1-1	Brown	3305	4	6	5				10			1		12	2	7	9		8				3	11			
45	7	Exeter City	2-0	Morrell, O'Driscoll	2790	4	6	5							1		10	2	7	9		8				3	11			
46	12	BRADFORD CITY	4-1	* see below	3608	4		5							1		10	2	7	9		8				3	11			
					Apps	45	44	23	7	1	6	30	18	7	41	29	22	46	19	17	4	23	10	3	1	46	44	9	7	26
					Goals	3	6	2			1	4		2		13	2	2	1	5		5				2	12			

Scorers in game 46: Campbell (og), Morrell, Rafferty, Nightingale

MR Lewis played at 6 in game 46

Three own goals

F.A. Cup

	Date	Opponent	Score	Scorers	Att	Beck JA	Brignull PA	Brown RW	Carter SC	Dawtry KA	Duffield MJ	Graham MM	La Ronde E	Lee TC	Leigh IR	Morgan TJ	Morrell PDP	Nightingale MB	O'Driscoll SM	Rafferty WH	Ramsbottom N	Savage RJ	Schiavi MA	Shaw CJ	Smeulders J	Sulley CS	Thompson IP	Thompson MS	Train R	Williams KD
R1	Nov 19	WALSALL	4-0	I Thompson, Beck, Morgan, Lee	4298	4	5					10	2	12	1	9	8	6								3	11		7	
R2	Dec 13	Windsor & Eton	0-0		3451	4	6	5				10		12	1	9	8	2								3	11		7	
rep	19	WINDSOR & ETON	2-0	Beck, I Thompson	6006	4	6	5	10						1	9	8	2								3	11		7	
R3	Jan 7	MANCHESTER UNITED	2-0	Graham, I Thompson	15000		6	5				10	2		1	9		8				4				3	11		7	
R4	31	Middlesbrough	0-2		20175	4	6	5	12				2		1	9	10	8				7				3	11			

F.L. Cup (Milk Cup)

	Date	Opponent	Score	Scorers	Att	Beck JA	Brignull PA	Brown RW	Carter SC	Dawtry KA	Duffield MJ	Graham MM	La Ronde E	Lee TC	Leigh IR	Morgan TJ	Morrell PDP	Nightingale MB	O'Driscoll SM	Rafferty WH	Ramsbottom N	Savage RJ	Schiavi MA	Shaw CJ	Smeulders J	Sulley CS	Thompson IP	Thompson MS	Train R	Williams KD
R1/1	Aug 30	BRISTOL ROVERS	1-2	Morgan (p)	3473	6	4			11				12	1	9	3	2								8	10	5		7
R1/2	Sep 13	Bristol Rovers	2-2	Graham. Brignull	4564	6	4		10		11	8				9		2			1					3		5		7

A.M. Cup

	Date	Opponent	Score	Scorers	Att	Beck JA	Brignull PA	Brown RW	Carter SC	Dawtry KA	Duffield MJ	Graham MM	La Ronde E	Lee TC	Leigh IR	Morgan TJ	Morrell PDP	Nightingale MB	O'Driscoll SM	Rafferty WH	Ramsbottom N	Savage RJ	Schiavi MA	Shaw CJ	Smeulders J	Sulley CS	Thompson IP	Thompson MS	Train R	Williams KD
R1	Feb 21	ALDERSHOT	4-0	Williams, Morgan, La Ronde, Savage	1706	8			12				2		1	9	6	5	10			4				3	11			7
R2	Mar 13	Millwall	2-2	Shaw, Beck	2099	4		5	11			9	6				10	2	7					12	1	3				8
QF	Apr 3	WREXHAM	2-0	I Thompson, Savage	1909	4	6					10			1		5	2	7	9		8				3	11			
SFS	May 14	BRISTOL ROVERS	1-0	Savage (p)	2810	4	6	5				9			1		10	2	7			8				3	11			
FS	21	MILLWALL	2-1	I Thompson, O'Driscoll	4058	4	6	5							1		10	2	7	9		8				3	11			
F	24	Hull City	2-1	Graham, Morrell	6544	4	6	5				9			1		10	2	7			8				3	11			

R2 won 7-6 on penalties a.e.t. Final at Boothferry Park, Hull.

Played in R1: P Jones (at 13)

1984/85

10th in Division Three

							Beck JA	Brignull PA	Brown RW	Claridge SE	Clark WR	Graham MM	Howlett GP	La Ronde E	Leigh IR	Lewis MR	Morrell PDP	Nightingale MB	O'Driscoll SM	Rafferty WH	Russell C	Savage RJ	Schiavi MA	Shaw CJ	Smeulders J	Sulley CS	Thompson IP	Williams KD
1	Aug	25	DERBY COUNTY	1-0	Brown	7794	4	6	5			12			1		8	2	7	9			11			3	10	
2	Sep	1	Hull City	0-3		4828	4		5						1		8	2	7	9	11	6	12			3	10	
3		8	ROTHERHAM UNITED	3-0	Rafferty 3	3106	4		5						1		8	2	7	9		6	11	12		3	10	
4		15	Plymouth Argyle	0-0		4933	4		5						1		8	2	7	9		6	11			3	10	
5		18	Newport County	1-1	Brown	2288	4		5						1		8	2	7	9		6	11	12		3	10	
6		22	DONCASTER ROVERS	1-3	Thompson	3662	4								1		8	2	7	9		5	11	6		3	10	
7		29	Bristol Rovers	0-1		5216	4					12					8	2	7	9		5	11	6	1	3	10	
8	Oct	2	SWANSEA CITY	1-2	Graham	2847	4		5			11						2	7	9	8	6			1	3	10	
9		6	BURNLEY	1-1	Savage	3180	4										5	2	7	9	8	6	11		1	3	10	
10		13	Bolton Wanderers	1-2	Russell	4651	4		5								11	2	7	9	8	6			1	3	10	
11		20	Lincoln City	0-0		2340	4		5								11	2	7	9	8	6			1	3	10	
12		23	YORK CITY	4-0	Russell 2, Thompson 2	2987	4		5								11	2	7	9	8	6	12		1	3	10	
13		27	PRESTON NORTH END	2-0	Rafferty 2	3509	4		5								11	2		9	8	6	7	12	1	3	10	
14	Nov	3	Reading	2-0	Thompson 2	4193	4		5								11	2	7	9	8	6			1	3	10	
15		6	WIGAN ATHLETIC	1-0	Rafferty	3276	4		5								11	2	7	9	8	6	12		1	3	10	
16		10	Walsall	0-0		4519	4		5								11	2	7	9	8	6	12		1	3	10	
17		24	BRENTFORD	1-0	Thompson	4113			5								11	2	7	9	8	6			1	3	10	4
18	Dec	1	Bradford City	0-1		5580			5			12					11	2	7	9	8	6			1	3	10	4
19		15	BRISTOL CITY	2-1	Graham, Savage	4987			5			9	6				11	2	7		8	3			1		10	4
20		21	ORIENT	1-0	Savage	3709			5			9	6				11	2	7		8	3			1		10	4
21		26	Cambridge United	0-1		2158						9	6	5			11	2	7		8	3		12	1		10	4
22		29	Millwall	1-2	Howlett	5000			5			12	6	10			11	2	7	9	8	3			1			4
23	Jan	1	GILLINGHAM	2-0	Savage 2 (1p)	5305			5	12			6	4			11	2	7	9	8	3			1		10	
24		12	HULL CITY	1-1	Rafferty	4454	4		5				6				11	2	7	9	8	3			1		10	
25		19	Rotherham United	0-1		4568	4		5	12			6				11	2	7	9		3			1	8	10	
26		26	PLYMOUTH ARGYLE	1-0	Thompson	3695			5				6				11	2	7	9	8	4			1	3	10	
27		30	Derby County	3-2	Burns (og), Savage, Thompson	9181			5				6				11	2	7	9	8	4			1	3	10	
28	Feb	2	BRISTOL ROVERS	1-0	Savage	5167			5				6				11	2	7	9	8	4			1	3	10	
29		9	Doncaster Rovers	0-3		2338	11	12	5				6					2	7	9	8	4			1	3	10	
30		12	Swansea City	0-0		4121	4		5				6				11	2	7	9	8	3			1		10	
31		23	READING	0-3		5115	4	5		12		9	6				11	2	7		8	3			1		10	
32	Mar	2	Preston North End	1-2	Howlett	2974	4	5		8			6				3	2	7	9			11	12	1		10	
33		5	York City	1-4	Thompson	4532	4	5		8		11	6				3	2	7	9				12	1		10	
34		9	LINCOLN CITY	3-1	Rafferty 2, Savage (p)	2955	4	5					6				11	2	7	9	8	3			1		10	
35		16	BOLTON WANDERERS	4-0	Brignull, O'Driscoll, Rafferty, Thompson	2715	4	5				12	6				11	2	7	9	8	3			1		10	
36		23	Burnley	1-1	Thompson	2784	4	5				8					6	2	7	9	11	3			1		10	
37		30	Wigan Athletic	2-1	Graham, Morrell	2402	4	5				6					11	2	7	9	8	3	12		1		10	
38	Apr	6	CAMBRIDGE UNITED	0-0		3716	4	5				6					11	2	7	9	8	3		12	1		10	
39		9	Gillingham	2-3	Savage, Thompson	5157	4					6		5			11	2	7	9	8	3			1		10	
40		13	WALSALL	4-1	Brazier (og), Rafferty, Russell 2 (1p)	2954	4					6				3	11	2	7	9	8	5			1		10	
41		20	Brentford	0-0		3559	4					6				5	11	2	7		8	3	9		1		10	
42		26	BRADFORD CITY	4-1	Rafferty 2, Russell, Thompson	3827	4					6				5	11	2	7	9	8	3			1		10	
43	May	4	Bristol City	0-2		7083	4									5	11	2		9	8	3	6	7	1		10	
44		8	MILLWALL	1-2	Beck	2983	4							3			11	2	7	9	8	5	6		1		10	
45		11	Orient	0-0		3574	4							5			11	2	6	9	8	3	7	12	1		10	
46		13	NEWPORT COUNTY	3-0	Carter (og), Russell, Thompson	2511	4			8	5						11	2	7	9		3	10	6	1			

	Beck JA	Brignull PA	Brown RW	Claridge SE	Clark WR	Graham MM	Howlett GP	La Ronde E	Leigh IR	Lewis MR	Morrell PDP	Nightingale MB	O'Driscoll SM	Rafferty WH	Russell C	Savage RJ	Schiavi MA	Shaw CJ	Smeulders J	Sulley CS	Thompson IP	Williams KD
Apps	36	10	26	6	1	18	17	6	6	4	44	46	44	41	36	43	19	12	40	23	44	6
Goals	1	1	2	1		3	2				1		1	13	6	9					13	

Four own goals

F.A. Cup

							Beck JA	Brignull PA	Brown RW	Claridge SE	Clark WR	Graham MM	Howlett GP	La Ronde E	Leigh IR	Lewis MR	Morrell PDP	Nightingale MB	O'Driscoll SM	Rafferty WH	Russell C	Savage RJ	Schiavi MA	Shaw CJ	Smeulders J	Sulley CS	Thompson IP	Williams KD
R1	Nov	17	Kettering Town	0-0		2867			5								11	2	7	9	8	6			1	3	10	4
rep		20	KETTERING TOWN	3-2	Savage, Russell, Thrower (og)	3286			5								11	2	7	9	8	6			1	3	10	4
R2	Dec	8	Dartford	1-1	Savage	3884			5			12					11	2	7	9	8	6			1	3	10	4
rep		11	DARTFORD	4-1	Williams, Savage (p), Russell, Rafferty	4811			5			12					11	2	7	9	8	6			1	3	10	4
R3	Jan	5	Manchester United	0-3		32080	12		5				6	4			11	2	7	9	8				1	3	10	

F.L. Cup (Milk Cup)

							Beck JA	Brignull PA	Brown RW	Claridge SE	Clark WR	Graham MM	Howlett GP	La Ronde E	Leigh IR	Lewis MR	Morrell PDP	Nightingale MB	O'Driscoll SM	Rafferty WH	Russell C	Savage RJ	Schiavi MA	Shaw CJ	Smeulders J	Sulley CS	Thompson IP	Williams KD
R1/1	Aug	28	Aldershot	0-4		2678	4	6	5						1		8	2	7	9	11		12			3	10	
R1/2	Sep	4	ALDERSHOT	0-1		2415	4		5			12			1		8	2	7		11	6	9			3	10	

A.M. Cup (Freight RoverTrophy)

							Beck JA	Brignull PA	Brown RW	Claridge SE	Clark WR	Graham MM	Howlett GP	La Ronde E	Leigh IR	Lewis MR	Morrell PDP	Nightingale MB	O'Driscoll SM	Rafferty WH	Russell C	Savage RJ	Schiavi MA	Shaw CJ	Smeulders J	Sulley CS	Thompson IP	Williams KD
R1/1	Jan	22	Plymouth Arg	1-2	Rafferty	2995	12		5	8			6				11	2	7	9		4			1	3	10	
R1/2	Feb	5	PLYMOUTH ARGYLE	2-0	Russell 2	2748	11	5					6					2	7	9	8	4			1	3	10	
R2		19	TORQUAY UNITED	2-1	Beck 2	2637	4	13	5			9	6				11	2	7		8	3	12		1		10	
QF	Apr	18	WALSALL	2-1	Graham, Thompson	2567	4					6				5	11	2	7	9	8	3	12		1		10	
SFS		30	BRENTFORD	2-3	Thompson, Russell (p)	4657	4					6				5	11	2	7	9	8	3	12		1		10	

1985/86

15th in Division Three

							Beck JA	Brown RW	Claridge SE	Clark WR	Clarke CJ	Coleman DH	Heffernan TP	Howlett GP	Keane TJ	Leigh IR	Lewis MR	Morrell PDP	Newson MJ	Nightingale MB	O'Connor MA	O'Driscoll SM	Randall AJ	Russell C	Shaw CJ	Smeulders J	Sulley CS	Thompson IP	White AJ	Williams KD
1	Aug	17	Derby County	0-3		11324	11	5			9		2	8					4	6		7		12		1	3	10		
2		24	BRISTOL CITY	5-0	Clarke 3, Russell 2	4969		5			9		2					11	4	6		7		8		1	3	10		
3		26	Brentford	0-1		4283	12	5			9		2					11	4	6		7		8		1	3	10		
4		31	NEWPORT COUNTY	0-1		3381	12	5			9		2					11	4	6		7		8		1	3	10		
5	Sep	7	Chesterfield	1-0	Clarke	3207		5			9		2					11	4	6		7		8		1	3	10		
6		14	NOTTS COUNTY	0-0		4235	2	5			9							11	4	6		7		8	3	1		10		
7		17	BLACKPOOL	1-4	Morrell	3039	3	5			9		2					11	4	6		7		8		1		10		
8		21	Wigan Athletic	0-3		2657	12	5			9		2					11	4	6		7		8		1	3	10		
9		28	DARLINGTON	4-2	Newson 2, Clarke, Thompson	2755	6	5			9		2					11	4	12		7		8		1	3	10		
10	Oct	2	Lincoln City	2-3	Clarke, Shaw	1862	6	5			9		2					11	4	12		7		8	10	1	3			
11		5	Cardiff City	1-0	Shaw	2156	6	5			9		2					11	4			7		8	10	1	3			
12		12	BURY	2-1	Russell (p), Heffernan	3122	6	5			9		2					11	4			7		8	10	1	3			
13		19	GILLINGHAM	2-3	Russell, Clarke	3561	6	5			9		2	12				11	4	3		7		8	10	1				
14		22	York City	1-2	Russell	4194	6	5			9		2	10			11		4	3		7		8		1				
15		26	BRISTOL ROVERS	6-1	Russell 2, Clarke 2, Beck, O'Driscoll	3798	6	5	12		9		2	10			11		4			7		8		1	3			
16	Nov	2	Bolton Wanderers	0-1		3800	6	5			9		2	10			11		4			7		8		1	3			
17		5	Plymouth Argyle	1-2	Newson	6186	6	5			9		2	10			11	12	4			7		8		1	3			
18		9	WOLVERHAMPTON W.	3-2	Heffernen, Clarke, Beck	4126	6	5			9		2	10				11	4			7		8		1	3			
19		23	Doncaster Rovers	1-1	Russell	2390	12	5			9		2					11	4	6		7		8		1	3	10		
20	Dec	14	Walsall	2-4	O'Driscoll, Clarke	4460	6	5			9		2					11	4			7		8		1	3	10		
21		17	ROTHERHAM UNITED	1-2	Brown	2489	6	5			9		2					11	4			7		8		1	3	10		
22		21	Bristol City	3-1	Heffernan, Howlett, Newson	5621	6	5			9		2	8		1		11	4			7					3	10		
23		26	READING	0-1		6105	6	5			9		2			1		11	4			7		8			3	10		
24		28	BRENTFORD	0-0		4006	6	5			9		2					11	4			7		8		1	3	10		
25	Jan	1	Swansea City	1-1	Clarke	6994	6	5			9		2					11	4			7		8		1	3	10		
26		11	Newport County	1-2	Thompson	2333	6	5			9		2					11	4	12		7		8		1	3	10		
27		18	DERBY COUNTY	1-1	Howlett	4223	6				9		2	8		1		11	4	5		7					3	10		
28		31	CHESTERFIELD	3-2	Clarke, Newson, Heffernan	2347	6				9		2	8		1		11	4	5		7			12		3	10		
29	Feb	4	YORK CITY	2-0	Clarke 2	2476	6				9		2	8		1		11	4	5		7					3	10		
30		8	Gillingham	0-2		3890	6				9		2	8		1		11	4	5		7					3	10		
31		22	WIGAN ATHLETIC	0-2		2949	6				9		2	8		1		11	4	5		7		12			3	10		
32	Mar	1	Darlington	0-0		2576	6	5			9		2	12		1		11	4	8		7					3	10		
33		4	LINCOLN CITY	2-2	O'Driscoll, Clarke (p)	1873	6	5			9		2	11		1			4	8		7					3	10		
34		8	CARDIFF CITY	1-1	Clarke	2707	6	5			9			11		1			4	2		7		8	12		3	10		
35		15	Bury	0-3		2097	6	5			9			11		1			4	2		7			8		3	10		
36		18	BOLTON WANDERERS	2-1	Clarke 2	2063	6	5			9		2						4	8		7				1	3	10		11
37		22	Bristol Rovers	3-2	Thompson, Clarke 2	3296	6				9		2	12				5	4	8		7				1	3	10		11
38		29	SWANSEA CITY	4-0	Clarke, Thompson, Beck, O'Driscoll	3328	6				9		2					5	4		11	7				1	3	10		8
39		31	Reading	2-1	Clarke, Beck	7342	6				9		2					5	4		11	7				1	3	10		8
40	Apr	5	PLYMOUTH ARGYLE	1-3	Beck	5351	6				9		2					5	4	12	11	7				1	3	10		8
41		12	Wolverhampton Wan.	3-0	O'Driscoll, Thompson, Clarke	3382	6				9							5	4	2	11	7				1	3	10		8
42		15	Notts County	1-3	O'Connor	2423	6	5			9							3	4	2	11	7		12		1		10		8
43		19	DONCASTER ROVERS	1-1	Clarke	2796				5	9					1		3	4	2	11	7	6	8						10
44		26	Rotherham United	1-4	Clarke	2101	6				9			10				5	4	2	11	7		8		1			3	
45		29	Blackpool	0-2		2259		5			9	6		10				3	4	2	11	7		8		1				
46	May	3	WALSALL	0-1		3047		5			9				12			3	4	2	11	7	6	8		1				10
						Apps	41	34	1	1	46	1	37	20	1	12	4	38	46	32	9	46	2	32	8	34	37	33	1	9
						Goals	5	1			26		4	2				1	5		1	5		8	2			5		

F.A. Cup

							Beck JA	Brown RW	Claridge SE	Clark WR	Clarke CJ	Coleman DH	Heffernan TP	Howlett GP	Keane TJ	Leigh IR	Lewis MR	Morrell PDP	Newson MJ	Nightingale MB	O'Connor MA	O'Driscoll SM	Randall AJ	Russell C	Shaw CJ	Smeulders J	Sulley CS	Thompson IP	White AJ	Williams KD
R1	Nov	16	DARTFORD	0-0		3499		5			9		2	10				11	4			7		8	6	1	3			
rep		19	Dartford	2-0	Clarke, Newson	2555		5			9		2					11	4	6		7		8		1	3	10		
R2	Dec	7	DAGENHAM	4-1	O'Driscoll, Thompson, Brown, Clarke	3336	6	5			9		2					11	4			7		8		1	3	10		
R3	Jan	4	Wigan Athletic	0-3		4185	6	5			9		2					11	4			7		8	10	1	3	12		

F.L. Cup (Milk Cup)

							Beck JA	Brown RW	Claridge SE	Clark WR	Clarke CJ	Coleman DH	Heffernan TP	Howlett GP	Keane TJ	Leigh IR	Lewis MR	Morrell PDP	Newson MJ	Nightingale MB	O'Connor MA	O'Driscoll SM	Randall AJ	Russell C	Shaw CJ	Smeulders J	Sulley CS	Thompson IP	White AJ	Williams KD
R1/1	Aug	21	Reading	3-1	Clarke 2, Thompson	2614		5			9		2					11	4	6		7		8		1	3	10		
R1/2	Sep	3	READING	2-0	Thompson, Russell (p)	2590	12	5			9		2					11	4	6		7		8		1	3	10		
R2/1	Sep	25	Everton	2-3	Clarke, Russell	13930	6	5			9		2					11	4			7		8		1	3	10		
R2/2	Oct	8	EVERTON	0-2		8081	6	5			9		2					11	4			7		8	10	1	3			

A.M. Cup (Freight Rover Trophy)

							Beck JA	Brown RW	Claridge SE	Clark WR	Clarke CJ	Coleman DH	Heffernan TP	Howlett GP	Keane TJ	Leigh IR	Lewis MR	Morrell PDP	Newson MJ	Nightingale MB	O'Connor MA	O'Driscoll SM	Randall AJ	Russell C	Shaw CJ	Smeulders J	Sulley CS	Thompson IP	White AJ	Williams KD
R1	Jan	14	Orient	1-3	Shinners (og)	947	6				9		2	8		1		11	4	5		7	13		12		3	10		
R1		21	READING	5-0	Clarke 4 (2p), O'Driscoll	1974	6				9		2	8		1		11	4	5		7					3	10		

Did not qualify for quarter-final.

1986/87

Champions of Division Three: Promoted

No.	Month	Day	Opponent	Score	Scorers	Att.	Aylott TKC	Brown RW	Coleman DH	Cooke RE	Heffernan TP	Howlett GP	Lewis MR	Morrell PDP	Newson MJ	O'Connor MA	O'Driscoll SM	Peyton GJ	Puckett DC	Pulis AR	Richards CL	Savage RJ	Sealy AJ	Whitlock M	Williams KD	Williams WJ
1	Aug	23	Brentford	1-1	Newson	3856	9					8		3	5		7	1	11	2	10	4		6		
2		30	NEWPORT COUNTY	2-1	Puckett, Richards	2799	9				8			3	5		7	1	11	2	10	4		6		
3	Sep	6	Notts County	1-1	Puckett	3619	9					8		3	5	12	7	1	11	2	10	4		6		
4		13	BOLTON WANDERERS	2-1	Savage (p), Morrell	3031	9					8		3	5	12	7	1	11		10	4		6	2	
5		16	CHESTER CITY	2-0	Howlett, Puckett	3027	9					8		3	5	10	7	1	11			4		6	2	
6		20	Mansfield Town	1-1	O'Connor	2841	9					8		3	5	10	7	1	11		12	4		6	2	
7		27	BRISTOL CITY	2-0	Savage 2 (2p)	5975						8		3	5	10	7	1	11		9	4		6	2	
8		30	York City	0-2		3770						8		3	5	10	7	1	11	12	9	4		6	2	
9	Oct	4	Darlington	3-0	O'Driscoll, Puckett, Newson	2006						8		3	5	10	7	1	11	2	9	4		6		
10		18	Bury	1-0	Puckett	2452	9					8		3	5	2	7	1	11		10	4		6		
11		21	DONCASTER ROVERS	3-2	Savage (p), Puckett, Morrell	4195	9					8		3	5	2	7	1	11		10	4		6		
12		25	WIGAN ATHLETIC	3-1	Richards, Howlett, Puckett	4911	9					8		3	5	2	7	1	11		10	4		6		
13	Nov	1	Middlesbrough	0-4		10702	9					8		3	5	2	7	1	11	12	10	4		6		
14		4	Walsall	0-2		5056	9				2	8		3	5	12	7	1	11		10	4		6		
15		8	CARLISLE UNITED	2-1	Newson, Richards	4284	9				2	8			5	10	7	1	11	3	12	4		6		
16		22	CHESTERFIELD	2-0	Puckett, O'Connor	4312	9				2	8		3	5	4	7	1	11		10			6		
17	Dec	2	GILLINGHAM	0-2		7756	9				2	8		3	5	4	7	1	11		10	12		6		
18		13	Rotherham United	2-4	Puckett 2	2092		12			2	8		3	5	4	7	1	11		10			6	9	
19		26	Bristol Rovers	3-0	O'Connor, Richards, J Williams	3573					12	8		3	2	4	7	1	11	9	10			6		5
20		27	FULHAM	3-2	O'Connor, Newson, J Williams	6670					2	8	11	3	10	4	7	1		9				6		5
21	Jan	1	SWINDON TOWN	1-0	Richards	10537					2	8	12	3	11	4	7	1		9	10			6		5
22		3	Chesterfield	1-1	Howlett	3029			12		2	8	6	3	11	4	7	1		9	10					5
23		10	BRENTFORD	1-1	O'Driscoll	4682					2	8		3	11	4	7	1		9	10			6		5
24		24	NOTTS COUNTY	3-0	Cooke, Aylott, Richards	6022	9			11	12			3	2	4	7	1		8	10			6		5
25		31	Bolton Wanderers	1-0	Aylott	4219	9			11				3	2	4	7	1		8	10			6		5
26	Feb	3	BLACKPOOL	1-1	Cooke	6242	9			11		12		3	2	4	7	1		8	10			6		5
27		7	Chester City	2-2	O'Driscoll, Cooke	2846	9			11				3	2	4	7	1		8	10			6		5
28		14	MANSFIELD TOWN	4-1	Aylott 2, Richards 2	5261	9			11				3	2	4	7	1		8	10			6		5
29		21	Bristol City	0-2		14538	9			11	12			3	2	4	7	1		8	10			6		5
30		24	Newport County	1-0	O'Driscoll	2142	9			11				3	2	4	7	1		8	10			6		5
31		28	YORK CITY	3-0	Cooke, Richards 2	5805	9			11				3	2	4	7	1		8	10			6		5
32	Mar	3	MIDDLESBROUGH	3-1	Newson, O'Driscoll, Aylott (p)	13835	9			11				3	2	4	7	1		8	10			6		5
33		14	BURY	1-0	Whitlock	6806	9			11				3	2	4	7	1		8	10		12	6		5
34		17	Doncaster Rovers	3-0	O'Connor, Aylott, Sealy	1777	9			11	5			3	2	4	7	1		8			10	6		
35		21	Gillingham	1-2	Heffernan	7577	9			11	5			3	2	4	7	1		8	12		10	6		
36		28	DARLINGTON	1-0	Hine (og)	6370	9			11				3	2	4	7	1		8	12		10	6		5
37		31	Port Vale	2-1	Newson 2	3228	9			11				3	2	4	7	1		8	12		10	6		5
38	Apr	4	Carlisle United	0-0		2005	9			11				3	2	4	7	1		8	12		10	6		5
39		11	WALSALL	1-0	Cooke	8626	9			11				3	2	4	7	1		8	10			6		5
40		14	Wigan Athletic	2-0	O'Connor 2	4672	9			11				3	2	4	7	1		8	10		12	6		5
41		18	Swindon Town	1-1	J Williams	14302	9			11				3	2	4	7	1		8	10		12	6		5
42		20	BRISTOL ROVERS	2-0	Aylott, Cooke	10034	9			11				3	2	4	7	1		8	10		12	6		5
43		25	Blackpool	3-1	Richards, Jones (og), Cooke	2866	9			11				3	2		7	1		8	10		4	6		5
44	May	2	PORT VALE	0-0		9559	9			11				3	2	4	7	1		8	10		12	6		5
45		4	Fulham	3-1	Aylott 2 (1p), Sealy	9239	9			11				3	2	12	7	1		8	10		4	6		5
46		9	ROTHERHAM UNITED	2-0	Aylott, Richards	11310	9			11				3	2	12	7	1		8	10		4	6		5
						Apps	37	1	1	23	15	23	3	45	46	43	46	46	19	35	43	16	13	45	6	26
						Goals	10			7	1	3		2	7	7	5		10		12	4	2	1		3

Two own goals

F.A. Cup

Rd	Month	Day	Opponent	Score	Scorers	Att.	Aylott TKC	Brown RW	Coleman DH	Cooke RE	Heffernan TP	Howlett GP	Lewis MR	Morrell PDP	Newson MJ	O'Connor MA	O'Driscoll SM	Peyton GJ	Puckett DC	Pulis AR	Richards CL	Savage RJ	Sealy AJ	Whitlock M	Williams KD	Williams WJ
R1	Nov	15	FAREHAM TOWN	7-2	Aylott, Richards 2, Puckett 3, Davies (og)	4759	9				2	8		3	5	4	7	1	11		10	12		6		
R2	Dec	6	ORIENT	0-1		4353					2	8		3	5	4	7	1	11		10	9		6		

F.L. Cup (Littlewoods Challenge Cup)

Rd	Month	Day	Opponent	Score	Scorers	Att.	Aylott TKC	Brown RW	Coleman DH	Cooke RE	Heffernan TP	Howlett GP	Lewis MR	Morrell PDP	Newson MJ	O'Connor MA	O'Driscoll SM	Peyton GJ	Puckett DC	Pulis AR	Richards CL	Savage RJ	Sealy AJ	Whitlock M	Williams KD	Williams WJ
R1/1	Aug	26	BRISTOL CITY	0-1		2631	9				5	8		3			7	1	11	2	10	4		6		
R1/2	Sep	2	Bristol City	1-1	(a.e.t.) Aylott	4776	9				4	8	12	3			7	1	11	2	10	6		5		

A.M. Cup (Freight Rover Trophy)

Rd	Month	Day	Opponent	Score	Scorers	Att.	Aylott TKC	Brown RW	Coleman DH	Cooke RE	Heffernan TP	Howlett GP	Lewis MR	Morrell PDP	Newson MJ	O'Connor MA	O'Driscoll SM	Peyton GJ	Puckett DC	Pulis AR	Richards CL	Savage RJ	Sealy AJ	Whitlock M	Williams KD	Williams WJ
PR	Dec	16	Wolverhampton Wan.	3-4	Puckett 3	1923					2		9	3	5	8	7	1	11		10			6		
PR	Jan	6	CARDIFF CITY	1-0	O'Driscoll	1482			11		2		6	3	12	4	7	1		9	10				5	
R1		29	Swindon Town	2-2	Williams, Cooke	4524	9			11	2	12		3	5	4	7	1		8	10				6	

R1 lost 2-4 on penalties a.e.t.

Played on Jan. 6: TJ Keane (at 8), L Bolson (at 13)
Played on Dec 16: AJ Randall (at 4)

1987/88

17th in Division Two

No.	Month	Day	Opponent	Score	Scorers	Att.	Armstrong D	Aylott TKC	Brooks S	Clark WR	Close SC	Coleman DH	Cooke RE	Goulet B	Heffernan TP	Keane TJ	Langan DF	Morrell PDP	Newson MJ	O'Connor MA	O'Driscoll SM	Peyton GJ	Puckett DC	Pulis AR	Randall AJ	Richards CL	Shearer DJ	Smeulders J	Whitlock M	Williams WJ
1	Aug	15	Sheffield United	1-0	Brooks	9757	10	9	4									3	2	11	7	1		12		8			6	5
2		22	BRADFORD CITY	2-0	Armstrong (p), Richards	7407	10	9	4				11					3	2		7					8		1	6	5
3		29	Birmingham City	1-1	Armstrong	8284	10	9	4				11					3	2		7	1				8			6	5
4		31	BARNSLEY	1-2	Richards	7486	10	9	4				11					3	2		7	1		12		8			6	5
5	Sep	5	Hull City	1-2	Brooks	5807	10	9	4				12					3	2	11	7	1				8			6	5
6		12	READING	3-0	Aylott, Newson, O'Connor	7597		9	4	5								3	2	11	7	1		10		8			6	
7		15	Middlesbrough	0-3		9660		9	4	5			12					3	2	11	7	1		10		8			6	
8		19	West Bromwich Albion	0-3		7749			4				9			8		3	2	11	7	1		10		12			6	5
9		26	LEICESTER CITY	2-3	Aylott, Newson (p)	7969		9	4				10		12			3	2	11	7	1				8			6	5
10		29	PLYMOUTH ARGYLE	2-2	Aylott, Brooks	6491		9	4				10		8	12		3	2	11	7	1							6	5
11	Oct	3	Stoke City	0-1		8104		9	4				11					3	2	12	7	1		10		8			6	5
12		10	BLACKBURN ROVERS	1-1	O'Driscoll	6789		9	4						6			3	2	11	7	1	12	10			8			5
13		17	Aston Villa	1-1	Aylott	15145		9	12				10		14			3	2	11	7	1		4			8		6	5
14		20	SHREWSBURY TOWN	2-0	O'Driscoll, Aylott	5587		9					10		2			3		11	7	1		4		12	8		6	5
15		24	Leeds United	2-3	Heffernan (p), Richards	15288		9	12				10		2			3		11	7	1		4		14	8		6	5
16		31	IPSWICH TOWN	1-1	Brooks	8105		9	4						2			3		11	7	1		8		10	12		6	5
17	Nov	3	Millwall	2-1	O'Driscoll, Shearer	5734		9	4						2			3		11	7	1		8			10		6	5
18		7	CRYSTAL PALACE	2-3	O'Driscoll, Williams	9083		9	4				14		2			3		11	7	1	12	8			10		6	5
19		21	HUDDERSFIELD T	0-2		6415		9	4				10	12				3		11	7	1	8	2					6	5
20		28	Swindon Town	2-4	O'Connor, Puckett	7934		9					10		2			3		11	7	1	8	4					6	5
21	Dec	1	MANCHESTER CITY	0-2		9499		9	14			4	12	10			2	3		11	7	1	8						6	5
22		5	OLDHAM ATHLETIC	2-2	Puckett 2 (1p)	5377		9				4	12				2	3		11	7	1	8				10		6	5
23		12	Bradford City	0-2		10763		9				3	10	12			2			11	7	1	8	4					6	5
24		19	MIDDLESBROUGH	0-0		6392		9	4				10				2	3		11	7	1	8						6	5
25		26	Leicester City	1-0	Cooke	11452		9	4				10				2	3		11	7	1	8				12		6	5
26		28	WEST BROMWICH ALB.	3-2	Pulis, Aylott, Shearer	8969		9					10		5		2	3		11	7	1	8	4			12		6	
27	Jan	1	BIRMINGHAM CITY	4-2	Cooke 2 (1p), Shearer, Puckett	7963		9	4				10				2	3		11	7	1	14	12			8		6	5
28		16	SHEFFIELD UNITED	1-2	Williams	6466		9	4		8		10				2	3		11	7	1	14	12					6	5
29	Feb	6	HULL CITY	6-2	* see below	5901		9	4		11		10				2	3	8		7	1							6	5
30		13	Manchester City	0-2		16161	12	9	4		11		10				2	3	8		7	1							6	5
31		27	STOKE CITY	0-0		6871	12	9	4		11		10				2	3	8		7	1							6	5
32	Mar	5	ASTON VILLA	1-2	A Gray (og)	10057	14	9	4		11		10				2	3	8	12	7	1							6	5
33		8	Barnsley	1-2	Richards	6140	10	9	4					12			2	3	8	7		1				11			6	5
34		12	Blackburn Rovers	1-3	Close	10807		9	4		11			14			2	3	8	12		1		7		10			6	5
35		19	Ipswich Town	2-1	Aylott, Close	10335		9	4		11		10				2	3	8	7		1		6						5
36		26	LEEDS UNITED	0-0		9147		9	4		11		10				2	3	8	7		1		6					5	
37	Apr	2	Crystal Palace	0-3		9557		9	4		11	3	10				2		8	7		1		6		12				5
38		8	Shrewsbury Town	1-2	Cooke (p)	7106		9	12		11		10				2	3	8	7	4	1		6		14			5	
39		13	Reading	0-0		10274		9			11		10				2	3	8	7	4	1		6		12			5	
40		19	MILLWALL	1-2	Pulis	14423		9			11		10					3	8	7	4	1		2		12			6	5
41		26	Plymouth Argyle	2-1	Pulis, Brooks	6310		9	4		11		10				14	3	8		7	1		2		12			6	5
42		30	Huddersfield Town	2-1	Close, Aylott	2794		9	4		11							3	8	10	7	1		2					6	5
43	May	2	SWINDON TOWN	2-0	Newson (p), Close	9212		9	4		11							3	8	10	7	1		2					6	5
44		7	Oldham Athletic	0-2		6009		9	4		14	12		11				3	8	10	7				2			1	6	5
						Apps	9	43	37	2	16	5	34	6	11	2	20	42	29	37	39	42	12	29	1	20	11	2	41	38
						Goals	2	9	6		6		5		1				3	2	4		4	3		4	3			2

Scorers in game 29: Close 2, Brooks, Aylott, Cooke (p), Norman (og)

Two own goals

F.A. Cup

Rd	Month	Day	Opponent	Score	Scorers	Att.	Armstrong D	Aylott TKC	Brooks S	Clark WR	Close SC	Coleman DH	Cooke RE	Goulet B	Heffernan TP	Keane TJ	Langan DF	Morrell PDP	Newson MJ	O'Connor MA	O'Driscoll SM	Peyton GJ	Puckett DC	Pulis AR	Randall AJ	Richards CL	Shearer DJ	Smeulders J	Whitlock M	Williams WJ
R3	Jan	9	Brighton & Hove Albion	0-2		14411		9					11		12		2	3		10	7	1	14	4			8		6	5

F.L. Cup (Littlewoods Challenge Cup)

Rd	Month	Day	Opponent	Score	Scorers	Att.	Armstrong D	Aylott TKC	Brooks S	Clark WR	Close SC	Coleman DH	Cooke RE	Goulet B	Heffernan TP	Keane TJ	Langan DF	Morrell PDP	Newson MJ	O'Connor MA	O'Driscoll SM	Peyton GJ	Puckett DC	Pulis AR	Randall AJ	Richards CL	Shearer DJ	Smeulders J	Whitlock M	Williams WJ
R1/1	Aug	18	EXETER CITY	1-1	Armstrong (p)	4094	8	9	4				12					3	2	11		1		7		10			6	5
R1/2		26	Exeter C	3-1	Cooke, Newson, Aylott	4094	10	9	4				11					3	2	12	7	1				8			6	5
R2/1	Sep	22	SOUTHAMPTON	1-0	Cooke	10364			4				9		10			3	2	11	7	1		12		8			6	5
R2/2	Oct	6	Southampton	2-2	Newson, O'Driscoll	13429		9	4				11					3	2	12	7	1		10		8			6	5
R3		27	Arsenal	0-3		26050		9	4				10		2			3		11	7	1	8	12		14			6	5

F.M. Cup (Simod Cup)

Rd	Month	Day	Opponent	Score	Scorers	Att.	Armstrong D	Aylott TKC	Brooks S	Clark WR	Close SC	Coleman DH	Cooke RE	Goulet B	Heffernan TP	Keane TJ	Langan DF	Morrell PDP	Newson MJ	O'Connor MA	O'Driscoll SM	Peyton GJ	Puckett DC	Pulis AR	Randall AJ	Richards CL	Shearer DJ	Smeulders J	Whitlock M	Williams WJ
R1	Nov	10	Sheffield Wednesday	0-2		3756		14				2	11	9				3			7	1	8	4	12				6	5

Played at 10: GP Howlett

1988/89

12th in Division Two

							Aylott TKC	Barnes DO	Bishop IW	Blissett LL	Bond KJ	Brooks S	Clarke CJ	Close SC	Coleman DH	Cooke RE	Holmes MJE	Morrell PDP	Mundee DWJ	Newson MJ	O'Connor MA	O'Driscoll SM	Peyton GJ	Puckett DC	Pulis AR	Richards CL	Shearer PA	Smeulders J	Teale S	Whitlock M	Williams WJ
1	Aug	27	Sunderland	1-1	Close	17998	9		10		4	8		11		7		3		2			1							6	5
2	Sep	3	CHELSEA	1-0	Cooke	8763	9		10		4	8				7		3		2		12	1			11				6	5
3		10	Brighton & Hove Albion	2-1	Newson, Brooks	8247	9		10		4	8						3		2	7		1			11				6	5
4		17	LEEDS UNITED	0-0		7922	9		10		4	8						3		2	7		1			11				6	5
5		20	Swindon Town	1-3	Bond	8055	9		10		4	8		14				3		2	7	12	1			11				6	5
6		24	OXFORD UNITED	2-1	Aylott, Newson	6532	9		10		4	8		12				3		2	7		1			11				6	5
7	Oct	1	Stoke City	1-2	Brooks	7485	9		10		4	8		12				3		2	11		1			7				6	5
8		5	West Bromwich Albion	0-0		7248	9		10		4	8		14				3		2	11	12	1			7				6	5
9		8	BIRMINGHAM CITY	0-1		6186			10		4	8		11		12		3				2	1	9		7				6	5
10		15	Portsmouth	1-2	Close	12801	9		10		4	8		11				3		2	14	7	1	12						6	5
11		21	SHREWSBURY TOWN	0-1		5449	9		10		4	12			14	11		3		2		7	1	8	5					6	
12		25	Oldham Athletic	0-2		4522	9		10		4	8		11	3				14		7	2	1	12	5					6	
13		29	IPSWICH TOWN	1-0	Bishop	6648	9		10		4			11	3					2	7	8	1		6						5
14	Nov	5	Bradford City	1-0	Brooks	9069	9		10		4	8		11				3		2	7	6	1								5
15		12	CRYSTAL PALACE	2-0	Aylott, O'Connor	8697	9		10		4	8		11				3		2	7	6	1								5
16		19	MANCHESTER CITY	0-1		9874	9		10		4	8		11		12		3		2	7	6	1								5
17		26	Barnsley	2-5	Aylott, Blissett	4937	9		10	11	4	8						3		2	7	6	1							12	5
18		29	HULL CITY	5-1	Blissett 4, Aylott	5420	9		10	11	4	8		12				3		2	7	6	1								5
19	Dec	3	BLACKBURN ROVERS	2-1	Clarke, Blissett	8418	9		10	11	4	8	12					3		2	7	6	1								5
20		10	Plymouth Argyle	1-1	Blissett	10619	9		10	11	4	6	8					3			7	2	1								5
21		17	WALSALL	2-1	Aylott, Blissett	6985	9		10	11	4	6	8					3			7	2	1								5
22		26	Leicester City	1-0	Clarke	13896	9		10	11	4	6	8					3			7	2	1								5
23		31	Watford	0-1		14006	9		10	11	4	8						3		2	7	6	1								5
24	Jan	2	BRIGHTON & HOVE ALB	2-1	Blissett, Newson	10627	9		10	11	4	8						3		2	7	6	1								5
25		14	Hull City	0-4		5690	9		10	11	4	8		12		14		3		2	7	6	1								5
26		21	SUNDERLAND	0-1		9032	9		10	11	4	8		12		14		3		2	7	6	1								5
27	Feb	4	WEST BROMWICH ALB.	2-1	Cooke, Coleman	11571	9		10	11	4				8	7		3		2		6	1						12		5
28		11	Birmingham City	1-0	Newson	6444	10		6	9					8	7		3		2		5	1						11		4
29		25	PORTSMOUTH	1-0	Newson	9959			10	11				9		7		3		2	8	6	1						4		5
30		28	OLDHAM ATHLETIC	2-2	Blissett 2	7783			10	11				9		7		3		2	8	6	1						4		5
31	Mar	4	Crystal Palace	3-2	Williams, O'Connor, Cooke	10022			10	11				9		7		3		2	8	6	1						4		5
32		11	BRADFORD CITY	3-0	Blissett 2 (1p), Bishop	8122	9		10	11				12		7		3		2	8	6	1						4		5
33		14	Ipswich Town	1-3	Blissett	10824	9		10	11				12	14	7		3		2	8	6	1						4		5
34		18	SWINDON TOWN	2-3	Blissett, Newson	9752	9		10	11		12				7		3		2	8	6	1						4		5
35		25	Chelsea	0-2		22467	14	7	10	11		12		9				3		2	8	6	1						4		5
36		27	LEICESTER CITY	2-1	Blissett, Newell (og)	8913	9	7	10	11								3		2		6	1		8				4		5
37	Apr	1	Leeds United	0-3		21114	9	7	10	11								3		2	12	6	1		8				4		5
38		4	Walsall	1-1	Williams	3619	9	7	10	11		12						3		2		6	1		8				4		5
39		8	WATFORD	0-1		9766	9	7		11		8						3		2	10	6			5			1	4		
40		11	Shrewsbury Town	0-1		2457	9	7		11		8			2			3			12	6			5		10	1	4		
41		15	STOKE CITY	0-1		6834	9	7	10	11		12						3		2	14	6	1		5		8		4		
42		22	Oxford United	1-3	Aylott	5684	9	7	10	11		8						3		2		6			5			1	4		
43		29	BARNSLEY	3-2	Blissett 2 (1p), Newson	5520	9	7	10	11		12					8	3		2		6						1	4		5
44	May	1	Blackburn Rovers	0-2		9345		7	10	11		12		9	5		8	3		2		6						1	4		
45		6	Manchester City	3-3	Shearer, Holmes, Blissett (p)	30564	9		10	11		8		12	14		7	3		2		6					5	1	4		
46		13	PLYMOUTH ARGYLE	0-0		7230			10	11		8					7	3	9	2		6					5	1	4		
						Apps	40	10	44	30	27	36	4	23	9	15	4	44	2	40	33	41	39	4	10	8	4	7	20	13	37
						Goals	6		2	19	1	3	2	2	1	3	1			7	2						1				2

One own goal

F.A. Cup

							Aylott TKC	Barnes DO	Bishop IW	Blissett LL	Bond KJ	Brooks S	Clarke CJ	Close SC	Coleman DH	Cooke RE	Holmes MJE	Morrell PDP	Mundee DWJ	Newson MJ	O'Connor MA	O'Driscoll SM	Peyton GJ	Puckett DC	Pulis AR	Richards CL	Shearer PA	Smeulders J	Teale S	Whitlock M	Williams WJ
R3	Jan	7	Blackpool	1-0	Blissett	5317	9		10	11	4	8						3		2	7	6	1								5
R4		28	Hartlepool United	1-1	Blissett (p)	6240	9		10	11	4					12		3		2	7	6	1		8						5
rep		31	HARTLEPOOL UNITED	5-2	* see below	10142	9		10	11	4				8	7		3		2		6	1								5
R5	Feb	18	MANCHESTER UNITED	1-1	Aylott	12500	9		10	11	4					7		3		2	8	6	1								5
R5		22	Manchester United	0-1		52422	9		10	11	4			12		7		3		2	8	6	1								5

Scorers in R4 replay: Baker (og), Stokes (og), Newson, Morrell, Cooke

F.L. Cup (Littlewoods Challenge Cup)

							Aylott TKC	Barnes DO	Bishop IW	Blissett LL	Bond KJ	Brooks S	Clarke CJ	Close SC	Coleman DH	Cooke RE	Holmes MJE	Morrell PDP	Mundee DWJ	Newson MJ	O'Connor MA	O'Driscoll SM	Peyton GJ	Puckett DC	Pulis AR	Richards CL	Shearer PA	Smeulders J	Teale S	Whitlock M	Williams WJ
R1/1	Aug	30	BRISTOL ROVERS	1-0	Aylott	4601	9		10		4	8		11		7		3		2			1			12				6	5
R1/2	Sep	7	Bristol Rovers	0-0		4057	9		10		4	8						3		2		7	1			11				6	5
R2/1		27	COVENTRY CITY	0-4		6543	9		10		4	8		11		7		3		2		14	1			12				6	5
R2/2	Oct	11	Coventry City	1-3	Cooke	7212			10		4	8		7	11	14		3			12	2	1	9	6						5

F.M. Cup (Simod Cup)

							Aylott TKC	Barnes DO	Bishop IW	Blissett LL	Bond KJ	Brooks S	Clarke CJ	Close SC	Coleman DH	Cooke RE	Holmes MJE	Morrell PDP	Mundee DWJ	Newson MJ	O'Connor MA	O'Driscoll SM	Peyton GJ	Puckett DC	Pulis AR	Richards CL	Shearer PA	Smeulders J	Teale S	Whitlock M	Williams WJ
R1	Nov	9	Derby County	0-1		7847	9		10		4			11		12	8	3			7	6	1							2	5

1989/90

22nd in Division Two: Relegated

						Att	Aylott TKC	Barnes DO	Blissett LL	Bond KJ	Brooks S	Cadette RR	Coleman DH	Holmes MJE	Kite PD	Lawrence GR	Miller PR	Morrell PDP	Moulden PA	Mundee DWJ	Newson MJ	O'Connor MA	O'Driscoll SM	Peacock GK	Peyton GJ	Redknapp JF	Shearer PA	Slatter NJ	Teale S	Williams WJ
1	Aug	19	Brighton & Hove Albion	1-2	Newson	9719		12	11					10	1	7	5	3	8		2		9	6					4	
2		22	WEST BROMWICH ALB.	1-1	Moulden	8226			11					10		7	5	3	8		2		9	6	1				4	
3		26	HULL CITY	5-4	Swan (og), Moulden 3, Blissett	6454			11					12		7	5	3	8		2	10	9	6	1				4	
4	Sep	2	Ipswich Town	1-1	Shearer	11474			11							7	5	3	8		2	10	9	6	1		12		4	
5		9	NEWCASTLE UNITED	2-1	Moulden 2	9882			11		10					7	5	3	8				9	6	1		2		4	
6		16	Middlesbrough	1-2	Blissett	16077		12	11		10					7	5	3	8				9	6	1		2		4	
7		23	BLACKBURN ROVERS	2-4	Peacock, Blissett (p)	7409		12	11		10					7	5	3	8				9	6			2		4	
8		26	PORT VALE	1-0	Blissett	6511			11	14	10					7	5	3	8		2		9	6	1		12		4	
9		30	Oxford United	2-1	Lawrence, Moulden	5325			11	14	10					7	5	3	8		2		9	6	1		12		4	
10	Oct	7	Sunderland	2-3	MacPhail (og), Blissett	15933		7	11	14	10						5	3	8		2		9	6	1		12		4	
11		14	OLDHAM ATHLETIC	2-0	Moulden, Peacock	6796			11	12	10			7			5	3	8		2		9	6	1				4	
12		17	Watford	2-2	Brooks, Blissett	9013			11	2	10		12	7			5	3	8				9	6	1				4	
13		21	PORTSMOUTH	0-1		9353			11	2	10		14				5	3	8			7	9	6	1		12		4	
14	Nov	1	WEST HAM UNITED	1-1	Blissett	9970			11	2	10		3						8			7	9	5	1		6		4	
15		4	Leeds United	0-3		25965			11	2	10		3		1				8	14		7	9	6			5		4	12
16		11	SHEFFIELD UNITED	0-1		8481			11	2	10		3			7	5		8				9		1		6		4	12
17		18	STOKE CITY	2-1	Brooks, Moulden	6412			11	2	10		3			7	12		8			14	9	6	1				4	5
18		25	Bradford City	0-1		7436			11	2	10		3			12			8		7		9	6	1				4	5
19	Dec	2	BRIGHTON & HOVE ALB	0-2		6890			11	2	10		3			7			8				9	6	1				4	5
20		5	Swindon Town	3-2	Lawrence, Blissett 2	7326			11	2	10		3			7			8		12		9	6	1				4	5
21		9	West Bromwich Albion	2-2	Blissett 2	8568			11	2	10		3			7			8				9	6	1				4	5
22		16	BARNSLEY	2-1	Moulden, Blissett	5506			11	2	10		3			7			8		12		9	6	1				4	5
23		26	Leicester City	1-2	Williams	14128			11	2	10		3			7			8		9			6	1				4	5
24		30	Wolverhampton Wan.	1-3	Shearer	15421			11	2	10		3			7	14		8		9			6	1		12		4	5
25	Jan	1	PLYMOUTH ARGYLE	2-2	Holmes, Williams	6939			11	2	10			9		7		3			12			6	1		8		4	5
26		13	Hull City	4-1	Holmes, Lawrence, Shearer, Blissett	4673			11	2				10		7		3	8					6	1	12	9		4	5
27		20	IPSWICH TOWN	3-1	Blissett 3 (1p)	7464			11	2				10		7		3	8		12			6	1	14	9		4	5
28	Feb	3	Blackburn Rovers	1-1	Moulden	7950	14		11	2				10		7		3	8		12			6	1		9		4	5
29		10	MIDDLESBROUGH	2-2	Moulden, Peacock	7630	12		11	2				10	1	7		3	8					6			9		4	5
30		24	BRADFORD CITY	1-0	Moulden	6206	14		11	2				10		7		3	8				12	6	1		9		4	5
31		28	Newcastle United	0-3		15163	12		11	2						7	5	3	8				10	6	1		9		4	
32	Mar	3	Stoke City	0-0		10978	14		11	2	12					7	5	3	8				10	6	1		9		4	
33		6	OXFORD UNITED	0-1		6319	14		11	2	7		3	10			5		8				12	6	1		9		4	
34		10	Port Vale	1-1	Brooks	7131	9		11		7		3	10		12	5			2			6		1		8		4	
35		17	SUNDERLAND	0-1		6328	9		11	4	7		3	10		12	5			2			6		1		8			
36		20	Oldham Athletic	0-4		10109			11	4	7		3	10		9	5						2	6	1	12	8			
37		24	WATFORD	0-0		6737	9		11	4	7	14	3	10		12	5						6		1		8	2		
38		31	Portsmouth	1-2	Brooks	8836	14		11	4	8	9	3	10	1	7	5						6				12	2		
39	Apr	3	WOLVERHAMPTON W.	1-1	Shearer	7448	9		11		8		3	10	1					4			7	6			5	2		
40		7	SWINDON TOWN	1-2	Blissett	7772	9		11		8		3	12			5			4			7	6	1		10	2		
41		11	West Ham United	1-4	Coleman	20202	9		11			14	3	10			5			12			7	6	1	8	4	2		
42		14	Plymouth Argyle	0-1		7520	9		11		8	12	3	10			5			2			7	6	1		4			
43		17	LEICESTER CITY	2-3	Peacock, Aylott	6781	12		11		8	9	3	10	1		5			2			7	6			4			
44		21	Barnsley	1-0	Aylott	7415	9		11		8	10	3				5			2			7	6	1		4	12		
45		28	Sheffield United	2-4	Cadette, Blissett (p)	20994	9		11		8	10	3			12	5			2			7	6	1		4			
46	May	5	LEEDS UNITED	0-1		9918	9		11	2	8	12	3			10	5						7	6	1		4			
						Apps	18	4	46	31	35	8	27	22	6	33	31	21	32	10	16	6	39	41	39	4	34	6	34	16
						Goals	2		18		4	1	1	2		3		13			1			4			4			2

Two own goals

F.A. Cup

						Att	Aylott TKC	Barnes DO	Blissett LL	Bond KJ	Brooks S	Cadette RR	Coleman DH	Holmes MJE	Kite PD	Lawrence GR	Miller PR	Morrell PDP	Moulden PA	Mundee DWJ	Newson MJ	O'Connor MA	O'Driscoll SM	Peacock GK	Peyton GJ	Redknapp JF	Shearer PA	Slatter NJ	Teale S	Williams WJ
R3	Jan	6	Sheffield United	0-2		11944			11	2				9		7	10	3	12					6	1		8		4	5

F.L. Cup (Littlewoods Challenge Cup)

						Att	Aylott TKC	Barnes DO	Blissett LL	Bond KJ	Brooks S	Cadette RR	Coleman DH	Holmes MJE	Kite PD	Lawrence GR	Miller PR	Morrell PDP	Moulden PA	Mundee DWJ	Newson MJ	O'Connor MA	O'Driscoll SM	Peacock GK	Peyton GJ	Redknapp JF	Shearer PA	Slatter NJ	Teale S	Williams WJ
R2/1	Sep	19	Crewe Alex.	1-0	Moulden	3504			11		10					7	5	3	8				9	6	1		2		4	
R2/2	Oct	3	CREWE ALEXANDRA	0-0		5343		7	11								5	3	8		2		9	6	1		10		4	
R3		24	Sunderland	1-1	Shearer	12595			11	2	10		3				5		8			7	9		1		6		4	
rep	Nov	7	SUNDERLAND	0-1		7349			11	2	10		3		1				8			7	9	6			5		4	12

F.M. Cup (Zenith Data Systems Cup)

						Att	Aylott TKC	Barnes DO	Blissett LL	Bond KJ	Brooks S	Cadette RR	Coleman DH	Holmes MJE	Kite PD	Lawrence GR	Miller PR	Morrell PDP	Moulden PA	Mundee DWJ	Newson MJ	O'Connor MA	O'Driscoll SM	Peacock GK	Peyton GJ	Redknapp JF	Shearer PA	Slatter NJ	Teale S	Williams WJ
R2	Nov	28	CHELSEA	2-3	(a.e.t.) Blissett, Shearer	6214			11	2	10		3			7			8			14	9	6	1		12		4	5

1990/91

9th in Division Three

							Aylott TKC	Blissett LL	Bond KJ	Brooks S	Coleman DH	Cooke RE	Ekoku EG	Fereday W	Guthrie PJ	Holmes MJE	Jones AM	Lawrence GR	Miller PR	Morrell PDP	Morris DK	Mundee DWJ	O'Driscoll SM	Peacock GK	Peyton GJ	Pulis AR	Redknapp JF	Shearer PA	Teale S	Watson AF	Wood PA
1	Aug	25	Brentford	0-0		5669	9	11	6		12		14		1	10				3			7	8				5	4		
2	Sep	1	BURY	1-1	O'Driscoll	5285	9	11	6						1	10		14		3			7	8			12	5	4		
3		8	Wigan Athletic	0-2		1972	9	11	6		10				1	12		14		3		2	7				8	5	4		
4		15	STOKE CITY	1-1	Blissett (p)	6374	9	11	6				12		1	10		7		3			2	8				5	4		
5		18	BRADFORD CITY	3-1	Teale, Blissett (p), Oliver (og)	4942	9	11	6		14		12		1	10		7		3			2	8				5	4		
6		22	Exeter City	0-2		6145	9	11	6		3		12		1	10		7				2	5	8					4		
7		29	FULHAM	3-0	Bond, Blissett, Ekoku	5885	9	11	6		3		12		1	10		7				2	5	8					4		
8	Oct	2	Reading	1-2	Mundee	5431		11	6		14		9		1	10		7	12	3		2	5	8					4		
9		5	Southend United	1-2	Ekoku	5255	14	11	6		3		9			10		7	12	5		2		8	1				4		
10		20	CREWE ALEXANDRA	1-1	Blissett (p)	5548	9	11	6	14						10		7	2	3			5	8	1		12		4		
11		23	Huddersfield Town	3-1	Teale, Blissett, Peacock	5373		11	6	9						10		12	2	3		7	5	8	1				4		
12		27	Preston North End	0-0		4921		11	6	7						10	9	14	2	3			5	8	1		12		4		
13		30	TRANMERE ROVERS	1-0	Jones	6268		11	6	10						7	9	12	2	3			5	8	1				4		
14	Nov	3	SHREWSBURY TOWN	3-2	Blissett, Peacock 2	5561		11	6	10						7	9		2	3			5	8	1				4		
15		10	ROTHERHAM UNITED	4-2	Peacock, Blissett 3 (2p)	5442		11		10						7	9		2	3			5	8	1		6		4		
16		24	Birmingham City	0-0		7416		11		10						7	9	12	2	3		14	5	8	1		6		4		
17	Dec	1	Chester City	0-0		995		11		10				6		7	9	12	2	3			5		1		8		4		
18		14	SWANSEA CITY	1-0	Blissett (p)	5031		11		10				8		7	9	12	2	3		6	5		1				4		
19		22	Grimsby Town	0-5		5651		11		10			14	8		7	9		2	3		6	5		1		12		4		
20		26	MANSFIELD TOWN	0-0		5280		11		10			14	6		12	9	7	2	3			5		1		8		4		
21		29	LEYTON ORIENT	2-2	Miller, Teale	6139		11					9	3		7	12	10	2			6	5		1	8			4		
22	Jan	1	Bolton Wanderers	1-4	Blissett (p)	7639		11					9	3		7	12	10	2			6	5		1	8			4		
23		12	Bury	4-2	Holmes, Blissett, Lawrence, Ekoku	2761		11	12				14	8		7	9	10	2	3			5		1	6			4		
24		19	BRENTFORD	2-0	Teale, O'Driscoll	7167		11	2				12	8		7	9	10		3			6		1				4	5	
25	Feb	2	Bradford City	0-3		4914		11		8				2	1	7	9	10		3		14	6						4	5	12
26		5	EXETER CITY	2-1	Jones, Blissett	4982		11		8				2	1	12	9	10		3		14	6						4	5	7
27		16	BIRMINGHAM CITY	1-2	Watson	6330		11						2		8	9	10		3		12	6		1				4	5	7
28		23	Rotherham United	1-1	Jones	4112		11								8	9	12		3		2	6		1	10			4	5	7
29		27	Stoke City	3-1	Jones, Lawrence, Blissett	7815		11								8	9	12		3		2	6		1	10			4	5	7
30	Mar	2	CHESTER CITY	1-0	Blissett (p)	4669		11					12			8	9	10		3		2	6		1				4	5	7
31		5	WIGAN ATHLETIC	0-3		4662		11					12			8	9	14		3		2	6		1	10			4	5	7
32		9	Swansea City	2-1	Pulis, Mundee	3086		11	10					8				12		3		2	6		1	9			4	5	7
33		12	READING	2-0	Jones 2	5921			8					10			9	12		3		2	6		1	11			4	5	7
34		16	Fulham	1-1	Jones	4085		11	10					8			9	12		3			6		1	2			4	5	7
35		18	Tranmere Rovers	0-1		5420		11	8					10			9	12		3			6		1	2			4	5	7
36		23	SOUTHEND UNITED	3-1	Blissett, Prior (og), Watson	7421		11	2					8		10	9	12		3			6		1				4	5	7
37		30	Mansfield Town	1-1	Holmes	2665		11	2			8				10	9	12		3	14		6		1				4	5	7
38	Apr	2	GRIMSBY TOWN	2-1	Jones, Cooke	7021		11	2			8				10	9			3			6		1	12			4	5	7
39		6	Leyton Orient	0-2		4294		11	2			8				10	9			3			6		1				4	5	7
40		13	BOLTON WANDERERS	1-0	Cooke	7159		11	2			8		12		10		9		3			6		1				4	5	7
41		16	CAMBRIDGE UNITED	0-1		7156		11	2			8				10	9			3			6		1				4	5	7
42		20	Crewe Alexandra	2-0	Blissett 2	2892		11	2			8	14			10	9			3			6		1	12			4	5	7
43		24	Cambridge United	0-4		6433		11	2			8	9			14	12			3			6		1	10			4	5	7
44		27	HUDDERSFIELD T	3-1	Watson, Blissett, Bond	6888		11	2			8	14			10	9			3			6		1	12			4	5	7
45	May	2	PRESTON NORTH END	0-0		7257		11	2			8	12			10	9			3			6		1				4	5	7
46		11	Shrewsbury Town	1-3	Morrell	5016		11				8	12	2		10	9			3		14	6		1	7			4	5	
						Apps	9	45	30	13	7	10	20	18	10	42	33	34	16	42	1	21	45	15	36	15	9	5	46	23	21
						Goals		19	2			2	3			2	8	2	1	1		2	2	4		1			4	3	

PR Mitchell played in games 1 and 2 at 2

Two own goals

F.A. Cup

							Aylott TKC	Blissett LL	Bond KJ	Brooks S	Coleman DH	Cooke RE	Ekoku EG	Fereday W	Guthrie PJ	Holmes MJE	Jones AM	Lawrence GR	Miller PR	Morrell PDP	Morris DK	Mundee DWJ	O'Driscoll SM	Peacock GK	Peyton GJ	Pulis AR	Redknapp JF	Shearer PA	Teale S	Watson AF	Wood PA
R1	Nov	17	GILLINGHAM	2-1	Teale, Jones	6113		11	6							7	9		2	3			5	8	1		10		4		
R2	Dec	8	HAYES	1-0	Brooks	6510		11	6	10						7	9	12	2	3			5		1		8		4		
R3	Jan	5	Chester City	3-2	Jones 2, Ekoku	1833		11					14	3		7	9	10	2			12	5		1	6	8		4		
R4		26	Portsmouth	1-5	Fereday	15800		11	2				14	12		7	9	10		3			6		1	8			4	5	

F.L. Cup (Rumbelows Cup)

							Aylott TKC	Blissett LL	Bond KJ	Brooks S	Coleman DH	Cooke RE	Ekoku EG	Fereday W	Guthrie PJ	Holmes MJE	Jones AM	Lawrence GR	Miller PR	Morrell PDP	Morris DK	Mundee DWJ	O'Driscoll SM	Peacock GK	Peyton GJ	Pulis AR	Redknapp JF	Shearer PA	Teale S	Watson AF	Wood PA
R1/1	Aug	28	Birmingham City	1-0	Blissett	5110	9	11	6				12		1	10				3			7	8			2	5	4		
R1/2	Sep	4	BIRMINGHAM CITY	1-1	Blissett	4490	9	11			6				1	10				3		2	7				8	5	4		
R2/1		25	MILLWALL	0-0		4911	9	11	6		3		12		1	10		7				2	5	8					4		
R2/2	Oct	10	Millwall	1-2	Aylott	7702	9	11	6		3							7	2				5	8	1		10		4		

A.M. Cup (Leyland DAF Cup)

							Aylott TKC	Blissett LL	Bond KJ	Brooks S	Coleman DH	Cooke RE	Ekoku EG	Fereday W	Guthrie PJ	Holmes MJE	Jones AM	Lawrence GR	Miller PR	Morrell PDP	Morris DK	Mundee DWJ	O'Driscoll SM	Peacock GK	Peyton GJ	Pulis AR	Redknapp JF	Shearer PA	Teale S	Watson AF	Wood PA
PR	Nov	6	GILLINGHAM	0-0		2784		11		7						10	9		2	3			5	8	1		6		4		
PR	Dec	11	Maidstone United	1-3	Jones	1009		11	6	8			14				9	10	2	3		12	5		1		7		4		

Did not qualify

1991/92

8th in Division Three

	Date	Opponent	Score	Scorers	Att	Baker S	Bartram VL	Bond KJ	Brooks S	Case JR	Cooke RE	Ekoku EG	Fereday W	Holmes MJE	Jones AM	Lawrence GR	McGorry BP	Mitchell PR	Morrell PDP	Morris MJ	Mundee DWJ	O'Driscoll SM	Puckett DC	Pulis AR	Quinn JM	Rowland K	Shearer PA	Statham B	Watson AF	Wood PA
1	Aug 17	DARLINGTON	1-2	Morris	6210	2	1			10	7			11	8				3	4	14	6			9	12			5	
2	24	Stoke City	1-1	Quinn	9999	2	1	7		10	12			11	8				3	4	14	6			9				5	
3	31	HULL CITY	0-0		5015	7	1	2		10	12			11	8				3	4	14	6			9				5	
4	Sep 3	Preston North End	2-2	Holmes, Case	3170	2	1			10	12		7	11	8				3	4	14	6			9				5	
5	7	Chester City	1-0	O'Driscoll	1117	7	1			10				11	8	12		2	3	4	14	6			9				5	
6	14	BOLTON WANDERERS	1-2	Quinn	5690		1	2		10	12			11	8	7			3	4	14	6			9				5	
7	17	SHREWSBURY TOWN	1-0	Morris	4454		1	2		10				11	12	7				4	8	6			9	3			5	
8	21	Huddersfield Town	0-0		6802		1	2		10	7			11		12				4	8	6			9	3			5	
9	27	FULHAM	0-0		6450		1	2		10	7		14	11		12				4	8	6			9	3			5	
10	Oct 5	Reading	0-0		4033	12	1	2						11			10			4	8	6			9	3			5	7
11	12	HARTLEPOOL UNITED	2-0	Holmes, Quinn	4817		1	2			10			11			12			4	8	6			9	3			5	7
12	19	Leyton Orient	1-1	Quinn	3876		1	2		10	7			11			12			4	5	6			9	3				8
13	26	BRADFORD CITY	1-3	Quinn	4445		1	2		10	7			11			6			4	12	5			9	3				8
14	Nov 1	STOCKPORT COUNTY	1-0	Morris	4649		1			10			7	11			6			4	2	5			9	3				8
15	6	Torquay United	0-1		1884		1	2		10			7	11			12			4	5	6			9	3				8
16	8	Swansea City	1-3	Quinn	2698		1	2		10	14		12	11			6			4	7	5			9	3				8
17	22	BRENTFORD	0-0		6035		1	2		10				11						4	7	6			9	3		5		8
18	30	Bury	1-0	Mundee	1886		1	2		10		12		11						4	7	6			9	3		5		8
19	Dec 14	BIRMINGHAM CITY	2-1	Wood, Quinn	6048		1	2		10	12	7		11						4	5	6			9	3				8
20	21	STOKE CITY	1-2	Wood	5436		1	2		10	7			11		12		14		4	5	6			9	3				8
21	26	Hull City	1-0	Quinn	4741		1	2	7	10	12	14		11						4	5	6			9	3				8
22	28	Darlington	0-0		3162		1	2	7	10		12		11						4	5	6			9	3				8
23	Jan 1	PRESTON NORTH END	1-0	Wood	5508		1	2	11	10	12	7		14						4	5	6			9	3				8
24	11	West Bromwich Albion	0-4		10932		1	2	7	10		9		11		12				4	5	6				3				8
25	18	WIGAN ATHLETIC	3-0	Bond, Wood, Quinn	4338		1	2	7	10		11		6						4	5	12			9	3				8
26	Feb 1	LEYTON ORIENT	0-1		6544		1	2	7	10	12	11		8					14	4	5	6			9	3				
27	8	Bradford City	1-3	Quinn	5820		1	2		10	12	7		14					3	4	5	6			9	11				8
28	11	BURY	4-0	Quinn, Mundee, Ekoku 2	3558		1	2	12		7	14		10					5	4	11	6			9	3				8
29	15	Birmingham City	1-0	Quinn	10898		1	2		12	7	11		10				14	5		4	6			9	3				8
30	22	WEST BROMWICH ALB.	2-1	Wood, Ekoku	7721		1	2		10	7	9		11		12		14	5	4		6				3				8
31	29	Exeter City	3-0	Quinn 2 (1p), Morrell	4539		1	2			7	11		6					5	4	14	10			9	3	12			8
32	Mar 3	Wigan Athletic	0-2		1790		1				7	11		6			14	12	5	4	2				9	3	10			8
33	7	PETERBOROUGH UTD.	1-2	Shearer	5379		1	2			7	11		6					5	4	8		12		9	3	10			
34	10	TORQUAY UNITED	2-1	Quinn, Ekoku	4083		1	5		12	7	11		6						4	2	10			9	3				8
35	13	Stockport County	0-5		3576		1	5		10		11		6						4	2	7	12	14	9	3				8
36	20	SWANSEA CITY	3-0	Ekoku 2, Wood	4385		1	2		10		11		6					5	4		12	7		9	3				8
37	24	EXETER CITY	1-0	Quinn	4959		1	2		10	7	11		6					5	4		12			9	3				8
38	29	Brentford	2-2	Holmes, Ekoku	7605		1	2		10	12	11		6					5	4		7			9	3				8
39	31	Bolton Wanderers	2-0	Ekoku, Wood	4905		1	2		10	7	11		6					3	4	14	5			9	12				8
40	Apr 3	CHESTER CITY	2-0	Wood, Ekoku	5974		1	2		10	7	11		6					3	4	12	5			9					8
41	8	Peterborough United	0-2		4910		1	2		10		11		6					3	4		5			9	12	7			8
42	11	Shrewsbury Town	2-1	Quinn, Ekoku	2586		1			10		11		6					3	4	12	5			9		7		2	8
43	14	HUDDERSFIELD T	1-1	Wood	7655		1			10		11		6					3	4	2	7	12				9		5	8
44	20	Fulham	0-2		7619		1			10	6	11		14					3	4	12	5			9		7		2	8
45	25	READING	3-2	Quinn 2 (2p), Ekoku	6486		1	4		10	7	11		6							2	12			9	3			5	8
46	May 2	Hartlepool United	0-1		2612		1	4		10	7	11		6					5		12	2			9	3	14			8
					Apps	6	46	38	7	40	31	28	5	46	7	8	8	5	24	43	41	44	4	1	43	37	8	2	15	35
					Goals			1		1	11			3					1	3	2	1			19		1			9

F.A. Cup

	Date	Opponent	Score	Scorers	Att	Baker S	Bartram VL	Bond KJ	Brooks S	Case JR	Cooke RE	Ekoku EG	Fereday W	Holmes MJE	Jones AM	Lawrence GR	McGorry BP	Mitchell PR	Morrell PDP	Morris MJ	Mundee DWJ	O'Driscoll SM	Puckett DC	Pulis AR	Quinn JM	Rowland K	Shearer PA	Statham B	Watson AF	Wood PA
R1	Nov 16	BROMSGROVE ROVERS	3-1	Bond, Mundee 2 (2p)	4301		1	2		10	6		4	11			12				7	5			9	3				8
R2	Dec 7	BRENTFORD	2-1	Quinn 2	6538		1	2		10	14	7		11			12			4	5	6			9	3				8
R3	Jan 4	NEWCASTLE UNITED	0-0		10651		1	2	7	10	12	11		14						4	5	6			9	3				8
rep	22	Newcastle United	2-2	Wood, Bond	25954		1	2	12	10	14	11		7						4	5	6			9	3				8
R4	Feb 5	Ipswich Town	0-3		17193		1	2	7	10		11		14					12	4	5	6			9	3				8

R3 replay won 4-3 on penalties a.e.t.

F.L. Cup (Rumbelows Cup)

	Date	Opponent	Score	Scorers	Att	Baker S	Bartram VL	Bond KJ	Brooks S	Case JR	Cooke RE	Ekoku EG	Fereday W	Holmes MJE	Jones AM	Lawrence GR	McGorry BP	Mitchell PR	Morrell PDP	Morris MJ	Mundee DWJ	O'Driscoll SM	Puckett DC	Pulis AR	Quinn JM	Rowland K	Shearer PA	Statham B	Watson AF	Wood PA
R1/1	Aug 21	Cardiff City	2-3	Morrell, Cooke	3439	2	1			10	12			11	8				3	4		6			9	7			5	
R1/2	27	CARDIFF CITY	4-1	Jones 2, Quinn, Watson	4489	2	1	7		10				11	8				3	4		6			9				5	
R2/1	Sep 24	Middlesbrough	1-1	Lawrence	10577		1	2		10	7		14	11		12				4	8	6			9	3			5	
R2/2	Oct 8	MIDDLEBROUGH	1-2	Quinn	5528		1	2			7		12	11			10			4	14	6			9	3			5	8

A.M. Cup (Autoglass Trophy)

	Date	Opponent	Score	Scorers	Att	Baker S	Bartram VL	Bond KJ	Brooks S	Case JR	Cooke RE	Ekoku EG	Fereday W	Holmes MJE	Jones AM	Lawrence GR	McGorry BP	Mitchell PR	Morrell PDP	Morris MJ	Mundee DWJ	O'Driscoll SM	Puckett DC	Pulis AR	Quinn JM	Rowland K	Shearer PA	Statham B	Watson AF	Wood PA
PR	Oct 22	SWANSEA CITY	3-0	Wood 2, McGorry	1814		1			10	7		12	11			6	14		4	5	2			9	3				8
PR	Dec 10	Cardiff City	3-3	Mundee, Ekoku, Quinn	1337		1				10	7	12	11			8			4	2	6			9	3		5		
R1	Feb 18	WREXHAM	1-2	Case	2279		1			10	7	9		11				4	5		2	6				3				8

1992/93

17th in Division Two

	Date	Opponent	Score	Scorers	Att	Bartram VL	Beadle PCWJ	Butler S	Cooke RE	Ekoku EG	Fletcher SM	Lovell SJ	Masters NB	McGorry BP	Mean SJ	Mitchell PR	Morgan N	Morrell PDP	Morris MJ	Moss NG	Mundee DWJ	Murray RJ	O'Driscoll SM	Pennock AB	Regis DR	Rowland K	Scott PR	Shearer PA	Smith D	Watson AF	Wood PA
1	Aug 15	Preston North End	1-1	Rowland	4763	1			12		9			10	7			3			14		2	5	8	11	6			4	
2	22	PORT VALE	2-1	Fletcher, Watson	4825	1			12		9			10	14			3	5				7	2	8	11	6			4	
3	29	West Bromwich Albion	1-2	Regis	12563	1			12		9			10	6			3	5				7	2	8	11				4	
4	Sep 1	Mansfield Town	2-0	Regis, Fletcher	3031	1			12		9			10	7			3	5				6	2	8	11				4	
5	5	HARTLEPOOL UNITED	0-2		4446	1			7		9			10				3	5		12		6	2	8	11				4	
6	12	FULHAM	2-1	McGorry 2	5398	1			7		9			10	12			3	5				6	2	8	11				4	
7	15	Blackpool	0-2		3455	1			7		9			10	8				5		3	12	6	2		11				4	
8	19	Bolton Wanderers	1-1	Morris	4623	1			7		9			10					5		3		6	2		11		8		4	
9	26	HUDDERSFIELD T	1-1	Rowland	4447	1			7		9			10	12				5		3		6	2		11		8		4	
10	Oct 3	Exeter City	1-1	Shearer	3653	1			10		9			8	12			14	4		3		7	2		11		6		5	
11	10	ROTHERHAM UNITED	0-0		4233	1			10		9			8	7			4			3			2		11		6		5	
12	17	Leyton Orient	0-1		4528	1			10		9			8	12				4		3		7	2		11		6		5	
13	24	STOCKPORT COUNTY	1-0	Morgan	4058	1					9			8			10		4		3		7	2		11		6		5	
14	31	Wigan Athletic	0-0		1803	1					9		11	8	12		10	3	4				7	2			14	6		5	
15	Nov 3	BRIGHTON & HOVE ALB	1-1	Mundee (p)	4828	1							11	8				3	4		9	14	7	2		12	10	6		5	
16	7	Stoke City	0-2		15133	1						9	12	8				3	4		2	14	7			11	10	6		5	
17	21	READING	1-1	McGorry	4418	1						9		6			10	3	4		8		2			11				5	7
18	28	Plymouth Argyle	1-2	Burrows (og)	6408	1						9		6			10	3	4		12	14	8	2		11				5	7
19	Dec 12	Bradford City	1-0	McGorry	5011	1							3	9			10		4		11			2			6	8		5	7
20	19	HULL CITY	0-0		4486	1		9					3	6			10		4		11		14	2		12		8		5	7
21	26	SWANSEA CITY	0-2		4995	1								9	12				4		11	14	10	2		3	6	8		5	7
22	Jan 9	BLACKPOOL	5-1	Ekoku 2, Murray 2, Wood	3807	1				10			3	9					4		6	11		2				8		5	7
23	16	Huddersfield Town	1-0	Ekoku	4316	1				10			3		12				4		6	14	9	2			11	8		5	7
24	26	WEST BROMWICH ALB.	0-1		5687	1				10	9		3						4		2	12	11	6				8		5	7
25	30	Port Vale	0-3		6834	1				10			3	9					4				6	2				8	11	5	7
26	Feb 6	PRESTON NORTH END	2-1	Ekoku, McGorry	3601	1				10	11		3	9					4		2	12	14	6				8		5	7
27	13	Hartlepool United	1-0	Ekoku	2197	1				10	11		3	9					4		2		8	6						5	7
28	20	MANSFIELD TOWN	4-1	McGorry, Fletcher, Ekoku, Wood	3987	1				10	11		3	9					4			12	2	6		8				5	7
29	26	Rotherham United	2-1	McGorry, Wood	4388	1				10	11		3	9					4				2	6		12		8		5	7
30	Mar 2	Fulham	1-1	Wood	3424	1				10			3	9					4			12	2	6		11		8		5	7
31	6	EXETER CITY	1-3	Pennock	4948	1				10			3	9					4			12	2	6		11		8		5	7
32	9	Chester City	0-1		1614	1				10	11		3	9					4			12	14	6		2		8		5	7
33	13	STOKE CITY	1-1	Ekoku	7129	1				10	9		3	6					4		2	12	14			11		8		5	7
34	16	Burnley	1-1	Mundee	8601	1					10		3	9					4		7	12	2	6		11		8		5	
35	20	Brighton & Hove Albion	0-1		7059	1				10	9		3						4		7	12	2	6		11		8		5	
36	23	PLYMOUTH ARGYLE	1-3	Fletcher	4150	1				10	9		3								2	12	4	6		11		8		5	7
37	27	Reading	2-3	Shearer, Beadle	5978	1	9				12					14			4		3	7	2	6		11		8		5	10
38	Apr 3	CHESTER CITY	0-0		2829	1	10				9					11			4			12	2	6		3		8		5	7
39	6	BRADFORD CITY	1-1	Murray	2851	1	10				9					12		3	4			7	2	6		11		8		5	
40	10	Swansea City	1-2	Mean	5101										12	11		10	4	1		9	2	6		3		8		5	7
41	13	BURNLEY	1-1	Shearer	4456	1	10				9							3	4			12	2	6			11	8		5	7
42	17	Hull City	0-3		3442	1	10				9			12				3	4				2	6			11	8		5	7
43	24	LEYTON ORIENT	3-0	McGorry, Shearer, Beadle	4595	1	10							9				3	4			12	2	6		11		8		5	7
44	27	BOLTON WANDERERS	1-2	Murray	4434	1	10							9				3	4			12	2	6		11		8		5	7
45	May 1	Stockport County	0-0		5446	1	10				11			9				3	4				2	6		12		8		5	7
46	8	WIGAN ATHLETIC	0-0		3838	1	10				12			9	8	2		3	4			11		6						5	7
					Apps	45	9	1	12	14	31	3	20	37	15	5	6	21	43	1	26	25	42	43	6	35	10	34	1	46	27
					Goals		2			7	4			8	1		1		1		2	4		1	2	2		4		1	4

Played in one game: DG Holmes (7, at 14), MT McElhatton (46, 14), DM Williams (44, 14)

One own goal

F.A. Cup

	Date	Opponent	Score	Scorers	Att	Bartram VL	Beadle PCWJ	Butler S	Cooke RE	Ekoku EG	Fletcher SM	Lovell SJ	Masters NB	McGorry BP	Mean SJ	Mitchell PR	Morgan N	Morrell PDP	Morris MJ	Moss NG	Mundee DWJ	Murray RJ	O'Driscoll SM	Pennock AB	Regis DR	Rowland K	Scott PR	Shearer PA	Smith D	Watson AF	Wood PA
R1	Nov 14	BARNET	0-0		4688	1						9	12					3	4		8		2			11	10	6		5	7
rep	25	Barnet	2-1	Lovell, Mundee	3731	1						9	14	8				3	4		2	12	7	6		11				5	10
R2	Dec 5	Cheltenham Town	1-1	Shearer	4100	1								9			10	3	4		12		6	2		11		8		5	7
rep	16	CHELTENHAM TOWN	3-0	Mundee, McGorry, Morgan	5100	1							3	6			10		4		9		11	2				8		5	7
R3	Jan 2	Blackburn Rovers	1-3	Ekoku	13773	1				10			3	6					4		11		9	2				8		5	7

F.L. Cup (Coca Cola Cup)

	Date	Opponent	Score	Scorers	Att	Bartram VL	Beadle PCWJ	Butler S	Cooke RE	Ekoku EG	Fletcher SM	Lovell SJ	Masters NB	McGorry BP	Mean SJ	Mitchell PR	Morgan N	Morrell PDP	Morris MJ	Moss NG	Mundee DWJ	Murray RJ	O'Driscoll SM	Pennock AB	Regis DR	Rowland K	Scott PR	Shearer PA	Smith D	Watson AF	Wood PA
R1/1	Aug 19	Walsall	1-1	Morris	3001	1					9			10	7			3	5		12		8	2		11	6			4	
R1/2	25	WALSALL	0-1		3567	1			12		9			10	7			3	5				8	2		11	6			4	

A.M. Cup (Autoglass Trophy)

	Date	Opponent	Score	Scorers	Att	Bartram VL	Beadle PCWJ	Butler S	Cooke RE	Ekoku EG	Fletcher SM	Lovell SJ	Masters NB	McGorry BP	Mean SJ	Mitchell PR	Morgan N	Morrell PDP	Morris MJ	Moss NG	Mundee DWJ	Murray RJ	O'Driscoll SM	Pennock AB	Regis DR	Rowland K	Scott PR	Shearer PA	Smith D	Watson AF	Wood PA
R1	Dec 9	Brighton & Hove Albion	2-3	Morgan, Mundee	1607	1							3	6	11		10		4		9			2				8		5	7
R1	Jan 5	READING	1-1	Ekoku	1218	1				10			3	9	6				4		11	12		2			14	8		5	7

Did not qualify

1993/94

17th in Division Two

	Date		Opponent	Score	Scorers	Att	Aspinall WG	Bartram VL	Beardsmore RP	Burns C	Chivers GPS	Cotterill SJ	Fletcher SM	Leadbitter CJ	Masters NB	McElhatton MT	McGorry BP	Mean SJ	Mitchell GL	Morris MJ	Moss NG	Murray RJ	O'Connor MA	O'Driscoll SM	Parkinson JS	Pennock AB	Russell KJ	Skinner JJ	Town DE	Watson AF	Wood PA
1	Aug	14	Bristol Rovers	1-0	Fletcher	7209		1	11			10	9		3		8			4		14	7		6	2				5	12
2		21	BRADFORD CITY	1-1	Cotterill	4589		1	11			10	9	14	3		8	12		4			7		6	2				5	
3		28	Hartlepool United	1-1	Parkinson	2482	12	1	11			10	9		3		8			4			7		6	2				5	
4		31	YORK CITY	3-1	McGorry 2, Cotterill	4113	12	1	11			10	9		3		8			4			7		6	2				5	
5	Sep	4	BURNLEY	1-0	Cotterill	5574	8	1	11			10	9	12	3					4			7		6	2				5	
6		11	Barnet	2-1	Masters (p), Fletcher	2979	8	1	11			10	9	12	3					4			7		6	2				5	
7		18	CAMBRIDGE UNITED	1-2	Cotterill	5417	8	1	11			10	9	14	3					4			7		6	2				5	12
8		25	Blackpool	1-2	Aspinall	4489	10	1	14				9	11	3		8			4			7		6	2				5	12
9	Oct	2	STOCKPORT COUNTY	1-1	Cotterill	4428		1	11			10	9	7	3		8			4					6	2				5	12
10		9	Fulham	2-0	Pennock, Fletcher	4004		1	12			10	9	11	3		8			4			7		6	2				5	
11		16	BRIGHTON & HOVE ALB	2-1	Masters. McGorry	5665		1	11			10	9	12	3		8			4			7		6	2				5	
12		23	Leyton Orient	0-0		3896		1	11				9	10	3		8			4			7		6	2				5	12
13		30	EXETER CITY	1-1	Wood	5155		1	11				9	3				8		4			7	12	6	2				5	10
14	Nov	6	Wrexham	1-2	Wood	3958		1	12		8		9	11	3					4			7		6	2				5	10
15		20	HULL CITY	0-2		4124		1	12		9			10	3		8			4			7		6	2				5	11
16		27	Reading	0-3		5549		1	12		2			10	3	14	8			4			7	9	6					5	11
17	Dec	7	PORT VALE	2-1	Cotterill, Wood	2954		1			4	10		11	3		8					12	7	2	6					5	9
18		11	Bradford City	0-0		4407		1			2	10			3		8			4			7		6	11				5	9
19		18	BRISTOL ROVERS	3-0	Pennock, Wood, Cotterill	4811		1			14	10	9		3		8			4		12	7		6	2				5	11
20		27	BRENTFORD	0-3		6422		1			14	10	9	3			8		4			12	7		6	2				5	11
21	Jan	1	PLYMOUTH ARGYLE	0-1		6990	11	1			4	10	9				8		3			12	7		6	2				5	
22		3	Huddersfield Town	1-1	Murray	6047	8	1	12		4	10	9	3		11						14	7		6	2				5	
23		15	Brighton & Hove Albion	3-3	Murray 2, Aspinall	9689	8	1			4	10		3					2		12	11	7		6	9				5	
24		22	FULHAM	1-3	Murray	4440	8		6		4		10	3				12	2		1	11	7			9				5	
25		29	Exeter City	2-0	Wood, Chivers	3602	8		12		4	10	14	3							1	11	7	6		2				5	9
26	Feb	5	LEYTON ORIENT	1-1	O'Connor	4084	8				4	10	12	3							1	11	7		6	2				5	9
27		12	Swansea City	1-1	Cotterill	3255	8	1			2	10		3						4		12	7		6	11				5	9
28		19	HARTLEPOOL UNITED	0-0		3201	8	1	11		2	10	9	3						4		12	7		6					5	
29		26	Burnley	0-4		9991	8	1	11		2	10	9	3				14		4		12	7		6					5	
30	Mar	5	BARNET	1-1	Aspinall	3407	8	1	12		2		10	3						4		14	7		6	9	11			5	
31		8	Rotherham United	2-1	Aspinall, Cotterill	2884	8	1			2	10		12		6				4		14	7			9	11	3		5	
32		12	Cambridge United	2-3	O'Connor 2	2836	8	1		5	2	10				6				4		12	7			9	11	3			
33		15	CARDIFF CITY	3-2	Cotterill 2, Chivers	2385				6	2	10	9			12				4	1		7			8	11	3		5	
34		19	BLACKPOOL	1-0	Cotterill	3335		1	12	6		10	8							4			7		9	2	11	3		5	
35		22	York City	0-2		3648		1	10	6			9							4		12	7		8	2	11	3		5	
36		26	Stockport County	2-0	Cotterill, Burns	5277	8	1		6	2	10	12			14				4			7			9	11	3		5	
37		29	HUDDERSFIELD T	1-2	Watson	3104	8	1		6	2	10	12							4			7			9	11	3		5	
38	Apr	2	Brentford	1-1	Fletcher	4305		1		6	2	10	8	12						4			7			9	11	3		5	
39		5	ROTHERHAM UNITED	0-0		3097		1		6	2	10	9	8						4		12	7				11	3		5	
40		9	Plymouth Argyle	0-2		7971		1		6	2	10				8		12		4		9	7				11	3		5	
41		16	Port Vale	1-2	Pennock	7603		1			2	10	9			8				4			7			6	11	3		5	
42		19	SWANSEA CITY	0-1		2465	9	1		2		10				8				4		12	7			6	11	3		5	
43		21	Cardiff City	1-2	Fletcher	3838	8	1		6		10	12							4			7	9		2	11	3		5	
44		23	WREXHAM	1-2	Aspinall	3290	10	1		8		12	9							4			7	6		2	11	3		5	
45		30	Hull City	1-1	Russell	4926	8	1		12		10	9							4			7	6		2	11	3		5	
46	May	5	READING	2-1	Fletcher, Cotterill	7106				8		10	9			12				4	1		7	6		2	11	3	14	5	
						Apps	24	41	24	14	26	37	36	27	18	10	16	5	4	38	6	20	45	8	30	40	17	16	1	45	16
						Goals	5			1	2	14	6		2		3					4	3		1	3	1			1	5

DJ Kevan played at 14 in game 44

F.A. Cup

	Date		Opponent	Score	Scorers	Att	Aspinall WG	Bartram VL	Beardsmore RP	Burns C	Chivers GPS	Cotterill SJ	Fletcher SM	Leadbitter CJ	Masters NB	McElhatton MT	McGorry BP	Mean SJ	Mitchell GL	Morris MJ	Moss NG	Murray RJ	O'Connor MA	O'Driscoll SM	Parkinson JS	Pennock AB	Russell KJ	Skinner JJ	Town DE	Watson AF	Wood PA
R1	Nov	13	BRIGHTON & HOVE ALB.	4-2	McGorry, Pennock, Masters, Wood	5223		1			9			10	3		8			4	12		7		6	2				5	11
R2	Dec	4	NUNEATON BOROUGH	1-1	Watson	5485		1	9		2	12		11	3		8			4			7		6					5	10
rep		15	Nuneaton Borough	1-0	Cotterill	4127		1				10	9		3		8			4		12	7		6	2				5	11
R3	Jan	8	Preston North End	1-2	Aspinall (p)	8457	8	1	11		4	10	9	3			12					14	7		6	2				5	

F.L. Cup (Coca Cola Cup)

	Date		Opponent	Score	Scorers	Att	Aspinall WG	Bartram VL	Beardsmore RP	Burns C	Chivers GPS	Cotterill SJ	Fletcher SM	Leadbitter CJ	Masters NB	McElhatton MT	McGorry BP	Mean SJ	Mitchell GL	Morris MJ	Moss NG	Murray RJ	O'Connor MA	O'Driscoll SM	Parkinson JS	Pennock AB	Russell KJ	Skinner JJ	Town DE	Watson AF	Wood PA
R1/1	Aug	17	CARDIFF CITY	3-1	Fletcher, Masters, Beardsmore	3054		1	11			10	9		3		8			4			7		6	2				5	
R1/2		24	Cardiff City	1-1	Parkinson	4459		1	11			10	9	12	3		8			4			7		6	2				5	
R2/1	Sep	21	Blackburn Rovers	0-1		10773		1				10	9	11	3		8			4			7		6	2				5	
R2/2	Oct	5	BLACKBURN ROVERS	0-0		10321		1	11			10	9	7	3		8			4			12		6	2				5	14

A.M. Cup (Autoglass Trophy)

	Date		Opponent	Score	Scorers	Att	Aspinall WG	Bartram VL	Beardsmore RP	Burns C	Chivers GPS	Cotterill SJ	Fletcher SM	Leadbitter CJ	Masters NB	McElhatton MT	McGorry BP	Mean SJ	Mitchell GL	Morris MJ	Moss NG	Murray RJ	O'Connor MA	O'Driscoll SM	Parkinson JS	Pennock AB	Russell KJ	Skinner JJ	Town DE	Watson AF	Wood PA
R2	Dec	21	LEYTON ORIENT	1-1	Murray	1383		1			12	10	9	3			8			4		14	7		6	2				5	11

Lost on 3-5 on penalties a.e.t.

1994/95

19th in Division Two

	Date		Opponent	Score	Scorers	Att	Andrews IE	Aspinall WG	Barfoot SJ	Beardsmore RP	Brissett JC	Chivers GPS	Cotterill SJ	Fletcher SM	Holland MR	Jones SG	Leadbitter CJ	McElhatton MT	Mean SJ	Morris MJ	Moss NG	Murray RJ	O'Connor MA	O'Driscoll SM	Pennock AB	Reeve JM	Robinson S	Russell KJ	Scully ADT	Town DE	Vincent JR	Watson AF	Young NA
1	Aug	13	Wrexham	0-2		3582		8		7			10	9			6		12	4	1		3	2				11				5	
2		20	BLACKPOOL	1-2	Cotterill	3098				7			10	9			6		8	4	1		3	2		12		11				5	
3		27	Rotherham United	0-4		2306				7			10	9			6		8	4	1		3	2				11				5	
4		30	PETERBOROUGH UTD.	0-3		2649		12		7			10	9			6	8		4	1	14	3	2				11				5	
5	Sep	3	YORK CITY	1-4	Aspinall (p)	3181		6		7			10	5			8	4	12		1	9	3	2		14		11					
6		10	Stockport County	0-1		4054	1	8		7			10	6			11	5	12				3	2				9		14			
7		13	Leyton Orient	2-3	Aspinall, Leadbitter	2540	1	8					10	6			11	7	12				3	2		14		9				5	
8		17	CHESTER CITY	1-1	Leadbitter	3025	1			7			10	6			11	2	8				3			12		9				5	
9		24	CARDIFF CITY	3-2	Beardsmore 2, Aspinall (p)	3177	1	9		7				6			11	4	8				3	2				10				5	
10	Oct	1	Hull City	1-3	Aspinall	3056	1	9	14	7				6			11	4	8				3	2		12		10				5	
11		8	Shrewsbury Town	0-3		3684	1	9	12	7				6			11	4	8					2		10						5	
12		15	BRENTFORD	0-1		4411	1	9		7		3		12				14	8	4					6	10			11			5	2
13		22	BRADFORD CITY	2-3	Mean (p), Morris	3037	1			7		3		12		9		14	8	4		5			6		10		11				2
14		29	Huddersfield Town	1-3	Jones	11251	1			7		3		5		10	6		8	4							12	9	11				2
15	Nov	2	Brighton & Hove Albion	0-0		5631	1			7		3				10	6		8	4							9	11	12			5	2
16		5	CAMBRIDGE UNITED	1-0	Robinson	3272	1			7		3				10	6	12	8	4		14					9		11			5	2
17		19	Birmingham City	0-0		15477	1			7						10	6	12	8	4					2		9		11			5	3
18		26	OXFORD UNITED	0-2		4277	1			7						10	6		8			12			4		9		11		3	5	2
19	Dec	10	Blackpool	1-3	Jones	3847	1			7						10	6		8	4			12		11		9		14		3	5	2
20		16	WREXHAM	1-3	Hughes (og)	2505				7						10			8	4	1				6		9	11	12		3	5	2
21		26	Bristol Rovers	1-2	Pennock	6937	1			7	8			12		10	6			4		5			11		9		14		3		2
22		27	CREWE ALEXANDRA	1-1	Beardsmore	3325	1			7	11			10			8			4		5	12		6		9			14	3		2
23		31	Wycombe Wanderers	1-1	Robinson	5990	1			7	11			10			9	14	12	4		5			6		8				3		2
24	Jan	2	SWANSEA CITY	3-2	Fletcher 2, Pennock	3816	1			7	11			10		14	9		12	4		5			6		8				3		2
25		7	Bradford City	2-1	Robinson, Leadbitter	5426	1			7	11			10		12	9			4		5			6		8				3		2
26		14	PLYMOUTH ARGYLE	0-0		4913	1				11			10		14		7	9	4		5	3		6		8					12	2
27		21	Cambridge United	2-2	Pennock, McElhatton	2832	1			3	11			10		7		14	9	4		5			6		8					12	2
28		28	HUDDERSFIELD T	0-2		4427	1			3	11			10	14	7	9	12		4		5			6		8						2
29	Feb	4	Oxford United	3-0	Jones 2, Fletcher	5473	1			3				10	11	7	9	12		4		5			6		8						2
30		11	BRIGHTON & HOVE ALB	0-3		5247	1			3	14			10	11	7	9		12	4		5			6		8						2
31		18	Plymouth Argyle	1-0	McElhatton	5435	1			3	11			10	7	9		2	12	4		5			6		8						
32		21	BIRMINGHAM CITY	2-1	Jones, Mean	6024				3	11			10	7	9		2	6	4	1	5					8					12	
33		25	HULL CITY	2-3	Jones, Pennock	4345					11			10	7	9		2	6	4	1	5			8					14		12	3
34	Mar	4	Cardiff City	1-1	Fletcher	3008	1			3	11			10	7	9		12	6	4		5			8		14						2
35		7	York City	0-1		2301	1			3	11			10	7	9		12	6	4		5			8								2
36		11	ROTHERHAM UNITED	1-1	Morris	5666	1			3	11			10	7		14		6	4		5			9		8					12	2
37		18	Peterborough United	0-0		4495	1			3	11			10	7		12		6	4		5			9		8						2
38		21	STOCKPORT COUNTY	2-0	Fletcher, Jones	2892	1			3	11			10		9		12	6	4		5			8		7						2
39		25	Chester City	1-1	Fletcher	1618	1			3	11			10	14	9			6	4		5			7		8			12			2
40	Apr	1	LEYTON ORIENT	2-0	Pennock, Holland	4118	1			3	11			10	12	9			6	4		5			7		8						2
41		8	WYCOMBE WANDERERS	2-0	Mean 2 (2p)	5816	1			3	11			10	12	9			6	4		5			7		8						2
42		15	Crewe Alexandra	0-2		3906	1			3	11			10	14	9			6	4		5			7		8			12			2
43		18	BRISTOL ROVERS	2-0	Morris, Mean	7020	1			3	11			10		9		12	6	4		5			7		8						2
44		22	Swansea City	0-1		2664	1			3	11			10	14	9		2	6	4		5			7		8					12	
45		29	Brentford	2-1	Mean, Jones	10079	1			3	11			10	14	9		12	6	4		5			7		8						2
46	May	2	SHREWSBURY TOWN	3-0	Robinson 2, Mean	10747	1			3	11			10		9		12	6	4		5			7		8						2
						Apps	38	9	2	43	25	5	8	40	16	30	27	27	40	38	8	31	13	10	31	7	32	13	10	5	8	22	32
						Goals		4		3			1	6	1	8	3	2	7	3					5		5						

Played in one game; SG Strong (46, at 14), D Wells (20, at 14), GJ Williams (8, at 14), S Brooks (11, at 3, subbed), CA Ferrett (11, at 14)

LE Russell played at 4 in three games 6, 7, and 8

One own goal

F.A. Cup

	Date		Opponent	Score	Scorers	Att	Andrews IE	Aspinall WG	Barfoot SJ	Beardsmore RP	Brissett JC	Chivers GPS	Cotterill SJ	Fletcher SM	Holland MR	Jones SG	Leadbitter CJ	McElhatton MT	Mean SJ	Morris MJ	Moss NG	Murray RJ	O'Connor MA	O'Driscoll SM	Pennock AB	Reeve JM	Robinson S	Russell KJ	Scully ADT	Town DE	Vincent JR	Watson AF	Young NA
R1	Nov	12	WORTHING	3-1	Morris, K Russell, McElhatton	3922	1			7		2					6	12	8	4		14			10		9	11				5	3
R2	Dec	3	Plymouth Argyle	1-2	Jones	6739	1			7						10	6	12	8	4		14			3		9	11				5	2

F.L. Cup (Coca Cola Cup)

	Date		Opponent	Score	Scorers	Att	Andrews IE	Aspinall WG	Barfoot SJ	Beardsmore RP	Brissett JC	Chivers GPS	Cotterill SJ	Fletcher SM	Holland MR	Jones SG	Leadbitter CJ	McElhatton MT	Mean SJ	Morris MJ	Moss NG	Murray RJ	O'Connor MA	O'Driscoll SM	Pennock AB	Reeve JM	Robinson S	Russell KJ	Scully ADT	Town DE	Vincent JR	Watson AF	Young NA
R1/1	Aug	16	NORTHAMPTON T	2-0	K Russell, Cotterill	2587		8		7			10	9			6		12	4	1		3	2				11				5	
R1/2	Sep	6	Northampton Town	1-0	Cotterill	3249	1	8		7			10	6			11	4				12	3	2				9		14		5	
R2/1		21	Chelsea	0-1		8974	1	9	12	7				6			11	4	8				3	2		14		10				5	
R2/2	Oct	4	CHELSEA	0-1		9784	1	9		7				6			11	4	8			12	3	2		10						5	

Played in R2/2 at 14: D Adekola

A.M. Cup (Auto Windscreens Shield)

	Date		Opponent	Score	Scorers	Att	Andrews IE	Aspinall WG	Barfoot SJ	Beardsmore RP	Brissett JC	Chivers GPS	Cotterill SJ	Fletcher SM	Holland MR	Jones SG	Leadbitter CJ	McElhatton MT	Mean SJ	Morris MJ	Moss NG	Murray RJ	O'Connor MA	O'Driscoll SM	Pennock AB	Reeve JM	Robinson S	Russell KJ	Scully ADT	Town DE	Vincent JR	Watson AF	Young NA
R1	Oct	19	Bristol Rovers	1-1	Murray	1725	1	9		7		3		10					8	4		12			6	14			11			5	2
R1	Nov	8	OXFORD UNITED	0-0		1374	1			7		12				10	6		8	4		14			3		9		11			5	2

Did not qualify

1995/96

14th in Division Two

	Date		Opponent	Score	Scorers	Att	Andrews IE	Bailey JA	Beardsmore RP	Brissett JC	Casper CM	Cureton J	Duberry MW	Fletcher SM	Glass JR	Holland MR	Howe EJF	Jones SG	McElhatton MT	Mean SJ	Morris MJ	Moss NG	Murray RJ	Ndah GE	Oldbury MJ	O'Neill JJ	Pennock AB	Rawlinson MD	Robinson S	Scott K	Town DE	Victory JC	Young NA
1	Aug	12	Bradford City	0-1		5107	1	14	3	11				10		7		9		6	4		5				12		8			13	2
2		19	PETERBOROUGH UTD.	3-0	Jones 3	4175	1	10	3	11						7		9		6	4		5						8				2
3		26	Wycombe Wanderers	2-1	Jones, Murray	4749	1	10	3	11						7		9		6	4		5				8	13			14	12	2
4		29	WREXHAM	1-1	Jones	4825	1	10	3	11						7		9		6	4		5				8				13	12	2
5	Sep	2	ROTHERHAM UNITED	2-1	Brissett, Holland	4906	1	10	3	11						7		9		6	4		5				8						2
6		9	Notts County	0-2		4875	1	10	3	11		14						9	13	6	4		5				8		12			7	2
7		12	Blackpool	1-2	Jones	3884	1	10	3	11		14						9	7	6	4		5				8		12			13	2
8		16	CREWE ALEXANDRA	0-4		4488	1	10	3	11		14				7		9	13	6	4		5				8		12				2
9		24	BRIGHTON & HOVE ALB	3-1	Robinson 2, Jones	4560	1	13	3	11		14				7		9		6	4		5				10		8			12	2
10		30	Stockport County	1-3	Bailey	5655	1	10	3	11		12	2			7		9			4		5		14			13	8			6	
11	Oct	7	Bristol Rovers	2-0	Brissett, Bailey	5165	1	10	3	11			6			7		9			4		5				2		8				
12		14	BURNLEY	0-2		4954	1		3	11			6	13		7		9			4		5	10	14		2		8				12
13		21	Swansea City	1-1	Jones	1988	1		3	11			6			7		9			4		12	10			5		8				2
14		28	CARLISLE UNITED	2-0	Brissett, Fletcher	4250		13	3	11			6	14		7		9			4	1	12	10			5		8				2
15		31	SWINDON TOWN	0-0		6352		8	3	11			6	12		7		9			4	1		10			5						2
16	Nov	4	Walsall	0-0		3626		8	3	11			6	14		7		9			4	1	12	10			5		13				2
17		18	BRENTFORD	1-0	Victory	3894		14	3	11				6		7		8				1	4	10	13		5		9			12	2
18		25	Chesterfield	0-3		4034		7	3	11				10				9	6		4	1			13		5	14	8			12	2
19	Dec	9	Brighton & Hove Albion	0-2		5414		12	3	11						7		9			4	1	5	10	13		6	14	8				2
20		16	STOCKPORT COUNTY	3-2	Ndah, Jones, Holland	3638		13	3	11						7		9			12	1	5	10	6			4	8				2
21		23	HULL CITY	2-0	Murray, Holland	3491	1	11	3							7	2	9			4		5	10				12	8			6	
22		26	Oxford United	0-2		6347	1	11	3							7	2	9			4		5	10	12			13	8			6	
23	Jan	2	SHREWSBURY TOWN	0-2		3245	1	10		11						7	3	9			4		5		12				8			6	2
24		6	BRISTOL CITY	1-1	Morris	3667	1	10	3	11						7		9		12	4		5	6					8				2
25		13	Peterborough United	5-4	* see below	4596	1	6	3	11	5					7		9		8	4			10	14				12			13	2
26		20	BRADFORD CITY	3-1	Jones, Holland, Robinson	3628	1	6	3	11	5					7		9		8	4				12				10			13	2
27	Feb	3	WYCOMBE WANDERERS	2-3	Bailey, Holland	4447	1	6	3	11	5					7		9		8	4								10				2
28		10	Bristol City	0-3		6217	1	6	3	11	5					7		9		8	4				2			14	10			12	
29		17	BLACKPOOL	1-0	Holland	4157	1	6	3	11	5					7		9										12	10	8			2
30		20	Rotherham United	0-1		2092	1	6	3	11	5					7		9			12							14	10	8	13		2
31		24	Crewe Alexandra	0-2		3535	1	6	3	11	5					7					4		12						10	8	13		2
32		27	NOTTS COUNTY	0-2		3191	1	6	3	11	5					7					4		12					14	10	8	13		2
33	Mar	2	OXFORD UNITED	0-1		3996	1	6	3	11	5					7		9					4					12	10	8	14		2
34		9	Hull City	1-1	Scott	2853		6	3	11					1	7	5	8					4					12	10	9			2
35		12	Wrexham	0-5		2003		6	3	11	5				1	7	14	9					4		13			12	10	8			2
36		16	YORK CITY	2-2	Robinson 2 (1p)	3505		6	3	11	5				1	7		9					4						10	8			2
37		23	Shrewsbury Town	2-1	Holland 2	2534		6	3	11	5				1	7		9					4					8	10				2
38		26	York City	1-3	Holland	2055		6	3	11	5				1	7		9					4		12			8			10	13	2
39		30	BRISTOL ROVERS	2-1	Robinson (p), Jones	4607		12	3	11	5				1	7		9											10				2
40	Apr	2	Burnley	0-0		7895		12	3	11	5				1	7		9								13			10				2
41		6	Carlisle United	0-4		5401		6	3	11	5				1	7		9								14		12	10				2
42		9	SWANSEA CITY	3-1	Jones, Bailey, Holland	4049		6	3	11					1	7		9					5						10				2
43		13	Swindon Town	2-2	Jones 2	10862		6	3	11					1	7		9					5			12			10				2
44		20	WALSALL	0-0		4380		6	3	11					1	7		9					5			13		12	10				2
45		27	CHESTERFIELD	2-0	Robinson, Jones	4483		6	3						1	7		9					5			11			10				2
46	May	4	Brentford	0-2		6091		6		11					1	7		9			13		5			3		12	10				2
						Apps	26	44	44	43	16	5	7	7	13	43	5	44	4	14	31	7	35	12	13	6	17	19	41	8	7	16	41
						Goals		4		3	1			1		10		17		1	1		2	2					7	1		1	

Scorers in game 25: Ndah, Casper, Mean, Jones 2

SG Strong played in game 38 at 14

YD Santos played at 13 in games 23, 24 and 28 (subbed)

PR Mitchell played in four games; 39 and 40 (at 6, subbed in both games), 41 and 43 (at 13)

MJ Dean played in five games; 29 and 30 (at 4), 31 and 32 (at 9), 33 (at 13). Subbed in all except game 32.

OO Coll played at 4 in the last 8 games, 39 to 46. IG Cox played at 8 in the same 8 games.

F.A. Cup

Round	Date		Opponent	Score	Scorers	Att	Andrews IE	Bailey JA	Beardsmore RP	Brissett JC	Casper CM	Cureton J	Duberry MW	Fletcher SM	Glass JR	Holland MR	Howe EJF	Jones SG	McElhatton MT	Mean SJ	Morris MJ	Moss NG	Murray RJ	Ndah GE	Oldbury MJ	O'Neill JJ	Pennock AB	Rawlinson MD	Robinson S	Scott K	Town DE	Victory JC	Young NA
R1	Nov	11	BRISTOL CITY	0-0		5304		8	3	11				10		7		9			4	1	5				6		12				2
rep		21	Bristol City	1-0	Robinson	5069		7	3	11				10				9		12	4	1	5				6		8				2
R2	Dec	2	BRENTFORD	0-1		4451		10	3	11						7			5		4	1			13		6	9	8				2

SG Strong played in R2 at 12

F.L. Cup (Coca Cola Cup)

Round	Date		Opponent	Score	Scorers	Att	Andrews IE	Bailey JA	Beardsmore RP	Brissett JC	Casper CM	Cureton J	Duberry MW	Fletcher SM	Glass JR	Holland MR	Howe EJF	Jones SG	McElhatton MT	Mean SJ	Morris MJ	Moss NG	Murray RJ	Ndah GE	Oldbury MJ	O'Neill JJ	Pennock AB	Rawlinson MD	Robinson S	Scott K	Town DE	Victory JC	Young NA
R1/1	Aug	15	Luton Town	1-1	Jones	2728	1	13	3	11				10		7		9	12	6	4		5						8				2
R1/2		22	LUTON TOWN	2-1	Jones, Morris	4884	1	10	3	11						7		9		6	4		5				8	14			13	12	2
R2/1	Sep	19	Watford	1-1	Jones	5037	1		3	11						7		9		6	4		5				10		8				2
R2/2	Oct	3	WATFORD	1-1	Oldbury	4365	1	10	3	11						7		9			4		5		13		2		8		12	6	

R2/2 lost 5-6 on penalties a.e.t.

A.M. Cup (Auto Windscreens Shield)

Round	Date		Opponent	Score	Scorers	Att	Andrews IE	Bailey JA	Beardsmore RP	Brissett JC	Casper CM	Cureton J	Duberry MW	Fletcher SM	Glass JR	Holland MR	Howe EJF	Jones SG	McElhatton MT	Mean SJ	Morris MJ	Moss NG	Murray RJ	Ndah GE	Oldbury MJ	O'Neill JJ	Pennock AB	Rawlinson MD	Robinson S	Scott K	Town DE	Victory JC	Young NA
R1	Sep	27	BRENTFORD	0-1		1092	1	12	3	11		14				7		9			4		5				10		8		13	6	2
R1	Nov	7	Exeter City	2-0	Brissett 2 (1p)	1898		4	3	11			6	2		7		9				1		10			5		8				
R2		28	Bristol Rovers	1-2	Robinson	1979		7	3	11									5		4	1			10		6	9	8			13	2

Played in R2: YD Santos (at 12), A Stephens (at 14)

1996/97

16th in Division Two

	Date	Opponent	Score	Scorers	Att	Bailey JA	Beardsmore RP	Brissett JC	Christie I	Coll OO	Cotterell LS	Cox IG	Dean MJ	Ferdinand RG	Fletcher SM	Glass JR	Gordon DA	Hayter JE	Holland MR	Howe EJF	Marshall AJ	Murray RJ	O'Brien RJ	Omoyimni E	O'Neill JJ	Rawlinson MD	Robinson S	Town DE	Vincent JR	Watson ML	Young NA
1	Aug 17	WATFORD	1-2	Brissett	7386	6	3	12		4		8			10	1	11		7			5			9						2
2	24	York City	2-1	Brissett, Fletcher	2804	6	3	11		4		8			10	1	9		7			5					12				2
3	27	Stockport County	1-0	Brissett	3446	6	3	11		4		8			10	1	9		7			5			12		13				2
4	31	PETERBOROUGH UTD.	1-2	Fletcher	4587		3	11		4		8			10	1	9		7			5			12		13		6		2
5	Sep 7	CREWE ALEXANDRA	0-1		3218	6	3			4		8			10	1	9		7			5			12		11				2
6	10	Bristol Rovers	2-3	Fletcher, Murray	4170	6	3			4	13	8			10		11		7		1	5			14		9		12		2
7	14	Preston North End	1-0	Fletcher	8268	6				4	8				10		9		7		1	5			11				3		2
8	21	NOTTS COUNTY	0-1		3678	6	12			4	8				10		9		7		1	5			11		13		3	14	2
9	28	Rotherham United	0-1		2629	6				4		8			10		9		7		1	5			13		12	11	3	14	2
10	Oct 1	WALSALL	0-1		2747					4	13	5	11		9		10		7	3	1			6			8	14		12	2
11	5	Gillingham	1-1	Holland	5966	10	3					5	11		9	1			7	14			4	6	12		8	13			2
12	12	WYCOMBE WANDERERS	2-1	Holland, Watson	3984	6	3			4		5	11		9		13		7	12	1			14			8			10	2
13	15	PLYMOUTH ARGYLE	1-0	Fletcher	3818		3			4		5	11		9		6			13	1	12		7		14	8			10	2
14	19	Wrexham	0-2		3945	6	3			4		5	11		9		12		7		1			10			8			13	2
15	26	Luton Town	0-2		6086	6	3			4		5	10		9				7	14	1			11	12		8			13	2
16	29	BRISTOL CITY	0-2		4197	6	3	12		4		5	11		9				7		1			13			8			10	2
17	Nov 2	BURY	1-1	Holland	3946	6	3			4		5	11		9		10		7		1	12					8				2
18	9	Blackpool	1-1	Cox	3744	6						5	11	4	9	1	10		7			12					8		3		2
19	19	BRENTFORD	2-1	Robinson 2 (1p)	2747	6		13	10			5		4	9	1			7			12			11		8		3	14	2
20	23	Burnley	0-1		8812	6		13	10			5		4	9	1			7			12			11		8		3	14	2
21	30	LUTON TOWN	3-2	Robinson 2, Cox	4322			10	14			5	6	4		1	9		7			12			11	13	8		3		2
22	Dec 3	Shrewsbury Town	1-1	Holland	1610	6		10	11			5		4		1			7			12				9	8		3		2
23	14	MILLWALL	1-1	Holland	4494	6	11	10				5		4		1			7			12				9	8	14	3	13	2
24	21	Chesterfield	1-1	Cox	4174	6	11					5		4		1			7			10				9		12	3	8	2
25	26	BRISTOL ROVERS	1-0	Watson	5036	6	11					5		4	12	1			7			8				9			3	10	2
26	28	Crewe Alexandra	0-2		3687	6	11	13				5		4	12	1			7			8				9		14	3	10	2
27	Jan 11	ROTHERHAM UNITED	1-1	Cox	3161	6	11	12				5		4	10	1			7							9	8	14	3	13	2
28	18	Walsall	1-2	Fletcher	3037	6	4	11				5			10	1			7			12				9	8	13	3		2
29	25	Bristol City	1-0	Cox	10434	6	4	11				5			10	1			7							9	8	12	3		2
30	Feb 1	BLACKPOOL	0-0		8201	6	4	11				5			10	1			7							9	8	12	3		2
31	4	Notts County	2-0	Cox, Town	2757	6	4	11				5			10	1			7							9	8	12	3		2
32	8	Bury	1-2	Robinson (p)	3599	6	4	11			13	5			10	1			7	14		12					8	9	3		2
33	11	PRESTON NORTH END	2-0	Brissett, Cox	4976	6	4	11				5			10	1			7								8	9	3		2
34	15	BURNLEY	0-0		6021	6	4	11				5			10	1			7			3				12	8	9			2
35	22	Brentford	0-1		6071		4	11			14	5	12		10	1			7	2		3			13	6	8	9			
36	Mar 1	SHREWSBURY TOWN	0-0		5810		4	11				5			10	1			7			2				6	8	9	3		
37	11	CHESTERFIELD	3-0	Fletcher, Robinson, Rawlinson	3368	6	4					5			10	1			7							11	8	9	3		2
38	15	Millwall	1-0	Bailey	8992	6	4	12				5			10	1			7							11	8	9	3		2
39	22	YORK CITY	1-1	Town	4367	6	4				12	5				1			7	13		10				11	8	9	3		2
40	29	Watford	1-0	Cox	10019	6	4	8			13	5			10	1			7			12				11	14	9	3		2
41	Apr 1	STOCKPORT COUNTY	0-0		5476	6	4	12				5				1			7			10				11	8	9	3		2
42	5	Peterborough United	1-3	Rawlinson	4223	6	4	12			13	5				1		14	7	3		10				11	8	9			2
43	12	GILLINGHAM	2-2	Murray, Robinson	5008	6	4					5				1		13	7	3		10			12	11	8	9			2
44	19	Wycombe Wanderers	1-1	Holland	6043	6	4					5				1			7	3		10			12	11	8	9			2
45	26	WREXHAM	2-1	O'Neill, Holland	4805	6	4					5	12			1			7	8					10	11		9	3		2
46	May 3	Plymouth Argyle	0-0		6507	6	4					5				1			7	10		12			13	11	8	9	3		2
					Apps	40	38	25	4	16	9	44	12	10	35	35	16	2	45	13	11	32	1	7	18	25	40	26	29	15	44
					Goals	1		4				8			7				7			2			1	2	7	2		2	

MJ Morris played in game 4 at 14

F.A. Cup

	Date	Opponent	Score	Scorers	Att	Bailey JA	Beardsmore RP	Brissett JC	Christie I	Coll OO	Cotterell LS	Cox IG	Dean MJ	Ferdinand RG	Fletcher SM	Glass JR	Gordon DA	Hayter JE	Holland MR	Howe EJF	Marshall AJ	Murray RJ	O'Brien RJ	Omoyimni E	O'Neill JJ	Rawlinson MD	Robinson S	Town DE	Vincent JR	Watson ML	Young NA
R1	Nov 16	Brentford	0-2		4509	6				4		5	11		10	1	9		7			12			14		8		3	13	2

F.L. Cup (Coca Cola Cup)

	Date	Opponent	Score	Scorers	Att	Bailey JA	Beardsmore RP	Brissett JC	Christie I	Coll OO	Cotterell LS	Cox IG	Dean MJ	Ferdinand RG	Fletcher SM	Glass JR	Gordon DA	Hayter JE	Holland MR	Howe EJF	Marshall AJ	Murray RJ	O'Brien RJ	Omoyimni E	O'Neill JJ	Rawlinson MD	Robinson S	Town DE	Vincent JR	Watson ML	Young NA
R1/1	Aug 20	Ipswich Town	1-2	Fletcher	6163	6	3	11		4		8			10	1	9		7			5			12						2
R1/2	Sep 3	IPSWICH TOWN	0-3		4119	6	3			4		8			10	1	9		7			5			14		11	12	13		2

A.M. Cup (Auto Windscreens Shield)

	Date	Opponent	Score	Scorers	Att	Bailey JA	Beardsmore RP	Brissett JC	Christie I	Coll OO	Cotterell LS	Cox IG	Dean MJ	Ferdinand RG	Fletcher SM	Glass JR	Gordon DA	Hayter JE	Holland MR	Howe EJF	Marshall AJ	Murray RJ	O'Brien RJ	Omoyimni E	O'Neill JJ	Rawlinson MD	Robinson S	Town DE	Vincent JR	Watson ML	Young NA
R1	Dec 10	Plymouth Argyle	0-2		944	6	12	10				5		4		1			7			9				11	8	13	3	14	2

1997/98

9th in Division Two

							Bailey JA	Beardsmore RP	Brissett JC	Cox IG	Dean MJ	Fletcher CN	Fletcher SM	Glass JR	Harrington JD	Hayter JE	Howe EJF	Jones SG	Murray RJ	O'Neill JJ	Rawlinson MD	Robinson S	Rolling FJ	Stein EMS	Teather P	Tomlinson GM	Town DE	Vincent JR	Warren C	Young NA
1	Aug	9	Northampton Town	2-0	Vincent, S Fletcher	6384	6	7		5			10	1						9	11	8	4			12		3		2
2		16	WIGAN ATHLETIC	1-0	Rolling	4194	6		12	5			10	1	13		7			9	11	8	4					3		2
3		23	Oldham Athletic	1-2	Robinson	4986	6		12	5			10	1			7			9	11	8	4					3		2
4		30	BLACKPOOL	2-0	Tomlinson, Robinson	4196	6	7	12	5				1						9	11	8	4			10		3		2
5	Sep	2	BRISTOL ROVERS	1-1	Robinson (p)	5550	6	7	12	5				1			13		14	9	11	8	4			10		3		2
6		5	Gillingham	1-2	S Fletcher	5167		7		5			10	1					12	6	11	8	4			9		3		2
7		13	LUTON TOWN	1-1	O'Neill	4561	6	7		5			10	1			12		13	11		8	4			9		3		2
8		20	Bristol City	1-1	Robinson	8330	6	7	13	5			10	1			4			9	12	8				11		3		2
9		27	GRIMSBY TOWN	0-1		3712	6	7	12	5			10	1			13			11		8	4			9		3		2
10	Oct	4	Chesterfield	1-1	Rolling	4481	6	7	13	5			10	1			12			9	11	8	4					3		2
11		11	Preston North End	1-0	Warren	8531	6	7		5			10	1			4				11	8						3	9	2
12		18	FULHAM	2-1	Cox 2	7484	6	7		5			10	1			4			12	11	8						3	9	2
13		21	MILLWALL	0-0		4752		7	12	5			10	1			4			6	11	8						3	9	2
14		25	Burnley	2-2	Howe, Vincent	9501		7	13	5			10	1			4			6	11	8	12					3	9	2
15	Nov	1	BRENTFORD	0-0		4772		7	11	5			10	1			6		14	12	13	8	4					3	9	2
16		4	Wrexham	1-2	Warren	2462		7	11	5			10	1			6			13	12	8	4					3	9	2
17		8	Plymouth Argyle	0-3		5067		7	13	5	14		10	1			4			6	11	8	12					3	9	2
18		18	SOUTHEND UNITED	2-1	S Fletcher, Warren	3019		7		5			10	1	11		4			6	12	8						3	9	2
19		22	CARLISLE UNITED	3-2	S Fletcher, Beardsmore, O'Neill	3709		7		5			10	1	11		4			6	12	8					13	3	9	2
20		29	Wycombe Wanderers	1-1	Robinson (p)	4340		7		5			10	1	11		4			6		8					12	3	9	2
21	Dec	2	YORK CITY	0-0		3365	12	7		5			10	1	11		4			6		8					13	3	9	2
22		13	Walsall	1-2	Robinson	3538	6			5			10	1		12	4			11	7	8						3	9	2
23		20	WATFORD	0-1		6231	6			5			10	1	13		4			7		8	12		11			3	9	2
24		26	GILLINGHAM	4-0	Jones 2, Robinson, Young	5672				5			10	1		13	4	9		7	12	8			6			3	11	2
25		28	Bristol Rovers	3-5	Jones, Cox, Robinson (p)	7256				5	14		10	1		13	4	9		6	7	8	12					3	11	2
26	Jan	10	NORTHAMPTON T	3-0	Jones, S Fletcher, Young	4257				5			10	1			4	9		7		8			6			3	11	2
27		17	Blackpool	0-1		4550	12		13	5			10	1	14		4	9		7		8	3		6				11	2
28		24	OLDHAM ATHLETIC	0-0		4079	6		11	5			10	1			4	9		7		8						3	12	2
29		31	Luton Town	2-1	Brissett, S Fletcher	6062	6		11	5			10	1			4			7		8			12			3	9	2
30	Feb	7	BRISTOL CITY	1-0	S Fletcher	6673	6		11	5			10	1						7		8	4		12			3	9	2
31		14	CHESTERFIELD	2-0	Warren 2	4271	6		11	5			10	1	12					7	14	8	4		13			3	9	2
32		21	Grimsby Town	1-2	Warren	5715	6		11	5		14	10	1		12				7	3	8	4		13				9	2
33		24	Fulham	1-0	Robinson	7708	6		11	5			10	1		12	13			7		8	4					3	9	2
34		28	PRESTON NORTH END	0-2		5009	6		11	5			10	1			12			7		8	4				13	3	9	2
35	Mar	3	PLYMOUTH ARGYLE	3-3	S Fletcher 2, Vincent	3545	6		11	5	13		10	1			14			7		8	4		9		12	3		2
36		7	Brentford	2-3	Rolling 2	4973	6		12	5			10	1			14			7		8	4	9	13			3	11	2
37		14	WREXHAM	0-1		5512	6	11	12	5			10	1			14			7	13	8	4	9				3		2
38		21	Southend United	3-5	Stein, Bailey, S Fletcher	4884	6	11	13	5			10	1			7			14	12	8	4	9				3		2
39		28	Carlisle United	1-0	Stein	4951		11		5	6		10	1			7					8	4	9				3		2
40	Apr	4	WYCOMBE WANDERERS	0-0		4281		11	3	5	6		10	1			7			13	2	8	4	9			14	12		
41		7	Wigan Athletic	0-1		2798	6	11	10	5				1			7			13		8	4	9			12	3		2
42		11	York City	1-0	O'Neill	2840	6	12	10	5	8			1			7			4				9				3	11	2
43		14	WALSALL	1-0	S Fletcher	3404	6	7	13	5	14		10	1			4			12		8		9				3	11	2
44		25	BURNLEY	2-1	Robinson (p), S Fletcher	6592	6	7	12	5			10	1			4			13		8	2	9				3	11	
45		28	Watford	1-2	Stein	12834	6	7	14	5	13		10	1			4					8	2	9				3	11	12
46	May	2	Millwall	2-1	Witter (og), Stein	7872	6	7	12	5			10	1			4			13		8		9				3	11	2
						Apps	32	29	31	46	8	1	42	46	8	5	40	5	4	43	25	45	30	11	10	7	7	44	30	44
						Goals	1	1	1	3			12				1	4		3		10	4	4		1		3	6	2

One own goal

F.A. Cup

							Bailey JA	Beardsmore RP	Brissett JC	Cox IG	Dean MJ	Fletcher CN	Fletcher SM	Glass JR	Harrington JD	Hayter JE	Howe EJF	Jones SG	Murray RJ	O'Neill JJ	Rawlinson MD	Robinson S	Rolling FJ	Stein EMS	Teather P	Tomlinson GM	Town DE	Vincent JR	Warren C	Young NA
R1	Nov	15	HEYBRIDGE SWIFTS	3-0	Beardsmore, Robinson 2	3385		7		5			10	1	13		4			6	11	8	12					3	9	2
R2	Dec	7	BRISTOL CITY	3-1	Carey (og), O'Neill, Fletcher	5687	6	7		5			10	1			4			11	12	8						3	9	2
R3	Jan	13	HUDDERSFIELD TOWN	0-1		7385	14		9	5			10	1	6		4		12	7		8	13					3	11	2

F.L. Cup (Coca Cola Cup)

							Bailey JA	Beardsmore RP	Brissett JC	Cox IG	Dean MJ	Fletcher CN	Fletcher SM	Glass JR	Harrington JD	Hayter JE	Howe EJF	Jones SG	Murray RJ	O'Neill JJ	Rawlinson MD	Robinson S	Rolling FJ	Stein EMS	Teather P	Tomlinson GM	Town DE	Vincent JR	Warren C	Young NA
R1/1	Aug	12	TORQUAY UNITED	0-1		3215	6		13	5			10	1			7		12	9	11	8	4				14	3		2
R1/2		26	Torquay United	1-1	Rolling	2278	6	7	13	5			10	1	12		14			9	11	8	4					3		2

A.M. Cup (Auto Windscreens Shield)

							Bailey JA	Beardsmore RP	Brissett JC	Cox IG	Dean MJ	Fletcher CN	Fletcher SM	Glass JR	Harrington JD	Hayter JE	Howe EJF	Jones SG	Murray RJ	O'Neill JJ	Rawlinson MD	Robinson S	Rolling FJ	Stein EMS	Teather P	Tomlinson GM	Town DE	Vincent JR	Warren C	Young NA
R2	Jan	6	LEYTON ORIENT	2-0	Jones, Robinson (p)	1732			13	5	6		10	1			4	9		12		8			7			3	11	2
R3		27	BRISTOL CITY	1-0	Vincent	2124	6		11	5			10	1		13	4			7		8			12			3	9	2
SFS	Feb	17	LUTON TOWN	1-0	Rolling	5367	6		11	5			10	1						7	3	8	4						9	2
FS1	Mar	10	Walsall	2-0	Rolling, Beardsmore	6017	6	11		5			10	1			12			7		8	4	9				3		2
FS2		17	WALSALL	2-3	Evans (og), Rolling	8972	6	11		5			10	1			12			7		8	4	9				3		2
F	Apr	19	Grimsby Town	1-2	Bailey	62432	6	7		5			10	1			4			12		8		9				3	11	2

Final at Wembley , lost in sudden-death extra time

1998/99

7th in Division Two

	Date	Opponent	Score	Scorers	Att	Bailey JA	Berthe M	Boli R	Cox IG	Day JR	Dean MJ	Fletcher CN	Fletcher SM	Griffin AR	Hayter JE	Howe EJF	Huck WRF	Hughes RD	Jenkins J	Lovell S	O'Neill JJ	Ovendale MJ	Rawlinson MD	Robinson S	Rodriguez D	Stein EMS	Tindall J	Town DE	Vincent JR	Warren C	Young NA
1	Aug 8	LINCOLN CITY	2-0	Cox, Stein	5573	6	5		7				10			4		11				1		8		9	12		3		2
2	15	Notts County	2-1	Berthe, Robinson	5269	6	5		7				10			4		11				1		8		9	12		3		2
3	22	MILLWALL	3-0	Cox, Tindall (p), O'Neill	6956	6	5		7				10			4		11			12	1				9	8		3		2
4	29	Fulham	0-0		12107		5		7		12		10			4		11				1		8		9	6		3		2
5	Sep 1	BLACKPOOL	1-1	Stein	6785	6	5		7		13		10			4		11			12	1		8		9	14		3		2
6	5	Stoke City	0-2		13443	6	5		7		12		10			4		11				1		8		9	14	13	3		2
7	8	Manchester City	1-2	S Fletcher	26696	6			7		12		10			4		11				1		8		9	5	13	3	14	2
8	12	WIGAN ATHLETIC	1-0	Berthe	5151	6	5		7				10			4		11				1		8		9			3		2
9	19	Wycombe Wanderers	2-0	S Fletcher, O'Neill	4267	6			7				10			4		11			5	1		8		9	12		3		2
10	26	OLDHAM ATHLETIC	2-0	Robinson, Stein	5877	6			7				10			4		11			5	1		8		9	3	12		13	2
11	Oct 3	Bristol Rovers	0-1		7526	6	12		7				10			4		11			5	1		8		9	3	13		14	2
12	10	Macclesfield Town	2-2	Robinson (p), Stein	2974	6	5		7							4		11			10	1		8		9	3	12		13	2
13	17	NORTHAMPTON T	1-1	Stein	6362		5		7							4		11				1		8		9		10	3	6	2
14	20	GILLINGHAM	3-3	Young, Hughes, Stein	5183	6	5		7							4		11				1		8		9		12	3	10	2
15	Nov 7	Reading	3-3	Warren, Stein 2 (1p)	13004	6	5	10	7							4		11			8	1			13	9	12			3	2
16	10	Chesterfield	1-3	Curtis (og)	3797	6	5	10	7							4		11			8	1				9	13	14	12	3	2
17	21	BURNLEY	5-0	* see below	5907	6			7					13		4		11			5	1		8	12	9			3	10	2
18	28	Walsall	0-1		3895	6	12		7				13			4		11			5	1		8		9			3	10	2
19	Dec 12	YORK CITY	2-1	Robinson, S Fletcher	4863	6	12	14	7				10			4					11	1	2	8	13	9			3	5	
20	19	Wrexham	1-0	S Fletcher	2716			11	7				10			4						1	6	8	12	9			3	5	2
21	26	Millwall	2-1	Warren, Stein	7807	6		11	7				10			4		12				1		8		9			3	5	2
22	28	LUTON TOWN	1-0	Cox	8863	6			7				10			4		11				1		8		9			3	5	2
23	Jan 9	Lincoln City	1-2	S Fletcher	3141	6			7				10			4		11				1		8	12	9			3	5	2
24	16	NOTTS COUNTY	2-0	Stein, Cox	5968	6			7				10			4		11			12	1		8		9			3	5	2
25	26	PRESTON NORTH END	3-1	O'Neill, Howe, Stein	6170	6			7				10			4		11			5	1		8		9			3		2
26	30	Luton Town	2-2	Robinson, Vincent	5426	6			7				10			4		11			5	1		8		9			3		2
27	Feb 6	STOKE CITY	4-0	S Fletcher 2, Robinson, Hayter	7637	6		9	7				10		13	4		11	14		5	1		8					3	12	2
28	13	MANCHESTER CITY	0-0		10946	6			7				10		9	4		11			5	1		8				12	3	13	2
29	20	Wigan Athletic	1-2	Robinson	4144	6			7		13		10		14	4		11				1		8		9	12		3	5	2
30	27	WYCOMBE WANDERERS	2-0	Robinson 2	6693	6			7		12		10		13	4		11				1		8		9			3	5	2
31	Mar 2	FULHAM	1-1	Vincent	9928	6			7				10		12	4		11				1		8		9			3	5	2
32	6	Oldham Athletic	3-2	Cox, Stein, Warren	4453				7		13		10		6	4		11				1		8		9	12		3	5	2
33	9	BRISTOL ROVERS	1-0	Howe	7181				7				10		6	4		11				1		8		9			3	5	2
34	13	READING	0-1		9445	12			7				10		6	4		11			5	1		8		9			3		2
35	16	Blackpool	0-0		3186				7				10	12	6	4		11			5	1		8		9			3		2
36	20	Preston North End	1-0	S Fletcher	12882				7		4		10	14	6			11			5	1	13	8		9		12	3		2
37	27	COLCHESTER UNITED	2-1	Warren, Hughes	6447	6			7		12				10	4	8	11			5	1	2			9				3	
38	Apr 2	Northampton Town	1-2	Robinson	6858				7	13			10		5	4	6	11			12	1		8		9				3	2
39	6	MACCLESFIELD TOWN	1-0	Stein	8033				7	14			10		5	4	6	11		13	12	1		8		9				3	2
40	9	Gillingham	1-2	Robinson	7813				7				10		5	4		11		13		1	6	8		9	12			3	2
41	13	WALSALL	0-1		8390				7				10	13	5	4		11		14	6	1	12	8		9				3	2
42	17	Burnley	0-0		9802				7				10		5	4	12	11		13		1	6	8		9				3	2
43	24	CHESTERFIELD	0-0		6890				7			13	10	6	5	4	3	11		9		1		8			12				2
44	27	Colchester United	1-2	Greene (og)	3550				7				10	12	5	4	6	11		13		1		8		9				3	2
45	May 1	York City	1-0	Hayter	3503	12			7				10		5	4	6	11				1		8		9				3	2
46	8	WREXHAM	0-0		8439	6			7				10		5	4	14	11		13	12	1		8		9				3	2
					Apps	32	15	6	46	2	9	1	39	6	20	45	8	44	1	7	24	46	7	42	5	43	17	10	32	32	44
					Goals		2		5				8		2	2		2			3			13		15	1		2	5	1

Scorers in game 17: Warren, Robinson 2 (1p), Stein 2

Two own goals

F.A. Cup

	Date	Opponent	Score	Scorers	Att	Bailey JA	Berthe M	Boli R	Cox IG	Day JR	Dean MJ	Fletcher CN	Fletcher SM	Griffin AR	Hayter JE	Howe EJF	Huck WRF	Hughes RD	Jenkins J	Lovell S	O'Neill JJ	Ovendale MJ	Rawlinson MD	Robinson S	Rodriguez D	Stein EMS	Tindall J	Town DE	Vincent JR	Warren C	Young NA
R1	Nov 14	Basingstoke Town	2-1	O'Neill, Stein	3830	6	5		7							4		11			12	1		8		9			3	10	2
R2	Dec 5	Torquay United	1-0	Robinson	2929	6			7				10			4		11			12	1		8		9			3	5	2
R3	Jan 2	WEST BROMWICH ALBION	1-0	Howe	10881	6		12					10			4		11			5	1		8		9			3	7	2
R4	23	Barnsley	1-3	Howe	11982	6		12	7				10			4		11			13	1		8		9			3	5	2

F.L. Cup (Worthington Cup)

	Date	Opponent	Score	Scorers	Att	Bailey JA	Berthe M	Boli R	Cox IG	Day JR	Dean MJ	Fletcher CN	Fletcher SM	Griffin AR	Hayter JE	Howe EJF	Huck WRF	Hughes RD	Jenkins J	Lovell S	O'Neill JJ	Ovendale MJ	Rawlinson MD	Robinson S	Rodriguez D	Stein EMS	Tindall J	Town DE	Vincent JR	Warren C	Young NA
R1/1	Aug 11	COLCHESTER UNITED	2-0	Robinson, Howe	3745	6	5		7				10			4		11				1		8		9	12	13	3		2
R1/2	18	Colchester United	2-3	Stein, S Fletcher	2550	6	5		7				10			4		11			12	1		8		9	13		3		2
R2/1	Sep 15	WOLVERHAMPTON W.	1-1	Stein	7096	6	5		7				10			4		11			14	1		8		9		13	3	12	2
R2/2	22	Wolverhampton Wan.	2-1	Stein 2	15431	6			7				10			4		11			5	1				9	8		3	12	2
R3	Oct 27	Barnsley	1-2	Stein	8560	6	5	12	7							4		11			10	1		8		9		14	3	13	2

A.M. Cup (Auto Windscreens Shield)

	Date	Opponent	Score	Scorers	Att	Bailey JA	Berthe M	Boli R	Cox IG	Day JR	Dean MJ	Fletcher CN	Fletcher SM	Griffin AR	Hayter JE	Howe EJF	Huck WRF	Hughes RD	Jenkins J	Lovell S	O'Neill JJ	Ovendale MJ	Rawlinson MD	Robinson S	Rodriguez D	Stein EMS	Tindall J	Town DE	Vincent JR	Warren C	Young NA
R1	Dec 8	READING	2-0	S Fletcher, Cox	2666	6	12		7				10			4		11			14	1		8	13	9			3	5	2
R2	Jan 5	PETERBOROUGH UTD.	5-1	S Fletcher, Stein 3, Robinson	3398	6		14	7				10			4		11			12	1		8	13	9			3	5	2
R3	Feb 2	MILLWALL	1-1	Stein	5339	6			7				10			4		11			5	1		8		9			3		2

Lost on 3-4 on penalties a.e.t.

1999/2000

16th in Division Two

							Att	Betsy K	Broadhurst KM	Cox IG	Day JR	Elliott ST	Elliott W	Fenton NL	Fletcher CN	Fletcher SM	Hayter JE	Howe EJF	Huck WRF	Hughes RD	Jorgensen C	Mean SJ	O'Neill JJ	O'Shea J	Ovendale MJ	Rawlinson MD	Robinson S	Sheerin JE	Stein EMS	Tindall J	Warren C	Watson GWG	Young NA
1	Aug	7	CAMBRIDGE UNITED	2-1	Mean, Howe		5552			5						10	8	4			7	6	12		1	11			9		3		2
2		14	Bristol City	1-3	O'Neill		11315			5						10	8	4	13	14	7	6	12		1	11			9		3		2
3		21	COLCHESTER UNITED	4-0	Stein, Jorgensen, S Fletcher 2		4508			5						10	12	4	13	11	7	6			1		8		9		3		2
4		28	Scunthorpe United	1-3	Stein		3376			5	14					10		4	12	11	7	6			1		8		9		3	13	2
5		31	LUTON TOWN	1-0	S Fletcher		4797			5						10		4	7	11		6			1		8		9		3	12	2
6	Sep	3	Burnley	1-2	Stein		10223	14		5	7					10		4	11		12	6	13		1				9	8	3		2
7		11	READING	3-1	Grant(og), Hughes, Casper(og)		6007	13		5						10		4	7	11	12	6			1		8		9		3		2
8		18	Blackpool	0-0			4471	12	3	5						10		4		11	7	6			1		8		9				2
9		25	BURY	1-1	Stein		4208	10	3	5								4	13	11	7	6			1		8		9		12		2
10	Oct	2	Chesterfield	1-0	Jorgensen		2775	12	3	5						10		4		11	7	6			1		8		9				2
11		16	STOKE CITY	1-1	Robinson		5990		11	5						10		4	12		7	6	13		1		8		9		3		2
12		19	BRISTOL ROVERS	0-1			5613			5						10			11		7	6			1		8		9		3	12	2
13		23	Bury	2-2	Warren, Robinson		3701			5	6				11	10					7				1		8		9		3		2
14	Nov	3	Preston North End	0-3			9630			5	6				11	10			12		7		14		1		8		9		3	13	2
15		6	CARDIFF CITY	1-0	Stein		4471			5					6	10	4				7		12		1		8		9		3	11	2
16		12	Gillingham	1-4	Robinson		6336			5					6	10	4		12		7				1		8		9		3	11	2
17		16	Wigan Athletic	1-3	S Fletcher		4338		4	5	6				11	10	12		13		7						8		9		3		2
18		23	BRENTFORD	4-1	Warren, Jorgensen, Stein 2		4202		4	5	6				11	10			12		7				1		8		9		3		2
19		27	MILLWALL	1-2	C Fletcher		5121		4	5	6				11	10	12		14		7				1	13	8		9		3		2
20	Dec	4	Cambridge United	2-0	Robinson (p), Day		3579		4	5	11	6				10	13				7	12			1		8		9		3		2
21		11	Notts County	1-5	O'Neill		4199		4	5	6	2			11	10	13				7	12	14		1		8		9		3		
22		18	OXFORD UNITED	4-0	* see below		4443		2	5	13	14			11	10	4		12		7		6		1		8		9		3		
23		26	Wycombe Wanderers	1-2	Hayter		5656		2	5		12			11	10	4				7		6		1		8		9		3		
24		28	WREXHAM	1-0	Stein		5394		2			5			11	10	4		12		7	13	6		1		8		9	14	3		
25	Jan	3	Oldham Athletic	0-1			5160			5		2			10		4				7	6	11		1		8		9		3		
26		8	NOTTS COUNTY	1-1	Stein		4344		2	5		6			10		4				7	12	11		1		8		9		3		
27		15	BRISTOL CITY	2-3	Robinson, O'Neill		5425		2	5	4	7			13		10				12	6	11				8		9		3		
28		22	Colchester United	1-3	Robinson		3767		3	5					10		4			11	12	6	13	7	1		8		9				2
29		29	SCUNTHORPE UNITED	1-1	Stein		4802			5							10			11	12	6	7	4	1		8		9		3		2
30	Feb	5	Luton Town	2-1	Mean, Watts (og)		5961										10	5		11	12	6	7	4	1		8		9		3		2
31		12	BURNLEY	0-1			5804		2						13		10	5		11	12	6	7	4	1		8		9	14	3		
32		19	Millwall	1-3	O'Shea		8463								10		2	5	14	11	12	6	7	4	1		8		9	13	3		
33		26	BLACKPOOL	2-0	Mean, Robinson (p)		4464										10	5		11	7	6		4	1		8		9	3			2
34	Mar	4	Reading	0-2			10551						14			12	10	5		11	7	6	13	4	1		8		9	3			2
35		7	Cardiff City	2-1	Stein, Hughes		4389						13			10	3	5		11	7	6	14	4	1		8		9		12		2
36		11	PRESTON NORTH END	0-1			5317								14	10	12	5		11	7	6	13	4	1		8		9		3		2
37		18	Brentford	2-0	Jorgensen, Robinson (p)		4578						13			9	10	5		11	7		6	4	1		8			12	3		2
38		21	GILLINGHAM	0-1			4443						13			9	10	5		11	7	12	6		1		8			4	3		2
39		25	WYCOMBE WANDERERS	2-0	W Elliott, Mean		4393						10	4		9	13	5		11	7	12	6		1		8				3		2
40	Apr	1	Oxford United	0-1			5214						10	4	12	9	7	5				6	11		1		8	13			3		2
41		8	OLDHAM ATHLETIC	3-0	Sheerin, S Fletcher, W Elliott		3808						10	4	14	9	13	5		11	12	6			1			8			3		2
42		15	Wrexham	0-1			2597						10	4	11	9	13	5			12	6	14		1			8			3		2
43		22	Stoke City	0-1			15022						12	4	11	9		5			7		6		1		8	13			3		2
44		25	CHESTERFIELD	1-1	C Fletcher		3481						13	4	11	9	12	5			7		6					8			3		2
45		29	Bristol Rovers	2-2	C Fletcher, S Fletcher		8847						10	4	11	9		5			7		6		1		8				3		2
46	May	6	WIGAN ATHLETIC	2-2	W Elliott, Jorgensen		6512						10	4	11	9		5			7		6		1		8	13			3		2
							Apps	5	16	28	11	8	12	8	25	36	31	28	17	21	44	32	30	10	43	3	40	6	36	8	41	6	37
							Goals				1		3		3	7	2	1		2	6	4	3	1			9	1	11		2		

Three own goals

Scorers in game 22: S Fletcher, Robinson (p), Jorgensen, Hayter
Played in one game: JA Bailey (7, at 14), S Lovell (1, 13) and DL Smith (43, 4).
JA Ford played at 14 in game 44 and 13 in game 45.
GJ Stewart played at 1 in three games 17, 27 and 44
T Forbes played at 4 in three games 12, 13 and 14
J Keeler played in three games; 39 (at 14), 45 and 46 (at 12)
BB Stock played in five games; 28 (at 14), 41 and 42 (at 7), 43 and 44 (at 10, subbed in both games)

F.A. Cup

						Att	Betsy K	Broadhurst KM	Cox IG	Day JR	Elliott ST	Elliott W	Fenton NL	Fletcher CN	Fletcher SM	Hayter JE	Howe EJF	Huck WRF	Hughes RD	Jorgensen C	Mean SJ	O'Neill JJ	O'Shea J	Ovendale MJ	Rawlinson MD	Robinson S	Sheerin JE	Stein EMS	Tindall J	Warren C	Watson GWG	Young NA
R1	Oct	30	Notts County	1-1	Warren	3674			5	6				11	10					7				1		8		9		3	12	2
rep	Nov	9	NOTTS COUNTY	4-2	S Fletcher 2, Stein, Robinson(p)	4026			5					6	10	4				7	12			1		8		9		3	11	2
R2		20	BRISTOL CITY	0-2		5223		4	5	6				11	10					7				1		8		9		3	12	2

T Forbes played at 4 in R1

F.L. Cup (Worthington Cup)

						Att	Betsy K	Broadhurst KM	Cox IG	Day JR	Elliott ST	Elliott W	Fenton NL	Fletcher CN	Fletcher SM	Hayter JE	Howe EJF	Huck WRF	Hughes RD	Jorgensen C	Mean SJ	O'Neill JJ	O'Shea J	Ovendale MJ	Rawlinson MD	Robinson S	Sheerin JE	Stein EMS	Tindall J	Warren C	Watson GWG	Young NA
R1/1	Aug	10	BARNET	2-0	Hayter, Huck	3281			5						10	8	4	13	12	7	6	14		1	11			9		3		2
R1/2		24	Barnet	2-3	Stein 2	1697			5	13					10	12	4		11	7	6			1		8		9		3	14	2
R2/1	Sep	14	Charlton Athletic	0-0		10346		7	5						10		4		11		6			1		8		9		3		2
R2/2		21	CHARLTON ATHLETIC	0-0		4369		3	5	11					10		4	12		7	6			1		8		9				2
R3	Oct	13	West Ham United	0-2		22067		11	5						10		4	12		7	6	13		1		8		9		3		2

R2/2 won 3-1 on penalties a.e.t.

JA Bailey played at 12 in R2/1

A.M. Cup (Auto Windscreens Shield)

						Att	Betsy K	Broadhurst KM	Cox IG	Day JR	Elliott ST	Elliott W	Fenton NL	Fletcher CN	Fletcher SM	Hayter JE	Howe EJF	Huck WRF	Hughes RD	Jorgensen C	Mean SJ	O'Neill JJ	O'Shea J	Ovendale MJ	Rawlinson MD	Robinson S	Sheerin JE	Stein EMS	Tindall J	Warren C	Watson GWG	Young NA
R2	Jan	11	BRIGHTON & HOVE ALB.	1-0	Hayter	4325		2		5				10		4				12	6	11		1	7	8		9	3			
R3		25	Bristol City	1-1	Stein	4291			5							10			11	7	6		4	1		8		9		3	12	2

R2 won in sudden-death extra time. R3 lost 1-4 on penalties a.e.t.

J Keeler played in R3 at 13

2000/01

7th in Division Two

	Date		Opponent	Score	Scorers	Att	Angus SD	Bernard N	Broadhurst KM	Cummings W	Day JR	Defoe J	Elliott W	Eribenne CY	Feeney W	Fenton NL	Fletcher CN	Fletcher SM	Grant P	Hayter JE	Howe EJF	Huck WRF	Hughes RD	Jorgensen C	Menetrier M	O'Connor G	Purches SR	Smith DL	Stewart GJ	Tindall J	Woozley DJ	Young NA
1	Aug	12	Bristol Rovers	1-1	Eribenne	8046	6				7		12	8		4	5	10					11	9	1		3					2
2		19	CAMBRIDGE UNITED	1-1	S Fletcher	4869	6				7			8		4	5	10		12		14	11	9	1		3			13		2
3		26	Luton Town	0-1		6013	13							8		6	5	10	4	14		12	11	9	1		3			7		2
4	Sep	2	Colchester United	1-3	Jorgensen	3459	2				12			8		6	5	10	4			11		9	1	13	3	14		7		
5		9	PORT VALE	1-1	C Fletcher	3859								8		12	5	10	4	13			11	9	1	14	3	6		7		2
6		12	SWINDON TOWN	3-0	S Fletcher 2, Hayter	3673	12						14				5	10	4	8			11	9		13	3	6	1	7		2
7		16	Walsall	1-1	Elliott	5054	6						13	12			9	10	4	8			11			14	3		1	7	5	2
8		23	OLDHAM ATHLETIC	1-1	S Fletcher	3976	6						12	14			9	10	4	8			11			13	3		1	7	5	2
9		26	WREXHAM	1-2	Jorgensen	3004	6						13	14			3	10	4	8			11	9		12			1	7	5	2
10		30	Brentford	2-3	Jorgensen, Hughes (p)	4210	6						8				2	10	4			13	11	9			3	14	1	7	5	
11	Oct	6	Bristol City	3-3	C Fletcher, Jorgensen, O'Connor	8938			13		11						2	10	4	8				9		14	3	6	1	7	5	
12		14	ROTHERHAM UNITED	0-1		3878			3				13				2	10	4				11	9		8		6	1	7	5	
13		17	WIGAN ATHLETIC	0-0		3035							8				5	10	4	2			11	9		13	3	6	1	7		
14		21	Bury	5-2	Jorgensen, Hayter 4	2892				2			12				5	10	4	8		14	11	9			3	6	1	7		
15		24	NOTTS COUNTY	0-1		3556				2							5	10	4	8	13	14	11	9			3	6	1	7		
16		28	Stoke City	1-2	Defoe	11572				2		7	14	12			5	10		8	4	13	11	9			3		1	6		
17	Nov	4	PETERBOROUGH UTD.	2-1	Defoe, Cummings	3936				2		7	8				5	10		13	4	12	11	9			3		1	6		
18		11	Northampton Town	3-0	S Fletcher, Defoe 2	5692			12	2		7	8				5	10			4		11	9		13	3		1	6		
19	Dec	2	Wycombe Wanderers	3-0	C Fletcher 2, Defoe	5185			13	2		7	10	8			5		14	12	4		11	9			3		1	6		
20		16	SWANSEA CITY	2-0	Hughes (p), Defoe	3738			12	2	5	7	8					10		13	4		11	9		14	3		1	6		
21		23	MILLWALL	1-2	Defoe	6843				2		7	8	12			5	10			4		11	9		13	3		1	6		
22		26	Oxford United	2-1	Defoe 2	6200			12	2	5	7	8					10		13	4		11	9			3		1	6		
23	Jan	1	LUTON TOWN	3-2	S Fletcher, Hughes (p), Defoe	5411			2			7	8					10	4	13	5		11	9		12	3		1	6		
24		13	Wrexham	2-2	Defoe, Hayter	2852			3	2		7					5	10		8	4		11	9					1	6		
25		23	Cambridge United	2-0	Defoe, Hayter	3027		3	2			7	8				5	10		13	4		11	9				12	1	6		
26		27	Millwall	1-0	Jorgensen	12713		3	2			7	8				5	10		13	4		11	9				12	1	6		
27	Feb	3	COLCHESTER UNITED	2-2	Hughes (p), C Fletcher	4407		3	2			7	8				5	10		13	4		11	9		12		14	1	6		
28		10	Port Vale	1-2	Tindall	3956		3	4			7	8				5	10					11	9		14	2	13	1	6		
29		17	WALSALL	2-2	Howe, Defoe	4564			2			7					5	10		8	4		11	9			3		1	6		
30		20	Swindon Town	1-1	Hughes	6455			2			7		13			5	10		8	4		11	9		12	3	14	1	6		
31		24	Oldham Athletic	1-2	Hayter	4845		3	2			7	14	13			5	10		8	4		11	9	12				1	6		
32		27	BRISTOL ROVERS	1-2	Jorgensen	3466		3	2				8	13			5	10		7	4		11	9	1	12				6		
33	Mar	3	BRENTFORD	2-0	S Fletcher, Elliott	4438		13	2		3	12	8				5	10		7	4		11	9	1					6		
34		6	Rotherham United	1-3	Hayter	6488		12	3			7	8				5	10		2	4		11	9	1					6		
35		10	BRISTOL CITY	4-0	Elliott 2, Hughes, C Fletcher	4028		14	3			7	8				5	10		2	4		11	9	1	12	13			6		
36		17	Wigan Athletic	1-1	Howe	5878		13	3			7	8				5	10		2	4		11	9	1	12				6		
37		24	BURY	1-0	Defoe	3325		12	3			7	8		13		5	10		2	4		11	9					1	6		
38		31	Swansea City	3-0	Hayter, Elliott, Feeney	4013		12	3			7	8		14		5	10		2	4		11	9			13		1	6		
39	Apr	3	OXFORD UNITED	4-3	Hayter, Hughes 2(1p), Feeney	3747		14	3			7	8		13		5	10		2	4		11	9			12		1	6		
40		10	READING	1-2	Defoe	6603			3			7	8	12	13		5	10		2	4		11	9					1	6		
41		14	Notts County	2-0	S Fletcher 2	5186			3			7	8	12	9		5	10		2	4		11				13		1	6		
42		17	STOKE CITY	1-0	Defoe	5373			3			7	8		13		5	10		2	4		11	9			12		1	6		
43		21	Peterborough United	2-1	Feeney, Defoe	6318			3			7	8		12		5	10		2	4		11	9		13	14		1	6		
44		23	WYCOMBE WANDERERS	2-0	Feeney, Elliott	5026			3				8	13	7		5	10		2	4		11	9		14	12		1	6		
45		28	NORTHAMPTON T	2-0	Elliott, Jorgensen	6511		14	3			13	8		7		5	10		2	4		11	9			12		1	6		
46	May	5	Reading	3-3	Elliott 2, Defoe	20589			3			7	8		14		5	10		2	4		11	9		13	12		1	6		
						Apps	9	14	30	10	7	29	37	17	10	5	43	45	15	39	31	8	44	43	11	22	33	14	36	45	6	8
						Goals				1		18	9	1	4		6	9		11	2		8	8		1				1		

Played in one game: J Keeler (28, at 12), BB Stock (18, at 14)

JA Ford played at 12 in three games; 10, 11 and 15 (subbed in 15)

JJ O'Neill played in three games; 12 and 13 at 12, 14 at 13

F.A. Cup

	Date		Opponent	Score	Scorers	Att	Angus SD	Bernard N	Broadhurst KM	Cummings W	Day JR	Defoe J	Elliott W	Eribenne CY	Feeney W	Fenton NL	Fletcher CN	Fletcher SM	Grant P	Hayter JE	Howe EJF	Huck WRF	Hughes RD	Jorgensen C	Menetrier M	O'Connor G	Purches SR	Smith DL	Stewart GJ	Tindall J	Woozley DJ	Young NA
R1	Nov	18	SWANSEA CITY	2-0	Elliott, Hayter	3422		5			2		8	13				10		7	4		11	9		12	3		1	6		
R2	Dec	9	NUNEATON BOROUGH	3-0	Hughes, Elliott, O'Connor	5835			2		12		8	13			5	10		7	4		11	9		14	3		1	6		
R3	Jan	6	GILLINGHAM	2-3	Defoe, C Fletcher	7403			2		5	7	8	13			3	10		11	4			9		14		12	1	6		

F.L. Cup (Worthington Cup)

	Date		Opponent	Score	Scorers	Att	Angus SD	Bernard N	Broadhurst KM	Cummings W	Day JR	Defoe J	Elliott W	Eribenne CY	Feeney W	Fenton NL	Fletcher CN	Fletcher SM	Grant P	Hayter JE	Howe EJF	Huck WRF	Hughes RD	Jorgensen C	Menetrier M	O'Connor G	Purches SR	Smith DL	Stewart GJ	Tindall J	Woozley DJ	Young NA
R1/1	Aug	22	Norwich City	0-0		12224							12	8			5	10	4			13	11	9	1		3	6		7		2
R1/2	Sep	5	NORWICH CITY	1-2	Jorgensen	3634								8			5	10	4	12		13	11	9	1		3	6		7		2

A.M. Cup (LDV Vans Trophy)

	Date		Opponent	Score	Scorers	Att	Angus SD	Bernard N	Broadhurst KM	Cummings W	Day JR	Defoe J	Elliott W	Eribenne CY	Feeney W	Fenton NL	Fletcher CN	Fletcher SM	Grant P	Hayter JE	Howe EJF	Huck WRF	Hughes RD	Jorgensen C	Menetrier M	O'Connor G	Purches SR	Smith DL	Stewart GJ	Tindall J	Woozley DJ	Young NA
R1	Dec	5	DOVER ATHLETIC	1-1	Huck	2171		8	3		5	10		9					4	14	2	6			1	7		11				
R2	Jan	9	SWANSEA CITY	0-1		3810		7		4			13	9			12	10				6	11		1	8		2		5		

R1 won 4-2 on penalties a.e.t.

J Keeler played at 13 in R1 and 14 in R2

BB Stock played at 12 in R1 and 3 (subbed) in R2

Bernard also known by his given name, Narada

2001/02

21st in Division Two: Relegated

						Bernard N	Broadhurst KM	Cooke S	Elliott W	Eribenne CY	Feeney W	Fletcher CN	Fletcher SM	Ford JA	Foyewa A	Hayter JE	Holmes D	Howe EJF	Huck WRF	Hughes RD	Kandol T	Maher S	McAnespie K	Melligan JJ	O'Connor G	Purches SR	Stewart GJ	Stock BB	Thomas D	Tindall J	Young NA
1	Aug 11	Huddersfield Town	0-1		10137		4		9	10	11	8			12	6		2		7					13	5	1			3	
2	18	BLACKPOOL	0-1		3709		4		11	9	10	8		7	13	6		2				3			14	5	1				
3	25	Cardiff City	2-2	Tindall, Feeney (p)	13383		4		11		10	8			9	6		2	13			3			12	5	1			7	
4	Sep 1	Cambridge United	2-2	Elliott 2	2754		4		11	10		8		12		6		2	14			3			9	5	1	13		7	
5	8	SWINDON TOWN	0-0		3770		4		11	10	9	7				8		2	13			3			12	5	1			6	
6	15	BURY	3-2	Hayter, Feeney (p), Stock	3004				8	12	10	7				9	11	3				4			5	6	1	13		2	
7	18	Peterborough United	0-6		3445				8	14	9	7				11	10	3		6		4			13	5	1	12		2	
8	22	Brighton & Hove Albion	1-2	Howe	6714				8	13	9	7		6		11	10	3				4			12	5	1			2	
9	25	READING	1-0	Hayter	3691		12		8	13	9	7		6		11	10	3				4				5	1			2	
10	29	Stoke City	0-2		14803				8	13	9	7		6		11	10	3	14			4			12	5	1			2	
11	Oct 5	OLDHAM ATHLETIC	3-2	Elliott, Holmes, Hayter	3312	5	4		8	12		7		6		11	10	3	14								1	9		2	
12	9	WIGAN ATHLETIC	2-0	Elliott, Hayter	2908	12	4		8	6		7				11	10	3	13						5		1	9		2	
13	13	Wycombe Wanderers	1-1	Holmes	6810	5	4		8	6		7				11	10	3			12				13		1	9		2	
14	20	BRENTFORD	0-2		3934	12	4		8	13		7				11	10	3	14		6				5		1	9			
15	23	Bristol City	0-1		9972	6	4		8	14		7				11	10	3			12				13	5	1	9		2	
16	27	NOTTS COUNTY	4-2	C Fletcher, Elliott 2 (2p), Feeney	3209	6	4		8	13	12	7				11	10	3		14						5	1	9		2	
17	Nov 3	Colchester United	2-1	Howe, Feeney	4369	13	4		8	12	6	7				11	10	3		14						5	1	9		2	
18	10	WREXHAM	3-0	Tindall, Stock, Hayter	5220	12	4		8		6	7				11	10	3		14					13	5	1	9		2	
19	20	PORT VALE	0-0		4428		4		8		6		12			11	7	3		10					13	5	1	9		2	
20	24	Chesterfield	1-2	Feeney	4353		4		8	13	6		11				7	3		10	12					5	1	9		2	
21	Dec 1	TRANMERE ROVERS	0-2		6035		4		8	14						11	7	3		10	13			6	12	5	1	9		2	
22	15	Northampton Town	0-1		3909		4		12	13	7	8				11	9	3		10				6	14	5	1			2	
23	22	QUEEN'S PARK RANGERS	1-2	C Fletcher	8147		4		9		7	8				11	12	3		10				6		5	1			2	
24	26	Swindon Town	0-0		6790		4		9		7	8				11		3		10	13	12		6		5	1			2	
25	29	Wigan Athletic	0-0		5011				9		7	8				11	12	3				4		6			1	10		2	
26	Jan 12	Blackpool	3-4	C Fletcher 2, Hayter	4583				9	12	7	8				11						4		6		3	1	10		2	
27	19	HUDDERSFIELD T	2-3	Feeney, Holmes	5307		4		9		7	8				11	13			12				6		3	1	10		2	
28	22	Queen's Park Rangers	1-1	Feeney	10901		4		12		7	8				11	9	5		6		13				3	1	10		2	
29	26	Oldham Athletic	3-3	Howe, Hughes, Feeney (p)	4853		4		10		7	8				11	9	5		6		14			12	3	1			2	
30	Feb 2	STOKE CITY	3-1	Purches, Hughes, Feeney	6027				12		7	8			13	11	9	5		6		4			10	3	1	14		2	
31	5	CARDIFF CITY	1-3	Holmes	4336				14		7	8			13	11	9	5				4		12	10	3	1	6		2	
32	9	Brentford	0-1		6698				14		7					12	9	5		6	8	4			10	3	1	11	13	2	
33	16	WYCOMBE WANDERERS	1-2	Howe	5807				9	12		8			13	11		5		6	7	4			10	3	1		14	2	
34	23	Bury	1-2	Holmes	4218				13		7	8				11	9	5		6		4	14		10	3	1		12	2	
35	26	BRIGHTON & HOVE ALB	1-1	Holmes	6337				7					12		11	9				13	4	6		10	3	1		8	2	5
36	Mar 2	PETERBOROUGH UTD.	0-2		5163				7		13					11	9	5				4	6		10	3	1		8	2	12
37	5	Reading	2-2	Holmes, Hayter	13538				7	13	8					11	9	5				4	12		10	3	1			2	6
38	9	NORTHAMPTON T	5-1	* see below	6322			10	7	13	8					11	9	5				4	14			3	1		12	2	6
39	16	Tranmere Rovers	0-0		7829			10	7		8					11	9	5		12	13	4				3				2	6
40	19	CAMBRIDGE UNITED	2-2	Elliott (p), Feeney	7082			10	7	14	8					11	9	5		12		4	13			3	1			2	6
41	23	BRISTOL CITY	1-3	McAnespie	7033			10	7		8					11		5			13	4	6			3	1	12	9	2	
42	30	Notts County	0-2		9014			10	7		8	6			12		9			11		4				3	1	14	13	2	5
43	Apr 2	COLCHESTER UNITED	0-1		5908			12	7		8	6			13	11	9			10		4				3	1		14	2	5
44	6	Port Vale	0-0		3514			10	7		8	6				11	9					4				3	1	12	13	2	5
45	13	CHESTERFIELD	3-1	Elliott (p), Feeney, Holmes	6068				7		8	6				11	9				14	4			13	3	1	10	12	2	5
46	20	Wrexham	1-2	C Fletcher	4289				7		8	6				11	9					4			12	3	1	10	13	2	5
					Apps	8	23	7	46	24	37	35	2	7	8	44	37	38	7	22	12	31	7	8	28	41	45	26	12	44	11
					Goals				8		13	5				7	9	4		2						2		2		3	

Home games before November 10 played at Dorchester Town
Scorers in game 38: Tindall, Purches, Feeney 2, Holmes
M Menetrier played at 1 in game 39.
DP Birmingham played in four games; 2 (at 12), 25, 26 and 27 (at 5, subbed in games 26 and 27)
DL Smith played in three games; 11 (at 13), 14 (at 2, subbed) and 29 (at 13)

F.A. Cup

						Bernard N	Broadhurst KM	Cooke S	Elliott W	Eribenne CY	Feeney W	Fletcher CN	Fletcher SM	Ford JA	Foyewa A	Hayter JE	Holmes D	Howe EJF	Huck WRF	Hughes RD	Kandol T	Maher S	McAnespie K	Melligan JJ	O'Connor G	Purches SR	Stewart GJ	Stock BB	Thomas D	Tindall J	Young NA
R1	Nov 17	WORKSOP TOWN	3-0	Hughes, Hayter, S Fletcher	4414		4		8		6	7	12			11		3		10	14				13	5	1	9		2	
R2	Dec 8	Peterborough United	0-1		4773		4		8		7	12				11	14	3		10	13			6		5	1	9		2	

F.L. Cup (Worthington Cup)

						Bernard N	Broadhurst KM	Cooke S	Elliott W	Eribenne CY	Feeney W	Fletcher CN	Fletcher SM	Ford JA	Foyewa A	Hayter JE	Holmes D	Howe EJF	Huck WRF	Hughes RD	Kandol T	Maher S	McAnespie K	Melligan JJ	O'Connor G	Purches SR	Stewart GJ	Stock BB	Thomas D	Tindall J	Young NA
R1	Aug 21	TORQUAY UNITED	0-2		2556		12		11		10	9		8	13	7		2	14			3			6	5	1				

DP Birmingham played at 4 (subbed)

A.M. Cup (LDV Vans Trophy)

						Bernard N	Broadhurst KM	Cooke S	Elliott W	Eribenne CY	Feeney W	Fletcher CN	Fletcher SM	Ford JA	Foyewa A	Hayter JE	Holmes D	Howe EJF	Huck WRF	Hughes RD	Kandol T	Maher S	McAnespie K	Melligan JJ	O'Connor G	Purches SR	Stewart GJ	Stock BB	Thomas D	Tindall J	Young NA
R1	Oct 16	Barnet	1-2	Kandol	789	12	4		8	14						11	10	3	7		6				5			9		13	

DL Smith played at 2 (subbed)

2002/03

4th in Division Three: Promoted after play off

	Date	Opponent	Res	Scorers	Att	Bernard N	Broadhurst KM	Browning M	Buxton L	Connell A	Cummings W	Elliott W	Eribenne CY	Feeney W	Fletcher CN	Fletcher SM	Gulliver P	Hayter JE	Holmes D	Maher S	McDonald S	Moss NG	O'Connor G	Purches SR	Ridgewell L	Stock BB	Tardif C	Thomas D	Tindall I	Young NA
1	Aug 10	Boston United	2-2	Maher, Stock	4184		4	12				7		9				10	13	5			11	3		8	1		6	2
2	13	KIDDERMINSTER HARR.	0-0		4771			12		14		7		9	8			10	13	5			11	3		4	1		6	2
3	17	CAMBRIDGE UNITED	1-1	Feeney	4315	2		4		13		12		9	8			10	7	5			11	3			1	14	6	
4	24	Swansea City	0-2		4325		5	4		12		7		9	8			10					11	3		13	1		6	2
5	27	OXFORD UNITED	1-1	Holmes	4842		5	4		10		7			8			12	9					3				11	6	2
6	31	Macclesfield Town	1-0	Connell	1795		5	4		10		7			8			12	9	14			13	3				11	6	2
7	Sep 7	Exeter City	3-1	Connell, Elliott (p), O'Connor	4466		2	4		10		7	14		8			13	9	5			12	3			1	11	6	
8	14	BURY	1-2	O'Connor	4851			4		10		7			8			14	9	5		1	13	3		12		11	6	2
9	17	RUSHDEN & DIAMONDS	3-1	Purches, Maher, Connell	4527			4		10		7	12		8				9	5		1		3				11	6	2
10	21	Darlington	2-2	Holmes, Connell	2950		14	4		10		7			8			13	9	5		1		3		12		11	6	2
11	28	CARLISLE UNITED	3-1	Tindall, Connell (p), Stock	5103		7	4		10			12		5			13	9			1	8	3		14		11	6	2
12	Oct 5	Lincoln City	2-1	Purches, Connell	3273	14	6	4		10		7	13		5	12		9				1		3		8		11		2
13	13	HARTLEPOOL UNITED	2-1	Elliott, Widdrington (og)	5998		6	4		10		7			5	12		9				1	13	3	14	8		11		2
14	19	Leyton Orient	0-0		5622		6	4		10		7			5	12		13				1	14	3	9	8		11		2
15	26	YORK CITY	1-0	S Fletcher	5755		6	4				7		12	5	9		10				1	13	3	14	8		11		2
16	29	Torquay United	0-4		3543		6	4				14		13	5	9		10				1	8	3	7	12		11		2
17	Nov 2	BRISTOL ROVERS	1-0	S Fletcher	6924	14	6	4				7		13	5	9		10	12			1	8	3				11		2
18	9	Wrexham	2-3	Thomas, Hayter	3105		6	4				7		13	5	9		10	14			1	8	3	12			11		2
19	23	Southend United	1-0	O'Connor (p)	4221	2	6	4				7			5	9		10				1	8	3				11	12	
20	30	SCUNTHORPE UNITED	2-1	Broadhurst, Hayter	6527		6	4				7			5	9		10	13			1	8	3				11	12	2
21	Dec 14	Shrewsbury Town	0-0		2869	13	6	4				7		12	5	9		10				1	8	3				11		2
22	21	HULL CITY	0-0		6098	14	6	4				7		13	5	9		10					8	3			1	11	12	2
23	26	Oxford United	0-3		8349			4				7		12	5	9		10	13				8	3		14		11	6	2
24	28	ROCHDALE	3-3	Browning, S Fletcher, O'Connor(p)	6240			4				7		12	5	9		10					8	3				11	6	2
25	Jan 18	MACCLESFIELD TOWN	2-2	Elliott, Hayter	5840	2		4	14			7		13	5	9		10					8	3		12	1	11	6	
26	Feb 1	BOSTON UNITED	2-1	Redfearn (og), Feeney	5180			12	2			7		14	5	9		10	13				8	3		4	1	11	6	
27	4	Kidderminster Harriers	0-1		2157		5				2	7	13			9		10	14				8	3		4	1	11	6	
28	8	WREXHAM	2-0	Feeney 2	5445		5		7		2	12		11		9		10	13			1	8	3		4			6	
29	11	SWANSEA CITY	3-0	Hayter, O'Connor 2 (2p)	5511		11	4	3		2	7			5	9		10	13			1	12			8			6	
30	15	Bristol Rovers	0-0		6347			4	3		2	7		11	5	9		10	12			1	14			8		13	6	
31	22	EXETER CITY	2-0	Holmes, O'Connor	6674			4	3		2	7		11	5	13		10	9			1	12	14		8			6	
32	Mar 1	Bury	1-2	Feeney	2914				4		2	13		11	5	9		10				1	7	3		8		12	6	
33	4	Rushden & Diamonds	1-2	Feeney	4353			4	13		2	7		11	5	9		10	14			1	8	3				12	6	
34	8	DARLINGTON	2-0	O'Connor, Hayter	5758			4	6		2	7			5	9		10	14			1	8	3		12		11		13
35	11	Rochdale	1-1	C Fletcher	1958			4	6		2	7			5	9		10	12			1	8	3				11		
36	15	York City	0-1		3642			4	6		2	7	14		5	13		10	9			1	8	3		12		11		
37	18	LEYTON ORIENT	3-1	Jones (og), Hayter, Feeney	5078			4	6		2			11	5	9		10	14			1	8	3		12			7	13
38	22	TORQUAY UNITED	1-1	Young	7181			4	6		2	7		11		9		10	14			1	8	3				13	5	12
39	25	Cambridge United	1-2	S Fletcher	2885			4	6		2	12			5	9		10	13			1	11	8		7				3
40	29	Hartlepool United	0-0		5625			4	6		2	7			5	9		10			12	1	11	8				13		3
41	Apr 5	Scunthorpe United	2-0	Hayter, Thomas	4488			4	6		2	7			5	9	14	10			13	1	11	8				12		3
42	12	SOUTHEND UNITED	1-0	Purches	6767			4	6		2	7			5	9	13	10			12	1		8		14		11		3
43	19	Hull City	1-3	S Fletcher	15816			4			2	7			5	9	6	10			14	1	13	8		12		11		3
44	21	SHREWSBURY TOWN	2-1	McDonald, Elliott	7102			4			2	7			5	9	6	12	14		10	1	11	8		13				3
45	26	LINCOLN CITY	0-1		7578			4			2	7			5	12	6	13	9		10	1	14	8				11		3
46	May 3	Carlisle United	2-0	Hayter 2	7402			4			2	7			5	9	6	14			10	1	13	8				11		3
					Apps	7	21	43	17	13	20	44	6	21	42	35	6	45	29	8	7	33	41	44	5	27	9	37	27	32
					Goals		1	1		6		4		7	1	5		9	3	2	1		8	3		2		2	1	1

JL Ashdown played at 1 in two games, 5 and 6
A Blayney played at 1 in two games, 23 and 24
A Foyewa played at 12 in game 27. GJ Stewart played at 12 in game 46.

Browning went in goal when Tardif was injured in game 22

Three own goals

Play Offs

	Date	Opponent	Res	Scorers	Att	Bernard N	Broadhurst KM	Browning M	Buxton L	Connell A	Cummings W	Elliott W	Eribenne CY	Feeney W	Fletcher CN	Fletcher SM	Gulliver P	Hayter JE	Holmes D	Maher S	McDonald S	Moss NG	O'Connor G	Purches SR	Ridgewell L	Stock BB	Tardif C	Thomas D	Tindall I	Young NA
SF1	May 10	Bury	0-0		5782						2	7			5	9	6	10	13		14	1	12	8		4		11		3
SF2	13	BURY	3-1	O'Connor, Hayter 2	7945			4			2	7			5	9	6	10				1	11	8		12				3
F	24	Lincoln City	5-2	* see below	32148			4			2	7			5	9	6	10	13			1	11	8		12		14		3

Final at the Millennium Stadium, Cardiff. Scorers S Fletcher, C Fletcher 2, Purches, O'Connor

F.A. Cup

	Date	Opponent	Res	Scorers	Att	Bernard N	Broadhurst KM	Browning M	Buxton L	Connell A	Cummings W	Elliott W	Eribenne CY	Feeney W	Fletcher CN	Fletcher SM	Gulliver P	Hayter JE	Holmes D	Maher S	McDonald S	Moss NG	O'Connor G	Purches SR	Ridgewell L	Stock BB	Tardif C	Thomas D	Tindall I	Young NA
R1	Nov 16	DONCASTER ROVERS	2-1	Thomas, Elliott	5371		6	12				7		8	5	9		10				1	4	3				11		2
R2	Dec 7	Southend United	1-1	Broadhurst	5721		6	4				7			5	9		10				1	8	3				11	12	2
rep	17	SOUTHEND UNITED	3-2	S Fletcher, Holmes, Browning	5456		6	4				7		13	5	9		10	14				8	3			12	11		2
R3	Jan 4	CREWE ALEXANDRA	0-0		7252	14		4				7		12	5	9		10	13				8	3			1	11	6	2
rep	14	Crewe Alexandra	2-2	Hayter, S Fletcher	4540	2						7		12	5	9		10	13				8	3		4	1	11	6	
R4	26	Stoke City	0-3		12004				2			7		13	5	9		10	14				8	3		4	1	11	6	

R3 replay won 3-1 on penalties a.e.t.

A Foyewa played at 13 in R1 and 14 in R3 replay
GJ Stewart played at 1 (subbed) in R2 replay and 12 in R3 replay

F.L. Cup (Worthington Cup)

	Date	Opponent	Res	Scorers	Att	Bernard N	Broadhurst KM	Browning M	Buxton L	Connell A	Cummings W	Elliott W	Eribenne CY	Feeney W	Fletcher CN	Fletcher SM	Gulliver P	Hayter JE	Holmes D	Maher S	McDonald S	Moss NG	O'Connor G	Purches SR	Ridgewell L	Stock BB	Tardif C	Thomas D	Tindall I	Young NA
R1	Sep 10	BRENTFORD	3-3	Browning, Connell, Thomas	3302		6	4		10		7			8			14	9	5			13	3			1	11	2	12

Lost 2-4 on penalties a.e.t.

Browning went in goal when Tardif injured

A.M. Cup (LDV Vans Trophy)

	Date	Opponent	Res	Scorers	Att	Bernard N	Broadhurst KM	Browning M	Buxton L	Connell A	Cummings W	Elliott W	Eribenne CY	Feeney W	Fletcher CN	Fletcher SM	Gulliver P	Hayter JE	Holmes D	Maher S	McDonald S	Moss NG	O'Connor G	Purches SR	Ridgewell L	Stock BB	Tardif C	Thomas D	Tindall I	Young NA
R1	Oct 22	Oxford United	3-2	S Fletcher, Hayter, Purches	4663	2	6	4				13		12	5	9		10				1	8	3		7		11		
R2	Nov 12	LEYTON ORIENT	1-0	Feeney	2724	2	6					7		8	5	12		10	9			1	4	3				11		
QF	Dec 10	CARDIFF CITY	2-1	Elliott, Hayter	3615	2	6	4				7		13	5	9		10				1	8	3				11	12	
SFS	Jan 21	BRISTOL CITY	1-3	C Fletcher	5125	2		4				7		8	5	14		13	9				10	3		11	1	12	6	

QF won on golden goal in extra time

BOURNEMOUTH AGAINST OTHER CLUBS (IN THE FOOTBALL LEAGUE)

	Home:						Away:					Totals:		
	p	*w*	*d*	*l*	*f*	*a*	*w*	*d*	*l*	*f*	*a*	*f*	*a*	*% won*
Aberdare Athletic	8	3	0	1	9	2	0	1	3	6	10	15	12	37.50
Accrington Stanley	4	2	0	0	8	3	0	0	2	3	5	11	8	50.00
Aldershot	56	15	8	5	54	27	10	7	11	29	29	83	56	44.64
Aston Villa	4	1	0	1	4	2	0	1	1	2	3	6	5	25.00
Barnet	2	0	1	0	1	1	1	0	0	2	1	3	2	50.00
Barnsley	32	8	5	3	29	16	2	4	10	15	29	44	45	31.25
Barrow	8	2	2	0	4	0	2	2	0	6	3	10	3	50.00
Birmingham City	10	3	0	2	9	7	2	3	0	3	1	12	8	50.00
Blackburn Rovers	14	3	2	2	10	8	0	1	6	7	15	17	23	21.43
Blackpool	24	6	3	3	16	10	2	3	7	13	18	29	28	33.33
Bolton Wanderers	18	5	1	3	16	10	3	2	4	7	11	23	21	44.44
Boston United	2	1	0	0	2	1	0	1	0	2	2	4	3	50.00
Bradford City	46	13	7	3	48	23	6	7	10	23	40	71	63	41.30
Bradford PA	4	0	2	0	4	4	1	1	0	3	2	7	6	25.00
Brentford	82	20	9	12	55	42	8	15	18	46	58	101	100	34.15
Brighton & Hove Alb.	88	19	16	9	57	44	13	8	23	55	81	112	125	36.36
Bristol City	66	16	10	7	62	28	3	7	23	28	60	90	88	28.79
Bristol Rovers	96	27	10	11	80	41	14	7	27	62	95	142	136	42.71
Burnley	18	4	3	2	11	6	0	5	4	6	16	17	22	22.22
Bury	34	11	4	2	29	17	5	3	9	22	32	51	49	47.06
Cambridge United	24	5	4	3	15	9	4	2	6	15	18	30	27	37.50
Cardiff City	30	9	3	3	31	21	2	5	8	13	29	44	50	36.67
Carlisle United	12	5	0	1	15	9	4	1	1	10	7	25	16	75.00
Charlton Athletic	22	7	1	3	22	15	4	4	3	18	23	40	38	50.00
Chelsea	2	1	0	0	1	0	0	0	1	0	2	1	2	50.00
Chester City	12	4	2	0	9	2	1	3	2	6	8	15	10	41.67
Chesterfield	32	10	5	1	25	10	3	7	6	10	19	35	29	40.62
Colchester United	48	11	10	3	48	27	6	5	13	28	44	76	71	35.42
Coventry City	42	9	7	5	32	25	6	2	13	28	52	60	77	35.71
Crewe Alexandra	28	5	5	4	15	11	3	3	8	11	17	26	28	28.57
Crystal Palace	64	21	8	3	75	31	6	7	19	29	60	104	91	42.19
Darlington	26	7	3	3	21	13	5	4	4	11	12	32	25	46.15
Derby County	4	1	1	0	2	1	1	0	1	3	5	5	6	50.00
Doncaster Rovers	26	6	3	4	26	16	1	6	6	11	19	37	35	26.92
Exeter City	80	27	9	4	78	39	14	8	18	53	72	131	111	51.25
Fulham	24	7	3	2	22	14	3	5	4	12	16	34	30	41.67
Gillingham	78	21	7	11	74	45	9	11	19	44	55	118	100	38.46
Grimsby Town	30	7	4	4	18	14	3	4	8	10	21	28	35	33.33
Halifax Town	32	8	5	3	20	10	4	3	9	16	26	36	36	37.50
Hartlepool United	26	10	1	2	26	8	3	6	4	9	11	35	19	50.00
Hereford United	12	3	3	0	10	7	3	1	2	6	4	16	11	50.00
Huddersfield Town	30	6	3	6	16	17	3	7	5	12	16	28	33	30.00
Hull City	38	8	7	4	35	23	3	4	12	21	42	56	65	28.95
Ipswich Town	28	8	5	1	28	13	3	2	9	13	20	41	33	39.29
Kidderminster Harriers	2	0	1	0	0	0	0	0	1	0	1	0	1	0.00
Leeds United	6	0	2	1	0	1	0	0	3	2	9	2	10	0.00
Leicester City	6	1	0	2	6	7	2	0	1	3	2	9	9	50.00
Leyton Orient	66	21	6	6	63	28	4	10	19	20	56	83	84	37.88
Lincoln City	22	5	4	2	15	6	3	2	6	10	23	25	29	36.36
Luton Town	46	12	6	5	44	32	6	5	12	22	40	66	72	39.13
Macclesfield Town	4	1	1	0	3	2	1	1	0	3	2	6	4	50.00
Manchester City	6	0	1	2	0	3	0	1	2	4	7	4	10	0.00
Mansfield Town	38	11	6	2	42	21	5	7	7	26	24	68	45	42.11
Merthyr Town	14	5	2	0	17	8	3	1	3	13	13	30	21	57.14
Middlesbrough	8	1	3	0	6	4	0	0	4	2	12	8	16	12.50

	Home:					Away:					Totals:		
	p	w	d	l	f	a	w	d	l	f	a	f	a	% won
Millwall	62	14	7	10	53	26	9	2	20	28	61	81	87	37.10
Newcastle United	2	1	0	0	2	1	0	0	1	0	3	2	4	50.00
Newport County	82	19	13	9	74	43	6	10	25	42	91	116	134	30.49
Northampton Town	86	23	13	7	82	41	12	8	23	54	86	136	127	40.70
Norwich City	50	8	7	10	31	29	9	6	10	40	54	71	83	34.00
Nottingham Forest	4	1	0	1	4	4	0	0	2	0	4	4	8	25.00
Notts County	50	12	7	6	36	23	10	2	13	37	44	73	67	44.00
Oldham Athletic	36	11	6	1	31	12	2	7	9	23	37	54	49	36.11
Oxford United	24	6	3	3	18	12	3	1	8	14	22	32	34	37.50
Peterborough Utd	36	6	6	6	28	25	3	1	14	15	41	43	66	25.00
Plymouth Argyle	60	8	11	11	37	42	3	6	21	18	57	55	99	18.33
Port Vale	58	17	10	2	54	20	7	10	12	29	36	83	56	41.38
Portsmouth	14	3	1	3	6	5	1	2	4	6	13	12	18	28.57
Preston North End	22	7	1	3	15	6	4	3	4	10	15	25	21	50.00
QPR	68	18	7	9	62	39	7	7	20	29	57	91	96	36.76
Reading	100	24	15	11	70	48	11	9	30	54	93	124	141	35.00
Rochdale	26	9	3	1	27	13	3	7	3	14	13	41	26	46.15
Rotherham Utd.	30	9	4	2	27	11	3	3	9	17	28	44	39	40.00
Rushden & Diamonds	2	1	0	0	3	1	0	0	1	1	2	4	3	50.00
Scunthorpe United	32	5	9	2	20	17	4	6	6	14	19	34	36	28.12
Sheffield United	10	0	2	3	1	4	1	2	2	5	8	6	12	10.00
Shrewsbury Town	58	19	7	3	53	23	5	9	15	27	44	80	67	41.38
Southampton	14	4	1	2	14	11	0	2	5	6	19	20	30	28.57
Southend United	96	28	9	11	82	49	8	19	21	50	84	132	133	37.50
Southport	16	6	1	1	20	7	2	3	3	5	7	25	14	50.00
Stockport County	36	15	2	1	27	5	5	4	9	15	24	42	29	55.56
Stoke City	20	4	4	2	14	8	1	2	7	6	14	20	22	25.00
Sunderland	4	0	0	2	0	2	0	1	1	3	4	3	6	0.00
Swansea City	42	13	3	5	32	15	4	5	12	16	31	48	46	40.48
Swindon Town	90	25	14	6	88	39	9	10	26	51	92	139	131	37.78
Thames	4	1	1	0	7	5	1	0	1	6	5	13	10	50.00
Torquay United	80	16	13	11	75	48	9	13	18	40	65	115	113	31.25
Tranmere Rovers	32	9	5	2	28	16	6	5	5	21	17	49	33	46.88
Walsall	86	19	13	11	69	41	6	18	19	37	65	106	106	29.07
Watford	94	20	16	11	83	54	14	10	23	46	65	129	119	36.17
West Bromwich Alb.	10	3	1	1	8	6	0	2	3	3	11	11	17	30.00
West Ham United	2	0	1	0	1	1	0	0	1	1	4	2	5	0.00
Wigan Athletic	34	8	5	4	21	14	5	4	8	14	20	35	34	38.24
Wimbledon	8	0	0	4	4	8	0	0	4	3	12	7	20	0.00
Wolverhampton W.	4	1	1	0	4	3	1	0	1	4	3	8	6	50.00
Workington	12	3	2	1	8	4	1	3	2	6	7	14	11	33.33
Wrexham	38	8	4	7	24	18	5	3	11	20	31	44	49	34.21
Wycombe Wan.	16	5	1	2	13	6	3	4	1	12	7	25	13	50.00
York City	42	11	6	4	40	22	6	4	11	18	31	58	53	40.48

TOTALS TO END 2002/03:

	Home:					Away:					Totals:		
	p	w	d	l	f	a	w	d	l	f	a	f	a	Points
	3276	842	449	347	2764	1611	379	418	841	1694	2744	4458	4355	3684
Comprising:														
New 1st/Old 2nd	136	28	16	24	98	81	15	14	39	68	125	166	206	159
New 2nd/Old 3rd	1518	383	211	165	1170	715	179	206	374	773	1172	1943	1887	1830
New 3rd/Old 4th	414	110	64	33	328	162	49	68	90	173	252	501	414	493
Div 3 (South)	1208	321	158	125	1168	653	136	130	338	680	1195	1848	1848	1202

1981/82 Division 4

1	Sheffield United	46	15	8	0	53	15	12	7	4	41	26	96
2	Bradford City	46	14	7	2	52	23	12	6	5	36	22	91
3	Wigan Athletic	46	17	5	1	47	18	9	8	6	33	28	91
4	BOURNEMOUTH	46	12	10	1	37	15	11	9	3	25	15	88
5	Peterborough United	46	16	3	4	46	22	8	7	8	25	35	82
6	Colchester United	46	12	6	5	47	23	8	6	9	35	34	72
7	Port Vale	46	9	12	2	26	17	9	4	10	30	32	70
8	Hull City	46	14	3	6	36	23	5	9	9	34	38	69
9	Bury	46	13	7	3	53	26	4	10	9	27	33	68
10	Hereford United	46	10	9	4	36	25	6	10	7	28	33	67
11	Tranmere Rovers	46	7	9	7	27	25	7	9	7	24	31	60
12	Blackpool	46	11	5	7	40	26	4	8	11	26	34	58
13	Darlington	46	10	5	8	36	28	5	8	10	25	34	58
14	Hartlepool United	46	9	8	6	39	34	4	8	11	34	50	55
15	Torquay United	46	9	8	6	30	25	5	5	13	17	34	55
16	Aldershot	46	8	7	8	34	29	5	8	10	23	39	54
17	York City	46	9	5	9	45	37	5	3	15	24	54	50
18	Stockport County	46	10	5	8	34	28	2	8	13	14	39	49
19	Halifax Town	46	6	11	6	28	30	3	11	9	23	42	49
20	Mansfield Town	46	8	6	9	39	39	5	4	14	24	42	47
21	Rochdale	46	7	9	7	26	22	3	7	13	24	40	46
22	Northampton Town	46	9	5	9	32	27	2	4	17	25	57	42
23	Scunthorpe United	46	7	9	7	26	35	2	6	15	17	44	42
24	Crewe Alexandra	46	3	6	14	19	32	3	3	17	10	52	27

1982/83 Division 3

1	Portsmouth	46	16	4	3	43	19	11	6	6	31	22	91
2	Cardiff City	46	17	5	1	45	14	8	6	9	31	36	86
3	Huddersfield Town	46	15	8	0	56	18	8	5	10	28	31	82
4	Newport County	46	13	7	3	40	20	10	2	11	36	34	78
5	Oxford United	46	12	9	2	41	23	10	3	10	30	30	78
6	Lincoln City	46	17	1	5	55	22	6	6	11	22	29	76
7	Bristol Rovers	46	16	4	3	55	21	6	5	12	29	37	75
8	Plymouth Argyle	46	15	2	6	37	23	4	6	13	24	43	65
9	Brentford	46	14	4	5	50	28	4	6	13	38	49	64
10	Walsall	46	14	5	4	38	19	3	8	12	26	44	64
11	Sheffield United	46	16	3	4	44	20	3	4	16	18	44	64
12	Bradford City	46	11	7	5	41	27	5	6	12	27	42	61
13	Gillingham	46	12	4	7	37	29	4	9	10	21	30	61
14	BOURNEMOUTH	46	11	7	5	35	20	5	6	12	24	48	61
15	Southend United	46	10	8	5	41	28	5	6	12	25	37	59
16	Preston North End	46	11	10	2	35	17	4	3	16	25	52	58
17	Millwall	46	12	7	4	41	24	2	6	15	23	53	55
18	Wigan Athletic	46	10	4	9	35	33	5	5	13	25	39	54
19	Exeter City	46	12	4	7	49	43	2	8	13	32	61	54
20	Orient	46	10	6	7	44	38	5	3	15	20	50	54
21	Reading	46	10	8	5	37	28	2	9	12	27	51	53
22	Wrexham	46	11	6	6	40	26	1	9	13	16	50	51
23	Doncaster Rovers	46	6	8	9	38	44	3	3	17	19	53	38
24	Chesterfield	46	6	6	11	28	28	2	7	14	15	40	37

1983/84 Division 3

1	Oxford United	46	17	5	1	58	22	11	6	6	33	28	95
2	Wimbledon	46	15	5	3	58	35	11	4	8	39	41	87
3	Sheffield United	46	14	7	2	56	18	10	4	9	30	35	83
4	Hull City	46	16	5	2	42	11	7	9	7	29	27	83
5	Bristol Rovers	46	16	5	2	47	21	6	8	9	21	33	79
6	Walsall	46	14	4	5	44	22	8	5	10	24	39	75
7	Bradford City	46	11	9	3	46	30	9	2	12	27	35	71
8	Gillingham	46	13	4	6	50	29	7	6	10	24	40	70
9	Millwall	46	16	4	3	42	18	2	9	12	29	47	67
10	Bolton Wanderers	46	13	4	6	36	17	5	6	12	20	43	64
11	Orient	46	13	5	5	40	27	5	4	14	31	54	63
12	Burnley	46	12	5	6	52	25	4	9	10	24	36	62
13	Newport County	46	11	9	3	35	27	5	5	13	23	48	62
14	Lincoln City	46	11	4	8	42	29	6	6	11	17	33	61
15	Wigan Athletic	46	11	5	7	26	18	5	8	10	20	38	61
16	Preston North End	46	12	5	6	42	27	3	6	14	24	39	56
17	BOURNEMOUTH	46	11	5	7	38	27	5	2	16	25	46	55
18	Rotherham United	46	10	5	8	29	17	5	4	14	28	47	54
19	Plymouth Argyle	46	11	8	4	38	17	2	4	17	18	45	51
20	Brentford	46	8	9	6	41	30	3	7	13	28	49	49
21	Scunthorpe United	46	9	9	5	40	31	0	10	13	14	42	46
22	Southend United	46	8	9	6	34	24	2	5	16	21	52	44
23	Port Vale	46	10	4	9	33	29	1	6	16	18	54	43
24	Exeter City	46	4	8	11	27	39	2	7	14	23	45	33

1984/85 Division 3

1	Bradford City	46	15	6	2	44	23	13	4	6	33	22	94
2	Millwall	46	18	5	0	44	12	8	7	8	29	30	90
3	Hull City	46	16	4	3	46	20	9	8	6	32	29	87
4	Gillingham	46	15	5	3	54	29	10	3	10	26	33	83
5	Bristol City	46	17	2	4	46	19	7	7	9	28	28	81
6	Bristol Rovers	46	15	6	2	37	13	6	6	11	29	35	75
7	Derby County	46	14	7	2	40	20	5	6	12	25	34	70
8	York City	46	13	5	5	42	22	7	4	12	28	35	69
9	Reading	46	8	7	8	31	29	11	5	7	37	33	69
10	BOURNEMOUTH	46	16	3	4	42	16	3	8	12	15	30	68
11	Walsall	46	9	7	7	33	22	9	6	8	25	30	67
12	Rotherham United	46	11	6	6	36	24	7	5	11	19	31	65
13	Brentford	46	13	5	5	42	27	3	9	11	20	37	62
14	Doncaster Rovers	46	11	5	7	42	33	6	3	14	30	41	59
15	Plymouth Argyle	46	11	7	5	33	23	4	7	12	29	42	59
16	Wigan Athletic	46	12	6	5	36	22	3	8	12	24	42	59
17	Bolton Wanderers	46	12	5	6	38	22	4	1	18	31	53	54
18	Newport County	46	9	6	8	30	30	4	7	12	25	37	52
19	Lincoln City	46	8	11	4	32	20	3	7	13	18	31	51
20	Swansea City	46	7	5	11	31	39	5	6	12	22	41	47
21	Burnley	46	6	8	9	30	24	5	5	13	30	49	46
22	Orient	46	7	7	9	30	36	4	6	13	21	40	46
23	Preston North End	46	9	5	9	33	41	4	2	17	18	59	46
24	Cambridge United	46	2	3	18	17	48	2	6	15	20	47	21

1985/86 Division 3

1	Reading	46	16	3	4	39	22	13	4	6	28	29	94
2	Plymouth Argyle	46	17	3	3	56	20	9	6	8	32	33	87
3	Derby County	46	13	7	3	45	20	10	8	5	35	21	84
4	Wigan Athletic	46	17	4	2	54	17	6	10	7	28	31	83
5	Gillingham	46	14	5	4	48	17	8	8	7	33	37	79
6	Walsall	46	15	7	1	59	23	7	2	14	31	41	75
7	York City	46	16	4	3	49	17	4	7	12	28	41	71
8	Notts County	46	12	6	5	42	26	7	8	8	29	34	71
9	Bristol City	46	14	5	4	43	19	4	9	10	26	41	68
10	Brentford	46	8	8	7	29	29	10	4	9	29	32	66
11	Doncaster Rovers	46	7	10	6	20	21	9	6	8	25	31	64
12	Blackpool	46	11	6	6	38	19	6	6	11	28	36	63
13	Darlington	46	10	7	6	39	33	5	6	12	22	45	58
14	Rotherham United	46	13	5	5	44	18	2	7	14	17	41	57
15	BOURNEMOUTH	46	9	6	8	41	31	6	3	14	24	41	54
16	Bristol Rovers	46	9	8	6	27	21	5	4	14	24	54	54
17	Chesterfield	46	10	6	7	41	30	3	8	12	20	34	53
18	Bolton Wanderers	46	10	4	9	35	30	5	4	14	19	38	53
19	Newport County	46	7	8	8	35	33	4	10	9	17	32	51
20	Bury	46	11	7	5	46	26	1	6	16	17	41	49
21	Lincoln City	46	7	9	7	33	34	3	7	13	22	43	46
22	Cardiff City	46	7	5	11	22	29	5	4	14	31	54	45
23	Wolverhampton W.	46	6	6	11	29	47	5	4	14	28	51	43
24	Swansea City	46	9	6	8	27	27	2	4	17	16	60	43

1986/87 Division 3

1	BOURNEMOUTH	46	19	3	1	44	14	10	7	6	32	26	97
2	Middlesbrough	46	16	5	2	38	11	12	5	6	29	19	94
3	Swindon Town	46	14	5	4	37	19	11	7	5	40	28	87
4	Wigan Athletic	46	15	5	3	47	26	10	5	8	36	34	85
5	Gillingham	46	16	5	2	42	14	7	4	12	23	34	78
6	Bristol City	46	14	6	3	42	15	7	8	8	21	21	77
7	Notts County	46	14	6	3	52	24	7	7	9	25	32	76
8	Walsall	46	16	4	3	50	27	6	5	12	30	40	75
9	Blackpool	46	11	7	5	35	20	5	9	9	39	39	64
10	Mansfield Town	46	9	9	5	30	23	6	7	10	22	32	61
11	Brentford	46	9	7	7	39	32	6	8	9	25	34	60
12	Port Vale	46	8	6	9	43	36	7	6	10	33	34	57
13	Doncaster Rovers	46	11	8	4	32	19	3	7	13	24	43	57
14	Rotherham United	46	10	6	7	29	23	5	6	12	19	34	57
15	Chester City	46	7	9	7	32	28	6	8	9	29	31	56
16	Bury	46	9	7	7	30	26	5	6	12	24	34	55
17	Chesterfield	46	11	5	7	36	33	2	10	11	20	36	54
18	Fulham	46	8	8	7	35	41	4	9	10	24	36	53
19	Bristol Rovers	46	7	8	8	26	29	6	4	13	23	46	51
20	York City	46	11	8	4	34	29	1	5	17	21	50	49
21	Bolton Wanderers	46	8	5	10	29	26	2	10	11	17	32	45
22	Carlisle United	46	7	5	11	26	35	3	3	17	13	43	38
23	Darlington	46	6	10	7	25	28	1	6	16	20	49	37
24	Newport County	46	4	9	10	26	34	4	4	15	23	52	37

1987/88 Division 2

1	Millwall	44	15	3	4	45	23	10	4	8	27	29	82
2	Aston Villa	44	9	7	6	31	21	13	5	4	37	20	78
3	Middlesbrough	44	15	4	3	44	16	7	8	7	19	20	78
4	Bradford City	44	14	3	5	49	26	8	8	6	25	28	77
5	Blackburn Rovers	44	12	8	2	38	22	9	6	7	30	30	77
6	Crystal Palace	44	16	3	3	50	21	6	6	10	36	38	75
7	Leeds United	44	14	4	4	37	18	5	8	9	24	33	69
8	Ipswich Town	44	14	3	5	38	17	5	6	11	23	35	66
9	Manchester City	44	11	4	7	50	28	8	4	10	30	32	65
10	Oldham Athletic	44	13	4	5	43	27	5	7	10	29	37	65
11	Stoke City	44	12	6	4	34	22	5	5	12	16	35	62
12	Swindon Town	44	10	7	5	43	25	6	4	12	30	35	59
13	Leicester City	44	12	5	5	35	20	4	6	12	27	41	59
14	Barnsley	44	11	4	7	42	32	4	8	10	19	30	57
15	Hull City	44	10	8	4	32	22	4	7	11	22	38	57
16	Plymouth Argyle	44	12	4	6	44	26	4	4	14	21	41	56
17	BOURNEMOUTH	44	7	7	8	36	30	6	3	13	20	38	49
18	Shrewsbury Town	44	7	8	7	23	22	4	8	10	19	32	49
19	Birmingham City	44	7	9	6	20	24	4	6	12	21	42	48
20	West Bromwich Albion	44	8	7	7	29	26	4	4	14	21	43	47
21	Sheffield United	44	8	6	8	27	28	5	1	16	18	46	46
22	Reading	44	5	7	10	20	25	5	5	12	24	45	42
23	Huddersfield Town	44	4	6	12	20	38	2	4	16	21	62	28

1988/89 Division 2

1	Chelsea	46	15	6	2	50	25	14	6	3	46	25	99
2	Manchester City	46	12	8	3	48	28	11	5	7	29	25	82
3	Crystal Palace	46	15	6	2	42	17	8	6	9	29	32	81
4	Watford	46	14	5	4	41	18	8	7	8	33	30	78
5	Blackburn Rovers	46	16	4	3	50	22	6	7	10	24	37	77
6	Swindon Town	46	13	8	2	35	15	7	8	8	33	38	76
7	Barnsley	46	12	8	3	37	21	8	6	9	29	37	74
8	Ipswich Town	46	13	3	7	42	23	9	4	10	29	38	73
9	West Bromwich Albion	46	13	7	3	43	18	5	11	7	22	23	72
10	Leeds United	46	12	6	5	34	20	5	10	8	25	30	67
11	Sunderland	46	12	8	3	40	23	4	7	12	20	37	63
12	BOURNEMOUTH	46	13	3	7	32	20	5	5	13	21	42	62
13	Stoke City	46	10	9	4	33	25	5	5	13	24	47	59
14	Bradford City	46	8	11	4	29	22	5	6	12	23	37	56
15	Leicester City	46	11	6	6	31	20	2	10	11	25	43	55
16	Oldham Athletic	46	9	10	4	49	32	2	11	10	26	40	54
17	Oxford United	46	11	6	6	40	34	3	6	14	22	36	54
18	Plymouth Argyle	46	11	4	8	35	22	3	8	12	20	44	54
19	Brighton & Hove Alb.	46	11	5	7	36	24	3	4	16	21	42	51
20	Portsmouth	46	10	6	7	33	21	3	6	14	20	41	51
21	Hull City	46	7	9	7	31	25	4	5	14	21	43	47
22	Shrewsbury Town	46	4	11	8	25	31	4	7	12	15	36	42
23	Birmingham City	46	6	4	13	21	33	2	7	14	10	43	35
24	Walsall	46	3	10	10	27	42	2	6	15	14	38	31

1989/90 Division 2

1	Leeds United	46	16	6	1	46	18	8	7	8	33	34	85
2	Sheffield United	46	14	5	4	43	27	10	8	5	35	31	85
3	Newcastle United	46	17	4	2	51	26	5	10	8	29	29	80
4	Swindon Town	46	12	6	5	49	29	8	8	7	30	30	74
5	Blackburn Rovers	46	10	9	4	43	30	9	8	6	31	29	74
6	Sunderland	46	10	8	5	41	32	10	6	7	29	32	74
7	West Ham United	46	14	5	4	50	22	6	7	10	30	35	72
8	Oldham Athletic	46	15	7	1	50	23	4	7	12	20	34	71
9	Ipswich Town	46	13	7	3	38	22	6	5	12	29	44	69
10	Wolverhampton W.	46	12	5	6	37	20	6	8	9	30	40	67
11	Port Vale	46	11	9	3	37	20	4	7	12	25	37	61
12	Portsmouth	46	9	8	6	40	34	6	8	9	22	31	61
13	Leicester City	46	10	8	5	34	29	5	6	12	33	50	59
14	Hull City	46	7	8	8	27	31	7	8	8	31	34	58
15	Watford	46	11	6	6	41	28	3	9	11	17	32	57
16	Plymouth Argyle	46	9	8	6	30	23	5	5	13	28	40	55
17	Oxford United	46	8	7	8	35	31	7	2	14	22	35	54
18	Brighton & Hove Alb.	46	10	6	7	28	27	5	3	15	28	45	54
19	Barnsley	46	7	9	7	22	23	6	6	11	27	48	54
20	West Bromwich Albion	46	6	8	9	35	37	6	7	10	32	34	51
21	Middlesbrough	46	10	3	10	33	29	3	8	12	19	34	50
22	BOURNEMOUTH	46	8	6	9	30	31	4	6	13	27	45	48
23	Bradford City	46	9	6	8	26	24	0	8	15	18	44	41
24	Stoke City	46	4	11	8	20	24	2	8	13	15	39	37

1990/91 Division 3

1	Cambridge United	46	14	5	4	42	22	11	6	6	33	23	86
2	Southend United	46	13	6	4	34	23	13	1	9	33	28	85
3	Grimsby Town	46	16	3	4	42	13	8	8	7	24	21	83
4	Bolton Wanderers	46	14	5	4	33	18	10	6	7	31	32	83
5	Tranmere Rovers	46	13	5	5	38	21	10	4	9	26	25	78
6	Brentford	46	12	4	7	30	22	9	9	5	29	25	76
7	Bury	46	13	6	4	39	26	7	7	9	28	30	73
8	Bradford City	46	13	3	7	36	22	7	7	9	26	32	70
9	BOURNEMOUTH	46	14	6	3	37	20	5	7	11	21	38	70
10	Wigan Athletic	46	14	3	6	40	20	6	6	11	31	34	69
11	Huddersfield Town	46	13	3	7	37	23	5	10	8	20	28	67
12	Birmingham City	46	8	9	6	21	21	8	8	7	24	28	65
13	Leyton Orient	46	15	2	6	35	19	3	8	12	20	39	64
14	Stoke City	46	9	7	7	36	29	7	5	11	19	30	60
15	Reading	46	11	5	7	34	28	6	3	14	19	38	59
16	Exeter City	46	12	6	5	35	16	4	3	16	23	36	57
17	Preston North End	46	11	5	7	33	29	4	6	13	21	38	56
18	Shrewsbury Town	46	8	7	8	29	22	6	3	14	32	46	52
19	Chester City	46	10	3	10	27	27	4	6	13	19	31	51
20	Swansea City	46	8	6	9	31	33	5	3	15	18	39	48
21	Fulham	46	8	8	7	27	22	2	8	13	14	34	46
22	Crewe Alexandra	46	6	9	8	35	35	5	2	16	27	45	44
23	Rotherham United	46	5	10	8	31	38	5	2	16	19	49	42
24	Mansfield Town	46	5	8	10	23	27	3	6	14	19	36	38

1991/92 Division 3

1	Brentford	46	17	2	4	55	29	8	5	10	26	26	82
2	Birmingham City	46	15	6	2	42	22	8	6	9	27	30	81
3	Huddersfield Town	46	15	4	4	36	15	7	8	8	23	23	78
4	Stoke City	46	14	5	4	45	24	7	9	7	24	25	77
5	Stockport County	46	15	5	3	47	19	7	5	11	28	32	76
6	Peterborough United	46	13	7	3	38	20	7	7	9	27	38	74
7	West Bromwich Albion	46	12	6	5	45	25	7	8	8	19	24	71
8	BOURNEMOUTH	46	13	4	6	33	18	7	7	9	19	30	71
9	Fulham	46	11	7	5	29	16	8	6	9	28	37	70
10	Leyton Orient	46	12	7	4	36	18	6	4	13	26	34	65
11	Hartlepool United	46	12	5	6	30	21	6	6	11	27	36	65
12	Reading	46	9	8	6	33	27	7	5	11	26	35	61
13	Bolton Wanderers	46	10	9	4	26	19	4	8	11	31	37	59
14	Hull City	46	9	4	10	28	23	7	7	9	26	31	59
15	Wigan Athletic	46	11	6	6	33	21	4	8	11	25	43	59
16	Bradford City	46	8	10	5	36	30	5	9	9	26	31	58
17	Preston North End	46	12	7	4	42	32	3	5	15	19	40	57
18	Chester City	46	10	6	7	34	29	4	8	11	22	30	56
19	Swansea City	46	10	9	4	35	24	4	5	14	20	41	56
20	Exeter City	46	11	7	5	34	25	3	4	16	23	55	53
21	Bury	46	8	7	8	31	31	5	5	13	24	43	51
22	Shrewsbury Town	46	7	7	9	30	31	5	4	14	23	37	47
23	Torquay United	46	13	3	7	29	19	0	5	18	13	49	47
24	Darlington	46	5	5	13	31	39	5	2	16	25	51	37

1992/93 New Football League Division 2

1	Stoke City	46	17	4	2	41	13	10	8	5	32	21	93
2	Bolton Wanderers	46	18	2	3	48	14	9	7	7	32	27	90
3	Port Vale	46	14	7	2	44	17	12	4	7	35	27	89
4	West Bromwich Albion	46	17	3	3	56	22	8	7	8	32	32	85
5	Swansea City	46	12	7	4	38	17	8	6	9	27	30	73
6	Stockport County	46	11	11	1	47	18	8	4	11	34	39	72
7	Leyton Orient	46	16	4	3	49	20	5	5	13	20	33	72
8	Reading	46	14	4	5	44	20	4	11	8	22	31	69
9	Brighton & Hove Alb.	46	13	4	6	36	24	7	5	11	27	35	69
10	Bradford City	46	12	5	6	36	24	6	9	8	33	43	68
11	Rotherham United	46	9	7	7	30	27	8	7	8	30	33	65
12	Fulham	46	9	9	5	28	22	7	8	8	29	33	65
13	Burnley	46	11	8	4	38	21	4	8	11	19	38	61
14	Plymouth Argyle	46	11	6	6	38	28	5	6	12	21	36	60
15	Huddersfield Town	46	10	6	7	30	22	7	3	13	24	39	60
16	Hartlepool United	46	8	6	9	19	23	6	6	11	23	37	54
17	BOURNEMOUTH	46	7	10	6	28	24	5	7	11	17	28	53
18	Blackpool	46	9	9	5	40	30	3	6	14	23	45	51
19	Exeter City	46	5	8	10	26	30	6	9	8	28	39	50
20	Hull City	46	9	5	9	28	26	4	6	13	18	43	50
21	Preston North End	46	8	5	10	41	47	5	3	15	24	47	47
22	Mansfield Town	46	7	8	8	34	34	4	3	16	18	46	44
23	Wigan Athletic	46	6	6	11	26	34	4	5	14	17	38	41
24	Chester City	46	6	2	15	30	47	2	3	18	19	55	29

1993/94 Division 2

1	Reading	46	15	6	2	40	16	11	5	7	41	28	89
2	Port Vale	46	16	6	1	46	18	10	4	9	33	28	88
3	Plymouth Argyle	46	16	4	3	46	26	9	6	8	42	30	85
4	Stockport County	46	15	3	5	50	22	9	10	4	24	22	85
5	York City	46	12	7	4	33	13	9	5	9	31	27	75
6	Burnley	46	17	4	2	55	18	4	6	13	24	40	73
7	Bradford City	46	13	5	5	34	20	6	8	9	27	33	70
8	Bristol Rovers	46	10	8	5	33	26	10	2	11	27	33	70
9	Hull City	46	9	9	5	33	20	9	5	9	29	34	68
10	Cambridge United	46	11	5	7	38	29	8	4	11	41	44	66
11	Huddersfield Town	46	9	8	6	27	26	8	6	9	31	35	65
12	Wrexham	46	13	4	6	45	33	4	7	12	21	44	62
13	Swansea City	46	12	7	4	37	20	4	5	14	19	38	60
14	Brighton & Hove Alb.	46	10	7	6	38	29	5	7	11	22	38	59
15	Rotherham United	46	11	4	8	42	30	4	9	10	21	30	58
16	Brentford	46	7	10	6	30	28	6	9	8	27	27	58
17	BOURNEMOUTH	46	8	7	8	26	27	6	8	9	25	32	57
18	Leyton Orient	46	11	9	3	38	26	3	5	15	19	45	56
19	Cardiff City	46	10	7	6	39	33	3	8	12	27	46	54
20	Blackpool	46	12	2	9	41	37	4	3	16	22	38	53
21	Fulham	46	7	6	10	20	23	7	4	12	30	40	52
22	Exeter City	46	8	7	8	38	37	3	5	15	14	46	45
23	Hartlepool United	46	8	3	12	28	40	1	6	16	13	47	36
24	Barnet	46	4	6	13	22	32	1	7	15	19	54	28

1994/95 Division 2

1	Birmingham City	46	15	6	2	53	18	10	8	5	31	19	89
2	Brentford	46	14	4	5	44	15	11	6	6	37	24	85
3	Crewe Alexandra	46	14	3	6	46	33	11	5	7	34	35	83
4	Bristol Rovers	46	15	7	1	48	20	7	9	7	22	20	82
5	Huddersfield Town	46	14	5	4	45	21	8	10	5	34	28	81
6	Wycombe Wanderers	46	13	7	3	36	19	8	8	7	24	27	78
7	Oxford United	46	13	6	4	30	18	8	6	9	36	34	75
8	Hull City	46	13	6	4	40	18	8	5	10	30	39	74
9	York City	46	13	4	6	37	21	8	5	10	30	30	72
10	Swansea City	46	10	8	5	23	13	9	6	8	34	32	71
11	Stockport County	46	12	3	8	40	29	7	5	11	23	31	65
12	Blackpool	46	11	4	8	40	36	7	6	10	24	34	64
13	Wrexham	46	10	7	6	38	27	6	8	9	27	37	63
14	Bradford City	46	8	6	9	29	32	8	6	9	28	32	60
15	Peterborough United	46	7	11	5	26	29	7	7	9	28	40	60
16	Brighton & Hove Alb.	46	9	10	4	25	15	5	7	11	29	38	59
17	Rotherham United	46	12	6	5	36	26	2	8	13	21	35	56
18	Shrewsbury Town	46	9	9	5	34	27	4	5	14	20	35	53
19	BOURNEMOUTH	46	9	4	10	30	34	4	7	12	19	35	50
20	Cambridge United	46	8	9	6	33	28	3	6	14	19	41	48
21	Plymouth Argyle	46	7	6	10	22	36	5	4	14	23	47	46
22	Cardiff City	46	5	6	12	25	31	4	5	14	21	43	38
23	Chester City	46	5	6	12	23	42	1	5	17	14	42	29
24	Leyton Orient	46	6	6	11	21	29	0	2	21	9	46	26

1995/96 Division 2

1	Swindon Town	46	12	10	1	37	16	13	7	3	34	18	92
2	Oxford United	46	17	4	2	52	14	7	7	9	24	25	83
3	Blackpool	46	14	5	4	41	20	9	8	6	26	20	82
4	Notts County	46	14	6	3	42	21	7	9	7	21	18	78
5	Crewe Alexandra	46	13	3	7	40	24	9	4	10	37	36	73
6	Bradford City	46	15	4	4	41	25	7	3	13	30	44	73
7	Chesterfield	46	14	6	3	39	21	6	6	11	17	30	72
8	Wrexham	46	12	6	5	51	27	6	10	7	25	28	70
9	Stockport County	46	8	9	6	30	20	11	4	8	31	27	70
10	Bristol Rovers	46	12	4	7	29	28	8	6	9	28	32	70
11	Walsall	46	12	7	4	38	20	7	5	11	22	25	69
12	Wycombe Wanderers	46	9	8	6	36	26	6	7	10	27	33	60
13	Bristol City	46	10	6	7	28	22	5	9	9	27	38	60
14	BOURNEMOUTH	46	12	5	6	33	25	4	5	14	18	45	58
15	Brentford	46	12	6	5	24	15	3	7	13	19	34	58
16	Rotherham United	46	11	7	5	31	20	3	7	13	23	42	56
17	Burnley	46	9	8	6	35	28	5	5	13	21	40	55
18	Shrewsbury Town	46	7	8	8	32	29	6	6	11	26	41	53
19	Peterborough United	46	9	6	8	40	27	4	7	12	19	39	52
20	York City	46	8	6	9	28	29	5	7	11	30	44	52
21	Carlisle United	46	11	6	6	35	20	1	7	15	22	52	49
22	Swansea City	46	8	8	7	27	29	3	6	14	16	50	47
23	Brighton & Hove Alb.	46	6	7	10	25	31	4	3	16	21	38	40
24	Hull City	46	4	8	11	26	37	1	8	14	10	41	31

1996/97 Division 2

1	Bury	46	18	5	0	39	7	6	7	10	23	31	84
2	Stockport County	46	15	5	3	31	14	8	8	7	28	27	82
3	Luton Town	46	13	7	3	38	14	8	8	7	33	31	78
4	Brentford	46	8	11	4	26	22	12	3	8	30	21	74
5	Bristol City	46	14	4	5	43	18	7	6	10	26	33	73
6	Crewe Alexandra	46	15	4	4	38	15	7	3	13	18	32	73
7	Blackpool	46	13	7	3	41	21	5	8	10	19	26	69
8	Wrexham	46	11	9	3	37	28	6	9	8	17	22	69
9	Burnley	46	14	3	6	48	27	5	8	10	23	28	68
10	Chesterfield	46	10	9	4	25	18	8	5	10	17	21	68
11	Gillingham	46	13	3	7	37	25	6	7	10	23	34	67
12	Walsall	46	12	8	3	35	21	7	2	14	19	32	67
13	Watford	46	10	8	5	24	14	6	11	6	21	24	67
14	Millwall	46	12	4	7	27	22	4	9	10	23	33	61
15	Preston North End	46	14	5	4	33	19	4	2	17	16	36	61
16	BOURNEMOUTH	46	8	9	6	24	20	7	6	10	19	25	60
17	Bristol Rovers	46	13	4	6	34	22	2	7	14	13	28	56
18	Wycombe Wanderers	46	13	4	6	31	14	2	6	15	20	42	55
19	Plymouth Argyle	46	7	11	5	19	18	5	7	11	28	40	54
20	York City	46	8	6	9	27	31	5	7	11	20	37	52
21	Peterborough United	46	7	7	9	38	34	4	7	12	17	39	47
22	Shrewsbury Town	46	8	6	9	27	32	3	7	13	22	42	46
23	Rotherham United	46	4	7	12	17	29	3	7	13	22	41	35
24	Notts County	46	4	9	10	20	25	3	5	15	13	34	35

1997/98 Division 2

1	Watford	46	13	7	3	36	22	11	9	3	31	19	88
2	Bristol City	46	16	5	2	41	17	9	5	9	28	22	85
3	Grimsby Town	46	11	7	5	30	14	8	8	7	25	23	72
4	Northampton Town	46	14	5	4	33	17	4	12	7	19	20	71
5	Bristol Rovers	46	13	2	8	43	33	7	8	8	27	31	70
6	Fulham	46	12	7	4	31	14	8	3	12	29	29	70
7	Wrexham	46	10	10	3	31	23	8	6	9	24	28	70
8	Gillingham	46	13	7	3	30	18	6	6	11	22	29	70
9	BOURNEMOUTH	46	11	8	4	28	15	7	4	12	29	37	66
10	Chesterfield	46	13	7	3	31	19	3	10	10	15	25	65
11	Wigan Athletic	46	12	5	6	41	31	5	6	12	23	35	62
12	Blackpool	46	13	6	4	35	24	4	5	14	24	43	62
13	Oldham Athletic	46	13	7	3	43	23	2	9	12	19	31	61
14	Wycombe Wanderers	46	10	10	3	32	20	4	8	11	19	33	60
15	Preston North End	46	10	6	7	29	26	5	8	10	27	30	59
16	York City	46	9	7	7	26	21	5	10	8	26	37	59
17	Luton Town	46	7	7	9	35	38	7	8	8	25	26	57
18	Millwall	46	7	8	8	23	23	7	5	11	20	31	55
19	Walsall	46	10	8	5	26	16	4	4	15	17	36	54
20	Burnley	46	10	9	4	34	23	3	4	16	21	42	52
21	Brentford	46	9	7	7	33	29	2	10	11	17	42	50
22	Plymouth Argyle	46	10	5	8	36	30	2	8	13	19	40	49
23	Carlisle United	46	8	5	10	27	28	4	3	16	30	45	44
24	Southend United	46	8	7	8	29	30	3	3	17	18	49	43

1998/99 Division 2

1	Fulham	46	19	3	1	50	12	12	5	6	29	20	101
2	Walsall	46	13	7	3	37	23	13	2	8	26	24	87
3	Manchester City	46	13	6	4	38	14	9	10	4	31	19	82
4	Gillingham	46	15	5	3	45	17	7	9	7	30	27	80
5	Preston North End	46	12	6	5	46	23	10	7	6	32	27	79
6	Wigan Athletic	46	14	5	4	44	17	8	5	10	31	31	76
7	BOURNEMOUTH	46	14	7	2	37	11	7	6	10	26	30	76
8	Stoke City	46	10	4	9	32	32	11	2	10	27	31	69
9	Chesterfield	46	14	5	4	34	16	3	8	12	12	28	64
10	Millwall	46	9	8	6	33	24	8	3	12	19	35	62
11	Reading	46	10	6	7	29	26	6	7	10	25	37	61
12	Luton Town	46	10	4	9	25	26	6	6	11	26	34	58
13	Bristol Rovers	46	8	9	6	35	28	5	8	10	30	28	56
14	Blackpool	46	7	8	8	24	24	7	6	10	20	30	56
15	Burnley	46	8	7	8	23	33	5	9	9	31	40	55
16	Notts County	46	8	6	9	29	27	6	6	11	23	34	54
17	Wrexham	46	8	6	9	21	28	5	8	10	22	34	53
18	Colchester United	46	9	7	7	25	30	3	9	11	27	40	52
19	Wycombe Wanderers	46	8	5	10	31	26	5	7	11	21	32	51
20	Oldham Athletic	46	8	4	11	26	31	6	5	12	22	35	51
21	York City	46	6	8	9	28	33	7	3	13	28	47	50
22	Northampton Town	46	4	12	7	26	31	6	6	11	17	26	48
23	Lincoln City	46	9	4	10	27	27	4	3	16	15	47	46
24	Macclesfield Town	46	7	4	12	24	30	4	6	13	19	33	43

1999/2000 Division 2

1	Preston North End	46	15	4	4	37	23	13	7	3	37	14	95
2	Burnley	46	16	3	4	42	23	9	10	4	27	24	88
3	Gillingham	46	16	3	4	46	21	9	7	7	33	27	85
4	Wigan Athletic	46	15	3	5	37	14	7	14	2	35	24	83
5	Millwall	46	14	7	2	41	18	9	6	8	35	32	82
6	Stoke City	46	13	7	3	37	18	10	6	7	31	24	82
7	Bristol Rovers	46	13	7	3	34	19	10	4	9	35	26	80
8	Notts County	46	9	6	8	32	27	9	5	9	29	28	65
9	Bristol City	46	7	14	2	31	18	8	5	10	28	39	64
10	Reading	46	10	9	4	28	18	6	5	12	29	45	62
11	Wrexham	46	9	6	8	23	24	8	5	10	29	37	62
12	Wycombe Wanderers	46	11	4	8	32	24	5	9	9	24	29	61
13	Luton Town	46	10	7	6	41	35	7	3	13	20	30	61
14	Oldham Athletic	46	8	5	10	27	28	8	7	8	23	27	60
15	Bury	46	8	10	5	38	33	5	8	10	23	31	57
16	BOURNEMOUTH	46	11	6	6	37	19	5	3	15	22	43	57
17	Brentford	46	8	6	9	27	31	5	7	11	20	30	52
18	Colchester United	46	9	4	10	36	40	5	6	12	23	42	52
19	Cambridge United	46	8	6	9	38	33	4	6	13	26	32	48
20	Oxford United	46	6	5	12	24	38	6	4	13	19	35	45
21	Cardiff City	46	5	10	8	23	34	4	7	12	22	33	44
22	Blackpool	46	4	10	9	26	37	4	7	12	23	40	41
23	Scunthorpe United	46	4	6	13	16	34	5	6	12	24	40	39
24	Chesterfield	46	5	7	11	17	25	2	8	13	17	38	36

2000/01 Division 2

1	Millwall	46	17	2	4	49	11	11	7	5	40	27	93
2	Rotherham United	46	16	4	3	50	26	11	6	6	29	29	91
3	Reading	46	15	5	3	58	26	10	6	7	28	26	86
4	Walsall	46	15	5	3	51	23	8	7	8	28	27	81
5	Stoke City	46	12	6	5	39	21	9	8	6	35	28	77
6	Wigan Athletic	46	12	9	2	29	18	7	9	7	24	24	75
7	BOURNEMOUTH	46	11	6	6	37	23	9	7	7	42	32	73
8	Notts County	46	10	6	7	37	33	9	6	8	25	33	69
9	Bristol City	46	11	6	6	47	29	7	8	8	23	27	68
10	Wrexham	46	10	6	7	33	28	7	6	10	32	43	63
11	Port Vale	46	9	8	6	35	22	7	6	10	20	27	62
12	Peterborough United	46	12	6	5	38	27	3	8	12	23	39	59
13	Wycombe Wanderers	46	8	7	8	24	23	7	7	9	22	30	59
14	Brentford	46	9	10	4	34	30	5	7	11	22	40	59
15	Oldham Athletic	46	11	5	7	35	26	4	8	11	18	39	58
16	Bury	46	10	6	7	25	22	6	4	13	20	37	58
17	Colchester United	46	10	5	8	32	23	5	7	11	23	36	57
18	Northampton Town	46	9	6	8	26	28	6	6	11	20	31	57
19	Cambridge United	46	8	6	9	32	31	6	5	12	29	46	53
20	Swindon Town	46	6	8	9	30	35	7	5	11	17	30	52
21	Bristol Rovers	46	6	10	7	28	26	6	5	12	25	31	51
22	Luton Town	46	5	6	12	24	35	4	7	12	28	45	40
23	Swansea City	46	5	9	9	26	24	3	4	16	21	49	37
24	Oxford United	46	5	4	14	23	34	2	2	19	30	66	27

2001/02 Division 2

1	Brighton & Hove Alb.	46	17	5	1	42	16	8	10	5	24	26	90
2	Reading	46	12	7	4	36	20	11	8	4	34	23	84
3	Brentford	46	17	5	1	48	12	7	6	10	29	31	83
4	Cardiff City	46	12	8	3	39	25	11	6	6	36	25	83
5	Stoke City	46	16	4	3	43	12	7	7	9	24	28	80
6	Huddersfield Town	46	13	7	3	35	19	8	8	7	30	28	78
7	Bristol City	46	13	6	4	38	21	8	4	11	30	32	73
8	Queen's Park Rangers	46	11	10	2	35	18	8	4	11	25	31	71
9	Oldham Athletic	46	14	6	3	47	27	4	10	9	30	38	70
10	Wigan Athletic	46	9	6	8	36	23	7	10	6	30	28	64
11	Wycombe Wanderers	46	13	5	5	38	26	4	8	11	20	38	64
12	Tranmere Rovers	46	10	9	4	39	19	6	6	11	24	41	63
13	Swindon Town	46	10	7	6	26	21	5	7	11	20	35	59
14	Port Vale	46	11	6	6	35	24	5	4	14	16	38	58
15	Colchester United	46	9	6	8	35	33	6	6	11	30	43	57
16	Blackpool	46	8	9	6	39	31	6	5	12	27	38	56
17	Peterborough United	46	11	5	7	46	26	4	5	14	18	33	55
18	Chesterfield	46	9	3	11	35	36	4	10	9	18	29	52
19	Notts County	46	8	7	8	28	29	5	4	14	31	42	50
20	Northampton Town	46	9	4	10	30	33	5	3	15	24	46	49
21	BOURNEMOUTH	46	9	4	10	36	33	1	10	12	20	38	44
22	Bury	46	6	9	8	26	32	5	2	16	17	43	44
23	Wrexham	46	7	7	9	29	32	4	3	16	27	57	43
24	Cambridge United	46	7	7	9	29	34	0	6	17	18	59	34

2002/03 Division 3

1	Rushden & Diamonds	46	16	5	2	48	19	8	10	5	25	28	87
2	Hartlepool United	46	16	5	2	49	21	8	8	7	22	30	85
3	Wrexham	46	12	7	4	48	26	11	8	4	36	24	84
4	BOURNEMOUTH	46	14	7	2	38	18	6	7	10	22	30	74
5	Scunthorpe United	46	11	8	4	40	20	8	7	8	28	29	72
6	Lincoln City	46	10	9	4	29	18	8	7	8	17	19	70
7	Bury	46	8	8	7	25	26	10	8	5	32	30	70
8	Oxford Uunited	46	9	7	7	26	20	10	5	8	31	27	69
9	Torquay United	46	9	11	3	41	31	7	7	9	30	40	66
10	York City	46	11	9	3	34	24	6	6	11	18	29	66
11	Kidderminster Harr.	46	8	8	7	30	33	8	7	8	32	30	63
12	Cambridge United	46	10	7	6	38	25	6	6	11	29	45	61
13	Hull City	46	9	10	4	34	19	5	7	11	24	34	59
14	Darlington	46	8	10	5	36	27	4	8	11	22	32	54
15	Boston United	46	11	6	6	34	22	4	7	12	21	34	54
16	Macclesfield Town	46	8	6	9	29	28	6	6	11	28	35	54
17	Southend United	46	12	1	10	29	23	5	2	16	18	36	54
18	Leyton Orient	46	9	6	8	28	24	5	5	13	23	37	53
19	Rochdale	46	7	6	10	30	30	5	10	8	33	40	52
20	Bristol Rovers	46	7	7	9	25	27	5	8	10	25	30	51
21	Swansea City	46	9	6	8	28	25	3	7	13	20	40	49
22	Carlisle United	46	5	5	13	26	40	8	5	10	26	38	49
23	Exeter City	46	7	7	9	24	31	4	8	11	26	33	48
24	Shrewsbury Town	46	5	6	12	34	39	4	8	11	28	53	41

SENDINGS-OFF 1979/80 to 2002/03

There have been 56 Bournemouth players sent off since the first of the tougher guidelines were issued to referees in July 1979. Two Bournemouth players were sent off in the same match on four occasions.

Brian Chambers	25/08/79	Newport County	h	3-2	
Ian Cunningham	18/09/79	Portsmouth	a	0-4	
Phil Ferns	11/10/80	Darlington	a	2-1	
Jon Moore	20/12/80	Lincoln City	a	0-2	
Phil Ferns	17/04/81	Southend United	a	1-2	
Brian Smith	17/10/81	Peterborough United	a	0-1	
Trevor Morgan	24/04/82	Sheffield United	a	0-0	
Max Thompson	06/09/83	Wimbledon	a	2-3	
Chris Sulley	02/10/85	Lincoln City	a	2-3	
John Beck	02/11/85	Bolton Wanderers	a	0-1	
John Williams	26/08/87	Exeter City	a	3-1 aet	FL Cup
Tom Heffernan	28/11/87	Swindon Town	a	2-4	
Paul Morrell	28/11/87	*ditto*			
Tony Pulis	21/10/88	Shrewsbury Town	h	0-1	
Mark Newson	26/11/88	Barnsley	a	2-5	
Paul Morrell	08/09/90	Wigan Athletic	a	0-2	
Jimmy Case	17/09/91	Shrewsbury Town	h	1-0	
Paul Wood	11/01/92	West Bromwich Albion	a	0-4	
Denny Mundee	05/02/92	Ipswich Town	a	0-3	FA Cup
Mark Morris	08/04/92	Peterborough United	a	0-2	
Brian McGorry	21/08/93	Bradford City	h	1-1	
Steve Cotterill	08/01/94	Preston North End	a	1-2	FA Cup
Scott Mean	16/08/94	Northampton Town	h	2-0	FL Cup
Alex Watson	27/08/94	Rotherham United	a	0-4	
Russell Beardsmore	30/08/94	Peterborough United	h	0-3	
Adrian Pennock	15/10/94	Brentford	h	0-1	
Scott Mean	10/12/94	Blackpool	a	1-3	
Alex Watson	10/12/94	*ditto*			
Neil Moss	16/12/94	Wrexham	h	1-3	
Jamie Vincent	26/12/94	Bristol Rovers	a	1-2	
Adrian Pennock	16/09/95	Crewe Alexandra	h	0-4	
Neil Young	16/09/95	*ditto*			
Neil Young	09/12/95	Brighton & Hove Albion	a	0-2	
Keith Scott	09/03/96	Hull City	a	1-1	
Russell Beardsmore	20/04/96	Walsall	h	0-0	
John Bailey	16/11/96	Brentford	a	0-2	FA Cup
Jason Brissett	03/12/96	Shrewsbury Town	a	1-1	
Jamie Vincent	22/03/97	York City	h	1-1	
Jamie Vincent	12/09/98	Wigan Athletic	h	1-0	
Jon O'Neill	06/02/99	Stoke City	h	4-0	
Carl Fletcher	20/11/99	Bristol City	h	0-2	
Christer Warren	26/12/99	Wycombe Wanderers	a	1-2	
Peter Grant	02/09/00	Colchester United	a	1-2	
Danny Smith	02/09/00	*ditto*			
Carl Fletcher	04/11/00	Peterborough United	h	2-1	
Wade Elliott	23/01/01	Cambridge United	a	2-0	
Jason Tindall	05/10/01	Oldham Athletic	h	3-2	Played at Dorchester
Warren Feeney	03/11/01	Colchester United	a	2-1	
Eddie Howe	17/11/01	Worksop Town	h	1-0	FA Cup
Richard Hughes	26/12/01	Swindon Town	a	0-1	
Carl Fletcher	22/01/02	Queen's Park Rangers	a	1-1	
Warren Feeney	20/04/02	Wrexham	a	1-1	
Neil Young	24/08/02	Swansea City	a	0-2	
Wade Elliott	14/09/02	Bury	h	1-2	
Marcus Browning	26/12/02	Oxford United	a	0-3	
Marcus Browning	21/01/03	Bristol City	h	1-3	LDV Vans

Name		D.O.B	Place of Birth	Died	First Season	Last Season	Previous Club	Next Club	Appearances				Goals			
									Lge	FAC	FLC	Oth.	Lge	FAC	FLC	Oth.
Adams RL	Rodney	15/09/1945	Bath		1966	1968	Frome Town	Weymouth	17	1	1	0	4	0	0	0
Aimson PE	Paul	03/08/1943	Macclesfield		1972		York City	Colchester Utd.	9	0	0	0	2	0	0	0
Aitken PG	Peter	30/06/1954	Cardiff		1982		Bulova (HK)	Bath City	1	0	0	0	0	0	0	0
Akers WWG	Wally	1917	West Auckland	1975	1935		Wolverhampton W.	Newport County	15	0	0	0	4	0	0	0
Allen DJ	Denis	02/03/1939	Dagenham	1995	1970		Reading	Ostend (Belgium)	17	1	1	0	3	0	1	0
Allen JC	Ian	27/01/1932	Paisley		1954	1955	QPR	Salisbury	52	3	0	0	11	1	0	0
Allen K	Kevin	22/03/1961	Ryde		1979		Juniors	Oxford City	1	0	0	0	0	0	0	0
Allen KR	Kenny	12/01/1949	Thornaby		1978	1982	Bath City	Bury	152	8	9	5	0	0	0	0
Anderson TC	Tommy	24/09/1934	Edinburgh		1958		Watford	QPR	5	0	0	0	1	0	0	0
Andrews IE	Ian	01/12/1964	Nottingham		1994	1995	Southampton	Leicester City	64	2	7	3	0	0	0	0
Angus SD	Stevland	16/09/1980	Westminster		2000		West Ham U (loan)		9	0	0	0	0	0	0	0
Archer J	John	18/06/1941	Biddulph		1961	1965	Port Vale	Crewe Alexandra	139	9	10	0	37	2	1	0
Armstrong D	David	26/12/1954	Durham		1987		Southampton	Retired - injury	9	0	2	0	2	0	1	0
Armstrong JD	Jimmy	12/06/1899	Chester-le-Street		1925	1926	Barnsley	Accrington Stanley	15	0	0	0	0	0	0	0
Armstrong JW	Joe	10/10/1892	Blaydon	1966	1923		Norwich City	Portsm'th Tramways	29	0	0	0	2	0	0	0
Arnott JH	John	06/09/1932	Sydenham		1956	1961	Shrewsbury Town	Gillingham	173	9	6	0	21	1	0	0
Ashdown JL	Jamie	30/11/1980	Wokingham		2002		Reading (loan)		2	0	0	0	0	0	0	0
Ashworth JM	Joe	06/01/1943	Huddersfield	2002	1965	1966	York City	Southend Utd.	60	5	1	0	2	0	0	0
Ashworth PA	Phil	04/04/1953	Burnley		1975		Blackburn Rovers	Workington	31	4	0	0	2	3	0	0
Aspinall WG	Warren	13/09/1967	Wigan		1993	1994	Portsmouth (loan)	Carlisle Utd.	33	1	4	1	9	1	0	0
Aylott TKC	Trevor	26/11/1957	Bermondsey		1986	1990	Crystal Palace	Birmingham City	147	7	13	3	27	2	4	0
Bailey DS	Danny	21/05/1964	Leyton		1980		Apprentice	Dagenham	2	0	0	0	0	0	0	0
Bailey JA	John	06/05/1969	Lambeth		1995	1999	Enfield	Brockenhurst	149	10	13	12	6	0	0	1
Bain AE	Alex	22/01/1936	Edinburgh		1961		Falkirk	Poole Town	8	1	2	0	4	0	1	0
Baker KR	Kieron	29/10/1949	Ryde		1969	1978	Fulham	Ipswich Town	217	14	19	0	0	0	0	0
Baker S	Steve	02/12/1961	Wallsend		1991		Leyton Orient	Aldershot	6	0	2	0	0	0	0	0
Barclay JM	John	08/09/1921	Mid Calder		1947	1948	Haddington	Chippenham Utd.	5	0	0	0	2	0	0	0
Barfoot SJ	Stuart	10/12/1975	Southampton		1994		Trainee	Torquay United	2	0	1	0	0	0	0	0
Barnes DO	Bobby	17/12/1962	Kingston		1988	1989	Swindon Town	Northampton Town	14	0	1	0	0	0	0	0
Barrow WH	Billy	Q1 1911	Cardiff		1935		Southend Utd.	Wrexham	26	4	0	3	4	2	0	2
Barry PP	Pat	25/10/1920	Southampton	1994	1950		Blackburn Rovers	Yeovil Town	4	0	0	0	0	0	0	0
Barton F	Frank	22/10/1947	Barton-on-Humber		1976	1977	Grimsby Town	Hereford Utd.	88	7	6	0	15	1	2	0
					1978		Hereford Utd.	Seattle Sounders								
Bartram VL	Vince	07/08/1968	Birmingham		1991	1993	Wolverhampton W.	Arsenal	132	14	10	6	0	0	0	0
Baynham DM	David	12/06/1902	Aberdare	1974	1927		Aberdare Ath.	Yeovil & Petters	7	0	0	0	0	0	0	0
Beadle PCWJ	Peter	13/05/1972	Lambeth		1992		Tottenham H (loan)		9	0	0	0	2	0	0	0
Beardsmore RP	Russell	28/09/1968	Wigan		1993	1997	Manchester Utd.	Retired - injury	178	9	14	9	4	1	1	1
Beck JA	John	25/05/1954	Edmonton		1982	1985	Fulham	Cambridge Utd.	137	7	7	13	13	2	0	3
Bedford NB	Brian	24/12/1933	Ferndale		1956	1958	Southampton	QPR	75	8	0	0	32	6	0	0
Bellis GA	George	08/06/1904	Khadki, India	1969	1935	1936	Burnley	Wellington Town	56	4	0	4	0	0	0	0
Benjafield BJ	Brian	02/08/1960	Barton-on-Sea		1978		Juniors	Oxford City	2	0	0	0	0	0	0	0
Bennett DM	Dave	05/03/1939	Southampton		1960	1961	Southampton	Guildford City	12	0	0	0	2	0	0	0
Bennett KE	Ken	02/10/1921	Wood Green	1994	1948		Southend Utd.	Guildford City	19	1	0	0	1	0	0	0
Benson JH	John	23/12/1942	Arbroath		1970	1973	Torquay United	Norwich City	149	12	17	0	0	0	0	0
					1974	1978	Norwich City	Norwich City (Scout)								
Bernard N	Narada	30/01/1981	Bristol		2000	2002	Arsenal		29	3	0	7	0	0	0	0
Berry WG	Bill	10/08/1904	Hackney	1972	1933		Crystal Palace	Lille (France)	13	1	0	0	2	0	0	0
Berthe M	Mohamed	12/09/1972	Conakry, Guinea		1998		West Ham Utd.	Hearts	15	1	4	1	2	0	0	0
Best D	David	06/09/1943	Wareham		1960	1966	Juniors	Oldham Athletic	232	9	13	0	0	0	0	0
					1975		Portsmouth	Dorchester Town								
Best G	George	22/05/1946	Belfast		1982		Golden Bay (USA)	Brisbane Lions (Aus)	5	0	0	0	0	0	0	0
Beswick SMcA	Sammy	08/03/1903	Macclesfield	1966	1929	1932	Tranmere Rovers	Poole Town	54	8	0	0	11	5	0	0
Betsy KEL	Kevin	20/03/1978	Seychelles		1999		Fulham (loan)		5	0	0	0	0	0	0	0
Bimpson JL	Louis	14/05/1929	Rainford		1960		Blackburn Rovers	Rochdale	11	0	0	0	1	0	0	0
Birch J	Joe	Q3 1904	Hednesford		1929	1931	Birmingham	Fulham	26	1	0	0	0	0	0	0
Bird KB	Ken	25/09/1918	Norwich	1987	1938	1952	Wolverhampton W.	Dorchester Town	249	15	0	2	0	0	0	0
Birmingham DP	David	16/04/1981	Portsmouth		2001		Portsmouth	Bognor Regis	4	0	1	0	0	0	0	0
Bishop IW	Ian	29/05/1965	Liverpool		1988		Carlisle Utd.	Manchester City	44	5	4	1	2	0	0	0
Blair J	Jimmy	11/05/1888	Glenboig	1964	1926	1927	Cardiff City	Retired	61	6	0	0	0	0	0	0
Blair JA	Jimmy	06/01/1918	Whiteinch	1983	1947	1949	Blackpool	Leyton Orient	80	4	0	0	8	1	0	0
Blakeman AG	Alec	11/06/1918	Oxford	1994	1948	1949	Sheffield Utd.	March Town	25	2	0	0	8	0	0	0
Blayney A	Alan	09/10/1981	Belfast		2002		Southampton (loan)		2	0	0	0	0	0	0	0
Blezzard RJ	Rupert	Q4 1912	Manchester		1935		Kells		1	0	0	0	0	0	0	0
Bliss H	Bertie	29/03/1890	Willenhall	1968	1925		Clapton Orient	Retired	6	0	0	0	0	0	0	0
Blissett LL	Luther	01/02/1958	Jamaica		1988	1990	Watford	Watford	121	10	8	3	56	2	2	1
Blizzard LWB	Les	13/03/1923	Acton	1996	1947		QPR	Yeovil Town	1	0	0	0	0	0	0	0
Boli RZ	Roger	26/09/1965	Adjame, Ivory Coast		1998		Dundee United	Retired - injury	6	2	1	1	0	0	0	0
Bolton R	Ronnie	21/01/1938	Golborne		1958	1965	Crompton R.	Ipswich Town	264	15	10	0	48	5	1	0
					1967	1968	Ipswich Town	Durban City (SA)								
Bond KJ	Kevin	22/01/1957	West Ham		1988	1991	Southampton	Exeter City	126	14	12	3	4	2	0	0
Book KA	Kim	12/02/1946	Bath		1967	1968	Frome Town	Northampton Town	2	1	0	0	0	0	0	0
Borthwick GM	Gary	30/11/1955	Slough		1977	1979	Barnet	Yeovil Town	74	3	1	0	4	0	0	0
Bow WJ	William	Q4 1900	Penrhiwceiber		1925		Merthyr Town	Coventry City	1	0	0	0	0	0	0	0
Boxshall D	Danny	02/04/1920	Bradford		1950	1951	Bristol City	Rochdale	51	2	0	0	8	1	0	0
Boyer PJ	Phil	25/01/1949	Nottingham		1970	1973	York City	Norwich City	140	9	9	0	46	4	0	0
Bradford J	Jack	09/04/1895	Paisley	1969	1927	1930	Wolverhampton W.	Letchworth Town	113	16	0	0	1	0	0	0
Brignull PA	Phil	02/10/1960	Stratford		1981	1984	West Ham Utd.	Cardiff City	129	8	7	9	11	0	2	0
Brissett JC	Jason	07/09/1974	Wanstead		1994	1997	Peterborough Utd.	Walsall	124	4	7	7	8	0	0	2
Broadhurst KM	Karl	18/03/1980	Portsmouth		1999	2002	Trainee		90	8	5	6	1	1	0	0
Brooks LW	Len	1914	Manningtree		1937	1938	Fulham	Colchester Utd.	39	3	0	1	0	0	0	0
Brooks S	Shaun	09/10/1962	London		1987	1991	Leyton Orient	Wimborne Town	129	5	12	3	13	1	0	0
					1994		Dorchester Town	Leyton Orient								

Name		D.O.B	Place of Birth	Died	First Season	Last Season	Previous Club	Next Club	Appearances Lge	FAC	FLC	Oth.	Goals Lge	FAC	FLC	Oth.
Brown BR	Bertie				1937			Barrow	3	0	0	0	0	0	0	0
Brown I	Irvin	20/09/1935	Lewes		1958	1962	Brighton & Hove Alb.	Poole Town	65	5	3	0	2	1	0	0
Brown J	Joe	26/04/1929	Cramlington		1954	1959	Burnley	Aldershot	215	15	0	0	5	0	0	0
Brown KG	Kenny	21/03/1952	Barnsley		1978	1979	Barnsley	Frickley Athletic	32	1	2	0	4	0	1	0
Brown KJ	Ken	18/10/1933	Coventry		1957		Nottm. Forest	Torquay United	6	0	0	0	1	0	0	0
Brown KJ	Keith	29/01/1942	Bournemouth		1963	1964	Pokesdown	Poole Town	15	0	1	0	0	0	0	0
Brown RW	Roger	12/12/1952	Tamworth		1977	1978	AP Leamington	Norwich City	147	16	8	6	8	1	0	0
					1983	1986	Fulham	Weymouth								
Brown S	Sam		Glasgow		1929	1930	Third Lanark	Brighton & Hove Alb.	59	6	0	0	0	0	0	0
Browning MT	Marcus	22/04/1971	Bristol		2002		Gillingham		43	4	1	5	1	1	1	0
Bryant JS	Jeff	27/11/1953	Redhill		1979		Wimbledon	Gravesend & Nth.	16	0	2	0	2	0	0	0
Bryce RS	Bob	17/11/1904	Grangemouth	1970	1928	1929	Grange Rovers	Luton Town	63	12	0	0	24	3	0	0
Buchanan CC	Cameron	31/07/1928	Holytown		1949	1954	Wolverhampton W.	Norwich City	83	5	0	0	18	0	0	0
Buchanan J	Jim		Winchburgh		1924	1927	Hibernian	East Stirling	65	10	0	0	10	0	0	0
Bucknall W	Wilf		Lichfield		1935	1936	Wellington Town		5	0	0	0	0	0	0	0
Budden WL	Wilf	12/02/1902	Southampton	1971	1923	1924	Bournemouth FC		10	0	0	0	1	0	0	0
Bugg AA	Alec	27/11/1948	Needham Market		1969		Ipswich Town (loan)		4	0	0	0	0	0	0	0
Bumstead RG	Ray	27/01/1936	Ringwood		1958	1969	Ringwood Town	Weymouth	415	28	22	0	55	6	4	0
Burgess MR	Mike	17/04/1932	Montreal, Canada		1957	1960	Newport County	Halifax Town	109	6	0	0	34	2	0	0
Burgin M	Meynell	29/11/1911	Sheffield		1935		Tranmere Rovers	Nottm. Forest	5	2	0	1	1	1	0	1
Burke C	Charlie	13/09/1921	Arran	1995	1946		Ardeer Recreation	Weymouth	25	3	0	0	7	0	0	0
Burns C	Chris	09/11/1967	Manchester		1993		Portsmouth (loan)		14	0	0	0	1	0	0	0
Burns DG	Derek	23/01/1950	Bournemouth		1968		Apprentice	Poole Town	4	0	0	0	0	0	0	0
Burns R	Roy	1916	Wolverhampton		1936		Wolverhampton W.		18	2	0	1	3	0	0	0
Bushby DC	Dennis	25/12/1933	Poole		1957			Peterborough Utd.	6	0	0	0	0	0	0	0
Butler G	Geoff	29/09/1946	Middlesbrough		1975	1980	Norwich City	Peterborough Utd.	119	6	8	0	1	0	0	0
Butler MA	Mick	27/01/1951	Worsborough Bridge		1978	1979	Huddersfield Town	Bury	69	5	4	0	19	1	0	0
Butler S	Steve	27/01/1962	Birmingham		1992		Watford (loan)		1	0	0	0	0	0	0	0
Butt LG	Len	20/12/1893	Freemantle		1923	1927	Southampton	Cowes	136	11	0	0	2	1	0	0
Buttle SA	Steve	01/01/1953	Norwich		1973	1976	Ipswich Town	Seattle Sounders	139	10	14	0	12	0	0	0
Buxton L	Lewis	10/12/1983	Newport		2002		Portsmouth (loan)		17	1	0	0	0	0	0	0
Cadette RR	Richard	21/03/1965	Hammersmith		1989		Brentford (loan)		8	0	0	0	1	0	0	0
Cameron WT	Bill	11/04/1914	Glasgow		1934		Middlesbrough	Stenhousemuir	1	0	0	0	0	0	0	0
Carter SC	Steve	23/04/1953	Great Yarmouth		1981	1983	Notts County	Torquay United	46	3	4	3	1	0	0	0
Case JR	Jimmy	18/05/1954	Liverpool		1991		Southampton	Halifax Town	40	5	3	2	1	0	0	1
Casey T	Tommy	11/03/1930	Comber, Co Down		1950	1951	Leeds United	Newcastle United	66	2	0	0	1	0	0	0
Casper CM	Chris	28/04/1975	Burnley		1995		Manchester U (loan)		16	0	0	0	1	0	0	0
Cave MJ	Micky	28/01/1949	Weymouth	1985	1971	1973	Torquay United	York City	141	10	8	0	20	2	0	0
					1976	1977	York City	Seattle Sounders								
Chadwick DE	Dave	19/08/1943	Ooctamund, India		1971	1973	Halifax Town	Gillingham	36	0	1	0	4	0	0	0
Chalk SR	Steve	15/10/1957	Southampton		1975	1977	Apprentice	Charlton Ath.	11	0	0	0	0	0	0	0
Chalmers WR	William	1912	Kirkcaldy		1932	1937	Raith Rovers	Barrow	153	10	0	8	17	5	0	2
Chambers BM	Brian	31/10/1949	Newcastle		1979	1980	Millwall	Halifax Town	42	2	2	0	7	0	1	0
Charleston T	Tom				1924		Wrexham	Poole	7	0	0	0	0	0	0	0
Charlton KP	Kevin	12/09/1954	Atherstone		1973	1974	Wolverhampton W.	Hereford Utd.	21	3	2	0	0	0	0	0
Cheney D	Denis	30/06/1924	Coalville		1948	1953	Leicester City	Aldershot	158	8	0	0	47	2	0	0
Cherrett PAM	Percy	12/09/1899	Christchurch	1984	1928		Bristol City	Cowes	36	7	0	0	19	2	0	0
Chivers GPS	Gary	15/05/1960	Stockwell		1993	1994	Brighton & Hove Alb.	Stamco	31	4	0	3	2	0	0	0
Chivers W	William		Merthyr Tydfil		1927		Swindon Town		1	0	0	0	0	0	0	0
Christie I	Iyseden	14/11/1976	Coventry		1996		Coventry City (loan)		4	0	0	0	0	0	0	0
Claridge SE	Steve	10/04/1966	Portsmouth		1984	1985	Fareham Town	Weymouth	7	0	0	1	1	0	0	0
Clark BD	Brian	13/01/1943	Bristol		1972	1973	Cardiff City	Millwall	30	4	0	0	12	3	0	0
Clark WR	Billy	19/05/1967	Christchurch		1984	1987	Trainee	Bristol Rovers	4	0	0	0	0	0	0	0
Clarke CJ	Colin	30/10/1962	Newry		1985		Tranmere Rovers	Southampton	50	4	4	2	28	2	3	4
					1988		Southampton (loan)									
Clayton L	Lew	07/06/1924	Royston, West Yorks		1955	1956	QPR	Swindon Town	40	4	0	0	1	0	0	0
Clifford P	Pat		Pontlottyn		1924	1929	Merthyr Town	Chester	189	20	0	0	16	7	0	0
Close SC	Shaun	08/09/1966	Islington		1987	1988	Tottenham H	Swindon Town	39	1	3	1	8	0	0	0
Coen JL	Joe	04/12/1911	Glasgow	1941	1932	1933	Guildford City	Luton Town	36	2	0	1	0	0	0	0
Coleman DH	David	08/04/1967	Hackney	1997	1985	1990	Juniors	Farnborough Town	50	1	6	3	2	0	0	0
Coley WE	Bill	17/09/1916	Wolverhampton	1974	1937		Wolverhampton W.	Torquay United	13	0	0	0	0	0	0	0
Coll OO	Owen	09/04/1976	Donegal		1995	1996	Tottenham H	Barnet	24	1	2	0	0	0	0	0
Collin G	George	13/09/1905	Oxhill	1989	1925	1926	Arsenal	Derby County	48	8	0	0	0	0	0	0
Collins AD	Des	15/04/1923	Chesterfield		1950		Barrow	Shrewsbury Town	5	0	0	0	1	0	0	0
Compton JF	John	27/08/1937	Poplar		1964		Ipswich Town	Retired - injury	27	1	1	0	1	0	0	0
Compton PD	Paul	06/06/1961	Stroud		1980	1982	Trowbridge Town	Aldershot	64	2	5	5	0	0	1	0
Connell A	Alan	05/02/1983	Enfield		2002		Ipswich Town		13	0	1	0	6	0	1	0
Cooke RE	Richard	04/09/1965	Islington		1986	1988	Tottenham H	Luton Town	125	9	12	6	28	1	4	1
					1990	1992	Luton Town	Bashley								
Cooke S	Stephen	15/02/1983	Walsall		2001		Aston Villa (loan)		7	0	0	0	0	0	0	0
Cooke TV	Thomas	07/03/1919	Melton Mowbray		1936	1937	Mansfield Town	Luton Town	19	0	0	1	0	0	0	0
Cotterell LS	Leo	02/09/1974	Cambridge		1996		Ipswich Town	Rushden & D.	9	0	0	0	0	0	0	0
Cotterill SJ	Steve	20/07/1964	Cheltenham		1993	1994	Wimbledon	Sligo Rovers (Mgr)	45	3	6	1	15	1	2	0
Coughlin DM	Denis	26/11/1937	Houghton-le-Spring		1962	1965	Yeovil Town	Swansea Town	88	6	5	0	40	5	1	0
Cox IG	Ian	25/03/1971	Croydon		1995	1999	Crystal Palace	Burnley	172	10	14	11	16	0	0	1
Coxford J	Jack	25/07/1901	Seaton Hirst	1978	1930	1933	Birmingham	Poole Town	134	9	0	2	3	0	0	0
Coxon WG	Billy	28/04/1933	Derby		1958	1965	Lincoln City	Poole Town	200	13	10	0	37	1	2	0
Craig FG	Frank		Swansea		1926		Fulham		7	1	0	0	1	0	0	0
Crawford A	Andy	30/01/1959	Filey		1981	1982	Blackburn Rovers	Cardiff City	33	4	2	2	10	1	0	0
Crawford GW	George	1906	Sunderland		1929		Gillingham	Northampton Town	4	0	0	0	0	0	0	0
Crickmore CE	Charlie	11/02/1942	Hull		1962	1965	Hull City	Gillingham	128	8	6	0	17	2	0	0
Crosland JR	Johnny	10/11/1922	St Annes		1954	1956	Blackpool	Wisbech Town	106	4	0	0	0	0	0	0

Name		D.O.B	Place of Birth	Died	First Season	Last Season	Previous Club	Next Club	Appearances				Goals			
									Lge	FAC	FLC	Oth.	Lge	FAC	FLC	Oth.
Cross J	Jack	05/02/1927	Bury		1947	1953	Guildford City	Northampton Town	136	6	0	0	64	3	0	0
Crumley JB	James	17/07/1890	Dundee	1981	1926	1928	Darlington		51	6	0	0	0	0	0	0
Crump LV	Leslie		Wolverhampton		1927		Kilmarnock		4	0	0	0	0	0	0	0
Cummings W	Warren	15/10/1980	Aberdeen		2000		Chelsea (loan)		30	0	0	4	1	0	0	0
					2002		Chelsea									
Cunningham I	Ian	06/09/1956	Glasgow		1974	1980	Apprentice	Swanage T & H	188	10	11	0	4	0	0	0
Cunningham L	Laurie	20/10/1921	Consett		1948	1956	Barnsley	Dorchester Town	273	12	0	0	0	0	0	0
Cureton J	Jamie	28/08/1975	Chippenham		1995		Norwich City (loan)		5	0	0	1	0	0	0	0
Currie JE	John	18/03/1921	Liverpool	1984	1946		Stafford Rangers	Port Vale	7	0	0	0	1	0	0	0
Curwood A	Albert		Bridgwater		1934		Blackpool	Swansea Town	7	0	0	0	0	0	0	0
Cutler RV	Reg	17/02/1935	Blackheath, Worcs		1956	1958	West Bromwich A.	Portsmouth	96	8	0	0	21	2	0	0
Davey HH	Hugh	14/06/1898	Belfast		1923	1924	Glentoran	Reading	43	6	0	0	22	2	0	0
Davidson I	Ian	31/01/1947	Goole		1971		York City	Stockport County	9	0	1	0	0	0	0	0
Davies F	Fred	22/08/1939	Liverpool		1970	1973	Cardiff City	Norwich City	134	10	8	0	0	0	0	0
Davies T	Tommy		Troedyrhiw		1925		Luton Town	Chelsea	5	1	0	0	0	0	0	0
Davis E	Eric		Sheffield		1936		Bangor City	Bath City	2	0	0	0	0	0	0	0
Dawkins DA	Derek	29/11/1959	Edmonton		1981	1982	Mansfield Town	Weymouth	8	3	1	1	0	0	0	0
Dawtry KA	Kevin	15/06/1958	Southampton		1980	1983	Crystal Palace	RS Southampton	65	4	5	4	11	0	0	3
Day JR	Jamie	13/09/1979	Sidcup		1998	2000	Arsenal	Dover Athletic	20	5	2	2	1	0	0	0
Dean MJ	Mike	09/03/1978	Weymouth		1995	1998	Trainee	Weymouth	34	1	0	1	0	0	0	0
Defoe J	Jermaine	07/10/1982	Beckton		2000		West Ham U (loan)		29	1	0	1	18	1	0	0
De Garis JF	Jim	09/10/1952	Worcester		1971	1973	Arsenal	Torquay United	12	3	1	0	0	0	0	0
Delaney JJ	John	03/02/1942	Slough		1973	1974	Wycombe Wan.	Wycombe Wan.	25	2	7	0	0	0	3	0
Dickie MMcF	Murdoch	28/12/1919	Dumbarton		1946	1947	Chelsea	Tonbridge	17	0	0	0	1	0	0	0
Dixon CH	Charlie	16/06/1903	Ansley	1983	1928		Sunderland	Connah's Quay BS	25	7	0	0	0	0	0	0
Donowa GW	George	31/12/1900	Southampton	1973	1923		Harland & Wolff	Salisbury	1	0	0	0	0	0	0	0
Dowsett GJ	Dickie	03/07/1931	Chelmsford		1957	1962	Southampton	Crystal Palace	169	9	6	0	79	3	2	0
Drummond IP	Ian	27/08/1923	Brechin		1949	1955	Portsmouth	Poole Town	265	13	0	0	2	0	0	0
Drummond RC	Bob	1898	Dalmeny		1927		Bristol City	Bathgate	7	0	0	0	1	0	0	0
Duberry MW	Michael	14/10/1975	Enfield		1995		Chelsea (loan)		7	0	0	1	0	0	0	0
Dudley SM	Sam	1905	Tipton		1928		Preston NE	Coleraine	2	0	0	0	0	0	0	0
Duff TE	Tommy		West Cornforth		1928		Huddersfield Town	Darlington	3	0	0	0	0	0	0	0
Duffield MJ	Martin	28/02/1964	Park Royal		1983		QPR (loan)		6	0	1	0	1	0	0	0
Duke GE	George	06/09/1920	West Hampnett	1988	1949		Luton Town	Guildford City	10	0	0	0	0	0	0	0
Dumbrell G	George		Catford		1933		Leicester City	Brentford	13	1	0	0	2	0	0	0
East KMG	Keith	31/10/1944	Southampton		1967	1969	Stockport County	Northampton Town	94	8	3	0	34	1	0	0
Edmunds P	Paul	02/12/1957	Doncaster		1981		Leicester City	Bentley Victoria	14	0	1	3	2	0	0	0
Ekoku EG	Efan	08/06/1967	Manchester		1990	1992	Sutton United	Norwich City	62	7	2	4	10	2	0	2
Ellaway WJ	Bill	12/10/1932	Crediton		1956	1957	Exeter City	Poole Town	4	0	0	0	0	0	0	0
Elliott RM	Mark	20/03/1959	Rhondda		1979		Cardiff City (loan)		4	0	0	0	0	0	0	0
Elliott ST	Stuart	27/08/1977	Hendon		1999		Newcastle U (loan)		8	0	0	0	0	0	0	0
Elliott W	Billy	23/10/1961	Poole		1980		Plymouth Argyle	Weymouth	11	1	1	0	1	0	0	0
Elliott W	Wade	14/12/1978	Southampton		1999	2002	Bashley		139	11	3	9	24	3	0	1
Elliott WB	Billy	06/08/1919	Harrington	1966	1938		Wolverhampton W.	West Bromwich A.	10	2	0	0	1	2	0	0
Eribenne CY	Chukki	02/11/1980	London		2000	2002	Coventry City		47	3	2	3	1	0	0	0
Evans GH	Hugh	12/12/1919	Ynysybwl		1950		Birmingham City	Walsall	22	1	0	0	8	0	0	0
Evans RP	Ray	21/06/1933	Preston		1959	1960	Preston NE	Morecambe	36	5	0	0	9	2	0	0
Evanson JM	John	10/05/1947	Newcastle-u.-Lyme		1979	1980	Fulham	Poole Town	53	3	4	0	2	1	0	0
Eyre CR	Ron	26/11/1901	Skegby	1969	1924	1932	Sheffield Wed.	Christchurch	304	33	0	0	202	27	0	0
Eyre EL	Les	07/01/1922	Ilkeston	1991	1951	1952	Norwich City	Chelmsford City	38	2	0	0	10	2	0	0
Falconer H	Harry	22/12/1954	Newcastle		1974		Burnley	Wimbledon	7	0	0	0	0	0	0	0
Farmer FBW	Brian	29/07/1933	Wordsley		1961	1964	Birmingham City	Christchurch	132	4	5	0	0	0	0	0
Farrow GH	George	04/10/1913	Whitburn	1980	1933	1935	Wolverhampton W.	Blackpool	107	7	0	7	12	0	0	2
Feely PJ	Peter	03/01/1950	City of London		1972	1973	Chelsea	Fulham	9	1	1	0	2	0	0	0
Feeney W	Warren	17/01/1981	Belfast		2000	2002	Leeds United		68	7	1	4	24	0	0	1
Fenton NL	Nicky	23/11/1979	Preston		1999	2000	Manchester C (loan)		13	0	0	0	0	0	0	0
Ferdinand RG	Rio	07/11/1978	Peckham		1996		West Ham U (loan)		10	0	0	1	0	0	0	0
Fereday W	Wayne	16/06/1963	Warley		1990	1991	Newcastle United	West Bromwich A.	23	3	2	2	0	1	0	0
Ferns P	Phil	14/11/1937	Liverpool		1965		Liverpool	Mansfield Town	46	5	2	0	0	0	0	0
Ferns PD	Phil	12/09/1961	Liverpool		1978	1980	Poole Town	Charlton Ath.	95	4	3	0	6	0	0	0
Ferrett CA	Chris	10/02/1977	Poole		1994		Trainee	Fleet Town	1	0	0	0	0	0	0	0
Fidler F	Frank	16/08/1924	Middleton		1952	1954	Leeds United	Yeovil Town	61	3	0	0	31	2	0	0
Finnigan TT	Trevor	14/10/1952	Bedlington		1977	1978	Blackpool	Yeovil Town	25	0	0	0	5	0	0	0
Fisher JA	Jackie	19/06/1925	Bermondsey		1949	1952	Millwall	Ramsgate Ath.	52	5	0	0	0	0	0	0
Flaherty J	Jack		Mexborough		1935		Wolverhampton W.		1	0	0	0	0	0	0	0
Fletcher AF	Alan	28/10/1917	Pendleton	1984	1938		Port Vale	Bristol Rovers	12	2	0	0	0	1	0	0
Fletcher CN	Carl	07/04/1980	Camberley		1997	2002	Trainee		147	13	4	9	15	1	0	3
Fletcher J	Jack	1910	Tyne Dock		1933	1934	Guildford City	QPR	26	1	0	2	3	0	0	1
Fletcher SM	Steve	26/06/1972	Hartlepool		1992	2002	Hartlepool Utd.		348	24	26	20	65	6	3	4
Flood JE	John	21/10/1932	Southampton		1958		Southampton	Headington United	17	1	0	0	3	0	0	0
Foote CRT	Chris	19/11/1950	Bournemouth		1968	1969	Apprentice	Cambridge United	45	2	4	0	2	0	0	0
Forbes AS	Alex		Bo'ness		1929	1931	Luton Town	Gillingham	47	7	0	0	1	0	0	0
Forbes T	Terrell	17/08/1981	Southwark		1999		West Ham U (loan)		3	1	0	0	0	0	0	0
Ford JA	James	23/10/1981	Portsmouth		1999	2001	Trainee		12	0	1	0	0	0	0	0
Foster CL	Cliff	1904	Rotherham		1925		Rotherham Utd.	Morecambe	4	0	0	0	0	0	0	0
Foyewa A	Amos	26/12/1981	Nigeria		2001	2002	West Ham Utd.		9	2	1	0	0	0	0	0
Friar J	John	22/07/1911	Newmains	1979	1933		Portsmouth	Port Vale	34	2	0	2	11	0	0	2
Funnell A	Tony	20/08/1957	Eastbourne		1981	1982	Brentford	Poole Town	64	5	3	3	22	2	1	0
Gabriel J	Jimmy	16/10/1940	Dundee		1972	1973	Southampton	Brentford	53	6	5	0	4	0	0	0
Gallacher P	Paddy	09/01/1913	Glasgow	1983	1938	1947	Blackburn Rovers	Weymouth	35	3	0	0	3	1	0	0
Gater R	Roy	22/06/1940	Chesterton		1962	1968	Port Vale	Crewe Alexandra	216	12	9	0	3	0	0	0
Gaynor LA	Len	22/09/1925	Ollerton		1951	1953	Hull City	Southampton	51	3	0	0	12	0	0	0

Name		D.O.B	Place of Birth	Died	First Season	Last Season	Previous Club	Next Club	Appearances Lge	FAC	FLC	Oth.	Goals Lge	FAC	FLC	Oth.
George FC	Charlie	10/10/1950	Islington		1981		Bulova (HK)	Derby County	2	0	0	0	0	0	0	0
George RS	Ricky	28/06/1946	Barnet		1965		Watford	Oxford United	3	0	0	0	0	0	0	0
Gibbs BR	Brian	06/10/1936	Gillingham, Dorset		1957	1962	Gosport Borough	Gillingham	58	2	4	0	15	0	2	0
Gibson IS	Ian	30/03/1943	Newton Stewart		1972	1973	Cardiff City	Berea Park (SA)	20	4	0	0	0	1	0	0
Gilmore HP	Henry 'Mike'	1913	Hartlepool		1936		Mansfield Town	Runcorn	13	2	0	0	0	0	0	0
Girling HM	Dickie	24/05/1922	Birmingham	1992	1951		Brentford	Hastings Utd.	4	0	0	0	0	0	0	0
Givens DJ	Don	09/08/1949	Limerick		1979		Birmingham C (loan)		5	0	0	0	4	0	0	0
Glass JR	Jimmy	01/08/1973	Epsom		1995	1997	Crystal Palace	Swindon Town	94	4	4	7	0	0	0	0
Gledstone PH	Peter	04/04/1934	Ferndown		1957	1963	B'mouth Gasworks	Retired - injury	131	7	4	0	2	0	0	0
Goddard HJ	Howard	10/05/1957	Over Wallop		1972	1975	Apprentice	Swindon Town	73	8	8	1	20	5	3	0
					1981	1982	Newport County	Aldershot								
Godwin TF	Tommy	20/08/1927	Dublin	1996	1952	1961	Leicester City	Dorchester Town	357	27	3	0	0	0	0	0
Golac I	Ivan	15/06/1950	Yugoslavia		1982		Southampton (loan)		9	1	0	0	0	0	0	0
Gold W	Billy		Birkenshaw		1931	1936	Baillieston Jnrs	Wolverhampton W.	77	3	0	3	0	0	0	0
Gordon DA	Dale	09/01/1967	Caister		1996		West Ham Utd.	Great Yarmouth	16	1	2	0	0	0	0	0
Goulet B	Brent	19/06/1964	Tacoma, USA		1987		Seattle Sounders	(United States)	6	0	0	1	0	0	0	0
Graham GK	George		Glasgow		1928		Morton	Caernarvon Town	17	5	0	0	2	1	0	0
Graham MM	Milton	02/11/1962	Hackney		1981	1984	Apprentice	Chester City	72	6	3	9	12	1	1	3
Grant P	Peter	30/08/1965	Bellshill		2000		Reading	(coaching staff)	15	0	2	1	0	0	0	0
Grapes SP	Steve	25/02/1953	Norwich		1975		Norwich City (loan)		7	0	0	0	1	0	0	0
Gray H	Harry	26/10/1918	Hemsworth	1989	1946	1947	Barnsley	Southend Utd.	30	1	0	0	7	0	0	0
Green RE	Bob		Tewkesbury		1929	1930		Derby County	6	0	0	0	0	0	0	0
Greenhalgh BA	Brian	20/02/1947	Chesterfield		1973	1974	Cambridge Utd.	Watford	24	3	0	0	7	1	0	0
Gregory JL	Jack	25/01/1925	Southampton		1959		Leyton Orient	Ashford Town	17	0	0	0	0	0	0	0
Griffin AR	Anthony	22/03/1979	Bournemouth		1998		Trainee	Cheltenham Town	6	0	0	0	0	0	0	0
Gripton EW	Bill	02/07/1920	Tipton	1981	1950	1951	Luton Town	Worcester City	79	1	0	0	0	0	0	0
Gritt SJ	Steve	31/10/1957	Bournemouth		1976		Apprentice	Charlton Ath.	6	0	2	0	3	0	0	0
Groves AJ	Alan	24/10/1948	Ainsdale	1978	1972	1973	Shrewsbury Town	Oldham Athletic	36	4	0	0	4	1	0	0
Groves J	John	16/09/1933	Derby		1963	1964	Luton Town	Retired - injury	54	2	4	0	0	1	0	0
Gulliver P	Philip	12/09/1982	Bishop Auckland		2002		Middlesbrough (loan)		6	0	0	3	0	0	0	0
Gulliver TR	Terry	30/09/1944	Salisbury		1966	1971	Weymouth	Capetown C (SA)	164	12	10	0	2	0	0	0
Gunn AR	Alistair	02/11/1924	Broughty Ferry		1954		Huddersfield Town	Arbroath	27	1	0	0	2	0	0	0
Guthrie PJ	Peter	10/10/1961	Newcastle		1990		Barnet	Sing Tao (HK)	10	0	3	0	0	0	0	0
Haddington WR	Ray	18/11/1923	Scarborough	1994	1952		Stockport Co.	Rochdale	2	0	0	0	0	0	0	0
Hague N	Neil	01/12/1949	Thurcroft		1974	1975	Plymouth Argyle	Huddersfield Town	89	6	9	0	7	1	0	0
Haigh G	Gordon	18/08/1921	Barnsley		1949	1950	Burnley	Watford	17	1	0	0	3	0	0	0
Hall RF	Richard	03/07/1945	Weymouth		1967		Weymouth	Weymouth	11	1	3	0	0	0	0	0
Halliwell JC	Cliff	20/05/1898	Sheffield	1984	1926	1931	Sheffield Utd.		216	27	0	0	2	0	0	0
Hampson RG	Ray	27/07/1932	Manchester		1957	1958	Aldershot	Folkestone Town	15	0	0	0	2	0	0	0
Hanlon W	Wally	23/09/1919	Glasgow		1948		Brighton & Hove A.	Crystal Palace	19	0	0	0	3	0	0	0
Hardy GD	Bob	23/05/1923	Kingston		1951	1953	Southport	Yeovil Town	76	5	0	0	0	0	0	0
Harman PR	Peter	11/10/1950	Guildford		1969		Apprentice	Reading	1	0	0	0	0	0	0	0
Harrington JD	Justin	18/06/1975	Truro		1997		Leicester City	Porthleven	8	2	1	0	0	0	0	0
Harrison HF	Frank		Bournemouth		1923		Bournemouth Trams	Bournemouth Trams	4	0	0	0	0	0	0	0
Harrison P	Peter	25/10/1927	Sleaford		1952	1956	Leeds United	Reading	173	10	0	0	34	2	0	0
Hartley TJ	Trevor	16/03/1947	Doncaster		1969	1970	West Ham Utd.	(coaching staff)	43	3	2	0	2	1	0	0
Harvey J	Joe	11/06/1918	Doncaster	1989	1937		Wolverhampton W.	Bradford City	1	0	0	1	0	0	0	0
Hayter JE	James	09/04/1979	Sandown		1996	2002	Trainee		186	12	5	12	31	3	1	5
Hayward DW	Doug		Bournemouth		1924				1	1	0	0	0	0	0	0
Hayward JW	Jack	Q4 1903	Warsop Vale		1925	1932	Bradford City	Crystal Palace	247	31	0	0	26	4	0	0
Heath WHM	Bill	15/04/1934	Bournemouth		1956	1957	Juniors	Lincoln City	34	1	0	0	0	0	0	0
Heffernan TP	Tom	30/04/1955	Dublin		1979	1982	Tottenham Hotspur	Sheffield Utd.	217	13	17	11	27	0	0	1
					1985	1987	Sheffield Utd.	Swanage T & H								
Heron AA	Alec		Worcester		1923	1925			26	12	0	0	0	0	0	0
Hill JE	John	29/11/1948	Yeovil		1967		Apprentice	Weymouth	4	0	0	0	0	0	0	0
Hobbs JE	Jack	17/04/1930	Swanage		1953	1954	Swanage	Weymouth	6	0	0	0	1	0	0	0
Hodgson K	Ken	19/01/1942	Newcastle		1964	1965	Scunthorpe Utd.	Colchester Utd.	78	7	1	0	24	4	0	0
Hold JD	John	28/03/1948	Southampton		1965	1970	Apprentice	Northampton Town	85	11	9	0	24	3	5	0
Holder P	Phil	19/01/1952	Kilburn		1978	1979	Crystal Palace	Tonbridge	58	2	2	0	4	0	0	0
Holland KA	Ken	18/04/1922	Doncaster		1948		Bury	Shrewsbury Town	3	0	0	0	0	0	0	0
Holland MR	Matt	11/04/1974	Bury		1994	1996	West Ham Utd.	Ipswich Town	104	3	6	3	18	0	0	0
Holland PG	Pat	13/09/1950	Poplar		1970		West Ham U (loan)		10	0	0	0	0	0	0	0
Holmes D	Derek	18/10/1978	Lanark		2001	2002	Ross County		66	5	1	5	12	1	0	0
Holmes DG	Danny	13/06/1972	Clophill		1992		Middlesbrough	Farnborough Town	1	0	0	0	0	0	0	0
Holmes MJE	Matt	01/08/1969	Luton		1988	1991	Trainee	West Ham Utd.	114	10	7	5	8	0	0	0
Hooton A	Alf		Hythe		1935		Howard's Ath.	Poole Town	4	0	0	0	0	0	0	0
Howard TE	Trevor	02/06/1949	King's Lynn		1974	1975	Norwich City	Cambridge Utd.	86	7	7	0	11	0	1	0
Howarth J	Jack	27/02/1945	Stanley		1976	1977	Aldershot	Southport	42	3	4	0	6	1	1	0
Howe EJF	Eddie	29/11/1977	Amersham		1995	2001	Trainee	Portsmouth	200	12	13	10	10	2	1	0
Howe RJ	Bobby	22/12/1945	Chadwell St Mary		1971	1973	West Ham Utd.	(coaching staff)	100	7	8	0	6	0	0	0
Howlett GP	Gary	02/04/1963	Dublin		1984	1987	Brighton & Hove Alb.	York City	60	4	2	7	7	0	0	0
Huck WRF	Willie	11/03/1979	Paris, France		1998	2001	Arsenal	Angers (Fr)	40	0	6	3	0	0	1	1
Hughes HJ	Harry	08/10/1929	Nuneaton		1952	1957	Chelsea	Gillingham	77	9	0	0	2	0	0	0
Hughes RD	Richard	25/06/1979	Glasgow		1998	2001	Arsenal	Portsmouth	131	8	10	5	14	2	0	0
Hughes W	Billy	09/05/1929	Ballymena		1953		Bolton Wanderers	Rhyl	16	0	0	0	1	0	0	0
Hunt RRA	Ralph	14/08/1933	Portsmouth	1964	1953	1954	Portsmouth	Norwich City	33	3	0	0	7	1	0	0
Hutchinson JA	Jimmy	28/12/1915	Sheffield		1946		Sheffield Utd.	Lincoln City	8	0	0	0	3	0	0	0
Hutchinson WL	Billy		Chester-le-Street		1930		Birmingham	Leeds United	2	0	0	0	0	0	0	0
Hutchison D	Davie	29/10/1908	Shotts		1936		Airdrie		2	0	0	0	1	0	0	0
Impey JE	John	11/08/1954	Minehead		1975	1982	Cardiff City	Torquay United	284	17	13	4	7	0	0	0
Isherwood H	Harry	01/01/1901	Darwen		1928		Birmingham	Worcester City	18	6	0	0	0	0	0	0
Jenkins J	Jamie	01/01/1979	Pontypool		1998		Trainee	Barry Town	1	0	0	0	0	0	0	0
Johnson JC	Jack	03/10/1905	South Kirkby	1991	1928	1929	Sheffield Wed.	Rotherham Utd.	12	0	0	0	4	0	0	0

Name		D.O.B	Place of Birth	Died	First Season	Last Season	Previous Club	Next Club	Appearances				Goals			
									Lge	FAC	FLC	Oth.	Lge	FAC	FLC	Oth.
Johnson PJ	Peter	18/02/1954	Hackney		1976	1978	Crystal Palace	Weymouth	107	5	8	0	11	0	1	0
Johnstone TC					1927				1	0	0	0	0	0	0	0
Jones AM	Andy	09/01/1963	Wrexham		1990	1991	Charlton Ath.	Leyton Orient	40	4	2	2	8	3	2	1
Jones BR	Bryn	20/05/1931	Swansea	1990	1959	1963	Newport County	Northampton Town	118	5	8	0	5	0	0	0
Jones DE	David	11/02/1952	Gosport		1970	1973	Apprentice	Nottm. Forest	134	10	7	0	5	0	0	0
Jones E	Emlyn 'Mickey'	29/11/1907	Merthyr Tydfil		1927		Merthyr Town	Everton	6	0	0	0	2	0	0	0
Jones G	Glan	27/02/1921	Merthyr Tydfil	1956	1948		Hull City	Crewe Alexandra	9	0	0	0	3	0	0	0
Jones GA	Gareth	18/06/1952	Cardiff		1973	1974	Torquay United	Weymouth	4	0	2	0	0	0	0	0
Jones JL	Jack		Penrhiwceiber		1938		Torquay United	Chester	12	0	0	2	1	0	0	1
Jones R	Roger	08/11/1946	Upton-on-Severn		1965	1969	Portsmouth	Blackburn Rovers	160	9	8	0	0	0	0	0
Jones SG	Steve	17/03/1970	Cambridge		1994	1997	West Ham Utd.	West Ham Utd.	79	3	4	4	29	1	3	1
Jorgensen C	Claus	27/04/1976	Holstebro, Denmark		1999	2000	AC Horsens	Bradford City	87	6	6	2	14	0	1	0
Kandol TO	Tresor	30/08/1981	Zaire		2001		Cambridge Utd.	Chesham Utd.	12	2	0	1	0	0	0	1
Keane TJ	Tommy	16/09/1968	Galway		1985	1987	Apprentice	Colchester Utd.	3	0	0	1	0	0	0	0
Keating RE	Reg	14/05/1904	Halton	1961	1936		Doncaster Rovers	Carlisle Utd.	11	2	0	0	5	0	0	0
Keeler J	Justin	17/04/1978	Hillingdon		1999	2000	Christchurch	Dorchester Town	4	0	0	3	0	0	0	0
Keeley A	Arthur			1942	1937		Wolverhampton W.	Chester	2	0	0	0	0	0	0	0
Keetley EA	Albert	22/02/1930	Nottingham		1953	1957	Bury	Weymouth (trainer)	86	5	0	0	0	0	0	0
Keith RM	Dick	15/05/1933	Belfast	1967	1963	1965	Newcastle United	Weymouth	47	3	2	0	0	0	0	0
Kelly EP	Eddie	07/02/1951	Glasgow		1981		Notts County	Leicester City	13	0	1	2	0	0	0	0
Kevan DJ	David	31/08/1968	Wigtown		1993		Notts County (loan)		1	0	0	0	0	0	0	0
Kilcar SP	Steve	22/12/1907	Bo'ness		1936		Burnley	Watford	6	2	0	1	0	1	0	0
King JA	Johnny	15/04/1938	Liverpool		1960		Everton	Tranmere Rovers	21	1	2	0	1	0	0	0
King TP	Tom	29/06/1909	Woolsthorpe	1993	1935	1936	Notts County	Luton Town	66	7	0	5	0	0	0	0
Kinghorn HMcG	Harry	1886	Midlothian		1928		(trainer)	(manager)	1	0	0	0	0	0	0	0
Kirkham RJ	Jack	16/06/1918	Ellesmere Port	1982	1938	1946	Wolverhampton W.	Wellington Town	48	4	0	1	27	3	0	0
Kirkpatrick E	Ernie	27/02/1899	Farnworth	1971	1929		Chorley	Chorley	2	0	0	0	0	0	0	0
Kitchener WH	Bill	03/11/1946	Arlesey		1971	1972	Torquay United	Cambridge City	36	3	3	0	2	0	0	0
Kite PD	Phil	26/10/1962	Bristol		1989		Gillingham	Sheffield Utd.	6	0	1	0	0	0	0	0
Lamb JF	James		Fulham		1923	1924			63	14	0	0	0	0	0	0
Lampard AJ	Alf		Nailsworth		1929		Nailsworth	Barnsley	2	0	0	0	0	0	0	0
Langan DF	Dave	15/02/1957	Dublin		1987		Oxford United	Peterborough Utd.	20	1	0	0	0	0	0	0
Langley WE	Bill		Wolverhampton		1938		Wolverhampton W.	Yeovil & Petters	22	2	0	0	12	3	0	0
La Ronde E	Everald	24/01/1963	East Ham		1983	1984	West Ham Utd.	Kalmar FF (Swe)	24	4	0	2	0	0	0	1
Lawrence E	Eddie	24/08/1907	Cefn Mawr		1936		Notts County	Clapton Orient	39	3	0	1	1	0	0	0
Lawrence GR	George	14/09/1962	Kensington		1989	1991	Millwall	Mikkellin Pallo (Fin)	75	4	4	2	5	0	1	0
Lawson HT	Herbert	12/04/1905	Sunderland		1934		Reading	Barrow	3	1	0	0	0	0	0	0
Lax G	George	1905	Pontefract		1933		Barnsley	Worcester City	7	0	0	0	1	0	0	0
Leadbitter CJ	Chris	17/10/1967	Middlesbrough		1993	1994	Cambridge Utd.	Plymouth Argyle	54	5	7	2	3	0	0	0
Leaver D	Derek	13/11/1930	Blackburn		1955		Blackburn Rovers	Crewe Alexandra	29	1	0	0	5	0	0	0
Ledwidge J	John				1932		Bray Unknowns		17	2	0	0	7	0	0	0
Lee TC	Trevor	03/07/1954	Lewisham		1982	1983	Gillingham	Cardiff City	35	2	1	0	9	1	0	0
Leigh IR	Ian	11/06/1962	Ilfracombe		1981	1985	Swaythling	Hamrun Sprtns (Mal)	123	9	4	8	0	0	0	0
Leitch W	Billy		Glasgow		1923	1925	Coventry City		81	1	0	0	1	0	0	0
Lennard DH	Dave	31/12/1944	Manchester		1977	1978	Stockport County	Salisbury	59	6	0	0	4	0	0	0
Lewis J	Jack	26/08/1919	Walsall		1949	1950	Crystal Palace	Reading	45	4	0	0	1	0	0	0
Lewis MR	Morgan	08/09/1965	Bournemouth		1983	1986	Juniors	Weymouth	12	0	1	4	0	0	0	0
Liddle TB	Tom	22/04/1921	Middleton	1994	1947		Hartlepools Utd.	Yeovil Town	1	0	0	0	0	0	0	0
Lister JS	Jim		Glasgow		1923		Hearts	Aberdare Ath.	28	0	0	0	7	0	0	0
Littlejohn RD	Roy	02/06/1933	Bournemouth		1952	1955	Juniors	Portsmouth	22	3	0	0	2	0	0	0
Littlewood SC	Stewart	1906	Treeton		1933		Port Vale	Altrincham	18	0	0	2	11	0	0	2
Livermore DE	Doug	27/12/1947	Liverpool		1974		Norwich C (loan)		10	0	0	0	0	0	0	0
Lock H	Herbert	22/01/1887	Southampton	1957	1923		Southampton	Retired	13	0	0	0	0	0	0	0
Longdon CW	Charlie	06/05/1917	Mansfield	1986	1946		Brighton & Hove Alb.	Rochdale	9	0	0	0	1	0	0	0
Longhorn D	Dennis	12/09/1950	Hythe, Hampshire		1967	1971	Apprentice	Mansfield Town	30	3	1	0	1	1	0	0
Loughnane JB	Brian	16/06/1930	Manchester		1956	1958	Shrewsbury Town	Wellington Town	43	2	0	0	5	0	0	0
Lovell SJ	Steve	16/07/1960	Swansea		1992		Gillingham	Sittingbourne	3	2	0	0	0	1	0	0
Lovell SWH	Steve	06/12/1980	Amersham		1998	1999	Trainee	Portsmouth	8	0	0	0	0	0	0	0
Lovery JB	Jimmy	26/07/1915	Stockport		1937	1938	Wolverhampton W.	Bradford City	30	3	0	1	9	0	0	0
Lovie JTH	Jim	19/09/1932	Peterhead		1960		Bury	Chesterfield	9	0	0	0	0	0	0	0
Lowson EB	Edmund	21/03/1903	Evenwood	1955	1924	1925	Doncaster Rovers	Poole	4	1	0	0	0	0	0	0
Lumsden JB	James		West Calder		1929		Preston NE		2	0	0	0	0	0	0	0
Lunn WJ	Billy	08/05/1923	Lurgan		1947	1949	West Bromwich A.	Newport County	47	3	0	0	19	0	0	0
Lynne MGA	Mike	20/03/1938	Kettering		1959	1960	Preston NE	Brighton & Hove A.	17	0	0	0	0	0	0	0
Lyons MC	Mike	31/01/1932	Iron Acton		1956	1958	Bristol Rovers	Swindon Town	105	9	0	0	0	1	0	0
McAlinden RJ	Bobby	22/05/1946	Salford		1976		Los Angeles Aztecs		1	0	0	0	0	0	0	0
McAnespie K	Keiran	11/09/1979	Gosport		2001		Fulham (loan)		7	0	0	0	0	0	0	0
McCulloch MJ	Mike	26/04/1900	Denny		1924		Chesterfield	St Bernards	10	0	0	0	1	0	0	0
McCulloch RG	Bob	20/04/1900	Glasgow	1964	1924		Kilmarnock	Watford	38	1	0	0	4	1	0	0
McDonald JC	Jack	27/08/1921	Maltby		1946	1947	Wolverhampton W.	Fulham	80	8	0	0	36	2	0	0
McDonald S	Scott	21/08/1981	Melbourne, Aus		2002		Southampton		7	0	0	1	1	0	0	0
MacDonald M	Martin	05/09/1931	Kilsyth		1952	1955	Portsmouth	Dorchester Town	51	3	0	0	1	0	0	0
MacDonald R	Bob	26/10/1935	Kilpatrick		1963		Manchester City	Weymouth	1	0	0	0	0	0	0	0
MacDougall EJ	Ted	08/01/1947	Inverness		1969	1972	York City	Manchester Utd.	198	13	12	0	119	19	6	0
					1978	1979	Southampton	Blackpool								
McElhatton MT	Mike	16/04/1975	County Kerry		1992	1995	Trainee	Scarborough	42	3	4	1	2	1	0	0
McGarry WH	Bill	10/06/1927	Stoke-on-Trent		1960	1962	Huddersfield T	Watford (Mgr)	78	2	0	0	2	0	0	0
McGibbon D	Doug	24/02/1919	Netley		1948	1950	Fulham	Lovells Ath.	103	3	0	0	65	0	0	0
McGorry BP	Brian	16/04/1970	Liverpool		1991	1993	Weymouth	Peterborough Utd.	61	10	7	5	11	2	0	1
McGowan RN	Robert	1906	Sanquhar	1984	1932		Glasgow Rangers	Queen of the South	6	0	0	0	1	0	0	0
McGrath ML	Martin	15/10/1960	Hendon		1980		Southampton	Oxford City	22	0	2	0	0	0	0	0
Machin M	Mel	16/04/1945	Newcastle-u.-Lyme		1970	1973	Gillingham	Norwich City	110	8	8	0	7	1	0	0
McInally TB	Tom	18/04/1900	Partick	1955	1929		Sunderland	Morton	10	4	0	0	1	0	0	0

Name		D.O.B	Place of Birth	Died	First Season	Last Season	Previous Club	Next Club	Appearances Lge	FAC	FLC	Oth.	Goals Lge	FAC	FLC	Oth.
McKay N	Norman	01/01/1905	Poole		1927				1	0	0	0	0	0	0	0
McKechnie TS	Tom	09/02/1940	Milngavie		1966		Luton Town	Colchester Utd.	14	1	1	0	2	0	1	0
McKenzie JA	Johnny	04/09/1925	Glasgow		1947		Partick Thistle (loan)		38	3	0	0	9	0	0	0
McKinney WE	Bill	20/07/1936	Newcastle		1965		Newcastle United	Mansfield Town	17	1	1	0	0	0	0	0
McManus EJ	Eddie	08/08/1937	Ramsgate		1958	1959	Dover	Gillingham	4	0	0	0	0	0	0	0
McPhail DD	Don	17/02/1911	Dumbarton	1992	1932		Middlesbrough	Barnsley	14	0	0	0	0	0	0	0
McSevich P	Peter	14/05/1902	Stevenston	1979	1928	1931	Aberdeen	Coventry City	142	16	0	0	1	0	0	0
Madden DJ	David	06/01/1963	Stepney		1982		Southampton (loan)		5	0	0	0	0	0	0	0
Maher SP	Shaun	20/06/1978	Dublin		2001	2002	Bohemians		39	0	2	0	2	0	0	0
Maidment HW	Harry	20/09/1901	Bournemouth		1924	1927		Thames	71	4	0	0	16	1	0	0
Mardon HJ	Harry	08/06/1914	Cardiff	1981	1937	1938	Notts County	Bristol City	25	0	0	0	14	0	0	0
Marsden F	Fred	06/09/1911	Blackburn	1989	1936	1948	Wolverhampton W.	Weymouth	194	17	0	3	1	2	0	0
Marsh C	Cliff	29/12/1920	Atherton	1990	1949	1951	Leeds United	Worcester City	39	0	0	0	2	0	0	0
Marshall AJ	Andy	14/04/1975	Bury		1996		Norwich City (loan)		11	0	0	0	0	0	0	0
Marshall GH	George	03/03/1896	Walker		1924		Reading	Darlaston	20	0	0	0	0	0	0	0
Marshall KC	Ken		Bournemouth		1923			Poole	2	3	0	0	0	0	0	0
Martin DV	Dennis	08/11/1928	Southampton		1948	1953	Juniors	Poole Town	23	0	0	0	0	0	0	0
Massey RW	Bob	06/04/1940	Marylebone		1959	1960	Juniors	Guildford City	5	0	0	0	0	0	0	0
Massey S	Steve	28/03/1958	Denton		1978	1980	Stockport County	Peterborough Utd.	97	4	5	0	19	2	1	0
Masters NB	Neil	25/05/1972	Lisburn		1992	1993	Trainee	Wolverhampton W.	38	7	4	2	2	1	1	0
Meadows JR	Ron	04/12/1920	Lancaster		1950	1951	Burnley	Accrington Stanley	16	0	0	0	0	0	0	0
Mean SJ	Scott	13/12/1972	Crawley		1992	1999	Trainee	West Ham Utd.	106	4	13	6	13	0	0	0
Melligan JJ	John 'JJ'	11/02/1982	Dublin		2001		Wolves (loan)		8	1	0	0	0	0	0	0
Mellors RD	Dick	17/03/1905	Mansfield		1934	1937	Reading	Queen of the South	116	8	0	5	0	0	0	0
Melville L	Les	29/11/1930	Ormskirk		1956	1957	Everton	Oldham Athletic	25	2	0	0	0	0	0	0
Menetrier M	Michel	23/08/1978	France		2000	2001	Metz	(France)	12	0	2	3	0	0	0	0
Meredith JF	John	23/09/1940	Hatfield, S Yorks		1969	1970	Gillingham	Hastings Utd.	51	2	6	0	1	0	0	0
Merrick NG	Neil	06/04/1952	Birmingham		1974		Worcester C	Johannesburg (SA)	15	1	1	0	0	0	0	0
Messer AT	Alf	08/03/1900	Deptford	1947	1934	1935	Tottenham H	(coaching staff)	10	0	0	0	0	0	0	0
Meyer HJ	Henry 'Porky'	04/03/1893	Christchurch		1924		Bournemouth Trams	Bournemouth Trams	2	12	0	0	0	5	0	0
Miles SG	Sid	16/05/1934	Bournemouth		1957		Army	Peterborough Utd.	1	0	0	0	0	0	0	0
Miles WP	William 'Dossie'	19/02/1898	Bournemouth	1971	1924	1928	Bournemouth Trams	Watford	94	10	0	0	10	1	0	0
Millar NH	Norman	30/11/1908	Dunadry	1998	1937	1938	Linfield		22	3	0	2	1	2	0	0
Miller J	Jimmy	10/05/1889	Tynemouth		1923		Chesterfield	Swansea Town	38	0	0	0	0	0	0	0
Miller J	Joe		Belfast		1931	1933	Hibernian	Ballymena	75	5	0	1	0	0	0	0
Miller KR	Keith	26/01/1948	Lewisham		1970	1979	West Ham Utd.	Dorchester Town	383	27	23	0	19	0	0	0
Miller PR	Paul	11/10/1959	Stepney		1989	1990	Watford	Swansea City	47	4	4	2	1	0	0	0
Miller RE	Ralph	22/06/1941	Slough		1968	1970	Gillingham	Weymouth	72	4	1	0	1	0	0	0
Milligan D	Dudley	07/11/1916	Johannesburg, SA		1947	1948	Chesterfield	Walsall	45	3	0	0	25	2	0	0
Milne AS	Alec	1915	Glasgow		1937		Third Lanark		3	0	0	0	0	0	0	0
Mitchell GL	Graham	16/02/1968	Shipley		1993		Huddersfield T (loan)		4	0	0	0	0	0	0	0
Mitchell PR	Paul	20/10/1971	Bournemouth		1990	1992	Trainee	West Ham Utd.	16	0	0	2	0	0	0	0
					1995		West Ham Utd.	Torquay United								
Mitchinson TW	Tommy	24/02/1943	Sunderland		1971	1972	Torquay United	Retired - injury	32	0	1	0	1	0	0	0
Monaghan P	Peter		Stevenston	1944	1937	1938	Ardeer Recreation	Killed in WWII	63	6	0	2	1	0	0	0
Mooney DF	Dean	24/07/1956	Paddington		1980	1981	GAIS (Swe)	Vasawands (Swe)	27	0	2	3	10	0	0	0
Moore J	Jon	17/11/1955	Cardiff		1979	1980	Millwall	Poole Town	36	2	2	0	2	0	0	0
Moore TD	Tommy	Q2 1910	Dudley Port		1934		Stourbridge	Stourbridge	6	0	0	1	2	0	0	0
Moralee WE	Bill	03/05/1906	Crook	1967	1928	1935	Huddersfield Town	QPR	189	15	0	6	6	0	0	0
Morgan MBB	Matthew	24/01/1900	Glasgow	1985	1930		St Mirren		6	0	0	0	0	0	0	0
Morgan N	Nicky	30/10/1959	East Ham		1992		Bristol City (loan)		6	2	0	1	1	1	0	1
Morgan R	Ron	06/09/1915	Twynrodyn	1990	1935		Wolverhampton W.	Doncaster Rovers	2	0	0	2	1	0	0	1
Morgan SE	Stuart	23/09/1949	Swansea		1974	1976	Colchester Utd.	Weymouth	81	4	2	0	5	0	0	0
Morgan TJ	Trevor	30/09/1956	Forest Gate		1980	1981	Leytonstone/Ilford	Mansfield Town	141	8	8	6	46	3	3	2
					1981	1983	Mansfield Town	Bristol City								
Morrell PDP	Paul	23/03/1961	Poole		1983	1992	Weymouth	Bashley	343	29	26	20	21	1	1	1
Morris DK	David	19/11/1971	Plumstead		1990		Trainee	Hereford Utd.	1	0	0	0	0	0	0	0
Morris MJ	Mark	26/09/1962	Morden		1991	1996	Sheffield Utd.	Brighton & Hove Alb.	194	17	15	9	8	1	2	0
Mortimer R	Bob	Q2 1908	Bolton		1934		Brentford	Accrington Stanley	18	0	0	2	3	0	0	0
Moss NG	Neil	10/05/1975	New Milton		1992	1995	Trainee	Southampton	55	6	1	8	0	0	0	0
					2002		Southampton									
Moulden PAJ	Paul	06/09/1967	Farnworth		1989		Manchester City	Oldham Athletic	32	1	4	1	0	0	1	0
Mundee BG	Brian	12/01/1964	Hammersmith		1982		Hungerford T	Northampton Town	4	0	1	1	0	0	0	0
Mundee DWJ	Denny	10/10/1968	Swindon		1988	1992	Salisbury	Brentford	100	11	5	6	6	4	0	2
Murphy VJ	Vincent		Limerick		1928		Grimsby Town	Walsall	6	0	0	0	0	0	0	0
Murray RJ	Rob	31/10/1974	Hammersmith		1992	1997	Trainee	Richmond K. (USA)	147	9	9	6	12	0	0	2
Murray T	Terry	22/05/1928	Dublin		1953	1954	Hull City	King's Lynn	13	0	0	0	1	0	0	0
Naylor TV	Tommy	01/04/1946	Blackburn		1964	1970	Apprentice	Hereford Utd.	143	11	5	0	3	1	0	0
Ndah GE	George	23/12/1974	Dulwich		1995		Crystal Palace (loan)		12	0	0	1	2	0	0	0
Neave IJG	Gordon	10/10/1924	Glasgow		1950	1953	Portsmouth	Aldershot	85	4	0	0	0	0	0	0
Neighbour JE	Jimmy	15/11/1950	Chingford		1982		West Ham U (loan)		6	0	0	0	0	0	0	0
Nelson JA	Tony	12/04/1930	Cardiff		1956	1964	Bristol City	(coaching staff)	194	9	8	0	1	0	0	0
Newsham S	Stan	24/03/1931	Farnworth		1952	1956	Bolton Wanderers	Notts County	142	10	0	0	74	4	0	0
Newson MJ	Mark	07/12/1960	Stepney		1985	1989	Maidstone United	Fulham	177	11	12	5	23	2	2	0
Newton GW	Graham	22/12/1942	Bilston		1964	1966	Coventry City	Port Vale	28	2	1	0	3	0	0	0
Nichol WB	William		Lochgelly		1928		Lochgelly Celtic	Gillingham	2	0	0	0	0	0	0	0
Nicholson S	Sid	1912	Shildon		1931	1932	Merthyr Town	Scunthorpe Utd.	8	0	0	0	0	0	0	0
Nightingale MBD	Mark	01/02/1957	Salisbury		1974	1975	Apprentice	Crystal Palace	199	15	13	13	8	0	0	0
					1982	1985	Norwich City	Peterborough Utd.								
Norris OP	Ollie	01/04/1929	Derry		1955	1958	Worcester City	Northampton Town	96	8	0	0	34	6	0	0
Norton P	Peter	11/11/1947	Manchester		1966	1967	Juniors	Crewe Alexandra	19	1	1	0	1	0	0	0
Norton R	Ralph	11/10/1942	Aylesham		1966	1967	Reading	Poole Town	47	2	1	0	4	0	0	0
O'Brien RJ	Roy	27/11/1974	Cork		1996		Wigan Ath.	Dorchester Town	1	0	0	0	0	0	0	0

Name		D.O.B	Place of Birth	Died	First Season	Last Season	Previous Club	Next Club	Appearances				Goals			
									Lge	FAC	FLC	Oth.	Lge	FAC	FLC	Oth.
O'Brien W	William		Glasgow		1936	1937	St Anthony's	Port Vale	16	0	0	0	5	0	0	0
O'Connor G	Garreth	10/11/1978	Dublin		2000	2002	Bohemians		91	10	2	10	9	1	0	2
O'Connor MA	Mark	10/03/1963	Rochford		1985	1989	Bristol Rovers	Gillingham	186	11	16	6	15	0	0	0
					1993	1994	Gillingham	Gillingham								
O'Donnell BF	Brian	08/08/1957	Port Glasgow		1981	1982	Blacktown C (Aus)	Torquay United	14	0	1	2	0	0	0	0
O'Driscoll SM	Sean	01/07/1957	Wolverhampton		1983	1994	Fulham	(coaching staff)	423	31	33	24	19	1	1	3
Oldbury MJ	Marcus	29/03/1976	Bournemouth		1995		Norwich City	Bashley	13	1	1	1	0	0	1	0
Oliver K	Ken	26/11/1938	Pelton		1966		Workington	Retired - injury	14	0	0	0	4	0	0	0
Omoyimni E	Manny	28/12/1977	Nigeria		1996		West Ham U (loan)		7	0	0	0	0	0	0	0
O'Neill A	Alan	13/11/1937	Leadgate		1963	1965	Plymouth Argyle	Cambridge Utd.	37	1	1	0	8	0	0	0
O'Neill JJ	Jon	02/01/1974	Glasgow		1995	2000	Celtic	Ross County	124	8	10	10	10	2	0	0
O'Rourke J	John	11/02/1945	Northampton		1973	1974	QPR	Rangers FC (SA)	22	1	0	0	4	0	0	0
O'Shea JF	John	30/04/1981	Waterford		1999		Manchester U (loan)		10	0	0	1	1	0	0	0
Ovendale MJ	Mark	22/11/1973	Leicester		1998	1999	Northampton Town	Luton Town	89	7	10	5	0	0	0	0
Parker ESH	Ernie	18/12/1913	Anerley	1983	1936		Mansfield Town	Bristol Rovers	7	0	0	0	0	0	0	0
Parker RW	Reg	1913	Reading		1931	1934	Tilehurst Wed.	West Ham Utd.	49	1	0	0	0	0	0	0
Parkinson JS	Joe	11/06/1971	Eccles		1993		Wigan Ath.	Everton	30	4	4	1	1	0	1	0
Parodi LV	Les	01/04/1954	Lambeth		1973	1974	Slough T	Christchurch	49	3	8	0	2	0	0	0
Parris JE	Eddie	31/01/1911	Pwllmeyric	1971	1934	1936	Bradford	Luton Town	103	8	0	6	23	10	0	4
Parsons JS	John	10/12/1950	Cardiff		1972	1974	Cardiff City	Newport County	7	0	1	0	1	0	0	0
Paterson T	Tommy	30/03/1954	Ashington		1976	1977	Middlesbrough	Darlington	57	3	4	0	10	0	1	0
Paton TG	Tommy	22/12/1918	Saltcoats	1991	1938	1947	Swansea Town	Watford	46	4	0	1	8	2	0	2
Payne CE	Clive	02/03/1950	Aylsham		1973	1975	Norwich City	Aylsham (p/m)	101	7	9	0	3	0	0	0
Peacock GK	Gavin	18/11/1967	Eltham		1989	1990	Gillingham	Newcastle United	56	2	6	2	8	0	0	0
Peed FE	Frank	27/06/1905	Vernado Tuerto (Arg)	1967	1930		Aston Villa	Norwich City	2	0	0	0	0	0	0	0
Pennock AB	Adrian	27/03/1971	Ipswich		1992	1995	Norwich City	Gillingham	131	12	9	8	9	1	0	0
Percival J	Jack	16/05/1913	Patrington	1979	1947	1948	Manchester City	Murton (p/m)	52	3	0	0	1	0	0	0
Peters RD	Roger 'Lou'	05/03/1944	Cheltenham		1968	1969	Bristol City	Bath City	37	2	1	0	3	0	0	0
Peyton GJ	Gerry	20/05/1956	Birmingham		1986	1990	Fulham	Everton	202	13	15	8	0	0	0	0
Phillipson-Masters	Forbes	14/11/1955	Bournemouth		1977		Southampton (loan)		7	0	0	0	2	0	0	0
Picton HV	Henry 'Taffy'	29/06/1915	Trehafod	1974	1936	1937		Crewe Alexandra	7	0	0	0	0	0	0	0
Pike TE	Theo 'Tot'	25/03/1907	Sunderland	1967	1927		Fulham	Birmingham	16	4	0	0	3	3	0	0
Pincott FC	Fred	19/03/1913	Bristol		1934	1938	Wolverhampton W.	Newport County	196	14	0	8	0	0	0	0
Pound JHK	Ken	24/08/1944	Portsmouth		1966	1968	Swansea Town	Gillingham	102	7	4	0	24	2	0	0
Powell A	Tony	11/02/1947	Severn Beach		1968	1973	Bath City	Norwich City	219	16	12	0	10	1	1	0
Priscott AJ	Tony	19/03/1941	Portsmouth		1965	1966	Aldershot	Aldershot	61	1	1	0	7	0	0	0
Proctor JR	Jack	1911	New Delaval		1932	1933	Huddersfield Town	Hartlepools Utd.	53	4	0	1	0	0	0	0
Prosser NA	Neil	08/03/1957	Edmonton		1980		Harlow Town	Tranmere Rovers	2	0	0	0	0	0	0	0
Prudham CE	Eddie	12/04/1952	Gateshead		1980		Stockport County		4	0	2	0	0	0	0	0
Puckett DC	Dave	29/10/1960	Southampton		1986	1988	Southampton	Aldershot	39	3	4	2	14	3	0	3
					1991		Aldershot	Woking								
Pugh GK	Gary	11/02/1961	Ramsgate		1980		Dover	Gravesend & Nth.	3	0	0	0	1	0	0	0
Pulis AR	Tony	16/01/1958	Newport		1986	1991	Newport County	Gillingham	90	4	7	3	4	0	0	0
Purches SR	Stephen	14/01/1980	Essex		2000	2002	West Ham Utd.		118	10	4	7	5	0	0	2
Quinn JM	Jimmy	18/11/1959	Belfast		1991		West Ham Utd.	Reading	43	5	4	2	19	2	2	1
Rafferty WH	Billy	30/12/1950	Glasgow		1983	1984	Portsmouth	Farense (Por)	58	5	1	6	18	1	0	1
Rampling DW	Dennis	25/11/1923	Gainsborough		1948		Fulham	Brentford	24	1	0	0	4	0	0	0
Ramsbottom N	Neil	25/02/1946	Blackburn		1983		Bradford City	Chorley	4	0	1	0	0	0	0	0
Randall AJ	Adrian	10/11/1968	Amesbury		1985	1987	Apprentice	Aldershot	3	0	0	3	0	0	0	0
Randle J	Jackie	23/08/1902	Bedworth	1990	1933		Birmingham	Guildford City	28	2	0	2	0	0	0	0
Ranson R	Ronnie		Felton		1938		Portsmouth	Clapton Orient	1	0	0	1	0	0	0	0
Rattray HW	Hardie		Glasgow		1924		Kilmarnock	Arthurlie	11	1	0	0	1	1	0	0
Rawlinson MD	Mark	09/06/1975	Bolton		1995	1999	Manchester Utd.	Exeter City	79	3	4	4	2	0	0	0
Readman JA	Joe	1905	West Hartlepool		1924	1926	Bolton Wanderers	Brighton & Hove Alb.	48	2	0	0	20	0	0	0
Redfern R	Bob	03/03/1918	Crook		1936	1946	Wolverhampton W.	Brighton & Hove Alb.	89	3	0	3	4	0	0	0
Redknapp HJ	Harry	02/03/1947	Poplar		1972	1982	West Ham Utd.	Brentford	102	6	8	0	5	0	1	0
Redknapp JF	Jamie	25/06/1973	Barton-on-Sea		1989	1990	Trainee	Liverpool	13	3	3	2	0	0	0	0
Reeve JM	Jamie	26/11/1975	Weymouth		1994		Trainee	Hereford Utd.	7	0	2	1	0	0	0	0
Reeves DB	Derek	27/08/1934	Poole	1995	1962	1964	Southampton	Worcester City	35	0	3	0	8	0	0	0
Reeves KP	Kevin	20/10/1957	Burley		1974	1976	Apprentice	Norwich City	63	5	3	0	20	0	0	0
Regis DR	Dave	03/03/1964	Paddington		1992		Plymouth Argyle (loan)		6	0	0	0	2	0	0	0
Reid MJ	Micky	07/08/1927	Wolverhampton	1975	1948		Wolverhampton W.	Portsmouth	5	0	0	0	2	0	0	0
Rhodes A	Arthur	1920	Devon		1937		Stockport Co.	Torquay United	8	0	0	0	3	0	0	0
Richards CL	Carl	01/12/1960	St Mary's, Jamaica		1986	1988	Enfield	Birmingham City	71	2	10	3	16	2	0	0
Richardson GWR	George	1899	Gainsborough	1963	1924		Sheffield Utd.	Boston Town	9	1	0	0	0	0	0	0
Richardson J	Jack				1934		Kettering		1	0	0	0	0	0	0	0
Richardson, John	(Jock)	11/11/1906	Motherwell	1986	1934		Reading	Folkestone Town	7	0	0	1	0	0	0	0
Richmond WC	Bill	01/03/1900	Kirkcaldy		1932	1934	Ayr United	Walsall	27	0	0	0	0	0	0	0
Rickard DBP	Derek	01/10/1947	Plymouth		1974	1975	Plymouth Argyle	Falmouth Town	32	0	5	0	6	0	2	0
Ridgewell L	Liam	21/07/1984	London		2002		Aston Villa (loan)		5	0	0	0	0	0	0	0
Riley HW	Hughen	12/06/1947	Accrington		1976	1977	Bury	Dorchester Town	72	4	5	0	7	0	0	0
Riley J	Joe	1908	Sheffield		1935	1937	Bristol City	Notts County	93	7	0	5	58	3	0	3
Ritchie AW	Alex	1907	Airdrie		1934		Raith Rovers	Third Lanark	33	1	0	0	12	0	0	0
Roberts CL	Leslie	28/02/1901	Halesowen	1980	1924	1925	Merthyr Town	Bolton Wanderers	51	5	0	0	11	2	0	0
Roberts WE	Wally	23/11/1917	Wrexham		1948	1949	Wrexham	Ellesmere Port	15	1	0	0	0	0	0	0
Robinson F	Foster	1901	South Shields		1923		Coventry City	Luton Town	31	0	0	0	1	0	0	0
Robinson S	Steve	10/12/1974	Lisburn		1994	1999	Tottenham H	Preston NE	240	16	14	16	51	5	1	3
Robinson SH	Sam	1910	Hucknall		1929	1930	Luton Town	Derby County	11	0	0	0	1	0	0	0
Robson JH	Jock	1898	Innerleithen		1926	1927	Arsenal	Montrose	42	6	0	0	0	0	0	0
Rodriguez DF	Dani	03/03/1980	Madeira, Portugal		1998		CS Farense (loan)		5	0	0	2	0	0	0	0
Roe A	Arthur	1892	South Normanton		1925	1926	Arsenal	Mansfield Town	50	5	0	0	2	0	0	0
Rolling FJ	Franck	23/08/1968	Colmar, France		1997		Leicester City	Gillingham	30	2	2	3	4	0	1	3
Rose JW	John	12/08/1920	Woolwich		1946		Salisbury		1	0	0	0	0	0	0	0

Name		D.O.B	Place of Birth	Died	First Season	Last Season	Previous Club	Next Club	Appearances Lge	FAC	FLC	Oth.	Goals Lge	FAC	FLC	Oth.
Rowell JF	Fred	31/12/1918	Dawdon		1946	1947	Army	Wrexham	31	3	0	0	11	0	0	0
Rowland K	Keith	01/09/1971	Portadown		1991	1992	Trainee	West Ham Utd.	72	8	5	3	2	0	0	0
Rowles AEJ	Eddie	10/03/1951	Gosport		1967	1970	Apprentice	York City	66	6	3	0	12	1	0	0
Rowley JF	Jack	07/10/1920	Wolverhampton	1998	1936	1937	Cradley Heath	Manchester Utd.	23	0	0	1	11	0	0	0
Rudge JR	John	21/10/1944	Wolverhampton		1974	1976	Bristol Rovers	Torquay United	21	0	0	0	2	0	0	0
Rule AH	Alan	10/01/1930	Southampton		1957		Norwich City	Swaythling Ath.	25	1	0	0	0	0	0	0
Rushworth PT	Peter	12/04/1927	Bristol		1953	1956	Leicester City	Salisbury	88	6	0	0	1	0	0	0
Russell C	Colin	21/01/1961	Liverpool		1984	1985	Huddersfield Town	Doncaster Rovers	68	9	6	4	14	2	2	3
Russell CJ	Jack	19/06/1904	Northfield		1930	1933	Worcester City	Luton Town	138	8	0	2	43	3	0	1
Russell KJ	Kevin	06/12/1966	Portsmouth		1993	1994	Burnley	Notts County	30	2	3	0	1	1	1	0
Russell LE	Lee	03/09/1969	Southampton		1994		Portsmouth (loan)		3	0	0	0	0	0	0	0
Russo G	Gary	02/08/1956	Hemsby		1975		Ipswich Town	Maidstone United	1	0	1	0	0	0	0	0
Rutter JT	John	13/09/1952	Warrington		1973		Wolverhampton W.	Exeter City	4	0	0	0	0	0	0	0
Sainty JA	John	24/03/1946	Poplar		1969	1973	Reading	Aldershot	118	6	10	0	20	0	3	0
Sanaghan J	Joe	12/12/1914	Motherwell	1951	1937	1948	Bradford	Stockport County	169	12	0	1	0	0	0	0
Santos YD	Ali	30/07/1975	Jersey, USA		1995		Jersey Scots (USA)		3	0	0	1	0	0	0	0
Saunders RC	Robbie	26/08/1945	Poole		1965		Apprentice	Poole Town	3	0	0	0	0	0	0	0
Savage RJ	Robbie	08/01/1960	Liverpool		1983	1986	Stoke City	Bradford City	82	8	3	10	18	3	0	3
Saxton E	Edgar	1896	Carlton, West Yorks		1923	1927	Barnsley	(coaching staff)	77	15	0	0	0	1	0	0
Schiavi MA	Mark	01/05/1964	City of London		1983	1984	West Ham Utd.	Northampton Town	29	0	2	3	0	0	0	0
Scott AJE	Tony	01/04/1941	Edmonton		1970	1971	Torquay United	Exeter City	62	4	3	0	6	0	0	0
Scott J	Joey	11/01/1953	Plymouth		1978	1979	Falmouth Town	Yeovil Town	21	0	1	0	4	0	0	0
Scott K	Keith	10/06/1967	Westminster		1995		Norwich City (loan)		8	0	0	0	1	0	0	0
Scott PR	Peter	01/10/1963	Notting Hill		1992		Fulham	Barnet	10	1	2	1	0	0	0	0
Scott WH	Harry	1908	St Helens		1929	1931	Pilkingtons	Swindon Town	81	5	0	0	36	0	0	0
Scully ADT	Tony	12/06/1976	Dublin		1994		Crystal Palace (loan)		10	0	0	2	0	0	0	0
Sealy AJ	Tony	07/05/1959	Hackney		1986		Crystal Palace (loan)		13	0	0	0	2	0	0	0
Sellars W	William		Glasgow		1937	1938	St Anthony's	Wolverhampton W.	23	3	0	0	0	0	0	0
Shanahan TC	Terry	05/12/1951	Paddington		1977		Millwall	Aldershot	18	0	1	0	1	0	0	0
Shaw CJ	Chris	23/08/1965	Bournemouth		1982	1985	Juniors	Bath City	25	2	0	2	2	0	0	1
Shaw TF	Fred	27/03/1909	Hucknall		1938		Mansfield Town	Ollerton Colliery	10	0	0	1	1	0	0	1
Shearer DJ	David	16/10/1958	Caol		1987		Gillingham	Scunthorpe Utd.	11	1	0	0	3	0	0	0
Shearer PA	Peter	04/02/1967	Birmingham		1988	1992	Cheltenham Town	Birmingham City	85	5	6	3	10	1	1	1
Sheerin JE	Joe	08/11/1977	Hammersmith		1999		Chelsea	Kingstonian	6	0	0	0	1	0	0	0
Sherman FH	Harry	16/10/1906	Edmonton	1985	1930	1931	Hampstead Town		25	0	0	0	4	0	0	0
Showers D	Derek	28/01/1953	Merthyr Tydfil		1977	1978	Cardiff City	Portsmouth	60	5	6	0	19	0	1	0
Sibley ES	Eric	17/11/1915	Christchurch		1937		Tottenham H	Blackpool	7	0	0	0	0	0	0	0
Siddall AB	Brian	02/05/1930	Northwich		1953	1956	Stoke City	Ipswich Town	85	3	0	0	16	1	0	0
Sille LT	Les	12/04/1928	Liverpool		1946		Tranmere Rovers	Ipswich Town	1	0	0	0	0	0	0	0
Simmonds MR	Mel	20/12/1951	Reading		1969		Reading	Guildford City	6	0	0	0	0	0	0	0
Simmons DJ	Dave	24/10/1948	Gosport		1968		Arsenal (loan)		7	0	0	0	3	0	0	0
Simpson A	Albert		Salford		1923		Manchester City	Peterborough Utd.	12	0	0	0	3	0	0	0
Singer DJ	Jimmy	30/08/1937	Fleur-de-Lys		1962	1963	Birmingham City	Newport County	59	1	1	0	22	0	0	0
Skinner JJ	Justin	17/09/1972	Dorking		1993		Wimbledon (loan)		16	0	0	0	0	0	0	0
Slatter NJ	Neil	30/05/1964	Cardiff		1989		Oxford Utd. (loan)		6	0	0	0	0	0	0	0
Smeulders J	John	28/03/1957	Hackney		1979	1980	Orient	Trowbridge Town	98	9	4	6	0	0	0	0
					1983	1985	Weymouth	Torquay United								
					1987	1988	Poole Town	Retired - injury								
Smith AWT	Bertie	22/04/1900	Camberwell		1928		Bangor City	(coaching staff)	28	1	0	0	0	0	0	0
Smith B	Brian	12/09/1955	Bolton		1980	1981	Blackpool	Bury	40	4	2	3	2	0	0	0
Smith CF	Charles		Newcastle		1923	1928	Bolton Wanderers		173	11	0	0	6	0	0	0
Smith D	David	29/03/1968	Stonehouse, Gloucs		1992		Coventry City (loan)		1	0	0	0	0	0	0	0
Smith DL	Danny	17/08/1982	Southampton		1999	2001	Bashley	Manchester City	18	1	2	3	0	0	0	0
Smith G	George	1910	Connah's Quay		1934		Wolverhampton W.	Bath City	16	0	0	2	0	0	0	0
Smith JW	Jack	28/10/1898	Whitburn	1977	1934	1935	Portsmouth	Clapton Orient	41	4	0	1	2	0	0	0
Smith R	Ron	07/06/1936	Garston		1959	1960	Liverpool	Crewe Alexandra	36	3	1	0	6	1	0	0
Smith W	Willie		Cellardyke		1934	1938	Wolverhampton W.		154	9	0	3	8	0	0	0
Southren T	Tommy	01/08/1927	Sunderland		1958	1959	Aston Villa	Retired - injury	64	4	0	0	11	1	0	0
Spackman NJ	Nigel	02/12/1960	Romsey		1980	1982	Andover	Chelsea	119	7	5	5	10	0	0	2
Spelman RE	Ron	22/05/1938	Blofield		1961	1963	Northampton Town	Watford	28	0	1	0	4	0	0	0
Standley TL	Tommy	23/12/1932	Poplar		1958	1964	QPR	Retired	159	6	7	0	5	0	0	0
Stanners W	Wally	02/01/1921	Carriden		1947		Bo'ness	Rochdale	3	0	0	0	0	0	0	0
Statham B	Brian	21/05/1969	Zimbabwe		1991		Tottenham H (loan)		2	0	0	1	0	0	0	0
Steele WM	Billy	16/06/1955	Kirkmuirhill		1975		Norwich City (loan)		7	0	0	0	2	0	0	0
Stein MES	Mark	28/01/1966	Cape Town, SA		1997	1999	Chelsea	Luton Town	90	7	10	8	30	2	7	5
Stephens AE	Arnold	31/01/1928	Ross-on-Wye	1955	1948	1953	Wolverhampton W.	Deceased	70	6	0	0	12	1	0	0
Stevens G	George		London		1932		Chelsea		1	0	0	0	0	0	0	0
Stewart GJ	Gareth	03/02/1980	Preston		1999	2002	Blackburn Rovers		85	7	1	0	0	0	0	0
Stiffle NE	Nelson	30/07/1928	India		1955	1957	Chesterfield	Exeter City	35	6	0	0	7	1	0	0
Stirling JR	Jim	23/07/1925	Airdrie		1947	1949	Coltness Utd.	Birmingham City	73	4	0	0	1	0	0	0
Stock BB	Brian	24/12/1981	Winchester		1999	2002	Trainee		59	4	0	8	4	0	0	0
Stocks DH	David	20/04/1943	Dulwich		1966	1971	Gillingham	Torquay United	220	12	13	0	2	0	0	0
Stringfellow JF	Frank		Sutton-in-Ashfield		1925	1928	Portsmouth	Scunthorpe Utd.	117	16	0	0	30	3	0	0
Strong SG	Steve	15/03/1978	Watford		1994	1995	Trainee	Bashley	2	1	0	0	0	0	0	0
Stroud DNL	Derek	11/02/1930	Wimborne		1950	1952	Poole Town	Grimsby Town	79	3	0	0	17	1	0	0
Stuckey BG	Bruce	19/02/1947	Torquay		1976		Reading (loan)		5	0	0	0	0	0	0	0
Sulley CS	Chris	03/12/1959	Camberwell		1980	1985	Chelsea	Blackburn Rovers	206	19	14	14	3	0	0	0
Summerhill A	Alan	25/11/1950	Liss		1969		Juniors	Crewe Alexandra	28	2	3	0	0	0	0	0
Surtees JW	Jack	02/07/1911	Percy Main	1992	1933		Portsmouth	Northampton Town	21	2	0	1	4	1	0	1
Tagg E	Ernie	15/09/1917	Crewe		1946	1948	Wolverhampton W.	Carlisle Utd.	80	7	0	0	8	1	0	0
Tait J	Jimmy		Edinburgh		1923		Hearts		12	0	0	0	4	0	0	0
Tait T	Tommy	20/11/1908	Hetton-le-Hole	1976	1934		Luton Town	Reading	12	0	0	2	5	0	0	2

Name		D.O.B	Place of Birth	Died	First Season	Last Season	Previous Club	Next Club	Appearances Lge	FAC	FLC	Oth.	Goals Lge	FAC	FLC	Oth.
Talkes WN	Wayne	02/06/1952	Ealing		1974		Southampton	Totton	5	0	2	0	0	0	0	0
Tardif C	Chris	20/06/1981	Guernsey		2002		Portsmouth (loan)		9	4	1	1	0	0	0	0
Tarrant H	Harold	1916	New Milton		1936		New Milton	Poole Town	1	0	0	0	0	0	0	0
Taylor E	Eden	1916	Sheffield		1937		Wolverhampton W.	Portsmouth	4	2	0	0	2	0	0	0
Taylor FE	Frank	16/07/1901	Wolverhampton	1973	1926	1927	Newport County	Gillingham	61	9	0	0	21	5	0	0
Taylor RV	Rod	09/09/1943	Corfe Castle		1965	1966	Gillingham	Poole Town	30	1	0	0	0	0	0	0
Taylor TWJ	Tommy	10/09/1946	Wandsworth		1966	1967	Gillingham	Bath City	26	0	1	0	8	0	0	0
Teale S	Shaun	10/03/1964	Southport		1988	1990	Weymouth	Aston Villa	100	5	8	3	4	1	0	0
Teather P	Paul	26/12/1977	Rotherham		1997		Manchester U (loan)		10	0	0	2	0	0	0	0
Thain AC	Albert	20/04/1900	Southall	1979	1931		Chelsea		20	1	0	0	6	0	0	0
Thomas B	Barrie	27/08/1954	Merthyr Tydfil		1979		Merthyr Tydfil	Bath City	3	0	1	0	0	0	0	0
Thomas D	Danny	01/05/1981	Leamington Spa		2001	2002	Leicester C (loan)		49	6	1	6	2	1	1	0
Thomas J	Jack	28/05/1936	Poole		1958		Poole Town	Parley Sports	4	0	0	0	0	0	0	0
Thomas R	Rees	03/01/1934	Aberdare		1957	1958	Brighton & Hove A.	Portsmouth	48	1	0	0	0	0	0	0
Thompson C	Cyril				1935		Crittall Ath.		5	0	0	0	1	0	0	0
Thompson IP	Ian	08/06/1958	Dartford		1983	1985	Salisbury	Salisbury	121	13	6	12	30	4	2	4
Thompson MS	Max	31/12/1956	Liverpool		1983		Swansea City	Baltimore Blast	9	0	2	0	0	0	0	0
Thompson P	Peter	16/02/1936	Blackhall		1961	1962	Derby County	Hartlepools Utd.	39	0	0	0	14	0	0	0
Thompson WG	Bill	10/08/1921	Glasgow		1952	1953	Portsmouth	Guildford City	46	3	0	0	0	0	0	0
Thomson D	Dan	10/08/1891	Dundee		1926		Bristol City	Torquay United	20	5	0	0	2	0	0	0
Threlfall W	Wilf	1901	Morecambe		1927		Birmingham	Morecambe	3	0	0	0	0	0	0	0
Tilsed RW	Ron	06/08/1952	Weymouth		1969		Apprentice	Chesterfield	2	0	0	0	0	0	0	0
Tindall J	Jason	15/11/1977	Stepney		1998	2002	Charlton Ath.		141	9	6	5	6	0	0	0
Tippett TJ	Tommy	04/08/1924	Gateshead		1951	1952	Southend Utd.	Dartford	37	1	0	0	10	0	0	0
Tomlinson GM	Graeme	10/12/1975	Keighley		1997		Manchester U (loan)		7	0	0	0	1	0	0	0
Town DE	David	09/12/1976	Bournemouth		1993	1998	Trainee	Rushden & D.	56	0	8	2	2	0	0	0
Townsend NR	Neil	01/02/1950	Long Buckby		1979	1980	Weymouth	Retired - injury	34	2	3	0	2	0	0	0
Train R	Ray	10/02/1951	Nuneaton		1983		Oxford United (loan)		7	4	0	0	0	0	0	0
Trevisone RR	Robert		Bournemouth		1933		B'mouth Gasworks	Poole Town	1	0	0	0	0	0	0	0
Trim RF	Reg	10/10/1913	Portsmouth		1930	1932	B'mouth Postal	Arsenal	22	3	0	0	0	0	0	0
Tunnicliffe WF	Bill	05/01/1920	Stoke-on-Trent	1997	1938	1946	Port Vale	Wrexham	50	6	0	1	7	1	0	0
Tunstall WH	Bill	19/01/1905	St Helens	1983	1933		Aston Villa		8	0	0	0	2	0	0	0
Turner HL	Harold		Desborough		1930		Harborough Town		9	0	0	0	0	0	0	0
Turner JT	John	30/10/1915	Wednesbury		1934	1935	West Bromwich A.	Chester	40	1	0	1	1	0	0	0
Twiss R	Dickie	11/11/1909	Ashton-in-Makerfield	1970	1934	1938	Port Vale		4	0	0	2	0	0	0	0
Tyler W	Billy	28/05/1900	Bradford, Lancashire	1974	1927		Bradford City	Grimsby Town	1	0	0	0	0	0	0	0
Tyrrell JJ	Joe	21/01/1932	Stepney		1957	1958	Millwall	Folkestone Town	3	0	0	0	1	0	0	0
Victory JC	Jamie	14/11/1975	Hackney		1995		West Ham Utd.	Cheltenham Town	16	0	2	2	1	0	0	0
Vincent JR	Jamie	18/06/1975	London		1994	1998	Crystal Palace (loan)		113	8	8	9	5	0	0	1
Voisey WT	Bill	19/11/1891	Millwall	1964	1923		Millwall	Leytonstone	26	0	0	0	2	0	0	0
Walker JH	Harry	1891	Wirksworth	1934	1923		Aberdare Ath.	Chesterfield	1	0	0	0	0	0	0	0
Walker R	Bob	23/07/1942	Wallsend		1965	1966	Margate	Colchester Utd.	10	0	0	0	0	0	0	0
Walker RG	Robert		Southampton		1926	1928	Cowes		21	1	0	0	0	0	0	0
Walker RW	Robert	21/05/1922	Bournemouth		1946		Aberdeen	Wrexham	2	1	0	0	2	0	0	0
Wallbridge T	Trevor	08/02/1959	Southampton		1977		Totton		1	0	0	0	0	0	0	0
Warren C	Christer	10/10/1974	Bournemouth		1997	1999	Southampton	QPR	103	10	7	7	13	1	0	0
Watson AF	Alex	05/04/1968	Liverpool		1990	1994	Liverpool	Torquay United	151	12	14	5	5	1	1	0
Watson GWG	Gordon	20/03/1971	Sidcup		1999		Bradford City	Hartlepool Utd.	6	3	1	1	0	0	0	0
Watson ML	Mark	28/12/1973	Birmingham		1996		West Ham Utd.	Welling United	15	1	0	1	2	0	0	0
Waugh WL	Billy	27/11/1921	Edinburgh		1953		QPR	Chelmsford City	18	0	0	0	3	0	0	0
Webb DJ	David	09/04/1946	Stratford		1980	1982	Derby County	Torquay United	11	2	0	0	0	1	0	0
Webb WG	Willie	12/07/1906	Glasgow		1930	1932	St Johnstone	Ramsgate PW	57	5	0	0	6	1	0	0
Webster E	Ernie	15/09/1903	Leigh	1989	1931		Brighton & Hove A.	Ramsgate	6	1	0	0	0	0	0	0
Weeks GJ	Graham	03/03/1958	Exeter		1978		Exeter City	Taunton Town	3	0	1	0	0	0	0	0
Weigh RE	Ray	23/06/1928	Flint		1949	1950	Shrewsbury Town	Stockport County	28	4	0	0	8	1	0	0
Weller CW	Chris	25/12/1939	Reading		1960	1964	Reading	Bristol Rovers	115	4	6	0	25	3	2	0
					1965	1966	Bristol Rovers	Yeovil Town								
Wells DP	David	29/12/1977	Portsmouth		1994		Trainee	Barry Town	1	0	0	0	0	0	0	0
Welsh A	Alan	09/07/1947	Edinburgh		1973	1974	Plymouth Argyle	Millwall	35	3	1	0	3	0	0	0
Whelpton JI	James	1887	Sheffield	1944	1923		Guildford Utd.		1	0	0	0	0	0	0	0
White A	Alfie	1910	Spennymoor		1931	1935	Derby County	Wrexham	124	9	0	2	33	3	0	0
White AJ	Tony	03/11/1966	Clacton		1985		Dorchester Town	Dorchester Town	1	0	0	0	0	0	0	0
White J	Jimmy	13/06/1942	Poole		1957		Juniors	Portsmouth	176	12	9	0	5	1	0	0
					1966	1970	Gillingham	Cambridge Utd.								
White KN	Kevin	26/06/1948	Poole		1966	1968	Apprentice	Bath City	49	5	4	0	6	1	0	0
Whitehouse JC	Jack	04/03/1897	Smethwick	1948	1930	1932	Sheffield Wed.	Folkestone Town	105	8	0	0	17	0	0	0
Whitelaw R	Bobby	02/11/1907	Stonehouse		1932		Celtic	Glentoran	10	0	0	0	2	0	0	0
Whiteside EK	Ken	11/12/1929	Liverpool		1955		York City		1	0	0	0	0	0	0	0
Whitlock M	Mark	14/03/1961	Portsmouth		1986	1988	Southampton	Reading	99	3	10	3	1	0	0	0
Whittam EA	Ernie	07/01/1911	Wealdstone		1936	1938	Wolverhampton W.	Reading	106	5	0	0	27	2	0	0
Whittle A	Alan	10/03/1950	Liverpool		1980		Orient	Preston Rams (Aus)	9	0	0	0	0	0	0	0
Wilkinson DL	David	28/05/1928	Sunderland		1950	1951	Blackburn Rovers	Berwick Rangers	8	0	0	0	3	0	0	0
Wilkinson E	Eric	06/03/1931	Sheffield		1955		Sheffield Utd.	Hastings Utd.	4	0	0	0	0	0	0	0
Williams DM	David	11/03/1955	Cardiff		1992		Norwich City	Everton (Ass. Mgr)	1	0	0	0	0	0	0	0
Williams E	Emlyn	1903	Aberaman		1931		Merthyr Town	Ramsgate	6	0	0	0	2	0	0	0
Williams GJ	Gareth	12/03/1967	Cowes		1994		Wolverhampton W.	Northampton Town	1	0	0	0	0	0	0	0
Williams KD	Keith	12/04/1957	Burntwood		1981	1986	Northampton Town	Bath City	102	9	8	9	1	2	0	2
Williams LS	Len	02/05/1910	Cefn-y-Bedd	1990	1929	1932	Wrexham	Portsmouth	90	6	0	0	18	0	0	0
Williams WJ	John	03/10/1960	Liverpool		1986	1989	Port Vale	Cardiff City	117	7	10	3	9	0	0	0
Wilson CH	Charlie	10/02/1904	Cleethorpes	1994	1933		Grimsby Town	Grantham	11	0	0	0	0	0	0	0
Wilson FC	Fred	10/11/1918	Nottingham	1994	1938	1950	Wolverhampton W.	Weymouth	98	6	0	2	0	0	0	0
Wilson FW	Fred		Windermere		1933		Bolton Wanderers	Barnsley	3	0	0	0	1	0	0	0
Wilson GR	George		Dublin		1924	1925	Clapton Orient	Boston Town	81	6	0	0	0	0	0	0

Name		D.O.B	Place of Birth	Died	First Season	Last Season	Previous Club	Next Club	Appearances				Goals			
									Lge	FAC	FLC	Oth.	Lge	FAC	FLC	Oth.
Wingate J	John	19/12/1948	Budleigh Salterton		1974		Exeter City	Exeter City	33	2	7	0	3	0	0	0
Wingham HC	Harry	25/06/1895	Selsey	1969	1923		Thornycrofts	Clapton Orient	18	6	0	0	0	0	0	0
Wood PA	Paul	01/11/1964	Middlesbrough		1990	1993	Sheffield Utd.	Portsmouth	99	13	2	5	18	2	0	2
Woods CMP	Charlie	18/03/1941	Whitehaven		1962	1964	Newcastle United	Crystal Palace	70	2	2	0	26	0	0	0
Wood J	Jimmy		Royston		1926		Hyde United	Hyde United	7	0	0	0	1	0	0	0
Woodward L	Laurence 'Dai'	05/07/1918	Troedyrhiw		1946	1953	Walsall	(coaching staff)	272	14	0	0	7	0	0	0
Woollard AJ	Arnold	24/08/1930	Bermuda		1956	1961	Newcastle United	Northampton Town	159	10	5	0	0	0	0	0
Woozley DJ	David	06/12/1979	Berkshire		2000		Crystal Palace (loan)		6	0	0	0	0	0	0	0
Wright R	Reg	17/01/1901	Dronfield	1973	1928	1930	Blackpool	Chesterfield	31	0	0	0	0	0	0	0
Young A	Andrew	17/09/1896	Darlington	1964	1927		Arsenal	Kidderminster H.	2	0	0	0	0	0	0	0
Young CR	Ron	22/07/1925	Bournemouth		1948	1949	Southampton	Chelmsford C	18	0	0	0	0	0	0	0
Young NA	Neil	31/08/1973	Harlow		1994	2002	Tottenham H		293	20	20	18	4	0	0	0
Young RG	Bob	24/12/1923	Bournemouth		1947		Juniors	Crewe Alexandra	1	0	0	0	0	0	0	0

Played in FA Cup and League Cup only

Name		D.O.B	Place of Birth	Died	First Season	Last Season	Previous Club	Next Club	Lge	FAC	FLC	Oth.	Lge	FAC	FLC	Oth.
Green APC	Alan	19/04/1951	Fordingbridge		1970		Local	Mansfield Town	0	1	2	0	0	0	0	0

Played in League Cup only

Name		D.O.B	Place of Birth	Died	First Season	Last Season	Previous Club	Next Club	Lge	FAC	FLC	Oth.	Lge	FAC	FLC	Oth.
Adekola D	David	19/05/1968	Liverpool		1994		Bury	Wigan Athletic	0	0	1	0	0	0	0	0
Hall P	Peter	29/09/1939	Stoke on Trent		1961		Port Vale	Yeovil Town	0	0	1	0	0	0	0	0
Massey RL	Ray	@1942			1961				0	0	1	0	0	0	0	0

Played in Miscellaneous Games only

Name		D.O.B	Place of Birth	Died	First Season	Last Season	Previous Club	Next Club	Lge	FAC	FLC	Oth.	Lge	FAC	FLC	Oth.
Adkins CR	Charles	@1914	Bishop Auckland		1935		Wolverhampton W.	Released	0	0	0	1	0	0	0	0
Bolson L	Lee				1986				0	0	0	1	0	0	0	0
Bright P	Percy	@1920			1938		B'mouth Gas Works		0	0	0	1	0	0	0	0
Cooke W	William	07/03/1919	Whittington		1938			Luton Town	0	0	0	2	0	0	0	0
Jones P	Paul				1983				0	0	0	1	0	0	0	0
Pearson H	Harold 'Tich'	1910	Birkenhead		1935		Tranmere Rovers	Birkenhead	0	0	0	1	0	0	0	0
Stephens A	Tony	12/01/1977	Portsmouth		1995		Trainee	Weymouth	0	0	0	1	0	0	0	0
Townsend EE	Eric	14/02/1914	Hove	1976	1934		Brighton & Hove Alb.	Shoreham	0	0	0	1	0	0	0	1

Played in 1939/40 only

Name		D.O.B	Place of Birth	Died	First Season	Last Season	Previous Club	Next Club
Wilkinson CE	Charlie	07/04/1907	Medomsley	1985			Southampton	

Club Managers

Harry Kinghorn	June 1923 - July 1925
Leslie Knighton	July 1925 - July 1928
Frank Richards	Aug 1928 - Oct 1930
Billy Birrell	Nov 1930 - May 1935
Bob Crompton	June 1935 - Feb 1936
Charlie Bell	June 1936 - June 1939
Harry Kinghorn	June 1939 - May 1947
Harry Lowe	July 1947 - Feb 1950
Jack Bruton	March 1950 - March 1956
Freddie Cox	April 1956 - July 1958
Don Welsh	July 1958 - Feb 1961
Bill McGarry	March 1961 - July 1963
Reg Flewin	Aug 1963 - April 1965
Freddie Cox	April 1965 - May 1970
John Bond	May 1970 - Nov 1973
Trevor Hartley	Nov 1973 - Jan 1975
John Benson	Jan 1975 - Jan 1979
Alec Stock	Jan 1979 - Dec 1980
David Webb	Dec 1980 - Dec 1982
Don Megson	Jan 1983- Oct 1983
Harry Redknapp	Nov 1983 - June 1992
Tony Pulis	June 1992 - Aug 1994
Mel Machin	Aug 1994 - Aug 2000
Sean O'Driscoll	Aug 2000 to date

Boscombe Southern League Appearances 1920/21 to 1922/23

	From	*To*	*Apps*	*Gls*
Armstrong J *	1922		23	6
Bailey WG	1921		22	8
Barnes F	1920		3	
Brighton HG	1920	1921	5	1
Brown EA	1922		1	
Budden WL *	1922		12	1
Butt LG *	1922		31	1
Cartmell JR	1921		30	4
Cherrett PAM *	1920		9	3
Cobb HG	1921		6	
Colbourne WR	1920	1921	50	1
Cornick	1920		2	
Davey HH *	1922		33	23
Dempsey	1920		3	1
Diaper	1920		7	
Drinkwater	1922		1	
Duff D	1922		1	
Dunford ER	1920		14	3
Ferguson CF	1920		6	
Frost HV	1921		4	
Garrett A	1920		8	1
Green J	1922		1	
Guy M	1922		1	
Harrison HF *	1921	1922	6	1
Hayward DW **	1922		0	
Heron AA *	1920	1922	84	
Heron W	1920		1	
Hillier	1920		1	
James WE	1922		38	12
Kelsall A	1922		3	1
Kirkpatrick	1922		1	

	From	*To*	*Apps*	*Gls*
Lamb JF *	1920	1922	95	
Lawson MB	1920		6	
Leavey HJ	1920	1921	41	7
Lewry WG	1921		13	1
Manson G	1920	1921	5	
Marshall E	1920	1921	5	
Marshall G	1920		3	
Marshall KC *	1920	1922	12	
Martland R	1920		18	3
Matthews VE	1921	1922	43	3
Mavin FJ	1921		4	1
Meader E	1921		20	5
Meyer HJ *	1920	1922	47	18
New JP	1920	1922	18	
Noble AH	1921		25	4
Parsley G	1920	1922	31	
Perrett F	1920			
Phillips H	1921	1922	7	
Ramsay EE	1920	1921	4	
Saxton E *	1921	1922	60	
Sharp	1920		3	
Smith CF *	1922		17	2
Smith G	1920	1922	31	8
Turner F	1922		4	3
Wakeley F	1920	1922	68	4
Watts AG	1921	1922	16	1
Whitcher	1920		10	1
White H	1920	1921	3	
Wilson	1920		4	
Wingham HC *	1921	1922	56	2
Young W	1921	1922	2	

** also made a Football League appearance*
*** played for Boscombe in FA Cup (and Football League)*

An unnamed Boscombe team group from 1908, when the club was playing in local football competitions